THE FUTURE

Fifth Generation of computers,
artificial intelligence, advanced
telecommunications, natural
language processing (p. 18, Point/
Counterpoints)

1956

FORTRAN language
developed (p. 245)

1981

IBM PC released

1979

Apple II computer desktop model
which runs Visicalc, becomes
available (p. 408)

1958

Integrated Circuit
developed by Jack S.
Kilby (p. 121)

1978

Visicalc, first business/professional
application program for
microcomputers (p. 408)

1959

COBOL language developed
by team including Grace
Murray Hopper (p. 247)

1978

First Apple built (p. 7)

1963

John Kemeny and
Thomas Kurtz develop
BASIC. TrueBASIC,
a structured version
of the language,
developed in 1984.
(p. 249)

1971

First integrated circuit on a
microchip developed by Ted
Hoff at Intel (p. 121)

Using Computers in
an Information Age

Dedication

The authors and the people at Delmar Publishers dedicate this book to the memory of Kip Sears, editor, gentleman, and friend.

Using Computers in an Information Age

RICHARD W. BRIGHTMAN

JEFFREY M. DIMSDALE

DELMAR PUBLISHERS INC.

Cover Photographs by: Ted Kurihara Photography, Charles Feil / FPG International, Campbell-Boulanger / FPG International

Administrative Editor: Christina Gallagher
Associate Editor: Karen Lavroff
Production Editor: Patricia O'Connor-Gillivan
Design Coordinator: John Orozco
Project Management, Design, and Production: Delgado Design, Inc.
Typesetting and Artwork: Burmar Technical Corporation
Color Separator: State Color
Printer: R.R. Donnelly & Sons Company, Willard, Ohio Manufacturing Division

For information address Delmar Publishers Inc.,
2 Computer Drive West, Box 15-015,
Albany, New York 12212

Printed in the United States of America
Published simultaneously in Canada
by Nelson Canada,
a division of International Thomson Limited

10 9 8 7 6 5 4 3 2 1

Library of Congress Cataloging in Publication Data

Brightman, Richard W.
  Using computers in an information age.

  Bibliography: p. N-1
  Includes index.
  1. Microcomputers.   I. Dimsdale, Jeffrey M.
II. Title.
QA76.5.B755 1986   004.165   85-15952
ISBN 0-8273-2372-7
ISBN 0-8273-2394-8 (instructor's guide)

Brief Contents

Contents

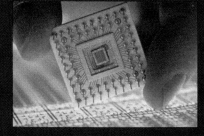

SECTION TWO *The Complete Computer System*

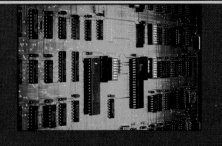

SECTION THREE Software Applications:
Tools in an Information Age

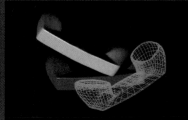

Data Communication   297

C H A P T E R 12

Word Processing 343

C H A P T E R 13

Accounting Systems 373

C H A P T E R 14

Spreadsheet Programs 407

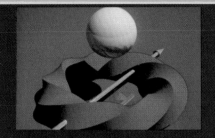

Preface

Can there be a teaching field more challenging than information processing and computers? Here is a field that changes significantly almost every month, a field that combines a half-dozen or more disciplines. It is a field of which virtually everybody needs a working knowledge because virtually everybody, from the corner-office-with-a-view executive and his or her secretary to the warehouse worker and the salesclerk, now uses a computer. Beyond using computers at work, almost everybody will also use them for personal applications — managing household finances, writing, learning, entertainment, and even shopping.

As teachers, we must prepare our students for this reality. We must anticipate, as best we can, our students' future. How do we see them using computers when they leave school for the high-tech world a few years after they complete our introductory course?

Until 1980 we were confident that they would be clients of corporate information systems departments. We would serve them best by introducing the complexities of information processing tasks, making them as comfortable as possible with the stringent logic of computer operation and programming and acquainting them with the exigencies of looking to the information systems department as the source of information and data processing. An important part of our task has been teaching a vocabulary our students could use to communicate with the professionals.

Now our crystal ball tells us that most of our students will use individually controlled computer resources. These resources will take the form of microcomputers, both standing alone and connected to other computers, including mainframes and minicomputers.

As we look over our students on the first day of class, we ask ourselves how many will ever work directly with a mainframe computer? Not many. Almost all will see the mainframe as a source of data and as a resource having the immense computing power required for jobs best left to the professionals.

Aside from those whom we inspire to join the profession, most of our students will use microcomputers for their day-to-day processing tasks. How will they use them? The patterns are clear: for word processing, spreadsheets, accounting, communications, graphics, and data base management. But also for such applications as resource management, analysis, and for increasing their personal creativity.

How to best serve these students, then? It's tempting to discard all we've done in the past and teach only about microcomputers and their most popular application programs. To do so, however, would ignore the fact that mainframe computer installations and information processing departments are not fading away. On the contrary, they continue to play increasingly influential roles in the working situations into which our students will graduate.

We need a balanced approach — one that will both introduce students to the skills they will use with their independent computing resources and acquaint them with the realities of information systems management in medium and large organizations.

Designed with this balance in mind, *Using Computers in an Information Age* closes the conceptual gap between such required information processing topics as hardware, systems development, and programming and such new topics as spreadsheet analysis, data base management, and word processing. These new topics focus on the computer user as one with direct control over the application. The new topics have become vital to our students' professional futures.

ORGANIZATION

The first two parts of the text concentrate on what many consider to be the traditional subject matter of introductory courses: data and information processing, systems development, computer systems, and programming. Traditional, perhaps—but this material is vital not only to those who find themselves working in a large organization but for all others who would understand the role that information and information processing systems play in the modern world.

When discussing computer hardware and software, we recognize that there are few conceptual differences among mainframes, minicomputers, and microcomputers. Therefore, the microcomputer, as the tool that our students are most likely to use as students and professionals is discussed throughout the text. We find this to be a more satisfying approach than treating microcomputers in a separate chapter as if the material were added to the book at the last minute.

Appendix A provides students with an understanding of the internal operation of computers. It uses a simple but operational computer called the DELRAM. Students can write programs for the DELRAM and execute them with either an Apple or an IBM PC computer. When running on these computers, DELRAM displays the contents of memory and the several registers as each program instruction executes.

Chapter Nine examines computer program development, for instructors who wish to emphasize good programming technique, but not a particular language. Appendix B provides students with a gentle but thorough introduction to BASIC, using structured programming techniques.

The third part of the text gives thorough treatment to the fifteen most popular types of applications programs used by business people today. Of these, the Big Six, as we refer to them, include word processors, spreadsheets, accounting programs, graphics programs, data base managers, and communication programs. Each of the Big Six is presented in a separate chapter. A final chapter in this section reviews nine additional programs that have, in the past few months, earned permanent places in the modern office. They include such applications as project management, idea processing, expert systems, and integrated systems.

Throughout the book, we approach the reader as a user of information systems. Not only is this the best way to interest and motivate students, but it also prepares them to become professionals and full participants in the information society.

HISTORY, SOCIAL ISSUES, AND CAREERS

In keeping with this user orientation, *Using Computers in an Information Age* treats several topic areas in special ways. Some texts place history, information processing careers, and societal and ethical issues in completely separate sections or chapters. We have found that this reduces the importance of these topics in the minds of our students. They finish those books with too little appreciation for how those topics link to the more practical aspects of computers and information processing which they see as the core of the course.

This observation led us to integrate historical material throughout the text so that students can easily grasp how past developments in hardware, operating systems, applications programs, and other aspects of the field have led to the present. Chapter One presents some overriding considerations of the effects of computer technology on society. Further aspects of that topic appear in *Point/Counterpoint* material placed at the end of several chapters where the ethical and controversial issues are in context with chapter material. Topics concerning careers in information processing are similarly treated and appear at the end of early chapters in sections entitled *New Professions*. This reflects our conviction that students should begin thinking about careers in the field at the outset of the course, not as an afterthought.

The material about social issues, history, and careers, as required by the DPMA and ACM curriculum guidelines for a first course in computing, is crucial for thorough preparation of our students. We find that integrating the material throughout the course is a more effective way of presenting it.

APPLICATIONS

Most texts that cover applications at all cover no more than three in depth: spreadsheets, data base managers, and word processors. These three programs are the most widely used today, yet familiarity with accounting, graphics, and communications programs has recently become equally important. The additional tools found in Chapter Sixteen round out the full range of modern computer applications, including many, such as expert systems and program generators, that will see increased use in the future. For our students, the computer users of tomorrow, it makes sense to teach the software of tomorrow.

LEARNING AIDS

Using Computers in an Information Age approaches the student as one who needs the vocabulary and knowledge required to work with information systems professionals. It also approaches the student as one who will use personal computing resources for many professional and personal data processing activities.

The text includes the following features to help students learn the vocabulary and gain the knowledge.

■ *Chapter Outlines* Each chapter begins with an outline of key points as an overview of the material to follow. This will help the student to develop his or her own learning objectives. Detailed learning objectives for each chapter appear in the *Instructor's Guide*. These can be shared with students as necessary.

- *Vocabulary* When a new term is introduced, it appears in italic type and is defined immediately. Key terms then appear again in a list for review at the end of each chapter.

  A computer game, called HangProgrammer, is included with the software package for the text. Played like the familiar hangman game, Hang-Programmer uses technical terms taken from the book. We find that students enjoy the game and learn the vocabulary more quickly when they play it.

  Finally, a comprehensive glossary of computer and information processing terms appears at the end of the text.

- *Review Questions* Questions at the end of each chapter allow you and your students to gauge the knowledge they have gained. Answers to the questions appear in the *Instructor's Guide.*

- *Discussion Questions* Comprehensive questions at the end of each chapter may be used in class or treated as short essay assignments or quizzes. These require students to work with the knowledge gained from the specific chapters as well as more general knowledge of business, ethics, and human nature. Answers to these questions appear in the *Instructor's Guide.*

- *Follow-up Questions to the End of Chapter Features* To help instructors assess students' understanding and to serve as a basis for class discussion, we follow *Point/Counterpoint* and *New Professions* with questions that require students to read, comprehend, and think—much as they will need to in later college courses and as professionals. Approaches for answering the questions are in the *Instructor's Guide.*

- *Case Studies* In Section III, Software Applications, each specific chapter ends with a case study. In each case a business professional in businesses ranging from small to very large, uses a popular application package to solve problems ranging from the spending of the advertising budget to the formatting and keyboarding of an important document. We designed the cases to appeal to students and to take into account the levels of business sophistication that students in a first course are likely to have.

- *Use of Color* Because it is a four-color book, students will find *Using Computers in an Information Age* enjoyable and interesting. To emphasize the input-processing-output cycles of data processing, we have color coded most of the book's diagrams so as to help students identify those processes: ▓▓▓▓ for input, ▓▓▓▓ for processing, and ▓▓▓▓ for output.

THE TEACHING PACKAGE

Teaching an introductory course in which the core knowledge changes almost daily is difficult. Recognizing that supporting materials can help, we have assembled a teacher's tool kit including an instructor's guide, a student guide, transparency masters, several types of software, a printed test bank, and a computerized test bank. Each element of the package meshes with the others to provide maximum support for instructor and student. The specifics follow:

- *Instructor's Guide* The *Instructor's Guide* is designed to make implementation of a user-oriented course as easy as possible. To that end, it includes sample lecture schedules, lecture outlines including teaching hints, instructional objectives for each chapter, and answers to in-text questions.

We have inserted a number of interesting anecdotes and unusual facts about computers in the lecture outlines. These add humor and interest to lecture presentations. Additional activities for students appear on a chapter-by-chapter basis.

- *Test Bank* A bank of over 3,000 test questions, including true-false, multiple choice, fill-in, short essay, and pencil and paper flowcharting and programming problems is available to adopters of the text. A computerized version of the test bank for popular microcomputers is also available to qualified adopters.

- *Student Study Guide* The *Student Study Guide* contains pre- and post-tests for every chapter of the text, as well as chapter overviews and key terms. All questions and terms are page-referenced to the text. Laboratory activities to accompany the software are found in Part II.

- *Transparencies* Masters of over 150 key figures from the text are available in the *Instructor's Guide*. We have referred to these in the lecture outlines to make them easy to use.

- *Software for Student Use* Because it is difficult to teach a user-oriented course without user software, and because different teachers and different institutions will have different software requirements, we have developed four levels of software support for Part III of this text. The software is available to qualified adopters.

  1. *Tutorial overview of application programs* A single disk walks students through five of the Big Six applications: word processing, data base management, spreadsheets, telecommunications, and graphics. It acquaints students with typical business uses in two to three hours.

  2. *Full function word processor, spreadsheet, and data base programs* For instructors who wish to spend more time on laboratory exercises in the three primary areas of computer applications, Delmar Publishers will provide completely functional versions of these microcomputer programs.

  3. *Generic Laboratory Exercises* We know that many instructors have favorite word processor, spreadsheet, and data base management programs available in their computer laboratories. For those who wish their students to continue using these packages but also wish to tie student work directly with the text and the *Student Study Guide*, Part II of the study guide provides exercises that the students can use successfully with any program. The *Instructor's Guide* explains where in the course particular laboratory exercises are most appropriate.

  4. *Computerized Learning Aids* Five interactive software modules support the material in Parts I and II of the text. Laboratory examples to accompany the software are included in Part II of the *Student Study Guide*.

We wrote this preface for teachers, although we suspect that other readers will find it of value too. Comments about this book that are of immediate interest to the students appear in Chapter One.

We close these prefatory remarks with the observation that teaching and learning should both be fun. We hope, while using this book, that you and your students have as much fun reading it as we had in writing it and testing its exercises and case problems with our students.

R.W.B.
J.M.D.

ACKNOWLEDGEMENTS AND APPRECIATION

Writing a book of the scope of *Using Computers in an Information Age* is no little undertaking. Although the book's cover shows the names of just two authors, you should know that, in fact, it is the fruit of the labors of many. Here, then, follows a brief and inadequate acknowledgement and expression of gratitude to those who helped us.

Howard L. Dimsdale, author Jeff Dimsdale's father and a professional writer in Hollywood, reviewed and critiqued the final version of the manuscript. His cogent suggestions have improved many aspects of a manuscript that we thought was finished at the time.

Edward Martin, Professor at Kingsborough Community College in New York, wrote the *Student Study Guide*. He also reviewed and critiqued every aspect of the manuscript and made an enormous contribution to the project. Jeff Denham, a writer from New York, made many helpful suggestions about the book's first chapter. William J. Moon, Professor at Palm Beach Junior College (North), wrote the *Test Bank* of over 3000 questions. He also reviewed and critiqued the entire manuscript.

Donald A. Ackley, librarian at Orange Coast College in California, gave generously of his time and expertise in helping us with the endless data base researches needed to gather information. Kevin Shannon, also of Orange Coast College, contributed heavily in working out the software requirements for the book. Other Orange Coast College faculty members who helped with advice, computer lore, and programming expertise include Sandra Savage, John R. Clark, Ronald Schryer, Olney Stewart, and Donald B. Rueter.

At Golden West College, Orange Coast's sister institution, various members of the computer science faculty and staff helped by giving advice about software and hardware systems. These include Donovan Nielson, Edwin Campbell, Michael Cox, and John Hanna.

The team at Delmar Publishers comes in for its share of the credit, too. Our main editor in Albany, Karen Lavroff, managed to encourage us, correct us, and console us as necessary. With others at Delmar's main offices, Karen assured that all our efforts would result in a final product that would make us all proud. Tina Gallagher, our editor in California, held our hands through the last agonizing stages of the book's production and promotion. Others of the Delmar team include Pat Gillivan, Sharon Rounds, John Orozo, and Greg Spatz. They are not the only ones who took a direct interest in the project. Virtually everyone at Delmar showed great interest and expended much effort to produce this book. To them belong the kudos for bringing off a very complex project.

The foundation of our success in preparing this book takes the form of the support and tolerance of those closest to us: our family and friends. It is they who must tolerate a room full of computers, books, papers, and arguing authors and editors. It is they who must understand distracted responses to questions and the irritability that comes from spending too many hours before a computer terminal. It is they to whom we owe our greatest gratitude. To you, Harriet and Howard Dimsdale, Kay, Shannon, and Alison Brightman, and our dear friends Bob and Nancy Rubinstein, we say thank you.

Finally, we pay tribute to an army of reviewers and corresponding faculty, none of whom can be thanked adequately enough for their contributions to this book.

The following people read and commented on major portions of the manuscript, as well as graciously and thoughtfully answering assorted frantic questions about hardware, their own courses, and the future of information processing.

Ronald Cerruti
City College of San Francisco

Cristanna Cook
University of Maine at Orono

John DiElsi
Mercy College

George Fowler
Texas A & M University

Jim Kasum
University of Wisconsin at Milwaukee

Terry Lundgren
Utah State University

Edward Martin
Kingsborough Community College

Judy Mondy
Northeast Louisiana State University

William J. Moon
Palm Beach Junior College (North)

Donovan Nielsen
Goldenwest College

Maria Rynn
Northern Virginia Community College

Robert Smith
Kent State University

Ronald Stearns
Miami-Dade Community College

Eileen Wrigley
Community College of Allegheny County

Those listed below also provided excellent and helpful advice on various parts of the manuscript and ancillary package:

Kuriahose Athapilly
Western Michigan University

Leonard Clark
San Diego City College

William Cornette
Southwest Missouri State University

Alex Ephrem
Monroe Business Institute, Bronx

Ray K. Fanselau
American River College

Richard Fleming
North Lake College

Mark Fletcher
Control Data Institute

Steven Friedman
Queensborough Community College

Paula Funkhouser
Truckee Meadows Community College

Stanley Gabis
Newbury Junior College

Nancy T. Chilson Grzesik
National Education Centers

Rod Heisterberg
Austin Community College

Peter Irwin
Richland College

James Kriz
Cuyahoga Community College

Corneilus R. Kucius
Merced College

Robert Leonard
Bunker Hill Community College

Dennis Lundgren
McHenry County College

C. Gardner Mallonee II
Essex Community College

Steven Mansfield
McHenry County College

Gary Martin
Solano College

Sharon McFall
Mesa Community College

Jerry Meyer
LaGuardia College

Wesley Nance
Cerritos College

R. W. Pew
Valencia Community College

Albert Polish
Macomb Community College

Bonita C. Sabo
Carbon County AVTS

W. L. Schlegel
Community College of Aurora

Willis Shockly
Seattle Central Community College

Larry Sieford
University of Texas, Austin

William R. Smith
Sinclair Community College

Arta Szathmary
Bucks County Community College

Eileen Trauth
Boston University

Jacque B. Vail
Burlington County College

James A. Wynne
Virginia Commonwealth University

Frank Yost
Mesa College

ALABAMA
D. Gates
Alabama A & M University

Ava Honan
Auburn University at Montgomery

Frank Scruggs
Troy State University, Montgomery

F. H. Wood
Troy State University, Montgomery

ARIZONA
Charles D. Bedal
Maricopa Technical College

Warren F. Buxton
Maricopa Technical College

Sharon R. McFall
Mesa Community College

ARKANSAS
Cary Hughes
University of Arkansas at Little Rock

Barbara Lewis
Draughon's School of Business,
Little Rock

Donna Satterfield
East Arkansas Community College

CALIFORNIA
Linda Avelar
Skyline College

R. K. Fanselau
American River College

Norman Jacobson
University of California, Irvine

David R. Lee
John F. Kennedy University

Gary Martin
Solano Community College

Richard M. Meyer
Hartnell College

Badis Mostefa
Long Beach College of Business

Wesley E. Nance
Cerritos College

Allan K. Orler
City College of San Francisco

Kevin Shannon
Orange Coast College

Ron Troyer
MTI Business College

Clark E. Williams
Kings River Community College

Louis A. Wolff
Moorpark College

Frank L. Yost
Mesa College

G. Goodrich
Aurora Technical Center

COLORADO
Cathy Hall
Aims Community College

Harris Robnett
Denver [Auraria] Community College

Walter L. Schlegel
Community College of Aurora

CONNECTICUT
Sharon J. Huxley
Post College

H. Stegenga
Housatonic Community College

DELAWARE
Hans J. Haal
Delaware Technical and Community
College

Philip A. Mackey
Delaware Technical and Community
College

FLORIDA
Dayle Coxen
Lively Vo-Tech Center

M. A. McGrath
Santa Fe Community College

William J. Moon
Palm Beach Junior College (North)

Murrell M. Gillan
Florida Southern College

Carol A. O'Dell
Joe Hernoon AVTS

R. W. Pew
Valencia Community College

Cathy Race
Lee Vo-Tech

Gary Taylor
Lindsey Hopkins Technical Educational
Center

GEORGIA
Norman L. Eaton
Griffin Tech

Paul T. Edenfield
Augusta Tech

Edward Marshall
Thomas Area Technical School

J. McNeil
Savannah State College

Roy W. Reach
Brenau College

Elizabeth Sappington
Augusta Area Technical School

Dwight Watt
Swainsboro Tech

HAWAII
G. Ron Jongeward
Hawaii Pacific College

IDAHO
Marian K. Bortnem
Mitchell Vo-Tech School

Milan Kaldenberg
Northwest Nazarene College

Kay V. Nelson
North Idaho College

Colin Randolph
College of Southern Idaho

ILLINOIS
Seth Carmody
Illinois State University

C. B. Garcia
University of Chicago

Jane Garvey
Loyola University

George M. Gintowt
William Rainey Harper College

Barbara T. Grabowski
Loyola University of Chicago

J. M. Hynes
University of Illinois at Chicago

Larry Jeralos
Southern Illinois University

Dennis Lundgren
McHenry County College

Stephen Mansfield
McHenry County College

James R. Moore
Moraine Valley Community College

Linda Oldham
Danville Area Community College

Heidi Perreault
Southern Illinois University

Michele S. Reznick
Oakton Community College

David M. Stettler
Northern Illinois University

Bernard J. Taheny
Moraine Valley Community College

Lawrence Waldrop
Loop College

IOWA
John Breshears
Southeastern Community College

Kay Carter
Simpson College

Ralph W. Christison
Scott Community College

Sheila McCartney
Iowa Central Community College

Sylvia Moore
Spencer School of Business

Allen Rager
Southwestern Community College

Kevin V. Rostenbach
AIC

INDIANA
Byung T. Cho
University of Notre Dame

Harvey L. Omstead
Indiana Institute of Technology

Julie Tinsley
Indiana Central University

KANSAS
G. H. Anderson
Cowley County College

Randy Johnston
Hutchinson Community College

Gary King
Southwestern College

KENTUCKY
Barbara Doyle
Cumberland College

M. Louise Hickman
Morehead State University

Charles Kimble
Jefferson Community College

Paul J. Mulcahy
Morehead State University

Ronald J. Nichols
Alice Lloyd College

James Sherrard
Jefferson Community College

Gladys F. Smith
Lexington Community College

Robert VanCamp
Southeast Community College

LOUISIANA
Ruby B. Holliday
Delgado Junior College

John C. Malley
Louisiana Technical University

Judy Bandy Mondy
Northeast Louisiana University

Jeanette E. Sciara
Louisiana Business College, Monroe

MAINE
Cristanna Cook
University of Maine at Orono

Jean Gutmann
University of Southern Maine

F. Hastings
University of Maine at Machias

MARYLAND
Martin Cronlund
Anne Arundel Community College

Bernadine Kolbet Esposito
University of Baltimore

Trudy Gift
Hagerstown Junior College

Alan R. Hevner
University of Maryland

C. Gardner Mallonee II
Essex Community College

Richard Yankosky
Frederick Community College

MASSACHUSETTS
Donna Akerley
North Shore Community College

Paul Chase
Becker Junior College

William J. Horne
Boston College

Robert J. Leonard
Bunker Hill Community College

Spencer E. Martin
Bentley College

Richard C. Maybury
Berkshire Community College

Alfred C. St. Onge
Springfield Technical Community
College

Eileen M. Trauth
Boston University

MICHIGAN
Kuriakose Athappilly
Western Michigan University

Gerald Gibbs
Wayne County Community College

Diane Krasnewich
Muskegon Community College

Albert Polish
Macomb Community College

Megan Roberts
Northwestern Michigan College

Andrew Suhy
Ferris State College

MINNESOTA
Edward R. Dutton
Itasca Community College

Mark Fletcher
Control Data Institute

Marjorie Frost
Red Wing Area Vocational Technical
Institute

Lisa Hokanson
Hutchinson Area Vocational Technical
Institute

Marge Petkovsek
Minnesota School of Business

Nancy Sams
Lowthian College

Maureen Thommes
Bemidji State University

MISSOURI
Tom Boyer
Lincoln University

William R. Cornette
Southwest Missouri State University

Kenneth A. Smith
Southwest Missouri State University

Kim Thorn
Ozark Bible College

B. Venz
William Woods College

NEBRASKA
J. Max Hoffman
Southeast Community College

Doris Lux
Central Community College

K. L. Maiwald
Nebraska Western College

Michael Overton
Lincoln School of Commerce

NEVADA
Pamela Beer
Nevada Vocational

Paula S. Funkhouser
Truckee Meadows Community College

NEW HAMPSHIRE
Bill G. Jenkins
Hesser College

NEW JERSEY
Sallyann Z. Hanson
Mercer County Community College

Dennis Kelly
Trenton State College

Daniel McGraw
The Cittone Institute

Robert Saldarini
Bergen Community College

H. Terry Reid
Saint Peters College

Jacque B. Vail
Burlington County College

R. Wallerstein
Union County College

NEW MEXICO
Linda Bock
Albuquerque Technical Vocational
Institute

NEW YORK
W. J. Abbott
Broome Community College

Roy Alvarez
Cornell University

Barry Appel
Queensborough Community College

John C. Beers
Rockland Community College

Chester J. Burton
SUNY at Cobleskill

Robert P. Cerveny
SUNY at Buffalo

Alex Ephrem
Monroe Business Institute, Bronx

Susan W. Friedlander
Broome Community College

Jerome Grumet
Queensborough Community College

Eli Gladstein
Queensborough Community College

Thaddeus A. Jones
Jefferson Community College

NEW YORK (Continued)

S. Klotz
Onondaga Community College

Edward Martin
Kingsborough Community College

Gerald H. Meyer
LaGuardia Community College

Shirley Nagg
Rochester Business Institute

Mitchell Redisch
Bramson ORT

Milton L. Reynolds
Ulster County Community College

Joseph Riley
SUNY at Cobleskill

Eugene F. Stafford
Iona College

Arthur A. Strunk
Queensborough Community College

David Sweeney
Hilbert College

Nora Teter
SUNY Plattsburgh

S. Tuohy
Iona College

Thomas M. Veeder
Elmira Business Institute

Raymond F. Vogel
Schenectady County Community College

Henry Weiman
Bronx Community College

David Witkowski
Orange County Community College

Richard L. Wolfe
Elmira Business Institute

NORTH CAROLINA

David Cooke
Campbell University

Leslie B. Davis
University of North Carolina at Wilmington

Gail Lee Elmore
Mitchell College

Hattie R. Jones
Chowan College

Chris Koone
Isothermal Community College

Zaki F. Rachmat
Appalachian State University

John Roberts
Stanley Technical College

Judith A. Smith
Anson Technical College

Robert C. Tesch, Sr.
University of North Carolina at Greensboro

NORTH DAKOTA

Robert Bloomquist
University of North Dakota

OHIO

Rich Bialac
Xavier University

Thomas A. Emch
Youngstown College of Business

James G. Kriz
Cuyahoga Community College

Martha Loughlin
Terra Technical College

John M. McKinney
University of Cincinnati

D. Michalke
Wright State University

Joyce Mirman
University of Akron

Terry Alan Obrock
Northwest Technical College

Stephen L. Props
Columbus Paraprofessional Institute

Howard W. Pullman
Youngstown State University

Elaine M. Shillito
Clark Technical College

Robert D. Smith
Kent State University

W. R. Smith
Sinclair Community College

Erwin C. Vernon
Sinclair Community College

OKLAHOMA

Richard Aukerman
Oklahoma State University

James R. Coffee
Central Area Vo-Tech

Anthony D. Krehbiel
Tulsa Junior College

Ralph H. Mengel
Central State University

Joan K. Pierson
Oklahoma State University

OREGON

James W. Cox
Lane Community College

Jerry DeMoss
Blue Mountain Community College

George F. Farrimond
Southern Oregon State College

David John Marotta
Lane Community College

David Sullivan
Oregon State University

PENNSYLVANIA

F. R. Cannon
Shippensburg University

Joyce Cook
Franklin County AVTS

Frank D. Cristillo, Jr.
Greater Johnstown AVTS

Carl E. Huth
Dauphin County Vo-Tech

William C. Koffke
Pennsylvania Institute of Technology

Michael Koplite
York College of Pennsylvania

Robert S. Law
Monroeville School of Business

Carl Lisowski
Luzerne County Community College

Alan Russell
Pinebrook Junior College

Bonita C. Sabo
Northampton County Area Community College

Arta Szathmary
Bucks County Community College

Charles Taylor
University of Scranton

Susan Traynor
Clarion University of Pennsylvania

Beverly I. White
Lackawanna Junior College

Eileen Wrigley
Community College of Allegheny County

RHODE ISLAND

Anthony Basilco
Community College of Rhode Island

Louise Perl
Roger Williams College

SOUTH CAROLINA

L. Edward Judice
Columbia Junior College

Alice Markwalder
University of South Carolina—Aiken

Linda J. Metcalf
Trident Technical College

Mark W. Smith
Trident Technical College

TENNESSEE

Linda H. Hasty
Motlow State Community College

Chang-Tseh Hsieh
Tennessee Technical University

David Hume
Tennessee Technical University

Janet Stockett
State Technical Institute

TEXAS

Glen R. Barnard
San Antonio Junior College

Ida Mae Baxter
Southwest Texas Junior College

Josephine Brunner
College of the Mainland

Pat Crude
Tarleton State University

Richard Fleming
North Lake College

Robert W. Hamilton
Amarillo College

Rodney J. Heisterberg
Austin Community College

Susan Helms
Hardin-Simmons University

D. Hughes
North Harris County College

Peter Irwin
Richland College

R. M. Richards
North Texas State University

Barbara W. Scofield
Midland College

UTAH
Terry Lundgren
Utah State University

R. Kenneth Walter
Weber State University

VIRGINIA
Charles E. R. Bamford
Virginia Western Community College

R. F. Brogan
Piedmont Virginia Community College

Donald L. Champion
Radford University

Jim Finn
Piedmont Virginia Community College

Willard H. Keeling
Blue Ridge Community College

Elizabeth W. Payne
Virginia Western Community College

Maria S. Rynn
Northern Virginia Community College

WASHINGTON
Howard Bullpitt
Olympia Technical Community College

William Burrows
University of Washington

Esther Harmon
Northwest College

R. Hirschfelden
University of Puget Sound

Suzanne Lybecker
Bellingham Vo-Tech Institute

Rebecca Montgomery
Edmonds Community College

Edryce A. Reynolds
Tacoma Community College

Larry Richards
Eastern Washington University

James Richardson
Ft. Steilacoom Community College

Willis E. Shockley
Seattle Central Community College

Darlene M. Wall
Lower Columbia College

Alfred Willis
Skagit Business College

WASHINGTON D.C.
Martin Fritts
George Washington University

E. Marshall Wick
Gallaudet College

WEST VIRGINIA
Mark E. Adams
Southern West Virginia Community College

WISCONSIN
Kathleen Bates
Milwaukee Area Technical College—West Campus

Lou R. Goodman
University of Wisconsin, Madison

Steve Hakes
District One Technical Institute

Lou Kassera
District One Technical Institute

James Kasum
University of Wisconsin at Milwaukee

Richard A. Magyar
Mount Senario College

John Moseng
District One Technical Institute

Carolyn Regner
University of Wisconsin at Oshkosh

Janet Valentine
Milwaukee Area Technical College—Watertown

William Van Donger
University of Wisconsin at Oshkosh

Jim Renner
NWCC

VIRGIN ISLANDS
John Munro
College of the Virgin Islands

LINOTYPE is a registered trademark of Allied Corporation. PHOTONET is a registered trademark of Photonet Computer Corporation. UNINET is a registered trademark of United Computing Systems, Inc. SABRE is a registered trademark of American Airlines, Inc. AMA/NET is a registered trademark of American Medical Association. Apple, the Apple logo, LISA, and ProDos are registered trademarks of Apple Computer, Inc. dBASE III and FRIDAY! are registered trademarks of Ashton-Tate. VERSATELLER is a registered trademark of BankAmerica Corporation. SIDEKICK is a registered trademark of Borland International, Inc. COMPUSERVE is a registered trademark of Compuserve, Inc., THE LAST ONE is a registered trademark of "AI" Systems Limited. DIALOG is a registered trademark of Lockheed Missiles & Space Company, Inc. VAX is a registered trademark of Digital Equipment Corporation. CP/M and CP/M-86 are registered trademarks of Digital Research, Inc., DOW JONES NEWS/RETRIEVAL is a registered trademark of Dow Jones & Company, Inc. MYLAR is a registered trademark of E.I. du Pont de Nemours and Company. THOR is a registered trademark of Fastware, Inc. TELENET is a registered trademark of GTE Telenet Communications Corporation. Habadex is a registered trademark of Haba Systems, Inc. SELECTRIC is a registered trademark of International Business Machines Corporation. KOMSTAR is a registered trademark of Eastman Kodak Company. 1-2-3 is a registered trademark of Lotus Development Corporation. BUSINESS WEEK is a registered trademark of McGraw-Hill Publishing Company, Inc. MCI MAIL is a registered trademark of MCI Communications Corporation. WordStar is a registered trademark of Micropro International Corporation. R BASE SERIES 4000 is a registered trademark of Microrim, Inc. MS-DOS, Multiplan, Project, and Microsoft are registered trademarks of Microsoft Corporation. Mobil Travel Guide is a registered trademark of Mobil Oil Corporation. THE NATIONAL GEOGRAPHIC MAGAZINE is a registered trademark of National Geographic Society. NewsFlash and NewsNet are registered trademarks of NewsNet, Inc. PEACHPAK is a registered trademark of Peachtree Software, Inc. Fancy Font is a registered trademark of Softcraft. TK!SOLVER is a registered trademark of Software Arts, Inc. VISICALC, VISIPLOT, and VISITREND + VISIPLOT are registered trademarks of Personal Software, Inc. VISITREND/PLOT is a registered trademark of VisiCorp. OPEN ACCESS is a registered trademark of Software Products International, Inc. SUPERCALC is a registered trademark of Sorcim Corporation. THE SOURCE is a registered trademark of Source Telecomputing Corporation. SPRINT is a registered trademark of Southern Pacific Communications. UNIVAC is a registered trademark of Eckert-Mauchly Computer Corporation. DELTA DRAWING is a registered trademark of Computer Access Corporation. SPSS is a registered trademark of Norman H. Nie and C. Hadlai Hull. RADIO SHACK and TRS-80 are registered trademarks of Tandy Corporation. TIME is a registered trademark of Time, Inc. TYMNET is a registered trademark of Tymshare, Inc. ADA is a registered trademark of The United States Department of Defense. E-COM is a registered trademark of the United States Postal Service. ETHERNET and 9700 are registered trademarks of Xerox Corporation. Z-80 is a registered trademark of Zilog, Inc. Forth is a registered trademark of FORTH, Inc. Macintosh is a trademark licensed to Apple Computer, Inc. Ashton-Tate is a trademark of Ashton-Tate. Used by Permission. dBASE II is a registered trademark of Ashton-Tate. State of the Art with Logo is a registered trademark. State of the Art or State of the Art, Inc. is a trademark. Dow Jones Market Manager PLUS is a registered trademark of Dow Jones & Company, Inc. CHAMPION Business Accounting Software is a registered trademark of Champion Software Corporation. The Sales Edge is a trademark of Human Edge Software Corporation. PFS is a registered trademark of Software Publishing Corporation. ENABLE is a registered trademark of The Software Group. ThinkTank is a registered trademark of Living Videotext, Inc. IBM is a registered trademark of International Business Machines Corporation. DICOMED, DICOMED IMAGINATOR, and DICOMED Presenter are registered trademarks of DICOMED Corporation.

CREDITS

Figure 6-15 was reproduced with the permission of SoftCraft, Inc. Figures 9-12, 9-13, 9-21, and 15-10 were reproduced with the permission of International Business Machines Corporation. Figures 10-6 through 10-10 were reproduced with the permission of Software Publishing Corporation. Figures 10-11 through 10-20 were reproduced with the permission of Ashton-Tate. Figures 11-19 through 11-23 were reproduced with the permission of MCI Communications Corporation. Figures 11-25 through 11-27 were reproduced with the permission of NewsNet, Inc. Figures 11-31 through 11-34 and 11-44 through 11-46 were reproduced with the permission of Source Telecomputing Corporation. Figures 11-35 and 11-36 were reproduced with the permission of Source Telecomputing Corporation and Mobil Oil Corporation. Figures 11-37 through 11-43 were reproduced with the permission of Source Telecomputing Corporation and United Press International, Inc. Figures 12-13 and 12-15 through 12-19 were reproduced with the permission of Apple Computer, Inc. Figures 13-7 through 13-10 and 13-15 through 13-18 were reproduced with the permission of Champion Software Corporation. Figures 13-14 and 13-19 were reproduced with the permission of State of the Art, Inc. Figures 13-21, 13-22, 13-24 through 13-26, and 13-28 through 13-32 were reproduced with the permission of ProData. Figure 14-1 was reproduced with the permission of Lotus Development Corporation, Software Arts, Sorcim/IUS Micro Software Corporation, Microsoft Corporation, and Apple Computer, Inc. Figures 14-4 through 14-6, 15-30 through 15-50, and 16-27 through 16-31 were reproduced with the permission of Software Arts. Figures 14-7 through 14-10 were reproduced with the permission of Sorcim/IUS Micro Software Corporation. Figures 14-12 through 14-36 were reproduced with the permission of Microsoft Corporation and Apple Computer, Inc. Figures 16-1 through 16-8 were reproduced with the permission of Microsoft Corporation. Figures 16-9 through 16-26 were reproduced with the permission of Haba Systems and Apple Computer, Inc. Figures 16-32 through 16-40 were reproduced with the permission of Software Arts, Inc. Figures 16-41 through 16-46 were reproduced with the permission of Human Edge Software Corporation and Apple Computer, Inc. Figures 16-47 through 16-56 were reproduced with the permission of Dow Jones & Company, Inc. Figures 16-57 through 16-65 were reproduced with the permission of Living Videotext, Inc. Figures 16-66 through 16-79 were reproduced with the permission of "AI" Systems Limited. Figures 16-80 through 16-83 were reproduced with the permission of The Software Group.

ABOUT THE AUTHORS

Richard W. Brightman, Golden West College, has over 20 years of experience as a classroom instructor, division chairperson, and dean in the Coast Community College District. The author of books on data processing, information systems, and RPG programming, Richard Brightman received a Ph.D. degree from U.C.L.A., an M.B.A. from the Stanford Graduate School of Business, and an A.B. from Stanford University. He is a member of the American Association of Higher Education and has served on the National Advisory Committee for Computer Curriculum of the American Association of Community and Junior Colleges, and the California Association of Community Colleges, Commission on Instruction.

Jeffrey M. Dimsdale, professor of mathematics and computer science, Orange Coast College, has worked as a classroom instructor, associate dean, and director of instructional development. He spent five years writing telecommunication, data base, and scientifically oriented programs for IBM, and holds a Ph.D. from U.S.C. and M.A.T. and an A.B. from U.C.L.A. His previous publications include journal articles, conference presentations, and a multimedia teacher training program.

Richard Brightman and Jeffrey Dimsdale are also coauthors of USING MICROCOMPUTERS forthcoming from Delmar in January, 1986.

Computers and Society: The Information Revolution

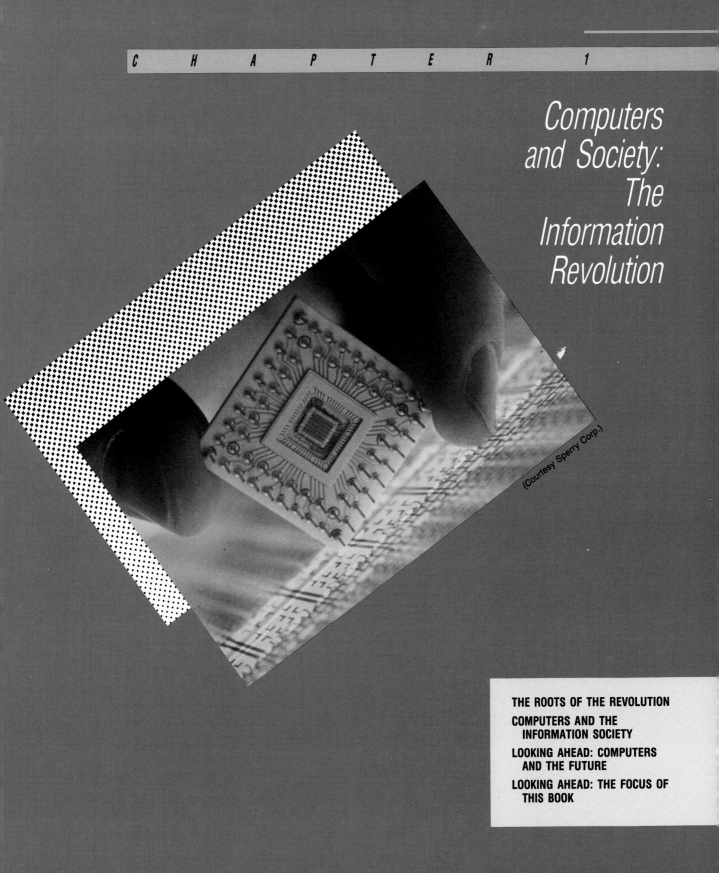

(Courtesy Sperry Corp.)

The wheel. The printing press. The steam engine and the power loom. The telegraph, telephone, and light bulb. The automobile, airplane, and assembly line. Radio, television, nuclear power, and the transistor. Such technical innovations have profoundly influenced the way we live today. Each such advance has spawned a technical revolution, and each revolution in turn has reached beyond the confines of technology to affect the ways we live, work, and see the world.

Using Computers in an Information Age introduces that most recent and exciting of revolutionary technical advances, the computer. More specifically, this book is about computers, business, and you. No matter what you plan to do, whether you will work with people or money, with words or numbers, computers will play an important role in how you do your job.

More than this, computers are changing the very nature of society itself. Such a development is indeed an important issue for all of us, and that's why this first chapter explores the revolutionary role of computers in our society— the *information revolution*.

Information is what computers process, transmit, and store. We use information, for example, to calculate, communicate, and make decisions. We use computers to create, manipulate, and manage information faster and more easily than with any system previously devised. So, the better you understand computers and what they can and cannot do, the more power you will have to put information to work for you.

You are on your way to becoming knowledgeable about computers and about how to use them. This chapter reviews how the Information Revolution is changing the world we live in, and not just the business world. In the chapters that follow, you will learn more about computers and their many applications in business. Once you've worked your way through this book, you'll be well on your way to becoming an active, informed member of the information society.

THE ROOTS OF THE REVOLUTION

Societies are complex structures of people and institutions that interact in a multitude of ways. The social and technological revolutions that alter these structures are no less complex. The information revolution, which has moved us from the industrial age to the information age, is no exception: it is the result of numerous developments in electronics and the information needs of our social institutions, from business and industry to medicine and law. Out of this complexity we can identify three general developments that are in large part responsible for the information revolution: the information explosion, the high-tech revolution in general, and the computer in particular.

Said one White House official at the President's State of the Union address in January, 1983: "Now we realize that this country is at a place in history comparable to when we went from being primarily an agricultural society to an industrial society."[1]

The Information Explosion

We have moved from the industrial age into the information age. Today, for the first time, we have an economy based on information. Between 6,000 and 7,000 new scientific articles are now written each day. John Naisbitt, in his

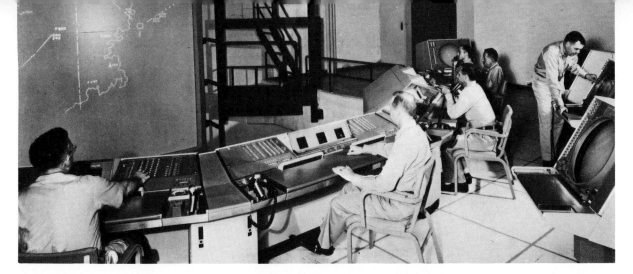

The IBM AN/FSQ-7 computer, one of the world's largest, is used for scientific and military purposes. (Courtesy International Business Machines Corp.)

1982 best-seller, *Megatrends*, predicted that the total amount of scientific information available in the world will double every twenty months. This means that every year and a half or so, we add an amount of scientific information equal to all that mankind has stored since the beginning of time.[2]

The explosion is not limited to scientific information. Massive collections of information, often called data banks, store facts about business, bank deposits movie reviews, criminals, legal precedents, economic statistics, and engineering data, just to name a few. These data banks are growing as fast as the scientific ones. Moreover, new data banks containing collections of information never before accumulated are being developed rapidly.

In 1983 there were nearly 1,500 data banks in operation. By 1985, this number had grown to more than 2,500. Today, physicians, for example, draw on the American Medical Association's AMA/NET which contains information, among other things, on over 1,500 drugs. Said one doctor: "One day I accessed...(it)...three times in twelve minutes. I needed information on arthritis and cancer in the leg. It saved me an hour and half of reading time."[3]

Law offices, in the past incomplete without extensive, not to mention expensive, law libraries now search electronic data banks such as Westlaw in St. Paul, Minnesota to find matters of law and court decisions. Some legal

Even Walt Disney's magic is controlled by computer; this one is at EPCOT Center in Florida. (©Walt Disney Productions)

Personnel directors use computers to organize employee data. (Courtesy Burroughs Corp.)

data banks can even provide the decision history of judges and transcripts of their written decisions, thus enabling lawyers to tailor their court presentations so as to best appeal to the presiding magistrate.

For business people, the Dow Jones News/Retrieval data bases, for example, offer a wide selection of services. The following is only a representative list of the kinds of information available from this data base:

- *The Dow Jones Business and Economic News* contains reports, from ninety-seconds to ninety-days old, from the *Wall Street Journal, Barron's,* and other financial periodicals.
- *The Weekly Economic Update* reviews each week's leading economic news.
- *Dow Jones Quotes* lists price and trading data for corporate and government securities.
- *Financial Investment Services* contains profiles and data on more than six thousand businesses.

The list of general and specialized data banks goes on—and is growing every day. The information explosion has something to offer nearly all of us—that is, if we have the equipment and know-how to retrieve the information we need.

The High-tech Revolution

The rapid growth of information does not depend solely on the development of the technology to process and transmit it. Scientists, historians, economists, and the rest would continue to conduct research and publish their findings, courts would continue to hand down their decisions, stock-market transactions would still be recorded, and world events would invariably inspire news stories whether or not the computers were available to process the information generated by these activities.

The explosion of information alone does not make a revolution. The information revolution has depended heavily on another, related revolution, namely the development of the technical tools to make information accessible to those who would use it. This is the *high-tech revolution.*

"High tech" is short for "high technology," the design and use of electronic devices such as the transistor and the silicon chip in computers and communications. We might trace the roots of the high-tech revolution back to 1828, when Charles Babbage produced the first programmable calculating device, the Analytical Engine. We might look to the more recent past, 1944, and mention Howard Aiken's Mark I, the first programmable computer. We might cite the first electronic computer, the slow, gigantic, but ground-breaking ENIAC, developed in 1946 by John Mauchly and Presper Eckert at the University of Pennsylvania. To be complete, we should also mention dozens of other major developments in computers and electronic communications—known together as *telecommunications*.

There seems to be no particular reason why technological developments involving communications devices and computers should be included in the high-tech revolution while similarly remarkable developments in agriculture, mining, oceanography, and transportation tend to be excluded from it. Possibly it is because computers and electronic communications get more press coverage, even more than the dramatic achievements of the space shuttle program and the philosophically and religiously sensitive research in genetic engineering.

The press coverage enjoyed by computers and telecommunications development provides a wealth of information illustrating this second aspect of the information revolution. The developments are indeed spectacular:

> If the aircraft industry had evolved as spectacularly as the computer industry over the past 25 years, a Boeing 767 would cost $500 today, and it would encircle the globe in 20 minutes on five gallons of fuel.[4]

We could hardly fail to notice such a remarkable aircraft if it existed, but there would still be an essential difference between our response to the jet and to the computer. No matter its sophistication, the plane would still require pilots with years of training to fly it; we would always remain as passengers, as passive riders on the aircraft revolution. With a computer and a little effort, we take an active part in the information revolution. For most of us, that part will make use of the tool that has made the information revolution a part of our everyday lives: the microcomputer.

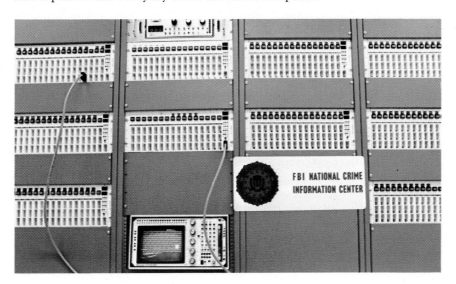

The National Crime Information Center links police departments throughout the country by computers connected to this telecommunications equipment. (Courtesy U.S. Dept. of Justice, Federal Bureau of Investigation)

Many people use computers for research at the Library of Congress. (Courtesy Library of Congress)

The Microcomputer Contribution

The high-tech revolution has turned the information explosion into the information revolution. The two developments are so firmly connected because it is technology that gives us the power to find and use information in ways never before possible. In other words, it is *access* to information that is so important. No other development has been as responsible for increasing our access to information as the microcomputer.

A *microcomputer* (or *micro*, for short) is a small, inexpensive, general-purpose computer that offers users most of the capabilities of its larger and more costly mainframe and minicomputer siblings. Indeed, the desk-top computer appears to be our best hope to make use of the information explosion for personal and economic enhancement or, for that matter, just to keep us from drowning in a flood of disorganized data. The microcomputer is making the information revolution a reality for all of us.

Within a few years, the personal computer has brought computing out of corporate data-processing departments and into the hands of the public, and with a vengeance. The best-known pioneer in the microcomputer field, Apple Computer, sold more than 300,000 of its products from its founding in 1977 to the middle of 1983, at which time it was shipping more than 20,000 units a month. At that time, Apple's share of the microcomputer market amounted to twenty-five percent, while its chief rival, IBM, accounted for an equal share with sales of its micro, the PC, first introduced in 1981. The entire market for desk-top computers exceeded 1.2 million units per year by July of 1983.

The growth of the personal computer market continues apace. By 1985, after only ten years on the market, yearly microcomputer sales were measured in billions of dollars. This remarkable growth can be attributed in part to rapidly dropping prices. In fact, one observer has predicted that by the year 2000 the cost of a personal computer system—including a processor, a video monitor, a data-storage device, a printer, and a communications link—will cost only about twice as much as a complete home entertainment center.[5]

This cost estimate is probably too high. Trade publications regularly point out the competitiveness of the micro market and its frequent price cuts. Today, you can buy a micro—albeit with limited processing capability—for as little as $100. A complete system, capable of performing the processing tasks discussed in this book, costs less than $3000.

You should not think that microcomputers are being purchased primarily by individuals for personal use such as home bookkeeping, hobbyist activities, and game playing. In 1983, two thirds of all microcomputers purchased found their way to the tops of business executives' desks. More than half of the $13 billion of microcomputers sold in 1985 went to businesses. In that same year, $63 billion was spent for all computing equipment, 20 percent for microcomputers. By 1995, it is expected that over 50 percent of the $313 billion spent to buy computers will be for micros.

The figures cited above tell us that the business community has recognized the competitive edge offered by the microcomputer. Fast and easy access to information is vital to good decision-making in business, and good decisions make for good business. "Time is money," they say, but today good information is money as well. Micros offer the most-affordable access to the benefits of the information explosion. This is so much the case that managers are flocking to crash courses on computing in such numbers that the American Management Association must offer its course, "Computers for Non-Computer Users," eighty times a year. Further advances in information technology—a term that encompasses data banks and the electronic equipment used to control and gain access to them—are inevitable. More databases, cheaper and more powerful equipment, and radically new approaches to computer technology loom on the near horizon.

COMPUTERS AND THE INFORMATION SOCIETY

Well, there you have it. The information revolution, a combination of massive increases in the world's inventory of information and the technical development of the means to cope with it, will, one way or the other, affect every segment of our lives. For most of us, participation in the technical aspects of the information society means using a telephone, a television or radio set, and a microcomputer. To be sure, millions will be employed professionally in the information processing and communications field as programmers, technicians, and analysts. All of us, the users of information services and computers, will use personal computer resources on our jobs and in our homes.

The first Apple computer was built in a garage using surplus parts mounted on a plywood board. (Courtesy Apple Computer, Inc.)

Computers at Work

Computers in commercial and industrial settings have been around for several decades—nothing new about that. What is new, however, is the availability of computing power at modest cost to managers and workers throughout business organizations. Thanks to the introduction of the microcomputer, the power to retrieve and process information no longer belongs exclusively to computer specialists. As the director of microcomputer research for International Data Corporation puts it:

> Microcomputers are primarily tools. They provide the means for accessing more information so the thinkers of the organization can make more informed decisions....Most importantly, though, microcomputers address certain needs and requirements in business that [larger computers] can't even come close to solving.[6]

Until recently, middle managers and specialized staff have handled much of the processing and analysis of operational data and information. Financial experts formulated recommendations and passed them on to corporate decision-makers. Industrial engineers studied work methods and manufacturing technologies in order to improve production processes. Data-processing experts designed new information systems to meet the organization's growing needs for information and operational control.

As a consequence, these middle managers have wielded control and authority far beyond that which their positions in the organization would justify. This has led to cumbersome decision-making processes and bureaucratic inflexibility that in turn has led to competitive disadvantages. One Xerox manager, for example, wanted to install brighter light bulbs in copying machines to be sold in Egypt. Much writing is done in pencil there and copying it requires stronger light. It took nine months to get approval from corporate product experts for this simple modification. Meanwhile, Xerox's competitors were moving ahead with product development. Xerox's total market share for copiers and supplies dropped from 98% in 1970 to less than 45% in 1982.

Corporate inefficiency has been characteristic of many industries in the

Robots are used for welding and other tasks that may be dangerous or boring and repetitive. (Courtesy Automatix, Inc.)

*The military uses computers for
training, planning, and
management.* (Courtesy Dept. of
the Army)

United States and American business is doing something about it. Firms are reducing their ranks of middle managers and staff experts, putting the full burden of operational decision-making on line managers and making those managers fully responsible for the success of their operations. Xerox, for example, has now eliminated most of its staff of corporate advisors. Individual product and development decisions are now made at the firm's twenty-four operational facilities, significantly decreasing the time required to make operational decisions.

The movement toward decentralized decision making and planning allows American business firms like Xerox to be more efficient and more responsive to market forces. This shift of responsibility also forces the decision makers to rely more and more on information delivered directly from operational sources without first being filtered through squads of staff advisors at headquarters. These managers must, therefore, have sources of information on site, where the decisions are now made.

Enter the computer. If managers are to make operational decisions independently from headquarters staff experts, they must have information. Fortunately, the information revolution now provides the means to make it available. The advent of the desk-top computer and its ability to retrieve needed information from many diverse sources, promises a huge increase in productivity of decision makers.

Business Week describes the advantages offered by these new resources as follows:

- Individual managers can now make decisions by combining information developed within their companies with outside databases, including economic and industry statistics. This allows them to assemble studies of markets, competition, pricing, and forecasts in hours rather than months.

- Electronic mail allows reports, memos, and other correspondence to be transmitted simultaneously to many people within the company as well as outside of it.

Air traffic is controlled with the help of the Sperry Arts III computer system. (Courtesy Sperry Corp.)

- New systems can turn reams of numbers into charts and colorful graphs. Information can thus be more quickly digested for faster action.

- Voice store-and-forward telephone systems let users send phone messages digitally by computer to any number of recipients within the company.

- Computerized scheduling systems make it possible to set dates for large meetings without consulting executives individually.

- Teleconferencing cuts travel time and expense by enabling managers in distant spots to talk "face-to-face" over television linkups.[7]

In these and other capacities, computers are appearing everywhere in the workplace. According to the editors of *InfoWorld,* "While it's still socially acceptable to admit you do not know how to operate a word processor or microcomputer, in the near future the picture will be different. The ability to operate a computer will be an assumed office skill much like typing is today."[8]

Recently, top management has embraced the hands-on use of computers as a fact of corporate life. Paul Strassman, Vice President of Xerox's Systems

The NCR 2820 Source Data Multifunction Terminal collects information on production, materials, and labor in factories. (Courtesy NCR Corp.)

*Technician checks magnified
schematic of a printed-circuit
board.* (Courtesy Sperry Corp.)

Program, uses his computer to increase his personal contacts with customers
and other Xerox executives:

> I accepted the chairmanship of the advisory group on the condition that all the
> group's meetings would be held electronically.... I'm doing five times as much work
> as I used to without the computer. It's so much easier to get involved, and in so
> much more detail.[9]

Roger Smith, Board Chairman of General Motors, encourages his top managers
to use personal computers on the job and has hired experts to train them.
American Motors, too, is providing its top managers with micros. So is Ford.
Mayford Roark, Executive Director of Systems there, sums up his company's
computing philosophy this way:

> The personal computer has at last presented us with a set of tools and technologies
> that are ideally suited to the office environment. Unlike earlier computers, it does
> not require access to an elite priesthood of programmers and analysts. The per-
> sonal computer is a tool anyone can use, for almost any kind of office work. It
> can eliminate a great deal of the tedious drudgery that used to be associated with
> office work, both at the professional and clerical levels. And it can make us more
> productive.[10]

The personal computer increases productivity, no doubt, but many would
disagree that anyone can use one. As with any other tool, its effectiveness
depends upon the skill with which it is used. Using a computer requires, first,
that one learn how. Almost anyone can learn to use a computer. Indeed, for
many the act of learning is addictive. The more one uses a computer the more
one wants to. In 1984, some Apple Macintosh dealers, trying to capitalize on
this phenomenon, offered to let prospective customers take a computer home
to "test drive" it for twenty-four hours. As many as 50% of the "drivers" bought
the machines.

Computers in Everyday Living

You'll find computers outside of your workplace as well. Computer manufacturers, for instance, are donating micros to primary and secondary schools by
the thousands every year, and more and more colleges and universities are
requiring incoming students to purchase micros. Within a decade, most
American homes of even modest means will have a computer that can easily

be connected to the same information sources used by professional researchers, scholars, and commentators. The infusion of technology portends many changes in society. What benefits and risks will the computerizing of American life bring?

Toward New Horizons

Some view the information revolution and its effect on society with enthusiasm often reserved for the naive. Robert Rosenblatt, writing colorfully in *Time* magazine, put it this way:

> Now I'll tell you something about machines in American history...What our forefathers (bless 'em) wanted was the land, not machines...When the machines came clanging along, they were supposed to let folks enjoy the land more...Only they got out of hand, you see, until all the lovely forever greens and blues got squeezed in a corner full of national parks and the sky choked black with factories. That isn't what we intended, though. Machines were meant to open the territory, not close it down.

> What's all this got to do with computers? you ask. I'll tell you. they reopen the territory, that's what they do. Oh, not the land, of course. That's gone like the topsoil...(They open the territory of the mind)...This here screen and keyboard might have come along any old decade, but it happened to pop up...because we were getting hungry to be ourselves again...

> What do you say? Are you ready to join your fellow countrymen (4 million Americans can't be wrong) and take home some bytes of free time, time to sit back after all the word processing and inventorying and dream the dear old dream?[11]

Computers are used to transact bank business from home.
(Courtesy Bank of America NT & SA)

Toward New Dangers

Not all observers share Robert Rosenblatt's rosy vision of the information society. Marvin Minsky of MIT, for one, has this to say: "The desktop revolution has brought tools that only professionals have had into the hands of the public. God knows what will happen now."[12]

Because information can be available to anyone with access to a computer and the necessary data transfer equipment, possibilities for misuse arise. News reports about computer buffs invading sensitive computer systems were illustrated eloquently in the 1983 film *War Games*. In the film, a high school student who is a computer buff breaks into the national defense computer system and nearly starts a nuclear war. Military authorities were quick to protest that such an invasion is impossible; but many people believe otherwise, if for no other reason than fear of technology and of being at the mercy of technologists.

Setting fictional disasters aside, we can easily identify two real dangers brought about by the rise of computers: computer crime and the abuse of privacy.

Computer Crime. These days, news reports frequently describe illegal electronic break-ins of computers and data banks. Indeed, computer crime has become the most-feared variety of white-collar crime. Little wonder. Benefits to the successful computer crook are often enormous. In 1983, an employee of the Wells Fargo Bank used its computer to embezzle $21 million.

In the same year, workers at a Florida welfare office were convicted for stealing $300,000 worth of food stamps by falsifying data in the agency's computer banks.

Most alarming, detected computer crimes are just the tip of the iceberg. The United States Chamber of Commerce estimates that detected computer crime alone costs the American business community more than $100 million a year. Most computer theft goes undetected, which means that the total loss to American businesses far exceeds that figure.

Not all computer crime involves stealing. Some computer enthusiasts, called *hackers*, need no more motive than the love of challenge to break into computer systems and data banks, either to damage them or simply to explore them. Perhaps best described as "computer trespass," such violations are illegal, too, and have stirred considerable national concern for the security of data banks. When a seventeen-year-old hacker who broke into computer systems throughout the country told the U.S. Congress that it was easy to do, computer managers began taking security measures more seriously.

By August of 1983, twenty states had enacted legislation aimed specifically at computer crime. California's statute, for instance, outlaws the "intentional accessing to defraud, extort, or obtain money, property, or services with fraudulent intent or malicious accessing, alterations or deletion, or a malicious accessing for a credit rating."[13] Even through the obscurity of their language, we can see that such laws are serious attempts to deal with the problem of computer crime.

Such laws, directed toward those who succeed in entering and using computer systems illegally, cannot address all varieties of criminal activity involving computers. Illegal copying of computer programs, or software, for example, costs the computer industry some $2 billion every year. Copying a computer program without the publisher's permission violates federal copyright laws and opens the perpetrator to civil suit. Lotus Development Corporation, among the most aggressive software firms in the pursuit of violators, sued Rixon, Inc. for making and distributing copies of Lotus' 1-2-3 program to its branch offices. "The suit, which was recently settled out of court for an undisclosed sum, has put companies on notice that the illegal duplication of personal programs can have painful consequences."[14]

Abuses of Privacy. In addition to computer crime, many people fear that the legal use of data banks threatens to violate individual privacy. Potential targets for abuse, such as data banks containing information about consumer credit, legal political activity, financial holdings, and the like have drawn important legislation aimed at protecting individual rights. The Fair Credit Reporting Act recognizes a citizen's right to examine and challenge data bank information on his or her credit rating. The Code of Fair Information Practices establishes guidelines for government data banks, although the code is not a matter of law. In 1974, however, the U.S. Congress approved the Privacy Act, which incorporates many features of the code. Other legislation, such as the Electronic Funds Transfer Act and the Financial Privacy Act, aims at the same general goal: to protect individuals and organizations from the undesirable use of data-bank information.

But abuses seem inevitable. Given a little ingenuity, almost anyone can find out what everyone else is doing or has done, if not in one place then in another. As of April 1984, each of our names, addresses, telephone numbers,

Computers control automated gas stations. (Courtesy NCR Corp.)

and other personal information appeared in no fewer than thirty-nine separate federal, state, and local data banks. These government data banks include information about our military service, arrest records, school records, family financial data, medical records and insurance claims, telephone bills (including details of every toll call), job applications and performance reviews, to name just a few. On a typical day, some of this information is passed from one computer system to another five times.

Beyond the considerable information kept by government agencies, yet more is maintained privately by banks, credit card companies, retail stores, credit unions and bureaus, and dozens, if not hundreds, of other organizations. After a year-long study of computer security and privacy, U.S. Congressman Dan Glickman of Kansas concluded that

> George Orwell missed the mark. The all-pervasive intrusion into our privacy which he envisioned is not just the [doing] of government. It's [the doing of] government, business, private organizations, and individuals who own computers.[15]

The potential for the abuse of information is enormous and its prevention seemingly impossible. It is this darker side of the information revolution that has spawned much understandable fear of computers.

Cyberphobia

Technical industries generally, and especially the information and data processing fields, are prone to coining words, to developing jargon. "Cyberphobia" is one such. It is new, not coming into vogue until late 1982. It is the combination of cybernetics and phobia.

The term *cybernetics* was introduced by Norbert Weiner of Massachusetts Institute of Technology in 1948. He gave the name to the study of control and communication that compares functions in animals (including humans) and machines (including computers). Its usage has changed over time, but its primary focus on communications and control remains intact. Some researchers have coined a variation, the "cybernetic society" as one in which people and computers interact in processing large amounts of information.

Because "phobia" means "fear of," the meaning of cyberphobia now becomes clear. It is the fear of interaction with computers. It is manifest in the anxiety of the inexperienced computer user who wonders as he or she has a first go at operating a computer, "Who's in control here?" It is not a trivial problem. Purveyors of computer systems are well aware of the pervasiveness of the feeling. Some business executives, partially from cyberphobia, partially from fear of losing status if seen working at a keyboard, shy away from desk-top computers. Others give persuasive reasons why computers are of no use to them: "A desk-top computer can't help me much. But they can help my staff members.... Managers must still make the decisions.... In the real world, managers don't simply manipulate data. Managers manage people, not numbers."[16]

Computer manufacturers understandably see cyberphobia as contrary to their best marketing efforts, and they're doing something about it. Apple Computer hired Dick Cavett for its commercials. Commodore used William Shatner and International Business Machines incorporated a likeness of Charlie Chaplin's tramp to promote its PC.

Few children suffer from cyberphobia. (Courtesy Apple Computer, Inc.)

Such efforts are directed at individuals who will make the decision to buy. As often as not, these people will find their way to a computer store, before any other place, for information. As a rule, computer stores are the last place cyberphobics should visit. *InfoWorld* quotes Murray Goralnick, operator of a Beverly Hills computer business:

> I would send my friends to a local computer store to get answers to questions they were asking me. They'd come back and say "Why'd you send me there, Murray?" They felt dumb and intimidated.[17]

The situation is improving. Computer retailers are making sincere efforts to improve communication between their salespeople and prospective customers. Many stores now offer free seminars especially for prospective business users so that they can learn to make informed decisions about the hardware and software they plan to purchase. Still other stores specialize in business applications, carry no computer games, employ expert salespeople and consultants, and actively discourage computer hobbyists, game enthusiasts, and other nonprofessionals from visiting their showrooms.

According to James Renier, President of Honeywell Information Systems, cyberphobics were typically born before 1954. Renier believes that schools and colleges should launch efforts to bring understanding of computers to that specific age group: "We can't wait for the next generation to come along...the arrival of computers in the workplace may be alienating workers who find computers enigmatic and threatening," he says.[18]

Cyberphobia is curable. Those who have been cured testify that the best treatment is to sit down in front of a computer and experiment, preferably alone, away from the danger of appearing inept in front of those who no longer suffer the affliction. There are many opportunities to do this. Libraries and schools have personal computers available, as do businesses devoted to providing computer time for individual users. Costs for computer time can range from nothing to ten dollars an hour. Hundreds of books and magazines provide guidance and information about what computers can do and how to make them do it. Finally, there are many people who are able and willing to help newcomers get started at computing. Only one thing is certain about curing cyberphobia: you must "get on" a computer for yourself, be forgiving of your mistakes, and be willing to spend some time at it. Familiarity with computers does not breed contempt, it breeds confidence.

LOOKING AHEAD: COMPUTERS AND THE FUTURE

Predicting the future these days is a risky business. The information revolution is moving so quickly that gazing into the crystal ball can actually endanger one's credibility. In early 1984, for example, David Winer, President of the software firm Living Videotext, described his ideal portable computer. It would take two to three years to develop, weigh as much as twenty-five pounds, and cost upwards of $5,000.[19] Eleven months later, Data General Corporation introduced a portable computer, the Data General/One, that surpassed all of Winer's ideal specifications. It weighed in at ten pounds, fit easily in a briefcase, and sold for $2,895.[20]

*Computers that fit in a briefcase
work just like larger models.*
(Courtesy Hewlett-Packard, Inc.)

Compaq produces a series of transportable and desk-top microcomputers that are compatible with the IBM PC. (Courtesy COMPAQ® Computer Corp.)

Generations Past and Present

Seeing where we are going, historians tell us, requires that we know where we've been—forecasts of the future must be based on the past. The historical development of the computer can be divided into four phases or generations. In the first of these, computers employed vacuum tubes and relays as switching devices. Assembled with care, these collections of switches—the ENIAC used 18,000 (see Chapter Five)—routed electrical impulses to produce calculated results. As it turns out, all digital computers today still perform calculations using switching techniques.

In the second generation of computers, tubes and relays were replaced by semiconductors, called transistors. These switching devices cost less, offered greater speed and reliability, used less energy, and produced less heat than vacuum tubes.

The third generation, born in 1964, used integrated circuits to replace transistors. An integrated circuit contains thousands of switches arranged on circuit boards small enough to be hidden by your fingertip. These became known as chips, and were cheaper, faster, and cooler still than their transistor forebears.

The fourth generation of computers saw components shrink to microscopic size. The chips became large scale integrated circuits (LSI) and then very large scale integrated circuits (VLSI), meaning that they contained a very large number of components on very small chips. Once again, the switches became smaller, less expensive, faster, and cooler.

These electronic developments have interesting consequences. As computer components shrink, they are located closer to one another. This means

AT&T entered the computer market in 1985 with a full line of equipment including the Model 3B2/300 super microcomputer. (Courtesy AT&T Information Systems)

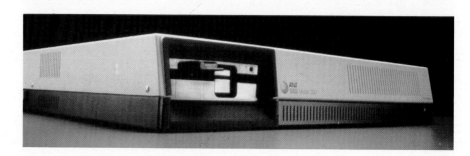

that electrons have shorter distances to travel from one component to another. As distances between components get shorter, they become critical in terms of increasing the speed of computer operations. But the closer the components are to each other, the hotter the computer runs—so much so that very high-speed computers will overheat and destroy their own components. Manufacturers of the largest, most powerful computing systems provide liquid cooling systems to prevent heat build up. This, in turn, reduces molecular activity, which also reduces the electrical resistance of the circuits, thus improving their performance and reliability even further.

The Fruits of Refinement

These technical developments are truly significant, but the key to anticipating the future has us focus on the results of technical change, not on the changes themselves. The results of the last four decades of technical refinement can be divided into four distinct trends concerning cost, availability, power, and applications of computers.

First, the cost of computing has dropped. This is true in two ways: both the purchase price for computers and the cost per unit of calculation have fallen dramatically. The decrease in the latter expense is particularly noteworthy. In 1950, the cost for performing 100,000 multiplications was about $1.25; today it's about five cents. Downward price trends should continue.

Second, thanks to their lower costs, computers are now readily available to almost anyone who would use them. In fact, most of us use computers without knowing it—they are in our wristwatches, our appliances, our automobiles, and our toys.

Third, computers have become more powerful. As you will see in Chapter Five, computer power is a matter of speed and memory capacity. Speed is measured by the number of instructions a computer can execute each second. Howard Aiken's Mark I computer of 1944 could add three 48-digit numbers in one second, a speed of about 300 instructions per second. Computer speeds

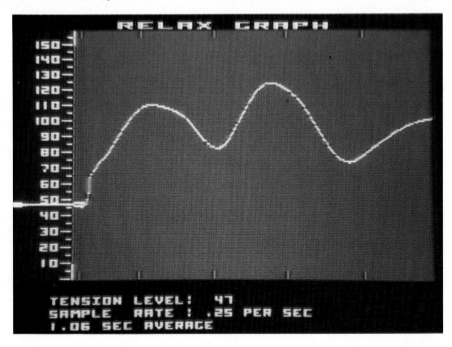

Computers can be used to create graphs and other pictorial data. (Courtesy Synapse Software)

have increased by several orders of magnitude since then and are measured today in millions of instructions per second (MIPS). Powerful computers operate at several hundred MIPS; the most powerful reach speeds of thousands of MIPS, that is, billions of instructions per second.

To illustrate the growth of memory capacity, we like to compare a popular second-generation (late-1950s) computer, the IBM 1401, with a modern microcomputer, the IBM PC AT (for Advanced Technology), introduced in 1984. The 1401 had a maximum internal memory capacity of 16,000 characters. The PC AT, in contrast, has a maximum capacity of more than three million characters, almost 200 times more than the 1401.

Fourth, more applications for computers are always being developed. At first used for governmental, military, and scientific purposes, they now are used for things ranging from guarding homes to helping salespeople be more convincing. They are used to pick mates and have been used to assist in marrying couples when the bride and groom and the minister were geographically separated. They control aircraft and ventures into space. They monitor biofeedback and help people learn how to relax. It would be impossible to compile an exhaustive list of different computer applications today. The number of things for which computers can be used is growing faster than one can write them down, even with a computer.

Generations to Come: The Intelligence Revolution

Taking these developments and trends into account, how do we picture the place of the computer five years from now? Already, the press is heralding the fifth generation of computers. This generation of computers will concentrate on advances in the way computers are used, not on the electronic refinements that characterized the previous four. Rather than processors of data, computers will be intelligent processors of knowledge. Already, a number of computer programs, called expert systems, are widely used. Physicians use computers to help diagnose disease, lawyers plan litigation, and scientists simulate biological growth, astronomical events, and social behavior.

In the future, we will see the dreams of the computer pioneers fulfilled as computers evolve the ability to "learn" from their own experiences. These pioneers saw the computer as a *heuristic* device, that is, as a machine that controls its own behavior based upon the results of its past activities. Today, research in this field, known as *artificial intelligence*, commands hundreds of millions of dollars annually. Far more than passive conduits of information, these intelligent computing machines will link information together, much as the human mind does, to arrive at logical conclusions.

Delicate manufacturing operations that require dust-free environments are often controlled by computer. (Courtesy E. Hartmann/Magnum Photos, Inc.)

The perfection of artificial intelligence devices will require new concepts in processing and memory design. Today, scientists are experimenting with computer processors that are grown biologically rather than manufactured as electronic components. Using living molecules that function as electronic components, a computer with the power of today's largest model would be microscopic in size.

Science fiction, you say? "Certainly, we're not dealing with science fiction in our research," claims James McAlear of Gentronix Laboratories. "Our civilization has the potential for creating a life-form vastly superior to that which has produced it."[21]

The largest memory storage devices available for the micros of today can accommodate up to 400 million characters, enough to store the names and addresses of over four million people. Artificially intelligent computers will require memory capacities far beyond these. Currently, researchers are perfecting a microcomputer storage device that will store three billion characters. That's enough room to store the names and addresses of 30 million people—more than the population of Canada.

Artificially intelligent computers are hardly of the microcomputer class. In Chapter Five, we call them "monster computers" because they tap into data-storage devices thousands of times larger than those available to any micro. Many industry observers expect these fifth-generation computers to be operating realities by the early 1990s.

On a more practical level for most of us, the cost of computing and computers will be much lower five years from now. We're reminded of the ball-point pen, which cost fifteen dollars when it first entered the marketplace in 1948. Today it is a give-away item. We remember pocket calculators selling for several hundred dollars in the early 1970s. Like ball-point pens, those small computers are now given away as promotional items. The drastic decline in computer hardware costs will continue for some time as new technological developments occur. Many of these developments are the by-products of artificial-intelligence research.

Computers will become increasingly available so that, by the turn of the decade, they will be as commonplace as the telephone. Already, communications devices that combine the functions of a television set, telephone, data terminal, and computer are being marketed.

In five years, computers will program themselves. The user will enter the specifications for a job to be done, and the computer will write its own program to do it. A great deal of work has already been done toward this end. Program generators—programs that write other programs—have been available for decades. We expect to see them perfected soon so that the layperson can develop specialized programs to satisfy unique needs.

We expect the large number of proprietary data banks that serve the public today to consolidate into an information utility, much like the telephone system. Like the telephone system, users of the utility will pay only for time spent using it or for the type and amount of information retrieved from it. Also, like the telephone system, electronic communications including electronic mail and teleconferencing will have replaced much of the paper mail system by 1990.

Soldering wires to chips requires a microscope. (Courtesy E. Hartmann/Magnum Photos, Inc.)

Living in the Electronic Future

We close this glance at the future of computers and computing by referring again to John Naisbitt's *Megatrends*, mentioned at the start of this chapter. His predictions forecast more than an age of miraculous new machines. Naisbitt foresees a society in which computers will exercise an ever-increasing influence on human affairs.

Our economy will evolve from a national one to an international one. Keeping track of international business transactions and monetary flow already is done largely by computer systems. The computer's ability to communicate financial data around the world almost instantaneously makes it a powerful force for bringing people closer together. Naisbitt suggests that to be really successful in the near future, you should be skilled in three languages: English, Spanish, and computer. By 1984, more people had become conversant in BASIC, a computer programming language, than spoke Norwegian, Swedish, and Danish combined.[22]

We find particularly significant another trend that has accompanied the high-tech revolution, the so-called high-touch trend toward increased human-to-human contact. The computer offers us the opportunity to tailor working, studying, and shopping arrangements to our personal needs and tastes. Increasing numbers of employees are working at home, using computers to transmit their day's production to the main office. Increasing numbers of students are taking high school and college courses over television and using computers to communicate with their school and instructors. More and more consumers are purchasing goods and services electronically, using computers to send in their orders and payments.

These increases in electronic communication have engendered rising expectations for increases in opportunities to communicate directly with people, as opposed to machines. Electronic funds transfer systems, which relieve us from the need to go to the bank, have disappointed the banking industry. It appears that many prefer visiting a bank if for no other reason than to say hello to someone. People enjoy going to a shopping center. It has become a form of family entertainment that electronic shopping will have a tough time replacing. Taking college courses electronically is fine for some, but most students prefer the campus experience. Going to college is a matter of human contact. For younger students, it is part of the transition to adulthood, as well.

The high-tech revolution can liberate us from traveling to distant job sites, difficulties in communication, and repetitive, manual tasks. But it is the ac-

What generation gap? Throughout the country, groups of children teach groups of senior citizens to use computers. (Courtesy James Balog/Black Star)

companying high-touch revolution that speaks most directly to our new sense of freedom, the freedom to use our newly found time to intensify our human-to-human contacts and seek new experiences for personal and social growth. Therefore, we offer one last prediction: that the high-tech revolution will result in a society more human, not less, more responsive to individual needs, not less, and more personally fulfilling, not less.

The future holds exciting prospects indeed, and the information revolution is still in its infancy. Changes in human and technical activities become revolutions inasmuch as they lead to solutions of the problems of the present and the future. As we cope today with the menace of computer crime, abuses of privacy, and threats of depersonalization, we are learning to apply these solutions to the larger, more complex problems promised by the decades ahead.

Many of these problems, of course, are beyond the exclusive reach of technical solutions. As Professor Joseph Weizenbaum of MIT tells us, "The assertion that all human knowledge is encodable in streams of zeros and ones—philosophically, that's very hard to swallow...There is a whole world of real problems, of human problems, which is essentially ignored."[23]

The future belongs to the problem-solvers, to those people who are able to combine knowledge and action in creative efforts to improve the quality of life for all.

LOOKING AHEAD: THE FOCUS OF THIS BOOK

How does this book fit into your role in the information society? Its title, *Using Computers in an Information Age*, tells the story. We concentrate on how to use computer systems in information processing applications. We take the view that professionals, whether responsible for very small enterprises or members of large corporate organizations, need to understand the role computers play in the business world. We recognize that managers generally do not wish to become computer experts, but, at the same time, we affirm that familiarity with computerized information processing is essential for success.

This text surveys the field of information and data processing. It reviews the needs organizations have for information and the systematic approaches they have developed to satisfy the needs. It also introduces the technical terms and concepts you will need to know to work productively with information-processing professionals and technicians.

You will find here a summary of technical information about computer operations, equipment, and programming. Consider the material here as a general education, as opposed to a technical education, because its goal is to foster computer literacy, not technical expertise.

The major portion of the book emphasizes the applications of computer systems to such tasks as accounting, database management, word processing, information analysis, decision-making, and communications. Most of you who will use computers in your careers will be using them in these areas of application.

This book recognizes that most users of computers will not be programmers, nor will they want to be. Designers of computers, for all their efforts to make computers simple to use, have yet to succeed in making them as simple to use as a telephone, television, or video recorder. As professionals, then, you must have more than a passing acquaintance with the technology of information processing. Having such technical knowledge is essential if you are to make intelligent decisions about the application of computers to business

Garages use computers to diagnose automobiles' ills.
(Courtesy Apple Computer, Inc.)

practices and problems. Technical knowledge will also serve you well as a consumer of information-processing equipment, systems, and services.

Throughout this text, we make little distinction among the various sizes of computers. What is true for large, multi-million dollar computer systems is generally true for desk-top computers costing a few hundred dollars. For most of us, intimate contact with a computer system will involve a microcomputer.

This last point is important because it acknowledges a persistent trend in the field of information processing. Large computer installations, with their large complements of personnel and bureaucratic procedures, have often disappointed management. Today, managers find that many applications can be implemented with microcomputers and commercially produced programs at a fraction of the time and cost required by the corporate data-processing department and its mainframe computer.

> The word is out: Corporate America is embracing personal computing. Backing up that conclusion is a recent survey...[that] produced some startling numbers. Personal computers have found a place in 57 percent of large and small business, and nearly one-third of the executives surveyed use personal computers. The biggest surprise? Of the business personal computer users, 93 percent say the machines met or exceeded their expectations.[24]

Many organizations are linking microcomputer work stations to their large central computers. As a result, more and more managers, and especially their clerical-support staffs, are finding micros atop their desks. Many managers, even though computer literate, still find their professional skills too valuable to be set aside while they work at a computer terminal. Immediate computing responsibilities, then, fall into the hands of others in the manager's office. These people also require skills in applying computers to professional tasks.

You can't, therefore, afford to read this book casually. Information processing is a technical field incorporating concepts from many disciplines: electronics, management, finance, statistics, mathematics, and communications, to name a few. At times, learning the vocabulary will seem like studying a foreign language. If you plan to succeed in your career, plan as well on making the concerted effort needed to succeed with this book.

In addition to your reading, you should have access to a computer. Direct contact is vital for your understanding of information processing, not to mention for curing cyberphobia. It will take time to learn computer skills; there are no shortcuts. A competent secretary working with a word-processing system for the first time, for instance, will require two or three weeks before realizing increased productivity. While studying the machinery and concepts of the information revolution, take time and have patience with yourself as you develop the technical skills that will make you a modern professional.

Wang, long a leader in office automation, has recently entered the general-purpose microcomputer field. (Courtesy Wang Laboratories, Inc.)

SUMMARY

We are in the midst of a revolution comparable to all other major developments in human history. We call it the *information revolution*, and it has two major components. The first is the *information explosion*, in which the amount of data accumulated by scholars and other professionals is increasing exponentially. The information available to humankind is more than doubling every two years. The second is the *high-tech revolution*, which will bring communications and data-processing equipment to every workplace and home. Thanks to the development of small and inexpensive computing devices, the ability to retrieve and process information from all over the world is now available to almost everyone.

Many people who could not conduct their affairs without it, see the information revolution as a blessing. Others fear that society is not ready for it. They voice apprehension about misuses of data banks and invasions of privacy. Still others, as they contemplate the technical changes occurring all around us, suffer from *cyberphobia*, the fear of computers.

There is little doubt that the information revolution will soon affect nearly everyone. As a result, many people are searching out technical information and education, which is available from a number of sources, such as schools and colleges, books and magazines, and computer manufacturers and dealers. The computer and communications industries are working to make their products and systems "user friendly," and manufacturers of microcomputers are giving their products to schools to encourage computer literacy, not to mention future sales.

Much attention today focuses on the information revolution. No wonder: we are on the verge of what many observers call the new American Frontier, the frontier of high technology. Many more add to this the hope that this revolution will result in changes for the better of human society itself.

artificial intelligence *cyberphobia* *information explosion*
computer crime *high-tech revolution* *information revolution*
cybernetics *high-touch trend* *telecommunications*

1. Identify two dangers of the computer revolution.
2. What equipment is necessary to have a complete personal computer system?
3. Define information revolution.
4. Why is there a move toward decentralized decision making in American business?
5. Name three acts that protect citizens against the abuse of data and information.
6. The _____ _____ _____ _____ _____ provides guidelines for government data banks.
7. What is the best way to overcome cyberphobia, the fear of computers?
8. Describe the first four generations of computers.
9. Identify four trends for the future of computers.
10. Characterize the fifth generation of computers.
11. What makes a program artificially intelligent?

1. Prepare a list of ways to use a microcomputer in the home.
2. Prepare a list of ways to use a microcomputer in the office or other business environment.
3. How is the computer used in the field in which you are majoring? (This may require you to visit the library.)
4. For two weeks, keep a journal describing how you interact with computers and the feelings you have about these interactions.
5. Discuss the computer, data bases, and their implications for privacy.
6. What are the implications of the extraordinary influence of middle management on data processing?

(Courtesy Batista-Moon Studio and MacConnection)

The New Profession

Thanks to the information revolution, an entire new profession has evolved over the last 40 years. The new profession requires high technical skills in computer and communication technology, great expertise in analyzing and designing information systems, considerable facility in working with people, and thorough knowledge of business operations. Meeting these requirements is no easy accomplishment. Professionals in the field of information processing combine diverse skills and are in great demand.

If demand is great now, it promises to become even greater in the future. The United States Department of Labor estimates that by 1990 more than 2 million people will be working in the computer field. Annual openings for entry-level positions such as computer programmers are projected to exceed 20,000. For other entry-level positions such as data entry operators and computer operators, more than 45,000 jobs will open each year in the next decade.

A RANGE OF OPPORTUNITIES

Corporate Positions

Besides increases in the number of people employed, the nature of the positions is changing, too. You'd expect that in a field in which technological change is so dramatic. Just a few years ago, computer installations were characterized by mainframe computers and centralized data processing operations. With the proliferation of microcomputers throughout the business world, programmers and analysts with combined experience with mainframes, minis, and micros were being sought in 1984 in four times the numbers than they were just two years earlier.

> The parallel trend toward greater in-house micro utilization is being driven by the relatively low cost, the attraction of personal and ready access, and the fact that many applications adapt well to these systems...we're observing a trend toward more entry level opportunities for individuals well trained in BASIC on the IBM Personal Computer...[25]

Opportunities in corporate and government organizations show every sign of continued growth for the remainder of this century. Forecasting International, Ltd., of Arlington, Virginia, predicts the numbers of workers in the following job areas by the year 2004: 8 million in telemarketing, 1.2 million in computer-aided design, and 1 million in software design. Growth in job titles shows the following annual increases: machine mechanics, 157%; systems analysts, 112.4%; computer operators, 91.7%; service technicians, 86.7%; and computer programmers, 77.2%.[26]

Other Opportunities

Doubtless, employment in large business and government organizations will offer the greatest number of employment opportunities in the immediate future. As computers invade more obscure corners of business and personal life, opportunities for employment will increase in numbers and diversity for more independent occupations.

Salespeople who are technically competent in matters of computer hardware and software are already in great demand in large and small retail stores. The need for skilled sales professionals, for all types and sizes of computer hardware and software products will increase along with the increase in the number of computer systems installed. Indeed, it has long been the case that salespeople for such organizations as IBM, Control Data Corporation, and Digital Equipment Corporation, to name but three, hold positions of considerable prestige, income, and opportunity.

Free-lance programmers, the subject of much attention for the vast fortunes they made during the first half of the 1980s, will continue to do well, particularly in the newer computer application areas. Many will serve as consultants or operate service bureaus to aid computer users, particularly small businesses. A *consultant* is one who helps others make the best use of their computer systems. A *service bureau* provides computer services to organizations that need them. The service bureau provides both the technical expertise and the computer system.

Computer technicians, those who are trained in digital electronics and who are competent to repair and service computer systems and peripheral devices, face enormous opportunities. Indeed, we observe that for all of the press coverage of new developments in computer and information processing technology, little attention has been given to maintenance of computer systems.

Educators who are technically competent and who can prepare others to be so are in great demand. High schools, colleges, and private computer training organizations cannot find enough teachers to do the job of preparing computer users to take best advantage of computer resources. Marvin Cetron, author of "Jobs for the Future: 500 Jobs, Where They'll Be and How to Get Them," points out that

> Our scarcest resource is kids,...(we must be)...preparing students for the jobs of tomorrow, jobs that the U.S. government may not even be currently listing as occupational titles.[27]

Recommending a 40% increase in salaries for teachers of math and science, Cetron voices the concerns of many that competent technical professionals will be attracted to the teaching profession only when it offers the same financial rewards as the industrial and commercial sectors.

Opportunities for the Nonprofessional

One need not be a professional data processor to take advantage of expertise with computers and information systems. Indeed, this book is addressed primarily to those who will not join the profession. We hope that it will persuade you that operational knowledge of microcomputer systems and understanding of the overall information needs of organizations are primary ingredients for success in most business occupations, especially those in management.

> It's remarkable how many decision-making officers use the personal computer. Industry observers assumed that computers would be used mainly by newly minted MBAs and that it should be a while before they showed up in executive suites. From all indications, personal computers are getting there a heck of a lot faster than we anticipated.[28]

Preparing to use computers in business occupations, managerial or otherwise, is a matter of learning how they may be applied to one's specialty. Accountants should have a firm grasp of accounting software. Office and clerical personnel should be skilled in word processing, database management, and communications. Skills in each of the Big Six application programs reviewed in the latter part of this text would seem to be of increasing importance to managers and prospective managers.

All personnel should have hands-on experience using either a microcomputer or a terminal. There seems to be no substitute for actually using a computer for gaining confidence with it. Experienced teachers in the field confirm that the confidence resulting from using computer resources personally does more for increasing understanding and the ability to communicate with professional data processors than any other single aspect of the education process.

QUESTIONS

1. If you were a computer expert, would you prefer working as a professional data processor for a large corporation or in one of the other opportunity areas outlined in this New Professions selection? Why?

2. Among the various occupations or professions you may be considering now, how does the information processing profession compare? Make a list ranking your possible careers in order of preference. What characteristics does each have that makes it attractive to you?

Data and Information Processing: The Essentials

(Courtesy AT&T)

DATA PROCESSING

INFORMATION PROCESSING

PROCESSING CYCLES

TECHNICAL TERMS AND CONCEPTS

Early in 1983, Apple Computers ran a four-page, fold-out advertisement for national distribution in *Time* magazine. It listed one hundred things that users of Apple computers were doing with their machines. Here's a sample:

- Talk with marine animals
- Catch crooks
- Diagnose disease
- Retrieve information
- Design aircraft
- Set type
- Teach CPR
- Help people meditate
- Design running shoes
- Marry people
- Cross-reference the Bible
- Help firemen locate hydrants
- Test beer recipes
- Choose grapes from the best vine
- Set off pyrotechnics
- Control sound systems
- Create sweater patterns
- Test tractor engines
- Maintain anesthesia in surgery
- Analyze Rorschach tests
- Animate movies
- Check spelling
- Detect lies
- Help a chimney sweep run his business

Indeed, it would seem that computers today can do almost anything. The fact is, computers are best at keeping track of things, performing calculations, and presenting information. They are not very good at making decisions, exercising judgement, providing kindness, and a number of other activities that require uniquely human capacities. Because computers are so effective at what they do best, they are particularly useful in business operations. In fact, in 1946 the UNIVAC (Universal Automatic Computer) was designed specifically for commercial applications. The first UNIVAC was installed at the U.S. Bureau of the Census in 1951 and another was installed in 1954 at General Electric's Appliance Park in Kentucky. Within ten years, the Smithsonian Institution exhibited UNIVAC as a relic, thus illustrating the speed, even then, at which the high-tech revolution was moving.

Most computers today are used for commercial and industrial purposes, with another large contingent occupied with the information processing needs of governmental agencies. The commercial and industrial applications are addressed here. Businesses use computers for data processing and information processing functions.

DATA PROCESSING

Data processing is the activity of converting raw facts (data) into information. We are surrounded by raw facts: the number of children attending school; the number of business firms grossing over $10 million per year; the number of telephones in operation; the names of those who contributed to the President's election campaign; and so on. The trick is to assemble raw facts into some useful form. Consider figure 2-1. It shows a scattering of raw facts about prices of securities traded on the New York Stock Exchange.

Even to those initiated in the shorthand used by securities exchanges, the facts shown in figure 2-1 are not very useful. These facts are raw, indeed. Given that each line contains facts about one security, we can make a little more

The New York Stock Exchange uses computers to conduct its daily business.
(Courtesy New York Stock Exchange)

FIGURE 2-1
Raw facts

```
AAPL 341/8 100 7/9 S C
200 S 7.9 ZOS E 211/8
7/9 E OXY 241/8 S 250
E 7/22 195/8 ZOS S
IBM C 1243/8 7/22  S
875/8 HWP C S  7/22
895/8 7/9 S C 100 HWP
7/9 S C 463/4 XRX 75
50 C  DEC 7/9 S 1161/4
DEC 7/22 112 S  C
C 321/2 7/22 AAPL S
GLM E  107/8 7/22 S
S IBM 7/9 50 C 1211/2
200 S 213/4 FLR 7/9 E
7/22 591/2 S CDA  C
7/22 C XRX 46 S
C CDA 7/9 563/8 S 200
S 300 GLM 7/9 113/8 E
211/4 S 7/22 E  FLR
OXY 7/22 E 241/8 S
```

FIGURE 2-2
Classified and formatted data

NAME	DATE	QUANTITY BOUGHT (SOLD)	PRICE	TYPE	PORTFOLIO
AAPL	7/9	100	34 1/8	S	C
ZOS	7/9	200	21 1/8	S	C
OXY	7/9	250	24 1/8	S	E
ZOS	7/22		19 5/8	S	E
IBM	7/22		124 3/8	S	C
HWP	7/22		87 5/8	S	C
HWP	7/9	100	89 5/8	S	C
XRX	7/9	75	46 3/4	S	C
DEC	7/9	50	116 1/4	S	C
DEC	7/22		112	S	C
AAPL	7/22		32 1/2	S	C
GLM	7/22		10 7/8	S	E
IBM	7/9	50	121 1/2	S	C
FLR	7/9	200	21 3/4	S	E
CDA	7/22		59 1/2	S	C
XRX	7/22		46	S	C
CDA	7/9	200	56 3/8	S	C
GLM	7/9	300	11 3/8	S	E
FLR	7/22		21 1/4	S	E
OXY	7/22		24 1/8	S	C

NAME	DATE	QUANTITY BOUGHT (SOLD)	PRICE	TYPE	PORTFOLIO
AAPL	7/9	100	34 1/8	S	C
AAPL	7/22		32 1/2	S	C
CDA	7/22		59 1/2	S	C
CDA	7/9	200	56 3/8	S	C
DEC	7/9	50	116 1/4	S	C
DEC	7/22		112	S	C
FLR	7/9	200	21 3/4	S	E
FLR	7/22		21 1/4	S	E
GLM	7/22		10 7/8	S	E
GLM	7/9	300	11 3/8	S	E
HWP	7/22		87 5/8	S	C
HWP	7/9	100	89 5/8	S	C
IBM	7/22		124 3/8	S	C
IBM	7/9	50	121 1/2	S	C
OXY	7/9	250	24 1/8	S	E
OXY	7/22		24 1/8	S	E
XRX	7/9	75	46 3/4	S	C
XRX	7/22		46	S	C
ZOS	7/9	200	21 1/8	S	E
ZOS	7/22		19 5/8	S	E

FIGURE 2-3
Classified, formatted, and sorted data

sense of figure 2-1 by *classifying* the data. This is done by creating a report showing columns with like data for each security in the appropriate column (see figure 2-2).

That helps. The column headings explain the various data items. Organizing data in this fashion is known as *formatting* it. By classifying and formatting the data, we have improved their usefulness substantially, although the facts have not yet been transformed into information. To make it easier to learn about the activity of a particular security, as identified by its stock symbol, it would help to sort the list alphabetically. Look at figure 2-3.

Much better. It now appears that the data represent prices for each security for each of two days, 7/9 and 7/22. *Sorting* the report by date so 7/9 always appears above 7/22 would improve things even more. If this were done, we could easily ascertain that all of these securities were purchased on 7/9. This would make it easier to compare the purchase price on that date with the price quotations for two weeks later, 7/22.

So far, we've seen classifying, formatting and sorting as valuable data processing techniques which help turn raw facts or raw data into information. While exploring these techniques, we have left unmentioned another important feature of the data with which we are working. This feature is called *encoding*. For the sake of convenience, people use shorthand notation to save space and time. Most people know, for example, that "IBM" stands for "International Business Machines" and they use the initials as a synonym for the full name of the company. The company is also known as Big Blue, in reference to the color scheme it uses for its computer products.

Sometimes encoding schemes are easy to interpret, sometimes not. On occasion, encoding not only saves space and time, but makes information more secure by limiting its understandability to those aware of the scheme. Any encoding scheme must assure that each code is unambiguous in its reference. Thus, "IBM" always refers to International Business Machines and "AAPL" always refers to Apple Computer, Incorporated. The codes used in figure 2-3 and the preceding figures are the official security exchange symbols for the company names of those firms with securities traded on the exchange. Here are the names and codes of the companies whose stocks appear in figure 2-3:

AAPL   Apple Computer, Inc.
CDA   Control Data Corporation
DEC   Digital Equipment Corporation
FLR   Fluor Corporation
GLM   Global Marine, Inc.
HWP   Hewlett-Packard, Inc.
IBM   International Business Machines, Inc.
OXY   Occidental Petroleum, Inc.
XRX   Xerox Corporation
ZOS   Zapata, Inc.

Other codes used in the table are fairly obvious: 7/22 refers to July 22, and 21 3/4, the price on 7/9 for FLR, represents $21.75 per share. Notice how formatting the price quotation by adding a blank between the whole dollar and fractional amount aids in interpretation. The Type codes describe the types of securities: *S* for common stock; *B* for bond; *P* for preferred stock; and so forth. The Portfolio code indicates which of two stock portfolios contains the issue: *C* stands for computers and office equipment; *E* stands for energy equipment, production, and exploration. Figure 2-3, then, is a list of securities held by an investor. Each security is classified by the type of industry in which the company operates, and a separate portfolio of security holdings is kept for each industry.

Encoding, then, is the process of reducing information into shorthand notation for the purpose of saving time and space. *Decoding*, its antonym, is the process of translating the code into meaningful words. Normally, most of us decode unconsciously, understanding the meanings of abbreviations without translating them first.

Data Collecting

Data collecting means gathering original data to be entered into the information system. Gathering the number of hours each week that hourly employees worked is essential to calculating the weekly payroll. Ordinarily, a time card, either prepared manually or with the aid of a time clock, is used for this purpose. The time card is known as the *source document*. The source document is the medium used to enter original data into the information processing system.

Designing source documents is challenging work. Almost all of us have been frustrated while trying to fill out such source documents as forms for insurance claims, passports, loan applications, and merchandise guarantee registrations. Preparation of such documents is known as *forms design* and is a critical aspect of data gathering. A poor source document form usually assures that the data gathered will be unreliable and it certainly slows down the data entry operations.

Other activities associated with the data gathering process include organizing procedures for handling source documents, initiating auditing and data entry or recording activities, and selecting mechanical and electronic devices to facilitate these tasks.

Verification is the process of ascertaining that the data have been entered accurately from the source documents into the information system. For example, if data were entered using a data entry keyboard, the verification process would involve having the data keyed a second time by a different data entry operator. The data entered at the first keying are then compared with those entered at the second. If they are not the same, something is amiss and must be repaired.

Recording

After data have been gathered, they must be recorded. Only then can processing begin. *Recording* is the process of expressing data in a form that is recognizable by either person or machine. Without it, no further data processing is possible. Henry Ford is reputed to have been able to keep most of the records of his Ford Motor Company in his head. Consequently, all of the processing had to take place there too. Modern businesspeople are more likely to use modern data recording and storage techniques.

When data are recorded for the first time, the process is called *origination*. A salesperson taking an order from a customer in the field will often prepare a sales order by preparing a form. This is origination. Recording data is accomplished through the use of paper and pencil, a typewriter (more paper), or devices that record data electronically or in some other machine-readable form. *Machine-readable* means that, once data are recorded, machines may be used for all subsequent data processing functions. In theory, once data are recorded in machine-readable form, they never again have to be entered manually into the data processing system.

Chapter Six describes a variety of data entry, or recording, equipment. Some equipment requires keying in data using a standard typewriter-like keyboard. Other equipment employs optical and electronic scanning devices. Barring Mr. Ford and others like him, of course, recording data in a form that is readable by humans or machines is necessary before any other data processing can take place.

Sorting

Sorting means putting data in order. They may be arranged numerically or alphabetically in ascending or descending order. Arrangement of data in descending order would be desirable if one wished to show the most recent transactions at the top of a list of transactions sorted by date. Newspaper listings of security transactions for the previous day are sorted alphabetically by the name of the company that has issued the security. Sorting follows no logical pattern, only the conventions of how we have memorized the letters of the alphabet—A, B, C,...,X, Y, Z—and of how we order numerals by the value they represent—0, 1, 2,...,8, 9, 10, 11.

Classifying

Unlike sorting, classifying is arranging data according to some logical relationship. The white pages of a telephone directory are sorted alphabetically by the names of telephone subscribers. The yellow pages, in contrast, classify telephone subscribers according to some characteristic. All the paint stores, for example, appear under the letter *P* and all the hobby shops appear under *H*, regardless of their names. To be sure, one could use the white pages to find the telephone numbers of all the hobby shops in town. It would only be a matter of reading every entry in the telephone book from A to Z. Having the data classified according to a particular characteristic makes the task of locating all entries with the desired characteristic, hobby shops in this example, much easier.

Establishing the classification scheme under which one will organize the data, however, is not always so easy. By definition, *classification* is the process of categorizing all items of data according to common characteristics and features. Scientists, for example, classify things as organic (living or having lived) and nonorganic (never having lived). Organic things are categorized further as animal or plant, and then into class, genus, species, and so forth. Businesses find it useful to classify customers by credit standing, type of merchandise most often ordered, geographical location, and volume of business done, to name a few examples. Figure 2-3 shows a classification of securities according to two industry-group portfolios: computers and office equipment versus energy exploration and equipment manufacture. The report, however, is not organized along those classification lines.

Calculating

Calculating is the process of performing mathematical operations on data. It is the only data processing function that produces new data. If our investor (figure 2-3) wished to determine whether or not a profit could be made by selling individual stocks or an entire portfolio, he or she could calculate the difference between the current stock price quotation and the purchase price, multiply that figure by the number of shares of each stock, and then add all of the profits and losses to make the desired determination.

It is the ability to perform calculations quickly that gives computers their reputation as miracle machines. After all, a device that can perform millions of multiplication problems per second commands some attention.

Calculating makes use of all mathematical operations. It also includes the ability to compare data to ascertain if one numerical value is equal to, greater than, or less than another. Comparisons extend to letters of the alphabet and words. Thus the word *under* is ranked greater than the word *over* because *u* comes later (greater) in the alphabet than *o*.

Storing and Retrieving

A box of cancelled checks in the hall closet is a commonplace example of data storage. In response to the accusation that the householder has not paid the rent, the box will be examined with some vigor to locate the cancelled check. This is an example of data retrieval. *Storing* data means recording them on storage media from which they may be retrieved when needed.

Retrieving is the process of locating the stored data and making them available for other processing activities. Paper is the most frequently used data storage device; filing systems designed to locate specific paper records abound in both number and variety. Even though paper remains the most popular data storage device, it is probable that more data are stored electronically than by any other medium. Chapter Ten discusses filing systems used to store and retrieve data in electronic information processing systems.

```
                    MIGHTY MIDGET WIDGET WORKS

                           Sales Report
                  Week Ending September 18, 1984


    TERRITORY:  Eastern
                                         Branch          Territory
    Branch        Salesperson    Sales   Totals          Total

    New York      R. Salver   $13,462.81  [Minor Total]
                  S. Magnum     8,391.69
                  T. Brown     18,925.84  $40,780.34
    Boston        Q. Adams      7,321.92
                  S. Peterson  10,391.46                 [Intermediate
                  D. Ostrach   14,382.61   32,095.99      Total]
    Norfolk       M. Browning   9,461.50
                  N. Long       7,392.85   16,584.35   $ 89,730.68


    TERRITORY:  Western
                                         Branch          Territory
    Branch        Salesperson    Sales   Totals          Total

    Los Angeles   B. Rasmin    13,561.28
                  G. Marshall   6,291.75
                  P. Manning    5,320.92   25,173.95
    San Francisco W. Sinclair  12,391.28
                  Y. Hennig     9,397.63
                  U. Undreth    4,921.82   26,710.73    51,884.68


    TERRITORY:  Central
                                         Branch          Territory
    Branch        Salesperson    Sales   Totals          Total

    Denver        D. Harper     7,822.50
                  G. Macy       9,391.73   17,214.23
    New Orleans   J. Lindsay   13,862.50
                  M. Hamilton   7,931.81
                  B. Smith      4,621.20   26,415.51    43,629.74

    COMPANY TOTAL                                     $185,245.10
                                                      ==========
                                      [Grand Total]
```

FIGURE 2-4
Sales summary report

Summarizing

Summarizing is the process of condensing data. An individual salesperson would be interested in the details and amounts of each sale during a weekly period. The branch sales manager would prefer that same information in summary form, showing the total sales for each salesperson for the same period. The territorial marketing manager would find a summary report of total sales for each branch most useful, and the corporate Vice President of Marketing would most likely opt for a report that shows sales per territory. In this fashion, a summary sales report prepared for the branch manager is summarized with other branch sales reports for the territorial managers, and the territorial sales reports are summarized for the Vice President of Marketing.

The business of summarizing data leads to the use of certain technical terms. Consider figure 2-4. The country is divided into three territories, each of which has two or three branches employing two or three salespeople. The column of figures showing sales per salesperson is known as the *detail listing*. The next column, Branch Totals, shows *minor* totals for each branch. The territory totals are known as *intermediate* totals and the sales total for the entire company is known as the *major,* or *grand,* total.

Communicating

Communicating is the process of transferring information from one place to another. We make a distinction between information and data. *Information* is organized data. Although raw data are communicated occasionally, communication operates primarily on information. Communicating data may take the form of transmitting instrument readings from a spacecraft to the space control center, or inventory counts from the warehouse to the purchasing department. Despite these important forms of data communication, communicating information is the more vital aspect of the function. Information communication takes place after the completion of the other data processing functions we have discussed.

The purpose of communicating is to inform the receiver. The sales report in figure 2-4 shows information resulting from the operation of all of the data processing functions. The data have been sorted to show the most active territory first in the report. They have been classified by territory and by branch, and they have been summarized by performing the calculations needed to show branch, territory, and company totals. They have been recorded on paper which can be stored in a file cabinet. Given an effective filing system, the paper can be retrieved on demand. This report could also be stored electronically and retrieved on demand from its storage device using techniques we will discuss in later chapters.

The report in figure 2-4 was produced by a computer system. It can be replicated at any time simply by causing a computer to display the report on a television screen or to print it again on paper. Alternatively, it can be transmitted to another computer anywhere in the world for viewing or printing. The computer instructions (known as the *programs*) that caused the computer to process the data and produce the reports can be executed again and again with new sets of data to produce subsequent versions of the same reports.

The Apple Lisa Computer, which is no longer manufactured, was one of the first commercially available microcomputers to run several programs simultaneously in separate windows. (Courtesy Apple Computer, Inc.)

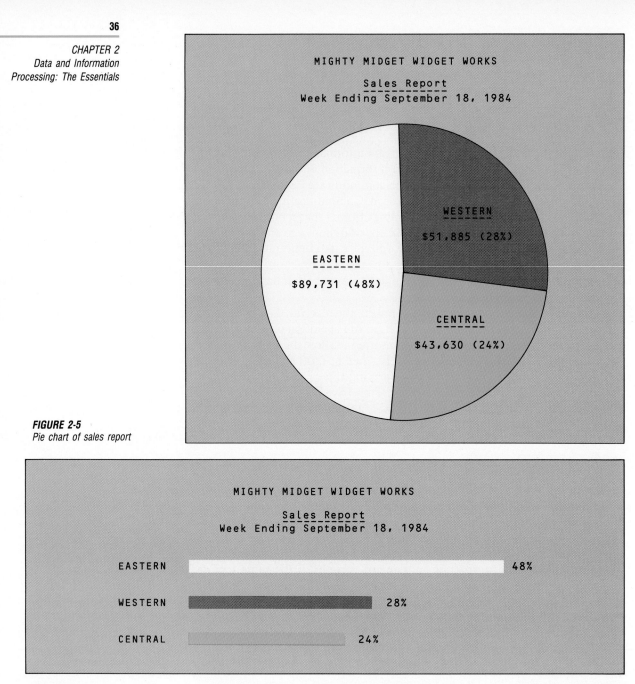

FIGURE 2-5
Pie chart of sales report

FIGURE 2-6
Bar graph of sales report

Earlier in this chapter, we observed that formatting data is an important aspect of the reporting function. The simple expedient of formatting and sorting the raw stock price data (figures 2-1 and 2-2) improved their usefulness considerably. The final reports, following classifying, summarizing and the rest, are even better. The adage has it that a picture is worth a thousand words. This applies to business information as well as other types of information. Consider figures 2-5 and 2-6. They present the same summary information for each territory as figure 2-4, but reporting that information graphically makes the presentation more effective. Figure 2-5 illustrates a *pie chart*; figure 2-6 a *bar graph*. Using computers to prepare graphs to present information is an important aspect of the communicating function. It has its own chapter in this book.

INFORMATION PROCESSING

As we've already observed, there is an important distinction between data and information. Information is data that have been processed using the data processing functions discussed in the previous section. There is also a distinction to be made between *data processing* and *information processing*. In data processing, the various functions apply to raw data. In information processing, these same functions apply to information. Obviously, this is not a rigid distinction because what is data to one person may be information to another. Those who watch the stock exchange ticker, for example, feel pretty well informed about the trading activities of the securities they follow. Those of us who do not spend a lot of time following the ticker view its output as little more than a stream of raw data; we would much prefer that the data be presented in a more informative manner.

Once data have been processed even a little, they become information. Figures 2-2 and 2-3 illustrate this transition. As a result, most activity in information systems amounts to information processing as opposed to data processing. Most needs for processing activities in the business world can be satisfied either by reworking existing information or by acquiring and working with additional information, i.e., data that have already been processed.

The ability to communicate information to those who need it and to process the information as required for its intelligent use is the foundation of the information revolution.

PROCESSING CYCLES

As activities, data processing and information processing are on-going. No sooner has the sales report for the week ending September 18 been delivered to management than another report like it must be prepared for the week ending September 25. Just as the mail must get through, the payroll must get out. The checks that the payroll department delivered last Friday must have their counterparts delivered next Friday. The work force is dynamic: employees resign; new ones are hired; pay raises are granted; and payroll deductions are modified. These and other changes to the payroll procedures have to be implemented. But the data processing functions — sorting, summarizing, calculating, and so forth — are static. For the new payroll, they need only be executed again, making use of current data.

The repetitive nature of data processing is best described in terms of a *processing cycle*: a sequence of procedures or steps required to perform a given task repetitively. Actually, all processing cycles are conceptually the same, that is, they all employ the same elements: origination, input, processing, output, and storage. To illustrate a processing cycle, let us consider an unrealistically simplified payroll cycle.

The payroll system for the Gunga Din Water Service uses two input files, and produces four outputs. The *master file* maintains records for all employees, which show their names, addresses and other vital information, and a running total of their year-to-date (YTD) earnings and withholdings. The *transaction file* contains information for each employee about the current pay period for which the payroll is to be produced, including the number of regular and overtime hours worked. The outputs of the payroll cycle include the paycheck,

```
                    GUNGA DIN WATER SERVICE
                    Payroll Files and Outputs

     MASTER FILE                    TRANSACTIONS FILE
     Employee Name                  Pay Period
     Address                        Regular Hours Worked
     Pay Rate                       Overtime Hours Worked
     S.S. No.                       Employee Name
     YTD Earnings                   S.S. No.
     YTD Withholding
     Date of Employment


     OUTPUT
     Paycheck
     Employee Statement
     Updated Master File
     Payroll Report
```

FIGURE 2-7
Files and output for processing
cycle

an employee pay statement which takes the form of a check stub, an updated master file, and a payroll report which is prepared for each pay period. Figure 2-7 shows the data available in the payroll files and a list of the outputs to be produced during every cycle, that is, once a week.

To keep things manageable, imagine that Gunga Din has only seven employees and that you are responsible for all payroll activities, that is, you are the payroll department. You keep a separate letter-sized payroll card for each employee filed alphabetically in a desk drawer by employee last name. This is the master file. You also keep copies of all the past weekly payroll reports in the same drawer filed by the date of the report.

Here's how the payroll processing cycle works. Each Friday at the close of the work day, the employees fill out time cards by writing their names, Social Security numbers, regular hours worked, and overtime hours worked for the past week. In doing this, the employees are said to be originating the data, and the time card on which they do it is known as the source document. After completing their time cards, the employees give them to you. Your responsibility is to have the checks and other output prepared before Friday of the next week.

Because you keep each of the seven employee pay records (the master file) in order alphabetically, the first thing you do is put the time cards (the transaction file) in the same order, so that you can process through both files alphabetically at the same time. This, of course, is an example of sorting. With only seven employees, having the master and transaction files in the same order is not critical, but if you had seven hundred employees, it would be essential.

Before data from the time cards can be used to calculate employees' pay, they must be verified. In a manual system, such as the one in this example, verification might involve checking the arithmetic and the daily entries on each card to make sure they are accurate and make sense. The supervisor's signature is usually required as another means of verification.

Now you are ready to calculate the pay for each employee. Working sequentially through both files, you pick up an employee's pay rate from the master record and the number of hours worked from the transaction record. You multiply the number of regular hours worked by the pay rate and the number of overtime hours worked by one and one-half the regular pay rate because Gunga Din pays time and one-half for overtime. Then you consult a table to ascertain the amount of withholding tax to deduct for the employee, based on his or her earnings for the week. Following this, you type the paycheck and the check stub, two of the required outputs. Finally, you add the total earned for the week in the year-to-date (YTD) earnings column on the master record for that employee. You do the same for the amount of withholding. Having finished with that employee you proceed to the next, and continue until you have processed all seven. Employees who did not work during the period have no time card or have one with zero hours recorded. Master record cards for these employees are skipped.

After all employee checks have been prepared, you process sequentially through the master file once more to prepare the weekly payroll report, a summary of the current pay period activity, and the YTD totals. Figure 2-8 illustrates the payroll summary report.

In this cycle, you've prepared paychecks, employee pay statements, and a summary payroll report, and you've updated each employee's YTD earnings and withholding information. Next Friday, the cycle will begin again with the origination of time cards for this week and end with the YTD information in the master file being updated by last week's activity.

Figure 2-9 shows a schematic diagram of Gunga Din's payroll procedure. Even this very simple system employs all of the stages of a processing cycle. Origination takes place when the employee fills out the time card. Input occurs when the source documents (time cards) prepared by the workers enter the system for processing. Processing is the performance of the activities — e.g., calculating, recording, and summarizing — required to accomplish the job. Output is manifest in the checks, check stubs, payroll summary report, and updated employee master pay records. Finally, storage is necessary to keep the master records safe until the start of the next cycle.

As you would expect, processing cycles are circular in nature. Figure 2-10 is a general diagram of all processing cycles. Observe that the cyclical aspect of the procedure involves processing and storing. Origination and input provide the system with the raw materials with which to work: raw facts or data. The output is the desired end product.

FIGURE 2-8
Gunga Din payroll report

```
                                    GUNGA DIN WATER SERVICE
                                    PAYROLL SUMMARY REPORT
                                 FOR THE WEEK ENDING OCTOBER 31, 1872


                                     HOURS              EARNINGS            WITHHOLDING         NET EARNINGS

   EMPLOYEE           S.S NUMBER  PAY RATE  REGULAR OVERTIME  REGULAR OVERTIME YEAR TO DATE  WEEK  YEAR TO DATE  WEEK   YEAR TO DATE

   FULTAH FISHER      652 51 9275    4.50    40.00    8.00    180.00   54.00    12321.18    31.25   1562.50    234.00   10758.68
   JULIAN VOUSE       831 40 3627    7.00    40.00    0.00    280.00    0.00    12380.70    48.92   2212.78    280.00   10167.92
   RUEBEN PAINE       462 79 3175    6.00    30.50    0.00    183.00    0.00    10821.82    21.12    948.16    183.00    9873.66
   DANNY DEEVER       833 22 6655    5.50    40.00   10.50    220.00   86.63    16417.22    98.71   4583.29    306.63   11833.93
   JUDY O'GRADY       128 78 4008    9.48    38.00    0.00    360.24    0.00    17849.32    74.38   4198.34    360.24   13650.98
   BABU CHUCKERBUTTY  567 41 8100    7.25    20.00    0.00    145.00    0.00     3010.00    12.81    550.83    145.00    2459.17
   BILL HAWKINS       929 61 4870    3.50    40.00   12.50    140.00   65.63    14837.18   121.72   5002.73    205.63    9834.45

   TOTALS                                  248.50   31.00   1508.24  206.26    87637.42   408.91  19058.63   1714.50   68578.79
```

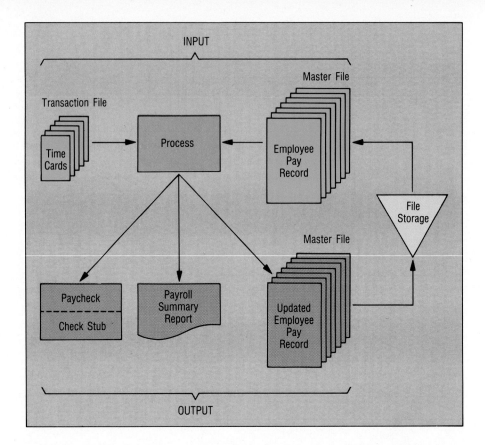

FIGURE 2-9
Gunga Din payroll cycle

What happens when an employee quits Gunga Din, or someone is added to the work force or gets a pay increase? You must update the master file with the new information. Updating, or *file maintenance*, is a cycle in itself, a cycle within a cycle. The term *maintenance* usually means processing a transaction, thereby changing the contents of some normally static field, or adding or deleting records from a normally static master file. Of course, with Gunga Din's simple payroll system, you just add a new employee record to the master file for a new worker, or remove a record from the file for a departed one, probably to be placed in a file of all records for former employees. With a hundred times that number of workers, substantially more elaborate procedures would be necessary.

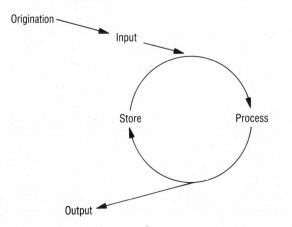

FIGURE 2-10
General processing cycle

Origination and input to the file maintenance cycles are similar to other data entry techniques. A new employee fills out a W–2 form and perhaps a couple of other documents, providing tax status and other information you need to establish the new payroll record. Mr. Din writes you a note explaining that he has just dismissed one of the employees, and another note instructing you to increase a worker's pay rate by seventy-five cents per hour. If workers get regular pay increases, say, every six months, then your file maintenance cycle must include a check of each worker's date of employment. You can see that Gunga Din's payroll system quickly gets complex as these routine adjustments are incorporated into it.

As a rule, processing cycles are complex. Consider a medium-sized distributor of industrial parts with eight sales representatives in the field taking orders from several hundred customers and persuading prospective customers to begin buying from the firm. Preparing a sales order in several copies (origination) and sending it to the marketing department (input) are probably the easiest parts of the system. On receipt of the order, the system must determine if the order is from a new or current customer, if the customer's credit standing will support the order, and if the merchandise ordered is in inventory. Then it must (1) prepare documents to ship the order to the customer; (2) update the customer's account so that the firm knows how much is owed to it by this customer; (3) prepare an invoice to be sent to the customer explaining the status of the order, the amount due for it, and the terms of payment; and (4) prepare monthly statements that detail the amount owed to the firm and give a summary of transactions over the past month, and send the statements to the customers.

That's only part of the story. The merchandise purchased, if taken from inventory, must sooner or later be replaced by sending a purchase order to the manufacturer. If the merchandise is not in inventory, it must be back ordered and the customer must be informed accordingly. Commissions must be calculated for the salesperson based on the amount of the sale, and payment must be made to the shipping firm that delivered the parts.

Procedures that accomplish these tasks are usually referred to as *systems*. In the next chapter, we will examine several basic processing systems found in most business operations.

Mainframe computers often use masses of data stored on magnetic tapes. (Courtesy Sperry Corp.)

In this brief review of business information systems and the basic activities incorporated in them, we have concentrated chiefly on ideas and relationships, and we have defined such terms as origination, summarizing, and formatting. Professionals in information and data processing, like professionals everywhere, have developed their own jargon, a lexicon of terms and abbreviations that have specialized and limited meanings. This section defines some of these.

Record

A *record* is a collection of data or information about someone or something of interest. Police agencies maintain records, sometimes known as "rap sheets," about people with histories of criminal activity. Gunga Din Water Service maintains a payroll record of each of its seven employees. Businesses ordinarily keep records of customers, vendors, inventory, and amounts owed to vendors or suppliers, and about events such as sales volume, bank deposits, and additions to inventory and equipment.

Field

Records are made up of fields. A *field* provides a specific item of data about the subject of a record. Gunga Din's transaction (time card) record of payroll information for each employee, for example, comprises these fields: Pay Period; Regular Hours Worked; Overtime Hours Worked; Name; and Social Security Number. Every record in the transaction file has the same fields because each record will be processed identically to produce the output of the payroll cycle. Thus, all of the records are identical in format. This need not always be the case, but in this simple example, the records are used only for the operation of the payroll system. Other systems, which use the same records for a number of different applications, may combine records of differing formats to produce the desired output.

Character

The term *character* refers to any one of the letters of the alphabet, the ten numerals in the decimal numbering system, and any number of symbols such as ?, %, ,, @, +, and). In data processing work, the blank, like the space between any two words on this page, is *not* the absence of a character. It is a character in its own right. The following two fields, for example, have the same number of characters.

    Field One: 558 7965
    Field Two: 789-2417

File

A *file* is a collection of records. The stack of time cards is called the transaction file, or payroll file. The master file contains a group of records, one for each worker. In most cases, each record in the file has exactly the same format. Figure 2-11 illustrates this consistency.

Name	SS Number	Rate	YTD Earnings	Address	Date
Bill Hawkins					
Babu Chuckerbutty					
Judy O'Grady					
Danny Deever	833 22 6655	00550	1641722	32 Asp, New Delhi	103172
Rueben Paine					
Julian Vouse					
Fultah Fisher					

FIGURE 2-11
Record layout for payroll file

Note that each record in the file is the same; each record contains the same fields, and the length of the fields, which is determined by the number of characters in each field, is consistent. In a manual system, such consistency is not necessary. The person processing the payroll can interpret, within limits, the data in each record, regardless of how they were recorded. Using computers to run the system, however, requires more rigidly enforced conventions: for example, the Social Security number is *always* nine characters (no blanks, slashes, or hyphens) long; the date of employment is always six characters; and the name is always twenty-five characters. Regardless of the length of the data to be recorded in a field, the field length remains as established. Thus the name, Danny Deever, which is only twelve characters long, still uses all of the twenty-five characters allocated for the name field. The remainder of the field is *padded* with blanks to the right, or *low-order*, positions in the field. This is known as *left-justifying* the data. In fields containing numeric data that will be used in calculations, excess character positions are padded with zeros or blanks to the left, or *high-order*, positions. For example, Danny's pay rate of $5.50 per hour, which uses only three of the five available positions, is padded with two zeros. Characters in numeric fields are normally *right-justified*, meaning that they are placed to the far right of the field. In this case, the field contains neither the dollar sign nor the decimal point. The computer will take care of those niceties when reports are prepared.

Airline reservationists work with massive real-time systems that link the world by telephone lines.
(Courtesy United Airlines)

The relationships among records, files, and fields has led to the use of the term *hierarchy of data* which is illustrated in figure 2-12. The top portion of the figure conforms to the manner in which most of us think of files, records, fields, and characters, and is based on the notion that a record looks like a sheet of paper containing two dimensions. A file, of course, is nothing more than a stack of such records. It may be sorted by some *control*, or *key*, field such as Social Security number or employee name. This way of viewing records and files is fine for manual systems and it serves pretty well for electronic systems that employ computers for keeping and processing files.

In electronic processing systems, the data take the form of one-dimensional strings of characters arbitrarily defined into records and files. The middle portion of figure 2-12 moves away from the two-dimensional paper record and considers the file as a stack of one-dimensional character strings called records. The strings of characters in each record are grouped into fields.

The bottom portion of the figure illustrates more accurately how a computer filing system treats the file: as a long string of characters. The definition of records and fields is usually established by the number of characters in each record, which is the sum of the number of characters in each field. There are computer filing systems that employ *variable-length* records by inserting record markers of one kind or another between each record, but a file is still considered a long line of characters.

In the chapter in this text that deals with data base management systems, we will meet the term *data base*. In many ways, a data base can be considered as a group of files, thus extending the concept of the hierarchy of data upward. We leave the discussion of data bases to that chapter.

FIGURE 2-12
Hierarchy of data

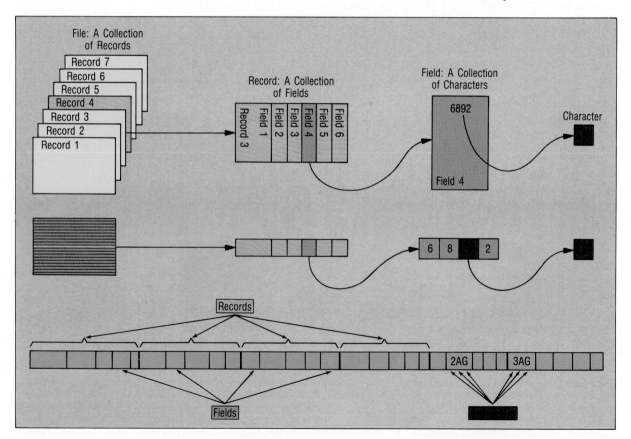

This chapter has reviewed many of the fundamental concepts and activities of data processing and information processing. Because most computers today are used for commercial and industrial purposes, the discussion has focused on those kinds of applications, as will the remainder of this book.

Data processing is the activity of converting raw facts into information. Information is the result of processing data so that they become useful, usually for some decision-making activity. The activities or functions of data processing include the following:

- *Data Collecting.* Gathering original data to be entered into the information system. Collecting new data is often called *origination* and may be recorded on a *source document.*
- *Recording.* Expressing data in some form that is recognizable by person or machine.
- *Sorting.* Arranging data alphabetically or numerically in ascending or descending order.
- *Classifying.* Arranging data according to some logical relationship. Classifying is based on some unifying characteristic of the data items.
- *Calculating.* Performing mathematical operations on data. Calculating produces new data.
- *Storing and retrieving.* Recording data or information on storage media from which they may be retrieved when needed and locating data and making them available for other processing activities.
- *Summarizing.* Condensing data and information.
- *Communicating.* Transferring information and data from one place to another. *Formatting* information and data makes communication more effective.

Information processing makes use of all the functions of data processing, but it uses them to process information, rather than data. Distinguishing between data and information is not a clear-cut proposition because what is data to one person may be information to another.

Almost all data and information processing take place as cyclical activities. A processing cycle is a sequence of procedures or steps required to perform a given task repetitively. A general model of a processing cycle includes five stages:

- *Origination.* Preparing new data to be entered into the processing cycle.
- *Input.* Entering data or information into the processing cycle.
- *Processing.* Exercising all of the data or information processing functions on the entered data. These functions include calculating, sorting, and classifying.
- *Output.* Producing the desired outcome of the processing cycle. The output may take the form of written reports, screen displays and graphical representations, updated data files, or preparation of information to be communicated to others.
- *Storage.* Saving some or all of the results of the processing cycle in a fashion that allows retrieval for subsequent cycles or for use by other data and information processing activities.

Certain technical terms and concepts are consistently employed by those who work in information processing and by those who use its results. These terms are:

- *File.* A collection of records. Each record in the file typically has the same format or layout as all the others.

- *Record.* A collection of data or information about someone or something.

- *Field.* A group of characters that provides a specific item of information about the subject of the record.

- *Character.* Any one of the letters of the alphabet, the ten numerals of the decimal numbering system, and a wide variety of special symbols such as $, #, and *.

KEY TERMS

calculating	file	processing cycle
character	file maintenance	program
classify	formatting	record
communicating	forms design	recording
control field	grand total	sorting
data	information	source document
data processing	information processing	summarizing
data retrieval	input	system
data storage	key field	transaction file
decoding	machine-readable	variable-length record
detail listing	master file	verifying
encoding	origination	
field	output	

REVIEW QUESTIONS

1. Name three types of things that computers do well.
2. Name three types of things that computers do poorly.
3. What are the nine processing functions?
4. Explain the difference between encoding and decoding.
5. What might an automobile repair shop use as a source document for an invoicing system?
6. Your address book is a file. Select one record from the book and identify each field.
7. What is the purpose of communicating?
8. What are the differences between files, records, fields, and characters?
9. How many characters are required to store a ZIP code?
10. How many characters are required to store the price of gasoline in 1984, $1.089? What is the second digit?
11. List five ways you (personally) might use a computer to make your work easier.

THOUGHT QUESTIONS

1. Differentiate between data and information.
2. The monthly household bill-paying cycle is a processing cycle the storage device for which is a checkbook. Describe this processing cycle using as many of the terms from this chapter as possible.
3. Suppose you maintained a phone book at home and one at the office. What are the advantages and disadvantages of this system? How can you use a computer system to maintain the advantages and eliminate the disadvantages? Describe the computer system you would need.

Computers May Be Sexless, But Humans Are Not

(Courtesy Rhiannon Computer Games for Girls/Addison-Wesley Publishing Co.)

To be perfectly accurate from a biological standpoint, machines are sexless things. After all, they do not reproduce themselves sexually; therefore, they cannot be characterized as male or female. To be sure, computers design other computers, undeniably a form of reproduction, but not many of us would go to the movies to watch it happen.

Humans assign human characteristics to inhuman and inanimate objects. Ships are female. Landlubbers condemn themselves as such by calling a ship *it* instead of *she*. Jimmy Doolittle and his crew named the B-25 they flew off the U.S.S. *Hornet* to bomb Tokyo in 1942 "Sweet Rosy O'Grady." Old Glory is feminine: "Long may she wave."

Chances are that feminine pronouns used in referring to aircraft, ships, the national flag, and the nation itself reflect the protective and nurturing nature of motherhood. A student's *alma mater*, which refers to his or her school or its anthem, means fostering mother.

Feminine anthropomorphisms do not always suggest fostering. The word *siren* harks back to Greek mythology. Siren was one of three sea nymphs who, with their singing, enticed sailors to their destruction on rocks. Today, a siren is a warning signal, but most have forgotten its original feminine reference.

The urge to attach feminine or masculine characteristics to inanimate things seems irrepressible. Observe children playing a game against a computer and you'll hear such comments as "Don't do that or he'll do this." The pronoun refers to the computer. Sargon, a popular chess-playing computer program, takes its name from a Mesopotamian king who conquered much of the known civilized world more than 4,000 years ago. Most computer games appeal to masculine interests—action, violence, speed, and risk—and more people use home computers to play games than for any other purpose. Occasionally, a game appeals blatantly to male interests. In 1982, Artworx began marketing one called Strip Poker. The user plays against Melissa or Suzi.*

If computers seem to appeal more to male than to female interests, it's because of how they are used. Aside from games, they are used for business, science, engineering, and other fields typically

*To be fair, we should observe that Artworx later introduced a version of the game in which the user played against male opponents.

dominated by males. School children believe that boys are better in science and math. That's where computers are often used. Parents contribute to the bias by encouraging boys to study those fields and discouraging girls from doing so.[1]

The separation of male and female interests begins with puberty. From then through the mid-twenties social distinction based on sex predominates. Boys are more aggressive than girls and push through to sign up for time in the computer lab. Girls protect their femininity by not competing for room on the sign-up sheet. Computers are machines and boys, not girls, like machines. "By male self selection and female default, the computer center becomes defined as 'male turf'—as socially inappropriate to girls as the boys' locker room."[2]

> The obvious irony is that the computer is intrinsically non-discriminatory.... It provides an opportunity for overcoming any unfair practices to interested users; yet as used in many schools, the computer is the object of selective access that favors some populations at the expense of others.[3]

In high school and college, beginning computer courses typically teach BASIC, a distinctly algorithmic language more akin to math than any other subject. Furthermore, BASIC courses emphasize business and computational applications, again, by tradition, areas of primarily male interest. Some argue that beginning computer courses should use Logo as well as BASIC. Logo, a language that facilitates computer production of graphic images, appeals more to feminine interests. "Our experience has been that there is much less male/female inequity in classes where Logo or other graphic approaches to programming are utilized."[4]

The United States' educational establishment is held by many as a chief hope in reducing sexual bias and stereotyping in all quarters—especially computer science. In 1984, the U.S. Department of Education's Women's Educational Equity Act Program funded a project involving three junior high schools. The project, called the Computer Equity Training Project, developed strategies to combat the propensity for girls to avoid computers. "We hope that by the end of this school year, teachers' efforts will succeed in reversing the computer avoidance tendency on the part of their female students."[5]

Reversing the tendency for females to leave computers to the boys promises important payoffs for the girls. On a national average, women earn about 60 percent as much as do men in the same occupations: "Put another way, the average female college graduate earns about the same income, about $12,000, as the average male high school dropout."[6] This discouraging statistic is not as severe in the management information systems (MIS) field.

> If you were to measure salaries of a class of people, such as women, and determine where they make the most money in their particular positions, I think you'd find it to be in a data processing area.[7]

The MIS field, however, is not without discrimination. Pay for women in MIS positions is 75 to 80 percent of what men earn,[8] higher than the national average, but still inequitable. Said one woman,

> Credibility was always a question, as for six of my eleven years, I was the only woman programmer or analyst on staff. I had to work harder to even approach the "equal" ranks.[9]

Nevertheless, the MIS field promises women rewarding careers and reduced discrimination if for no other reason than qualified personnel in MIS are very difficult to find. Reported Donald Hogan of Hitchcock Publishing Company:

> I had a position open for three months and rather than take a warm body, I just kept passing on it until I saw someone I thought was uniquely qualified. In this particular case, it happened to be a minority.[10]

The time to start preparing women for opportunities in MIS is when they are still in grammar school, as the first part of this Point/Counterpoint selection suggests. Combatting sexual stereotyping must begin at the time when sexual stereotyping begins.

QUESTIONS

1. Clip thirty or forty advertisements from computer magazines. Separate them by whether they appeal more to men or to women or depict males or females in dominant or authoritative positions. What is the ratio of male-centered to female-centered ads?
2. As a high school or junior high school teacher, what would you do to encourage girls to use the school's computer lab?
3. Interview a woman professional in MIS. Promise to keep her identity confidential and write a short report about her experiences with sex bias or the lack of it in her occupation.

Business Information Systems: The Essentials at Work

(Courtesy International Business Machines Corp.)

In 1964, *Time* magazine published these two paragraphs:

> The U.S. Government requires the business community to file no fewer than 5,455 different reports during the year on a variety of subjects, ranging from employment to industrial inventories. Small businessmen complain that they sometimes have to pay the accountants who handle their forms more than they make themselves, and some big businessmen spend as much as $300,000 a year just answering Defense Department questionnaires. In a single year, one Midwestern farm-products company handled 173 different federal forms, ranging in frequency of filing from daily to annually and finally turned in a total of 37,683 reports that involved 48,285 man-hours of work.
>
> When they looked out from under this mountain of paperwork and saw the President of the U.S. turning off unnecessary lights in the White House, a lot of businessmen decided that he was the kind of man who would understand their problem. So they began deluging him with letters asking that the Government also try to economize on the forms and questionnaires that they must deal with (sometimes under pain of stiff penalties). They read their man right. President Johnson has declared war on excessive paperwork for businessmen, promising to simplify reports, and eliminate them when possible....Last week, in fact, Government agencies were busily turning out reams of reports on how to eliminate unnecessary paperwork.[1]

THE NEED FOR INFORMATION

If there were no need for information, there would be no need for automated methods to produce it. Necessity has inspired us to develop the information and data processing techniques we now use in order to produce the required information as economically and quickly as possible. One early such effort took place in 1890 at the U.S. Bureau of the Census. Faced with the prospect of processing the 1890 census data, the Bureau determined that it would take twelve years to get the job done using its customary manual methods. This meant that the Bureau would still be processing 1890 data two years after the 1900 data were gathered. Using an electro-mechanical counting machine he had invented, Herman Hollerith, a statistician with the Bureau, tabulated the census data and completed the work in two and one-half years. Hollerith's census machine used cards into which the census data were recorded as punched holes. In that respect, Hollerith used punched cards to control machinery, much the same as had Joseph Marie Jacquard to control looms some ninety years before.

To best exploit his invention, Hollerith left the Bureau to form a company called the Tabulating Machine Company. Some years and mergers with other companies later, this firm became International Business Machines Corporation. The encoding scheme that Hollerith used to record census data into cards has endured to the present as the familiar (at least to data processing folks) punched-card code or, "IBM card" code, officially known as the Hollerith code, after its inventor.

Despite our best efforts to contrive better and faster ways to produce information, the need for more of it still outpaces us. From the point of view of the business enterprise, needs for information derive from external and internal demands. Requirements to produce reports for the government, for example, represent a substantial component of the total information needs of the firm, as the excerpt at the beginning of this chapter illustrates. Since that article was published, external requirements for information from American businesses have increased, not decreased. Public concern over affirmative ac-

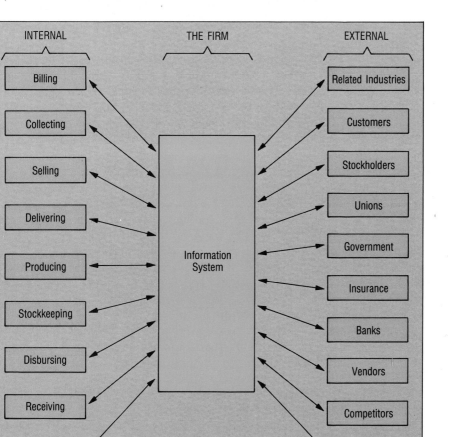

INTERNAL   THE FIRM   EXTERNAL

Billing   Related Industries

Collecting   Customers

Selling   Stockholders

Delivering   Unions

Producing   Information   Government
                   System

Stockkeeping   Insurance

Disbursing   Banks

Receiving   Vendors

Buying   Competitors

                                       World Events

FIGURE 3-1
Need for business information

tion, fair employment practices, environmental protection, and healthy working environments has spawned a number of federal and state regulatory agencies, all requiring information.

Figure 3-1 charts the basic information needs of business enterprises today. These needs derive from both internal and external sources.

This chapter covers the systematic flow of information within business organizations as it is needed to facilitate a number of business activities, both operational and managerial. First, the term *system* is defined and a few general characteristics of systems are reviewed. Because this is a book about using computers for information processing, we will consider information systems generally, and those information systems in which computers play an important, if not a dominant role, specifically.

SYSTEMS

If you're the person in your household who pays the bills, you probably have developed a consistent way to do it. As the bills arrive, you put them in one place to await the time when you are ready to work on them. When that moment arrives, you place your checkbook in front of you, the unpaid bills on your left, and a trash can nearby. You open a bill, throw the envelope away, sort out the advertising matter, and throw it away too. Next, you examine the bill for accuracy, write the check, record the check in the check register, stuff the check and the return portion of the bill in an envelope, seal it, stamp it, and place it on your right. Finally, you mark the stub of the bill as paid and file it among the other paid bills. Then you proceed to the next bill, and continue in this fashion until finished. Perhaps you've discovered that if you open all the bills at once and throw the advertising away, write all the checks at once, do all the stuffing at once, do all the stamping, and then the filing at once, it takes less time. You congratulate yourself on having devised a better bill-paying system.

Actually, however efficient it may be, this is not a system in the formal or official sense of the word. Instead, it is a *procedure*, the most elemental of all the components of a system. Let's say that you persuade two other members of your household to help. One opens and verifies accuracy, you write the check and record it, the other stuffs and files. *Now* you've got a *system*: a set of elements or components working together to achieve a common goal. There are three components in your system: you and your two helpers. Each of the components performs certain procedures—opening envelopes, filing, and so forth. The components of a system need not be human. You could install machines to help, too. The distinction between a system and a procedure is not always clear. It's a matter of one's point of view.

A component of a system may be a system itself, in which case we often call it a *subsystem*. Let's say the opener and verifier drafts another person to help. They divide their work so that one person opens the envelope, sorts the bill from the advertising matter, and passes it on to the other who verifies the bill's accuracy before giving it to you for check writing. These two people make up a subsystem of the bill-paying system.

This leads us to a more complete definition of the term *system*: a group of components, consisting of subsystems or procedures, that work in a coordinated fashion to achieve some objective. The most elemental activity of a system is the procedure, which specifies the detailed functions to be performed. As a component in this system, for example, you receive the bill from the verifier, write the check, update the check register, then pass the check and the bill to the stuffer and filer.

It is the coordination among the components that distinguishes a system from other ways of getting a job done. The components work together. Five individual basketball stars all making individual plays aren't nearly as effective as five players working as a team, that is, as a system. For this reason, systems are said to be *synergistic*, meaning that their total output exceeds the total of the sum of their individual outputs.

The total business enterprise may be, and usually is, described as a nesting of systems and subsystems. In this situation, each system in the firm is defined by a *boundary*, an area that separates it from the other systems, and through which communications with the other systems flow. As we will see later, the accounting system, which is bounded by its purpose of accomplishing accounting tasks, communicates with other systems such as the production and sales systems by receiving from them as input the information needed for accounting, and by providing them with the information they need for producing and selling. The formal channel through which information flows between systems is known as the *interface*. A monthly analysis of production costs represents one interface between the accounting and production systems. The weekly management meeting involving the vice presidents of marketing and personnel represents an interface between those two systems.

Multi-user word processing systems permit many people to use the same database.
(Courtesy Sperry Corp.)

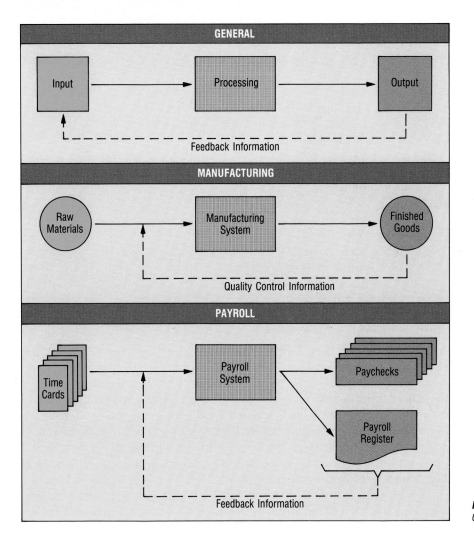

FIGURE 3-2
Operational features of systems

By their nature, systems are cyclical, repetitive. If one sets out to do something just once, it's unlikely that much effort will be spent devising the best system to do it. The payroll system is certainly a good illustration of the cyclical nature of systems. Not all systems, we should observe, are so rigidly tied to repetitive output. The marketing system, for example, sets more singular goals: win 35% of the national market for widgets; or penetrate the high-income consumer market for personalized stationery.

Whether more or less cyclical, all systems are characterized by four features: input, processing, output, and feedback. Figure 3-2 illustrates this idea. The top portion shows the relationship of the four features. Below that we see a manufacturing system with input consisting of raw materials. The materials are processed to produce, as output, the finished goods. The payroll system receives employee time cards as input and processes those data to produce the output of payroll checks and a payroll register.

In every case, there is a *feedback* loop, a formal or informal process by which the output of the system is evaluated and the results of the evaluation are returned to the system as one of the system's inputs. Each of these features deserves further comment.

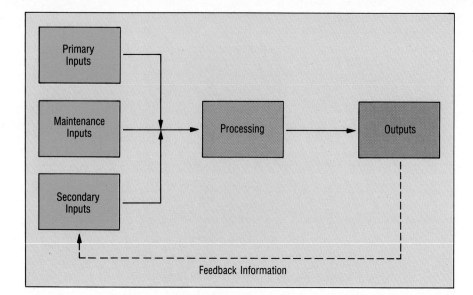

FIGURE 3-3
Types of system inputs

Input

A system's *input* consists of those things it receives from its environment that affect it or are necessary for its operation. By the system's *environment*, we mean anything outside the system that influences its operation. Obviously, the official inputs—raw materials and time cards—influence the manufacturing and payroll systems, and are necessary. Other inputs to these systems, such as changes in income tax withholding laws, product quality requirements, and environmental regulations, also represent inputs into these two systems. We may categorize system inputs into three varieties: primary, secondary, and maintenance, as shown in figure 3-3.

Primary inputs are the basic raw materials of the system: the time cards, the rolled steel, the foodstuffs delivered each day to the restaurant's kitchen, and the stock price quotations transmitted every fifteen minutes to the trader's market analysis computer program. During system analysis, the review of the operation of a system, the primary inputs may be considered to the detriment of the other two types of input. All types of system inputs are equally important and all can affect the system's operation.

Maintenance inputs consist of the deliberate mechanisms established by the organization to maintain the proper operation of the system. The formal feedback loop, such as the quality control department, is a typical example. Regular reviews of a system's operation to assure that it is meeting its objectives in the most effective manner is another way that organizations feed input into a system. Routine updating of information used by the system is yet another. For the payroll system, employee payroll records must often be updated as employees earn promotions, change names, are hired, and so forth.

Secondary inputs come to the system from diverse corners of the system's environment. We've mentioned product quality standards and environmental regulations for the manufacturing system. We should also include societal imperatives concerning working conditions, operational schedules, and business ethics, to name a few.

Other secondary inputs come from within the organization itself and include the personalities and foibles of individuals in the organization, the managerial and operational structure of the organization itself, and employee groups and cliques. The working environment of an organization with a strong, active union, for example, is different from the working environment of an organization that has no union. The environment affects the manner in which the firm's work is carried out.

Processing

Processing refers to the day-to-day work of the system. As we've observed, the most elemental unit of a system is the procedure. How the system goes about its work is the subject of Chapter Four which deals with systems analysis and design. There, we will examine procedures in some detail. For our purposes here, we will consider *processing* to be the execution of the set of procedures required of each component of the system for the successful attainment of the system's objectives.

Output

Output is the result of all of the system's activity: the paychecks, the finished goods, the current projections of stock prices, and so on. As with input, output is manifest in three forms: primary, maintenance, and secondary. The primary output of a system, such as the outputs mentioned in the first sentence of this paragraph, should meet the objectives of the system. Maintenance output contributes to the system's feedback loop and helps to assure that the primary outputs of the system are up to snuff.

Secondary outputs consist of those outputs, intentional or not, that affect the system's environment. Possibly the classic case of a secondary output affecting a system's environment negatively is that of the manufacturing plant that discharges chemicals and hot water into the river next to it.

Secondary outputs do not go unnoticed and can, in fact, be a primary objective of the system. Consider the traveler's check system offered by most banks. Those about to embark on a trip find it prudent to purchase traveler's checks because they offer protection against loss. Safety, then, is the primary output of the system from the viewpoint of the traveler. From the perspective of the banking industry, itself a system, there may be several hundred million dollars worth of unredeemed traveler's checks outstanding at any one time. Interest that the banks earn on this float can be enormous, on the order of millions of dollars each day. Now that's taking secondary output into account with a vengeance.

Feedback

Feedback is the process by which all of the outputs of a system are measured against required standards. Any differences between the standards and the outputs prompts the modification of the inputs or the system itself. Figure 3-4 completes our picture of a general system. The three varieties of input are processed into the three varieties of output. Information about the outputs is then returned to the system as maintenance inputs so that the system, or its primary and secondary inputs, can be modified or controlled to better assure the adequacy of the outputs.

Analysis of feedback information, although not an easy task, is usually abetted by those who benefit or suffer from the output. An underpaid employee will not tarry long before alerting us to a defect in the payroll system. Other

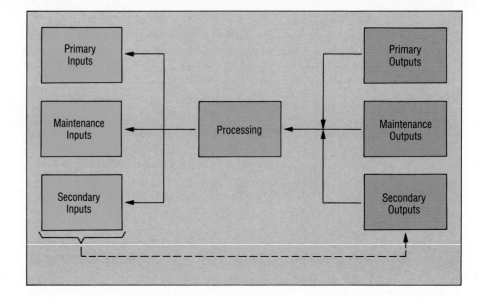

FIGURE 3-4
Total system overview

feedback information for the payroll system includes the degree to which the system produces forms and reports needed for the U.S. Internal Revenue Service, how effectively other payroll deductions are accounted for, and how well payroll costs are allocated to the firm's activity or profit center. Industrial pollution, a secondary output for some manufacturing concerns, attracts public outcries which signal a need to improve a particular industrial system.

We should acknowledge at this point that negative feedback seems to have more effect than positive. When things are going well, why change the system? This view ignores those secondary inputs to a system that try to anticipate the future. Legend has it that Henry Ford once said to his son Edsel, "They (meaning auto buyers) can have any color of car they want, so long as it's black." Henry was paying little attention to the changing tastes of the day (secondary input), and even less to Edsel (another secondary input).

All systems require constant evaluation to assure that they are satisfying current requirements and are preparing for the future as well. Feedback processes that pay as much attention to the secondary outputs and inputs as they do to maintenance outputs and inputs will serve the system better than those that do not.

So that's what a system is all about, at least in a general sense. We've reviewed the basic features of all systems: input, processing, output, and feedback. As a general discussion, we've considered different types of systems. Now it's time to turn to the systems that are of particular interest to those who use computers in business: information systems.

INFORMATION SYSTEMS

An information system is no different than any other system. It has all the features: input, processing, output, and feedback. If we must identify a difference, it lies in the nature of its input and output. Information systems receive, as input, data and information, and produce, as output, information. That's all there is to it. In fact, if we consider an enterprise as a system of subsystems, we can define an *information system* as a subsystem specializing in processing data and information to produce new information. Information, you will recall, is nothing more than data (or information) that is organized in a form that is useful in making decisions.

In doing its work, an information system performs several routine tasks. These include editing and checking data files for accuracy; updating data files, such as a file of data about employees; producing transaction documents, such as a listing of sales for the day (or other time period), called a sales register; and producing routine operational documents and various management reports. In short, an information system uses data and information as raw materials for its processing function which produces useful information.

For the sake of convenience, we break information systems into two types: *operational* information systems which produce the information and documents needed for the routine operations of the organization, and *management* information systems which produce information needed for effective decision making. The distinction is by no means clear. Many decisions must be based upon operational information, and most operations follow management decisions. With those admonitions in mind, we continue with an examination of operational information systems.

Operational Information Systems

Every organization, whether public agency, non-profit, or for-profit, provides goods or services to its clientele and receives income for doing so. The plumbing manufacturer, a for-profit business, produces pipes and fixtures which it sells to its customers. The United Way, a charitable, non-profit organization, supports needy community service agencies and receives income from its donors. Military organizations provide protection and receive income from the citizens of the community. Each of these organizations and all others operate in a cyclical fashion, repeating basic operational activities during the life of the organization. These are called *operating cycles*.

Mission control center at the Johnson Space Laboratory. (Courtesy National Aeronautics and Space Administration)

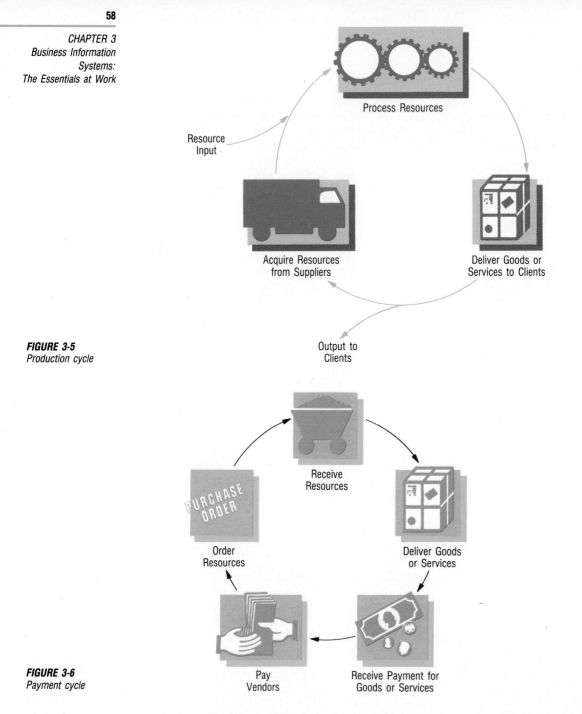

FIGURE 3-5
Production cycle

FIGURE 3-6
Payment cycle

To get started, it helps to consider operating cycles in two parts: the cycle that produces the goods or services and the cycle that reflects the payment for them. Figures 3-5 and 3-6 illustrate these cycles.

In figure 3-5, resources needed to produce the goods and services are acquired from the firm's suppliers. The resources take the forms of raw materials to be manufactured into products; merchandise to be stored, marketed, and sold; labor to be used in the firm's operation; physical facilities, such as a rented warehouse or a store; and services, such as trucking. Money, too, is a resource which organizations buy or rent from financial institutions for use in the firm's operation.

Figure 3-6 shows the cycle of payments. The firm orders resources from suppliers; receives them; delivers them to customers, often after processing them in activities such as manufacturing or storage; receives payment from the customers; and pays the vendors.

Business Operations

A few paragraphs from now, we will review the flow of information within an organization as it goes about its day-to-day work. In this overall picture, we consider the operations of the business to consist of nine key operations: purchasing, receiving, storing, producing, selling, delivering, billing, collecting, and disbursing.

Purchasing.   Purchasing is the activity of ordering resources from suppliers which are known as *vendors*. It makes use of a source document, known as a *purchase order*, which identifies the purchaser, lists the materials or merchandise to be purchased, and specifies quantities and delivery requirements, among other things. Purchasing and buying are synonymous. Firms maintain files containing information about amounts of money owed to vendors. Such files are known as *accounts payable* files.

Receiving.   After the vendor ships the materials or merchandise that have been purchased, the firm receives it. Except in very small organizations, the purchaser usually prepares a document called a *receiving report* which lists all of the items included in the shipment. The person preparing the receiving report does not have a copy of the purchase order; the receiving report is based entirely on the contents of the shipment. Later, the receiving report and the purchase order will be compared to check the shipment's accuracy.

Storing.   Having been received, the materials are stored as inventory until needed for the operations of the business. Information about the received

Many businesses use portable data entry devices to keep track of their inventory. (Courtesy INTERMEC Corp.)

Banks use computers to sort checks. (Courtesy NCR Corp.)

materials is entered into the firm's *inventory file,* a file of information about all material and merchandise being stored.

Producing. Producing modifies the materials in inventory to make them ready for selling to the firm's clients. Turning steel into carving knives, breaking barrels of dishwasher detergent into separate boxes, and detailing a new automobile for delivery to a customer are examples of production. For manufacturing firms, production may often be considered the process of turning raw materials inventory into finished goods inventory. When finished goods inventory for an item for sale falls below desirable quantities, a *production order* is frequently employed to signal the production facility to manufacture more.

Services are also produced. Janitorial firms, dry cleaners, and restaurants all have production activities. By renting funds, financial institutions are producing a service. In order to produce, organizations must purchase materials, labor, and services.

Disbursing. Disbursing means paying for materials, labor, and services purchased. Information about the amount of money owed to vendors of materials and services is kept in a file of *accounts payable* records, one for each vendor. Purchasing labor is a matter of hiring employees. Because employees are paid frequently, there is usually no need to maintain a record of how much is owed to them except when the accounting system closes the books at the end of an accounting period. Vendors, on the other hand, often allow payment some time after the materials were delivered. It is in the best interests of the firm to take advantage of this time period and to keep the money owed for its own use. For this reason, the accounts payable system must alert the disbursing department of the best time to pay the accounts. Because businesses tend to keep track of money more carefully than other assets, they employ a number of documents to control disbursements. These include *vouchers,* or authorizations to pay, *disbursement reports,* and a number of other documents that provide information on cash flow and balances, often on a daily basis.

Selling.   Selling means just what you think it does. For some organizations, selling amounts to waiting for customers to walk into the store and place an order. For others, such as catalog or mail-order businesses, the orders arrive by mail. Many others employ salespeople either on site or in the field. Salespeople who work in the field visit prospective customers and work out ways in which the firm's products or services can best meet the customers' needs. From the data processor's standpoint, sales activity is recorded originally on a source document called a *sales order* or a *customer order.* On it appear the customer's name and address, the materials or services to be purchased by the customer, delivery instructions, and so on.

It should be clear that a sales order for the seller is the same as a purchase order for the buyer. Many sales transactions are initiated at the seller's place of business by the receipt of a purchase order from the customer. Customer orders are not always initially recorded on paper. Increasing numbers of organizations use computer systems in which sales information is entered directly into the order-processing, or order-entry, system.

The order-processing, or order-entry, system consists of a series of subsequent data processing activities, including adjusting and replenishing inventory, billing customers, shipping and updating information in the customers' accounts receivable files.

Delivering.   Delivering means sending purchased materials to the customer. When a sale is made, procedures that cause the purchased goods to be packed and shipped are mobilized. A *shipping order* or *packing slip* accompanies the shipped goods. It describes the content of the shipment and the means of delivery used, refers to the customer's purchase order by date and purchase order number, and indicates, when appropriate, that the material ordered is out of stock and will be *back-ordered,* that is, shipped as soon as available.

Billing.   Except in cash-and-carry businesses, a sales transaction usually is accompanied by a credit transaction, that is, the seller loans the buyer the amount of the purchase for a given period of time. A firm purchases four gross of men's workshirts in assorted sizes and colors. The vendor specifies the *terms of sale* indicating, say, that if the total amount of the purchase is paid in ten days a two percent discount may be taken. Otherwise, the total amount of the purchase is due in thirty days.

The terms of sale, itemization of merchandise shipped or back-ordered, and other information appear on an *invoice.* An invoice is a bill. It tells the customer how much is owed and when payment is due. Usually, the invoice is mailed to the customer through first class mail, and arrives before the shipment. The shipment, you'll recall, is accompanied by the shipping order. The invoice is mailed separately.

Collecting.   When the firm mails the invoice to the customer announcing the shipment of merchandise, it records information about the transaction in the customer's account. The file of customer accounts contains a record for each customer which shows, among other things, the amount owed from prior transactions. This file is known as the *accounts receivable* file. Collecting is the activity of receiving payment from those who owe the firm money: the accounts receivable. Too often, collecting requires more than sitting back and waiting for the funds to roll in. Accounts become delinquent and customers pay slowly, despite the enticement to pay quickly offered by the cash discount.

Figure 3-7 illustrates, in a very simplified form, the basic operating cycles of any business. It combines the cycles shown in figures 3-5 and 3-6, and shows the three major external entities with which the firm must communicate: vendors, customers, and employees. In the interest of simplification, many other external entities such as the owners or stockholders, the government and taxing agencies, and the bank that the firm uses for deposit of operating funds (checks from its customers, for example) and for payment of checks given to vendors and employees are not included in this illustration. Figure 3-7 emphasizes communications with external entities. These communications typically take the form of delivering the forms and documents reviewed in the preceding paragraphs: invoices, shipping orders, and the like.

Although paper is still the most prevalent communication medium, it will eventually yield to the electronic forms of communication that characterize the information revolution. Already, customers can enter orders into their vendors' order-entry system electronically, thus initiating the order-delivery-invoicing-payment cycles with little or no human intervention. Electronic funds transfer systems in which funds from the customer's bank account are automatically transferred to the vendor's account in time to qualify for the cash discount are now in place and their widespread use is inevitable.

Communications within the firm are, if anything, considerably more complex than their external counterparts. The nine basic operations of business cannot be executed independently. The shipping department needs information from the sales department in order to do its job. Similarly, the production department needs information from the warehouse in order to produce finished goods before inventory runs out. Figure 3-8 illustrates the information flow among the firm's internal operations.

Although it is essential for an understanding of the firm's operations, figure 3-8's simplified view of internal communications is like a view of a forest from an aircraft at 30,000 feet. You know the forest is there, but you can't see the paths that lead through it.

Consider the events that must transpire every time a business makes a sale. The customer's purchase order comes into the sales department. The purchase order, considered to be a sales order by our business, is sent to the

FIGURE 3-7
Operating cycles

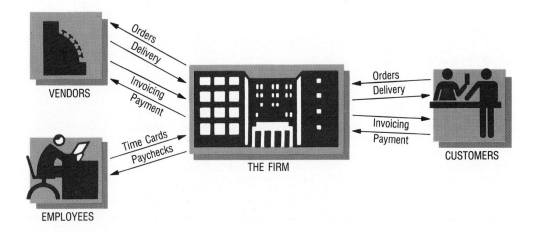

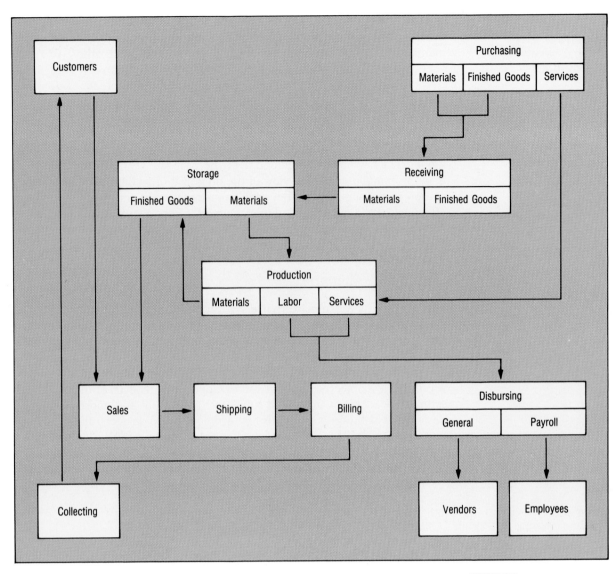

FIGURE 3-8
Intrafirm communications

accounting department which prepares a shipping order after investigating the customer's credit status and other matters, and sends the shipping order to the warehouse.

The warehouse ships the material with the shipping order and returns a copy of the shipping order, with a notation explaining what was actually shipped or back-ordered, to the accounting department. The accounting department then prepares and mails the invoice, and updates the customer's account receivable record by the amount of the sale.

Eventually, the customer returns a check in payment of the invoice. The accounting department records the payment in the accounts receivable record and deposits the check in the firm's bank account. Each month, the accounting department prepares and mails a statement to the customer that lists and summarizes outstanding, or unpaid, invoices.

There is a lot of information flowing among the various operational departments of any business. Paper communications media, thanks to the information revolution, are being replaced by electronic information processing systems, albeit not as quickly as some would like. Part of this relatively new development is the matter of rethinking how the various operating departments or functions in a business organization relate to each other. The concept of individual and fairly autonomous departments responsible for specialized business operations, such as storage, is giving way to broader notions of integrated systems connected by communication channels, such as the one in figure 3-9.

Figure 3-9 combines business operations into subsystems of the total firm based on information needs and especially on information processing techniques that have been developed over the past few years. Figure 3-9, then, is an *information processing* view of the organization, which focuses on information processing systems that enable management to operate the firm more effectively. Because successful management is dependent upon information, it is inevitable that managers' views of their organizations will be affected by the information processing tools most readily available to them.

Accounting Systems

It may come as no surprise that early information processing concentrated heavily on the accounting system. In the past, the accounting system provided management with much of its control information. The accounting system was then, and is now, rigorous and detailed. After all, when calculating profits and taxes, one insists on accuracy. Information from other company sources was much less objective. Market surveys, personnel reports, even production estimates were often laced with subjective judgement and, more often than desirable, wishful thinking. Thus management relied on accounting information as something tangible, an accurate determination of the "bottom line."

Because the accounting system produces a great deal of information about the operation of all of the firm's other systems, it is still considered by many

FIGURE 3-9
Operational information system

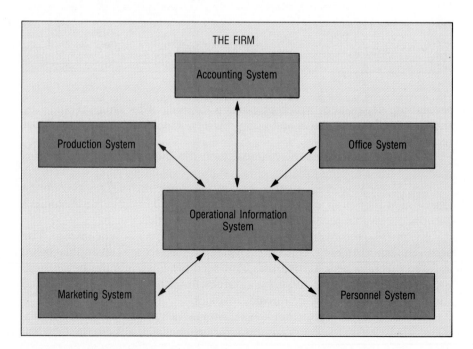

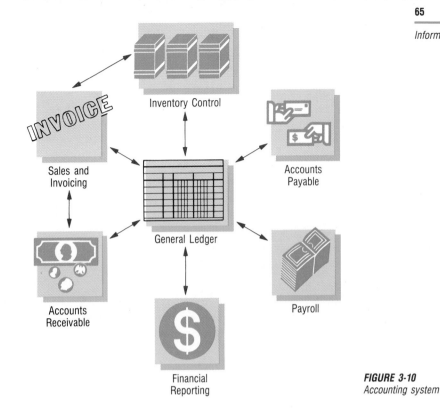

FIGURE 3-10
Accounting system

to be the heart of the total information system. Figure 3-10 shows a typical accounting system and its subsystems.

The heart of the accounting system is the *general ledger subsystem*. In it, all transactions are recorded. An order of supplies from a vendor, for example, in the form of the source document called the purchase order, is recorded in the general ledger. Information from the general ledger is then used to update other subsystems of the accounting system, in this case, the accounts payable and inventory control systems. The lines connecting the subsystems in figure 3-10 represent the flow of information among them. Periodically, the accounting system produces various financial documents such as balance sheets and statements of profit and loss.

Figure 3-10 shows an accounting system comprising six subsystems, all of which are interconnected through the general ledger and some of which are directly connected to each other (e.g., accounts receivable is connected to sales and invoicing). Accounting systems may have more or fewer subsystems, depending upon the needs of the organization. Cash and carry businesses would have little need for an accounts receivable subsystem. Other organizations might add subsystems such as financial modeling or personnel management.

Office Systems

Everybody complains about paperwork. Every business has lots of it, and it is typically performed in the office. Indeed, the office has long functioned as the focal point of communications within the organization and with outside organizations and individuals. Even today, most of this communication

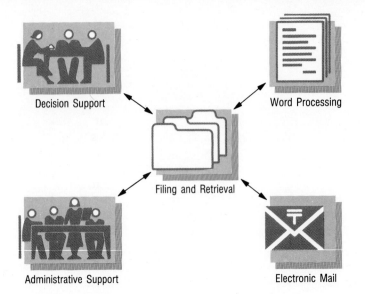

Decision Support

Word Processing

Filing and Retrieval

Administrative Support

Electronic Mail

FIGURE 3-11
Office system

uses paper media. Letters are dictated to secretaries who type them, file a copy or two, and mail the original to the addressee. Memoranda flow to and from offices and individuals within the firm. Telephone messages, often scribbled on small slips of paper, clutter desk tops or climb on spindles. Appointment calendars are kept, meetings are set up and then changed. Old correspondence is dug out of filing cabinets for review and reports are prepared and distributed.

Although electronic techniques are available to accomplish all of these tasks, they have not yet been as widely adopted by organizations as have electronic accounting systems. It is estimated that the total market for automated office equipment is less than ten percent saturated, meaning that efforts to automate office functions will see the same growth in the immediate future as have other systems that are amenable to computerization. In anticipation of this growth, a good deal has been written about *office automation*: the integration of office functions through electronic processes. Although it is still in a state of flux, the concept of the automated office system is evolving toward that illustrated in figure 3-11 as manufacturers develop equipment and processing techniques.

The heart of the automated office system is the record storage and retrieval subsystem, the counterpart of the rooms full of filing cabinets so familiar to all office workers. Because paper media have always been used for communications and record keeping, the first development in automating office procedures was *word processing*. Word processing, in fact, is a double system. It provides techniques for preparing correspondence and documents electronically, without the use of paper. Once the document is letter perfect, the word processing operator, a modern secretary, uses the system to print it on paper.

Of course, if the information is processed electronically before printing, it takes no great leap of imagination to see that it might as well be delivered electronically, too. Networks of computers are enjoying increased use in intrafirm communications (communicating among units *within* the firm) as the next step in automating the office. Similarly, many organizations are investigating interfirm communications (communicating with agencies *outside of* the firm), or *electronic mail*, as a more effective means of transmitting correspondence to entities outside the organization.

Other subsystems of the office system include administrative support systems which facilitate personal, group, and facility scheduling, electronic sign-in and sign-out procedures, and personnel directory services.

Manufacturing Systems

Twenty years ago, one could visit an automobile assembly plant and watch completed cars emerge from the end of the assembly line every sixty seconds or so. Walking down the line, one saw workers attaching parts and subassemblies to each auto as it passed by their work stations.

This was a marvel of production scheduling then as it is today. As the automobile frames move inexorably down the line, the correct parts are delivered to the workers just as each auto moves into the work station. Workers and supervisors can consult computer terminals to ascertain the exact equipment configuration for the car passing by.

The production scheduling system must be supported by subsystems that deliver the required materials, parts, and subassemblies to the worker at the time needed to put the automobiles together. Figure 3-12 illustrates how subsystems for product design, equipment control, inventory control, and cost accounting relate to the production scheduling system to form the overall manufacturing system.

The inventory control and cost accounting subsystems are closely related to the accounting system illustrated in figure 3-10. The product design and equipment control subsystems have made a remarkable technological breakthrough for manufacturing industries. Known as CAD/CAM systems, short for Computer-Aided Design and Computer-Aided Manufacturing, these systems permit designers to develop products by drawing them on a television monitor using an electronic pen. Then, using various product and material specifications, the CAD/CAM system completes the specifications of the items, prints up drawings if they are needed, and produces control tapes which are used to govern the operation of the equipment used to manufacture the part.

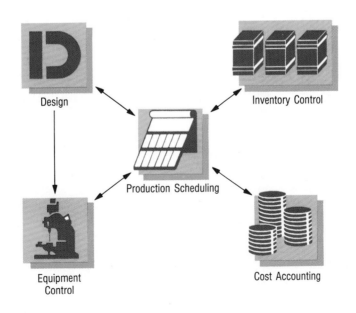

Design

Inventory Control

Production Scheduling

Equipment Control

Cost Accounting

FIGURE 3-12
Manufacturing system

Modern data processing techniques now make use of production control and scheduling methods that in the past were too cumbersome or esoteric, but that are usable now even by small manufacturing organizations. As we shall see in Chapter Sixteen, such methods are at the fingertips of the small job-shop operator, as well as the giant oil refinery.

Marketing Systems

The pattern for marketing systems follows the same lines as that for other operational systems in the enterprise. The marketing system's purpose is to assure that the firm's outputs are presented to potential customers in the most effective manner. To do this, marketing people must consider the nature of the product (output) and how it satisfies customer needs, the most effective pricing policies, the best distribution channels to use in moving the product to the place where customers will be most likely to purchase it, and the optimum promotion and advertising campaign to acquaint potential customers with the product and its availability.

Marketing professionals call these things the four Ps: Product, Price, Place, and Promotion. A marketing system, whether large or small, must include each of these components. Figure 3-13 illustrates the conceptual nature of a marketing system. In addition to those components taking care of the four Ps, another component, marketing research, is shown.

The information system must provide marketing managers with information about slow product lines, product profitability, and advertising effectiveness, to mention a few. Mail-order firms make heavy use of computers for order processing and merchandise shipping. Considerable interest is being shown systems that enable consumers to purchase products through their home computer systems as well as through computer systems installed in supermarkets.

FIGURE 3-13
Marketing system

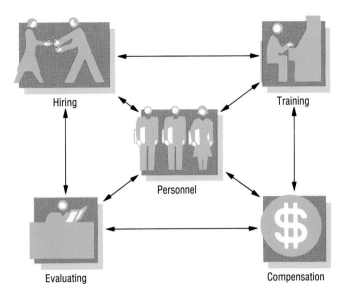

Hiring

Training

Personnel

Evaluating

Compensation

FIGURE 3-14
Personnel system

Personnel Systems

Personnel systems look after the people in the organization. They recruit needed talent, train employees, evaluate employees' performance, and determine compensation rates, sometimes in negotiation with employee collective bargaining organizations. Figure 3-14 illustrates a typical personnel system.

Computers' contributions to personnel systems are typically found in the record-keeping aspects of the operation. For example, large organizations, especially public agencies, must produce many analyses of the characteristics of their work force for government agencies responsible for enforcing affirmative action and fair employment practices. Even organizations of modest size must maintain information about each employee. Computerized personnel systems help keep track of it all.

To conclude this review of operational information systems, we should emphasize that the size of the organization does not determine the functions that each of these systems must perform. Every business, in one form or another, has accounting, producing, marketing, personnel, and office systems.

In small firms, one person may be responsible for several systems, possibly all in the case of sole proprietorships. In every case, the emphasis here is on the information that must flow within each system in order for it to operate effectively. Depending on the needs of the organization, the more-or-less separate systems making up the entire enterprise will vary. Taxicab operators have dispatch systems to keep track of available cabs. Hotels have room reservation systems. Airlines employ massive data banks for seat reservation purposes.

MANAGEMENT INFORMATION SYSTEMS

The distinction between operational information systems and management information systems lies more in their emphasis than in their operation. Operational information systems produce information needed to keep the basic business operations working effectively and efficiently. Management information systems produce information needed for effective and efficient decision making. Of course, operational information is needed by decision makers, too. The two types of information systems are not distinct in the real world, only in textbooks which try to separate things in order to make them easier to understand.

Our definition of a *management information system* goes like this: the system that stores and retrieves information and data, processes them, and presents them to management as information to be used in making decisions. Figure 3-15 shows the idea. The management information system provides managers with information that best serves management functions.

Management and Decision Making

Management Functions

Management information systems must serve the basic functions of management. Depending on which management textbook you consult, these functions vary. Most, however, agree that they include planning, organizing, staffing, directing, and controlling. Planning looks to the future and requires information that helps predict it. Organizing assembles the firm's resources—physical assets, personnel, financial assets, and other resources—to meet its objectives. Staffing recruits and assigns the best personnel to do the work. Directing, sometimes considered synonymous with leading, coordinates all of the firm's activities and resources. Controlling evaluates the results and makes adjustments accordingly. All of these functions require information. It is the job of the management information system to provide it.

Figure 3-16 shows how the operational information system and the management information system work together. Obviously, decisions must be made concerning not only day-to-day operations, but also broader areas. The firm's information system, comprised of its operational and management aspects, gives the decision makers the information they need.

FIGURE 3-15
Management information system

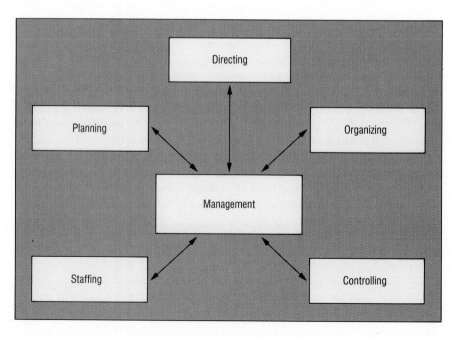

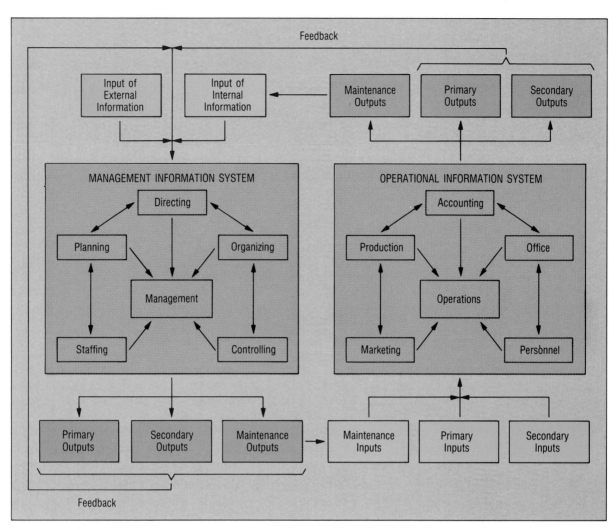

FIGURE 3-16
Relationship between operational and management information systems

Decision Making

Not all managers make the same level of decisions. Some are caught up in the day-to-day operations of producing the services and goods the firm offers to its clientele. Others devote their energies to working out how best to meet the changing conditions of the marketplace and how to maximize the economic security and influence of the organization. It is convenient and not at all pejorative to place managers at three levels of decision making: *top* management, *middle* management, and *lower* management.

Lower management makes *operational* decisions and relies most heavily on the operational information system. These decisions involve such things as how best to schedule the flow of orders through a job-shop manufacturing operation, or how best to schedule the flight attendants for an airline, or how to chase down customers who don't pay their bills promptly. Information needed for these kinds of decisions is detailed, technical, and is closely related to the operational information system.

Middle management makes *tactical* decisions such as how to conduct an advertising campaign to woo customers away from the competition. Apple Computer's announcement in early 1984 of the Macintosh computer, for example, involved a multi-page advertising spread in *Time* magazine, and clever,

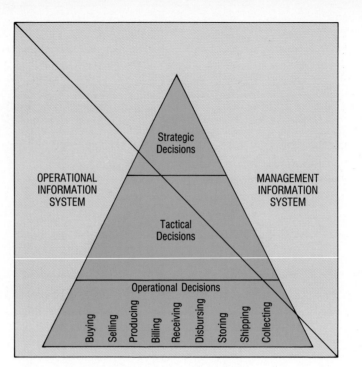

FIGURE 3-17
Decision pyramid and
information systems

if not insulting, comparisons of that computer with its major rival, the IBM PC, during the Super Bowl game. That was a tactic designed to improve Apple's share of the personal computer market.

Decisions to introduce a new product like the IBM PC or the Apple Macintosh are good examples of *strategic* decisions. These are made by top managers who rely heavily on the management information system to provide the external data and information needed to arrive at the best strategy to accomplish the organization's goals.

These types of decisions—operational, tactical, and strategic—lead to what some observers call the pyramid of decisions, with strategic at the top and operational at the base. This is shown in figure 3-17. Overlaying the pyramid is a diagram showing the contributions of the management information system and the operational information system to the three levels of decision making. You can see that operational decisions, at the base of the pyramid, are served primarily by the operational information system, while strategic decisions rely primarily on the management information system. In between, tactical decisions, which are made by middle managers, benefit from information from both the operational and management information systems.

Characteristics of Management Information Systems

Centralized, Hierarchical, and Decentralized

Let's consider some specific characteristics of management information systems. These systems must be designed to best fit the way the organization operates. Some organizations are very centralized, with most, if not all, decision-making power vested in a central decision-making body. Others are decentralized, with decision-making power distributed among those most closely related to the details of the operation. Management information systems serving these diverse organizational patterns must, perforce, be diverse.

Centralized decision-making processes demand centralized information systems. Organizations adhering to the centralized pattern have a centralized data processing department or division which gathers data and information into a centralized data bank and distributes it to those who need it for the decisions they must make.

Hierarchical organizations position decision makers, that is, managers, at various levels in the organization. Management information systems to serve these levels must be implemented by computer power at each level, under the independent control of the decision makers at that level.

Decentralized organizations require decentralized computer service, so that each independent decision-making unit can control its own data and information processing activities.

The degree to which an organization is geographically dispersed often affects the manner in which its information services are organized. Companies in which all of the physical facilities are at one location are prone to use centralized information processing techniques. Other companies that have widely dispersed facilities, often disperse information processing services too.

A recent development in management information systems practice recognizes that although independent decision making offers great advantages to the organization, centralization of information and data also has its advantages. Management information systems that try to take both of these factors into account are known as *distributed information systems*, or *DIS*. A distributed information system is one in which the decision maker acts independently, but does so with the full advantage of a centralized data bank. The computer power needed to process data and information from the data bank is distributed to the decision makers so that each can perform the analytical and processing tasks independently.

Distribution-oriented and Storage-oriented Systems

A *distribution-oriented* system is one whose operations emphasize the transmission of information to users throughout the organization. Its antithesis, the *storage-oriented* system, is more concerned with the safekeeping of data and information. An airline seat registration system is an example of the former, a library an example of the latter.

Computer operators control mainframe computers from a console. (Courtesy Sperry Corp.)

Sizes of Management Information Systems

Authorities in the field consider an information system with access to 50,000 or fewer records to be small. Medium-sized systems manage up to a million records. Large systems work with more than a million records.

Data-Retrieval and Document-Retrieval Systems

Data-retrieval systems store data and information using various storage devices. The digital computer, with its peripheral devices, forms an important element in such systems. Data-retrieval systems retrieve and manipulate data to produce information needed by the organization. Reports are prepared and computer terminal displays, among other things, are generated as a result of the data processing activities of these systems.

Document-retrieval systems store forms and documents, as opposed to data and information, and retrieve the documents without manipulating the data or information they contain. Computers are used in these systems to locate and retrieve entire documents, rather than to manipulate data.

Producers of automated
information systems foresee the
day of the paperless office.
(Courtesy AT&T Information
Systems)

Batch and Real-Time Processing

Information systems use batch and real-time processing techniques. *Batch* processing gathers transactions and saves them for processing all at once. A savings and loan company, for example, might process all of the deposits and withdrawals for the day after the close of business. That way, all of the routine updating of depositors' accounts is done at one time. As a consequence, the status of each account is ordinarily one day behind.

Real-time processing, by contrast, processes transactions as they occur. Thus the *electronic fund transfer* system, *EFT*, updates checking accounts at the moment of purchase, so that the accounts are always current. Airline seat reservation systems are the oldest example of real-time transaction processing, having been operational since the introduction of American Airlines' SABRE system in the late 1950s.

Real-time systems form the basis for a type of management information system known as the decision support system. Such systems depend upon immediate or near-immediate access to data stored in the computer system. The ability to retrieve information immediately is often called an *on-line query system*. As its name suggests, an on-line query system is connected to the computer system all of the time, meaning that a manager or other individual may retrieve data and information from the computer whenever they are needed.

Types of Reports

One way or another, all information systems prepare reports. These reports may be printed on paper, recorded on microfilm, displayed on video terminals, transmitted to other computers, or communicated by any of a host of other options. Typically, information systems produce four varieties of reports.

Monitoring, or *scheduled, reports* present information about the regular, day-to-day operations of the firm. Accounts receivable analyses, daily production reports, inventory status reports, and familiar financial statements such as the balance sheet and income statement are examples of monitoring reports.

Triggered reports, often called *exception reports*, are produced when something out of the ordinary takes place. An extraordinary number of depositors withdraw all of their savings in a day, or a sharp increase in rejected parts from a manufacturing process are examples of events that generate triggered reports. Exception reports most often signal that something is wrong and needs direct managerial attention, but that is not always the case. An investment management system would produce an exception report if the price of a security exceeded an established amount, indicating that the time to sell the security had arrived.

Demand reports are prepared to meet a specific need, usually on a one-time basis. The marketing manager may require an analysis of customers' purchasing decisions broken down by geographical area, or the purchasing officer may need an analysis of transportation costs associated with all of the firm's vendors.

Planning reports help management predict the future. For that reason, they are sometimes known as *predictive reports*. Often as not, data for planning reports originate outside of the organization, and may result from market research studies, industry reports, government publications, and the like. Ford Motor Company's decision to produce the Mustang, for example, resulted from extensive research that showed that a large number of youthful, moderately affluent people wanted a car with a youthful, vigorous, sporty image.

We should observe that these report categories are not always distinct in practice. A demand report for one organization may be a scheduled report for another. A scheduled report may become unscheduled, that is, its regular production may be suspended with the thought that if it is needed, it can be ordered. This converts it into a demand report.

Manual and Automated Systems

We finish this summary of the characteristics of a management information system by observing, again, that much of today's data processing is done using manual techniques. Letters are written in longhand, or are typed manually. Most businesses, because they are small, keep their records in the proprietor's head, with reenforcement provided by notes scribbled on scraps of paper. The operator of a small gardening service who buys supplies and equipment from three or four vendors doesn't need an automated accounting system and couldn't care less about retrieving information from a data bank halfway across the country. Automated information systems, that is, those that use computers, have not and will not replace manual systems categorically.

As the cost of computerized information systems continues to drop, however, more and more manual systems in small businesses will be replaced by those serviced by a computer. Already, thousands of households have found it expedient to use a personal computer for household financial accounting: keeping checking account records, preparing income tax returns, and so forth. Increasing numbers of small businesses now find using a computer to be an expeditious way of taking care of routine data processing chores. Sending statements to thirty or forty customers is a lot easier with a computer than doing the job by hand. For a modest investment, this operation becomes much less burdensome. Moreover, once purchased, it takes little time to recognize that the computer can not only perform that task, but many others as well.

A mouse increases computer efficiency. (Courtesy Apple Computer, Inc.)

Information Systems as a Management Tool

Managers view the information system as a tool that provides them with the information they need to do their jobs. As workers are said to be only as good as their tools, so too might managers be described.

As a tool, the management information system assists in decision making. Good decisions require good information. If the information system is good, its product—that is the information it provides—is accurate, timely, complete, and concise. Although these words need little explanation, their meaning is so obvious that their importance is often overlooked. Inaccurate information is often worse than no information at all. Incomplete information almost invariably leads to erroneous conclusions. Information that is not concise obscures the essentials, a condition known as *information overload.* Information that is too late is no help. The toughest job of the information system, in the final analysis, is not pumping out facts and figures, but producing information that has these four characteristics and that is easy to maintain.

MIS and DSS

The Management Information System

For several decades, forward-thinking managers have dreamed of a "total management information system," or MIS. If the means of communication within the various systems in the firm is electronic, why not connect all these systems electronically? That way, everyone in the organization can retrieve needed information from all of the firm's operations. Figure 3-18 illustrates how this would look.

Figure 3-18 shows a totally integrated management information system in which all of the organization's data and information is available to all who would use it. The information, contained in a central data bank, is under the control of the data processing department, which makes sense because consistency in data file organization and retrieval techniques makes for more efficient operations.

MIS sees most of the firm's information stored in a central data bank, as in figure 3-18. In this situation, all of the firm's systems are connected to a central computer system, providing information and data which are stored in a data base, or file system. Users, employing work stations that include a typewriter-like keyboard, a display screen, and other input-output devices, are able to retrieve data and enter new data, including changes, into the data bank. The collection of input-output devices at each work station is known as a *terminal.* In this system, all of the computer programs that serve the user terminals and the various information processing systems (accounting, manufacturing, etc.) are prepared and maintained by the firm's data processing department. Thus, the users have no ability to write their own programs, design their own output reports, or modify the data files in any way.

This situation has led to management's disenchantment with MIS. Operating departments believe themselves to be too dependent upon the data processing department. This department, because of the overall complexity of the total MIS, the conflicting requirements of the operating department users, and the inefficiencies caused by complex personnel (not to mention personal) relationships is hard pressed to serve the users effectively.

Decision Support Systems

Today, the concept of the total MIS has yielded to an idea that puts more control of data and information processing activities in the hands of the decision makers. This idea is known as the *decision support system,* or DSS. The object of a DSS is to maintain data and information files in consistent formats so as to facilitate just the sort of access to information that MIS advocates

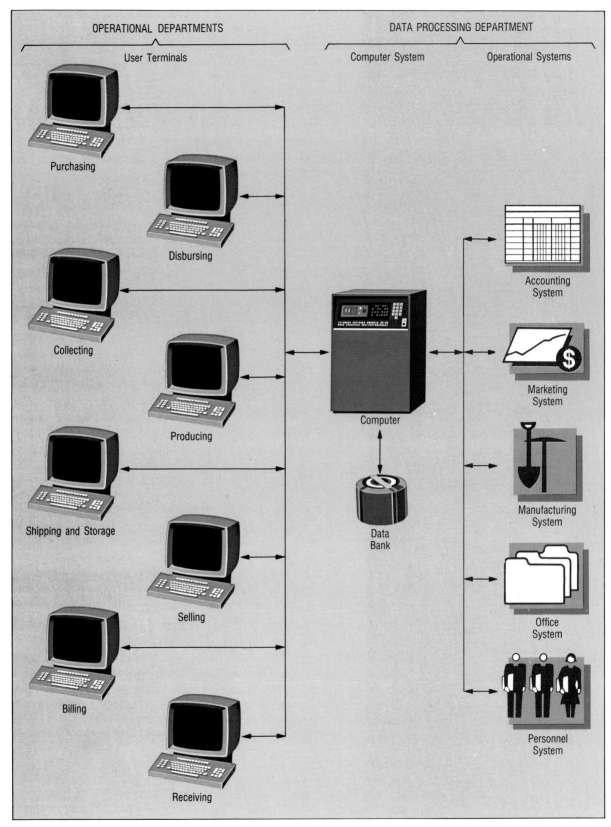

FIGURE 3-18
Management information system

promised. The set of files thus maintained is known as the *data base* or the *model base*.

A DSS consists of a set of computer programs and the hardware that allow decision makers to arrange data and information from various sources in ways that best serve their individual organizational responsibilities. The system employs a set of programs to analyze the data retrieved from the data base, and an interface, that is, a communication network in which a computer operated directly by decision makers is connected to the data base.

Figure 3-19 shows quite a different arrangement than that in figure 3-18. In figure 3-19, systems such as accounting, office, and production operate within the context of a network of operating department computer systems, each of which has its own data base, computer, and necessary input-output devices. Each department has wide latitude in designing and executing its own applications, and each has access to information from the systems being used by all the other departments.

Because each operating terminal has an independent computer, the terminal is said to be "intelligent," as opposed to the "dumb" terminals employed by the MIS shown in figure 3-18. In this situation, responsibility for writing computer programs to meet the needs of individual departments falls largely on the departments themselves. The role of the data processing department consists chiefly of assuring that equipment and file formats are compatible, so that everyone can use the system.

The system illustrated in figure 3-19 is often called a *distributed data processing* system because the facility to process data with a computer is distributed to the users, as opposed to being centralized. Such systems may be served by a central computer, as shown in the lower box in the illustration, in which case the central computer is known as a *slave* to the other computers.

Microcomputers and Decision Support Systems

Microcomputers used in decision support systems have proven to be a very economical way to provide managers with independent computing power and access to needed data and information. Because of this independence, the use of microcomputers has given managers a psychological boost by freeing them from the need to deal with a central data processing department in order to get service from the mainframe computer. A number of firms have developed comprehensive DSS systems which link mainframe computing and data base management power with individual processing stations. Managers who use DSS are often most enthusiastic. Bob Dembner, financial vice president for Omega Watch Company, for example, had this to say:

> I have been in finance for 18 years, and I've never come across a tool as valuable as a decision support system...I used to spend 150 hours preparing the budget for our company in Switzerland. Now the DSS does that for me in four minutes. And if I need to change one item—or 800 items—it gives me a new budget in four minutes. I'll never again be without it.[2]

The Information Center

Distributing computing power throughout the organization to the decision makers implies that they know how to use it. The very notion of distributed data processing and DSS requires managers and their support staffs to acquire new skills, namely computing skills. The growth of DSS as an information system *modus operandi* is accompanied by the growth of an organizational

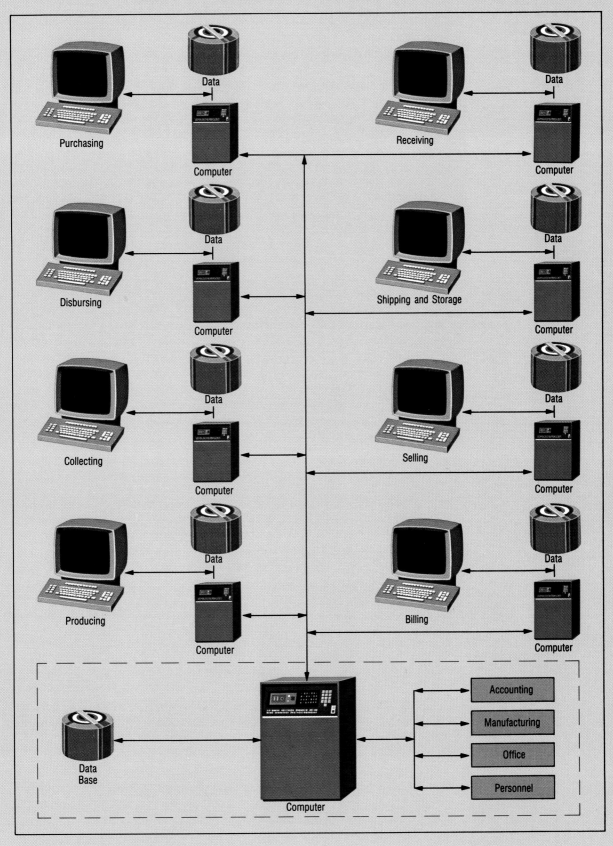

FIGURE 3-19 Decision support system

department that helps managers come up to speed. These are known as *information centers* or *strategic information centers*.

An information center is a place in the organization where managers and other end users can go to learn how to use computer resources to get and process the data and information they need. The information center encourages users to solve their own problems, quite a contrast to the MIS idea in which all of the problems were to have been solved by data processing department technicians. The center coordinates and controls user services, devices, and programs in order to assure consistency throughout the organization.

The information center considers information and data to be assets, just like all the other assets the organization has at its command. Managing these assets so that they will be most useful to decision makers is a task that requires considerable skill in dealing with people, as well as with technical details. This responsibility is being met through the introduction of the *chief information officers*, or *CIO*, a relatively new organizational position that assures the availability of necessary resources to decision makers.

Not a little of the growth of the information center has been in response to, if not defense from, individual managers who have been frustrated in their attempts to get needed service from the MIS department, and who have resorted to buying their own computers. It's too easy to acquire computing power for the office. A half-hour's visit to a computer store takes care of that. The trouble is, if all managers make their own decisions about individual computers and software, there is little chance for communication among these diverse systems. The chief information officer monitors this important matter.

In addition, because information is such an enormously valuable asset, the CIO is in an enormously powerful position. Martin Goetz, senior vice president of Applied Data Research observes that:

> Large organizations are trying to get a handle on all of the requests for information. Plus, with personal computers invading the office, there's more and more end-users saying 'I want certain kinds of data.' Because of that, there arises the question of having some kind of 'traffic cop' saying who can and who can't have the data—the chief information officer. The possibility for abuse of a position like that is tremendous. If a post like that got out of hand, the person in it could ruin the whole company through loss and theft of information.[3]

The great value of information to the organization gives rise to systems that deliver the information to those who need it. Modern information systems are a far cry from the systems used just a few decades ago.

SUMMARY

Information needs for modern businesses derive from internal and external demands. External demands come from such sources as stockholders, financial institutions, and government agencies. Internal demands are governed by the firm's operating characteristics. Modern management practice requires that operating information, as well as information from external sources, be immediately available to decision makers. Business information systems not only facilitate the day-to-day operation of the firm, but also provide information to those who need it to make intelligent decisions.

A *system*, whether it produces a manufactured product, does bookkeeping, or performs any other task, is a group of components consisting of *subsystems* and procedures that work in a coordinated fashion to achieve some objective(s). A *procedure*, which is the most elemental activity of a system, specifies the detailed functions to be performed. Every system consists of four parts: input, processing, output, and feedback.

Input refers to those things that the system receives from its environment that are necessary to, or affect its operation. System inputs come in three varieties: *primary*, the basic raw materials of the system; *maintenance*, the mechanisms used to maintain the effective operation of the system; and *secondary*, all the other inputs, internal or external, to the organization that affect the system's operation.

Output is the result of all the system's activity. It, too, has three forms: *primary*, *maintenance*, and *secondary*. Primary outputs are the official outputs of the system. Secondary outputs represent outputs, whether or not deliberate, that the system produces in addition to its main purpose. Maintenance outputs are used to assess the effectiveness of the system.

The *feedback* function uses maintenance outputs and other information from the system's environment to keep it operating effectively.

An *information system* is a system specializing in processing data and information to produce information as its output. The information serves the organization in two basic fashions: in its day-to-day operations, and as input to managerial and decision-making processes.

Business operations are cyclical in nature, repeating operational steps as the work of the firm proceeds. As the cycles operate, they require information and data flow among the operational units of the firm. All businesses are characterized by nine operational functions:

- *Purchasing*—locating and acquiring resources.
- *Receiving*—taking receipt of the resources purchased.
- *Storing*—keeping materials available for use by the firm.
- *Producing*—combining materials and labor to produce goods or services.
- *Selling*—promoting the firm's goods or services to its customers and potential customers.
- *Delivering*—moving the goods or services sold to the customer.
- *Billing*—telling customers how much is owed to the firm for the goods or services bought from it.
- *Collecting*—receiving the funds owed.
- *Disbursing*—paying vendors and others for goods and services received.

The firm can be considered as a system of interrelated systems: the accounting system, the manufacturing system, the office system, the marketing system, and the personnel system. When linked together, these systems make it possible to implement a *management information system*. Management information systems produce data and information needed by those who perform management functions (planning, organizing, staffing, directing, and controlling) for the organization. They also provide information for decision makers. Organizations require three types of decisions: *operational decisions* which are made by *low-level managers*; *tactical decisions* which are made by *middle managers*; and *strategic decisions* which are made by *top managers*.

Management information systems can be described by various characteristics. These include their degree of *centralization*, whether they are *distribution-* or *storage-oriented*; their *size*, whether they retrieve and process *data*, as opposed to retrieving *documents*; whether they use *batch* or *real-time* processing; the types of reports (*triggered*, *monitoring*, *demand*, and *planning*) they prepare; and the degree to which they use *manual* or *automated* processing techniques.

Because the information system is vital as a management tool, much effort has been spent in trying to perfect it. The *total management information system*, or *MIS*, centralizes all data and information storage, retrieval, and processing activities. Because of difficulties in implementing MIS and because of the availability of microcomputers, the concept of MIS has been replaced by the *decision support system*, or *DSS*. The distinction between MIS and DSS is primarily one of technique: MIS employs central processing and file storage; DSS distributes control of these matters to the users.

DSSs, then, employ *distributed data processing* techniques in which managers and other users of the information system are in direct control of processing activities. The DSS, because it requires its users to be at least moderately competent in the use of computers, gives rise to the *information center*, a place where users can learn how best to take advantage of the information processing resources available to them. The information center and the DSS are managed by a new position, the *chief information officer*, or *CIO*.

KEY TERMS

batch processing	exception report	planning report
chief information officer	information center	predictive report
data base	information system	procedure
data retrieval system	input	processing
decision support system (DSS)	interface	real-time processing
	management information system (MIS)	scheduled report
demand report		strategic information center
distributed data processing	model base	subsystem
distributed information system	monitoring report	system
	on-line query system	system environment
document retrieval system	operating cycle	terminal
	operational information system	text processing
electronic fund transfer		triggered report

REVIEW QUESTIONS

1. List at least four uses of the computer for information flow within a business.
2. List the nine key operations of a business.
3. What is the most prevalent business communication medium?
4. What will be the most prevalent business communication medium in the electronic age?
5. Identify two systems that require little or no human intervention between a business and its client.
6. Describe a firm in terms of systems and subsystems.
7. With which subsystems did early data processing products concern themselves? Why?
8. What is the heart of an office automation system?
9. List the two aspects of word processing.
10. What is the main disadvantage of MIS?
11. Describe a distributed data processing system.

THOUGHT QUESTIONS

1. Explain the differences and similarities between MIS and DSS. Which is more likely to include a distributed data processing system?
2. What are the implications of a changeover from paper as the principal medium of business communication to electronic signals?
3. Briefly describe the operating cycle of a flower shop.
4. Discuss the three types of decisions, who makes them, and what types of information systems are used for each. Give examples as appropriate.

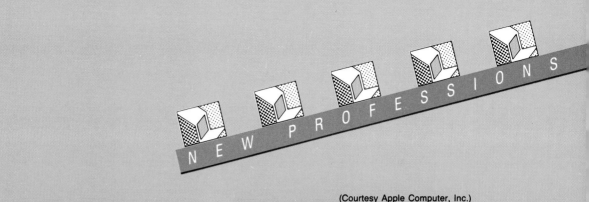

(Courtesy Apple Computer, Inc.)

Careers in the New Profession

A career in the information processing profession can be very exciting. There is no field that offers the excitement and challenge of change like this one. If you like waking in the morning with the question What'll happen to me today?, you'll like information processing. If you like the satisfaction that comes with conquering difficult technical concepts and putting them to work for the benefit of an organization or an individual, if you like to see the knowledge you've gained through hours of study made obsolete overnight, if you like learning new things, if you like teaching new things to others, then this is your field.

Because of the technical requirements of the work, it's unlikely that many information processing executives get their jobs without first working through the ranks of programming, systems analysis, supervisory, and operational management positions:

The ideal manager that companies seem to be searching for right now typically has an undergraduate technical degree and a postgraduate degree in business which expands his or her perspective.[4]

For most, the technical degree will be one in computer science. The postgraduate degree will be in management or business administration. Debra Zahay, now a consultant for Interactive Data Corporation, a division of Chicago's Chase Manhattan Bank tells of her experiences:

...I was a newly minted MBA with a concentration in MIS and a burning desire to save the world from information overflow. It took about six months of working in a large corporate data processing organization for me to realize that I needed some technical background if I was going to be more than a casual participant in the systems development process.

83

Zahay asked for a programming assignment just to gain technical experience. Seven months after starting she felt comfortable enough with her assignment to begin helping other programmers. In fifteen months, "...people began asking me questions. I had arrived."[5]

Entry-level Positions

For those just starting out, or for those who already have experience in the business world and wish to enter the field, there are but a limited number of entry-level positions. Zehay's experience illustrates the need for technical backgrounds. Entry-level positions typically include jobs as programmers, computer operators, and data entry operators, but some variations may be found in different organizations.

Programmers

Preparation for a first job as a programmer usually includes collegiate work in computer science or data processing with courses in such specific programming languages as COBOL, Assembly language, PL/1, ADA, and BASIC. Employers seek experienced programmers when they can find them, but ordinarily they cannot and will hire recent graduates with degrees in computer science or management information systems.

Beyond having academic preparation, programmers need additional skills. These include the ability to understand the logical flow of a program and the logical steps required to solve a problem. Programmers need the ability to ask questions and to make the best use of the resources available, resources that seldom seem adequate. Technical skill in one or more programming languages is essential, to be sure, but the programmer's most important asset is problem-solving ability.

Computer Operators

Academic preparation for positions as computer operators is not as demanding as for computer programmers. A high school diploma is required, augmented by additional specialized training. Often, companies will provide on-the-job training to promising personnel. Trade schools and community colleges often offer short courses for those who wish to apply for this position.

Many enter the information processing field as computer operators, attend college on a part-time basis while working and find that, thanks to their experience as operators and their tenure with their employer, they make attractive candidates for computer programming openings.

Data Entry Operators

The training requirements for data entry operators is fairly short, given basic keyboarding skills. Both proprietary trade schools and community colleges offer courses in preparation for these positions. The courses range in length from 8 to 15 weeks. Most positions require typing skills of 30 words per minute or greater.

Because data entry operators can frequently find part-time and temporary jobs, these positions are favorites with those who are working their way through a collegiate computer science curriculum. They offer direct experience in the field, which is important for finding jobs as programmers, and they also provide an opportunity to prove oneself to an organization, thus paving the way for promotion.

QUESTION

1. What programs or courses does your school or college offer that prepare students for the entry-level positions described above?

System Development: Building Information Systems

(Courtesy Gould AMI Semiconductors, 1985)

Computerizing requires you to look at your business in a new way. Rather than concentrating on customers, products, prices and so on, you emphasize data, forms, information flows, procedures and so on. This approach is necessary because computers are subordinate parts of information systems. This effort is usually productive, because a better information system (that is, an automated system) normally improves business results.[1]

The author of these remarks to small business people was encouraging them to recognize that a manager's job, even in a small organization, requires more attention to figuring out how things could best be done than toward actually doing them. It's the bane of anyone who strikes out as an expert craftsman, consultant, caterer, gardener, or whatever. As the business grows, it becomes more complex, requiring more complex systems to take care of its operational and management information needs.

IMPERATIVES FOR SYSTEM CHANGE

Most managers would like information systems to take care of themselves. They don't. As with anything complex, systems require attention lest they deteriorate. They need attention because of the many forces working both inside and outside the firm that require flexibility in the way things get done. That, after all, is really the essence of a system: a way to get something done.

Forces that press for modifications in the way things are done are many. *Technological changes*, as we saw in Chapter One, rank high as a cause of change in the way organizations go about their work. Inasmuch as this is a book about computers, we are most interested in the technical developments in using computers for data and information processing tasks. As computers change, so do the ways in which we use them. We've observed in Chapters One and Three how the availability of microcomputers to management personnel has forced organizations to revise their thinking about management information systems. The small computers meet productivity needs in a very cost-effective manner. There could be no more striking an example of how technological changes require changes in information systems.

Social changes also force organizations to adopt new information processing techniques. Legislation, such as the Freedom of Information Act, the Code of Fair Information Practices, and the Privacy Act, set controls and guidelines concerning data banks holding information about private citizens. These laws illustrate how social concern can force commercial and government organizations to mend their ways. Another social change, particularly pertinent here, is the acceptance of computers as an office tool by both managers and other office workers. Offices that do not employ this resource are considered backward by growing numbers of white collar workers who, consequently, prefer employment elsewhere. The same can be said of many manufacturing and service operations.

Economic changes represent perhaps the most obvious force for systems change. "If the way we've been doing things in the past reduces profits, then we'd better change" is an argument that cannot be easily denied. Changes in government fiscal policy to award substantial tax credits to firms that purchase computer equipment, for example, has done much to spur organizations to revise their information systems.

Internal changes, the last we'll consider in this list, include appointments of new management personnel, mergers with other firms, company reorganizations, and last, but not least, the ambitions of those in the business who wish to make a mark for themselves by inaugurating better ways of doing things.

FIGURE 4-1
Systems development cycle

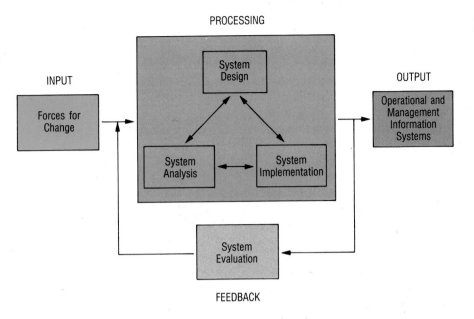

THE SYSTEM DEVELOPMENT CYCLE

So systems must change. Our purpose here is to outline orderly methods to design and effect such changes. The activity of changing systems is systematic in that it is a repetitive process. No sooner is a new or revised system put into operation, than forces for change demand continued review of its effectiveness. Thus all systems, especially information systems, have a life cycle. The process of reviewing and modifying them, called the *system development cycle*, is cyclical also. It is illustrated in figure 4-1.

Figure 4-1 shows the familiar input-processing-output-feedback pattern of all systems. In system development, the system's output consists of various organizational information systems. Its input comes from the forces for change that we've reviewed. The feedback component helps evaluate the effectiveness of the systems in terms of changing requirements.

The processing component has three parts: *system analysis, system design*, and *system implementation*. None of these parts can be considered apart from the other two. In fact, the process of system development is a closely interlinked set of activities. Nevertheless, it helps to categorize the parts into these broad areas to better understand what's going on. Later in this chapter, we will investigate the phases of the system development cycle in detail. First, let's look at the tools used by systems analysts and designers.

TOOLS OF SYSTEMS ANALYSIS AND DESIGN

Systems analysts work with the overall objectives of a system and the minute details of how each element or procedure of the system operates. They must consider the flow of information among the operating units of the organization and how the organization's parts fit together with the system being analyzed or designed. The distinction between system analysis and system design is more one of purpose than of technique. In fact, analysts do both kinds of work. *System analysis* refers to studying what a system does and why it should be done. *System design* involves studying how a system actually works or should work.

In order for analysis and design work to be useful, it must be expressed in a way that others can understand. One way to do this is to write it in formal English. To simplify things, analysts draw pictures, diagrams, and charts. These are the tools of the trade.

To get started, let's reconsider the bill-paying system in Chapter Three. You'll recall that bills were paid when those responsible for paying them decided to take on the task. Let's expand this system into one that is more typical of a business operation. In businesses, such an operation would be known as an *accounts payable* application and would function as part of the overall accounting system. Accounts payable, or A/P as it's usually called, is an elaborate system in most businesses. It maintains records of amounts due to the firm's vendors and assures that they are paid on time.

As bills, called invoices, are received from the firm's vendors, they are checked against purchase orders sent to the vendors and against receiving reports prepared by the firm's receiving department to assure that the invoices are correct. Thus approved for payment, the amount due each vendor is recorded in the accounts payable records so that the firm knows how much it owes to each. Then the invoices are filed according to the day they must be paid in order to qualify for cash discounts the vendors offer for prompt remittance.

Each day, the disbursing department pulls all the bills to be paid that day from the file, writes and mails the checks, and records the payments in the check register and the accounts payable records. The paid invoices are then filed in case they are needed later for reference.

Writing it like this is one way to describe this small system. Expressing it in pictorial form is usually more effective. Analysts use a number of pictorial forms and diagrams to analyze how systems operate. We turn to these now.

Computers are used to check stock and maintain inventory records at many firms. (Courtesy INTERMEC Corp.)

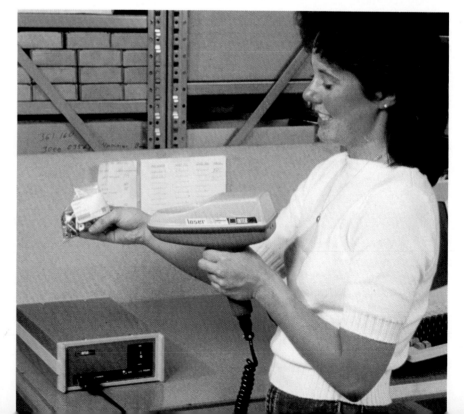

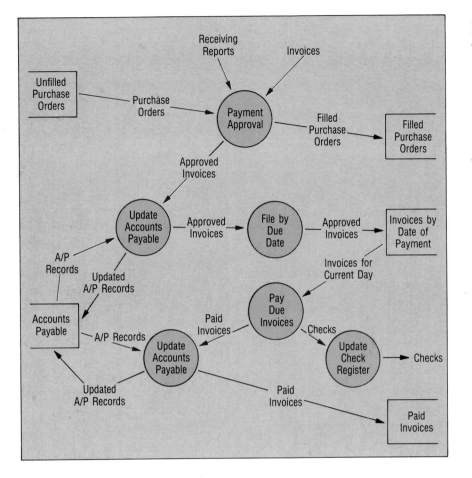

FIGURE 4-2
Data flow diagram of accounts
payable system

Data Flow Diagrams

Figure 4-2 shows a *data flow diagram* of the accounts payable system. A data flow diagram, known as a DFD, conforms to generally accepted conventions for its symbols. The open-ended rectangle, frequently referred to as a *sink*, signifies a file or other source of information. The circle, often called a *bubble*, is an operation or a procedure that transforms data. The arrows, which represent the flow of data, carry annotations to show exactly the data that are flowing. DFDs also conform to the *sandwich* principle, which means that every bubble falls between at least two data flow arrows.

System Flowcharts

DFDs concentrate on the flow of data and the general operations in using data to produce desired results. *System flowcharts* do much the same thing, but also suggest the specific data processing techniques to be employed. We cannot tell from figure 4-2 how the operations in the bubbles are carried out. System flowcharts provide more detail about that important matter. For that reason, system flowcharts are often said to be *device-specific*, particularly if automated processing techniques are employed. Figure 4-3 shows a system flowchart for our accounts payable application.

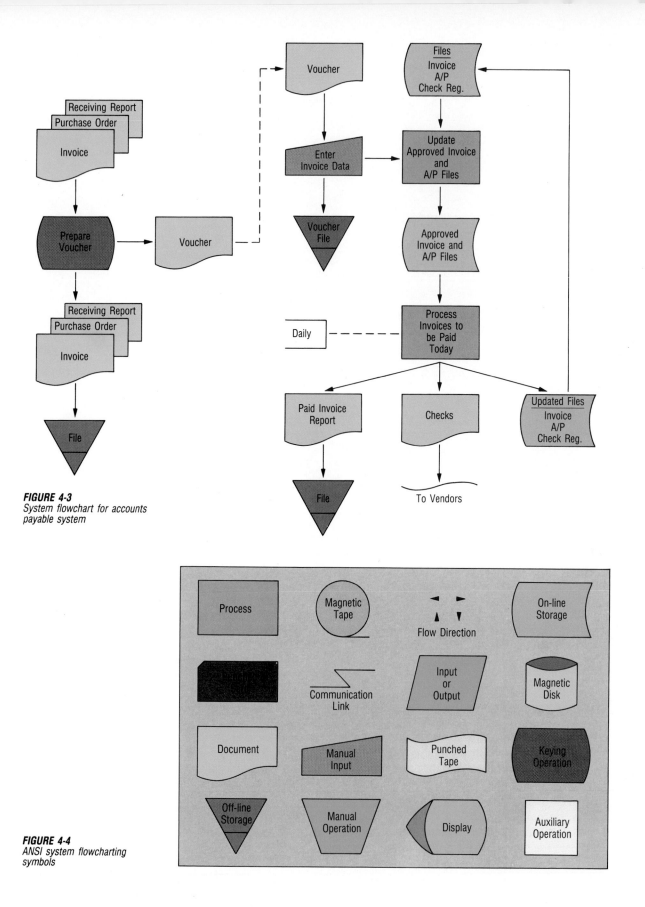

FIGURE 4-3
System flowchart for accounts payable system

FIGURE 4-4
ANSI system flowcharting symbols

Receiving Report
Purchase Order
Invoice

Prepare Voucher

Voucher

Receiving Report
Purchase Order
Invoice

File

Voucher

Enter Invoice Data

Voucher File

Files
Invoice
A/P
Check Reg.

Update Approved Invoice and A/P Files

Approved Invoice and A/P Files

Daily

Process Invoices to be Paid Today

Paid Invoice Report

Checks

Updated Files
Invoice
A/P
Check Reg.

File

To Vendors

Process

Magnetic Tape

Flow Direction

On-line Storage

Communication Link

Input or Output

Magnetic Disk

Document

Manual Input

Punched Tape

Keying Operation

Off-line Storage

Manual Operation

Display

Auxiliary Operation

In figure 4-3, we have modified our system to make use of a computer to identify those invoices to be paid each day. The computer maintains current files of invoices that are approved for payment, and of updated accounts payable records which are contained in an accounts payable file. These files are stored on magnetic disks. Input to the system is initiated when the person responsible for entering approved invoice data into the system uses vouchers, that is, authorizations to pay, as entry data. The data are keyed into the system which updates the approved invoice and accounts payable files. Each day, a computer program selects the invoices to be paid that day, prepares the vendors' checks, and updates each vendor's accounts payable record accordingly. The system also produces a daily report of all paid invoices.

Preparation of vouchers that authorize payment of individual invoices is done *off-line*, as shown in the figure. Off-line means that the operation is not directly connected to the computer system. The purchase order, receiving report, and invoice are compared to assure accuracy of the invoice. The voucher is then forwarded to the *data entry clerk* who enters the data in an *on-line operation*, one that is directly connected to the computer.

System flowcharting, like the preparation of DFDs, follows a number of conventions governing the use of symbols. In figure 4-3, for example, the rectangle indicates a major processing function; the triangle represents off-line storage; and the open-sided rectangle with dotted lines is used for annotation. The entire set of symbols, which has been adopted by the American National Standards Institute (*ANSI*), appears in figure 4-4.

Forms Flowcharts

As carriers of data and information, forms and documents flow hither and yon in the organization as needs dictate. The system flowcharts and DFDs we have discussed so far give little indication of which units in the organization perform the data processing work and which use the information. Forms flowcharting does this in terms of the documents and the operations performed with them. Granted that modern data processing methods can and should reduce the amount of paper shuffled about in organizations, much paper flow still exists. Therefore, it is a good idea to have a tool that will help in its analysis.

Figure 4-5 shows a forms flowchart of our accounts payable system. Each of the three organizational units responsible for paying invoices is awarded a column on the chart which shows the flow of documents used in the system. Ordinarily, forms flowcharts are accompanied by a narrative description. Points in the narration are identified by circled numerals on the chart. Here's the narration for figure 4-5:

1. On receipt of goods ordered, Receiving Department prepares the receiving report (RR), forwards it to Accounting.
2. On receipt of invoice from vendor, Accounting compares invoice with purchase order (PO) and receiving report, approves payment, and updates accounts payable file (A/P).
3. Each day, Disbursing pulls vouchers for invoices to be paid that day, prepares vendor checks, updates accounts receivable.
4. Disbursing prepares paid invoice report, forwards it to Accounting.

Forms flowcharts do not try to indicate how data are processed; they show only the flow of forms among the organizational units.

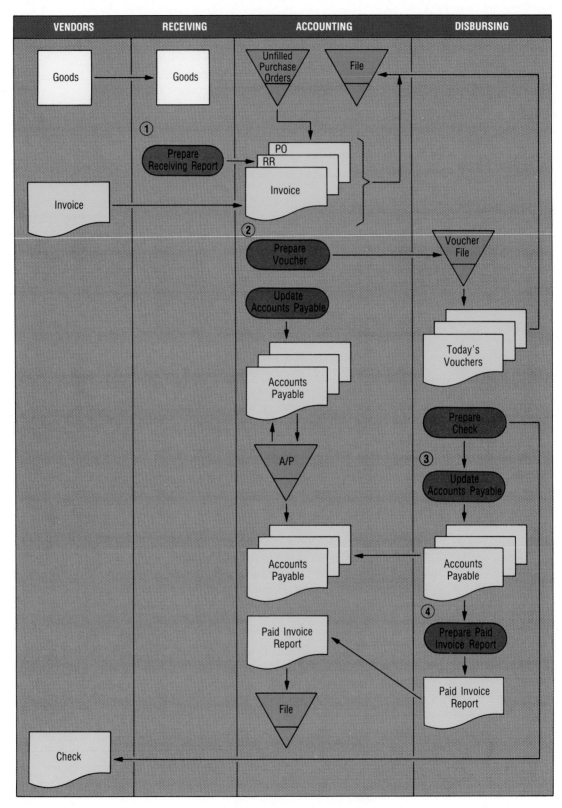

FIGURE 4-5
Forms flowchart for accounts payable system

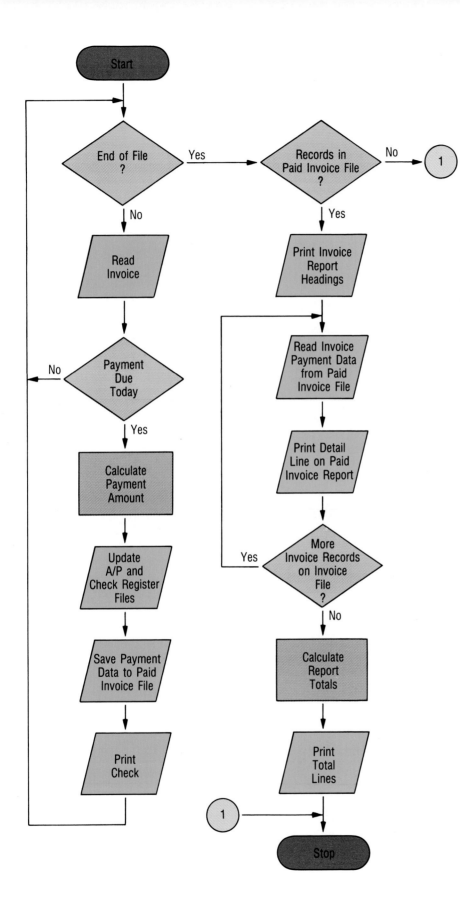

FIGURE 4-6
*Program flowchart for accounts
payable system*

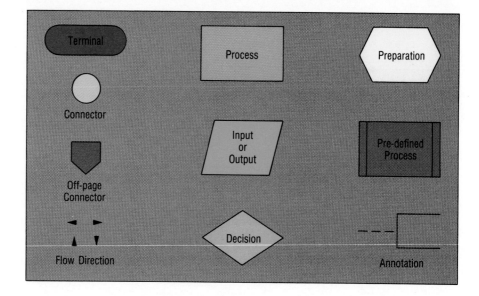

FIGURE 4-7
ANSI flowcharting symbols

Procedural or Program Flowcharts

You'll remember from Chapter Three that the elemental unit of any system is the procedure, the step-by-step activity followed by an element, or member, of the system. System flowcharts, DFDs, and forms flowcharts provide overviews of the flow of data and the assignment of functions among the actors in the system. If the actors are all human, the system is *manual*. When computers are introduced to perform certain procedures, the system is, at least in part, *automated*, or *computerized*.

The accounts payable procedure we've been examining is a prime candidate for computerization. Program flowcharts, often called *block diagrams*, depict the step-by-step procedures to be used by a computer system to process data. Figure 4-6 shows a program flowchart for the accounts payable system.

The program flowchart in figure 4-6 shows that the computer reads an invoice from the disk file containing all invoices and checks to see if it should be paid today. If it should not be paid today, the computer reads another and continues until it reads one that does require payment. When it finds one, the computer calculates the amount due the vendor, updates the accounts payable and check register files, and reads the next invoice. The information concerning the payment to that vendor is placed in a paid invoice file to be used later in producing the paid invoice report. The computer continues this process until the end of the invoice file is reached, and then examines the paid invoice file to determine if it has records for this day (after all, there may have been no invoices due for payment today). If there are records in the file, the computer prepares the paid invoice report and stops executing the program.

The program flowchart in figure 4-6 only makes sense in terms of the system flowchart in figure 4-3. As shown in figure 4-3, our computer system uses magnetic disks to store data files. Program flowcharts, such as the one in figure 4-6, do not typically provide information about what sort of data files are used and what the final reports look like. Those are other concerns of system analysis and system design.

As with system flowcharts, program flowcharts are read top to bottom and left to right. They use the standard ANSI flowcharting symbols which appear in figure 4-7 and which are reviewed in detail in Chapter Nine and Appendix B.

Hierarchy or Structure Charts

Block diagrams such as the one in figure 4-6 are not easy to read if one wants the overall picture of what's happening. They do, of course, specify the procedures to be followed and the sequence in which they must be executed. Systems analysts have devised other tools that do the same thing and take less effort to understand. Among these is the *hierarchy* or *structure chart,* a diagram that depicts the procedures of an operation in a hierarchical, or tree-like, fashion.

Figure 4-8 illustrates how a structure chart can be used to describe our invoice-paying system. Each rectangle on the diagram identifies a particular procedure, or *module,* that must be executed in order to accomplish the overall task. The diagram is hierarchical because the modules at the top of the chart control the modules beneath them. The module Invoice Payment controls the five modules beneath it. Each of those five modules must be accomplished before the total invoice payment task is finished. Similarly, two of the second-level modules control other modules. The Calculate Amount to be Paid module controls the two modules that calculate and deduct trade and cash discounts from the invoice amount. The Update module controls the three third-level modules which update the files used by the system.

Hierarchy charts, which are read from top to bottom and left to right, concentrate on those procedures that must be executed to accomplish each module's job. This is called *top-down analysis* because it starts with the overall job to be done, invoice payment in our case, and specifies each of the procedures required to do the job. These procedures may have subprocedures, as is the case with the Calculate Amount to be Paid and Update Files modules.

HIPO and VTOC

HIPO (pronounced "hypo") stands for Hierarchy plus Input-Processing-Output. As an analysis and design tool, its approach is very similar to that of structure charts. Like structure charts, in contrast to program flowcharts, HIPO is more concerned with *what* is done than with *how* it is done. When HIPO is used to design or analyze a procedure, visual representations are used in an effort

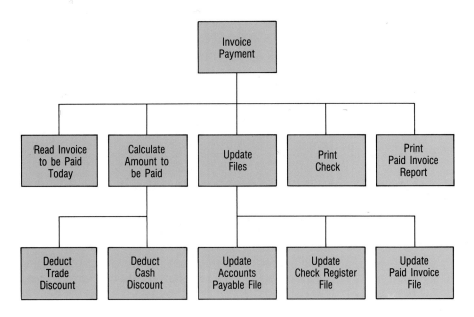

FIGURE 4-8
Hierarchy or structure chart for accounts payable system

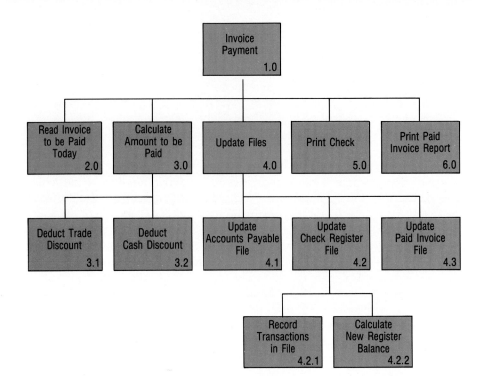

FIGURE 4-9
VTOC of accounts payable
system

to provide more detail than would ordinarily appear on a structure chart. The collection of visual and descriptive materials is known as the *HIPO package*.

A HIPO package usually contains a visual table of contents, called a *VTOC* (pronounced "veetok"), and one or more *IPO diagrams*. Figure 4-9 shows a VTOC for the accounts payable system. It looks almost identical to figure 4-8 because it is. We've added two additional modules supporting the Update Check Register module. We've also numbered the modules, which is typical of VTOCs, in order to clarify modular relationships and make them easier to describe.

The differences between hierarchy or structure charts and VTOCs are minor. The big difference comes with the addition of an IPO diagram to the VTOC. IPO diagrams express the input, processing, and output of the various modules in the VTOC. It is necessary to support each module with an IPO diagram. In particular, the high-level modules are usually fairly well described by their supporting modules. Lower-level modules, however, usually require detailed descriptions of their internal processes.

Figures 4-10 and 4-11 show IPO diagrams for modules 2.0 and 4.1 on the VTOC of the invoice payment system. The addition of IPO diagrams provides the same degree of detail found in program flowcharts but, thanks to the VTOC, the detail does not obscure the overall picture of the operation of the system.

Input/Output Analysis

In system analysis and design, a great deal of effort is spent analyzing the data that move through the system. This is called *input/output analysis*, or *I/O analysis*. Systems analysts use the diagrams and charts described in the preceding paragraphs to keep track of the flow of data through the system. They also use a number of other tools to provide very specific information about the data being processed.

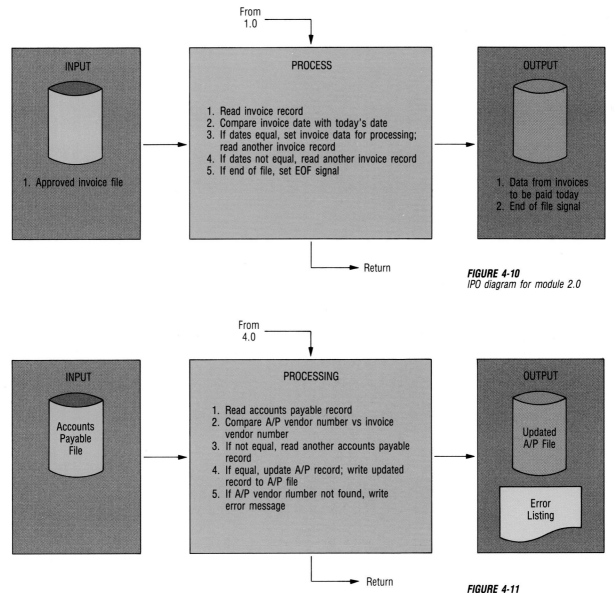

FIGURE 4-10
IPO diagram for module 2.0

INPUT

1. Approved invoice file

PROCESS

From 1.0

1. Read invoice record
2. Compare invoice date with today's date
3. If dates equal, set invoice data for processing; read another invoice record
4. If dates not equal, read another invoice record
5. If end of file, set EOF signal

→ Return

OUTPUT

1. Data from invoices to be paid today
2. End of file signal

FIGURE 4-11
IPO diagram for module 4.1

INPUT

Accounts Payable File

PROCESSING

From 4.0

1. Read accounts payable record
2. Compare A/P vendor number vs invoice vendor number
3. If not equal, read another accounts payable record
4. If equal, update A/P record; write updated record to A/P file
5. If A/P vendor number not found, write error message

→ Return

OUTPUT

Updated A/P File

Error Listing

Data Analysis Charts

Figure 4-12 shows a *data analysis chart* for the invoice-paying system. The chart, which is divided into three sections, shows each of the data elements used in the system. The term *data element* is synonymous with *field*, which we met in Chapter Two. It means an item of information about someone or something in which we are interested. The data elements, or fields, for the invoice-paying application are listed in the middle part of figure 4-12. The left part of the data analysis chart shows the *input files* from which each of the data elements may be retrieved for use in the system. The right side of the chart shows the *output files* which must include each of the data elements. Thus element 9, the Payment Date field, which comes from the Approved Invoice file, is required for use in each of the four output files, as indicated by the Xs. The use of the term *file* to refer to a printed report, by the way, reflects a common convention observed by data processing professionals.

Element Number	Invoice File	Accounts Payable File	Check Register File	DATA ELEMENT	Accounts Payable File	Check Register File	Paid Invoice File	Paid Invoice Register
1	X	X	X	Vendor Number	X	X		
2	X	X	X	Vendor Name	X	X	X	X
3	X	X	X	Vendor Address	X	X		
4	X	X		Transaction Date	X			
5	X			Purchase Order Number		X	X	X
6	X	X	X	Invoice Number	X	X	X	X
7	X			Terms of Trade				
8	X			Payment Terms				
9	X			Payment Date	X	X	X	X
10		X		Account Payable Balance	X			
11			X	Check Number		X	X	X
12	X			Invoice Amount			X	X
13	Calculated from #7, 8, 12			Discount Amount			X	X
14	Calculated from #12, 13			Payment Amount	X			

FIGURE 4-12
Data analysis chart for accounts payable system

The simple expedient of using a checklist chart such as the one in figure 4-12 often reveals opportunities for streamlining. For example, the Vendor Number, Vendor Name, and Vendor Address fields appear in each of the three input files. This is called *redundancy*. Confronted with this situation, we may well decide that those fields need only be maintained in the Accounts Payable file, thus reducing the amount of data storage and the opportunities for two or more files to contain inconsistent data.

Data Element Dictionaries

A *data element dictionary*, such as the one shown in figure 4-13, records the details of each data element used in an organization's information system. Figure 4-13 shows the element number and name, the length of the element in terms of characters, the type of data field used to hold the data in each record, and the format of each element.

File Formats

Data processors use the term *file format*, or *file structure*, to refer to the organization of data and data files. Analysts and designers use file layout sheets and record layout sheets as tools to help design records and data files. We leave the discussion of file organization and data retrieval systems to Chapter Ten which deals with data base management systems.

Output Formats

The end products of any system are its outputs. System analysis and design concentrate on the primary outputs of the system, but not always to the exclusion of the secondary outputs. The primary outputs, which include data and information written to files within the system, are described by the record format and file specifications for those files.

The predominant form of system output is still the report—either printed on paper or displayed on a computer video display screen, or *cathode ray tube* (*CRT*). Computer printouts are usually produced on paper of widths of either 8 1/2″ or 14 7/8″. The paper report must be laid out carefully, so as to present the information in the most useful manner to the reader.

When information is to be displayed on a CRT, each individual screen display must be designed in a manner that facilitates the use of the information. Screen design can be more difficult than report design because the screen is often used for inputting data into the application at the same time that it is displaying information.

To close this discussion of the tools of detailed analysis, we should observe that no analyst or organization uses all of them. In fact, many computer installations develop their own analytical tools to best fit their staff talents and the exigencies of their data processing organization. Data flow diagrams, structure charts, and HIPO charts are the most popular of these tools. Program flowcharting, once a standard tool for system analysts and computer programmers, has yielded to structure charts as a more feasible and workable way to analyze and design large, complex programs.

The tools presented here are not the only ones available. Many analysts have their favorite tools, and many organizations require standardized use of tools that are not described in these pages. Those that are described here, however, represent the most frequently used.

Other tools of procedural analysis, like program flowcharts and structure charts, present the logic of the processing task and are used largely as a means to communicate with those who design computer programs. These include, for example, decision tables, Nassi-Schneiderman charts, Warnier-Orr diagrams, and pseudocode.

FIGURE 4-13
Data element dictionary for accounts payable system

NUMBER	NAME	LENGTH	TYPE	FORMAT
1	VENDOR NUMBER	5	C	CCCCC
2	VENDOR NAME	20	C	CC -20- CC
3	VENDOR ADDRESS	30	C	CC -30- CC
4	TRANS. DATE	6	C	MMDDYY
5	P.O. #	7	C	CCCCCCC
6	INVOICE #	7	C	CCCCCCC
7	TERMS OF TRADE	5	N	99.99
8	PAYMENT TERMS	5	N	9.999
9	PAYMENT DATE	6	C	MMDDYY
10	A/P BALANCE	8	N	99999.99
11	CHECK #	4	C	CCCC
12	INVOICE AMOUNT	7	N	9999.99
13	DISCOUNT AMOUNT	6	N	999.99
14	PAYMENT AMOUNT	7	N	9999.99

Hospitals use computers in every aspect of their daily work. (Courtesy Burroughs Corp.)

The fundamental point of this discussion of analytical tools is that data processing work is complex and technical. Computers, being the most inflexible of devices, require careful and deliberate thought in the design of procedures for them to follow.

We turn now to the system development cycle and its four parts: analysis, design, implementation, and evaluation.

SYSTEM ANALYSIS

System analysis is the process of answering questions about how the system under investigation actually works. Answering questions, of course, must be preceded by gathering information. That starts with the preliminary investigation.

The Preliminary Investigation

In the preliminary investigation, enough information is gathered to answer the question, Should a full scale analysis of the system be launched? If the answer is yes, the information gathering continues with greater depth and with more detailed analysis. Probably the most important question to be answered by the preliminary investigation is just what is the problem anyway?

Problem Definition

It's easy to brush off the problem definition component of the preliminary investigation by observing that if we didn't know what the problem was, we'd have nothing to solve. As it turns out, more often than not we know there's a problem long before we know what it is, much less how to solve it. Most important, before we go to the time and expense of designing and implementing a new system, we'd better be sure that we're really solving the problem with it.

For this reason, a lot of effort should be devoted to defining the problem carefully. During the preliminary investigation, analysts use much information that is available. *Operational manuals* provide guidelines and instruct personnel who operate the system in the procedures of their jobs. *Documentation* provides descriptions, diagrams, and specifications prepared by the designers of the current system that detail exactly how it should work.

Recognizing that things, especially systems, rarely work the way they are supposed to, analysts do not rely solely on the official documentation of a system to determine the problem with it. Instead, they supplement this official description by gathering information from within and without the organization using questionnaires, personal interviews, and observation of the system in action.

Project Scope

Once they are satisfied that the problem has been identified and understood, analysts turn to estimating how big a task it will be to modify the present system or to design a new one, and the degree to which the new way of doing things will affect other operations and systems in the organization. It is rare, indeed, to be able to change the operations of one part of the organization without affecting other parts. As we saw in Chapter Three, the organization is a system of linked systems. One cannot change one without changing others. Determining the project scope, then, demands not only the effort required to change the one system, but the effort to change the others, as well.

Cost Benefit Analysis

The preliminary study roughs out the estimated costs and benefits of several alternatives to solving a problem. The alternatives are by no means thoroughly studied at this point, only the problem is. Nevertheless, some attention is spent on whether or not continued analysis of the situation is in order. Will the benefits of the new or modified system justify the expense of designing and implementing it? Although costs appear to be the relatively easy part of this question, they're not all that easy to determine. It is symptomatic of the complexity of system design work, be it for an information system, a weapons system, or a nuclear power system, that the costs of putting the system in place are almost always underestimated.

Benefit analysis is even tougher. A management information system, if it operates well, enables managers to make higher-quality decisions. An improved operating information system will result, for example, in more effective customer billing. This will result in better customer relations. Surely this is desirable, but how much is it worth? Suffice it to say that cost-benefit analysis is difficult at best, but must be done in order to estimate the financial and operational impact of the system development project on the organization.

Preliminary Report

The final product of the preliminary investigation is known as the preliminary report. The report

1. discusses the investigations that took place;
2. summarizes the operation of the current system;

3. defines the problems to be solved by the anticipated system development project;

4. suggests alternatives to be analyzed in the pursuit of solutions to the problems; and

5. hazards an estimate of the costs and expected benefits of the new system.

Detailed Investigation

Provided that the preliminary report justifies it, a full-scale analysis of the current system may be ordered. For organizations of substantial size, this may begin with the establishment of a *design team*, consisting of data processing and systems professionals, as well as operational personnel directly associated with the system being analyzed.

The analysis, whether done by a team or an individual, results in a complete documentation of the current system as it actually operates (one must recognize that few systems operate exactly as designed; they are modified informally by their operating personnel). It also produces a determination of alternate methods of achieving the system's tasks and an assessment of the relative costs and benefits of each alternative.

This information, which is contained in a final report called a *feasibility study*, is accomplished by a recommendation to leave the current system alone, modify it, or design a new one.

Data Gathering

When a system analysis project is at the detailed analysis phase, data are gathered and analyzed, and recommendations based upon the analysis are made. Clearly, the quality of the recommendations depends heavily on the quality of data gathered.

Few analysts feel hampered by a lack of information about the current system. The analyst's toughest problem in gathering data is sorting them all out, separating the important from the unimportant. It helps to break things down.

First, consider categorizing the information according to its source. *Internal sources* include all of the materials and personnel in the organization. The analyst collects all of the manuals, flowcharts, previous studies, and reports available concerning the system being studied. Often, people who work with the system can provide information of a higher quality than that obtained from official documents because those folks know how the system *actually* works, whereas the manuals and documentation express only how it is *supposed* to work.

External sources, easily overlooked by those concentrating on their internal organizational responsibilities, include customers, vendors, former employees, government agencies, computer manufacturers (interested, of course, in helping to install ever better computerized information systems), and last, but not least, professional consultants.

How then, does one gather information from these diverse sources? Analysts have settled on a handful of proven techniques. In the *documentation review*, all of the written materials pertaining to the system under study are examined. The manner in which the system is supposed to operate and the objectives it is to achieve are compared with how the system actually works, how well its objectives are being met, and whether or not those objectives serve the needs of the organization as well as they should.

Gathering information from individuals within the organization is accomplished through questionnaires and interviews. *Questionnaires* elicit written responses to questions about the system: how it operates, its faults, and its strengths. Some questions are *open-ended*—they invite essay answers and general comments. Others are *objective*—they require a yes or no, a true or false, or a choice among alternatives. If they are done well, *interviews* can usually provide great insights into the operation of the system. *Structured interviews* are much like questionnaires in that each interviewee is asked the exact same questions. This aids in assuring consistency in the information being gathered. *Unstructured interviews*, which give the respondent the opportunity to offer unsolicited information, often reveal unnoticed characteristics of the system.

Doubtless, no system study can be conducted well without observing the system in operation. *Observation*, then, is a key data gathering technique. An analyst brings an objective view toward what's going on. Days and weeks spent in close contact with all operational aspects of the system bring insights that all other data gathering techniques cannot. Frequently, analysts use simulated problems, unknown to the system's operators, to assess how well the system copes with extraordinary situations. Unusual customer complaints, faulty input data, requests for out-of-the-ordinary service, and simulated computer breakdowns can be particularly revealing.

Data should be gathered with some purpose in mind. Early in the detailed analysis phase of a system study, the study team or design team agrees on the kinds of information and data to be gathered and expresses this in a *checklist*. A checklist is a summary of the types of information to be collected during the data gathering activities. Typically, the checklist can be categorized into a few broad questions: What are the system's objectives? Do its objectives fit the needs of the organization well? What input data does it need to provide the required output? What are the strengths and weaknesses of the system? Under each of these rubrics follows a list of specific questions that will eventually appear on questionnaires and in interviews, and that will be researched from the written documentation available.

Analysis of Data

Analysis of the data gathered during a system study seeks to answer the sorts of questions outlined in the preceding paragraph. At this point, the tools of system analysis and design described earlier come in to play. Analysts collate and assemble information gathered from interviews and questionnaires and from observing the system in operation.

In the process, analysts are likely to uncover more questions, as well as aspects of the system that can benefit from improvement. They may detect, for example, that several of the system's tasks are duplicated elsewhere in the organization, or that some of the system's functions must be repeated because of faulty procedures or faulty data. They may find that the objectives of the system are not being met because the organization has outgrown them, or because the organization's operating environments now demand altogether different information services.

When it is finished with its analysis of the data, the project team should have extensive documentation of the current system and comprehensive information about what the information system should be doing to meet the needs of the organization, and how it can be improved.

System Specifications

After gathering and analyzing data, the team writes explicit *system specifications*, which set forth what the system *should* be doing. Almost always, system specifications begin with a detailed description of the required *outputs* of the system. Although this may seem backwards, system analysis and design work best when they start with the desired results.

Once the system's output is specified, the team determines the necessary input data, referred to as *input requirements.* These requirements specify the sources of the data needed by the system, as well as the formats in which the data are most easily and economically retrieved. Should we gather point-of-sale information from sales slips prepared by the salespeople, or should we use point-of-sale terminals and transmit the sales data electronically? Answers to such questions are the fundamental objectives of data gathering and analysis.

Analysis of Alternatives

Although the system analysis phase of the system development cycle is concerned primarily with the system's outputs and inputs, the manner in which the inputs are processed to produce the outputs is hardly ignored. In fact, as a result of the detailed analysis of the operating characteristics of the current system, the design team is in an excellent position to assess other methods of achieving the system's objectives. These alternate methods are analyzed in an effort to recommend a choice between the variety of ways to get the job done. Should we stick with manual data entry in our invoice-paying system, or should we automate that, as we have our procedures for writing checks? How much will it cost? What will be the long-run cost savings, if any? Perhaps we should engage a bookkeeping service and let it handle the entire procedure. Maybe we should purchase a large computer system to do not only the accounts payable application, but all other accounting tasks, too. Maybe we should use the computer system to develop a total management information system. Or maybe we should lease a computer like that....

The alternatives are endless. The design team, as it concludes its work in the detailed investigation, will formulate recommendations from the most promising alternatives. These will be presented to management as part of the final report of the system analysis phase: the feasibility report.

Modern mainframe computers can be connected to many terminals, allowing hundreds of users access to the computer at the same time. (Courtesy Sperry Corp.)

Feasibility Report

The feasibility report puts all of the system analysis work between two covers. Rarely, however, is the report delivered only in writing. Indeed, a well-developed feasibility report includes extensive presentations before management, operational personnel, and users of the system. Some call the feasibility report a *system proposal* because, in essence, it proposes to change things. It is rare indeed to find a system that can emerge faultless after careful scrutiny by experts. To be sure, changes can be proposed in writing. That's the report. Getting the changes accepted by those who must work with them, be served by them, and pay for them, however, requires personal attention and salespersonship.

The feasibility report always includes a summary of the reasons and objectives of the system analysis itself. What brought it about? What was it to achieve? It continues with a general description of the operation of the current system, an explanation of how it does and doesn't succeed in meeting its objectives, and a determination of how those objectives should change, if that's the case. If a system modification or a complete system redesign is recommended, the preferred alternative must be included in the recommendation. Finally, an estimate of the costs of installing and operating the new system, compared to maintaining the old system, must be carefully worked out.

SYSTEM DESIGN

We proceed with the discussion of the development cycle, assuming that all of the major decisions have been made in the design phase. These include, of course, decisions about what the new or modified system must do and how. The design phase takes these decisions as starting points and assembles all of the particulars of the new system. The end product of the design phase is a set of operating procedures, including computer programs and hardware specifications needed to implement the new system. This part of the design phase is described in the *design report*.

Design Approaches

Given the information from the feasibility report concerning the current system's required objectives and how it *does* work, the design phase concentrates on how it *should* work. This phase also develops the means to make it work that way. There are a number of approaches that organizations take in addressing this stage of the system development process.

The Expediency Approach

With the expediency, or *ad hoc*, approach, the company recognizes that immediate changes must be made and designs the changes with little or no concern for how they relate to the rest of the organization's systems. Using this approach, we could modify our accounts payable application by redesigning the operating files and procedures without concerning ourselves with how this one application fits in with the overall accounts payable system, the larger accounting system, or the overall information needs of the organization. Many would refer to such an approach as producing a "quick and dirty" solution: quick because it improves the specific situation right away, but dirty because it stands a great chance of fouling up other operations. The expediency approach is also inexpensive, at least in the short run, because it requires much less time and effort than do other approaches that take a larger view.

Often, the expediency approach is desirable. The problems to be solved may, in fact, be quite unrelated to any other operating features of the information system. The problems may be of such an emergency nature (regularly missing cash discount deadlines, for example) that an immediate patch of the system is imperative.

The expediency approach finds little favor with professional analysts. It results, they point out, in frequent, unrelated redesign projects and inconsistent file formats and data processing procedures. If used regularly, the approach makes data communications among operating units of the organization impossible. In the long run, this approach increases the expense of system maintenance.

The Bottom-Up Approach

The bottom-up approach takes a broader view of the information processing activities of the organization. In this approach, system analysts consider the specific outputs and processes required of the application under design, and then determine how larger units of the information system must be modified in order to best facilitate the total situation. This is a *modular* approach which involves breaking the entire system into a number of units or modules. Analysts use the *structured* methods illustrated in figure 4-14 in this approach. These methods resemble those shown in figure 4-8, but they are more comprehensive.

FIGURE 4-14
*Structure chart showing invoice
payment system as a module
controlled by other modules*

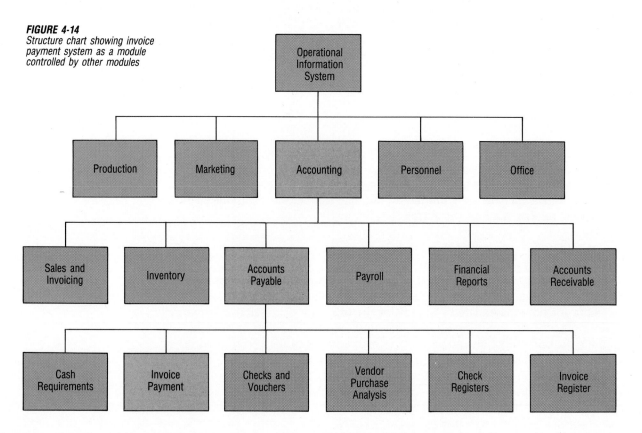

Figure 4-14 shows the Invoice Paying module as being one of several subsystems that are controlled by the more general Accounts Payable module, which is, itself, one of several modules controlled by the Accounting or General Ledger module, which, in turn, is controlled by the overall Operational Information System. When analysts use the bottom-up approach, they start with the Invoice Paying module and work up, modifying the controlling modules as necessary to facilitate the requirements of the situation.

Although the bottom-up approach is more comprehensive than the expediency approach, it is often criticized for being backward. It appears as if the tail is wagging the dog. Nevertheless, depending on the circumstances, this approach may be the most feasible. It does focus on the immediate operational changes needed in the module under question, and it does take into account the requirements of other modules in the system.

The Top-Down Approach

Analysts use the same modular techniques in the top-down approach as in the bottom-up approach except that, as you would suppose, the work in the top-down approach flows from the upper-level, controlling modules to the operating modules at the bottom (see figure 4-14). This approach is favored by most analysts because it results in the most comprehensive solutions to problems. It is, admittedly, more expensive in the short run and it requires much more time and effort to complete. However, in this approach, the objectives and operating requirements of the information system as a whole are considered *first*, and the operations of the subsystems, or modules, are subordinated to the overall goals. As a result, its advocates assert, the top-down approach is less expensive in the long run and it maximizes the productivity of the entire information system. It is criticized, nonetheless, for its slowness and for the consequent likelihood that the low-level operational modules will never become fully developed because the controlling modules will always be under study as the organization and its information requirements continue to change.

The Eclectic Approach

In the eclectic, or *combined*, approach, analysts try to use the best parts of the other approaches in the hope that their disadvantages will be minimized. They review the entire structured vision of the information system, as depicted in structure charts such as the one shown in figure 4-8, pick the best level at which to start, and work upward and downward. Thus, the approach is comprehensive but there is room to trade off the need for speed in design against the need for comprehensiveness.

Design Particulars

Using the tools covered earlier in this chapter, system designers assemble a complete working picture of the new or redesigned system in the design phase. This picture includes a number of particulars:

1. Design of forms and reports, the most evident of the system's outputs.
2. Design of files and data bases, the specifics of how data will be stored and retrieved by the system.
3. Design of personnel procedures which specify the responsibilities of those who operate the system or who will use it.

4. Design of computer programs, the detailed presentation of what the various computer programs will do as part of the system's operation.
5. Analysis of the alternatives reviewed during the design process and the choices made from among them.
6. Final analysis of the expected costs and benefits of the new system.
7. Preparation of the documentation of the new system. This material will serve as the design specifications for the implementation phase.

The Walkthrough

The final design step, just short of preparing the design report, "walks" all of the personnel associated with the system and all of those who will do the implementation work through it. The logic of the system is presented, the details of operating procedures are reviewed, and the outputs, both primary and secondary, are evaluated. Programs to be written for the system are examined by the programming staff, as are the data bases and file systems. Users of the system are given every opportunity to find fault with it and to make recommendations for its improvement.

The walkthrough is the last opportunity to catch mistakes that would be costly to correct once implementation work is under way. It involves personnel from every level in the organization. It not only serves as a double-check of the new system's operational validity, but it also sets the stage for that most difficult of the implementation phase's tasks: getting the people in the organization prepared and willing to adopt the new way of doing things.

The Design Report

The design report, like the feasibility report, documents all of the work of the design team and provides the details of the new system. It describes how the new system best and most economically fits the needs of the organization. It sets the timetable for the system's implementation, thus outlining the tasks that must be accomplished and their sequence of execution.

The design report, as a planning tool, requires approval from management before implementation work begins. This, like the preliminary and feasibility reports, is a decision-making point in the system design cycle.

SYSTEM IMPLEMENTATION

Changing over from one system to a new one is known as *conversion*. The date of conversion is the moment of truth for all of the work that has taken place in the system development project. The total conversion process may be considered in two parts: the preconversion work and the conversion itself.

Preconversion Work

Now that the new system has been designed and its implementation authorized, the design team, augmented by data analysts, computer programmers, and other technical staff, take on the tasks of bringing the system to life. These tasks are many. They include:

1. Deciding if software, that is computer programs, for the new system should be purchased or leased from commercial sources, or if it should be developed by the firm itself;

2. Deciding what hardware, that is, computing machinery and data processing peripheral equipment, should be purchased or leased;

3. Preparing the existing data files for conversion to the new system;

4. Preparing the physical site for the new system;

5. Training the personnel who are to be operatives in the new system and the users of the system;

6. Testing the new equipment, software, and operating procedures; and

7. Preparing the final documentation of the new system.

Conversion

The moment of truth has arrived. The system is designed and all the work necessary to make it operate has been done. Now we must convert from the old system to the new. We have several approaches.

The Crash Approach

In the crash conversion approach, we discard the old system and replace it with the new one overnight. In a twinkling of an eye, all of the new procedures, programs, data files, and inputs are made operational. Crash conversion, sometimes known as *direct* conversion, represents the ultimate confidence in the work done in designing and implementing the new system.

Given a preference, most analysts would probably opt for one of the more conservative approaches discussed in the following paragraphs. That's because the crash approach has great risks. No matter how carefully planned and tested, anything new, including a system, must stand the test of time before one is certain that is as good as it appears to be. It seems that no amount of forethought can anticipate all of the subtle problems that arise with the installation of a new system.

Nevertheless, the crash approach may be the only reasonable alternative. The new system may be such a departure from the old one that only a revolutionary turnover is possible. Perhaps the new equipment will not support the old system. Maybe a more conservative approach is so much more expensive that it's worth the risk of making mistakes to save the cost.

The Pilot Approach

In the pilot approach, we try out the new system somewhere. "Let's set this up in the Winnepeg branch and see if it works. If it does, we'll go ahead with the other branches." The pilot approach works best when the new system is small in scope or is one that operates as a number of identical systems in different parts of the organization. It minimizes the risk of changing everything at once and provides a good test of the system's operational reliability.

The pilot approach does not work very well with large comprehensive systems. A major revision in the Lockheed airline seat reservation system, for example, does not lend itself well to a pilot conversion.

The Phased Approach

In the phased approach, we implement the conversion in a piecemeal fashion. We implement small parts of the new system one at a time until the entire conversion is completed. Once proven, the new part is left operational and another new portion of the new system is implemented.

This approach is gradual. It moves step-by-step through the conversion process, implementing small parts of the new system as replacements for small parts of the old system, one at a time. It presumes that the new and old systems are similar enough that this will work. The outputs and inputs must not be radically different, and the processing components of the new system must be compatible with those of the old system.

The Parallel Approach

In the parallel approach, we operate the old and the new systems simultaneously for a time to make sure that the new system meets the requirements that the old system has been meeting all along. This approach is particularly appropriate for systems that produce routine output that users or recipients expect regularly. A new payroll system, for example, may be implemented in a parallel fashion. The outputs of the new and the old versions may be compared to make sure that the new is producing the required output.

Converting People

Inaugurating any new way of doing things is likely to meet with resistance from those who must change their working routines to fit the new system. Some resistance to change is normal; it's part of the human condition. Having established working patterns and relationships, most of us feel reluctant to change them. Resistance to changes involving the use of computers can often be greater than resistance to other changes. Perhaps the people involved suffer from cyberphobia, which we discussed in Chapter One. Maybe they see the installation of computers as a threat to their job security or to their feelings of self-esteem and job satisfaction.

It's easy to think that one can brush off these feelings as inconsequential. The logic that led to the decision to install the new system is so compelling that everyone in the organization will embrace it, if not wholeheartedly, at least with a willing spirit. The trouble is, the feelings of resistance toward new systems are not based upon logic and, therefore, cannot be coped with by using logical arguments. Resistance to change among employees is rarely covert. Instead, employees begin to show signs of aggression toward the new system. They withhold information that would make the system's design and operation more effective. They project their own mistakes onto the system, blaming it when things go wrong, or they avoid the system as much as possible, reverting to their old working patterns.

These well documented behavior patterns are normal. We mention them here to emphasize that no matter how well designed the system, no matter how much more effective the organization will be because of it, the system's operating personnel and users are likely to resist it. Chances are that many of them will do so even if shown, incontestably, that their personal performance will improve because of it.

Coping with this natural resistance cannot be left until the moment of conversion. Analysts agree that involving all of the personnel in the analysis, design, implementation, and evaluation of the new system does more to reduce

Considering the needs and desires of the people involved is an important part of managing the implementation of a new system. (Courtesy NCR Corp.)

resistance than anything else. Support from top management for the new system is a first prerequisite for its successful installation. That alone, however, it not enough. Support from the system's users and its operating personnel is gained through careful nurturing throughout the development cycle.

SYSTEM EVALUATION

The final phase of the system development cycle has a couple of stages. Immediately following conversion, and for a short (one hopes) period of time afterward, an initial evaluation, or *audit*, of the system is conducted. Thereafter, evaluation of the system is an on-going process, providing the *feedback* portion of the cycle.

Initial Audit

The initial audit involves examining the performance of the system against the standards and benchmarks established during the design phase. The technical performance of the software and the hardware is evaluated, and the degree to which the new system effectively meets its objectives is assessed. During the initial audit, we investigate how the system is used by its support staff and by the system's users. Often, this uncovers the need for additional personnel training, concerning the system's operation and its outputs. The system's documentation is reviewed once again and is modified as necessary so that it accurately reflects the system's actual operational characteristics. Finally, the project team and top management make a last calculation of the costs and benefits of the new system.

Feedback

During the life of the system, the feedback component of the development cycle provides a continuous flow of information about the system's effectiveness. As forces for change bear more heavily on the system with time, so too will the strength of the reasons to review its operation formally, in the initiation of a preliminary study. And so the cycle continues.

The most important single message offered by this chapter tells us that systems do not and cannot stay unchanged. The forces for change discussed at the outset can be ignored only at great peril to the organization. Excusing poor performance with the argument that "That's the way we've always done it" or "The computer won't let us do it any differently" is never received favorably by dissatisfied clients. It has been observed many times that the only thing that doesn't change is change itself.

SUMMARY

Responding to such imperatives for system modification and design as *technological development*, *social changes*, *economic changes*, and *internal changes*, organizations must employ systematic means of reviewing the way their information systems perform.

System analysis is the process of evaluating all aspects of a particular system and the situation in which it operates. System analysis goes on, or should go on, all of the time. Virtually everything that is done in the world of work is done according to some system, even if the system is bad or if it just happened, as workers fell into repetitive patterns in accomplishing their tasks.

As a formal activity, system analysis starts with the recognition that systems invariably offer opportunities to do things better and pose problems that are not easily solved. When the opportunities and problems grow to sufficient strength, management calls for a *preliminary investigation* to check things out. The result of this initial activity is often called a *preliminary report.* The preliminary report discusses the *problem,* the *scope* of the project needed to solve it, and includes an initial *cost benefit analysis.*

Provided the preliminary report indicates that it would be worthwhile to conduct a thorough and detailed study of the current system, a *detailed investigation* will be ordered. This study reviews all of the operating characteristics of the current system. The work is detailed, time consuming, and must be done meticulously. It requires *gathering data* and *analyzing* it, preparing *system specifications,* and *analyzing alternatives* available to meet the new requirements.

When the detailed investigation is completed, the organization has a document that describes its current system, including its advantages and disadvantages, and compares the current system to other alternatives, one of which is recommended for implementation. This document is a *feasibility report.*

If a system thus analyzed is to be modified or replaced on the basis of the recommendations in the feasibility study, the organization prepares a new way to get the system's job done. This is known as *system design.* In system design, we formulate exactly the procedures and subsystems that will operate in the new or modified system. We also specify how information and data are to be stored, retrieved, processed, and reported in the system. A number of methods are used in system design. These include the *expediency, bottom-up, top-down,* and *eclectic approaches.* The most desirable of these, in the long run, is the top-down procedure. Design of the new system concludes with the *walkthrough,* a dry-run or paper review of its operating characteristics. The final product of the design activity, the *design report,* is a detailed description of the ultimate output of the system development cycle—the new information system.

Finally, the new system is *implemented.* Introducing a new way of doing things is never easy. A primary concern of system implementation involves the people who will be operational team members in the new system.

Converting from the old system to the new can be accomplished in several ways. The *crash* or *direct* approach involves converting everything at once. The *pilot* approach tries out the new system in a small unit of the organization before installing it throughout. The *phased* approach eases the new system into place in parts. The *parallel* approach runs the new system concurrently with the old system for a time to test it by comparison before final conversion.

Last, but first in importance, is *system evaluation* which takes place during the analysis and design phases, as well as after the system has been implemented. System evaluation provides continuing information about the effectiveness of the system.

Systems analysts use a number of tools, including:

1. *Data flow diagrams* which show the flow of data through the system, using such symbols as *bubbles, sinks,* and *arrows.*

2. *System flowcharts* which also show the flow of data through the system and which suggest the specific data processing techniques to be used as well.

3. *Forms flowcharts* which depict the movement of forms and documents through the organization. They also specify the organizational units that use the information contained in the forms.

4. *Procedural,* or *program, flowcharts* which outline the step-by-step procedures to be used by a computer system to process data.

5. *Hierarchy* or *structure charts* which also specify the procedures a computer system is to follow but which do it in a hierarchical fashion. They break down computer programs into modules, thus making it easier to visualize the entire operation.

6. *HIPO* (Hierarchy plus Input-Processing-Output) charts which are similar to structure charts in that both show procedures in a hierarchical, or modular, fashion. HIPO packages include a VTOC, or Visual Table of Contents, and an IPO diagram. The package offers the advantage of an overall view of the procedure or system with the detail found in program flowcharts.

7. *Input/output analysis* techniques which provide specific information about the data being processed. Such tools as *data analysis charts, data element dictionaries, file format specifications,* and *output specifications* are used in input/output analysis.

In using these tools, analysts focus on how to make information systems serve the organization most effectively. Ultimately, the effectiveness of an information system is measured by the quality of information delivered by it to its decision makers.

ANSI	*design report*	*module*
automated system	*documentation*	*on-line operation*
block diagram	*feasibility study*	*operational manual*
conversion	*file structure*	*redundancy*
data analysis chart	*forms flowchart*	*system development cycle*
data element	*hierarchy chart*	*system flowchart*
data element dictionary	*HIPO diagram*	*visual table of contents*
data flow diagram	*input/output analysis*	*(VTOC)*
(DFD)	*IPO diagram*	*walkthrough*

1. Identify four imperatives for system change.
2. What are the three phases of system development?
3. Which phase of system development looks at the current situation?
4. Which phase of system development considers changes in the system?
5. Which analysis tool shows how data flows in a system?
6. Which analysis tool shows how paper flows in a system?
7. Which analysis tool shows the step-by-step procedures followed in a system?
8. What is the principal advantage of using a hierarchy chart?
9. What is the principal advantage of using a data analysis chart?
10. What information is provided in a data element dictionary?
11. What data gathering techniques are used in system analysis?
12. What is the result of a system analysis?
13. Why does the system analyst interview system users, as well as read system documentation?
14. Name four approaches to system design.
15. Identify four approaches to system implementation.

1. Discuss the human problems inherent in changing a system. Describe a process to minimize them.
2. Compare and contrast the four methods of system design.
3. Compare and contrast the four methods of system implementation.
4. Discuss the imperatives for system change, including examples where appropriate.

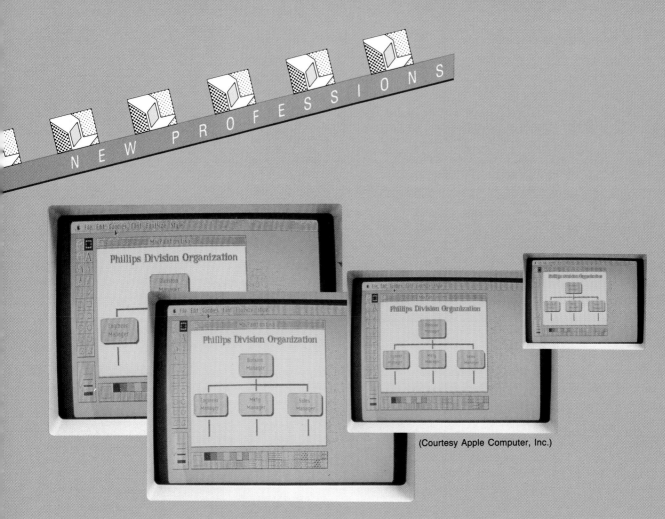

(Courtesy Apple Computer, Inc.)

Information Processing in the Organization

Despite the many independent opportunities in the information processing field described in the New Professions selection for Chapter One, most professionals find themselves in large organizations. Let's consider the variety of responsibilities and opportunities available in that quarter.

Responsibilities

The responsibilities for information processing managers and specialists, whether falling to an individual, a small group, or a specialized department in the firm are many and varied. In terms of the discussions of information systems in the first four chapters of this book, these brief descriptions of the responsibilities should be self-explanatory:

1. Organization planning and analysis

2. System analysis, design, implementation, and evaluation

3. Forms design and control

4. Preparation of written procedures and operations manuals

5. Analysis of information reports and system outputs

6. Design and maintenance of data files and file processing procedures

7. Equipment and software preparation and selection

8. Facilities layout

9. Maintenance of the physical security of the computer installation

10. Assurance of the security of personal rights to privacy in the use of data banks that store personal information

11. Establishment and maintenance of audit trials — the means by which individual transactions can be traced through the entire system

12. Protection and maintenance of computer and other data processing equipment and the library of computer software

13. Assurance of the integrity and accuracy of data through the exercise of various data control procedures

14. Maintenance of security procedures that prevent unauthorized access to and use of data

The Organization of Information Processing

In small organizations, the owner or manager shoulders the responsibility for managing information systems and processing along with all the other burdens of running the business. As the organization grows, it becomes economically feasible and desirable to employ specialists to do the work of systems analysis, design, computer programming, operations and all of the other functions needed to provide management with needed information. Sooner or later, the specialists are organized into a department known as the data processing or information systems department.

In Chapter Three, we examined several ways in which data processing activities are organized within a firm: centralized, hierarchical, and decentralized. The position of the information processing department within the firm is often related to the degree to which the provision of information services is centralized. The more decentralized the service, the more decentralized the information processing department. As a rule, centralized information service activities provide economies of scale, better integration of data and data processing systems, and the advantage of concentrating skilled technicians and managers in one place, thus taking better advantage of their talents.

Decentralized information processing activities are likely to win greater appreciation from users because with them, the users are more in control of things, as we saw in Chapter Three. Decentralized systems also provide better response to user needs and involve less risk to the entire organization in the case of computer failure. This is so because if several operating departments use identical computer installations, operations of one can be transferred to another.

Medium and large size organizations, even those embracing the decentralized decision support system concept, nevertheless have a centralized information services department. Even if information processing activities are decentralized, a central coordinating authority is found to be of great advantage in assuring consistency of data storage and processing techniques.

Large organizations with centralized data processing services seek employees with higher degrees of specialization in various aspects of the field — experience and training with a particular operating system or computer, for example. Organizations that use decentralized data processing generally prefer employees with more general preparation and experience because the data processing tasks are more varied at each of the locations where they are conducted. The same is true for small organizations which might look to a very small data processing staff for all of their information system activities.

Over the years, the position of the information processing department in the organization has changed, just as has everything else. In the early days, its services were more tightly linked to accounting than any other organizational function. Data processing departments (they were not called information processing departments until the mid-1960s) consequently reported to those in charge of accounting. As the data processing operation grew in importance, its supervisor or manager reported to more powerful corporate executives — from Manager of Accounting to Vice President for Finance, for example.

Today, in medium and large organizations, the information department is headed by its own *Vice President for Information Systems*, reporting to the President. Figure 4-15 shows a hypothetical organizational arrangement. Positions, titles, organizational charts, and working relationships vary considerably from one organization to the next. No one company is like another. Figure 4-15 is a rough, general representation of how information processing activities are organized in modern corporations.

In figure 4-15, the information systems department is broken into two subordinate departments: *systems* and *operations*. Each of these is further organized into separate functional specialty areas.

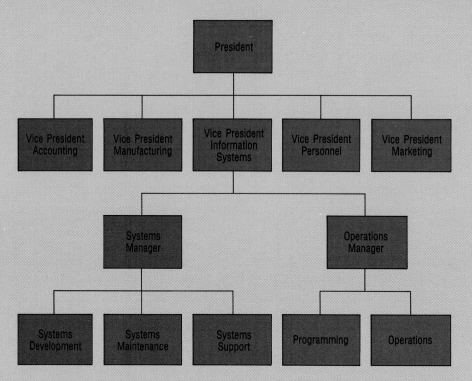

FIGURE 4-15
Organization chart showing position of the Information Processing Department in a large organization.

Systems

Broadly speaking, the systems department is responsible for three functional areas. *System development* encompasses all of the systems analysis, design, implementation, and evaluation activities discussed in this chapter. *System support* provides general operational service for all system activities. These services include maintaining and preparing organizational charts, designing and producing forms, preparing operating manuals for various application systems employed by the organization. *System maintenance* monitors the operation of current hardware and software systems as well as the day-to-day operation of all organizational systems. Personnel in this area often specialize in specific applications areas such as accounting, personnel, or production.

Operations

The operations branch of the information systems department is responsible for the operation of computing equipment. Because the operation of computing equipment depends heavily on the correct functioning of computer programs, the opera-

tions department is often in charge of all of the firm's computer programming activities, including both applications programming and systems programming.

Applications programming involves the preparation of programs to perform specific data processing tasks. System programming involves maintaining the operating system programs. In very large organizations, a separate programming department may be formed and in still others, programmers may be assigned to systems and operations activities.

The operations department is responsible for the performance of operating systems, the computer hardware, database management systems, and the purchase or lease of computing machinery.

QUESTION

1. Consider the responsibilities met by the data processing department in a large organization. What personal characteristics besides technical expertise must employees have to work successfully in information processing positions?

Computer Hardware: The CPU and Memory

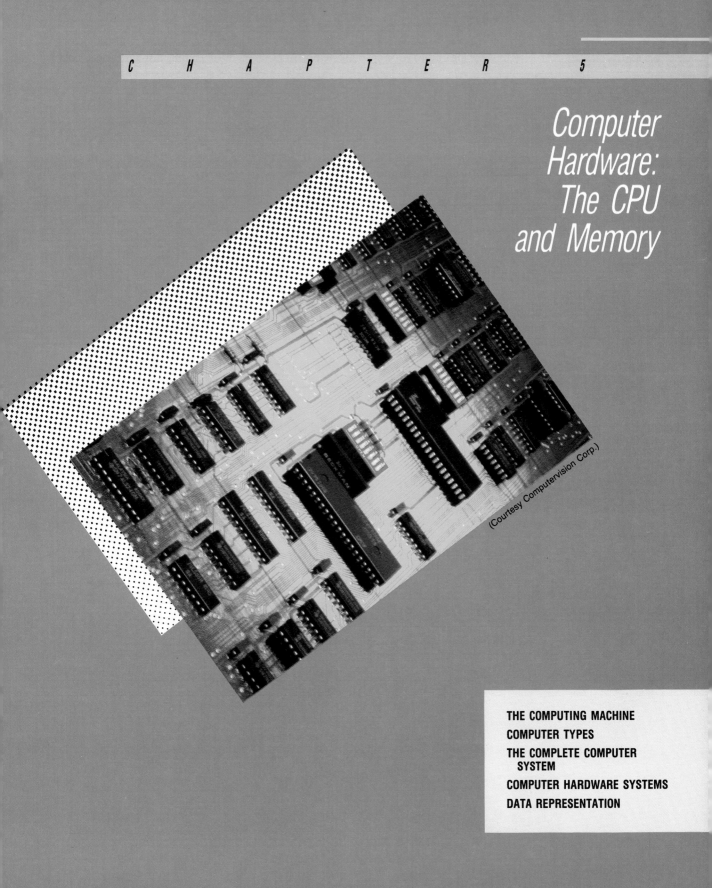

(Courtesy Computervision Corp.)

One evening I was sitting in the rooms of the Analytical Society at Cambridge, my head leaning forward on the table in a kind of dreamy mood, with a Table of logarithms lying open before me. Another member, coming into the room, and seeing me half asleep, called out, "Well, Babbage, what are you dreaming about?" to which I replied, "I am thinking that all these Tables (pointing to the logarithms) might be calculated by machinery."[1]

That was in 1812. Today, tables of logarithms are things of the past. To find the logarithm of a number, one now consults a computer far grander than Charles Babbage could have dreamed about. The computer might well fit loosely in a shirt pocket, a phenomenon that was not at all possible in Sir Charles' time when machinery was powered by steam.

THE COMPUTING MACHINE

Wishing for machinery to perform lengthy calculations started long before the turn of the nineteenth century. Some scholars mark the beginning of the history of calculators around 1617, with the invention of a device nicknamed "Napier's Bones," after its inventor John Napier. This was a calculating device that performed multiplication. In 1620, Edmund Gunther invented a forerunner of the slide rule, which was used for about two centuries for multiplication, division, and other mathematical operations. In 1642, Blaise Pascal assembled his "Machine Arithmetique," a calculator operated by turning dials. Plastic versions of the arithmetique could still be purchased in stationery stores as late as 1965.

Other observers might date the development of computing machinery with the abacus, a calculating device still widely used throughout the world. Its roots lie in antiquity. Its use depends on the calculating power of the human mind because the abacus is used primarily as a memory aid, to store intermediate results of a series of calculations. Skilled abacus users can perform complex problems more quickly than can users of pocket calculators because the mind works faster than the fingers.

A. Pascal's adding machine, the Arithmetique, was the first mechanical calculator. (Courtesy International Business Machines Corp.)

B. The Chinese abacus, an ancient adding machine still in use in much of the world. (Courtesy International Business Machines Corp.)

B.

A.

Charles Babbage is credited as the first pioneer in the development of modern computer machinery, even though his machine never worked during his lifetime. His mechanical Difference Engine and his Analytical Engine took advantage of techniques used by Joseph Jacquard to control patterns produced by looms. Augusta Ada Byron, Countess of Lovelace, and Sir Babbage's long-time colleague commented: "We may say most aptly that the Analytical Engine weaves *algebraic patterns* (Lady Lovelace's italics) just as the Jacquard-loom weaves flowers and leaves."[2]

The development of the modern computer awaited the use of electrical power. Earlier devices were hand-powered, using cranks and levers. Data were stored and calculated by gears and wheels. Electricity offered a way to store and calculate data using electrical signals. Herman Hollerith, a statistician with the U.S. Census Bureau, used the same punched-card idea as had Jacquard and Babbage, but he used electricity, too. He fed his cards under a set of contact brushes that completed electrical circuits. Other devices stored the number of times each circuit was completed. The technique compiled the country's census data in a fraction of the time initially estimated by the Census Bureau.

The "circuit complete" (on) versus "circuit not complete" (off) characteristic of computing with electricity remains the foundation of all modern digital computers. This is the *binary system*, about which more will be said later. Early computers used electrical relays to process binary data. A relay either completed a circuit or it didn't. *Relays* are electrical switches that are either on or off, a binary situation in which a circuit is either open or closed.

Howard Aiken of Harvard used relays and other electromechanical devices to produce the first machines that can properly be called *digital* because they processed digits of data. He completed his first computer, the Mark I, in 1944.

Charles Babbages's Difference Engine was the forerunner of modern computers. (Courtesy International Business Machines Corp.)

Herman Hollerith's tabulating machine was used to complete the 1890 U.S. census. (Courtesy International Business Machines Corp.)

The Mark I was one of the world's first electric computers. (Courtesy Harvard University, Cruft Photo Lab)

ENIAC, the world's first electronic computer is on display at the Smithsonian Institution. (Courtesy Sperry Corp.)

It was followed by four other Marks, II through V. The Mark I was controlled, or programmed, using a circular strip of punched paper, reminiscent of the punched cards of Hollerith, Babbage, and Jacquard. Because the paper was looped, the instructions punched into it were executed repeatedly as the strip fed through the reading device.

If we can make a machine do something once, we should be able to make it do it again and again, automatically. This idea was contributed about 130 years earlier than the Mark I. It is credited to Ada Lovelace who urged Babbage to use iterative processes in his Difference and Analytical Engines. Today, the term *looping* refers to computer programming techniques that cause computers to do the same thing many times over.

Use of electronic vacuum tubes, which performed the same function as relays, gave us the first *electronic digital computer*, the ENIAC (Electronic Numerical Integrator and Computer). Completed in 1945, it used 18,000 vacuum tubes and some 86,000 other electrical parts. It stood ten feet tall, 100 feet long, and three feet deep. Now displayed at the Smithsonian Institution, it could in its day multiply two ten-digit numbers more than 200,000 times faster than a human.

To put that into perspective, a modern jet airliner travels at about 500 miles per hour, which is about 100 times faster than an active person can walk. If a rocket ship were to carry us at 100,000 miles per hour, that would be 20,000 times faster than an active person can walk. ENIAC increased our ability to perform calculations by a factor of 200,000. Modern digital computers operate many times faster than the ENIAC.

Babbage's engines, the Mark I, and ENIAC must be counted as major milestones in the development of computing machinery. During the late 1940s, a different kind of milestone was passed. Computers, using vacuum tubes and relays, stored data internally in what became known as the computer's *memory*.

The program of instructions that controlled the computer's processing of data was external. It was recorded on a loop of paper tape, as for the Mark I, or as a setting of switches and wiring panels, as for the ENIAC. This was a very error-prone situation. One mis-set switch or incorrectly installed wire would result in an incorrect program. Moreover, each time the computer was to perform a task, such as calculating cannon shell trajectories or preparing weather forecasts, as the ENIAC did, the switches had to be set and the wires installed especially for that application. This was a very time-consuming task. In short, the computer program had to be prepared anew each time it was to be executed.

Improving the situation required a computer program that remained fairly permanent. The program could be stored in the memory of the computer, along with the data to be processed. That way, each time the computer was used for a particular application, the program had only to be loaded into the computer's memory so control of the machine could be turned over to the instructions stored electronically. This idea, as important in its way as the use of electricity, is known as the *stored program concept*. It was given to us by John von Neumann.

The stored program concept is a double-barrelled idea. Once the program is in memory, the computer can process it, just as any other data. Thus, the computer, based upon the results of processing data, can modify its own program. In a sense, it "learns" from the work it has been doing. Processes that learn in this fashion are known as *heuristic processes*, a subject in which von Neumann was keenly interested.

Later developments improved the technology with which we implement these fundamental ideas. The transistor, which was invented by William Shockley in 1948, and for which he earned the Nobel Prize in 1956, replaced the unreliable, power-hungry, heat-producing vacuum tubes used in earlier computers. In 1958, Jack S. Kilby invented the integrated circuit, thus paving the way for the miniaturization of electronic circuits and attendant reductions in power requirements, heat production, and cost of computer components. The devices, made of silicon, soon replaced transistors as the primary electronic component of computers. In 1971, Ted Hoff, an engineer at Stanford University, installed a complete computer processor on one integrated circuit, or "chip," about the size of a thumbnail.

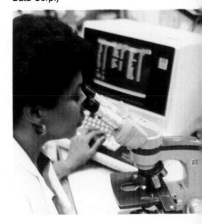

Scientists use the computer to control other tools and to analyze data. (Courtesy Control Data Corp.)

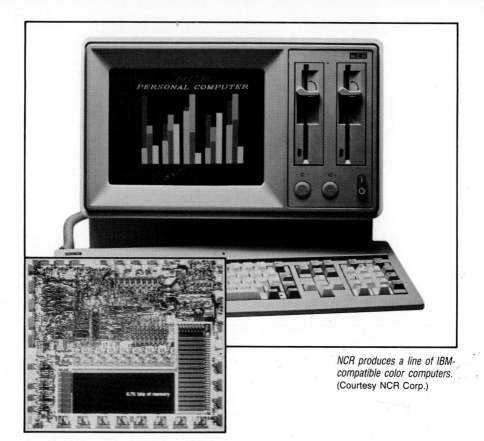

Single chips now contain complete central processing units. (Courtesy Intel Corp.)

NCR produces a line of IBM-compatible color computers. (Courtesy NCR Corp.)

In the quarter of a century that has elapsed since the invention of the integrated circuit, the development of computer machinery has moved toward producing smaller, faster, more powerful, and less expensive computers. The ENIAC cost $450,000 in 1944 dollars. Today, a pocket calculator purchased for less than fifty dollars is as powerful. A modern microcomputer, with its ability to retrieve data from massive data banks, is several generations beyond the first electronic computer. Comparing ENIAC with, say, an Alpha-Micro computer, which is a fast, powerful system for professional and commercial uses, is like comparing the rickshaw with the Enterprise of *Star Trek* fame.

COMPUTER TYPES

Computers can be categorized broadly by the way they process data and by their size. Computers process data as analog or digital data.

Analog versus Digital Computers

An *analog* computer processes data that vary continuously, such as variations in temperature, speed, the chemical composition of petroleum products, or the amount of current flowing through an electrical conductor. It's true that we often express continuous data in digital form. We say that a vehicle travels at 321 miles per hour. Actually, the velocity of a moving object varies continuously. As it accelerates, its speed doesn't jump discretely from 321 to 322 miles per hour. Instead, it gradually increases. Analog computers are used for a wide variety of industrial and scientific applications that require the processing of continuous data. The dial type automobile speedometer is an example of a continuous measure of speed. Digital speedometers round the actual speed to the nearest whole number.

Analog computers *measure* things. Digital computers, in contrast, *count* things. By far, the majority of computers in use today are digital. There are more counting applications than there are applications that require continuous measurement. Because of their pervasiveness in business settings, we will limit our attention here to digital computers.

Monsters, Mainframes, Minis, and Micros

Categorizing computers by size is not very easy. That's because the power of a computer that filled a room in 1970 can be carried about in a briefcase today. Nevertheless, those in the industry find it convenient to refer to computer systems as *mainframe* computers, *minicomputers*, and *microcomputers*. The term *monster computer* is reserved for computer systems of enormous power and size, which are employed for scientific research and military applications.

Monsters

Monster computers are also known as maxicomputers or supercomputers. The Cray and the CYBER computers are the best known examples of monster computers today. The Cray, for instance, sells for up to $20 million, depending on its configuration. Its installation requires specially prepared subflooring to carry its weight and special plumbing to carry the fluorocarbon fluid needed to cool it. The purchase price includes the services of two full-time engineers to maintain it—forever.

Relatively few monster computers (fewer than 150) have been installed, although in the next few years that number is expected to triple. Monster com-

The Cray-1 computer is one of the fastest, most powerful machines in the world. (Cray Research, Inc.)

puters are used in such applications as nuclear physics, meteorology, and petroleum engineering as well as in military applications. Today, weather forecasts for the entire globe can be predicted by one monster computer.

Mainframes

Mainframes make up the bulk of computer installations in large organizations, at least in the sense that they do more data processing work than any of the other types of computers. Typical mainframe computers cost over $400,000 and can exceed $1 million. Because they have special power and environmental control requirements, mainframes are housed in special rooms. This feature has added greatly to the mystique of computing as perceived by the uninitiated. Mainframes are manufactured by several United States companies, including IBM, Burroughs, Digital Equipment Corporation (DEC), and Control Data Corporation (CDC) which also manufactures the monster, CYBER.

Mainframe computers often serve more than one user at a time because they are able to support large networks of individual terminals and remote job-entry locations. Banks, large commercial and industrial companies, and government agencies all use mainframe computers. Most professional programmers work in a mainframe environment, preparing new programs and maintaining existing ones.

Minis

Minicomputers, more properly called medium-sized computers, are smaller, slower, and less expensive than mainframes. They have no special power or environmental control requirements, so they can be located conveniently throughout the organization's facilities. They cost between $20,000 and

Burroughs is one of the world's largest producers of mainframe computers. (Courtesy Burroughs Corp.)

Minicomputers often fit on a desktop. Many models can be linked to several work stations. (Courtesy Wang Laboratories, Inc.)

Microcomputers, which are typically designed for a single user, fit neatly on a desktop. (Courtesy Digital Equipment Corp.)

$40,000. Minis can perform many of the tasks that mainframes can, but on a reduced scale. They can support a network of user terminals, but not as many as mainframes can. They can store and retrieve data from the same types of input and output devices as mainframes, but they have a smaller storage capacity.

Micros

The microcomputer gets its name from the fact that its main computing component, the *microprocessor*, is located on one integrated circuit or chip. Larger computers use more than one chip for the various processing components. Of the four sizes of computers, micros are the slowest, but they more than offset that relative disadvantage with their ease of use and their low expense. Microcomputers fit nicely on desk tops; for that reason, they are sometimes known as desktop computers. Many individuals purchase microcomputers for personal use, either for their jobs or for other purposes. Micros, then, are also known as *personal computers*.

Introduction of microcomputers into the workplace, as we've seen in earlier chapters in this book, has led to increased productivity on the part of workers and management. It has also led to increased dissatisfaction with the services provided by the data processing department and its mainframe computer, as managers and other computer users find that they can perform data processing tasks independently from the data processing department.

Much progress has been made in linking managers' personal computers with the data bases and processing capabilities of the organization's mainframe computer. The ability to *download* data from one computer to another and to *upload* the results back has made distributive data processing systems and decision support systems possible and economically feasible.

As the computer technology continues to improve, it becomes possible to package increasing amounts of computing power in smaller packages. Desktop microcomputers now offer as much processing ability as mainframes

A. Portable computers can be linked by telephones to networks of other computers. (Courtesy Texas Instruments, Inc.)

B. Computers that fit in a briefcase can be used anywhere, even in a hotel room. (Courtesy Hewlett-Packard, Inc.)

C. Transportable computers provide all of the capabilities of any microcomputer, including hard disk drives. (Courtesy Panasonic Industrial Co.)

did ten years ago. Packaging computer components in ever smaller units has led to the development of transportable and portable computers. A *transportable* computer can be carried from place to place. Initially dubbed "portables," their weight (up to 40 pounds) and bulk made it unlikely that any but the strong would carry them about much. Nevertheless, they were found under airline seats and in hotel rooms as they travelled with their owners. More easily carried, truly *portable* computers fit in a briefcase and include video display screens and small printers. Such portability is made at little or no sacrifice to the computing power found in larger desktop units.

It's quite possible to design and manufacture a computer with all the power of a desktop computer that is too small to use physically. There's not much point in trying to reduce the size of the keyboard input device. Video display devices must be large enough to read comfortably. Rather than continued reduction in computer size, we expect to see continued increases in the computing power of devices that fit nicely on one's lap as well as on a desktop or aircraft courtesy tray.

THE COMPLETE COMPUTER SYSTEM

Doubtless because of the startling advances in computer hardware technology, people think of computers as hardware devices. The fact is, the hardware is only one part of the complete system. Without programs to tell computers what to do, they remain immobile and unproductive, like an automobile without fuel. For this reason, we define a *computer system* as a combination of hardware devices and programs assembled to accomplish some specific tasks.

Computer systems employ two broad categories of programs, both of which are necessary for the computer's operation. One category of programs is known as the *operating system*. As its name indicates, the operating system

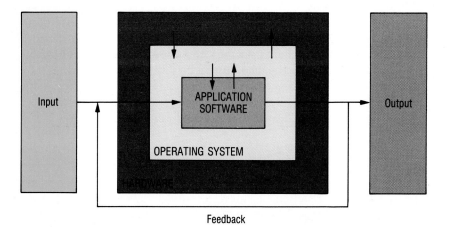

FIGURE 5-1
The complete computer system

controls basic aspects of the computer's operation. The other category consists of the *application program* which instructs the computer to perform those procedures necessary to get some job done: payroll, accounts payable, word processing, for example. Programs, as a group, are often called *software*. Figure 5-1 diagrams the relationship among these three components of a complete computer system: the hardware, the operating system, and the application software.

The rest of this chapter considers the hardware portion of the central processing unit, the part of the computer hardware system that performs the processing tasks. Chapter Six deals with data storage, input, and output devices. Operating systems and applications software are covered in Chapters Seven and Eight, respectively. The decision to describe the hardware of complete computer systems before the other two components is arbitrary. We have to start somewhere. We repeat, for emphasis, that all three components of the complete computer system are equally important.

COMPUTER HARDWARE SYSTEMS

The hardware components of a computer system consist of a system of interconnected electronic and mechanical devices. Any computing machine, be it a calculator carried about in a purse, a microcomputer sitting on a desk, or a large mainframe computer installed in its specially designed, air-conditioned quarters, has the same parts. Figure 5-2 shows the parts of a computer hardware system.

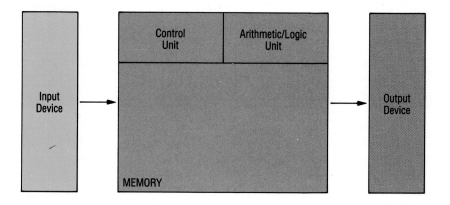

FIGURE 5-2
Parts of a computer hardware system

The parts of a computer hardware system are somewhat analogous to the human brain. The computer has a memory, as does the brain: each stores data. The computer's arithmetic/logic unit performs the calculations and logical operations needed to process the data, just as the brain does those things. In both cases, the control unit controls all of the operations—the functioning of memory and processing and the operation of peripheral devices such as arms, fingers, legs, printers, display screens, and data storage devices.

Computer Operation

A computer in operation follows instructions that have been placed in its memory. The set of instructions is known as a *program*. Each instruction in the set occupies one memory position; the control unit fetches the instructions one at a time from their sequentially-ordered memory locations and executes them.

In figure 5-3, data are read into memory from the input device. Typically, only a few records of data are read at once. They are stored in a data *buffer*, an area of memory set aside for input and output data. The control unit, fetching instructions in sequence from memory, executes the instructions, causing the data to be processed by the arithmetic/logic unit. The results of processing are then returned to another buffer from which they will eventually be transmitted to the output device.

When data are inputted into memory, they destroy whatever data may have already been stored there. This is called the *destructive-write* characteristic of memory devices. Because of it, one input data buffer may be used for all of the data input operations making it possible for the computer system to process much more data than can be stored in memory at one time. Data are input, processed, and output, then new data are placed into the input data buffer destroying the old. Processing then continues in the looping fashion first proposed by Ada Lovelace. The output data buffer works the same way. Data coming to it from the arithmetic/logic unit destroy the data that were already there, requiring that output operations be conducted before new results are produced.

On the other hand, once data are in memory, they may be read by the control unit without destroying them. This is known as *non-destructive read*. The program, for example, which is made up of data consisting of instructions to the computer, may be read as many times as necessary.

One can see from figure 5-3 that a computer system follows the same basic input-processing-output logic of all systems. The feedback component, which

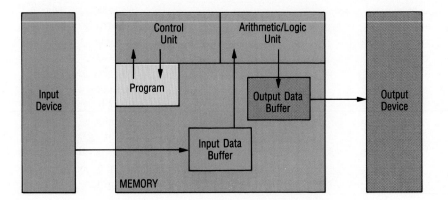

FIGURE 5-3
Data flow in a computer hardware system

is not shown in figure 5-3, is a process of reviewing the output with the object of modifying the program or the input data as necessary to produce the desired results.

Appendix A of this text presents a blow-by-blow description of a computer in operation, from the preparation of the set of program instructions through the final output of the application.

The Central Processing Unit

The main component of a computer hardware system is the *central processing unit*, usually called the *CPU*. It has three parts. The heart of the system is the *primary storage*, or *memory*, where data being processed and the programs controlling the computer are contained. The *arithmetic/logic unit* performs the calculations and makes comparisons between units of data. The *control unit* controls the operations of all the hardware as the programs in memory dictate. The CPU establishes the *power* of a computer hardware system, which is described in terms of the *size of memory*, that is, the number of characters of data it can store, and the *speed* of the control and arithmetic/logic units, which is measured in millions of instructions per second (*MIPS*).

Data come into the CPU from input devices such as terminal keyboards, disk storage units, and tape storage units. Output from the processing operations is delivered to output devices such as printers, video display screens, disk and tape units, and plotters. In Chapter Six, we will investigate the characteristics of these devices. Right now, let's consider the components of the CPU. They consist of the *processor*, which contains the arithmetic/logic and control units, and the *memory*, which stores the programs that control the computer and the data being processed.

Processors

From a technical standpoint, the control and arithmetic/logic units are usually considered to be a hardware device that is separate from the memory device. This is because the memory size may vary independently from the control and arithmetic/logic units. As a separate device, the control and arithmetic/logic units are known as the *processor*. Processors used in microcomputers are known as *microprocessors*, but there is no conceptual difference between microprocessors and processors found in mainframe and minicomputer systems.

The speed of the processor is governed by two things: the number of *operating cycles* it executes in a time period and the amount of data it can process in one cycle. During one operating cycle, the processor transfers an amount of data from memory to the arithmetic unit, performs a calculation on an amount of data, transfers an amount of data from memory to an output device, or receives data into memory from an input device. A *clock*, or timer, coordinates the activities of all of the devices controlled by the processor, so that, for example, data are not transferred from the arithmetic/logic unit until the unit has completed its calculation activity. The speed of the clock governs the number of cycles a processor can execute each second. Among the slowest processors are those that operate at about 1 million cycles per second. These are usually found in the CPUs of microcomputers, although many microcomputers boast processors that operate between 6 and 10 million cycles per second. The Cray computer executes about 30 million cycles per

Microprocessor
(Courtesy Fairchild)

second. The Hitachi-Hydra computer, which is used for experimentation in artificial intelligence, executes 200 million cycles per second.

Processor speed is also governed by the amount of data that can be processed in one cycle. This is measured in terms of *access width,* meaning the number of *binary digits,* or *bits,* that can be transferred or processed at one time. As we will see later in this chapter, computers represent data using binary coding schemes made up of zeros and ones. One character—a letter of the alphabet or a number, for example—requires eight bits, called a *byte.*

A processor with an access width of 8 bits transfers one byte or one character per cycle. A processor with a 16-bit access width transfers two bytes. The second is twice as fast as the first. Access width is governed by the *bus,* an electrical conductor that connects all of the hardware system components. Computer systems have two buses. One connects all of the peripheral input/output devices to the CPU and the primary storage to the processor. The other connects the internal parts of the processor. The IBM PC, for example, uses the 8088 processor which is manufactured by Intel. The 8088 has an *internal bus* of 16 bits, which means that data are transferred within the processor at a rate of two bytes per cycle. The 8088 has an *external bus* of 8 bits; therefore, it transfers data to and from memory and the computer's peripheral devices at a rate of one byte per cycle. IBM's PC AT uses the Intel 80286 processor which has both internal and external buses of 16 bits. The Apple Macintosh, which uses the Motorola 68000 processor, has an internal bus of 32 bits and an external bus of 16 bits. The Alpha Micro, another microcomputer, employs internal and external buses with access widths of 32 bits each. The IBM System 38, a mainframe computer, uses a 48-bit bus.

Most manufacturers of large computers, such as Digital Equipment Corporation (DEC) and IBM, manufacture their own processors. Producers of microcomputers and some minicomputers typically use processors manufactured by firms that specialize in the production of processors. In the United States, which dominates the market for these devices, there are but a few manufacturers of processors. Intel produces the 8088 (IBM PC), the 8086 (IBM Display Writer word processor), and several other more powerful processors. MOS Technology produces the 6502 processor, an 8-bit device used in the Apple II and Franklin computers. Motorola manufactures the 68000, a 32/16 (meaning 32-bit internal and 16-bit external bus) used in the Apple Macintosh. Zilog manufactures the Z80 processor, an 8-bit processor used in many microcomputers.

Processors used in computers today are thousands of times more powerful than those used in the early years of computer development. DEC, for example, produces a processor on a single chip that has virtually all of the computing power of its VAX-11/780 super-minicomputer, a system that serves multiple users with more power per user than large mainframe computers offered in the early 1970s. It is this continuing development of computer processing devices that makes it difficult, and pointless in the opinion of many experts, to differentiate between mainframes, micros, and other computer sizes. The mainframe of yesterday rides on your lap today.

Memory

A computer's memory stores all of the data currently being processed as well as the program that controls the processing. All digital computer memories consist of a number of cells, each of which has a unique address that is used to store and retrieve data to and from the cell. Most computers store only one character of data in each cell. In computers used for commercial applications, each memory cell stores one byte of data. The size of a computer's memory is measured in terms of *kilobytes* and *megabytes*. Because "kilo" stands for 1,000 and "mega" stands for 1,000,000, computer memory is measured by the thousands or millions of bytes that can be stored in memory at one time.

In computer usage, the prefix "kilo" actually stands for 1,024 bytes. Because computers are binary devices, most of the numbers found in the internal operations of computers are powers of 2. A kilobyte, then, is 2^{10} or 1,024 bytes. It is usually indicated with the initial K or, sometimes, KB. Thus, a computer with a memory size of 512K is said to have a 512,000 byte main storage. Really, it's 512 × 1,024, or 524,248 bytes. A memory with a capacity of one megabyte (abbreviated as 1M or 1MB) has 1,048,576 or 2^{20} memory locations.

Memory size is limited by the design of the silicon chips it uses and by the number of chips that are installed in the computer. That's why the same make of computer can offer a number of different memory sizes. An IBM PC AT, for instance, can have memory sizes ranging form 256K to 3000K, or 3M bytes.

Computer memory goes by a number of different names, including *storage, main storage, primary storage, main memory, primary memory,* and *RAM. RAM* stands for *random access memory* and also describes the way computers store and retrieve data from memory. It means that the processor has direct access to each memory cell; it doesn't have to work through any of the other cells to get to a specific one. Given the address of a memory location, the processor can move a character into that location or read one out of it without reference to any of the other cells in memory.

The development of RAM marked an important advance in computer technology because it increased the speed with which data can move about in the CPU by several orders of magnitude. Prior to RAM, computer memory devices typically took the form of magnetic drums on which were recorded the contents of each memory location. As the drum revolved under a set of read/write heads, identical in concept to the read/write head of your home tape recorder, the contents of memory were stored or retrieved. Because it was mechanical, as well as electronic, this process was relatively slow.

In the 1950s, Jay W. Forrester of Massachusetts Institute of Technology devised a type of memory that recorded bits magnetically on very small doughnut-shaped pieces of iron called cores. *Core memory,* as this memory device came to be known, could store and retrieve characters of data electronically and randomly. Since then, random access memory has remained the fastest and most effective memory device. Old-timers in the computer field still refer to memory as core sometimes, even though memory devices in computers today record data on silicon chips as patterns of positive and negative electrical charges. More recently, the term *RAM* has come to refer to memory chips because memory devices are manufactured as silicon chips. Increasing the memory of a microcomputer, for example, is a matter of adding RAM chips to it.

Data recorded in memory remain there as long as electrical current is available to sustain the memory's pattern of positive and negative charges. If the power drops because of power failure or because the computer was inadvertently turned off, all that is in memory is destroyed. A sudden surge in electrical power can also destroy memory because it changes the internal voltages of the computer. For this reason, memory devices are said to be *volatile,* that is, they are dependent upon a consistent source of electrical power. All mainframe and most minicomputer installations are equipped with backup power and surge suppression to protect against what otherwise might be disastrous loss of data. Power-loss and surge-protection devices are used similarly for microcomputer installations, particularly in business applications.

Not all memory is volatile. So-called *bubble memory* is independent of continuous electrical power because it, like core memory, records data magnetically. Unlike core memory, however, bubble memory is *sequential* rather than random in its method of data access. In order to retrieve or store data from or to a particular location, the processor must proceed through all of the memory cells in order by cell address until it reaches the one to use. Therefore, it is slower than RAM. Bubble memory is found in portable and lap-sized computers that are battery powered. One would not want to lose several hours work just because the batteries wore out. The safety factor is well worth the reduction in speed.

We've seen that computer memory is write-destruct and read non-destruct. Unlike RAM, the contents of which is under the control of the user, some varieties of memory cannot be written on at all. They are reserved for data and programs that must not be modified or inadvertently written over by the user. Most computers today have both kinds of memory. Read-only memory, or *ROM*, can only be read. It is protected by the manner in which it is manufactured. ROM is used to store programs and data that are essential for the proper operation of the computer system and of the application programs that are an integral part of its operation. ROM is non-volatile. The data in ROM, typically programs, remain there whether or not the computer is on. Many computers, especially microcomputers, come equipped with ROM chips that contain operation and application programs.

A type of ROM called *PROM* is programmable, hence its name: Programmable Read-Only Memory. Once programmed, PROM is unavailable to the user for modification. In a sense, once a PROM has been programmed, it becomes ROM. Essentially, ROM is a part of the hardware of the computer system. A variety of PROM allows this type of memory to be erased and reprogrammed to suit the needs of a particular application, but only if it is removed from the computer for that purpose. Such devices are known as Erasable Programmable Read-Only Memory, or *EPROM*. As a rule, users and programmers of computers do not concern themselves with modifying PROM or EPROM, even if they can. ROM, PROM, and EPROM are often called *firmware*, meaning software that is built into the hardware.

DATA REPRESENTATION

When entering data into a computer or reviewing output data from a computer, we ordinarily use the letters of the alphabet, various special symbols, and the numerals in the decimal numbering system. Computers work with *binary conditions*—a semiconductor is or isn't conducting; a relay is or isn't tripped; a switch is closed or open. Modern digital computers represent all data in binary form.

Numbering Systems

The Binary Numbering System

The binary numbering system is very simple, so simple that many of us find it confusing at first. This results primarily from our close acquaintance

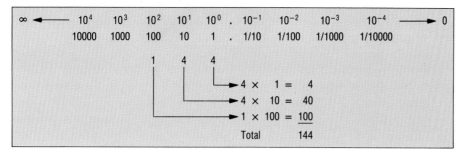

FIGURE 5-4
Decimal numbering system

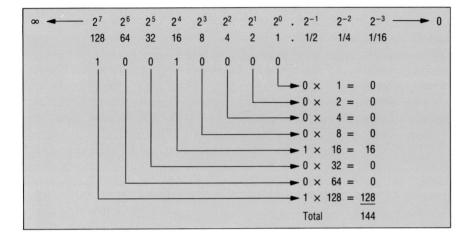

FIGURE 5-5
Binary numbering system

with the *decimal* numbering system. The fact is that both numbering systems operate in exactly the same manner. Consider the decimal number 144, which is a gross, that is, a dozen dozen. It consists of three digits. It also has a decimal point immediately to the right of the right-most 4, although, by convention, this is not shown if no digits are to appear to its right. The digit immediately to the left of the decimal point indicates the number of units, the one to the left of that the number of tens, the one to the left of that the number of hundreds. Thus each digit in the number has *place value*. Each place in any numbering system represents some power of the base of the system.

In figure 5-4, for example, our representation of a gross really means
$$1 \times 10^2 + 4 \times 10^1 + 4 \times 10^0.$$
The powers of the base increase by one as the places range to the left. Any number (except zero) raised to the zero power is equal to one. Any number raised to the one power is equal to itself. Any number raised to the second power, or squared, is that number times itself and so on leftward. To arrive at the value being represented, simply multiply the digits by their place values and add the products. The place values are always ascending powers of the base of the numbering system, in this case 10. The decimal point marks the place where whole numbers start.

The binary numbering system works in exactly the same fashion. In the decimal system, we use ten symbols—0 through 9. In the binary system, we use but two—0 and 1. Just as in decimal numbers, the place values in binary numbers are determined by ascending exponents of the base, which is 2.

Figure 5-5 shows the representation of a gross using the binary numbering system. The place positions have values determined by ascending powers of the base, 2. In the binary numbering system, there are only two possible symbols, 0 and 1, thus we represent a gross with the binary number 1001000.

Representing a dozen in the decimal system requires two digits which appear as 12, that is

$$1 \times 10^1 + 2 \times 10^0.$$

The binary system requires four digits to represent the same quantity. In the binary system a dozen appears as 1100:

$$1 \times 2^3 + 1 \times 2^2 + 0 \times 2^1 + 0 \times 2^0.$$

The Hexadecimal Numbering System

The hexadecimal numbering system, often abbreviated as "hex," employs 16 as its base and has sixteen symbols. Computers frequently use hexadecimal numbering systems, especially when outputting the exact binary configuration of the data being represented, because of the direct relationship between binary, base 2, and hexadecimal, base 16: $16 = 2^4$. The hexadecimal system is, in an important sense, shorthand for the binary system, the number system that computers actually use.

We are all familiar with the ten symbols in the decimal numbering system, 0 through 9. Understanding the symbols of a numbering system with a smaller base, such as binary, is easy because we use two of the symbols we already know: 0 and 1. The hexadecimal system uses sixteen symbols. Hexadecimal symbols 0 through 9 are equivalent to their decimal counterparts. In both systems, a half-dozen is represented by the symbol 6 in the unit's position of the number. (In the binary system, a half-dozen appears as 110). What happens, however, when we must represent a value greater than 9 in the hexadecimal system? In a base-16 system, we must have sixteen different symbols. To do this, we start with 0, count upward through 9, and then continue counting with letters of the alphabet: A, B, C, D, E, and F. In this scheme, A is equivalent to the decimal numeral 10, B to 11, C to 12, D to 13, E to 14, and F to 15. The decimal value 15 is the largest value that can be recorded by a single hexadecimal digit: F.

Before going any further, let's recognize a convention adopted by data processing professionals to differentiate a numeral used in one numbering system from the same numeral used in another. We wouldn't know, for example, whether the numeral 101 is binary, decimal, or hexadecimal by just looking at the digits. In the binary system, the numeral would represent the value five; in the decimal system it would represent one hundred one; and in the hexadecimal system, two hundred fifty-seven. The convention holds that the letter H or the dollar sign ($) precedes every hexadecimal numeral. Binary numbers are identified with the word *binary*. Some writers use a subscript 2 immediately to the right of the binary number. Decimal numbers have no identification. Using the convention, we can observe that $F = 15 = binary 1111$.

Now, representing a gross in hexadecimal appears as $90, that is,

$$9 \times 16^1 + 0 \times 16^0,$$

as in figure 5-6. As with all numbering systems, hexadecimal place values represent leftward ascending powers of its base, 16.

FIGURE 5-6
Hexadecimal numbering system

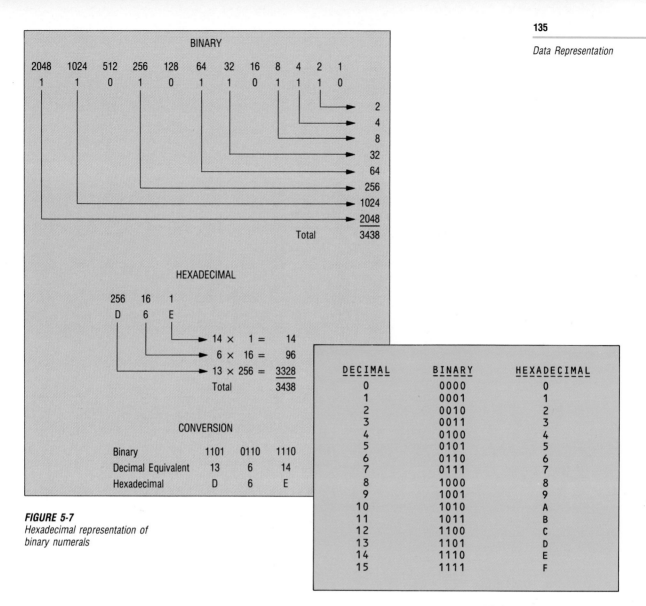

FIGURE 5-7
Hexadecimal representation of binary numerals

FIGURE 5-8
Decimal, binary, and hexadecimal equivalents

Let's look at a large number and see how the three numbering systems, decimal, binary and hexadecimal, relate to each other. Figure 5-7 shows that binary 110101101110 is equivalent to 3438. The hexadecimal representation of the same value is $D6E. At the bottom of the figure, note how the binary number can be broken into four-digit sections. Each of the sections can be represented by one hexadecimal symbol. It is in this fashion that hexadecimal serves as a shorthand for writing binary representations of data.

Figure 5-8 shows a conversion table for the decimal values 0 through 15 and their binary and hexadecimal equivalents. Observe that in every case, the binary equivalent of the decimal value can be represented by one hexadecimal symbol.

The hexadecimal shorthand for binary is of important use to professional programmers, computer hobbyists, and others who work with the details of computer operations. It is of great help when analyzing data that are represented in binary. Figure 5-9, for example, shows the binary contents of a portion of the memory of an Apple computer as represented in hexadecimal

```
0250-  F0 01 18 2C 81 C0 A0 12
0258-  90 CC A0 24 20 2C 02 20
0260-  DC 03 84 1E 85 1F A0 0E
0268-  B1 1E 48 C8 B1 1E 85 1F
0270-  68 85 1E 20 E3 03 84 08
0278-  85 09 A0 0C A9 01 91 08
0280-  A9 00 A0 03 91 08 A0 08
0288-  91 08 C8 A9 D0 91 08 A2
0290-  10 8A A8 2C 83 C0 B1 1E
0298-  F0 27 A0 04 91 08 8A A8                        ── The Letter H
02A0-  C8 B1 1E 2C 8B C0 A0 05
02A8-  91 08 8A (48) 20 E3 03 20
02B0-  D9 03 68 AA E8 E8 A0 09
02B8-  B1 08 18 69 01 91 08 D0
02C0-  D0 A9 02 8D ED 03 A2 00
02C8-  86 48 2C 89 C0 A9 20 4D
02D0-  05 C3 4D 07 C3 F0 03 8E
02D8-  00 D0 A2 46 BD 88 03 9D
02E0-  B3 B6 CA 10 F7 AD 00 E0
02E8-  8D C2 B6 A0 82 C9 4C F0
02F0-  02 A0 80 8C EE B6 A9 4C
02F8-  8D F5 03 8D F8 03 A9 B5
0300-  8D
```

FIGURE 5-9
ASCII memory listing

form. The left column shows the memory address of the left-most position in every row. Each row shows the content of eight memory positions. Both the memory addresses and the memory position contents are shown in hexadecimal form. Thus the address $0250 refers to memory position 592 in decimal. In binary form, the contents of that memory position is 11110000. Memory position $0251 contains binary 00000001. Memory position $0259 contains binary 11001100.

Coding Schemes

The binary numbering system works quite well for computers. After all, computers do calculations using binary arithmetic. Routines that automatically convert decimal numbers, which we like to use, into binary form for a computer's use relieve us of the necessity of converting the values ourselves. To be most effective, computers must also be able to process non-numeric characters such as letters of the alphabet and special symbols. Because digital computers record and process data only in binary form, we need binary coding schemes to represent non-numeric characters, too. Such coding schemes represent *all* characters within the scheme itself, that is, no distinction is made between numerals and non-numeric characters. This, too, is shown in figure 5-9.

Binary coding schemes separate the characters, known as the *character set*, into zones. A *zone* groups characters together so as to make the coding

CHARACTERS	ZONE	DIGIT
0 THROUGH 9	3	0 THROUGH 9
A THROUGH O	4	1 THROUGH 15
P THROUGH Z	5	0 THROUGH 10

FIGURE 5-10
ASCII zone and digit configurations

scheme easier to decipher and the data easier to process. Within each zone, the individual characters are identified by a *digit code*.

Figure 5-10 shows a typical arrangement. Zone 3 is used to represent all of the numerals in the decimal numbering system. Each numeral, 0 through 9, is identified by a digit code, also 0 through 9. Zone 4 is used to represent the first fifteen letters of the upper-case alphabet, A through O. Zone five contains the remainder of the upper-case letters, P through Z. In this scheme, the numeral 5 is represented by a 3 zone and a 5 digit; the letter C by a 4 zone and a 3 digit. All data coding schemes used by digital computers today employ the zone and digit system to represent characters.

ASCII

The coding scheme illustrated in figure 5-11 illustrates the most commonly used scheme today, the ASCII code. *ASCII* (pronounced "Askey") stands for

FIGURE 5-11
ASCII

CHARACTER	ZONE	DIGIT	HEXA-DECIMAL	DECI-MAL
blank	010	0000	20	32
!	010	0001	21	33
"	010	0010	22	34
#	010	0011	23	35
$	010	0100	24	36
%	010	0101	25	37
.	.	.	.	.
0	011	0000	30	48
1	011	0001	31	49
2	011	0010	32	50
.	.	.	.	.
9	011	1001	39	57
:	011	1010	3A	58
;	011	1011	3B	59
<	011	1100	3C	60
.	.	.	.	.
A	100	0001	41	65
B	100	0010	42	66
.	.	.	.	.
N	100	1110	4E	78
O	100	1111	4F	79
P	101	0000	50	80
Q	101	0001	51	81
.	.	.	.	.
Y	101	1001	59	89
Z	101	1010	5A	90
.	.	.	.	.
a	110	0001	61	97
b	110	0010	62	98
.	.	.	.	.
y	111	1001	79	121
z	111	1010	7A	122
.	.	.	.	.

American Standard Code for Information Interchange. The first three digits of an ASCII character code always represent the zone. The last four digits indicate the character within that zone. Thus the numeral 5 is in zone 3 (011) and is identified within that zone as the fifth character, digit 5 (0101). In this fashion it appears as 0110101. The letter C is represented as 1000011.

ASCII is a seven-digit code, meaning that all characters used by the computer system are represented by some combination of seven binary digits. The shorthand parlance for "binary digit" is *bit*. Therefore, ASCII is known as a "seven-bit" coding scheme. Because there are 128 (2^7) possible combinations of zeros and ones in a seven-bit binary number, ASCII has a maximum character set of 128 characters, enough to represent the 52 upper- and lower-case letters of the alphabet, the ten numerals in the decimal numbering system, and up to 66 other symbols.

Figure 5-11 shows the complete ASCII character representation scheme. Note the five basic zones: 0–9, zone 011; A–O, zone 100; P–Z, zone 101; a–o, zone 110; and p–z, zone 111. The special characters are scattered throughout the scheme so that the numerals and the alphabetic characters can be grouped together in logical sequence.

BCD

The initials *BCD* stand for Binary Coded Decimal. BCD was initially designed to encode numeric information in a manner that would be easier than straight binary to convert into decimal. Each decimal digit in a decimal value is translated into its binary equivalent and is recorded in one BCD position which contains four bits.

Another version of BCD adds zone bits so that non-numeric as well as numeric characters can be represented. This brings the total number of bits needed to record a character up to six and gives the scheme its name, "6-bit BCD." Figure 5-12 shows a listing of BCD and 6-bit BCD characters.

FIGURE 5-12
BCD and 6-bit BCD

CHARACTER	BCD	6-BIT BCD ZONE	6-BIT BCD DIGIT
0	0000	00	0000
1	0001	00	0001
.	.	.	.
.	.	.	.
8	1000	00	1000
9	1001	00	1001
A		11	0001
B		11	0010
.		.	.
.		.	.
H		11	1000
I		11	1001
J		10	0001
I		10	0010
.		.	.
.		.	.
Q		10	1000
R		10	1001
S		01	0010
T		01	0011
.		.	.
.		.	.
Y		01	1000
Z		01	1001

CHARACTER	EBCDIC ZONE	DIGIT
:	0111	1010
#	0111	1011
@	0111	1100
.	.	.
.		
a	1000	0001
b	1000	0010
.	.	.
.		
i	1000	1001
j	1001	0001
.	.	.
.		
r	1001	1001
s	1010	0010
.	.	.
.		
y	1010	1000
z	1010	1001
A	1100	0001
.	.	.
.		
I	1100	1001
J	1101	0001
.	.	.
.		
R	1101	1001
S	1110	0010
.	.	.
.		
Y	1110	1000
Z	1110	1001
0	1111	0000
1	1111	0001
2	1111	0010
.	.	.
.		
8	1111	1000
9	1111	1001

FIGURE 5-13
EBCDIC

EBCDIC

EBCDIC (pronounced "Ehbseedick") stands for Extended Binary Coded Decimal Interchange Code. It is an eight-bit code that accommodates as many as 256 (2^8) different characters. EBCDIC is the standard coding scheme for virtually all commercial computer installations using large and medium size computers. Figure 5-13 shows the EBCDIC character set.

Developed by IBM, EBCDIC stood for many years as the industry's standard data coding scheme. It is an accident of history, perhaps, that the makers of the Apple computer, the first commercially successful microcomputer, designed their machine to use a teletype keyboard. They did this because those keyboards were readily available through electronic retail stores, as were many of the other parts of the first Apple. Teletype keyboards used the ASCII code, then the standard for digital data transmission. Because the Apple was such a successful microcomputer, other micro manufacturers, including IBM some years later, also used the ASCII code even though their keyboards were more like standard typewriter keyboards.

Today, because more people use micros than any other kind of computer, ASCII is the predominant coding scheme and can be found on some mini and a few mainframe computers. Programs that convert data from one coding scheme to another are commonplace.

Bits, Bytes, and Nibbles

We've seen that data coding schemes use patterns of binary digits to represent characters of data to be processed. The term *bit* is used as shorthand for binary digit. Digital computer systems store one character of data in each memory cell. That's why, when we looked at figure 5-9, each memory cell contained a two-digit hexadecimal number. We saw that in position $028B the letter *H* was recorded as $48. Computers, even those that use the ASCII seven-bit coding scheme, record eight bits of information in each memory position. Each two-digit hexadecimal number requires eight binary digits, so everything works out very nicely. The letter *H*, as figure 5-14 illustrates, is configured as two patterns of four-bit binary numbers. The total of the eight-bit group is known as a *byte* (pronounced "bite"). Every byte represents one of the characters in the computer's character set. For this reason, the term *byte* and the word *character* are nearly synonymous. *Byte*, however, has the more technical connotation of "comprising eight bits."

Each byte consists of a zone and a digit which identify the character represented. A byte, therefore, consists of two four-bit parts, each called a *nibble*. Finally, as we know, each nibble is made up of four bits, the shorthand expression for binary digit.

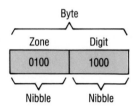

FIGURE 5-14
Bits, bytes, and nibbles

Parity

Computers, like any other electronic or mechanical device, do break down. One of the ways in which a computer can operate incorrectly is by transmitting data from one component to another inaccurately. If one bit is transferred incorrectly when transmitting data from primary storage to the accumulator, or from the magnetic disk to the memory, incorrect results are a certain outcome. It's only prudent to double-check each byte of data to be sure that it has been transferred or calculated correctly.

Parity systems are used just for this purpose. In computer lexicon, *parity* refers to the number of bits in a character configuration that are "on," that is, the number of ones. Parity checking systems assure that the number of ones in a byte is always even or always odd. Here's how it works. We'll add a ninth bit to the EBCDIC code for each character. We'll do this in a manner that establishes that the number of ones in each character is always odd. This is known as *odd* parity. We could just as well have decided upon even parity, it doesn't matter.

Figure 5-15 shows the result for the capital letters and the numerals. The ninth bit, called the *parity bit*, establishes the oddness of the number of ones in each nine-bit character code. Each time a character is to be transmitted, its parity is checked for oddness. If the number of ones in the character is even, something went wrong and a bit was dropped or added to the byte incorrectly. This might occur because of a fault in some data storage device or in memory, or because of a breakdown in one of the processing registers, such as the accumulator. This signals an error condition which will initiate a number of error checking and correcting routines. If the error cannot be repaired by the computer's correction routines, an error message will be delivered to the user or the operator of the computer system.

Of course, if an even number of bits is transmitted incorrectly, no parity error condition will arise. Other error checking routines must help in such an event.

All of this is done within the computer system. Ordinarily, we are unaware

CHARACTER	PARITY BIT	EBCDIC CODE
0	1	1111 0000
1	0	1111 0001
2	0	1111 0010
3	1	1111 0011
.	.	. .
.	.	
8	0	1111 1000
9	1	1111 1001
.	.	. .
.	.	
A	0	1100 0001
B	0	1100 0010
C	1	1100 0011
.	.	. .
.	.	
Y	1	1110 1000
Z	0	1100 1001

FIGURE 5-15
EBCDIC with odd parity

of all the error checking that takes place until the moment when an uncorrect-able error occurs, at which time the computer announces that it needs help. From our point of view, the computer works with eight-bit bytes. The computer actually works with nine, using the ninth bit to check the accuracy of the data being manipulated.

All large and medium computer systems employ parity checking and so do increasing numbers of microcomputers, including IBM's PC. Parity checking is important. The idea of a computer system designed so well that there is but one chance in a million that data will be transmitted or calculated incorrectly sounds pretty good. But if we use a data storage device that transmits 125 million bits per second into primary storage, for example, the odds of transmitting a bit incorrectly tell us to expect about 125 errors every second. Obviously, one chance in a million is not good enough. Parity checking is one of several ways in which computer systems double-check their own work. It is of particular importance in communications systems in which data are transmitted from one computer to another.

SUMMARY

The history of calculating devices is punctuated by a few major milestones:

1. The *looping* concept, thanks to Lady Lovelace, and Charles Babbage's development of calculating engines that would do the same thing over and over again. Much later, the Mark I used this same idea.

2. The introduction of electricity and electronic data representation methods that employ *binary conditions.*

3. The stored program concept, using the computer's memory to store both the data to be processed and the machine's controlling instructions.

4. The miniaturization of electronic circuitry, thanks to the invention of the transistor and integrated circuit which can be manufactured in the form of small silicon chips.

There are two basic types of computers, *analog* computers which measure and *digital* computers which count. Digital computers are often categorized by their power which is measured in terms of memory size and processing speed. The most powerful are *monsters. Mainframes, minicomputers,* and *microcomputers* range downward in power. Microcomputers can further be categorized into *desktops, transportables,* and *portables.*

The *complete computer system* consists of the *hardware*, that is, the physical electronic and mechanical devices, the *operating system*, the controlling programs that govern the hardware operation, and the *application programs*, the programs that cause the computer to perform its work. Operating system and application programs are usually known as *software*.

The hardware components of a computer system include the *CPU*, or central processing unit, *secondary storage*, and *peripherals*, or input/output devices. The CPU consists of the *memory*, or *primary storage*, which is used to store both data and programs. Memory size is measured in terms of the number of characters, or *bytes*, it can contain. The CPU also contains the *arithmetic/logic* and *control units*. Together, these are known as the *processor*. Processor power is measured in terms of the number of millions of operations it can perform each second. This is governed by the processor's *clock*, or timer, and its *access width*.

As used by computer systems, data are encoded into binary form using primarily the *ASCII* and *EBCDIC* coding schemes. Transfer of data within the CPU and to and from the peripherals is done in these binary forms.

KEY TERMS

access width	digital computer	non-volatile memory
analog computer	EPROM	operating cycle
binary system	firmware	primary storage
byte	heuristic program	processor
central processing unit	hexadecimal system	PROM
character set	kilobyte	random access memory (RAM)
computing power	megabyte	read-only memory (ROM)
data buffer	microprocessor	stored program
destructive write	non-destructive read	volatile memory

REVIEW QUESTIONS

1. Describe the binary nature of digital computers.
2. Looping is a _____ process which allows the computer to repeat the same procedure over and over.
3. Storing instructions in the computer electronically is called the _____ _____ _____.
4. Heuristic programs change themselves on the basis of _____.
5. Analog computers _____ things while digital computers _____ them. Which is most frequently used in a business setting?
6. Why are mainframe computers housed in special facilities?
7. Why will computers not get much smaller than briefcase size?
8. A complete computer system is made up of _____, _____, and _____.
9. The three parts of the CPU are _____, _____, and _____.
10. The only language a computer understands is its own unique _____ language.
11. The binary number 10011 equals _____ decimal.
12. The hexadecimal number $1C equals _____ decimal and _____ binary.
13. Most microcomputers encode data using the _____ scheme while mainframes generally use _____.
14. _____ is partially determined by access width in a CPU.

THOUGHT QUESTION

1. Explain the differences between the various types of computer memory: RAM, ROM, PROM, and EPROM.

Point Counterpoint

Will Computers Replace Books?

(Courtesy Hewlett-Packard Inc.)

"Reading rots the mind," warned an adage coined more than a century ago. One suspects it found its greatest favor among the nonliterate. As literacy increased, so did the practice of reading for fun, whatever the predicted effects on the mind. Sometimes the reading material was of literary merit, sometimes not. Dickens' *Oliver Twist* first appeared in serial form in popular periodicals, as did all of his other novels. So did C. S. Forrester's Horatio Hornblower series and Robert Louis Stevenson's *Kidnapped.* Edgar Rice Burrough's *Tarzan of the Apes,* first published in 1914, inaugurated a sequence of novels that has sold millions of copies and has been translated into more than 50 languages. Reading had found its place as an entertainment medium.

The introduction of the radio as an entertainment medium, contrary to dire predictions, did little to cool readers' ardor for books. Neither did movies. From the 1950s through the 1970s, television was hailed as the Great Mind Rotter. The TV set earned such sobriquets as "Boob Tube," "Idiot Box," and "One-eyed Monster." Cartoons depicted bleary-eyed watchers transfixed mindlessly before the glowing screen. Today, the stereotypical cartoon image of the slothful husband finds him, pot belly protruding, slouched before the TV with junk food at one hand and beer at the other. The pundits predicted the demise of reading for fun with great assurance. After all, with children spending an average of six hours per day watching TV, when would they learn to enjoy reading?

For nearly two generations, television has been the predominant home entertainment medium. Yet the popular press thrives. Slothful husbands subscribe to *Sports Illustrated.* The very people who schedule their daily activities around episodes of their favorite soap operas buy romance novels by the hundreds of thousands. Reading remains a very popular activity.

Now it's the computer's turn. Author Christopher Evans predicts that by 1990, books will have completed a "slow but steady slide into oblivion."[3] His reasons list the advantages that computers have over print:

1. Computers can store more characters per unit than books. Electronic devices no larger than a postage stamp can now store two copies of the Bible.

143

2. Because costs of computer storage are dropping so rapidly, it will soon be cheaper to store characters in electronic form than to print them on paper.

3. Computer display is more versatile than the printed page. It can combine text with computer graphics, including color and animation, and display several pages at once in screen windows.

4. Books are passive conveyors of information. Computers can be interactive. Electronic textbooks, for example, can present information passively, just like a book, but also can ask the reader questions, analyze the answers, and respond accordingly.

Physician Michael Crichton, author of the best-selling novels *The Andromeda Strain* and *The Great Train Robbery* sees the same potential.

> If there were (a computer powerful enough) right now, I would never do a novel again in the same way. I would do it as an illustrated novel.[4]

He describes an illustrated novel as an art form lying between a book and a movie, combining text with sound effects and high-quality graphics. That sounds just like a computer game. Well it should.

Crichton designed the game *Amazon*, which was released in late 1984 and which incorporates just those characteristics.

Computer adventure games often show the characteristics of a novel, including plot, locale, and characterization. *Executive Suite*, for example, puts the player in the employ of the Mighty Microcomputer Corporation. He or she deals with various corporate situations and personalities.

The future may well see the electronic novel in which the reader is a participant, interacting with and affecting the sequence of events. Will this replace the book? You be the judge.

QUESTIONS

1. Why do you think people both watch television and read books?
2. What advantages do books have today over computers in providing fictional entertainment?
3. Develop arguments that refute Evans' four points.
4. Describe evidence that people like to play games against people as much as against machines.

Computer Hardware: Secondary Storage and Input/Output

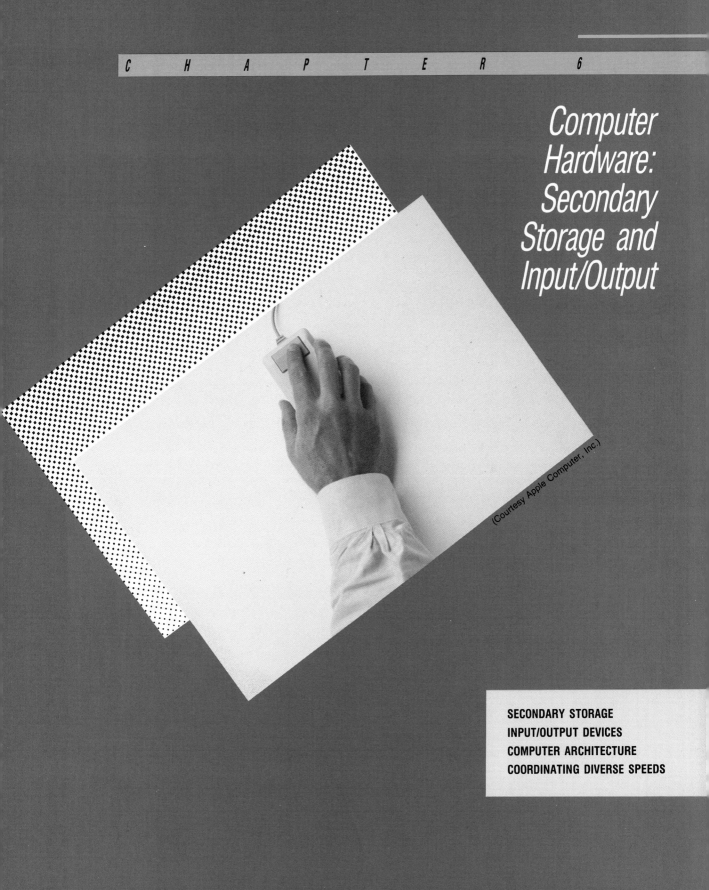

(Courtesy Apple Computer, Inc.)

SECONDARY STORAGE
INPUT/OUTPUT DEVICES
COMPUTER ARCHITECTURE
COORDINATING DIVERSE SPEEDS

In Chapter Five, we examined the central processing unit of the hardware components of the complete computer system. Other hardware devices needed to accomplish data processing tasks include those designed to enter data into the hardware system and to receive the results of data processing as output. These devices are known as *input/output devices*. Once data have been rendered machine-readable and entered into the computer system, data processing professionals are reluctant to enter them again. Besides being wasted effort, there's too great a chance that the second time they are entered, mistakes will be made.

For these reasons, data processing installations try to adhere to the write-it-once principle, which stipulates that once data are entered into a computing system, they should never be entered again. Moreover, the vast quantities of data that are processed by computer systems today make it necessary to avoid manual data entry to every extent possible. As a consequence, considerable effort has been devoted over the past few decades to develop automatic data entry devices and devices that will store data in machine-readable form more or less permanently, so that they are always available to computer systems.

These data storage units are known as *secondary storage devices*, as compared with primary storage which refers to the CPU's memory. Primary storage is fast, limited in capacity, and volatile. Secondary storage is not as fast, is almost unlimited in capacity, and does not depend upon a continuous supply of electrical power to sustain the data.

We turn first to those secondary storage devices most commonly found in computer installations today. Following that, we'll review the input and output devices that are most prevalent. This chapter does not give exhaustive information about every secondary storage and input/output device used today. That would be impossible because of their great variety. Those discussed here, however, illustrate the manner in which all such devices work.

SECONDARY STORAGE

As we saw in Chapter Five, primary storage, or RAM, is the workbench of the computer. All data to be processed must first be recorded in it and all output of results draws data from it. RAM has two crucial characteristics. First, data can be stored there only temporarily, thanks to RAM's volatility. Second, RAM cannot store a great deal of data. A 5 megabyte (5 million character) memory, for instance, may appear to be pretty large. A magazine publisher who must store some 200 characters of data for each of 300,000 subscribers can't fit the entire file in memory. Besides, the computer must be used for tasks other than processing this one file, so it can't occupy RAM all of the time.

These characteristics of primary storage give rise to the need for the ability to store large quantities of data in *machine-readable* form that can be read into RAM in small segments for processing. Units that do this are known as *secondary storage* devices. The two most prevalent of these are disks and magnetic tape. These media offer the ability to store data *off-line*, meaning that data to be processed from time to time by the computer system are not stored permanently as part of the hardware configuration. When needed, they are mounted on data reading and writing devices called *drives*, as required by the application programs.

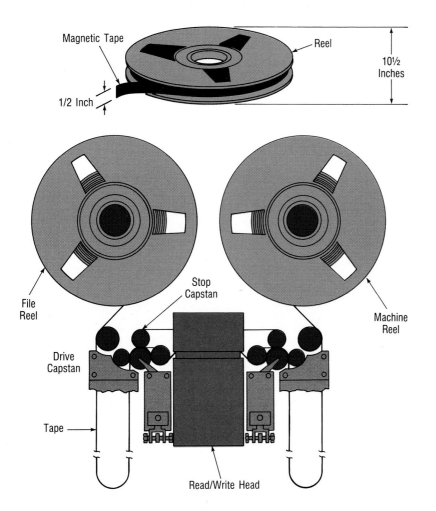

FIGURE 6-1
Magnetic tape

Magnetic Tape

In concept, magnetic tape storage devices used by computer systems are identical to the tapes you might have in your home video or music tape recorder. In fact, most microcomputer systems can use exactly those devices to store data.

Physically, magnetic tape consists of a long strip of Mylar that has been coated with an iron-oxide compound which is magnetizable. The strip, typically one-half inch wide for mainframe and minicomputer tape mechanisms* is wound on a *reel* in lengths of 2400 or 3600 feet, depending on the thickness of the tape. Most tape reels are ten and one-half inches in diameter. See figure 6-1.

Data are recorded on and read from tape using a *tape drive*. Tape to be processed moves from the file reel through a read/write mechanism and is rewound on the machine reel.

Data recorded on tape use the same coding schemes as those discussed in Chapter Five. Bits are represented as microscopic magnetic fields. Magnetization in one direction represents a zero, in the other direction a one. Thus

*Microcomputer systems can employ audio cassette tape devices for secondary storage, but these are too slow to be satisfactory.

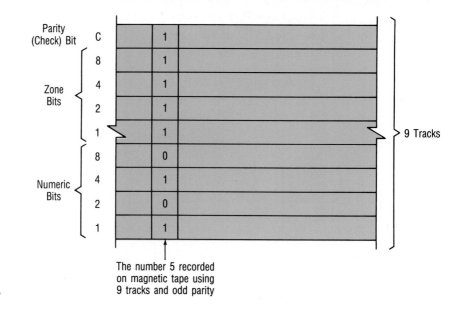

Parity (Check) Bit — C
Zone Bits — 8, 4, 2, 1
Numeric Bits — 8, 4, 2, 1
9 Tracks

The number 5 recorded
on magnetic tape using
9 tracks and odd parity

FIGURE 6-2
EBCDIC coding on magnetic tape

encoded, characters are recorded laterally across the width of the tape, as shown in figure 6-2. An eight-bit coding scheme such as EBCDIC, to which a parity bit is added, requires nine bits per character. A EBCDIC tape, then, is organized into nine *tracks* along its length. Because the tracks are parallel, this recording scheme is known as *parallel*. As data are read from or written to the tape, an entire character, consisting of nine bits, is transferred at once.

The number of characters that can be recorded on a reel of magnetic tape is governed nominally by the tape's *density*. Because characters are recorded laterally, they each occupy an amount of tape length equal to one bit. Thus, a tape density of 1600 bits per inch (bpi) means that 1600 characters can be recorded on each inch along the total length of the tape. A little arithmetic shows that over 46 million characters can be stored on a 2400 foot tape.

This is a theoretical number that, in practice, is never achieved. Data recorded on tape, as with all other recording media, are organized into characters, fields, records, and files. Thus, a tape file may be visualized as a sequential series of records. In processing, a number of records is read from the tape into RAM, where processing takes place. The results are then outputted, perhaps as a written report, perhaps as another tape file written on another drive. Because RAM capacity is limited, only a few records are read from the input tape at one time.

Some large mainframe installations include dozens of tape drives. (Courtesy Los Alamos National Laboratory)

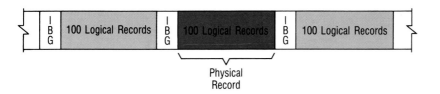

| | I B G | 100 Logical Records | I B G | 100 Logical Records | I B G | 100 Logical Records | |

Physical
Record

FIGURE 6-3
*Magnetic tape with blocking
factor of 100*

Here's what happens. First, the tape drive begins moving the tape from the file reel. It takes a certain amount of time for it to come up to speed. This requires space along the tape that cannot be used for data storage. Next, the records to be processed are read from the tape into RAM. Then the tape drive slows down and stops to await the next read operation. That, too, takes space that cannot be used for data storage (see figure 6-3).

This technique of storing records on tape in the form of groups that are read into or written from RAM all at once gives rise to a number of technical terms that are used concerning all types of secondary storage media. The group of records is called a *physical record* or *block*. Each record (the unit of information about something or someone) in the group is known as a *logical record*. The number of logical records in a physical record is referred to as the *blocking factor*. A blocking factor of ten indicates that ten logical records make up one physical record or block. The term *block*, then, refers to a group of logical records all of which are read into or written from RAM at once. The physical records, or blocks, are separated from each other by blank space on the tape, which is called the *interrecord gap* or the *interblock gap*.

As a recording medium, tape is also used for original data entry. This is accomplished through the use of *key-to-tape* units. One of these appears in figure 6-4. The operator enters data using a typewriter-like keyboard. The data are recorded on the tape using the appropriate coding scheme and the necessary blocking factor and record layout needed by the application programs that will process the tape records.

Magnetic tape is a *sequential* medium. This means that records appear on it in order—by employee number, account number, part number, etc. Because of this physical characteristic, the data on a tape must also be processed sequentially. If one has a file of 50,000 records on a tape, access to record number 45,567 can be had only by reading through all of the preceding 45,566 records. Other data file processing techniques will be discussed in Chapter Ten which is devoted to data base management systems. Suffice it to say here that because of its physical characteristics, magnetic tape can only be processed sequentially.

FIGURE 6-4
Key-to-tape unit (Courtesy Sperry
Corporation)

That is quite all right for many business applications. Producing the weekly payroll checks is better done using sequential methods, as is preparing a monthly inventory status report. Many applications are well suited to sequential or batch processing techniques. Magnetic tape is an economical and efficient way to store data for those applications.

Figure 6-5 shows the basic idea of processing data using magnetic tape. Assume that the firm's accounts receivable are maintained in a tape file, called the A/R file. Transactions involving each of the accounts—e.g., new purchases, payments, and address changes—are recorded on another tape file called the transactions file. The records in both files are in sequential order by account number and thus can be matched as records are read from each file. Data are read from each of these files into memory. The results of processing, that is, the updated accounts receivable records, are written on a third tape. This third tape becomes the new master tape when we repeat the processing cycle.

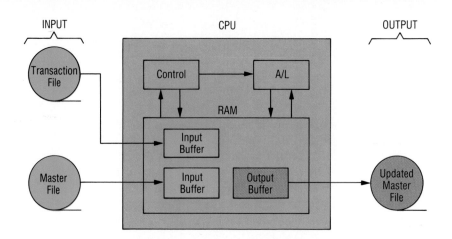

FIGURE 6-5
Tape processing

The RAM areas into which data are read from tape and from which data are written to tape are called *buffers*. The buffers are established by the application program. If each of the three tapes has a blocking factor of 20 and each logical record contains 300 characters of data, then each buffer requires 6000 characters. Thus 18,000 memory positions are used for input and output operations. Input/output buffers, called I/O buffers, are used with all types of secondary storage media. They speed I/O operations and conserve storage space on the secondary medium.

Disk Storage

Disk storage is the preferred medium for most secondary data storage today. Unlike magnetic tape files, disk files do not have to be processed sequentially, although they may be if the application calls for it. Any record stored on disk may be retrieved without having to process through all of the preceding records in the file. For this reason, a disk is known as a *direct-access storage device*, or *DASD*. The direct-access feature of magnetic disks makes this medium faster and more flexible than tape. As with magnetic tape, disks may also be used for original data entry purposes using *key-to-disk* devices.

To free-up larger machines, input is often done on a key-to-disk unit. (Courtesy Wang Laboratories, Inc.)

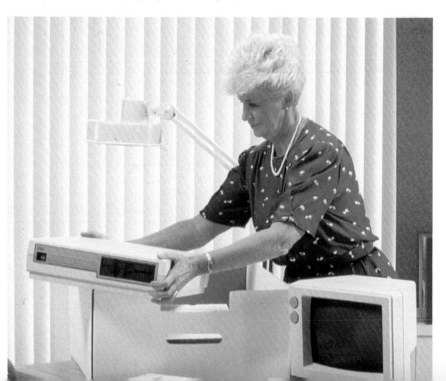

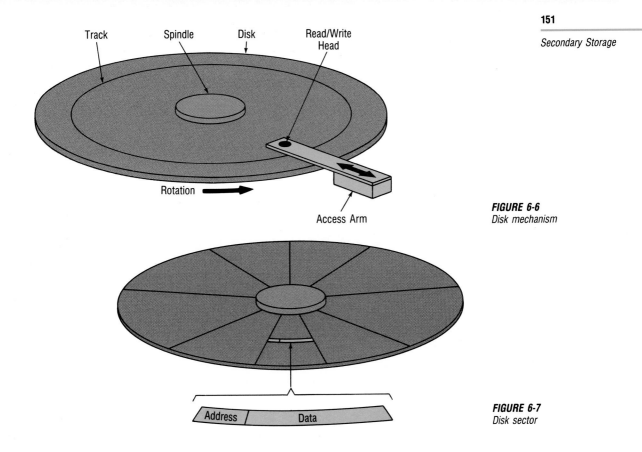

FIGURE 6-6
Disk mechanism

FIGURE 6-7
Disk sector

A magnetic disk consists of a circular platter of non-magnetic material, such as aluminum or Mylar, which is covered with the same sort of iron-oxide coating as that used with magnetic tape. As with tape, characters are recorded by magnetizing microscopic areas on the disk's surface using the usual data coding schemes. In operation, the disk is mounted on a spindle which causes it to rotate. A read/write head, similar to that used with magnetic tape, moves back and forth across the disk's radius, retrieving and storing data as required, much as a phonograph needle can move to different sections of a record without having to play all of it.

In figure 6-6, the *access arm* transports the read/write head across the disk which rotates past it. As data are recorded on the disk, they describe a circular *track* about its surface. If the access arm has 100 positions, the resulting disk has 100 concentric tracks. Unlike tape, which records characters of data in parallel along its surface, the bit configurations making up character codes on disk are recorded *serially* around the track, one bit after the other. Each track is divided into *sectors* for the purpose of increasing the speed with which small amounts of data can be recorded or retrieved. A track of data on the IBM PC disk drive, for example, holds 4,608 characters of data. Dividing the track into nine sectors provides access to 512 characters at a time. This is similar to tape processing operations. For this reason, a sector is often called a *block*, or *physical record*, which may contain several *logical records*. Data are stored and retrieved from the disk one block or sector at a time through the use of a *sector address* which identifies the specific track and sector containing the desired data (see figure 6-7).

Data may be recorded on both sides of a disk. A disk system, for example, that uses 40 tracks of nine sectors each, has 360 sectors available on each side

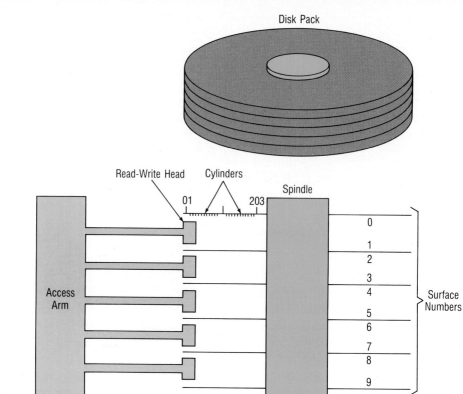

FIGURE 6-8
Disk pack and access mechanism

of a two-sided disk for a total of 720 sectors. If each sector contains 512 bytes, or characters, the disk offers a total data storage capacity of 368,640 bytes. Such a disk is said to be a 360K disk, following the convention that one K equals 1,024 bytes (360 × 1,024 = 368,640).

Many disk systems used with mainframe and minicomputers have several disks on one spindle, so that they all rotate together. Such a configuration is known as a *disk pack* (see figure 6-8). The *read/write* heads are mounted on *access arms*, all of which are attached to an *access mechanism*, which moves the arms and their read/write heads from one track to another. If the disk pack records data on 20 disk sides, one movement of the access mechanism makes 20 tracks of data available by electronically switching the individual read/write heads on and off, thus eliminating much physical movement. The total collection of tracks available on one movement of the access mechanism is known as a *cylinder*. Such devices store enormous amounts of data which are available to the computer at speeds that seem instantaneous. The IBM 3350 disk storage unit, for example, has a capacity of 317 million bytes, roughly equivalent to 160,000 double-spaced typewritten pages.

The amount of time it takes to retrieve (or store) data from (or to) disk is called the *disk access time*. What happens is this: when data are to be retrieved from a disk, the disk address is determined. This identifies the cylinder, disk surface, and sector. The access arm moves to the cylinder, the appropriate read/write head is switched on, and everything waits until the desired sector passes by the read/write head. Then the data are read and transmitted to memory. This action involves three kinds of delays: head switching delay, access arm movement delay, and rotational delay. Although disk access time is measured in thousandths of a second, the time it takes to retrieve data from disk is much longer than to retrieve it from primary storage.

Modern computers use disk drives for the bulk of their secondary storage. (Digital Equipment Corp.)

When in use, that is, when *on-line*, disks and disk packs are mounted in a *disk drive*. If they are removable, disks provide both on-line and off-line data storage capability. Most computer systems, including microcomputers, employ several disk drives, thus multiplying the amount of on-line data by the number of drives attached to the CPU. A system with, say, ten IBM 3350s on-line makes over three billion characters of data available to the CPU at once. It is just such configurations that make large-scale data base systems possible.

Disk storage media take several forms. *Hard disks*, which are rigid, contain the most data. They are used with drives that rotate them at a faster rate than other types of disks. Hard disks may be fixed in their drives or may be removable. They are usually about 14 inches in diameter, although smaller hard disks are commonplace in microcomputer systems. One such system is known as the *Winchester* because its prototype made use of two drives of 30 million bytes each and was affectionally dubbed the "30-30." It used a 14-inch platter. Later versions, called "mini-Winchesters" or "mini-Wins," use 8-inch or 6 1/4 inch platters that are sealed in their drives and can store up to 85 million bytes.

The disk pack looks like a stack of record albums. (Courtesy Control Data Corp.)

Flexible disks or *diskettes*, often called "floppy disks" or "floppies" because they use a thin sheet of Mylar as their base, are an important data storage medium for micro and minicomputers. Ranging in size from 8 inches to 3 1/4 inches, they offer the advantages of ease of transport and low expense. They are encased permanently in a protective envelope which is inserted into the disk drive. Figure 6-9 illustrates a disk drive in which a diskette is mounted.

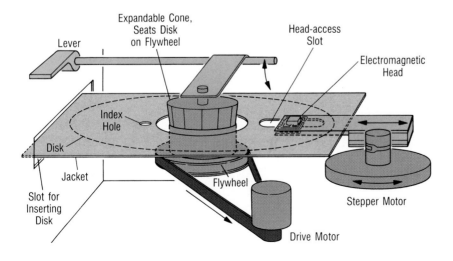

FIGURE 6-9
Diskettes and drive mechanism

154

CHAPTER 6
Computer Hardware:
Secondary Storage
and Input/Output

INPUT/OUTPUT

CPU

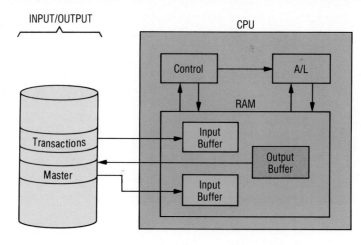

FIGURE 6-10
Disk processing

Disk storage media used today record data magnetically. Research has been underway for a number of years to perfect *optical* means of recording data on disks, similar to the laser digital audio disks that became available for home use in 1983. Radio Corporation of America, for example, has developed a laser disk that stores 10 billion bytes, which it produces exclusively for government markets. A billion bytes is called a *gigabyte*, so this is a 10G disk. By 1990, it is anticipated that 20G disks will be readily available for commercial applications at a cost of about $50 per disk.

Figure 6-10 shows the same accounts receivable application that appears in figure 6-5. In this case, both the transactions file and the master file are stored on the same device, the disk drive. Data are transmitted to input buffers in RAM and processed, and the results are stored in an output buffer for eventual recording back to disk. Using disk storage, the master file may be updated directly without preparing a new master file, as was required when using the tape system. Each record to be updated with a transaction may be retrieved *directly*, without reading through the entire file. Even though master files may be updated in this manner, backup versions of the master file should always be maintained as insurance against accidental loss.

Mass Storage Systems

Mass storage systems hold trillions of bytes of data. (Courtesy International Business Machines Corp.)

It has been estimated that industry's need for machine-readable data storage is increasing at the rate of 45 to 60 percent each year. This has inspired computer equipment manufacturers to develop storage devices with ever higher

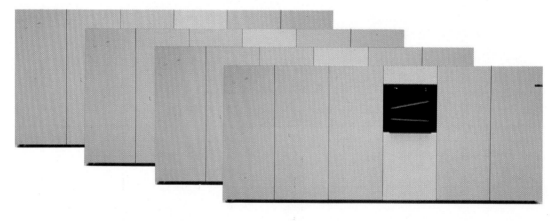

capacities. The top-of-the-line disk unit manufactured by IBM, for example, stores more than 2.5G bytes of data. *Data cartridge systems* store data in a series of 50M cartridges. Examples include Control Data's 38500 and IBM's 3850 Mass Storage System. These devices provide up to half a trillion bytes of on-line storage. They are slower than disk systems because they involve more physical movement. A cartridge is loaded into the read/write mechanism, the data are processed, and then the cartridge is replaced in its honeycomb-like storage bin. Then the read/write mechanism moves on to find the next cartridge to be processed.

INPUT/OUTPUT DEVICES

Secondary storage units perform both input and output functions, but they communicate with the CPU using machine-processable coding schemes such as ASCII and EBCDIC. No one wants to spend time deciphering ASCII codes to learn the results of a processing operation. Means must be available for people to enter data into the computer system and to receive information from it in an intelligible form.

Input/output, or I/O, devices are the means by which we communicate with computers. They translate between our language and the electronic signals needed by the CPU. Input/output devices are often called *peripherals* because they relate peripherally to the central processing unit. We've seen a couple already: key-to-tape and key-to-disk devices. We continue now with a look at other input/output units.

Cathode Ray Tubes

Cathode ray tubes (CRTs) go by a number of names, including *tubes, monitors, video display terminals (VDTs),* and *screens.* CRTs are used as primary output devices for microcomputer systems and as output media for *terminals* (I/O

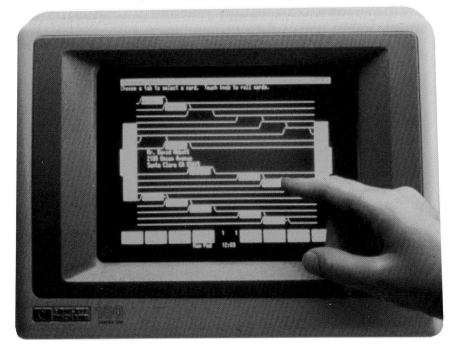

CRTs display both text and graphic data. (Courtesy Hewlett-Packard, Inc.)

```
<   Z Mem:23417 Len:23428 Pos:  2845 Tab:  529 File:  c5.5
a microcomputer, a\[Oterminal\[&is an input/output device which has no
independent computing power.  As a microcomputer output unit, the CRT displays
a portion of RAM known as the\[Odisplay memory\[&.  In order to view other
portions of memory, the operator can\[Oscroll\[&the screen up, down and
sideways to bring the desired information into view.
        A characteristic feature of CRTs is the\[Ocursor\[&which indicates to
the user where input data will next be entered into that portion of memory
being viewed.  Cursors appear in several forms depending on the computer being
used and the application being run at the time.  It may show as a blinking
rectangle, a blinking underscore, a checkered rectangle or in any of a number
of other configurations.  Figure 6-11, for example, shows a rectangular cursor
used by the word processing system used to prepare this chapter.  ▌It indicates
exactly where in the text the next character typed on the keyboard will appear.
.ff6
.li0
.cj
  :--------------------------------------:
  :          FIGURE 6-11                 :
  :--------------------------------------:
.lj
.li1
```

Cursor

FIGURE 6-11
Cursor

devices without independent computing power) attached to mainframes and minicomputers. As output devices, CRTs display data in text and in graphic form. Use of CRTs for graphics is discussed in Chapter Fifteen.

The term *text* refers to the display of characters of information. A typical screen displays 24 lines of text, each of which contains 80 characters. Some screens can display 80 lines of text with 132 characters each, thus making it possible to view an entire page as if it were typewritten. Although typically installed horizontally, like a home TV set, some CRTs can be rotated into a vertical position to facilitate the examination of full-page documents.

The CRT displays a portion of RAM known as the *display memory*. In order to view other portions of memory, the operator can *scroll* up, down, and sideways to bring the desired information into view.

A characteristic feature of CRTs is the *cursor* which indicates to the user where input data will next be entered into that portion of memory being viewed. Cursors appear in several forms, depending on the computer being used and the application being run. They may appear as a blinking rectangle, a blinking underscore, a checkered rectangle, or any of a number of other configurations. Figure 6-11, for example, shows a rectangular cursor used by the word processing system used to prepare a draft of this chapter. The cursor shows exactly where in the text the next character typed on the keyboard will appear.

CRTs may also serve as input devices through the use of *light pens* and *touch screens*. Light pens are often used in computer graphics work and are discussed in that chapter. They may also be used to select choices from a screen menu. Touch screens allow the operator to touch the screen with a finger or some other pointing device to make menu choices.

With Hewlett-Packard's touch screen, the user inputs by making choices on a CRT menu. (Courtesy Hewlett-Packard, Inc.)

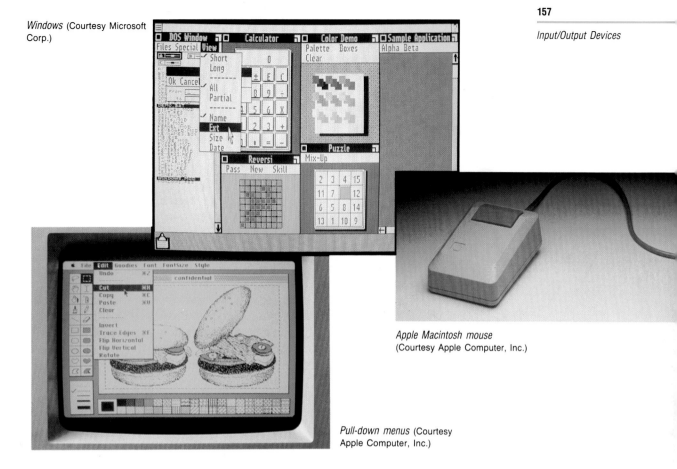

Windows (Courtesy Microsoft Corp.)

Apple Macintosh mouse
(Courtesy Apple Computer, Inc.)

Pull-down menus (Courtesy Apple Computer, Inc.)

Many application systems divide the CRT screen into *windows* which display the status of data files, correspondence, and calculations all at once. The user can adjust the size of the windows.

CRTs often display *menus* which offer the user a choice of functions that are available from the application program. To select an option, the user enters its identifying number or letter, or moves the cursor to it, and then presses the Enter Key. The use of *pull-down* menus by several application programs further adds to their flexibility. The menu of operations appears across the top of the screen. The user points to the menu choice with a finger or a light pen, or by moving the cursor, and "pulls" the menu down so that it fills the screen, or as much of it as is needed.

Cursor movement may also be controlled through the use of a *mouse*, a device that fits into the palm of the hand and is rolled about on the desk top to position the screen's cursor for menu selection, text editing, picture drawing, and other operations.

Keyboards

Data may be entered into a computer system by many means; however, the keyboard remains the predominant computer input device. A computer keyboard is used much like a typewriter's and has all of the expected alphabetic, numeric, and special characters found on a typewriter. Unlike the typewriter, which records the data on paper, each character keyed is encoded into the computer system's data coding scheme and is stored in memory.

Figure 6-12 shows a typical keyboard. In addition to the standard keys, one finds a *numeric keypad* which is essential for applications that require entry of large amounts of numeric information. *Function keys*, which are identified as F1 through F8 in figure 6-12, are used to call frequently used operations. *Cursor-control keys*, the ones with the arrows, move the cursor on the CRT. Other special keys delete and insert characters from the text, scroll the screen, clear the screen, and so on.

Computer keyboards employ one or more *control keys*. Control keys work just like the shift key on a typewriter in that they cause other keys on the keyboard to perform different functions than normal. If you hold the shift key down and press the letter e, you get a different character: E. Holding down the control key while you press one of the other keys causes a different character to be sent to memory. Control characters, like other characters, have their own code. The ASCII decimal code for control-P, for example, is 16. In many word processors, control-P causes the document in RAM to be printed. Some computers have more than one control key. The IBM PC, for instance, has a control key and an *alternate key*, both of which perform the function of transforming the normal use of the keys into some special purpose.

The *reset key* is used to reset the registers in the processor. It is used only to recover when for some technical reason the computer cannot perform a function called for by the user, such as trying to print when no printer is attached to the computer. In this circumstance, the computer is likely to "hang up" as its circuitry tries to send signals to a non-existent device.

Like the control keys, the *escape key* is used to cause other keys to perform special functions. Unlike the control keys, however, it is not held down while pressing another key. It is depressed once, sending a signal to the computer system for that purpose. The other keys then perform whatever function is called when in escape mode until that mode is turned off.

The traditional format of a computer or terminal keyboard follows the organization prescribed by the typewriter keyboard. This is known as the *QWERTY keyboard* because of the sequence of six letters in the upper left-hand corner of the alphabetic portion of the typewriter keyboard. In the past few years, considerable interest has been accorded the *DVORAK* keyboard which arranges keys differently. The DVORAK keyboard is designed for rapid data entry or typing and we should expect to see many more such keyboards in the near future.

FIGURE 6-12
Keyboard

Computer input is done on a variety of keyboards. (Courtesy International Business Machines Corp.)

Printers

CRTs are very useful for displaying the results of processing. Their images, however, are temporary. Sooner or later, printed versions, or *hard copies*, are needed. Statements must be sent to customers, checks must be prepared for employees and vendors, reports must be prepared for management, and so on. Although electronic means of transmitting and displaying information are growing in popularity, printed paper remains an essential communications medium.

Printers fall into three basic categories that are defined by the amount of printed output the device produces during one operation. *Page printers* print an entire page at once, *line printers* produce one line at a time, and *character printers* produce one character at a time. Printers can also be categorized by whether or not the print head strikes the paper: if it does, the printer is known as an *impact printer*; if not, it is a *nonimpact printer*.

Nonimpact printers are the fastest because they minimize the amount of physical movement required during the printing process. The Xerox 9700 Electronic Printing System, for example, uses laser beams to form character images on paper. It produces 120 pages per minute. Nonimpact printers are useful to commercial printers and to producers of catalogs and directories.

Other nonimpact printers use a variety of technologies. *Thermal printers*, the slowest of the nonimpacts, form characters by burning them on specially treated paper. Operating at about 30 characters per second, they are sometimes built into microcomputers, especially portable and lap-sized versions.

Electrostatic printers operate in a manner similar to thermal printers. They form the characters by charging the paper electrically. The paper then passes

*Laser printers connected to a
CPU provide letter-quality output
at a high rate of speed.
(Courtesy Xerox Corp.)*

through a toner solution. Particles of ink adhere to the charged areas of the paper. When the paper is heated, the particles melt, thus producing the characters. Electrographic printers can be quite fast. A Honeywell model, for example, prints up to 18,000 lines (about 300 pages) per minute.

Ink-jet printers squirt streams of ink to the surface of the paper. The ink dries almost immediately. These printers are fairly slow, producing from 50 to 100 characters per second, but they offer the advantages of low cost and multiple-color printing. We discuss color ink-jet printers in Chapter Fifteen of this book.

Impact printers involve more physical motion and, because the paper is struck by the printing device, are quite noisy. They can produce *multi-part reports*, meaning that through the use of carbon paper interleaves or chemical transfer methods, multiple copies can be printed at once. *Line printers* produce a line of characters all at once. The length of the line varies with the requirements of the application. Most line printers produce 120 to 144 characters per line, requiring a paper width of fourteen inches. The most common width is 132 characters. Printing is accomplished by passing the paper through the printer which uses a moving belt or chain containing the complete character set. A set of hammers, one for each of the printing positions on the line, strikes the paper from behind. This presses the paper against an inked ribbon, behind which is the character to be printed. Figure 6-13 illustrates this process.

*Ink-jet printers create images by
blowing ink onto paper.
(Courtesy Quadram Corp.)*

*Some transportable computers
have built-in printers.
(Courtesy Panasonic)*

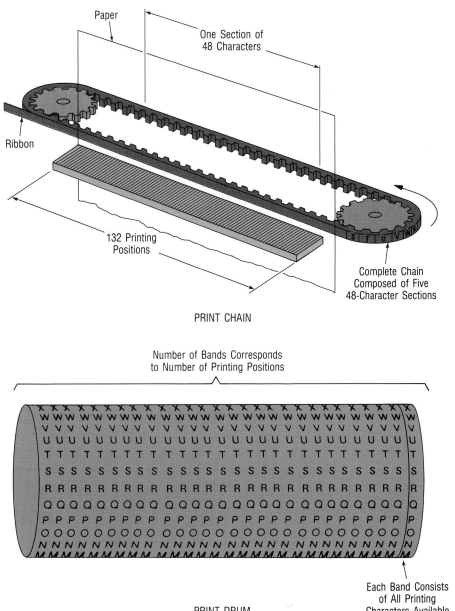

Paper

One Section of
48 Characters

Ribbon

132 Printing
Positions

Complete Chain
Composed of Five
48-Character Sections

S T U V W

PRINT CHAIN

Number of Bands Corresponds
to Number of Printing Positions

Each Band Consists
of All Printing
Characters Available

PRINT DRUM

FIGURE 6-13
*Line printers: chain and drum
units*

Some line printers employ a revolving drum to move the characters past the hammers. Such printers are known as *drum printers* as opposed to *chain* or *belt printers*. Because they involve fewer moving parts, drum printers are more reliable than chain or belt printers. Line printers are quite fast, producing up to 2000 lines (35 pages) per minute, but the quality of print is generally suitable only for internal uses.

Character printers form one letter at a time on the paper. Typically, they do this in one of two ways. *Dot-matrix* impact printers use a print head consisting of a column of vertical wires or pins, which passes along the length of the line being printed. Letters are formed by striking these wires against a ribbon which then strikes the paper. The characters appear as selected dots from among those in a rectangle or matrix, as shown in figure 6-14. Initially, the most common dimensions for the matrix were seven by nine, or 63 dots.

*Drum printers use a revolving
drum and an impact device to
create images on paper.
(Courtesy Dataproducts Corp.)*

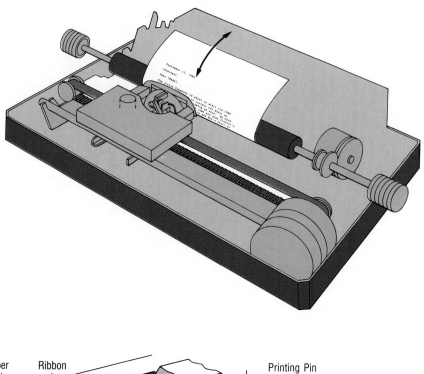

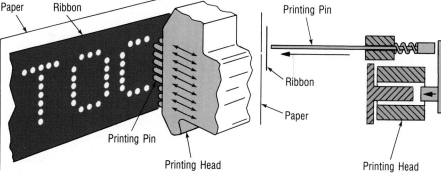

FIGURE 6-14
Dot-matrix printer

Recently manufacturers have substantially increased the number of pins and the number of dots per matrix. Increasing the *density* of the matrix, in this manner, improves the appearance of the document and increases the cost of the equipment. Nonimpact printers such as ink-jet, thermal, and electrostatic units also use the dot-matrix technique. Dot-matrix speeds range from 50 to 350 characters per second.

Because of their flexibility, dot-matrix printers can produce a wide variety of type and graphic effects, including color. Figure 6-15, for example, shows an advertisement that was printed by an inexpensive dot-matrix printer.

Letter-quality printers use fully formed metal or plastic casts of the letters to be recorded on paper. These operate in a manner very similar to the printing operation in an electric typewriter. The print head, which is equipped with a hammer, moves across the paper. In front of the head spins a *daisy wheel,* a *thimble,* or a similar element containing the character set (see figure 6-16). As the character to be printed comes into position, the hammer strikes it against the ribbon and the paper. The print head then moves on to the next character. Letter-quality printers produce faultless copy, but they are slow, ranging in speed from 12 to 50 characters per second.

FIGURE 6-15
Dot-matrix printing (Courtesy
SoftCraft)

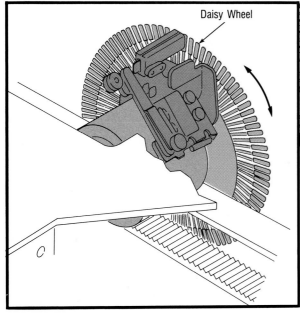

Daisy Wheel

FIGURE 6-16
Daisy wheel printing head

Data Entry Devices

If printers are slow data output devices, keyboards are even slower input devices because they depend on the keyboard skills of the operator. Data origination techniques that reduce or eliminate keyboarding will increase the speed of data entry and make it more accurate. Documents in machine-readable form reduce the possibility of human error in entering data from source documents. Thus, if we can devise a machine-readable form, the data on it can be read directly into the computer system without further human intervention.

A number of tools have been developed to make data input to computer systems independent of any human operator. These include *optical character*

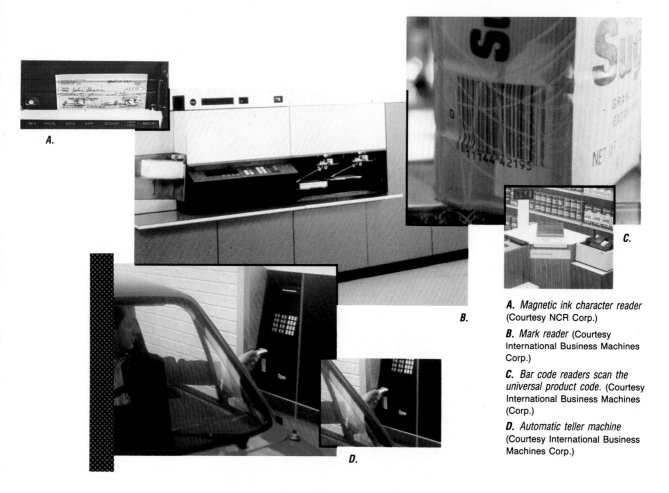

A. *Magnetic ink character reader* (Courtesy NCR Corp.)

B. *Mark reader* (Courtesy International Business Machines Corp.)

C. *Bar code readers scan the universal product code.* (Courtesy International Business Machines (Corp.)

D. *Automatic teller machine* (Courtesy International Business Machines Corp.)

readers (OCR), *magnetic ink character readers (MICR), optical mark readers (OMR),* and *bar code* or *line code readers.*

Character readers read optically (OCR) or with the use of machines that respond to magnetic ink (MICR). Mark readers interpret marks placed on forms used for data gathering purposes. Bar code readers sense price and inventory codes printed on products that are purchased frequently, such as products in supermarkets. This code is known as the *Universal Product Code (UPC).*

The bar code readers used in supermarkets are one of many types of remote data entry units. They are known as *point-of-sale* (POS) terminals. Remote data entry terminals permit the entry of data directly into the computer system for updating inventory files, preparing customers' bills, and other processing tasks. They are used in manufacturing and distribution, in warehouses, retail stores, bank teller windows, and business offices. Portable data entry terminals enable workers and executives in the field to enter data directly into the main computer system and to retrieve data. These terminals are usually connected to the computer center via telephone lines.

Voice Input and Output

Communicating with HAL, the computer on the spacecraft in *2001, A Space Odyssey,* was a matter of talking out loud and listening to it talk back. We are probably closer to that technological reality than we are to the year 2001. Com-

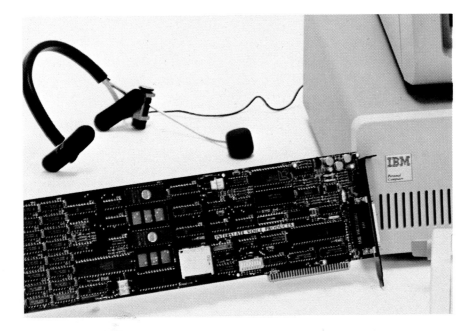

Specialized hardware can be used to provide voice input to the computer. (Courtesy Interstate Voice Products)

puter voice output is commonplace. Telephone information services frequently use computer voice output to provide directory service, time of day, and other information to inquirers. Programs that accept voice input to control their operation are available for all kinds of computers, from micros to monsters. To be sure, one cannot carry on a fluent conversation with a computer, but one can communicate the essentials. Typically, voice input systems require that the user pronounce the vocabulary of voice commands several times while the system "listens" and analyzes the voice patterns of the various words. Thereafter, using an average of the voice patterns, the system responds to the commands as directed. Once initialized with the voice pattern of one individual, such systems will often not respond to anyone else.

Communications

Making computers easier to use is a matter of making communication with them and between them easier. The development of input and output devices to facilitate this communication has, in its way, been as remarkable as the development of the central processor. As the use of touch screens and voice input and output, and the production of the printed word and document improve in efficiency, so too will the value of computer systems increase to those of us who use them.

The introduction of microcomputers to the corporate world has inspired the development of techniques that link them to mainframe computers, thus making distributed data processing a reality. It's not as easy as simply wiring the computers together or equipping them with modems, devices to connect computers to the telephone system. A mainframe using EBCDIC, for example, cannot communicate with a micro using ASCII, without software that translates from one coding scheme to the other. Giving diverse operational units in the organization the ability to update and otherwise manipulate data files risks destroying the consistency or integrity of that most important company asset: information. Managers of mainframe computer installations are understandably wary of micro-mainframe links.

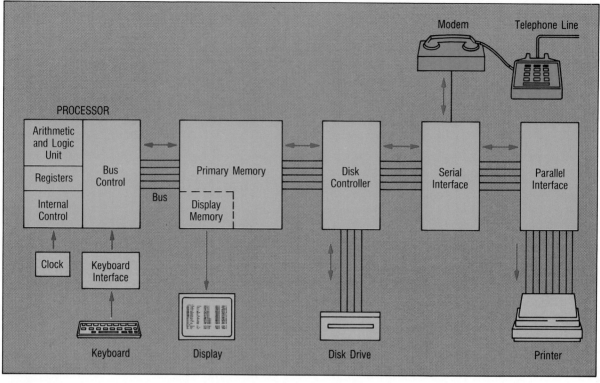

FIGURE 6-17
Computer architecture

COMPUTER ARCHITECTURE

Connecting the various secondary storage and input/output units to the central processing unit is accomplished through the use of a bus, as was mentioned earlier in this chapter. Most mainframe computers employ several buses, each specializing in a particular type of I/O device. Input/output units usually require special circuitry to connect them to the internal bus of the CPU. Known as *interfaces*, devices providing that circuitry can often be plugged into the computer in a matter of minutes in the case of microcomputers and

Interface boards connect
computers to peripheral devices.
(Courtesy Quadram Corp.)

FIGURE 6-18
IBM PC mother board (Courtesy
International Business
Machines Corp.)

hours in the case of mainframes. Figure 6-17 illustrates this idea for a typical microcomputer. Mainframe and minicomputers are somewhat more involved, but the concept is the same.

In figure 6-17, all of the components of the hardware system communicate with the processor through the bus. As we've seen, the access width of the bus is a crucial factor governing the speed, or *throughput,* of the total complex. We connect each of the peripheral devices to the bus through an interface. Depending upon the type of peripheral device, the *interface,* or *controller,* will transmit data either *serially* or in *parallel.* Because communicating data over the telephone requires sending them one bit at a time, the interface for a modem is a serial one. Disk units require parallel controllers, meaning that they receive data one byte, or eight bits, at a time. Printers, depending on their design, need either serial or parallel interfaces. Because the controlling circuitry is installed on printed-circuit boards or cards, we refer to peripheral control interfaces as "parallel cards," "serial cards," or, more generally, "controller cards."

The term *open architecture* refers to the ease with which various input/output peripherals and their associated controllers can be introduced into the hardware system. Many models of microcomputers offer open architecture through the use of *expansion slots* built into their main circuit boards. Figure 6-18, for example, shows the main circuit board, known as the *mother board,* for an IBM PC. The computer system is expanded by adding additional RAM and controller cards for various peripherals by installing the cards into the slots.

In the mid-1980s, producers of microcomputers began building the controlling circuitry for peripherals into the mother board itself, thus obviating the need to purchase additional circuitry to attach a printer, modem, or whatever to the system. These computers, such as the Apple IIc and Macintosh, and the IBM PC Jr., have *closed architecture,* meaning that the ability to attach peripherals is limited by the controlling circuitry built into the machine. Closed architecture is typical for lap-sized, or "knee-top," computers. In a recent

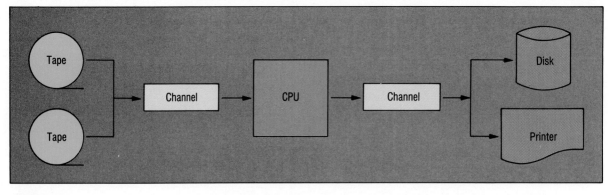

FIGURE 6-19
Input/output channels

development, devices are now being manufactured to convert closed architecture systems into open architecture ones, providing added flexibility to the user.

COORDINATING DIVERSE SPEEDS

The components of a computer hardware system operate at different speeds. The processor, involving only electronic activity, is the fastest. Disk drives are faster at transmitting data than are tape drives. Printers and data entry devices such as keyboards and bar code readers are the slowest. As a result, the processor spends most of its time waiting for the peripherals to do their work.

We've seen that the input and output of data involves areas of RAM known as buffers which are used as temporary holding areas until the data are ready to be transmitted or processed. By adding special-purpose processors, buffers can be made to work independently of the central processing unit. When this is done, the CPU can continue its work while the special-purpose processor controls input and output activity to and from the buffers. The combination of buffer and I/O processor is known as a *channel*. As is the case with all computers, the channel must be programmed to do its task. Figure 6-19 shows how channels intercede between I/O units and the CPU.

Each channel can handle several I/O devices, but only one I/O device per channel can transmit to or receive from RAM at one time. With more than one channel in operation, several I/O operations can take place at once while the CPU continues other processing tasks. This operation is known as *SPOOLing*, meaning Simultaneous Peripheral Operations On Line. In figure 6-19, three processors are in operation: one in the CPU and one in each of

Printer buffers store output data and release the computer for other tasks. (Courtesy Practical Peripherals)

the two channels. Coordinating the work of these computers and the flow of data is the job of the operating system, the topic of Chapter Seven.

For microcomputers, the chief need for SPOOLing relates to the slowness of printers. It is frustrating to lose the use of your computer while it prints a lengthy document. SPOOLing for these computers is accomplished in one of three ways. A peripheral card containing a processor that will set aside a portion of RAM as an output buffer may be installed. Another type of card includes the controlling interface for the printing device as well as additional memory to be used as an output buffer. This is often called a *buffer card*. Another technique attaches a buffer and its controlling processor between the computer and the printer. This is known as a *stand-alone buffer* because it does not require installation in one of the computer's expansion slots.

Technically speaking, a stand-alone buffer is a channel, inasmuch as it provides additional storage as well as a separate processor to control output. Microcomputer users, however, refer to it as a "buffer."

We close this second chapter about computer hardware with the observation that the development of the computing machine, starting with the ENIAC, has been a history of increasing power while decreasing size and cost. Computer processors now control appliances and monitor the operation of automobiles. They are worn in the pocket and on the wrist. They are more pervasive in Western society today than the telephone. Without them, modern airplanes could not fly, ships could not sail, millions of workers would not be given their paychecks, and most aspects of the modern commercial world would grind to a halt. To say that society is dependent on computers is surely an over-simplification. But our society, as an information society, recognizes that computers stand as a fundamental implement in our way of life.

Optical character readers make any typed page machine-readable. (Courtesy CompuScan)

SUMMARY

In Chapter Five, we studied the coding schemes used by computers to represent data. In this chapter, we covered some of the devices, called *secondary storage* devices, that are used to store those data. The most frequently used secondary storage devices are *magnetic tape* and *disk*. Because it is a *direct-access* device, disk is faster and more flexible than tape which is a *sequential* device.

We also examined some of the more common devices used to enter data into computer systems. In the entry process, these devices translate data from human-readable form to machine-readable form. Data entry devices include *keyboards, CRTs, printers, magnetic ink character readers (MICR), optical character readers (OCR), voice recognition units*, and devices used to transmit data over telephone lines.

Computer output devices include *CRTs* or *monitors* for visual output, and *printers* for hard copy. Output devices for communications and graphics are examined in the chapters devoted to those topics. As computer output devices, printers take several forms. These can be categorized as *impact versus nonimpact, dot-matrix versus letter-quality*, and *high-speed versus slow-speed*. Computerized *voice-output* units deliver information audibly.

Because the CPU operates so quickly and input/output devices so relatively slowly, hardware devices called *channels*, or *buffers*, are placed between the CPU and the input/output devices so that the CPU spends less time waiting for the input/output devices to catch up.

KEY TERMS

buffer
cathode ray tube
  (CRT)
computer architecture
controller
cursor
data cartridge
direct-access storage
  device (DASD)
disk drive
expansion slot
floppy disk
gigabyte
hard copy
hard disk drive
interface

I/O
light pen
machine-readable
magnetic ink character
  reader (MICR)
magnetic tape drive
monitor
mother board
mouse
off-line
on-line
optical character reader
  (OCR)
optical disk
optical mark reader
  (OMR)

parallel
peripheral device
point-of-sale terminal
secondary storage
serial
SPOOL
tape drive
terminal
throughput
touch screen
video display terminal
  (VDT)
voice input
voice output
window
write-it-once principle

REVIEW QUESTIONS

1. List two attributes of primary storage and two of secondary storage.
2. What are two main differences between disk and tape storage?
3. What is the relationship between physical and logical records in secondary storage?
4. Peripherals include _____ and _____ devices.
5. _____ _____ and _____ _____ turn the CRT into an input device.
6. The primary input device on a microcomputer is the _____.
7. _____ printers form images by spraying ink or burning the paper.
8. Printers may print a character, _____, or even _____ at a time.
9. What is the purpose of a printer buffer or SPOOLer?
10. A _____-_____ printer can be used for both text and graphics.

THOUGHT QUESTIONS

1. Describe the components of computer system hardware.
2. Compare and contrast Winchester and floppy disks.
3. Discuss the relative merits of open architecture versus closed architecture in microcomputers.

(Courtesy Gould AMI Semiconductor)

Information Processing Positions

Within any firm's information processing organization exists a number of positions, all of which have their individual challenges and responsibilities. We categorize them here into three sets: management, supervisory, and operational. The distinction among them is fairly conventional. Operational personnel do the actual work: operate computers, write and maintain programs, design systems, and the like. Supervisory personnel supervise operational personnel. Managers supervise supervisory personnel and establish policy.

Management Positions

The brief management job descriptions in the paragraphs that follow are more illustrative than definitive. The number and level of management positions is determined by the size of an organization. The responsibilities of management must be met by all firms, large or small. The degree to which the responsibilities are combined to define specific management positions depends on the needs of the organization, the abilities of the managers involved and, frequently, company politics.

Vice President of Information Systems

The vice president (VP) of Information Systems is responsible to the president for the effective operation of all of the organization's information processing activities. The person in this position supervises the executives in charge of the more specific areas of systems and operations. Whereas in the past the Information Systems VP position had

171

a *staff*, or advisory, relationship with corporate management, it has now moved into a more generally responsible *line*, or decision-making, responsibility in many organizations.

> The information position, which started out reporting to financial officers when computers were used as accounting machines, has been broadened to incorporate a full range of information systems. In enlightened companies this position now has a much closer relationship to operations or line management.[1]

As a result of this change in responsibility over the past decade, information processing managers need education and experience in general management areas, not just their own information processing specialties. The microcomputer revolution is contributing its share to the change in relationships:

> Thanks to the advent of decision support systems, many executives have been exposed to the once mysterious process of accessing raw data and playing with what-if variables. And thus they are more inclined to question information managers about the collection and dissemination of data—and the value of all this to the operation.[2]

Systems Manager

The systems manager supervises the entire systems development cycle as described in Chapter Four. Depending upon the organization, the systems department may be responsible for programming activities. If not, the programming function falls to the operations manager. Ordinarily these managers share responsibility for seeing to it that the applications and operating systems are maintained.

Operations Manager

The operations manager is responsible for the maintenance and operation of computer equipment, facilities, and operating systems programs. As compared with the systems manager who is responsible more for software considerations, especially applications systems, the operations manager is responsible for hardware.

This distinction, based on hardware versus software, is somewhat equivocal. Both managers have responsibilities for both hardware and software. The operations manager, however, is more concerned with operating hardware and software. The systems manager is more concerned with applications software and applications hardware such as the specialized input and output devices discussed in this chapter.

Other Management Specialty Areas

Figure 4-15 shows management function areas that report to the managers of systems and operations. Large organizations usually employ individuals in such management positions. Smaller firms leave the responsibilities of these positions to the systems and operations managers.

Systems development personnel look after the design and development of new information systems. This position plays a key role in the system development cycle. Systems development projects, as we've seen from Chapter Four, are most often worked on by a project team. A systems development manager may supervise several such teams, each headed by a project leader.

Systems maintenance staff monitors the performance of currently operating information systems. Staff members reporting to a systems maintenance manager will typically be experts in the various applications systems employed by the organization.

Systems support staff provides the day-to-day services that applications systems require for effective operation. Staff members reporting to the systems support manager will have special skills in forms design, records management, technical writing, and other matters needed to maintain the operating procedures of the company's systems.

The *programming manager* supervises the firm's computer programmers. Some firms may divide programmers into several specialty areas such as systems programming, applications programming, and communications programming and may assign a lead programmer to each area. Other firms may assign programming personnel directly to the systems and operations managers, thus avoiding the necessity for the programming management position. To the extent that programming activity is centralized in one management unit, it is often organized into projects, usually with a lead programmer or programmer/analyst in charge who reports to the programming manager.

Operations refers to the day-to-day work of the information processing department itself. The manager of operations is responsible for seeing that batch jobs are processed through the computer system as scheduled, that background or on-line support programs operate effectively, that libraries of data and programs are maintained and are available for use, and that the equipment is adequate and in operating order. Personnel reporting to the operations manager include those responsible for computer operations, data management, and equipment maintenance, to mention a few.

Supervisory Positions

First-line supervisory positions include those directly responsible for overseeing the work of operating personnel. Not all firms have the three layers of management depicted in figure 4-15. Many of those that do include supervisory personnel from the following representative list.

The *data base administrator* is responsible for the maintenance and organization of the firm's data bases. As increasing numbers of companies employ more sophisticated data bases and database management programs, this position will increase in importance. Applications programmers and programmers who are specialists in database management languages report to this supervisor.

The *data control supervisor* maintains records of all data and reports that enter and leave the information processing department. This person is responsible for the data control clerks in the organization. The data control operation, for example, would keep records of all paychecks by check number and employee number and would maintain control balances that would be used to verify the accuracy and integrity (meaning untampered with) of the data.

The *data entry supervisor* supervises those who prepare data for processing by the computer system. These personnel include *card punch operators, key-to-tape operators*, and *key-to-disk operators* as well as those who enter data using video data entry terminals.

The *operations supervisor* runs the computer room in mainframe computer installations. Computer operators report to this person as do, frequently, those responsible for routine maintenance of computer room equipment.

The *programming supervisor* reports to the programming manager and is often responsible for teams of programmers who specialize in particular applications or systems programs. In very large information processing organizations, a number of *lead programmers*, each of whom is in charge of a team, may report to the programming supervisor.

Operating Personnel

Our use of the term *operating personnel* here should not lead to confusion between those personnel involved with computer operations and those who are not. By operating personnel, we mean those employees who do the work as opposed to those who supervise its execution.

The following list, like the preceding ones, is representative. Actual positions in organizations depend upon the organization's size, structure, industry, management style, and a host of other factors. The list does, however, describe briefly the most common operating positions in the information processing field.

Applications programmers design and prepare programs for specific applications. They develop program logic charts, code and debug programs, and prepare final program documentation. Contrary to popular belief, programmers spend most of their time preparing documentation and searching out elusive errors in coding and logic. Comparatively little of their time is spent in developing innovative logic and coding patterns.

Systems programmers, like applications programmers, prepare computer programs. Systems programmers, however, specialize in those programs that make up the computer's operating system, the software that controls computer resources. Most of their efforts are devoted to maintaining the operating system, providing support services, and preparing system program routines (called "patches") for the specialized needs of applications programs and users. As a group, systems programmers are more technically oriented than are applications programmers because they require more detailed knowledge of how the computer hardware works and how the operating system controls the hardware.

Programmer/analysts occupy positions that lie between programmers and system analysts in terms of breadth of responsibility. Usually, the position of programmer/analyst is the first level of promotion from that of programmer, although in many organizations, the position of systems programmer represents a promotion from that of applications programmer. As its title suggests, the programmer/analyst is involved in both program and system design. This person, as compared with programmers, spends less time in program coding and debugging and more in defining the input and output requirements of the program and helping, if not supervising, those programmers who prepare the coding and do the debugging and documentation.

Systems analysts, as their title indicates, are the key operating personnel in the system development cycle. They work with users to define organizational needs for information, to identify problems with current systems, and to determine how best to meet the needs and solve the problems. The systems analyst is the key operative in organizations that provide users with information processing services through a mainframe computer. It is this person who communicates with users, defines users' needs, and translates those needs into recommendations for equipment and processing systems to meet them.

Librarians are responsible for the safekeeping and accessibility of the organization's data files when they are maintained on magnetic tape and removable disk packs. These secondary storage media are usually stored in a vault and require periodic physical maintenance even if the data are not routinely processed. Magnetic tapes, for example, should be rewound periodically to assure that magnetic fields recorded on areas of the tape wound over itself do not affect each other. Some installations maintain thousands of reels of tape and equivalent numbers of disk packs. All of these must be stored and records must be maintained of their storage locations so the data can be retrieved quickly when needed. It's a big job.

Computer operators as their title implies, operate the computer hardware system. As directed by a daily job sheet or log, the operator sets up jobs to be executed, mounts tapes and disk packs, loads paper and forms into printers, and monitors the operation of equipment in the computer room. Mainframe computers and minicomputers are controlled by entering instructions to the operating system through the computer's main console. This console also keeps a running log of all of the computer's activities during the day.

The computer operator is responsible for assuring that the jobs run according to plan and, if they don't, for alerting those responsible that something is amiss. This isn't as easy as it might seem to the uninitiated. Frequently, computers give no sign that all is not as it should be. Operators must be sensitive to what is and what is not reasonable output for various applications so that those responsible can be contacted when the output appears to be incorrect. The console must be closely monitored for unusual variances in computer activity which might signal incorrect operation. In general, the computer operator has the first responsibility for sounding the alarm when something seems wrong.

Data entry operators translate human-readable data into machine-readable form. Even though the industry has made great strides in devising means to collect data at their source in machine-readable form, there remains a great deal of data that must be converted before it is ready for processing. Data entry operators include *key-punch,* or *card-punch, operators* who record data and verify them as holes punched into cards. These operators also use key-to-disk and key-to-tape devices to record data magnetically on disk and tape media. In addition, they operate data entry terminals which enter data directly into the system on a real-time basis.

QUESTION

1. Plot out a career ladder for yourself as if you were planning a career in information processing. List the various positions you would expect to hold and, for each one, the skills you think you should develop for promotion to the next level.

Operating Systems: Managing Computer Resources

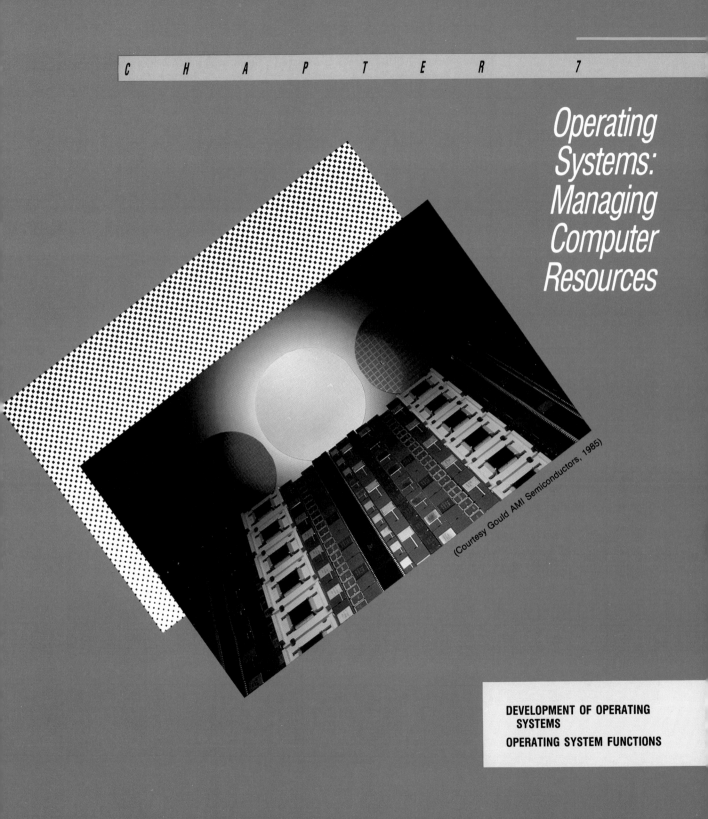

(Courtesy Gould AMI Semiconductors, 1985)

DEVELOPMENT OF OPERATING SYSTEMS

OPERATING SYSTEM FUNCTIONS

A complete computer system comprises three parts: the hardware, the application software, and the operating system. The hardware does the work, the application software defines the work to be done, and the operating system coordinates it all.

During their first decade or so of commercial use, complete computer systems involved only the hardware and the application software. Human operators controlled the operating details of the computer system. A *job sheet,* or *run sheet,* provided information about the various activities to be performed by the computer.

Consulting it, the operator would mount tapes on the specified drives, locate the punched data cards, stack them into card feeders, set switches, prepare wiring panels and, finally, press a button called "Start" or "Load" on the console of the computer. Having such an expensive resource standing idle while humans scurried about making things ready left much to be desired.

Programmers worked in machine language. What was worse, they also had to do detailed machine language programming to control the various peripheral devices called by their programs.

Preparing computer programs took extraordinary amounts of time. Programmers prepared them on paper using coding sheets. These were then delivered to cardpunch operators who recorded the programs as holes in cards. Thus rendered machine-readable, the programs to be tested and the test data for them were submitted to the computer center. Programs never executed properly the first time. Weeks and months were required to produce programs that, today, can be completed in a few days.

UNIVAC I was one of the first commercial computers. (Courtesy Sperry Corp.)

So what's different today? Three things. First, most programming today is done using terminals, thus enabling programmers to test their work, usually in parts or modules, as they go along. Second, programming has been made easier through the use of modern programming languages, the subject of Chapter Nine. Suffice it to say here that a programming system translates programs into machine language. Third, the work of the operator in setting up each application program has been largely automated through the use of operating systems.

DEVELOPMENT OF OPERATING SYSTEMS

It all got started in the mid-1950s. Storing programs on punched cards used considerable space and required considerable time to enter programs into primary storage, or RAM. Therefore, computer installations found it expedient to store all their operating programs on magnetic tape. This was called the *program library*. A short program would load specified programs from the library into RAM and set each one to executing. When one program was finished, the next one was "called" from the library. The program that "called" the application programs was called the *monitor*.

Input to the monitor program typically took the form of a deck of punched cards, called *job control cards*, which described the programs to be executed. The operator fed the deck into a card reader. If an application program required punched card input, these data cards were fed into the reader, too. The monitor would read the job control cards, load the required program into RAM, and set the program to executing.

Figure 7-1 illustrates the idea. The specifications in the job control cards followed the formats required by the monitor. In time, these specifications became known as the *Job Control Language*, or *JCL*, of the system. Because the entire process used sequential tape and card files, it was limited to *batch* or *stacked-job* processing applications. In stacked-job processing, several jobs

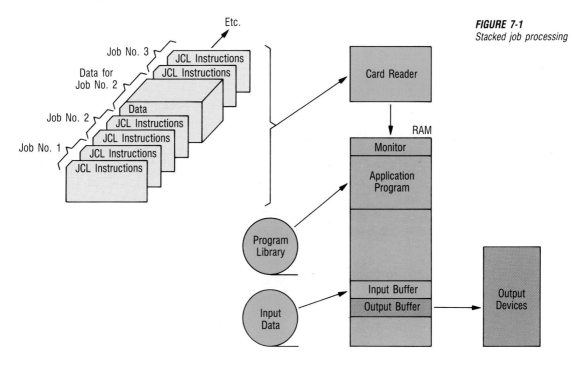

FIGURE 7-1
Stacked job processing

are loaded into the computer and executed one immediately after the other. Batch processing accumulates transactions to be processed at one time. It can be compared with *real-time* processing which processes transactions individually at the time they occur.

While techniques for using program libraries and monitors were being developed, programmers and managers recognized that the input/output (I/O) routines coded by each programmer were essentially identical. Why not develop standard I/O routines for all of the peripheral devices used in the computer system and require that all application programs use them? This would relieve programmers from having to rethink I/O coding for each program.

This worked very well, but each application program carried its own I/O routines which were identical with those in all of the other application programs. This unnecessarily increased the size of the program library, a problem data processors call *redundancy*. I/O routines, therefore, were stored separately in the program library. Another short program added them to the application programs when each was loaded into RAM for execution. This program was called the *link editor* because it linked each application program to the I/O routines. The set of I/O routines became known as the *Input/Output Control System,* or the *IOCS*.

Programmers no longer had to include I/O instructions in their programs. Instead they used general statements such as GET and PUT to retrieve a record from an input device or to write one to an output device. Known as *macro instructions,* or *macros*, these commands signaled the monitor to call the link editor to replace the macros with the necessary coding to accomplish an I/O operation. Eventually, IOCS would become an integral part of the operating system, thus eliminating altogether the need to insert I/O routines into application programs.

So long as the monitor controlled the IOCS and the execution of the link editor and application programs, it seemed logical that it should control the allocation of primary storage, or RAM, too. This relieved programmers of that responsibility, thus letting them concentrate even more on the logic of their programs, to the exclusion of the operating details of the computer system.

But controlling the allocation of RAM means controlling the location of data and programs stored in it. The introduction of magnetic disk, secondary storage media in the early 1960s had a profound impact on the way computers could be used and, consequently, on the nature of their operating systems. A *disk operating system (DOS)* maintains its program libraries on disk. Expanding the monitor program to include memory management and control of I/O operations from disk made it a much more useful tool for controlling the computer system's operation.

Data required for application programs could now be stored on disk; operators no longer had to mount and unmount reels of the tape for each job. Giving DOS control of memory and peripheral device management earned it the somewhat more authoritarian name of *supervisor* because it supervises virtually all of the computer's activities. Having the program library on disk allows the supervisor to look ahead at the jobs to be run and issue instructions through the computer's console to the operator indicating what that person should do to prepare the peripherals for upcoming operations.

If this looks like a case of a machine telling people what to do, you're correct. Having a computer system control itself through its supervisor program carries with it the consequence of having humans serve the machine. Be consoled, however. The benefits outweigh the psychological discomfort. Besides, we humans can always pull the plug. We remain the ultimate authorities.

*Fritz Lang's movie **Metropolis**
predicted that humans would
someday serve machines.
(Courtesy Museum of Modern
Art, Film Stills Archive)*

OPERATING SYSTEM FUNCTIONS

Today, an *operating system* is considered to be a set of programs that standardize the way a computer's resources are made available to the user and to applications software. The emphasis here is on the words "set of programs."

The computer system's peripheral devices include disks, tapes, and various other I/O units. One of the disk drives stores the operating system and the several application programs used by the system. As a physical unit, the disk drive containing these programs is known as the *system resident device*, which is sometimes abbreviated to *system device, resident device,* or just *sys-res.* Figure 7-2 shows what's happening.

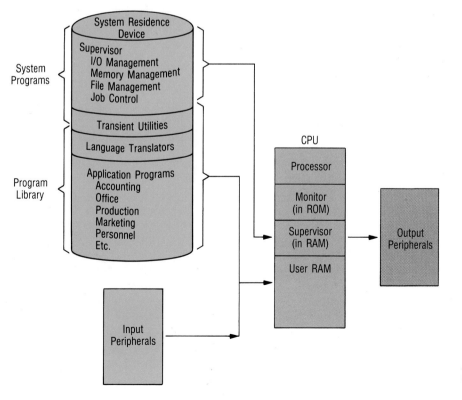

FIGURE 7-2
Operating system resources

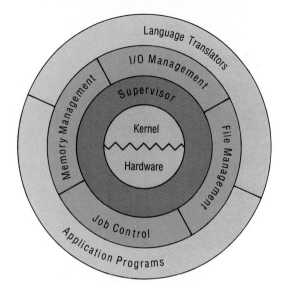

FIGURE 7-3
Operating system shell

At this point, we should mention some peculiarities about operating system terminology. Many consider "supervisor" and "monitor" to be synonyms, and for some computer systems, they are. In other systems, the monitor is separate from the supervisor and is limited to initial start-up operations and to programming in machine language. Inasmuch as almost all operating systems today are disk-based, they are known as disk operating systems, or DOS (rhymes with "hoss"). Some data processors use the more general acronym, *OS*, (pronounced "oh ess") for operating system.

These peculiarities of operation and semantics should not detract from the basic functions of all operating systems. These functions include input/output management, memory management, file management, and job control. Lumping all of these functions together as a group of programs known as system programs under the control of the supervisor yields the complete operating system.

In figure 7-3, we see the concept. The monitor, often called the *kernel*, is at the center. It is usually included in ROM as an integral part of the hardware system. The supervisor (OS or DOS) surrounds the kernel; the functions surround the supervisor; and other utilities and application programs surround the functions. This visual concept is known as a *shell*, a multi-layered set of programs in which the outer ones control the inner. Not all of the programs making up the shell are available in RAM at once. Those programs that are available in RAM are called *resident* system programs. They may be executed directly by the user or by the application program. Those programs that are not available in RAM must be loaded into RAM prior to their execution. These are called *transient system programs* or *transients* because they are loaded into RAM temporarily prior to execution.

Input/Output Management

As long as the machine is turned on, a computer system's processor is never idle. Even when the computer is apparently dormant, the processor loops through a short program which determines if something has been entered from the keyboard or other input device.

Imagine that you are using a minicomputer system terminal to design a report. As you ponder the format of your report, the processor spins through its loop waiting for you to enter a command. When you do, the processor performs a few functions and resumes waiting for you. Because your computer operates at, say, eight million cycles per second, the huge majority of cycles are wasted while you think and tap away at the keyboard.

You finish designing the report. You enter a final command which causes the report to be printed. The system's printer seems pretty fast: 150 characters per second. While it chatters away, you cannot use the computer because it is occupied with the printing operation. At the same time, the processor still spends most of its time waiting between each character that is printed and for data which is retrieved one buffer-full at a time from disk storage.

The disparity between the relatively slow speeds of peripherals and the fast speed of the processor calls for I/O management techniques that make better use of the speed of the processor.

SPOOLing and Buffering

We broached the subject of SPOOLing and buffering in Chapter Six. SPOOLing (Simultaneous Peripheral Operations On Line) refers to operations in which more than one peripheral device can operate at once. Buffering refers to the use of temporary data storage devices that receive output from or input to the CPU and store it until the CPU is ready to process it.

When the application program calls for an I/O operation, data are transferred to or from the buffers. Another program, the IOCS, is resident in RAM as well. When the processor is not otherwise occupied, the supervisor turns it to executing the IOCS. When the application program requires action, the supervisor *interrupts* the processor from executing IOCS and returns it to running the application program. When the application program pauses in its processing requirements (as when you ponder your next command), the supervisor returns the processor to the IOCS.

It's as if the computer is doing two things at once. Actually, it's not. Figure 7-4 shows three programs resident in RAM. The IOCS program inputs and outputs data to and from the buffers. The application program performs its work separately from the I/O operations. The supervisor program alternates the attention of the processor between the other two programs as needed. It's not unlike a juggler who appears to be moving three things at once, but really is moving his or her attention from one to another object in turn.

In a strict technical sense, SPOOLing operates with *one* processor trading its attention between IOCS and one or more application programs. Buf-

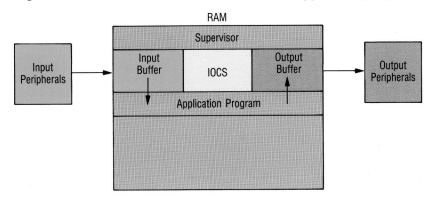

FIGURE 7-4
IOCS operation

fering, on the other hand, uses *two* processors. The second processor and the storage buffer are located in a channel, as described in Chapter Six. The technical distinction between SPOOLing and buffering, then, lies in the number of processors involved. SPOOLing uses one, the central processor; buffering uses two.

Multitasking and Overlapping

Different application programs have different I/O requirements. One way to balance the speed of the processor with the speed of the I/O peripherals is to put two or more application programs in RAM at once. Let's consider putting two application programs in RAM. Job A requires considerable input and output, but little calculation and manipulation of data. Job B requires little I/O, but much calculation and manipulation. Loading both into RAM promises increased productivity.

Figure 7-5 shows a multitasking environment. The computer system consists of three parts: an input channel, a processor, and an output channel. Time is measured in nominal intervals just to keep things simple. In reality, the intervals would be measured in *milliseconds* (thousandths of a second), *microseconds* (millionths of a second) or, on very fast computers, *nanoseconds* (billionths of a second). At the bottom of the figure, the input, processing, and output time requirements for the two jobs are listed. Job A, because it requires a total of eight units for I/O operations and one for processing, is said to be *I/O-bound*, meaning that its total productivity is bound by the maximum speed of the I/O units. If Job A were executing alone, the processor would wait most of the time while input and output took place. Job B is *process-bound*. If it were to execute alone, the I/O peripherals would be waiting for the processor to complete its work before input and output operations could take place.

Putting Job A and Job B in RAM at the same time and letting the supervisor control their execution makes better use of the system's resources. Operations proceed as follows. The initial input data for Job A (A1) are read into RAM (time interval 1). When this is accomplished, the processor begins working on the data (time interval 4). While that's taking place, the initial input

FIGURE 7-5
Overlapping

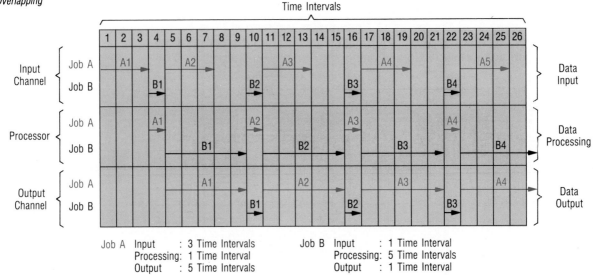

Job A Input   : 3 Time Intervals
        Processing: 1 Time Interval
        Output   : 5 Time Intervals

Job B Input   : 1 Time Interval
        Processing: 5 Time Intervals
        Output   : 1 Time Interval

data for Job B (B1) are read. After data A1 have been processed, the output channel begins outputting the results (time interval 5). While that's happening, the processor begins executing Job B on data B1. As execution of Job B continues, the input channel reads the second unit of data for Job A (A2). When processing of B1 finishes, the output channel begins outputting it (time interval 10). Meanwhile, the processor returns to Job A to process A2. While that's going on, the input channel reads B2, and so forth.

After the start-up period of five time intervals, the system is working as efficiently as possible. The processor and the output channel are working one hundred percent of the time, alternating between Jobs A and B. The input channel is idle for two time periods out of every six. Notice that input, output, and processing can take place at the same time in this system because the system uses three processors: one for each of the channels, and the central processor. Processing, of course, cannot take place until the required data have been inputted. Similarly, outputting requires that processing of the output data be complete.

Multitasking, then, is a matter of having more than one application program resident in RAM. The operating system turns the attention of the processor to the application programs as necessary to make the most effective use of the total system hardware resources. This is called *multiprogramming.* *Overlapping* is a process in which input, output, and processing activities take place at once. This is possible only when the system has more than one processor. Figure 7-5, which illustrates overlapping, shows a computer system with three processors: the CPU and two channels.

Multitasking can also refer to a computer system in which more than one processor is used to work on separate application programs. Such configurations are said to use *multiprocessing.* Although in a pure sense, multiprocessing refers to any procedure involving more than one processor (including overlapping) the term usually means multitasking with multiprocessing.

Multitasking, with many more than two application programs under execution, predominates in mainframe and minicomputer installations. Its use is growing with microcomputer systems, particularly those that remain connected to a communications network awaiting incoming data. As long as there is no input from the communications systems, the computer can be used for other purposes. As soon as a transmission signal is received from the communications system, the user's program is interrupted and control of the processor is turned over to the communications program. When communications have ceased, control returns to the user's program.

Integrated circuits are manufactured under sterile conditions much like those in a hospital operating room. (Courtesy Sperry Corp.)

Integrated circuits, smaller than a fingernail, contain a myriad of electronic components. (Courtesy Sperry Corp.)

Time-sharing

The operating system provides the facility to execute more than one program from RAM using multitasking techniques. There is no reason why users, whether individuals or units within an organization, cannot run their applications independently. This is called *time-sharing* because each of the users shares the computing time of one computer system.

In such a situation, the company controller could perform analyses of financial data, the sales department could develop a report on customer purchasing activity, and a secretary could prepare a written report at the same time. Now, we know that these things don't happen at the same time. The processor runs only one program at a time, but it switches so quickly among the programs in RAM that it appears to any one of the users that he or she has complete control of the system.

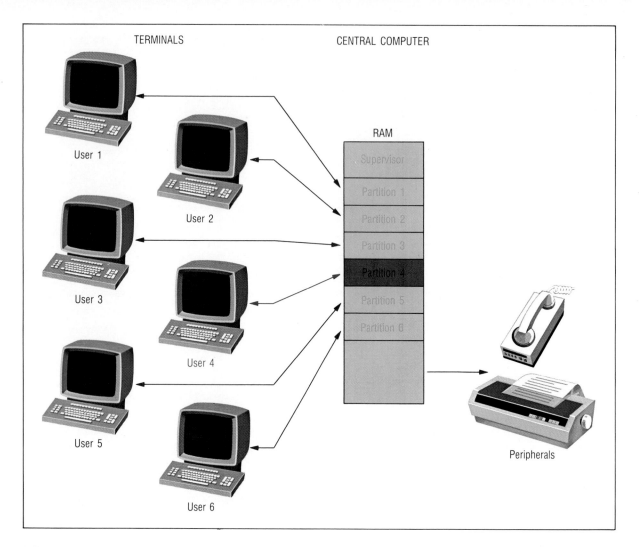

TERMINALS   CENTRAL COMPUTER

User 1

User 2

RAM

Supervisor

Partition 1

Partition 2

Partition 3

Partition 4

Partition 5

Partition 6

User 3

User 4

Peripherals

User 5

User 6

FIGURE 7-6
Partitioning

You may recall chess masters who would play several games at once against different opponents. Walking about the tables, they would allocate a small bit of their attention to each game, then move on to the next. From each opponent's perspective, he or she was playing the game against one person. That's how computer time-sharing works.

Setting up this arrangements is a matter of connecting a number of on-line terminals to the computer (see figure 7-6). The operating system allocates a portion of RAM called a *partition* or *work space* to each. The work space contains the user's program and associated data. OS then *polls* each of the terminals to determine whether or not a transaction awaits processing. If so, the processor is directed to that user's partition, the processing is accomplished, and the operating system continues polling until another transaction is ready from one of the terminals. As the term is used in time-sharing systems, a *transaction* is anything that requires the attention of the computer system.

Normally, each user is limited to a maximum amount of time to process any one transaction. This is called a *time slice* and may be the same for all users or may vary depending upon the relative importance or priority of the user activities. If a transaction from one user exceeds the amount of time in his or her time slice, processing is temporarily suspended while the operating system polls and processes transactions from other terminals.

As people use computer terminals, they spend most of their time thinking and keying in commands. The transaction is not sent to the computer system until the Return or Enter key is pressed. Even so, if there are a great number of users, the *response time* of the system may degrade to the point where users must wait noticeably after entering a transaction.

Networking

We can connect several computers in a *network*. This differs from time-sharing. Time-sharing uses *one computer* to which a number of terminals are connected. Networking links *a number of computers* for the purpose of communication and for the sharing of common data files and peripherals.

One such networking operating system is UNIX, which was developed by AT&T's Bell Laboratories. Initially designed as an operating system supporting time-sharing operations for minicomputers, UNIX now is used in mainframe, minicomputer, and microcomputer networks. Each unit or *node* in the network is an independent computer, that is, a "smart terminal." Within the limits set by the operating system, each node has access to all of the programs and data available to other nodes. Each node may have its own set of peripherals or it may use peripherals located elsewhere in the network.

Figure 7-7 shows a typical networking arrangement. Several computers are connected to a central, or slave, computer which serves them all. Usually, the service consists of access to data files and offers each computer the processing power and peripherals of the slave. Chapter Eleven examines networking as an aspect of communications.

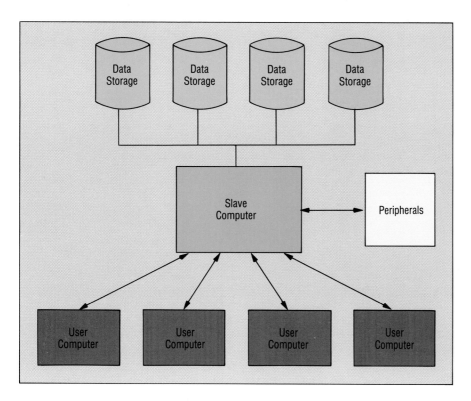

FIGURE 7-7
Networking

Memory Management

Computing environments today, which are characterized by multitasking, time-sharing, networking, and the like, cannot afford the risk of having individual programmers control memory allocation. A programmer, for example, might accidentally load a program right into someone else's partition, thus destroying that person's program and data. Besides, keeping track of memory when writing programs is a very tricky business.

For these and other reasons, memory management is left to the operating system. The OS allocates memory to itself and its resident system programs, sets aside areas for application programs and user partitions, arranges the I/O buffers, and reserves storage for specialized purposes.

Memory Allocation

Details about how OS allocates areas of RAM are provided in a *memory map* of the system. Two examples of memory maps appear in figure 7-8. On the left is the map established for the IBM PC by the operating system, PC-DOS, which was written by Microsoft Corporation for the PC. The total PC memory, including ROM and read/write, or R/W, RAM amounts to 1024K bytes, or one megabyte of primary storage. On the right, RAM for the Apple II computers is allocated by ProDOS. Thirty-six thousand memory positions are available to the user for application programs.

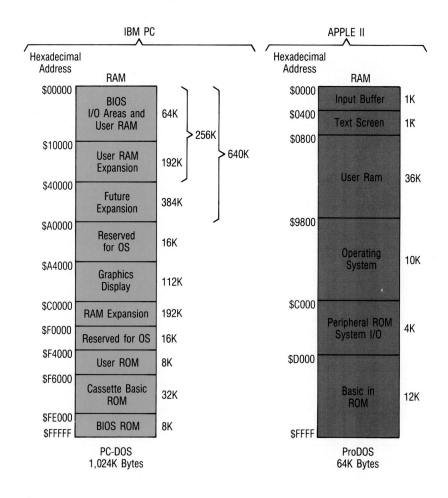

FIGURE 7-8
Memory maps

Operating systems are memory-consuming programs. In both the examples shown in figure 7-8, the operating system and its resident programs and reserved space use nearly half of the available RAM addresses. Operating systems, then, are expensive in terms of RAM. The efficiencies they offer, however, make them indispensable.

Background and Foreground

Operating systems that support multitasking assign priorities to the programs resident in RAM. This way, programs of particular importance take precedence over others. In one popular scheme, the OS sets up a program to be run as a *background* program, meaning that as long as nothing is required by any of the other resident applications, the processor will execute it.

Consider a situation in which point-of-purchase sales data are collected one transaction at a time for real-time updating of customer accounts and inventory files. During slow periods, the computer might be standing idle much of the time. Putting a batch program that prepares periodic reports or that writes payroll or vendor checks in RAM will give the computer something to do while it waits for sales transactions.

In this case, the operating system assigns a high priority to incoming sales transactions so that upon the input of a sales transaction, the system will interrupt the execution of the background program, process the transaction, and then return to the batch job. Several resident application programs are possible, each with its own level of *priority interrupt*.

Virtual Memory

One can load only so many programs into memory for multitasking execution before memory is exhausted. In fact, individual programs may be too large to be contained in memory. To solve this problem the OS loads only a part of each program into memory at one time. Operating systems that manage memory in this fashion are known as *virtual memory,* or VM, systems.

One way they do this is to divide the program into *segments.* Each segment is a logical entity in that it performs some well-defined function. This function might be a calculation procedure, an output formatting procedure, or a data file sorting operation. The entire program, consisting of such segments, is stored on disk. When a segment is ready for execution, it is loaded into memory for that purpose. If a segment in memory refers to other segments, those segments are loaded when they are required.

*The operating system controls
access to the printer by various
users in this multi-user system.
(Courtesy NCR Corp.)*

This gives every appearance of limitless memory space inasmuch as the length of a program is limited only by the amount of space on disk available for its storage. The top part of figure 7-9 shows the second segment of a three-segment program in RAM. After this segment has been executed, the next one will be loaded and executed.

Dividing RAM into *pages,* or *page frames,* and then dividing each program into pages of the same size accomplishes the same task. A program is loaded into RAM one page at a time. When execution of that page finishes, the operating system loads and executes the next page. A page may or may not contain a complete logical segment of the program.

Still a third way, called the *segmentation and paging system,* combines the characteristics of segmenting and paging. RAM is divided into page frames and each program is divided into logical segments that will ordinarily fit into

The AT&T 6300 computer is designed around the Microsoft-DOS operating system. (Courtesy AT&T Information Systems)

one page frame or less of memory. In those cases in which a segment is too large for one page, more than one page is assigned to it. This is illustrated in the bottom portion of figure 7-9. Note that segment 6 and 8 each require two pages.

Using virtual memory, many users can execute programs that require more RAM than is available in the computer system. Given a great number of users, the number of page or segment transfers between disk and RAM may become excessive. In this case, the computer spends most of its time transferring programs. This condition is known as *thrashing*. It signals that either more RAM is required or that fewer programs must be resident at one time.

Keeping track of memory addresses in VM systems is no mean trick for the operating system. In order to speed things up, many computer systems include VM routines as part of the hardware, in ROM. This technique has led to the development of *virtual machines*, computers that are designed specifically for VM systems.

From the user's point of view, a virtual machine offers the capability of a stand-alone computer system dedicated only to the user's tasks. The computer system, then, appears to consist of a number of computers acting as independent devices. In figure 7-10, for example, three individual user terminals, a point-of-sale terminal, and two batch applications are resident at once.

It should be pretty clear that virtual memory techniques and virtual machines would be impossible without high-speed, direct-access devices such as disk storage units. Some additional work has been done in which the operating system, while running a virtual memory system, will "remember" past

FIGURE 7-9
Virtual memory

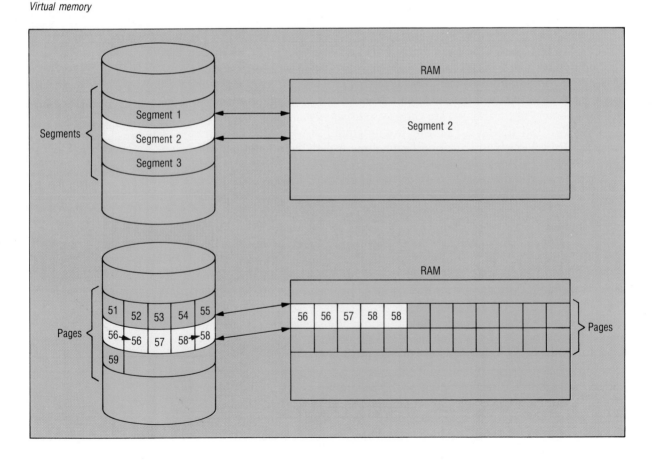

activities and the sequence of page and segment swaps during the execution of various application programs. Thus armed, it can anticipate page-frame and segment swaps and execute them prior to their need, thus reducing the amount of time spent waiting for swapping to finish. In a very practical sense, this is an heuristic system.

File Management

The preferred data storage medium today is disk, although many installations that employ batch processing methods use magnetic tape, too. The term "file" means, of course, a group of related records. The records may hold data about customers, employees, or whatever the organization needs to keep track of.

FIGURE 7-10
Virtual machine

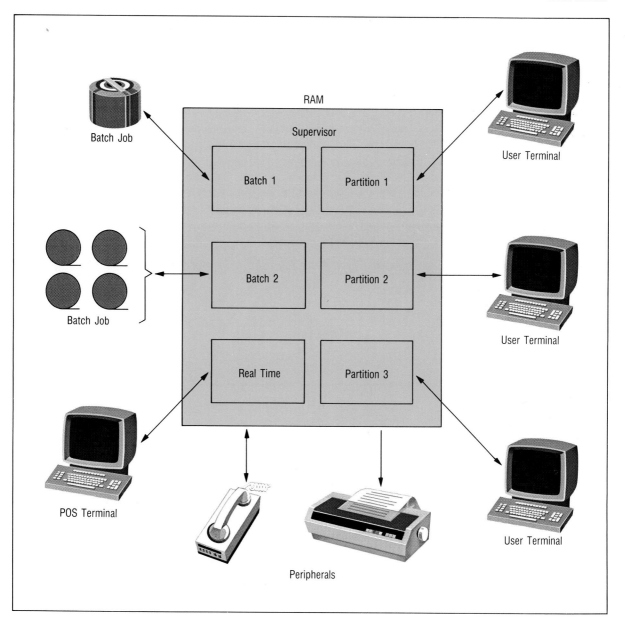

The records may also be computer instructions. Thus, the file, as a group of program instructions, is a computer program. Particularly as files are stored on secondary storage media, the term "file" refers to anything stored on the medium, be it a program or a data file.

Filenames and Directories

As we've seen in Chapter Six, files are stored on disk at particular sector or block addresses. The operating system maintains a *directory*, or *catalog*, of the addresses of each file. Each file must be assigned a name, called a *filename*. Notice the curious spelling. Data processing folk refer to the name of a file as its "filename," one word. The directory, in its simplest form, is nothing more than a list of filenames with the disk addresses at which the files may be found. In short, it is a table of contents. Referring to a filename causes the operating system to consult its directory of filenames, find the address of the required file, and make it ready for use.

Directory Hierarchies

So far, we've considered a directory as a list of files. A directory may also be a directory of other directories. Figure 7-11, for example, illustrates a situation in which a computer system is used to maintain files of written work by various authors. The works are categorized as poetry and prose. Works of prose, are further categorized as fiction or nonfiction. In this situation, the *root directory*, called WRITERS, yields two *subdirectories*; POETRY and PROSE. Under PROSE, there are two additional subdirectories, NFICTION and FICTION. Finally, under each of the three lowest-level subdirectories, the separate files for each author are listed. These are the data files.

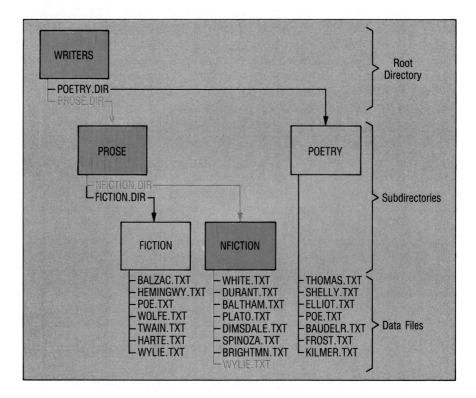

FIGURE 7-11
Directories

This whole arrangement is called a *tree*. It's really upside down, but that's what it's called. Finding a particular data file in the hierarchy of directories is a matter of specifying the *datapath*, or *path*, through the directories to it. To find the file about Philip Wylie, for example, the system must proceed through PROSE to NFICTION to WYLIE. The ".TXT" beside each filename, incidentally, identifies each as a text file. Many operating systems use such identifiers to indicate the type of file in the system.

Using hierarchical directories, consisting of the root and one or more levels of subdirectories, is very helpful with computer systems that enjoy considerable on-line secondary storage capacity. A microcomputer user with a hard disk containing several million bytes of storage will find the technique useful. Users of limited-capacity, floppy disks, on the other hand, will probably find it more trouble than it's worth. To minicomputer and mainframe installations, the use of hierarchical file directory systems is indispensable.

Volume Labels and Directories

Frequently, storage media can be removed from the hardware system. This is true of magnetic tapes, disk packs, and individual disks, both hard and floppy. It's always a good practice to attach a label to the disk or tape to easily identify its contents when it is not mounted, that is, when it is off-line.

Because we can have multiple disk and tape drives on-line at one time, it's important to provide a way for the operating system to determine what tapes or disks are actually mounted on the drives. This is accomplished by the *volume label*, or *volume directory*, a name assigned to each disk and tape used in the computer installation. The volume label identifies the storage medium as a physical unit while the filenames and the directory names identify the data stored on the unit.

Job Control

Figure 7-3 depicts the notion of the operating system as a shell of concentric programs centered on the hardware. When one of the application programs, or language translators is running, it interacts with the operating system to control the hardware functions. Many consider it an ideal system when that interaction makes details of the computer hardware and operating system *transparent*, or invisible, to the user.

According to the ideal view, when the user turns the computer on, the system should begin working on the user's application without further ado. That's fine if the computer does only one job, as is the case with stand-alone word processors and pocket calculators. Computers and their supporting operating systems, being the flexible tools they are, can perform a great number of different tasks. The user must be prepared to tell the operating system what task to perform at the moment.

Think of the operating system shell illustrated in figure 7-3 as an onion. When the computer system is complete, an application program is executing and the user communicates with it. When the application program finishes, it is no longer a part of the system: the outer layer has been peeled off. The user now must communicate with the supervisor or operating system to tell it what to do next. He or she does this by using the OS's *Job Control Language*, or *JCL*.

Operation	Unix	MS-DOS	ProDOS	AppleDOS	CP/M
Copy File	cp	copy	menu choice	menu choice	utility
Display Directory	ls -l	dir	CAT or CATALOG	CATALOG	dir
Rename File	mv	rename	RENAME	RENAME	ren
Execute Program Named "filenm"	filenm	filenm	-FILENM	RUN FILENM	filenm
Display Contents of Text File	cat	type	not available	not available	type
Compare Files	cmp	comp	menu choice	not available	utility

Note: AppleDOS, ProDOS, and CP/M include utility programs for copying files and comparing files. These operations cannot be executed with a direct DOS command.

FIGURE 7-12
Operating system commands

JCL Instructions

We've used the term *JCL instruction* to refer generically to an instruction to the operating system. In mainframe installations, JCL programming is important work. Some programmers, called system programmers, specialize in this activity alone. Most users and programmers use such terms as *system commands* and *DOS commands* when referring to instructions that tell the operating system what to do. In the UNIX operating system, such commands are called *shell commands*.

At its simplest level, using system commands is no more difficult than entering the command and pressing the Enter or Return key. Using commands in this fashion, one can copy files from one disk to another, change the name of files, delete files (a function to be exercised with great reservation and care), and cause an application program to begin executing. Figure 7-12 shows a comparative sample of frequently used system commands for MS-DOS, ProDOS, and UNIX. The words "menu choice" in the figure indicate that the operation is selected from a list of DOS functions shown on a screen menu.

Utilities

We would remind you at this point that an operating system is a *group of programs*. JCL instructions, or system commands, call upon the system to execute a program contained in its program library. In a sense, all programs are utilities inasmuch as they perform some useful work. Operating system libraries include a number of frequently used utility programs, some of which were written by the manufacturer, others of which were written by the installer or by the user. The distinction between *utilities* and other application programs is that utilities are general; they are not specific to any one application.

Utilities typically available with operating systems include those that sort files into ascending or descending order on one or more control fields, others that convert data from one storage medium to another, such as from punched cards to disk or magnetic tape to disk, and still others that manage communications operations.

Among the most important utilities are those that translate program coding into machine-executable instructions. These are called language translators, or programming systems, and are discussed in Chapter Nine. Another important utility is the program or set of programs that looks after the data base containing the information used most often by the organization's computer system. These programs are the topic of Chapter Ten.

Batch Files

System commands can be entered and executed one at a time from a computer keyboard. This is true, of course, for all types of computers: monsters, mainframes, minicomputers, and microcomputers. Rather than enter them individually, a sequential series of system commands may be stored as a separate file for execution by the simple expedient of running that file as a program. Such a file of system commands is known as a *batch file, EXEC file, shell program,* or *JCL program.*

Batch files are very useful for setting up memory configurations, I/O device identifiers, and other housekeeping chores that the computer operator must perform regularly. They are also used to establish a sequence of *application* programs to be run. In this sense, a batch file resembles the original monitor program discussed in the first part of this chapter.

System Disks

The programs making up the operating system are stored on the sys-res device. Because the storage device is almost always disk, it is known as a *system*

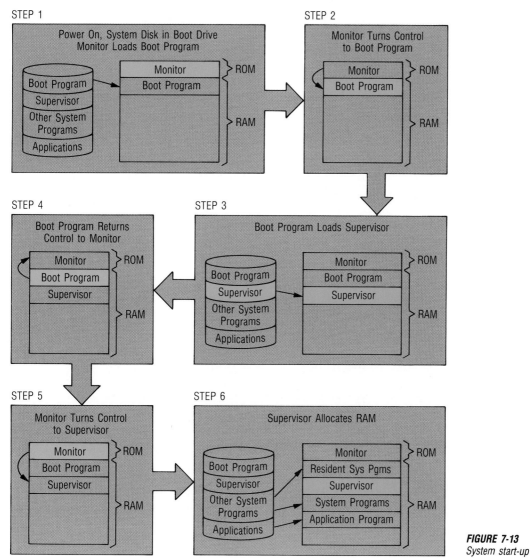

FIGURE 7-13
System start-up

disk, command disk, or *boot disk.* ("Boot" is short for "bootstrap;" it owes its origin to the phrase, "Pull yourself up by your bootstraps.") If the boot disk is in the default drive of the system (called the *boot drive*), turning the computer on automatically loads the operating system into RAM and turns control of the computer over to it.

A system disk contains at least two things: the supervisor and the program that loads the supervisor into RAM and starts it executing. A system disk may contain other operating system utility programs at the discretion of the user. The supervisor programs, because they are resident in RAM, are the internal, or resident, programs of the system, as we mentioned earlier. The remaining operating system programs, which must be brought into RAM from disk just prior to execution, are known as transient or external programs.

Figure 7-13 shows what happens when we start up a computer system. The monitor, or operating system kernel, which is resident in ROM, consults the boot drive for the command, or boot, program which will load the supervisor into RAM. Finding it, the monitor loads that program into RAM and starts it executing. The boot program loads the supervisor programs into RAM and returns control to the monitor which immediately transfers control to the supervisor. The supervisor then consults the JCL files for application programs to be processed. In microcomputer and distributed data processing systems, the supervisor displays the DOS prompt indicating to the user that it is ready for instructions.

Command-driven versus Menu-driven Operating Systems

The job control language we've discussed so far involves entering individual commands to the operating system either through the keyboard or by using batch files. These systems, then, are *command-driven.* This is the most flexible way to use an operating system. It's also the most difficult. Some operating systems, to make things easier for the user, employ menus which allow the operator to select operating system functions from a list of choices displayed on the monitor. These are called *menu-driven* systems.

Both ProDOS and UNIX employ menus for users who wish to use them. In addition to using menus, some operating systems offer on-screen help messages to remind users how to use the system's functions.

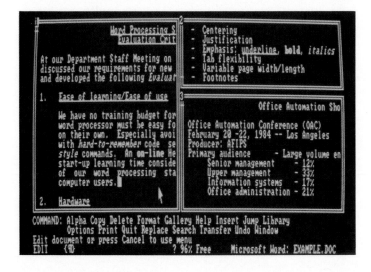

Some application programs use the operating system to display the contents of different files in windows. (Courtesy Microsoft Corp.)

Windows

Some operating systems employ windows as a means of displaying the operating system functions available and the status of the files on which the user is working.

A *window* is an area of the display screen set aside to show the contents or status of a file. Using such an operating system, for example, one can establish, say, three windows on the screen. One might show the contents of a memorandum being written, another an illustration to be included in the printed form of the memo, and the last a list of all the other illustrations available. Windows can be overlapped on the screen so that they appear to be stacked on top of each other, like sheets of paper on a desk.

SUMMARY

From its humble beginnings as a short program that read job control cards and summoned programs to be executed from the program library, the operating system has evolved into a comprehensive set of programs that provide indispensable functions. These functions include:

1. Input and output management which controls SPOOLing and buffering, multitasking and overlapping, time-sharing and networking.

2. Memory management including the allocation of RAM to various purposes, background and foreground program priorities, and virtual memory systems.

3. File management under which files stored on secondary storage can be copied, sorted, displayed, and removed, among other functions.

4. Job control functions which include executing programs on demand from the user, using utilities and other programs, and developing batch programs of command statements for automatic execution of operating system functions.

I/O management makes use of the *Input/Output Control System*, or *IOCS*. Under operating system control of input and output, all I/O operations are standardized from the programmer's viewpoint. Simultaneous I/O operations are facilitated through the use of *SPOOLing* and buffering. *Overlapping* of application programs balances *I/O-bound* and *process-bound* programs by having them both resident in RAM at once, a situation known as *multiprogramming* or *multitasking*. If the system configuration includes more than one processor, as when it uses I/O channels, it is said to use *multiprocessing*.

I/O control also facilitates *networking* and *time-sharing*, arrangements in which more than one user is on-line. Networking connects a number of computers for the purposes of communication and sharing of common data files. Time-sharing connects several terminals to one computer in such a manner that each user appears to have complete control over the computer system. To accomplish this, each user is allocated a RAM *partition* for programs and data, and enjoys periodic *time slices* of the processor's time.

Operating systems allocate memory to themselves and to the application programs, as described in a *memory map*. A substantial portion of RAM, which would otherwise be available to the user and to application programs, is consumed by OS programs stored in ROM. The use of *virtual memory* techniques relieves constraints on program size and on the number of concurrent users by loading *portions* of programs into RAM for execution.

File management operations use a *directory* of *filenames* which associates each file in disk storage (the preferred medium) with the disk addresses of the files. Every file contains data. Sometimes the data are text; sometimes programs. Larger computer systems, including microcomputers with large disk storage devices, use *subdirectories* as a means of file organization. These hierarchical file systems, which consist of a *root directory* and two or more subdirectories, are called *trees. Datapaths,* delineate the route that OS must follow to locate a file within a tree.

Job control language consists of *system commands* which are delivered to OS through a keyboard or through *JCL*, or *batch,* programs. The operating system can be visualized as a *shell* with the *monitor,* or *kernel,* at the center being directly associated with the hardware of the computer system. Surrounding that is the *supervisor;* surrounding the supervisor are the OS utilities, or functions; and surrounding the utilities are the application programs. When an application program is not executing, the outer layer of the shell is removed. The operating system awaits instructions and displays its *prompt,* at which time the user can communicate directly with OS and can use the utilities or execute a program.

KEY TERMS

background	memory map	resident device
batch processing	menu-driven	resident system program
command-driven	monitor	response time
directory	multiprocessing	shell
disk operating system (DOS)	multiprogramming	stacked-job processing
filename	multitasking	supervisor
foreground	operating system (OS)	system disk
input/output control system (IOCS)	overlap	system program
	partition	system resident device
interrupt	poll	time-sharing
job control language (JCL)	program library	tree
macro instruction	real-time processing	utility
		virtual memory (VM)

REVIEW QUESTIONS

1. The three parts of a complete computer system are the _____, _____ _____, and _____ _____.
2. What language is used to specify how a program is to be run?
3. What connects application programs to the IOCS?
4. An _____ _____ controls the computer resources.
5. The operating system is stored on a disk known as the _____ _____ _____.
6. Identify four major functions of an operating system.
7. Explain the difference between SPOOLing and buffering.
8. Differentiate between networking and time-sharing.
9. Does it make more sense to run two process-bound jobs, two I/O-bound jobs or one of each at the same time? Why?
10. Which program has first call on computer resources, a program in foreground or a program in background?
11. What is the major advantage of virtual memory?

THOUGHT QUESTIONS

1. What are the relative merits of menu-driven and command-driven systems?
2. Using as many words from the end of chapter list as possible, describe an operating system and what it does, in detail.
3. Explain how time-sharing works.

Point Counterpoint

Of Humans and Robots

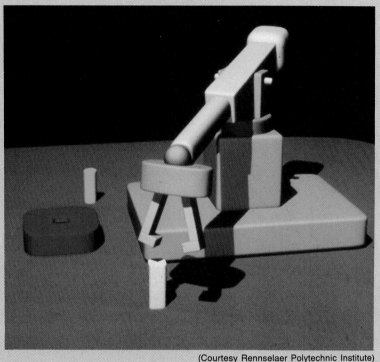

(Courtesy Rennselaer Polytechnic Institute)

The term *robot* is derived from the Czech word meaning compulsory service. It was made popular in 1921 by the Czech writer Karel Capek in his play *R.U.R.* which stands for "Rossum's Universal Robots." The play opens with a business executive dictating to a secretary who then types the document using an ordinary typewriter. The secretary is a robot with a fairly human appearance. She exhibits the stereotypical characteristics of female secretaries of the time.

The human-like (some writers have used the words *humanoid* and *android* as synonyms for robot) vision of robots has persisted over the years, culminating, perhaps, with the very human robot in the movie *The Alien*. The more human-like robots became in fiction, the more likely they were to take on such undesirable human qualities as avarice, thirst for power, and the will to do harm. Indeed, Capek's robots revolted—that's what the play is all about.

That kind of behavior hardly fits the official definition of the term *robot*: a mechanical or electronic device designed to perform work generally done by a human being. Keeping robots in line with their mission of compulsory service requires a sort of code of ethics, which was articulated by Isaac Asimov, author of more than 300 books on science and science fiction. Here's how they appeared in his book *I, Robot*:

THE THREE LAWS OF ROBOTICS
1. A robot may not injure a human being or, through inaction, allow a human being to come to harm.
2. A robot must obey the orders given it by human beings except where such orders would conflict with the First Law.
3. A robot must protect its own existence as long as such protection does not conflict with the First or Second Law.

– Handbook of Robotics
56th Edition, 2058 A.D.[1]

Today, few robots, with the exception of toys, take human form. Robots, in the form of word processing computers, do our typing—a far departure from Capek's mechanical secretary. Computer operating systems, the subject of this chapter, certainly do work previously and generally done by humans. For all practical purposes, they are invisible, but they are nonetheless robots. Other robots pilot airplanes, stuff chocolates into candy boxes, turn the oven off when the roast is medium rare, start the coffee in the morning, and call the police if an intruder breaks into the house, to mention a few examples.

All robots are controlled by computers, although it is unlikely that Capek and other early science-fiction writers conceived of robots' controlling units as such. The spaceships in the movies *2001* and *2010* were, in essence, giant robots under the control of the Hal 9000, a computer that went berserk and violated Asimov's Second Law.

Personal robots, as opposed to astronautical or industrial ones, are controlled by the same microprocessors found in personal computers. Androbot produces a line of robots called the TOPO. The most sophisticated of the line is a robot called B.O.B. (for Brains On Board). B.O.B. uses an Intel 8088 processor, the same as that used in the IBM PC. Says Bill Burton, Director of Androbot's sales and marketing:

> Forget the preconceived notion of Buck Rogers. Think of (the robot) as a PC with sensors and the ability to move. Instead of getting out of your chair and knocking out a letter, you would call B.O.B., take off his keyboard and type the letter, then tell B.O.B. to go away and mail (it) electronically. The robot can do everything your IBM PC can do. It can dial up Dow Jones, add up the gains and losses on your stock portfolio, then walk up to you at 5 p.m. with a report and a drink—champagne if the news is good, a scotch if it's bad.[2]

For all these positive aspects of robots, many believe that they threaten us today in the real world, just as they have in the world of fiction. Now, however, the threat is of a different order.

> A robot may have its eye on your job. Think it can't happen? Think that no machine could do what *you* do?
>
> Better reconsider. Robots are getting smarter and cheaper, and to hear employers talk, human labor is getting increasingly expensive and not a bit smarter.
>
> Robots can work day and night, year round with no weekends off, no vacations, no sick leave, no time out for meals or coffee breaks. They don't join unions. They don't bring lawsuits against their employers. And they don't expect to be paid a little more every year.[3]

As ideal employees, modern robots don't take human physical form any more than they take human psychological form. Robots shaped like snakes can burrow into caves and drill holes to bring geological samples to the surface for analysis. Humans couldn't do that without great danger. Many industrial robots look like long arms with tools at the end. They are impervious to poisonous fumes, excessive heat or cold, and other environmental factors. It is predicted that by the 1990s, robots will enter the construction trades to carry materials, cut boards, and lay bricks and stone. They won't wear hard hats or whistle at girls passing by.

But as robots become more powerful and pervasive, Asimov's laws loom important in the real world. In 1984, a Japanese worker was killed by a robot on an assembly line. Joe Bosworth, President of RB Robot Corporation, suggests that the laws will become necessary as robots become serious tools in the home. Without them, manufacturers will not produce robots that meet their full potential.

> I don't think you'll have robots with any strength or potentially dangerous capabilities until those three laws are clearly dealt with ... Before automobiles came along, we didn't worry about speeding or drunk driving. But we've built a body of law that creates liability. We may be headed for something similar with robots.[4]

QUESTIONS

1. Are there robots today that break one or more of Asimov's Laws of Robotics? If so, list a few examples.
2. Are Asimov's laws complete? Can you think of others that are necessary now that Asimov could not have anticipated in 1950?
3. When George Meany was President of the AFL/CIO, he visited an automobile assembly plant and heard many virtues of the completely automated factory, one without human workers at all. He asked, "Who will buy the cars?" What do you think will be the economic consequences of increased use of industrial robots?
4. Considering the types of things that computers do best, which of those do you feel humans, instead of robots, ought to do?

Application Programs

(Courtesy Harris Corp., Computer Systems Division)

Computers are used for scientific research. Among the most commonly used programs are those that complete statistical analyses. (Courtesy Control Data Corp.)

Man is a tool-using animal, without tools he is nothing, with tools he is all.[1]

Chuck and Shari Flaming run a 4000-head cattle feedlot in Nebraska. They monitor daily feed consumption with an IBM PC.[2] When consumption drops for a particular pen, they know that its cattle are ready for market. Detective Sergeant John Dextradeur of the New Bedford, Massachusetts Police Department uses an Apple IIe to analyze geographic patterns of burglaries and armed robberies to better know where to concentrate forces to apprehend culprits.[3] Jan Hoskins of Winnipeg, Canada designs textile patterns with an Apple II+. The computer, which is connected to her looms, also controls the weaving process.[4]

Stories such as these are not hard to find. What catches the eye is the name of the computer used in doing the work, probably because people like to think that a computer hardware system does it all alone. Computer manufacturers, understandably, make the most of this. The list of jobs being done by Apple Computers, which was shown at the beginning of Chapter Two, is a case in point.

APPLICATION SOFTWARE AND THE COMPLETE COMPUTER SYSTEM

Farmers control crops and livestock with computerized record keeping programs. (Courtesy U.S. Dept. of Agriculture)

We know that the work is actually done by a *complete computer system*, consisting of the hardware, the operating system, and the application program. All work to be performed by the hardware and operating system is governed by the application program. The Flamings use a program called The Heritage Feedyard System, Dextradeur uses PFS:File, and Hoskins uses a group of programs that she wrote herself and now markets under the name of Pattern Master I, II, and III.

Background

In the 1960s, computers and their accompanying operating systems were acquired as a package. Vendors of computing hardware *bundled* systems software and hardware together. There was little or no possibility that an application program or an operating system designed on a computer from one manufacturer would work on another's machinery. Computer installations wrote most of their own application programs, tailoring them specifically to the operating system that came with the bundle. Changing computer hardware, even to other models from the same manufacturer, required substantial re-programming of the applications programs so that they would operate on the new equipment. The situation was so severe that manufacturers provided *simulators*, or *emulators*, for their equipment to make a new computer operate as if it were the old. When IBM introduced the System/360 in 1964, for example, it provided an emulator that could run programs written for the IBM 1401 which was widely used by installations that IBM considered likely candidates to convert to the new computer.

In 1969, IBM, the leading practitioner of bundling, *unbundled* its hardware products from the software that supported them. This had both good and bad consequences. It was good because it allowed data processing managers more latitude in designing the operating environments of their installations. It was bad because it added to the existing confusion brought about by a lack of operating system standards as firms specializing in writing systems entered the market. This made the preparation and maintenance of application programs even more difficult because each application program could work only in conjunction with a particular operating system.

Today, an enormous number of organizations produce system and application software for computers. International Data Corporation maintains a file of all software vendors. Called "The Enterprise File," it contains data on more than 15,000 software firms which produce some 40,000 products. In terms of dollar volume, most of these products are leased or purchased by mainframe computer installations found in large business and government organizations. An application program that keeps track of bank transactions, for example, can lease for more than $200,000 per year. The annual market for mainframe and minicomputer application software exceeds $13 billion.

The proliferation of microcomputers in businesses and homes has given birth to more than 1,000 firms that specialize in application programs for that kind of computer. In 1980, sales of those products amounted to $260 million.

One of the most popular computers of the pre-micro era was the IBM 1401. It occupied a whole room and had less capacity for data storage than almost any micro available today. (Courtesy International Business Machines Corp.)

The IBM 701 mainframe was an early computer designed primarily for scientific, engineering, and statistical processing. (Courtesy International Business Machines Corp.)

By 1990, this figure will exceed $6 billion. The programs have sometimes made their producers rich. Bill Gates, for example, founder and chairman of Microsoft Corporation, amassed a personal fortune of $100 million by the ripe age of 28.

The purchase of a computer and an operating system inevitably leads to the acquisition of application programs. Because of the intimate relationships between the operating system, the hardware, and the application program, we must consider all three as we contemplate the tasks we wish our computer system to perform. Being ultimately interested in the application program as the tool that actually controls the work, we need to review the constraints that the hardware and the operating system place on our range of choices. After all, there's not much point in considering an application program that won't run on our machine.

Hardware Constraints

Some hardware constraints are pretty obvious. Word processing application systems are of little use without a printer. Communications programs only make sense if our computer has the requisite modem. After the obvious, more subtle considerations come into play. Will the communications program work with any modem, or with only a few, and which ones are they? Will the word processor include the printer control codes required to take full advantage of our printer's capability?

The capacity and flexibility of secondary storage devices is often a critical concern. Mainframe and most minicomputer installations enjoy considerable capacity. Most application programs will not require more. Even so, the matter cannot be taken for granted. A data base management program, the most popular type of application in large installations, must have sufficient disk storage capacity to maintain the files required by the organization. It's not only a matter of the minimum capacity required by the application program itself, but also of the capacity required by the size of the data files.

Most business users of microcomputers employ a system that has two floppy disk drives or a floppy disk drive and a hard disk. Many business application programs for micros are written with a minimum of two drives in mind. To be sure, some are not, but users of such programs soon learn that having two makes the work go much easier.

RAM capacity, as you might suspect, is crucial. The range of memory requirements for application programs varies widely. Finpac Corporation markets

Large computer systems store billions of bits of data on hundreds of disk drives. (Courtesy McAuto)

a financial reporting system that includes report writing, general ledger, accounts payable, and accounts receivable functions. The program runs on a powerful mini, the DEC VAX computer, and requires one megabyte of primary storage. The Peachtree Peachpak 4 program, which offers general ledger, accounts payable, and accounts receivable, requires 64K of RAM. Versions of it that will run on an Apple with 16K are available. The two products are really not comparable, the former being much more powerful and flexible, but they do illustrate the range of memory requirements for applications programs that perform similar functions.

As new microcomputer applications grow in performance, so too does their need for RAM. In the early 1980s, microcomputer users found 48K to 64K quite adequate for most available software. Now, 256K represents a more realistic bottom limit. It's not just the amount of RAM needed to contain the program itself that should concern us. The minimum RAM requirements for many programs provide only enough space for minimum performance. Getting the most out of an application means providing RAM capacity that is sufficient for data as well as the program to be stored in RAM.

The IBM 650 was an early computer designed for commercial operations. It was programmed, in part, by plugging wires into removable wiring panels. (Courtesy International Business Machines Corp.)

Operating System Constraints

During their development and for the first couple of decades of their use, operating systems were prepared for specific processors. IBM's OS/360 was designed to run only on the System/360 computer. The System/370's operating systems were designed specifically for that machine. CP/M (Control Program/Microprocessor), for many years the most popular operating system for microcomputers, was designed for the Intel 8080 and Zilog Z80 processors. Similarly, AppleDOS and ProDOS were designed for the MOS Technology 6502.

Application software producers wrote, and still write, their programs for specific operating systems; they have no choice. This means that an application program written under CP/M will not run under ProDOS, MS-DOS, or any other operating system. Regardless of its size, once a computer has been purchased, the choices of application programs are limited to those that will run in that hardware-operating system environment.

This situation leads to frustration in all quarters. Computer users find their range of application program choices severely reduced. Software producers lose sales because nobody will buy a program that won't run. Hardware manufacturers find their market restricted by the limited availability of application programs. There are four solutions.

First, the hardware can be changed. Because of the open architecture of most computers (see Chapter Five), users can add circuitry to the computer so that it includes the processor required by the operating system for which the desired application program was written. Apple II+ and IIe owners can install a card that contains the Z80 processor in their computers. This card is known as the Z80 card. Now, they can use the thousands of applications programs available under the CP/M operating system. Similarly, IBM PC owners can install a card containing the 6502 processor, thus gaining access to the thousands of AppleDOS programs. In effect, these computers become two computers in one because each has two processors. Some computers, such as the Franklin, come with two processors already installed, making the computer capable of working with more than one operating system and, consequently, expanding the available application software substantially. In order to make its popular word processing program WordStar available to millions of Apple owners, MicroPro marketed WordStar with a Z80 card and the requisite CP/M operating system.

Capabilities of open architecture microcomputers can be extended by using expansion cards. Some such cards increase the number of programs a computer can run. (Courtesy Microsoft Corp.)

The IBM 3081 is a large mainframe computer. (Courtesy International Business Machines Corp.)

Adding another processor is a Rube Goldberg solution at best. Often as not, the add-on processor cannot take full advantage of the features of the host computer. 6502 processor cards for the IBM PC, for example, don't make full use of that computer's keyboard, memory capacity, and disk storage space.

A solution that avoids these problems adds others. It requires that application software producers write their programs for several operating systems. While this expands the market for their products, it also increases their development costs and raises prices to prospective purchasers. Nobody likes that.

Another solution depends upon operating system producers to prepare separate versions of their programs for each processor. Several have already done so. Digital Research, for example, produces several versions of CP/M. CP/M-80 and CP/M-86 run on the Intel 8080 and 8086 processors. Versions of UNIX have been prepared for several mainframe processors, and for those used in most mini and microcomputers as well. This solution suffers the same drawback as that of requiring application program producers to prepare multiple versions of their wares. It increases the cost to the user.

The fourth solution addresses the heart of the problem: producers could develop a standard operating system for all computers under which all application programs would run. From the beginning of the development of operating systems, the computer industry has complained about the lack of standards. A standard OS would divorce decisions about hardware and application programs from constraints imposed by the operating system. Although movement toward this ideal can be seen, particularly with the UNIX operating system, the going is slow.

Each operating system vendor wants its product to become the standard. In the intensely competitive computer industry, no producer wants to discard all of its developmental work to adopt the new standard. Furthermore, few of the millions of operating computer installations are willing to reprogram their application programs or purchase new ones. Complaining about the lack of a standard is one thing. Making the financial sacrifice to adopt one is quite something else.

Firmware

One solution to the complex problems involved in assembling all three parts of the complete computer system puts the operating system and one or more application programs on ROM. When purchasing a computer, the user also

Large mainframe computers run complex programs which may have thousands of lines of code.
(Courtesy Burroughs Corp.)

purchases, as an integral part of the hardware, the system and the application software to be used with it. Inasmuch as the software is integrated with the hardware, it is known as *firmware*.

Because most users of microcomputers use their systems for only a handful of general application programs, this would seem to preclude a lot of agonizing over what kind of computer and operating system to get in order to run the application programs one wants. The manufacturer need only include the most popular applications as firmware.

So far, this approach has found its biggest success with portable and lap-sized computers, the users of which prefer not to carry about several application and system program disks. This advantage is outweighed, especially in larger computers, by the limitations it places on the user to select the application programs that best fit his or her individual needs. Nevertheless, increasing numbers of application programs may be delivered on ROM for installation by the user in the computer system.

The previous paragraphs suggest the relationships that must be taken into account by computer users. As a rule, application program selection begins with a definition of the work to be done. Well-managed organizations employ the tools described in Chapter Four of this book to define the work. After the work has been defined, decisions can be made about the programs to use, whether to write them in-house or to purchase them, and about hardware and operating system compatibility.

You can see that the hardware, the operating system, and the application program are so closely intertwined that decisions about one cannot be made separately from the others. That's why we emphasize so repeatedly the concept of the complete computer system.

SOURCES OF APPLICATION SOFTWARE

The term *software* is used most often to refer to application programs. Some authorities like to divide software into two categories: *system software*, meaning operating system programs; and *application software*, meaning the programs that control the actual work. For the remainder of this text, we shall use the term *software* in the latter sense unless indicated otherwise.

There is an enormous variety of software available to computer users. Later in this chapter, we'll review some broad categories of software to illustrate its diversity. Right now, let's look at where the software comes from.

Write Your Own

Through the 1970s, computer installations typically wrote their own software. These were mainframe installations served by crews of systems analysts, programmers, and other technical experts. Programming was, and still is, a highly technical skill requiring a knowledge of computer hardware and operating system specifics and a finely tuned sense of logic. In order to tell a computer what to do, one must think like a computer. The work is done using programming languages to create sequences of instructions which are then translated into the computer's machine language. Chapter Nine discusses the processes involved in computer programming.

Today, most users of computers are individuals working at microcomputers or terminals attached to mainframes and minis. In the past, a user was one

Word processing and spreadsheet programs are often included in ROM on lap-sized computers. (Courtesy Hewlett-Packard, Inc.)

served by a data processing department. Today, a *user* is one served by a computer system, sometimes through the services of a data processing department, but most often directly, using his or her computer or terminal.

Most users today prefer not to write their own programs. Indeed, most will never need to. Being concerned with using a computer as a tool, users rely on software prepared by others. This, of course, has led to the explosive growth of the software industry. This is not to say that no user will write programs. Many develop software to meet a unique need. Others do because they find programming fun. Almost anyone can learn to write computer programs. Most discover, however, that the time and effort required to program detracts from the time available to pursue their professional responsibilities. Programming for fun is a great hobby, but like all hobbies, it should not hamper one's other obligations.

Buy Someone Else's

Most mainframe installations today employ programmers in great numbers. There will probably always be a need for tailor-made programs because they can best meet the unique needs of the organization. For several years, however,

McAuto employs a large staff in their CAD/CAM facility. (Courtesy McDonnell Douglas Information Systems)

data processing managers have found that the advantages of tailor-made software are often outweighed by their high cost. Purchasing software prepared by software vendors is often a better alternative. The relatively high cost of programming personnel is frequently cited as the reason for the movement toward commercial software products: "We're writing less and less home-grown stuff," explains John Hargraves, Manager of Data Processing Systems at Travelers Insurance. He credits his company's freeze on hiring programmers as an important reason for purchasing commercial software.[5]

Users purchase commercial software packages from four sources: producers, computer stores, software stores, and mail-order houses. Software is also available from a number of non-commercial sources.

Producers

Mainframe installations usually purchase or lease software directly from the producer. This is especially true for large, expensive applications. The producer provides technical services in installing and testing the software and in training personnel in its use. This kind of service is a matter of vital concern to the purchaser. IC System's IC Dental Lab, a financial control and operational program for dental laboratories, can cost as much as $150,000. Software like that is not installed casually. It may consist of thousands of program modules and may require months of site preparation and personnel training before it is operational.

Mainframe installations that support distributed data processing networks also purchase software for individual nodes or microcomputers operating within the system directly from the producer.

Microcomputer users may also purchase software directly from the producer. Producers of microcomputer software do not ordinarily help with installing and implementing their programs. Many, however, maintain a telephone consulting service to aid those who encounter difficulty. When purchasing software directly from the producer, microcomputer users must rely heavily on the user's manuals and other documentation that comes with the package. While in the past these documents have been difficult to use, their quality has now improved to the point where most users have little trouble. Moreover, many software packages now come with tutorial materials in the form of books, audio tapes, and data diskettes which introduce the user to the operation of the program and give examples of its application. Still other producers operate retail stores that specialize in their computers and software. IBM's Product Centers and Tandy Corporation's Radio Shacks are cases in point.

Computer Stores

Many computer stores are full-service operations, which means that they offer training, after-purchase consultation, and the opportunity to try software packages before buying. Many computer stores specialize in business applications and the computers best suited to operate them. Others, much like discount stores, offer no support, but lower prices. Users patronizing such vendors must rely on themselves. Still other stores will sell software at lower prices if the purchaser needs no training or after-purchase help.

*Thousands of programs have
been made commercially
available in the past five years.*
(Courtesy Peachtree Software,
Inc., an MSA Company)

Software Stores

Growing markets for software have encouraged the establishment of stores
specializing in its distribution. Such organizations are usually full-service operations that include training and consultation with the purchase. Many conduct
classes for their customers or prospective customers. Some count the fees for
the classes toward the purchase price of software. Software stores often have
an advantage over computer stores because they carry a larger inventory of
application packages and owe no allegiance to any hardware manufacturers.

Mail-Order Houses

The chief advantage of purchasing software from mail-order houses lies
in reduced prices. Many offer very fast delivery. Telephone orders may be
shipped out the same day they are received. Purchasing software on this basis
is best practiced only by users who know exactly what they want and how
to use it. As a rule, mail-order houses provide no support to their customers.

Friends and Pirates

People who program, whether as a hobby or a profession, are understandably
proud of their accomplishments. Professionals, of course, sell their work. Others
usually give it away. As a rule, computer buffs are more than happy to help
others make the best use of computer systems. A colleague who has developed
a program to keep track of business correspondence, say, will usually want
to share it with others. Trading programs is a legitimate and valuable source
of acquiring software.

Less legitimate, in fact, illegal, is the practice of copying and giving away
or selling copyrighted commercial programs, a practice known as *pirating* or
bootlegging. Pirating, which is a euphemism for *stealing*, is a serious problem.
Ric Giardina, general counsel for MicroPro, estimates that for every copy of
a commercial program sold, twenty copies are distributed fraudulently.[6] In

addition to the immediate loss of revenue that results from illegal program copying, there is a long-term effect. If programmers perceive that their rewards for developing new programs will be reduced, they will be less willing to expend the effort. As a result, we all will have fewer software products.

Many commercial programs are *copy-protected*, meaning that the disks on which they are delivered have special codes that prevent users from copying them. This distresses many computer users who feel it a wise practice to make backup copies of all program disks. In answer, many software producers provide a backup copy along with the original. Others will replace programs for registered owners for a nominal fee.

Copy-protected programs cause other technical problems. When a disk is damaged, getting a replacement from the software vendor may take days or weeks. Meanwhile all production using that software comes to a halt. Users who wish to store a program on hard disk will need to copy it from the floppy disk on which it was delivered to the hard disk device. Such copying may be prevented by the copy-protection scheme. Organizations that wish to use one program on multiple work stations may find it necessary to purchase a separate copy for each station and see this as a prohibitive expense.

A few firms and individual programmers produce and market programs designed to "break" copy-protection schemes. Users purchasing these programs can then solve some of these technical problems, provided that the copying programs can, in fact, break the code. A purchaser of a program purchases the right to use it and is licensed by the software producer to do so. The license agreement often forbids the purchaser to copy the program either for his or her own use or for distribution to others, free or otherwise. Enforcing such licensing agreements is next to impossible, although a few software vendors have sued effectively when they have discovered violations.

It may be of some consolation to software vendors that much of the illegal copying that takes place is done by hobbyists, or *hackers*, who collect software much as others collect phonograph records. The copied programs are not often used for any productive purpose, they are just part of the collection and wouldn't have been purchased anyway. Breaking the copy-protection scheme was done just for the satisfaction of doing it, of meeting the challenge. Most business computer users don't move in hacker circles and, consequently, have little opportunity to copy programs illegally, even if so inclined. If they did, they would also have to copy the program documentation, often more difficult than copying the program itself. Without documentation, most software is useless.

Nevertheless, software producers are understandably concerned about the situation. They are promoting stronger legislation prohibiting illegal program copying and they are conducting advertising and public information campaigns against it. In the opinions of many users, reducing the price of software will combat illegal copying most effectively. By reducing the price, there is little economic incentive to copy the program. Increased sales would more than make up the price cut.

Users Groups, Bulletin Boards, and Publicly Supported Software

In addition to the thousands of commercially available software programs, thousands more, which are known as *public domain* programs, are available for free. Users frequently find that, for their purposes, such programs are equivalent to those available commercially. The two most important sources for public domain software are users groups and bulletin boards, although some writers of programs in the public domain will provide them for a small fee.

Users Groups

The United States is studded with computer users groups. Typically, a *users group* is a club made up of people who use a particular make of computer, although a few specialize in a single software product or operating system. For thirty years, Guide and Share, two users groups for IBM mainframe computers, have served as forums for sharing information among managers responsible for the use of those computers. Usually, however, mainframe and minicomputer users groups do not share software because it is considered to be proprietary to the installation that developed it.

Microcomputer users groups, on the other hand, share software as a matter of course. Such organizations maintain extensive public-domain software libraries from which members can copy programs to their own disks. Monthly newsletters describe new additions to the library; members may copy as many programs as they like, keeping those that serve a purpose and discarding those that do not.

Bulletin Boards

Any computer with a communications facility can retrieve public-domain software through any of hundreds of bulletin boards. A *bulletin board*, or BBS (Bulletin Board Service), is simply a computer that is accessible over telephone lines. Most users groups maintain bulletin boards which facilitate the distribution of software to the membership. Often, the bulletin board is open to anyone who knows the telephone number. BBSs also serve as centers for posting messages and for communicating technical help and information about commercial and public-domain software.

Bulletin boards typically serve users of microcomputers. The largest number of bulletin boards serves users of the CP/M operating system, probably because it was the first operating system used by computers from many

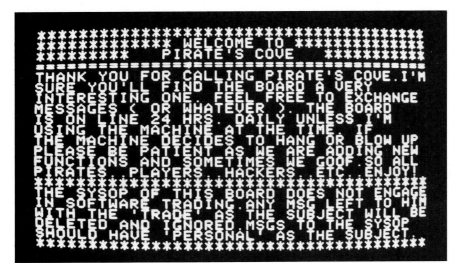

Bulletin boards provide free exchange of information among computer users. (Courtesy George Taber/TIME Magazine)

different manufacturers. The number of BBSs serving users of MS-DOS, IBM PCs, TRS-80s, and Apples is increasing rapidly.

One of the largest bulletin boards in the United States is A.P.P.L.E. Crate, run by Call A.P.P.L.E. of Seattle, Washington. Using a bulletin board such as this one is a matter of dialing the BBS and making a connection. Once this is done, bulletin board information is available and all of the programs on the host computer can be downloaded to the caller's computer.

Publicly Supported Software

Publicly supported software is a variety of public-domain software. The difference is that those who develop publicly supported software ask that its users donate a small amount to the producer. Excellent word processing and communications programs, to mention a couple, are available under this arrangement. The developer encourages users to copy the software and to distribute it freely. Users are asked to donate amounts ranging from $10 to $100, although there is no requirement to do so.

Books and Periodicals

The proliferation of microcomputers has been accompanied by a proliferation of books and periodicals that help users optimize their effectiveness. Hundreds of magazines are devoted to specific computers or operating systems. Books of program listings, such as *Some Common BASIC Programs, Apple II Edition*[7], are usually available in editions for all major makes of microcomputers. The authors of such works, or the publisher, will often sell a disk containing all of the programs to the reader, thus avoiding the necessity of keying the programs into the computer.

Computer magazines also provide program listings. Often, disks containing the programs are available. One can subscribe to electronic versions of periodicals, receiving disks containing dozens of programs through the mail. Other versions of electronic periodicals are distributed over communications networks such as Compuserve or may be retrieved directly by subscribers through the publisher's BBS.

Some computer stores provide equipment and supplies as well as training and technical support. (Courtesy Radio Shack, a division of Tandy Corp.)

COMMERCIAL SOFTWARE PACKAGES

The bewildering array of commercial software products available today makes the task of classifying them very difficult. We take our classification from *The Software Catalog*, a publication that lists and describes commercial software products for mini and microcomputers.[8] Our purpose here is to illustrate the variety of programs available by listing the types of programs in each of eight categories.

1. Commercial: Accounting-General Ledger; Accounting-Integrated Systems; Budgeting; Cost/Benefit Analysis; Information Retrieval; Invoicing/Billing; Marketing; Insurance; Personnel/Manpower; Mailing Lists; Payroll; Taxes; Word Processing.

2. Educational: Administration; Computer Assisted Instruction; Counseling; Laboratory Experiments; Languages; Libraries; Testing.

3. Industrial: Civil Engineering; Electrical Engineering; Mechanical Engineering; Manufacturing; Quality Control.

4. Personal: Astrology; Biorhythms; Financial; Games; Health and Diet; Household Management; Security Systems; Sports.

5. Professional: Accounting; Dental; Hospital Administration; Insurance; Medical; Legal; Veterinary Medicine.

6. Scientific: Aerospace; Agronomy; Astronomy; Biology; Chemistry; Computer Science; Electronics; Medicine; Oceanography; Operations Research; Physics; Social Science; Statistics.

7. Specific Industries: Architecture; Automotive; Aviation; Banking; Catering; Communications; Construction; Distribution/Wholesaling; Energy; Farming; Pharmaceutical; Publishing; Real Estate; Steel; Textiles; Utilities.

8. Systems: Language Translators; Communications; Data Base Management; Graphics; Operating Systems.

The entries in the preceding list do not include all of the types of software within each category, but they do illustrate their range. Perhaps a more useful way to categorize software is according to whether the program is *horizontal*, that is, used by a number of different industries, or *vertical*, serving the specific needs of a particular industry. Examples of vertical software in the preceding list include most of those in categories 2, 5, 6, and 7. These are programs designed to meet the unique needs of a particular kind of business or organization. Categories 1 and 3 are more general in nature and are used by firms in many different industries. Vertical software is sometimes called *industry-specific*; horizontal software, *industry non-specific*.

THE BIG SIX

A survey of what kinds of programs are most heavily used in the United States would undoubtedly show that programs serving personal needs are the most popular. This is not because they do the most work, but because more individual computer users employ them than any other kind. Categories 2 and 4 suggest some of the areas of personal use. Games are very popular, not only among the young set, but among adults as well. One of the most successful

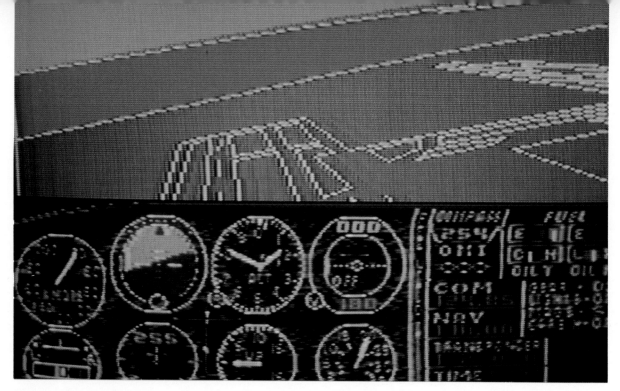

Microsoft's flight simulator is an extremely popular program that allows pilots and would-be pilots to hone their skills. (Courtesy Microsoft Corp.)

game programs of all time simulates flying an aircraft. Besides being fun, pilots and aspiring pilots find it useful for reviewing navigation, communication techniques, and actual flying skills. Educational programs which teach arithmetic, spelling, art, music, typing, and foreign languages are inexpensive and enjoyable to use.

But this is a book about using computers in business. From the business user's perspective, the big six includes data base management, word processing, spreadsheet analysis, communications, graphics, and accounting systems. This book discusses each of these in its own chapter. We look at them here only in the most general way, as a means of illustrating their importance. Each of the six is a horizontal, as opposed to vertical, program. It is partially because they can be used by a wide spectrum of business and other organizations that they are so popular. Their popularity also results from the fact that they meet fundamental data processing needs of all organizations and individuals.

Data Base Management

As we know, business data processing depends on files as a means to organize data. A *Data Base Management System (DBMS)* is a data-keeping system. Because mainframe and minicomputer installations depend so heavily on large data bases, a DBMS often serves as the heart of the installation's application software complex. The DBMS maintains the files, updates them, and makes data available to other application programs and individual users. Comprehensive data base managers will combine individual data elements from various files to organize information in ways to show different relationships.

Most DBMSs are general and will manage any kind of data. Others are more specific and are designed for vertical applications. Equine Management Systems, for example, markets the Equine Management program which runs on Digital Equipment Corporation (DEC) computers. *Equine Management*

Business graphics produced by a microcomputer linked to this company's mainframe enable these managers to conduct their business more effectively. (Courtesy Cullinet Software, Inc.)

is a very specialized data base management program indeed, serving the interests only of those who breed horses or buy and sell them.

For large computer systems, the capacity of the DBMS is usually governed by the capacity of the secondary storage complement. The same is true for many microcomputer DBMSs. Ashton-Tate's dBASE-III and Microrim's RBASE 4000 boast the ability to manage more than a billion records, a number that far exceeds current disk storage capacity for micros.

Word Processors

Word processors are used to enter text, edit it, save it electronically on disk, retrieve it, merge it with other text, and print it in acceptable document formats. Word processors are also used in conjunction with programs that check for spelling, grammar, and style errors, and with others that will prepare mass mailings of what appear to be individually typed and addressed letters.

More computers are used for word processing than for any other single application. Word processing software is not usually found in mainframe installations because the nature of word processing work wastes much of the

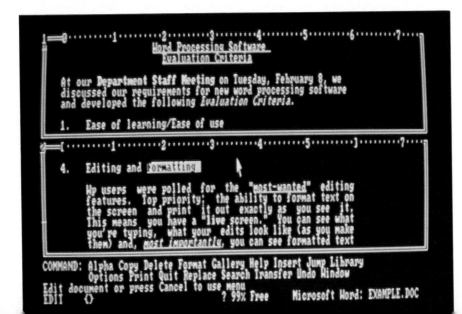

Microsoft Word allows word processing in as many as eight windows, for separate documents or for different parts of the same document. (Courtesy Microsoft Corp.)

mainframe's power. The UNIX operating system, however, which is used on computers of all sizes, includes a powerful system that rivals many individual word processing programs. When used in minicomputer installations, word processors often operate in a networked arrangement so that a number of operators have access to common data bases.

Spreadsheet Programs

A *spreadsheet,* sometimes called a *worksheet,* can be visualized as a rectangular sheet of paper broken into columns and rows, much like the familiar accounting columnar paper. The intersection of each column and row defines a *cell.* Working with a video display screen rather than a sheet of paper, the user enters values and formulas into the cells of the spreadsheet. A user who wishes, for example, to forecast cash flow for the organization would enter information concerning sources and uses of cash and the amounts expected. The spreadsheet program would then calculate the amount of excess cash or the amount of cash the firm needs to borrow at the end of every time period.

Because the spreadsheet contains formulas that interrelate various cells, the user can then pose "what if" questions. What if cash sales decline and credit sales increase? What if the union negotiates a pay increase for the work force? By adjusting one or two numbers, the entire spreadsheet is recalculated showing the new results.

Spreadsheet programs are enormously productive because they take over the calculations required for this kind of analysis. People have been known to purchase computers for the sole purpose of being able to use this tool. Apple Computer has estimated that the introduction of VisiCalc, the first electronic spreadsheet program, accounted for the sale of tens of thousands of its computers.

Communications

Communications programs are vital for sharing information among users and computer systems. As we've seen from Chapter Six, communication requires

Spreadsheets are among the most popular business productivity tools. (Courtesy Lotus Development Corp.)

AT&T consumer products microprocessor-based Sceptre home terminal allows customers to access videotex data base information, shop at home, banking, and other transactional services. (Courtesy AT&T Information Systems)

certain hardware devices. It also requires software to control the transmission and retrieval of data. The ability to download data from a mainframe computer to a micro for spreadsheet analysis, for example, depends upon the communications programs used by both computers. Networks, time-sharing, access to such public data bases as Compuserve and The Source, bulletin board operations, and electronic mail all require software for their effective operation.

The software is not complex because the hardware and its controlling operating system take care of the technical matters. In fact, it's possible to use communications devices without application software at all. As this requires the user to enter set-up codes and control the transfer of data directly, most prefer to use software that does that automatically. It's faster and more accurate.

Sometimes communications facilities are part of the operating system, as with UNIX's mail facility. Even under that system, however, transmission of data to and from external computer systems uses specialized communications programs.

Graphics

Computers are great devices for generating reams of paper full of numbers. Graphics programs translate those numbers into pictorial form which makes it much easier to understand the relationships involved. Graphics programs that produce business graphs such as line charts, bar graphs, and pie charts, are a boon to those who need to communicate the results of data processing activities to others. That, after all, is the purpose of analysis anyway.

Computer graphics, as a tool, goes beyond preparing business graphs. If a computer can draw a picture using the results of numerical calculations, it can also do the process in reverse, taking a picture and converting it to a set of numerical relationships. For example, the user can draw shapes on a video screen. The software will use the shapes to prepare specifications for parts to be manufactured, an activity called *Computer-Aided Design (CAD)*.

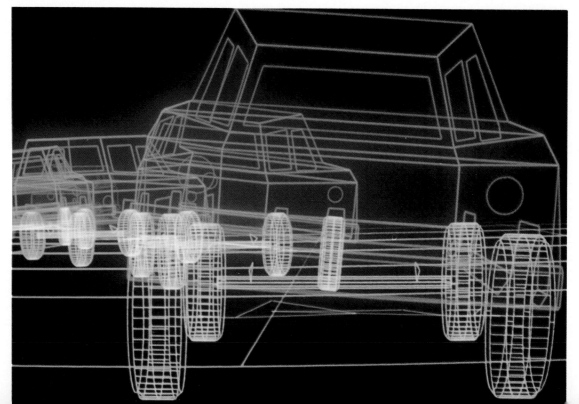

Many popular programs create business graphics from data produced by a spreadsheet program. (Courtesy Apple Computer, Inc.)

Moreover, the specifications can be produced in machine-readable form (e.g., on magnetic tape) for use in controlling the machine tool that will manufacture the parts. This is known as *Computer-Aided Manufacturing (CAM)*. Together, computer-aided design and computer-aided manufacturing, known as CAD/CAM, are revolutionizing such industries as manufacturing, architecture, and electronics.

Accounting Systems

Even automobiles are designed using computers and computer-aided design programs. (Courtesy Apple Computer, Inc.)

Accounting systems, more properly called bookkeeping systems, maintain the books of an enterprise and produce a number of reports needed for analysis of operations and financial condition. They also prepare documents required by the Internal Revenue Service and other government agencies.

The heart of the accounting system is the general ledger, or G/L. It maintains the basic set of books and produces fundamental financial statements. Added to the general ledger are a number of subsidiary systems for accounts receivable, accounts payable, payroll, and the like. The subsidiary systems produce data for the general ledger and prepare a number of reports peculiar to each subsidiary system.

Few business applications fit computerized processing methods as well as do accounting systems. The firm's accounting cycle is repeated frequently during the year in a well-defined series of repetitive operations. That's the kind of work that computers do best. Indeed, without computer accounting application programs, many organizations would find it impossible to complete their accounting tasks.

INTEGRATED SOFTWARE

As initially developed, the big six were *stand-alone* programs, meaning that they operated independently of any other application package. Each required separate data entry operations. Thus, the data maintained by a data base manager were not available directly to a spreadsheet program. They had to be entered into the spreadsheet manually. Numbers calculated by a spreadsheet program were not available to a graphing program. The graphs were not available to word processing programs; they had to be pasted into documents where they were to appear. Many versions of the big six still operate on this basis.

To cope with this difficulty, some software producers developed file transfer techniques that aided in making data from one program available to another. VisiCorp, for example, designed special file formats for its VisiCalc program that could be used by VisiPlot, a graphing program. Other producers began introducing limited versions of one program as part of another.

A number of software products that integrate several of the big six functions are currently available. An integrated software package, then, is one in which more than one of these functions operates on a more or less full-scale basis. Lotus Development Corporation's 1-2-3 was one of the first to do this. It integrates spreadsheet analysis, graphing, and data base management into one program. After its introduction in 1983, it quickly became the leading software package for the IBM PC and look-alike computers.

Since then, many other software producers have followed suit. The Software Group's Enable, Business Solution's Jack2, Context Management System's MBA, and Software International's Open Access are typical products. Open Access, for example, combines data management, spreadsheet analysis, graphics, word processing, communications, and time management into one program.

In order to make integrated programs easier to use, most producers have adopted the use of windows which display information from several of the programs on the screen at once. That way, while composing a report with the word processor, for example, one can view a graph to be included in it and the table of numbers that generated the graph all at once.

Integrated software often requires substantial computer hardware resources. 1-2-3 requires a minimum of 256K RAM storage. Apple's Appleworks

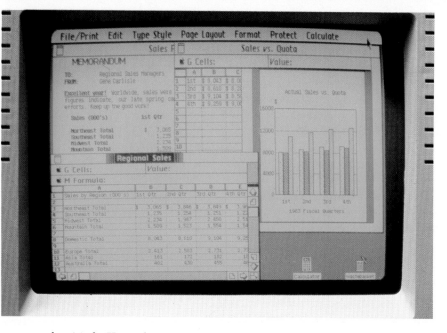

Computers such as the Apple
Macintosh XL run several
programs simultaneously.
(Courtesy Apple Computer, Inc.)

runs on the Apple IIe with 128K of storage and two disk drives. Lotus' Symphony, which adds word processing and communications to the programs in its 1-2-3, requires a minimum RAM capacity of 320K.

Having one program do so many things necessarily places limits on the capacity of its functions. The Lotus programs, 1-2-3 and Symphony, for example, offer enormous capacity in their spreadsheet functions, but limited facility in the others which are all operated within the context of the spreadsheets. As useful as integrated software may be, these limitations often suggest stand-alone packages as the best alternative to large-scale or specialized operations. Symphony's data base manager, for example, is limited to about 8,000 records and cannot compare with the capacity of RBASE 4000 or dBASE III. Professional writers will likely find the integrated word processor programs too limited for their work and will prefer stand-alone alternatives such as MicroPro's WordStar or Microsoft's Word. Graphics programs in integrated packages usually offer only a handful of rudimentary business graphs. Microsoft's Chart, in contrast, includes over 40 different graphing options.

Still another way to integrate the processing operations of a number of different microcomputer application programs makes use of special programs that work with the operating system to provide windows and a desk-top environment. These programs link application programs that would otherwise be unable to work together. The programs make it possible to transfer data files automatically among the applications, and give every appearance of a completely integrated package. IBM's Topview and Microsoft's Windows are examples. Using such programs permits the employment of full-powered application programs in a working environment that integrates them.

As a rule, microcomputer software, whether integrated or not, does not provide the capacity and flexibility required by mainframe computers. Most software used by mainframes is available in limited versions for micros and minis. These programs, because of their inherent limitations and because of constraints imposed by microcomputer operating systems and hardware, cannot handle the volume required by large-scale organizations. Nevertheless, managers in all sizes of organizations see microcomputers and the types of software tools reviewed in this chapter as fertile opportunities to improve the performance of the overall management information system.

SUMMARY

As that third of the complete computer system that controls the actual work of the system, *the application program,* or *software,* is constrained by limitations imposed by the other two parts, the hardware and the operating system. *Hardware constraints* include the kind and capacity of peripheral devices such as secondary storage, printers, and modems. RAM availability is also an important hardware constraint on the software.

Operating system constraints are just as serious. Because application programs must be written to run under particular operating systems, and because operating systems are designed for particular processors, the choice of application programs is often severely limited. Solutions to these problems may involve using multiple processors and operating systems, writing software for multiple operating systems, or adopting a standard operating system for all computers.

Users have a number of sources for obtaining software. They may write their own, a prevalent practice in mainframe installations, or they may purchase or lease software directly from its producer. Users of microcomputers acquire software by purchasing it through computer and software stores and mail-order houses. They may also avail themselves of the considerable library of public-domain software available through *users groups* and *bulletin boards. Publicly supported software,* which is frequently of high quality, is available for a modest cost. Finally, software is available free from those who have written it and are willing to provide copies. Copyrighted commercial software products, however, may not be copied legally without permission.

The variety of software available is staggering. Tens of thousands of programs are available for commercial, educational, industrial, personal, professional, and scientific applications. Software may be *horizontal,* that is, of use to all or most all organizations regardless of industry, or it may be *vertical,* useful to particular types of businesses.

The big six software products, especially for microcomputer users, are *data base management systems (DBMSs), word processors, spreadsheet programs, communications programs, graphics programs,* and *accounting systems.*

In order to make data processed under one of these programs readily available to others, many software producers have developed *integrated systems* which include two or more of these programs in one. Still others have developed programs that work with the operating system to integrate the operations and data files of application programs that otherwise would remain stand-alone programs.

KEY TERMS

application software	copy-protect	user
bootleg software	emulator	users group
bundled system	firmware	vertical program
cell	horizontal program	window
computer-aided design (CAD)	integrated software	
computer-aided manufacture (CAM)	public-domain program	
	publically supported software	

1. Why were emulators developed?
2. What type of programs limit the applications programs that can be run on a particular computer?
3. Business users of microcomputers frequently have a hardware configuration of _____ floppy drive(s) and _____ hard disk(s).
4. The primary use of mainframe computers is for _____ _____ _____ _____.
5. Identify four solutions to the application program/operating system/hardware matching problem.
6. Why do software vendors copy-protect their products?
7. Name two sources of public domain software.
8. How is publically supported software different from public domain software?
9. Software documentation has become more "user friendly" in the past few years. Now documentation in the form of tutorials is available in books, audio tapes, and _____.
10. What services does a full-service computer store offer?
11. A program written for the real estate industry is called a _____ program while an accounting program is a _____ one.
12. Identify the six major types of programs used in business.
13. What is the most common use of computers (particularly microcomputers)?
14. What is an integrated software program?
15. What is the primary advantage of using a program with window capabilities?

1. What are the advantages and disadvantages of writing your own programs?
2. Discuss the issues of software piracy and copy-protection.
3. Select one of the big six. Describe its uses in a business environment.

Home Computers Don't Need Software. They Need Weirdware.

(Courtesy AVL)

Chapter Two of this text began with a sample of some of more than 100 uses to which Apple computers were being put at the end of 1982. In the intervening years, television commercials have blitzed viewers with the virtues of one computer over another for use in the home. Some depict a despondent youngster, who has returned home after flunking out of college, and a pair of distraught parents. "If only we'd purchased Johnny (or Jill) a computer, he (she) would have been successful," implies the message. Advertisements show happy families clustered about the computer radiating togetherness, intellectual achievement, and fun.

In the early years of the microcomputer revolution, many affluent and not-so-affluent parents rushed out to buy computers for their children and for themselves only to find that after a few months, their interest had waned. A few more months passed and the computer was stashed ignominiously in the hall closet.

Computer programmer Galen Gruman explains that professionals, business managers, and scientists all have demonstrable needs for computing equipment. Asking parents what they or their children will use the computer for puts a blank look on their faces, he observes. Computers are useless to those without computing skills.

> ...learning computer skills is not achieved by spending $1,000 or $3,000 or even $7,000 on a home computer system. Classes at a school or local college are an appropriate start, for computing is like reading: You don't buy a small child a work of literature until after his reading skills are developed. You also needn't buy an expensive computer system until the child knows enough about both using programs and writing them...For most people, (computers) are a waste of money that could go to tutoring a child...or into a college fund.[9]

Home computer users, asserts writer Dan Gutman, need weirdware, not software, to make their computers do what they want.

> Joe America doesn't care about Framework or Symphony or Zork for that matter. He wants programs that help him plant his garden, chart his biorhythms,

plan the route of the family vacation, fix his car, choose a college or pick a career...The computer isn't going to become a common appliance in the American home until the manufacturers realize that the computer revolution must be fueled by weird-ware, not more word processors and spreadsheets.[10]

Of course, there are computer programs that do these things, continues Gutman. Some will help you study for your bar mitzvah, analyze your personality, mix drinks, practice I Ching, or administer self-hypnosis.

Whether the programs are weird or not, many computer users don't know where to find them. They are marketed by small companies that cannot afford splashy ads on television or in computer magazines. Instead, they are sold by mail order and advertised by word of mouth.

One of the caveats of this book holds that a computer cannot solve a problem that the user cannot solve himself or herself first. John Zussman, writing in A+ *Magazine*, a publication devoted to Apple users, adds a corollary: "People won't do anything with a computer that they didn't do without one."[11]

QUESTIONS

1. Make a list of software that you've heard about or seen advertised for the home or non-professional computer user.
2. What things do you do now that you would (or do) use a computer to do?
3. How would (or does) a computer help with the things in question 2?

Programming and Programming Languages

(Courtesy Cray Research, Inc.)

THE ART OF COMPUTER PROGRAMMING

THE PROGRAMMING PROCESS

STRUCTURED PROGRAMMING

LOGIC DESIGN TOOLS

COMPUTER LANGUAGES

DIAGNOSTIC PROCEDURES: DEBUGGING AND TESTING

DOCUMENTATION

As we have seen in the preceding chapters, a computer is not a useful tool by itself. It must be part of a larger system the three parts of which are in balance. The three parts of a complete computer system are the hardware, the operating system, and the application software. Application software comprises the set of programs that control the hardware and operating system to make them perform the required data processing tasks.

A great deal of application software is commercially available as ready-made programs. Many computer installations, particularly those that employ small hardware systems, use commercial software. Often, however, no suitable software exists for some of the applications needed by a particular organization. If software is available at all, it may require such substantial modification to tailor it to the needs of the organization that it is easier to prepare it from scratch. In these circumstances, data processing installations must consider writing their own software or contracting to have it written.

THE ART OF COMPUTER PROGRAMMING

Computer programming is the art of conceiving a problem in terms of the steps to its solution and expressing those steps as instructions for a computer system to follow. We stress the two parts to this definition. The first part focuses on defining the problem and the logical procedures to follow in solving it. The second introduces the means by which programmers communicate those procedures to the computer system that is to execute them.

Programmers use system analysis and design tools, particularly flowcharts and structure charts, to define the problem in terms of the steps to its solution. To communicate the logic of the solution to the computer, they use programming languages. A *programming language* is a collection of commands that direct the control of a computer system. Programming languages, like human-to-human languages, contain a number of rules of expression, called the *syntax* of the language. The syntax governs the manner in which the commands may be used. Just as faulty syntax will cause misunderstanding in English, it will cause computer systems to fail to respond properly to an instruction. Appendix B of this text reviews the world's most popular programming language, BASIC, its syntax, and many of its commands.

As we know, each computer responds only to its machine language, the collection of commands, expressed as binary numbers, that control its operation. Few programmers today prepare computer programs using machine language. Instead, they use one of several hundred programming languages that have been developed over the past forty years to make writing computer programs easier. Operation of these languages depends upon another program or set of programs that translates the program from the language used by the programmer (e.g., BASIC) into machine language for the particular computer to be used. Such *language translators* or *programming systems* convert the commands prepared by the programmer, called the *source program* into its machine language counterpart, called the *object program*.

Most professional programmers work in mainframe computer installations in large organizations. To be sure, a number of software development companies that produce commercial software packages employ programmers, but the majority are not involved in the development of new application programs. This does not mean that the life of a corporate programmer is one lacking in challenge and excitement. Quite the contrary, program maintenance and modification, the chief task of such programmers, is often more challenging than new development.

Data processing managers identify certain traits common to all good programmers. They are self-motivated, patient, and disciplined. They are logical thinkers who deal well with detail. They are creative problem solvers who are technically competent and know the capabilities and limitations of the computer systems with which they work.

This chapter considers various aspects of computer programming. It reviews the process of developing computer programs, describes the tools available to the programmer, and examines several of the most popular programming languages used today.

THE PROGRAMMING PROCESS

The programming process parallels the system development cycle described in Chapter Four. The phases include analysis, design, implementation, and evaluation. In the analysis phase, the problem is described and analyzed. In the design phase, programmers plan the logic of the solution. In the implementation phase, they *code, debug, test,* and *document* the program. Coding is converting the solution into symbols the computer can understand. Debugging and testing eliminate errors from the program. Finally, all of the materials used in designing and writing the program are gathered together and organized as its documentation. As with all systems or procedures (a program, after all, is a procedure), *evaluation* is an on-going process which assures that the program continues to meet the organization's needs.

Problem Analysis and Definition

It is not enough to say, We need a payroll program, when describing a business problem. Rather, we must be considerably more specific: We need a payroll program for up to 1000 salaried and hourly employees who may be paid weekly or monthly. In addition to withholding all federal, state, and city taxes correctly, the program must withhold voluntary deductions for payment to charities, credit unions, and retirement programs. It must also prepare tax reports as required. We could continue with many pages of problem definition. Payroll is one of the more difficult data processing operations, thanks to the complexities of pay withholding and the requirements for reporting payroll information to state and federal taxing authorities.

After defining the problem, we examine it for relationships among its various parts and for a logical structure into which a program design might fit. If we describe a problem carefully at the beginning of the programming process, our program will be better and will cost less to develop.

A world of information is available to the home computerist with a modem and communication software. (Courtesy Hayes Microcomputer Products, Inc.)

Logic Design

There are two aspects to designing program logic. First, we must design the *general logic* of the program. This can be done with the aid of a structure chart which shows the major elements of the program and their relationships to each other. Figure 9-1 shows a structure chart for a payroll problem. A structure chart describes the relationships among the components of the applica-

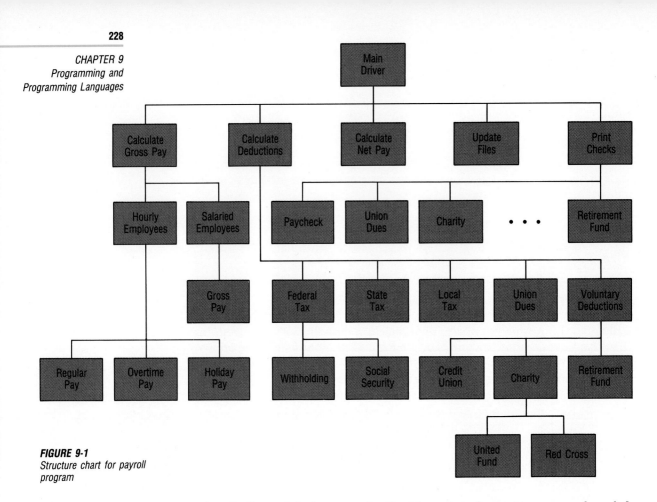

FIGURE 9-1
Structure chart for payroll
program

tion. In figure 9-1, for example, the hierarchy of priorities ranges from left to right and top to bottom. Thus, gross pay and deductions must be calculated before net pay can be determined.

Once we have completed the general logic description, we must deal with the *detailed logic* of the program: the step-by-step operation of each block in the structure chart. Flowcharts and pseudocode, two tools used by programmers, assist in the design of detailed logic. Figures 9-2 and 9-3 show these aids for one block of the structure chart in figure 9-1.

A detailed look at flowcharts and pseudocode appears later in this chapter.

Coding

After we have written detailed logic, we must render that logic understandable to the computer. We do this by *coding,* or converting, the logic into one of the computer languages available for a wide range of machines. Computer languages stand midway between our own *natural language* (the language we speak and write) and the zeros and ones required by the computer.

Debugging and Testing

After coding a program, the programmer must test it to be sure that it runs correctly. There are several steps in this process, starting with *desk checking* or reading through the code to be sure there are no omitted lines and no typographical errors. Desk checking is a matter of trying to think like a computer.

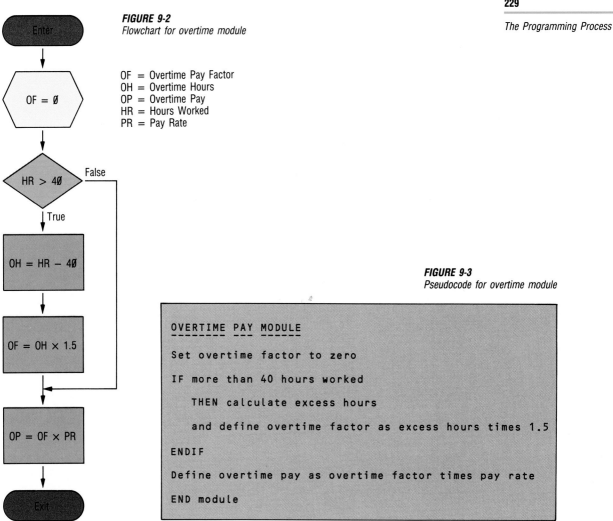

FIGURE 9-2
Flowchart for overtime module

OF = Overtime Pay Factor
OH = Overtime Hours
OP = Overtime Pay
HR = Hours Worked
PR = Pay Rate

FIGURE 9-3
Pseudocode for overtime module

```
OVERTIME PAY MODULE

Set overtime factor to zero

IF more than 40 hours worked

    THEN calculate excess hours

    and define overtime factor as excess hours times 1.5

ENDIF

Define overtime pay as overtime factor times pay rate

END module
```

We mentally execute each command or program instruction in an attempt to find fault with the program's logic. Eventually, we will test the program on the computer with data for which we know the correct answers. The results will tell us whether the program is behaving correctly.

Documentation

The final step in the development cycle, documentation, is one that actually continues throughout the process. Documentation is essential. It provides the installation with information needed to operate and maintain the program. Even for the individual programmer who writes programs for personal use, documentation is required as a reminder of what each step in the program accomplishes. Experienced programmers are quick to testify how quickly one forgets the details of a program's logic.

Most computer languages allow some documentation to be built into the code. In some languages, the code itself is documentation. Good documentation includes descriptions of the logic and coding, how to use the program, what input to provide, what output to expect, and other information of value to programmers who may modify the program and to users of the program.

Documentation is often ignored, with inevitable costly consequences. There are many horror stories about otherwise excellent software that has no usable documentation.

STRUCTURED PROGRAMMING

Structured program design is a tool developed in the 1960s to make it easier to define the elements of a problem. Today, it is the preferred approach to all computer programming projects, and, as we've seen from Chapter Four, for systems analysis and design work, too.

Modules

One form of *structured program* is one that has been designed in small independent parts called *modules*. The modules are linked together by *driver programs* which direct the computer to "enter" the appropriate module. When

FIGURE 9-4
Three structures

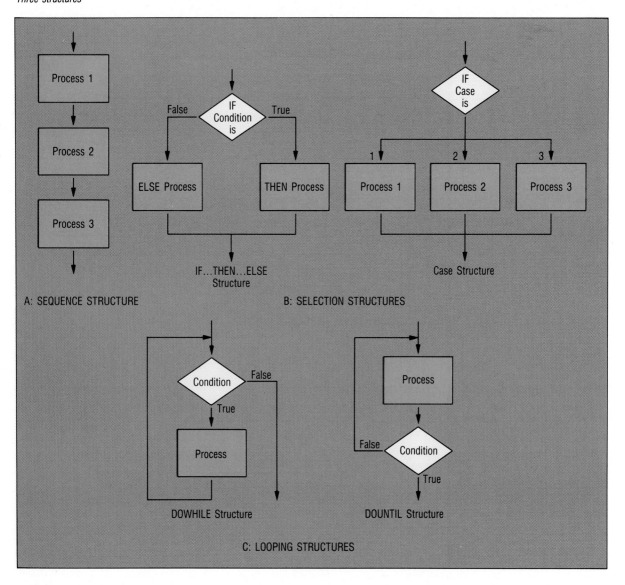

the computer "exits" the module, control is returned to the driver program. Each module has only one entry point and one exit point. A module may consist of several smaller modules.

Philosophically, structured programming adheres to advice proffered in the seventeenth century by French mathematician Rene Descartes. He suggested that the best way to solve a complex problem is to break it down into ever smaller parts and when no further breakdown is possible, to begin solving each of the parts. Together, the individual solutions to each part make up the solution to the whole.

Structures

The elemental unit of any system, as we saw in Chapter Four, is the procedure. In computer programming work, as in mathematics and other analytical pursuits, practitioners use the term *algorithm* to describe the specific method used to produce the results. An algorithm, then, is a method of solving a problem or executing a procedure.

Structured program design is relatively simple, even for very complex problems, because it breaks the entire project into a set of algorithms. Bohm and Jacopini showed that any algorithm could be expressed using only three mechanisms or structures.[1] A *structure*, as the term is used in computer programming, refers to one of three algorithms: the sequence structure; the selection structure; or the loop structure. Figure 9-4 illustrates them.

Sequence Structure

The *sequence structure*, which comprises one or more *process boxes*, represents serial operations: those that always follow one another. Each process box in the structure represents one of the steps in the procedure or algorithm. Figure 9-5 shows a sequence structure used in a payroll program.

Selection Structure

The *selection structure* requires the computer to make a decision based upon the comparison of some data. On the basis of the comparison, a specified condition will be true or false.

Figure 9-4 shows two variations of selection structures. The *IF...THEN...ELSE...* structure tests the condition and branches to one of two process boxes. Figure 9-6 illustrates this situation. If the condition (employee is paid on an hourly basis) is true, the hourly pay is calculated. This is the THEN action. If the condition is false, the salary is calculated; the ELSE action.

The other selection structure variation is the *case structure* which permits the selection of more than two alternative process boxes based upon the condition (see figure 9-4). Use of this structure would be appropriate, for example, when determining the trade discount for a customer, based upon the type of customer making the purchase. Wholesalers, retailers, mail-order firms, and membership stores, four types of customers, may require different methods of calculating trade discounts.

Looping Structure

Our payroll application might require the computer to calculate the pay of fifty employees. Because the same set of process boxes and selection structures would have to be executed for each of the fifty, we should be able to

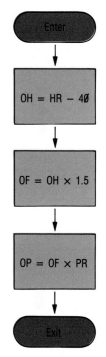

FIGURE 9-5
Sequence structure in payroll program

prepare one sequence of program instructions and execute it as many times as there are employees. This, of course, is called *looping,* one of the milestone concepts in the development of computing machines.

There are two kinds of loops, both of which are shown in figure 9-4. In the first, if a condition is true, the computer executes all of the procedures in the loop. This is called a *DOWHILE LOOP.* It's equivalent to saying, I'll walk while it is daylight. In the second, the computer executes the loop *before* checking the condition. This is called a *DOUNTIL LOOP.* It says, I'll walk until nightfall.

Figure 9-7 shows both looping structures at work in the payroll program. In the case of DOWHILE, the computer continues calculating employees' gross pay so long as the identification number of the last employee record read is not equal to zero. In the case of DOUNTIL, check preparation continues until the last check has been processed.

Proper Programs

In the language of structured programming, a *proper program* is one that has only one entry point and one exit point. Notice that each of the structures in figures 9-4 through 9-7 conforms to those criteria. A proper program usually consists of modules, each of which is also proper. This means that structured programming limits the use of unconditional branches. An *unconditional branch* is an instruction that causes the computer to skip instructions regardless of any conditions that might exist. A typical unconditional branch instruction is GOTO, which is used in both FORTRAN and BASIC, two old (more than 20 years) and popular languages. Structured programming is often called GOTO-less programming. The programming language Pascal, for example, still in its teens, has no GOTO command. Some computer languages, particularly the older ones, cannot be programmed without unconditional branches. They are called *unstructured languages.*

Structured Programming Technique

There are two approaches to writing a structured program. They are called *programming by level* and *programming by path.* In programming by level, all modules on level one, the top-most level, are written before anything is done on level two. Level two is programmed before level three and so forth. This

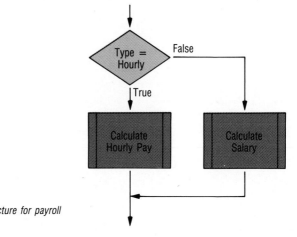

FIGURE 9-6
Selection structure for payroll
program

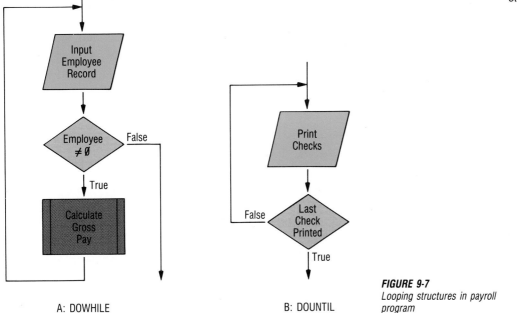

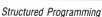

FIGURE 9-7
Looping structures in payroll program

A: DOWHILE B: DOUNTIL

is shown in figure 9-8. The numbers indicate the sequence in which the modules are programmed. Programming by level is also called *top-down programming*.

In the programming by path method, all modules along a logical path in the program are written in sequence. This is sometimes called *backtracking*. Following this method, the programmer then backtracks to the first unwritten module that is directly connected to the path being programmed. Eventually, all modules are completed. Programming by path is illustrated in figure 9-9.

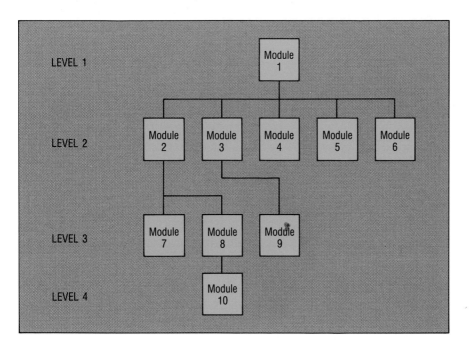

FIGURE 9-8
Programming by level

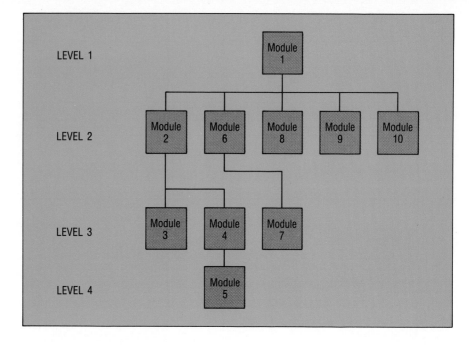

FIGURE 9-9
Programming by path

As a rule, large computer installations that employ many programmers use structured programming techniques. Such techniques make it much easier to keep track of the specific procedures or algorithms that make up the totality of the project. They also facilitate the specialization of effort required to coordinate all the aspects of a large programming project. After using structured programming, most programmers agree that it is the best approach to coping with the complex relationships found in preparing applications and systems programs. It makes programs easier to understand, edit, update, and correct. All too often, unstructured programs become a hodgepodge of branches and subbranches that become ever more complex as the program is modified and corrected.

LOGIC DESIGN TOOLS

Many believe that learning to become a computer programmer is a matter of learning a number of computer programming languages. If one can talk to computers, so goes the conventional wisdom, one is a programmer. Nothing could be further from the truth. Computer programming is a skill of problem solving. Facility with one or several computer languages is secondary. The definition of computer programming given at the outset of this chapter emphasizes the point: computer programming is the art of conceiving a problem in terms of the steps to its solution.

Once the problem has been analyzed into small units, or modules, and has been expressed as a structure chart, the programmer turns to the detailed logic of each module, using the three structures described in the preceding pages. Programmers use a number of tools to design detailed logic. In this book, we limit our attention to two: flowcharting and pseudocode. This is not to suggest that these are the only tools, but rather to illustrate the two most common.

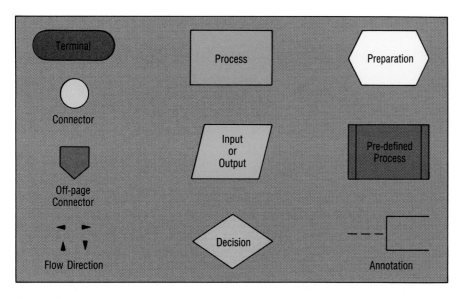

FIGURE 9-10
ANSI flowcharting symbols

Flowcharting

Chapter Four reviewed flowcharting as a technique of both system and computer program design. Program flowcharts present a pictorial description of the logical order of operations within a program module.

Flowcharting Symbols

As a pictorial representation, flowcharts make use of symbols that have specific meanings. The symbols, as adopted by the American National Standards Institute, appear in figure 4-7 and we repeat them in figure 9-10 for convenience.

The *rectangle* represents operations or processes such as calculations. It is typically used in sequence structures. If the rectangle has vertical bars in it, it represents a *predefined process,* one that has already been programmed. The predefined process might be in the program being developed or it might be in a library of frequently used program routines or modules.

The *diamond* represents a decision and is the key operating feature of the selection and looping structures illustrated in figures 9-6 and 9-7.

The *parallelogram* represents input or output.

The *hexagon* denotes program preparation. Often, for example, certain values must be established initially by the program before operations begin. A date may require specification, or various program counters must be initialized to zero.

Ovals are called *terminals* because they signify the two ends of a program, that is, where the program starts and where it stops.

Circles and *pentagons* are called *connectors.* They show the flow of logic from one symbol to another, without the use of flow lines. They are used for on-page (circle) and off-page (pentagon) connections. Connectors are used to keep the flow lines of a program from becoming too confusing. They are usually used with a letter or number that matches another letter or number elsewhere in the flowchart, thus indicating the destination of the leap.

Program flow is represented by lines that are parallel to the edges of the paper. Arrowheads show the direction of flow. Flow lines never cross each other. Instead, connectors are used to jump the flow of logic across other lines.

Finally, the *open rectangle,* which is connected to the flowchart with a dotted line, is used for annotation: notes and comments that help explain what's going on.

Types of Flowcharts

There are two basic types of flowcharts. *Macroflowcharts,* also known as *block diagrams,* show a general description of the steps of a program. *Microflowcharts* show the logic in full detail. A microflowchart is often represented as a predefined process symbol in another flowchart, thus indicating the use of a procedure common to several programs. Block diagrams fall between structure charts and microflowcharts in a hierarchy of detailed logic.

Flowcharting Rules

Flowcharts are used to describe the logic of a program. Because of the nature of the programming process, it is often necessary for the programmer to change that logic during the development process. Since the flowchart expresses the logic, it must be redrawn, at least in part. This can be a tedious task, but it is one made simpler by following a few basic rules.

1. Organize all flowcharts in modules. This is a basic tenet of structured programming.
2. Use the standardized symbols described here, which are approved by the American National Standards Institute (ANSI) and the International Standards Organization (ISO) for all flowcharts.
3. Vary symbol size but not shape.
4. Maintain consistent spacing between symbols. This makes the flowchart much more readable.
5. Arrange main program flow from top to bottom and from left to right. In fact, arrowheads are optional on flowlines in these directions. Even so, we recommend using arrowheads on all flowlines.
6. Do not use connectors unless it is absolutely necessary. The three reasons for using connectors are (1) flow continues to another page; (2) a flowline must cross another flowline; and (3) symbols representing consecutive operations are so far apart that a continuous flowline would make the chart confusing. Figure 9-11 illustrates the good use of a connector to avoid a long flowline.
7. Never cross flowlines.
8. Print, do not write, all information in a flowchart.
9. Label every flowchart with the name of the program, the name of the programmer, the date, and any other pertinent information.
10. Always draw flowcharts in pencil until the program is certified as correct and operational.
11. Make certain that all paths in the flowchart are accounted for. There must be no path that goes nowhere. This rule is consistent with the notion of the proper program that has one entry and one exit.

Flowcharting work goes more quickly when the programmer uses a couple of aids. A flowcharting template makes it easy to draw symbols quickly. The

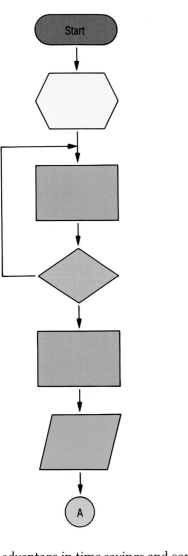

FIGURE 9-11
Use of connector to avoid long flowline

advantage in time savings and consistency of symbol shape is balanced against the disadvantage of having only one or two sizes for each symbol. Figure 9-12 shows a plastic template which can be purchased in most stationery stores.

The flowcharting form shown in figure 9-13 enables the programmer to produce a chart with symbols properly spaced. Its disadvantage is the limited symbol size. Flowcharting forms are produced in pads and can be obtained from computer supply firms.

Some computer installations use computer programs that produce flow-charts. These come in two varieties. One version examines a program that has already been written and describes its logic in the form of a flowchart. This type of flowcharting program is particularly valuable for analyzing programs that don't operate properly because of an error in logic and for preparing final program documentation. The other accepts program specifications and develops logic to meet the specifications. The resulting flowchart is then used as the basis for coding the program.

There we have flowcharting, the most widely used tool for logic design. Its advantages include the useful documentation it provides, the pictorialization of relationships within the program, and the ease with which a flowcharted program is coded, debugged, and tested. Because it is a graphical display, logical

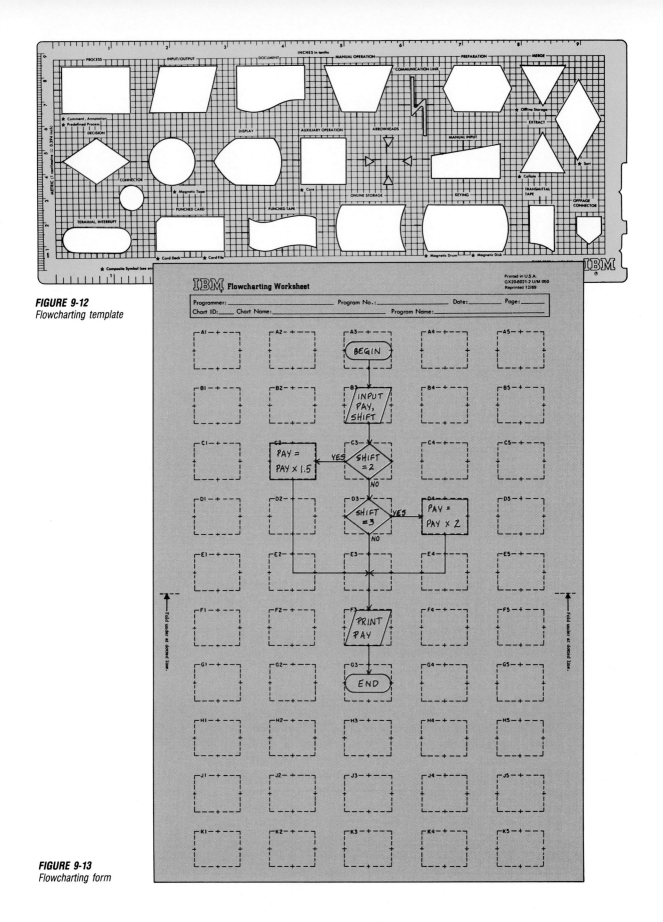

FIGURE 9-12
Flowcharting template

FIGURE 9-13
Flowcharting form

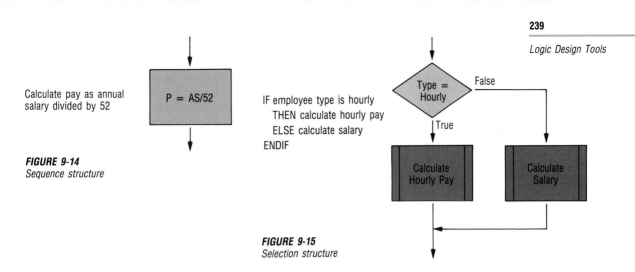

Calculate pay as annual salary divided by 52

P = AS/52

FIGURE 9-14
Sequence structure

IF employee type is hourly
   THEN calculate hourly pay
   ELSE calculate salary
ENDIF

FIGURE 9-15
Selection structure

errors are more easily detected and corrected. Its disadvantages are the difficulty and expense involved in constructing and modifying a flowchart. In addition, complex flowcharts are sometimes very hard to read and follow. Another tool, pseudocode, alleviates some of these problems.

Pseudocode

Pseudocode is a narrative description of the steps involved in executing a computer program in the order in which they will be executed. Pseudocode is written like an outline, with indentation showing the basic programming mechanisms of structured programming. Each structured mechanism in a program has its own level of indentation. The beginning and end of the mechanism are shown at one level of indentation while the steps within the mechanism are shown at the next level.

In figures 9-14 through 9-17, we repeat flowcharts of the basic mechanisms of structured programming, using the payroll example. With them, we show

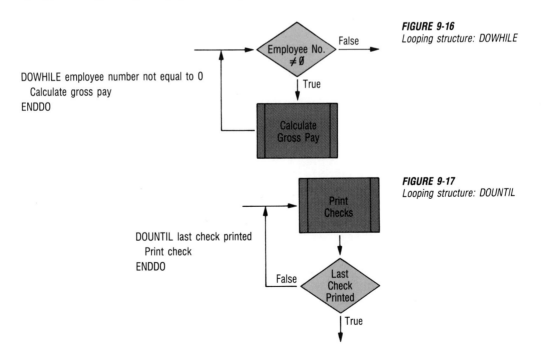

FIGURE 9-16
Looping structure: DOWHILE

DOWHILE employee number not equal to 0
   Calculate gross pay
ENDDO

FIGURE 9-17
Looping structure: DOUNTIL

DOUNTIL last check printed
   Print check
ENDDO

the corresponding pseudocode. Notice the use of the vocabulary of structured programming: DOWHILE and DOUNTIL.

Figure 9-18 shows a flowchart and the corresponding pseudocode for a program that combines several structured mechanisms.

It is easier to code a program from pseudocode than from a flowchart because of the code-like outline provided, but flowcharts are better for designing logically complex problems. For this reason, many programmers assert that the most effective way of programming is to use a flowchart at the macrolevel and pseudocode at the microlevel.

Coding

After a program has been designed using structure charts, flowcharts, and pseudocode, it must be coded, that is, specific computer instructions, which will cause the computer system to execute the program's operations, must be prepared. Coding can be done in any one of hundreds of computer languages. Selecting the proper language requires an understanding of the various languages and of the issues involved in language selection. It is also important to understand the language capabilities of the computer for which we are writing code.

COMPUTER LANGUAGES

Categorizing Languages

There are many ways of categorizing computer languages: by level, purpose, structure, orientation, and translation method.

Level

Computer languages are called *low-level* if they require the programmer to have detailed knowledge of the computer hardware system. A *high-level* language is one that is fairly machine-independent in that little or no knowledge of specific computing machinery is required. As a rule, the higher the level of a language, the more similar it is to English, or to the programmer's natural language.

Purpose

Languages are *general-purpose* if they can be used to solve a variety of types of problems. The lower the level, the more general-purpose the language. *Special-purpose* languages can be used for very narrow classes of problems. An example of a special-purpose language is WPL. Written by Apple for use with their word processor, Applewriter II, WPL only functions to control word processing functions for that one computer.

Structure

Early languages like FORTRAN, COBOL, and BASIC were not designed for structured programming. Programmers must struggle to write structured programs using these languages. A language is structured if it is relatively easy

DOWHILE employee number ≠ 0
  Input employee weekly work record
  IF employee is hourly
    THEN calculate gross
        pay based on reg,
        OT, weekend hours
    ELSE pay = annual salary/52
  ENDIF
  Record gross pay in payroll file
ENDDO

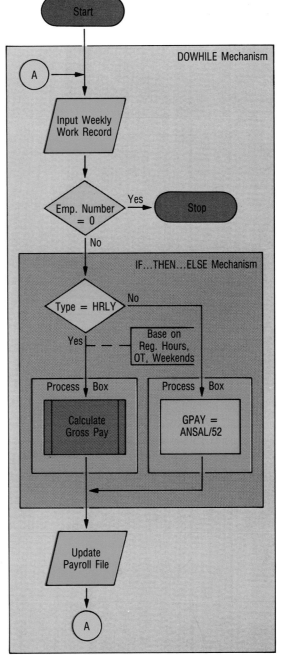

FIGURE 9-18
A structured flowchart

to implement the structure mechanisms described earlier in this chapter. Pascal, C, and Ada, for example, were designed with those structures in mind and, therefore, make structured programming easier. Several early languages have been modified recently to create structured forms. True BASIC is an example.

Orientation

Languages can be classified as *procedure-oriented* or *problem-oriented.* In a procedure-oriented language, programmers specify how to solve a problem by indicating the procedures or algorithms the computer is to use. In a problem-oriented language, programmers specify what is to be accomplished, leaving the development of procedures to the language. For example, BASIC is a procedure-oriented language. In BASIC, we must specify each step the computer must take to solve a problem. RPG (Report Program Generator), on the other hand, is a problem-oriented language designed for generating business reports. In RPG, we specify the format in which the report is to be printed, the format of the input data, and the calculations and other operations required to produce output data.

Translation Method

Except for machine language, which is already in machine-executable form, every computer language must be translated into the zeros and ones that the computer understands. The translation is performed by another computer program, called the language translator. The language translator uses the program prepared by the programmer as input and produces the machine language program as output. This is done in three ways.

Some languages are compiled. A *compiler* translates an entire program into machine language before the program is executed. The original program prepared by the programmer is called the *source* program. The machine language program that is the output of the translator program is called the *object program*. Once the object program is created, we never have to use the source program again except, perhaps, to modify it. This saves considerable computer time with programs that are run frequently. Compiled programs tend to run fast but must be debugged as a whole unit.

Other languages are interpreted. An *interpreter* converts the source program to machine language as the program is being executed. Interpreters translate code line-by-line. If a line of code is used one thousand times in a DOUNTIL loop, for example, that line is translated one thousand times. For this reason, interpreters tend to run more slowly than compilers. Interpreted languages are easier to debug, however, inasmuch as they allow each line of code to be checked for syntax as it is entered into the computer. Thus, programmers can edit and debug a problem as they create it. Interpreters never create object programs. Every time a program is run it must be retranslated into machine language.

Using an interpreted language can be compared with a conversation between two people who do not speak each other's language. Each of them must wait for an interpreter to translate the other's remarks. A compiled language, on the other hand, is like a memorandum written in German that is translated entirely into English before it is delivered to the English-speaking recipient.

Assembly language, which we describe later, is neither compiled nor interpreted. It is *assembled*. From our point of view, assembling a program is virtually the same as compiling one, although it is somewhat less time-consuming inasmuch as the assembly language source program is already close to machine language.

Some languages can be interpreted or compiled. BASIC is such a language. BASIC programs designed for frequent use are often written, debugged, and tested using an interpreter, then compiled for everyday use or *production runs*.

Interaction

Some languages are *interactive*. This means the programmer can conduct a dialog with the computer—enter a line of code, have the computer test it, do an arithmetic computation, and so forth in any order, at any time. Other languages are not interactive. Interactive languages tend to be interpreted rather than compiled.

Important Languages: A Baker's Dozen

Machine Language

Machine language is the fundamental language of computers. Instructions, made up of zeros and ones, tell the control unit of the computer CPU what to do and what data to use. A typical machine language instruction for a large computer looks like this:

ExperTelligence produced ExperList™, one of the first systems to provide for the development of artificial intelligence on the Macintosh. (Courtesy ExperTelligence)

```
0011101010010101011110010111101101010100110110
```

This instruction tells the computer what operation to perform, what pieces of data to use, as identified by the memory addresses where they are stored, and the length of those pieces of data. Some modern computers have hexadecimal converters built into their circuitry. In such computers, our machine language instruction would look like this:

```
3A95797B5536
```

We can interpret this instruction as follows, remembering that all the numbers are in hexadecimal.

```
Perform operation 3A
using 9 and 5 bytes of information
starting at memory locations 797B and 5536 respectively.
```

Machine language is the lowest level language. It was the first language available to programmers, and in fact, the only language until the early 1950s. It is very fast since no translation is needed, and it makes very efficient use of memory. The programmer has complete control of the computer and is able to use all of its capabilities. A machine language program is merely data to the computer. Therefore, the program can modify itself during execution.

Machine language has many disadvantages. It is difficult to learn. For example, the programmer might have to remember that 00110011 means add while 00110110 means subtract. There are many such codes. The programmer must keep track of every memory location, every register, and all other details about the machine.

It is very easy to make errors in a machine language program and very hard to correct them. For instance, if a programmer omits an instruction, every line following the omission will probably be wrong. Machine language programs can only be run on the machine for which they were written because machine language is directly related to the logic that is wired into each processor. Machine language programs are very slow to write because so much detail must be included. Therefore, they are expensive to develop. Finally, machine language programmers cannot use coding written for other programs in a new program. They must start over with each program.

As a result of these disadvantages, virtually nobody programs in machine language any more.

Figure 9-19 shows a sample machine language program.

Assembly Language

Assembly language was developed in the early 1950s to alleviate some of the difficulties in using machine language. It replaced the binary code of

```
20 58 FC          00100000  01011000  11111100        BEGIN
A9 C2             10101001  11000010                   01
8D 00 04          10001101  00000000  00000100         02
A9 C5             10101001  11000101                   03
8D 01 04          10001101  00000001  00000100         04
A9 C7             10101001  11000111                   05
8D 02 04          10001101  00000010  00000100         END
A9 C9             10101001  11001001                   (C)
8D 03 04          10001101  00000011  00000100
A9 CE             10101001  11001110
8D 04 04          10001101  00000100  00000100
A2 01             10100010  00000001
A9 8D             10101001  10001101
20 ED FD          00100000  11011010  11111101
8A                10001010
20 DA FD          00100000  11011010  11111101
E8                11101000
E0 06             11100000  00000110
D0 F2             11010000  11110010
A9 C5             10101001  11000101
8D 00 07          10001101  00000000  00000111
A9 CE             10101001  11001110
8D 01 07          10001101  00000001  00000111
A9 C4             10101001  11000100
8D 02 07          10001101  00000010  00000111
A9 8D             10101001  10001101
20 ED FD          00100000  11101101  11111101
60                01100000
    (A)                       (B)
```

FIGURE 9-19
Machine language program for
the Apple II+
(A) As entered
(B) As stored
(C) Output

machine language instructions with symbolic names, or *mnemonics*. The term *mnemonic* means memory aid. Thanks to their use, assembly language instructions are easier to remember than are their machine language counterparts. A sample instruction might look like this:

    PT1 ADD REG5,COST

where PT1 is a label or reference, ADD is the mnemonic that instructs the computer to add, and REG5 and COST represent a register and a storage location, respectively.

Assembly language programmers still need to know a great deal about the machines they are using. Assembly language programs are not transportable, that is, they can only be used on the machine for which they were written. A great deal of code must be written for any program because assembly language instructions are in essential one-to-one correspondence with machine language instructions.

Advantages of assembly language include relative addressing; instead of specifying every storage location, the programmer specifies only the first location used. The assembler assigns the rest. This makes an assembly language program much more correctable if an error has been made in coding. The assembler provides an error listing which also aids in the debugging process. Perhaps most important is the use of mnemonics which provides a memory aid to programmers as they write code. Since assembly language is very close to machine language, it is also quite fast.

Assembly language programming is presently losing its popularity except in special programs that require machine features that are unavailable in higher level languages. In earlier times, equipment was expensive and personnel was not. Today programming time is very costly while equipment is relatively inexpensive. Because of the high development costs of assembly language programs and the lack of transportability, end users are willing to use slightly slower programs written in higher level languages.

Figure 9-20 shows an assembly language version of the program in figure 9-19.

```
01 ;APPLE ASSEMBLY LANGUAGE PROGRAM          BEGIN
02 ;TO LIST 5 NUMBERS                        01
03            ORG     $300                    02
04            OBJ     $800                    03
05 CLR        EQU     $FC58                   04
06 PRNTA      EQU     $FDED                   05
07 PRNTN      EQU     $FFDA                   END
08 BEGIN      JSR     CLR                     (B)
09            LDA     #$C2
10            STA     $0400
11            LDA     #$C5
12            STA     $0401
13            LDA     #$C7
14            STA     $0402
15            LDA     #$C9
16            STA     $0403
17            LDA     #$CE
18            STA     $0404
19 NUMBRS     LDX     #$01
20 LOOP       LDA     #$8D
21            JSR     PRNTA
22            TXA
23            JSR     PRNTN
24            INX
25            CPX     #$06
26            BNE     LOOP
27 END        LDA     #$C5
28            STA     $0700
29            LDA     #$CE
30            STA     $0701
31            LDA     #$C4
32            STA     $0702
33            LDA     #$8D
34            JSR     PRNTA
35 DONE       RTS
           (A)
```

FIGURE 9-20
Apple assembly language
program
(A) Listing   (B) Output

FORTRAN

Early computer users were scientists and engineers. It is not surprising, therefore, that the first high-level language was designed to solve scientific problems. This language is FORTRAN, short for FORmula TRANslator. Scientific problems are characterized by complex arithmetic computation, minimal input and output, and limited use of data files.

FORTRAN was developed by an IBM group led by John Backus. It made its first appearance in 1956, but errors in its compiler led to a corrected version known as FORTRAN II which was released in 1959. It is the world's oldest high-level language. Since its introduction, many other versions of FORTRAN have been released. FORTRAN IV, for example, was designated as standard FORTRAN by ANSI in 1966. This was revised in 1977 as FORTRAN 77, the latest standard. Even with standards, compatibility among different versions is often a problem because so many software producers have released FORTRAN compilers. For this reason, transportability can be a problem for FORTRAN programs.

FORTRAN is still a very popular language because there are so many programmers familiar with it and because there are so many available programs written in it. Figure 9-21 shows the flowchart for a simple looping program. We will code this program in most of the higher level languages described in the pages to come. Figure 9-22 shows the coded FORTRAN program. Figure 9-23 shows the output for all of the sample programs.

FIGURE 9-21
Flowchart for sample programs

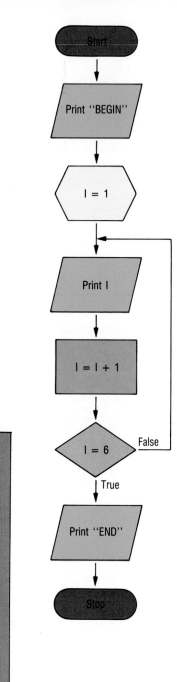

```
Print "BEGIN"
Set I = 1
DOUNTIL I = 6
  Print I
  Step I by 1
ENDDO
Print "END"
```

FIGURE 9-22
FORTRAN program

```
C       FORTRAN EXAMPLE - PROGRAM TO LIST 5 NUMBERS
10      FORMAT (1X, 'BEGIN')
20      FORMAT (1X, I2)
30      FORMAT (1X, 'END')
        WRITE (6, 10)
        DO 40 I = 1, 5
        WRITE (6,20) Z
40      CONTINUE
        WRITE (6,30)
        END
```

FIGURE 9-23
Output for sample programs

```
BEGIN
1
2
3
4
5
END
```

COBOL

In 1959, the Department of Defense sponsored the Conference on DAta SYstems Languages (CODASYL). Out of this conference grew the CODASYL committee. (Commodore Grace Hopper of the U.S. Navy, one of the first women to be successful in the computer field, served on the committee.) The committee undertook the development of a language suitable for business applications. Business applications are characterized by limited need for sophisticated computations, substantial demands on input and output, and heavy use of data files. The CODASYL committee named the language COBOL (COmmon Business Oriented Language). It was first published as COBOL-60 by the Government Printing Office in 1960. In 1968 and again in 1974, ANSI established standard versions of COBOL because of the large number of compilers being developed.

COBOL soon became an extremely popular procedure-oriented language, perhaps because government policy required that all computers bought or leased by the government be able to use a COBOL compiler. Even today, COBOL is heavily used in commercial and government computer installations. As much as 80 percent of government and business programming has been written in COBOL.

A look at the employment section of the want ads of any major newspaper will show how popular COBOL still is. We would be remiss if we did not observe that COBOL's popularity may be due to its advantages or may, instead, be due to the fact that so many programs are written in it. Computer installations may well be unwilling to rewrite programs using a more modern language because of the cost involved. The trade press occasionally carries articles debating whether or not COBOL is dead. The fact that one rarely sees such debates concerning FORTRAN, COBOL's predecessor, may suggest that FORTRAN has already met its demise, but that COBOL is still hanging on.

COBOL is more like English than FORTRAN. This is both an advantage and a disadvantage. It is easy to read and tends to be self-documenting, but it requires a very large compiler. For this reason, it has only recently become available on microcomputers. Also, coding is fairly slow because there is so much to write. COBOL is reasonably machine-independent, so programs are fairly transportable.

Grace Hopper, a true luminary in the modern era of computers, was a moving force behind the development of COBOL.
(Courtesy Sperry Corp.)

```
PROCEDURE DIVISION.

MAIN ROUTINE.

    DISPLAY "BEGIN".

    PERFORM PRINT-OUT-I VARYING I FROM 1 BY 1 UNTIL I > 5.

    DISPLAY "END".

    STOP-RUN.

PRINT-OUT-I.

    DISPLAY I.
```

FIGURE 9-24
COBOL procedure division

COBOL programs are constructed like an essay. There are divisions, sections, paragraphs, and sentences. The sentences correspond to FORTRAN statements. Programs consist of four divisions: the procedure division which specifies the processes to be performed; the environment division which describes the computer and its peripheral equipment; the data division which specifies the formats of input and output data; and the identification division which distinguishes the program from all other programs. Data processing people use the acronym IEDP, I Enjoy Data Processing, to help remember the names of the divisions.

Figure 9-24 shows the procedure division of our example program.

BASIC

BASIC (Beginner's All-purpose Symbolic Instruction Code) is probably the most popular computer language in the world today. Many commercial programs written for microcomputers have been coded in BASIC. The language is available on virtually every microcomputer because its interpreter requires very little memory. It is also widely used with mainframe and minicomputers, particularly those installed in educational institutions.

The language was developed by John Kemeny and Thomas Kurtz of Dartmouth College in the early 1960s. It was developed in conjunction with the world's first time-sharing system and served, as its first purpose, to make it easy for computer users to retrieve information from mainframe data files.

It was originally designed as a teaching language but has become much more with the advent of the microcomputer. ANSI has defined a small set of instructions that form standard BASIC. This list has been considerably extended, with Microsoft BASIC fast becoming the standard for personal computers. Although the many versions of BASIC are similar, there remain slight differences that require program revision when a program is run on a computer for which it was not initially designed.

BASIC is a general-purpose, procedure-oriented, interactive language that is normally interpreted, though many compilers are available. This allows programmers to write, debug, and test their programs using an interpreter and then compile their correct programs and enjoy the speed of object program execution. BASIC does not lend itself well to structured programming: unconditional branch statements must be used to implement some of the logical mechanisms.

```
10 REM BASIC PROGRAM TO LIST 5 NUMBERS

20 PRINT "BEGIN"

30 FOR I = 1 TO 5

40 PRINT I

50 NEXT I

60 PRINT "END"

70 END
```

FIGURE 9-25
BASIC program

```
/* SAMPLE PL/1 PROGRAM TO PRINT 5 NUMBERS */

START: PROCEDURE;

    WRITE LIST ('BEGIN');

    LOOP: DO I = 1 TO 5;

        WRITE LIST (I);

    END LOOP;

    WRITE LIST ('END');

    STOP;

END START;
```

FIGURE 9-26
PL/1 program

The advantages of programming in BASIC include ease of use, flexibility, good diagnostic messages, and its interactive nature. Its disadvantages include the lack of standardization and thus limited transportability, its slow execution speed, and its unstructured nature. A BASIC version of our sample program is shown in figure 9-25.

PL/1

Another general-purpose, procedure-oriented language developed in the 1960s is PL/1, or Programming Language 1. Developed by IBM, this language combines the best characteristics of FORTRAN and COBOL. It is a modular (structured) language that is both extensive and sophisticated. For this reason, its compiler is very large, a fact that has prevented its use on microcomputers. Figure 9-26 shows the example program written in PL/1.

RPG

RPG is a problem-oriented language whose purpose is to generate business reports. In fact, RPG stands for Report Program Generator. RPG pro-

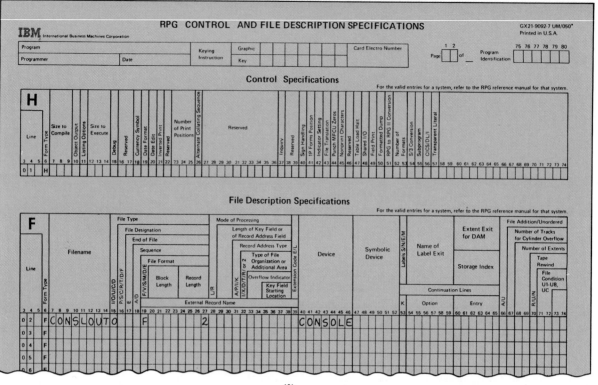

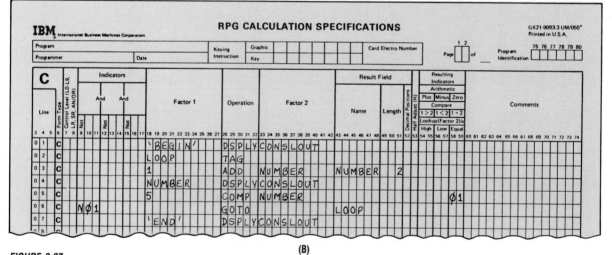

FIGURE 9-27
RPG coding sheets and program

grams are actually little more than descriptions of the reports to be generated. They are written using a series of coding forms which are shown in figure 9-27. The coding forms ask the following questions: (1) what records will be used to produce the report; (2) what fields will be read from each record; (3) what computations are to be done; (4) what subtotals and totals should be taken; and (5) how should the report be formatted.

RPG was designed for use on small computer systems but has not made an impact on the microcomputer market since most data base programs for microcomputers include their own report generators.

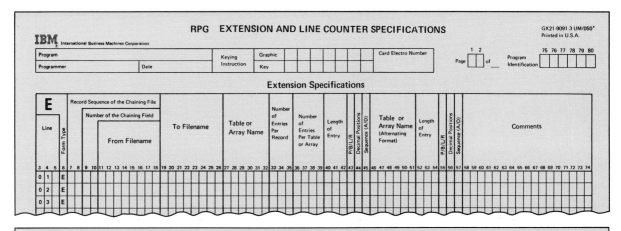

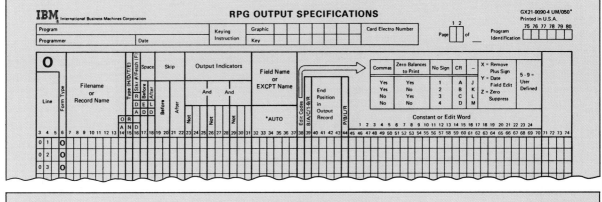

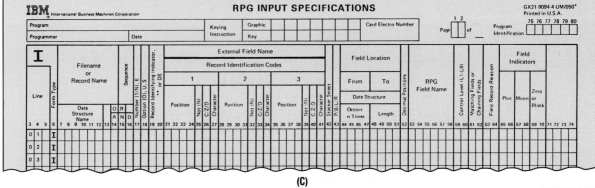

(C)

FIGURE 9-27
(Continued)

LISP

John McCarthy of Stanford University developed LISP, short for LISt Processor, in 1960. LISP is a special-purpose language designed to manipulate nonnumeric data. It offers a convenient way to represent sentences, formulas, computer programs, and similar data. LISP is a powerful tool for pattern recognition, simulation of human problem-solving processes, and heuristic programming (programs that modify themselves, or "learn," as they are executed). LISP is especially suitable for artificial intelligence applications.

APL

Conceived as a notation system for teaching mathematics in 1962 by Kenneth Iverson, APL (A Programming Language) became available as a com-

FIGURE 9-28
APL keyboard

```
   ▽ LISTNUMS

[1] 'BEGIN'

[2] 5 1 ⍴⍳5

[3] 'END'

   ▽
```

FIGURE 9-29
APL program

puter language through IBM in 1969. Originally, APL was known as Iverson's Language.

APL combines a freeform style with a lack of restrictions on input and output. It has extremely powerful mathematical capabilities, but it is very hard to read (there are no mnemonics) and it requires a special keyboard (shown in figure 9-28) and printer. The latter problem has been solved with the advent of daisy-wheel printers into which special type fonts can be placed. It is a fast language with fewer restrictions on data than exist in other languages. Its file handling capabilities are somewhat limited.

Because APL handles tables of information easily and many business applications deal with tabular data, some programmers have embraced APL as their language of choice. Because it requires a very large amount of storage, APL is not available on smaller microcomputers. In addition, APL uses nonstandard arithmetic, evaluating expressions from right to left with no hierarchy of operations. Thus, $3 \times 4 + 2$ equals 18 in APL when we expect it to equal 14.

Figure 9-29 shows the sample program in APL. Notice the brevity of coding.

Pascal

Like BASIC, Pascal was designed as a teaching language. It was written as a structured language by Nicklaus Wirth in 1971. The language was named after French mathematician and philosopher Blaise Pascal (1623–1662) who, you might remember, was the inventor of the first mechanical adding machine.

Pascal is well-suited for both batch and interactive uses. Although it is easy to use and powerful, it lacks sophisticated input and output capabilities which limits its use in business applications. It is not yet standardized so transportability can be a problem, although the UCSD (University of California at San Diego) version is recognized as a standard. Given the power of the language, its compiler is quite small. In an effort to improve Pascal, Wirth developed a modification called Modula 2 which was introduced in 1984.

Pascal is suitable for and popular on microcomputers, although it requires considerable memory to operate the fully implemented UCSD version. It uses an operating system especially designed for it called the P-system.

Figure 9-30 shows our looping program as written in Pascal.

Forth

Forth was designed as a "fourth generation computer language." The computer on which the language was developed limited filenames to five characters, thus Fourth became Forth. It is a fairly low-level language (higher than

```
        PROGRAM LISTNUM;

        VAR I: INTEGER;

        BEGIN

            WRITELN ('BEGIN');

            FOR I := 1 TO 5 DO WRITELN (I);

            WRITELN ('END');

        END.
```

FIGURE 9-30
Pascal program

assembly, lower than FORTRAN) which was developed for microcomputers in the late 1970s.

Forth's power is in the way it extends itself. It has a limited vocabulary of functions. When one programs a new function, it becomes part of the standard vocabulary of the language. Thus, Forth offers excellent control of the computer because it is close to assembly language in level, yet it allows us to use code written for previous projects.

Although it is a general-purpose language, Forth is particularly good for industrial process control applications. In fact, it is the standard control language for astronomical observatories around the world. It is also used by many industry leaders such as IBM and Hewlett-Packard for in-house development projects.

Figure 9-31 shows the looping program as it appears in Forth.

C

After concluding that system programming, meaning the development of operating system programs, was too time-consuming and difficult, AT&T set out to prepare a general, low-level language that would work on all computers. C is the third version of a language developed by Bell Laboratories in conjunction with its operating system UNIX. The earlier versions were A and B. With C, operating systems and application programs can be written in a matter of months rather than years. Many commercial application programs and operating systems for all sizes of computers are now prepared using the C language.

Also, like Forth, C is a lower level language than Pascal or PL/1 but higher than assembly language. It is machine-independent and transportable, yet it provides the control of an assembler. At the same time, it provides features

```
        :NUMLIST "BEGIN" CR

            5 0 DO I 1 + . CR LOOP

            "END" CR;
```

FIGURE 9-31
Forth program

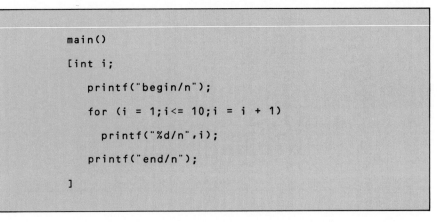

```
main()

[int i;

    printf("begin/n");

    for (i = 1;i<= 10;i = i + 1)

      printf("%d/n",i);

    printf("end/n");

]
```

FIGURE 9-32
C program

of high-level languages. Thus, C is user oriented and machine efficient.

Like Forth, C can extend itself as the programmer defines new functions. It is structured, allowing the programmer to build complex programs out of simple parts. It is fast and it requires little storage. It is a difficult language to code and hard to read.

C has been used to develop the special effects in many films such as the *Star Trek* series. It is fast becoming the *lingua franca* of professional programmers.

Figure 9-32 shows the loop program written in C.

Ada

The last of the languages we will discuss is Ada, named after the world's first programmer, Ada Lovelace, daughter of the poet Byron. Her work with Charles Babbage and his analytical engine led to the first concepts of programming.

Ada the programming language was developed around 1980 in response to Department of Defense demands for a standardized language. Up to that time, programming done for the Army was incompatible with programming done for the Navy and so forth. Ada was designed as a general-purpose language with exceptional capabilities. It included so much that the compiler became enormous. It was designed for use in environments of great complexity where reliability is paramount.

The name Ada is legally protected. Nobody may use it on a product without a license from the Defense Department. Thus, all Ada compilers are compatible.

It is likely that Ada will become a major programming language of the 1990s because of the support the government has placed behind it.

Figure 9-33 shows our example program in Ada.

Selecting a Language

As we have seen, computer languages fall into families. The hierarchy of languages is shown in figure 9-34.

Speed is an important criterion. The speed with which a program runs relates to its position on the chart. Generally, languages closer to machine language run faster, while higher level languages run slower. Programs that must execute quickly, because they control equipment in real time or because they are used so heavily, should be programmed in fairly low-level languages

Augusta Ada Byron, the world's
first computer programmer,
worked with Charles Babbage
over 150 years ago. (Courtesy
Culver Pictures Inc.)

FIGURE 9-33
ADA program

```
WITH IO;

PACKAGE BODY COUNT IS

USE IO;


BEGIN

  PUT ("BEGIN");

  NEW ← LINE;

  FOR I IN 1..5

    LOOP

      PUT (I);

      NEW ← LINE;

    END LOOP;

  PUT ("END");

  NEW ← LINE;

END COUNT;_ _
```

FIGURE 9-34
Hierarchy of languages

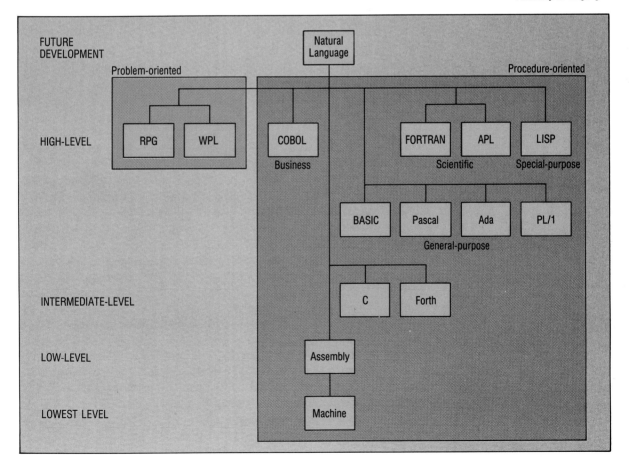

TABLE 9-1 CHARACTERISTICS OF MAJOR COMPUTER LANGUAGES

Language	Math Capability	English-Like	Character Manipulation	Availability	Standardized	Storage Needs	Interactive	Orientation	Level	Purpose	Notes
Ada	High	Yes	Yes	Low	Yes	High	No	Proc	High	Gen	Expected high impact in late '80s, '90s
APL	High	No	High	Low	No	High	Yes	Proc	High	Sci	Extremely abstract
Assembly	High	No	High	High	No	Low	No	—	Lo	Gen	Different on each machine
BASIC	High	Mod	High	High	No	Low	Yes	Proc	High	Gen	Universal among microcomputers
C	High	No	Yes	Low	No	Low	No	Proc	Mid	Gen	Used for system programming
COBOL	Low	Yes	High	High	Yes	High	No	Proc	High	Bus	The standard language for business
Forth	High	No	High	Low	No	Low	Yes	Proc	Mid	Sci	Transportable assembly language
FORTRAN	High	No	Low	High	Yes	Low	No	Proc	High	Sci	First high-level language
LISP	Low	No	High	Low	No	Low	Yes	Proc	High	AI	Good for artificial intelligence
Machine	High	No	High	High	No	Low	No	—	Low	Gen	Lowest possible level
Pascal	High	Yes	High	High	No	Low	Yes	Proc	High	Gen	Structured, weak input, output
PL/1	High	Yes	High	Low	Yes	High	No	Proc	High	Gen	Early structured language
RPG	Low	No	Low	Yes	No	Low	No	Prob	High	Bus	Unavailable on microcomputers

Abbreviations used:
AI   Artificial intelligence   Mod   Moderately
Bus   Business   Prob   Problem
Gen   General   Proc   Procedure
Mid   Middle   Sci   Scientific

such as assembly language, machine language, and the two "transportable assembly languages," C and Forth.

Another criterion is the purpose of the program. If it requires substantial computation, select a strong computational language such as FORTRAN, BASIC, or APL. If the program uses files heavily, select a language with good file-handling capabilities, COBOL for instance. If you need to quickly write a program for one-time use, select an interpreted general-purpose language like BASIC. A program that manipulates character data might be written in COBOL, Pascal, or PL/1. Table 9-1 shows some attributes of the languages we have discussed.

Other criteria to consider include the time and money required to design and code a program in a particular language, the availability of languages on the computer system available to us, what languages our programmers know and how easy it is to learn the language of choice, the storage requirements of the compiler, language standardization and program transportability, frequency of modification to the program, and potential equipment changes in the future.

Once a language has been selected and the program coded, the fun begins. The next step in completing the program is making sure it works as it is supposed to. This process is called debugging and testing.

DIAGNOSTIC PROCEDURES: DEBUGGING AND TESTING

It is a rare program that operates correctly the first time it is run. Almost all programs, then, must be debugged before they are released for normal use. *Debugging* is the process of finding and removing errors, both in syntax and in logic in a program.

According to legend, the name arose in the late 1940s when a MARK I program would not run correctly and Grace Hopper found a moth caught in a relay. This prevented the relay from closing and making electrical contact. When the moth was removed, the program worked as expected. Thus, the program was "debugged." Legends being what they are, there may be as much reason to attribute the term *debugging* to a small beetle, *le cafard*, which would crawl into the ears of French Legionnaires and penetrate their brains, thus driving them buggy. In the 1850s, when this malaise was believed to account for Legionnaires' grumpiness, the only cure was a rifle and the opportunity to use it, surely a form of debugging that many a frustrated programmer has contemplated.

It is unlikely that programmers will wait until a project is finished to begin debugging it. They probably will debug each module as it is written and then debug the entire program as well. In order to do this, we often have to write dummy code to simulate missing modules. This dummy code, which is just used temporarily, is called a *program stub*.

After desk checking, which was described earlier, the programmer orders a computer run. It is likely that syntax errors will be found in this run. In higher level languages, these errors are reported in an *error listing*. Figure 9-35 shows a typical error listing. The error listing provides only incidental information about logic errors.

FIGURE 9-35
Error listing from a BASIC compiler

```
*****FATAL ERROR
LINE NUMBER 1204 <----------------------- location in RAM
SYNTAX

!ERR!  = I

TYPE CNTRL-C TO ABORT,
ANY OTHER KEY TO CONTINUE:


    .   .   .   .


*****FATAL ERROR
UNDEFINED LINE NUMBER 200 <-------------- BASIC line number
REFERENCED LAST IN LINE 150 <----------- BASIC line number

TYPE CNTRL-C TO ABORT,
ANY OTHER KEY TO CONTINUE:

*****FATAL ERRORS ENCOUNTERED

*****COMPILATION TERMINATED
```

To find any logic errors that remain, programmers next *trace* through the program. This can be done several ways. Programmers often mentally "step through" a program, keeping track of variables, output, and input. Sometimes they use a trace function of their programming language, which shows each statement that is executed and what happened at that statement. Figure 9-36 shows a BASIC trace of our sample program. In this example, the line number of each statement executed is printed along with any data input or output. At the top of the figure, lines 10 and 20 are executed and the characters "BEGIN" are outputted.

Some languages like APL allow limited traces where only statements selected by the programmer are traced. This is particularly useful in modules with loops. When programmers use languages that do not have trace capabilities, they write dummy statements instead. These statements print information about the program on the CRT or a printer. It is important to remove all dummy statements when testing is complete.

Preparation of test data is a very demanding task. The data should anticipate all possible circumstances so that the program behavior can be assessed when they are encountered. Test data should help in the detection of logical errors, such as an incorrect arithmetic expression, which the computer system will take at face value without signalling an error condition. Incorrect branches and loops often cause no error condition, but do represent incorrect program operation.

Finally, all paths through the program's structure chart and subordinate flowcharts must be checked to assure that the program coding accomplishes the necessary processes. Program stubs and temporary execution of program execution to examine accumulators, counters, and registers helps in this type of examination.

When all else fails to locate the problem with a faulty program, programmers call for a dump such as the one shown in figure 9-37. The term *dump* means a listing of the contents of primary storage. It is sometimes called a *storage dump*, *memory dump*, or *core dump*, in remembrance of the first type of random access memory (see Chapter Five). The listing is used to determine the contents of memory at the time the program "blew up," or ceased operating. Dumps are usually printed in hexadecimal. They show what is stored in every computer memory location.

Only after all this checking and double-checking will the programmer have a successful program. It's been said that no program is ever completely correct. Although this assertion is something of an exaggeration, it points out the need to monitor computer output carefully for accuracy.

FIGURE 9-36
BASIC trace listing

```
#10  #20  BEGIN

#30  #40  1

#50  #40  2

#50  #40  3

#50  #40  4

#50  #40  5

#50  #60  END

#70
```

```
0370-  02  03  00  04  05  06  00  00
0378-  00  00  00  00  07  08  00  00
0380-  00  09  0A  0B  0C  0D  00  00
0388-  0E  0F  10  11  12  13  00  14
0390-  15  16  17  18  19  1A  00  00
0398-  00  00  00  00  00  00  00  00
03A0-  00  1B  00  1C  1D  1E  00  00
03A8-  00  1F  00  00  20  21  00  22
03B0-  23  24  25  26  27  28  00  00
03B8-  00  00  00  29  2A  2B  00  2C
03C0-  2D  2E  2F  30  31  32  00  00
03C8-  33  34  35  36  37  38  00  39
03D0-  3A  3B  3C  3D  3E  3F  00  00
03D8-  00  00  00  00  00  00  00  00
03E0-  00
```

FIGURE 9-37
Memory listing

DOCUMENTATION

As we suggested earlier, high-quality documentation is essential for a successful programming project. Documentation begins in the first phases of the project and continues until the end. There are several aspects of a good documentation package.

User documentation should be designed to make the program easy to use. All features of the program should be fully explained in language suitable for the end user. Care must be taken to insure that the programmer does not assume knowledge the user may not have and that technical jargon is kept to a minimum. Technical words, if they are used, must be defined clearly. All procedures must be described. The programmer must write the materials so that a user in trouble can solve his or her problem. User documentation for microcomputer software initially developed a reputation for failing to meet these criteria. Things are much better now.

Operator documentation must be written for mainframe programs. This documentation, sometimes known as a *run book*, provides the operator information for starting, running, and terminating a job. It provides information about file set-up and take-down. It alerts the operator to expect certain messages on the operator's console. In addition, operator documentation includes information about preparation for the run.

Programmer documentation includes a statement of the problem to be solved, the algorithm used to solve it, and any structure charts, flowcharts, or pseudocode that was developed. It also includes input and output samples, test data, a dictionary of the data elements required by the program, information about hardware needs for the program to run correctly, and maintenance information so that follow-up programming can be done easily.

SUMMARY

Programming is expensive and time consuming. Whenever possible we should use commercially available software. Prepackaged software generally provides reliable programs at minimal expense.

If writing a program is the only way to accomplish a goal, several steps must be followed rather carefully. The problem and its solution must be defined carefully. This may be accomplished by using a structure chart to show the general logic of the program and flowcharts and pseudocode to specify the detailed logic of the program.

Having defined the problem and the procedures for its solution, the language to be used must next be selected. The common ones include COBOL, BASIC, and FORTRAN. Using the selected language, the program is coded. It is best to code using structured mechanisms. After it has been coded, the program must be checked for logical and clerical errors. Error checking is called debugging. This process may be very easy, or we may have to redesign the entire program.

When the program is finally operational, documentation for it must be completed.

KEY TERMS

assembly language	flowchart	procedure-oriented language
batch entry	high-level language	process box
block diagram	interactive language	programming by level
code	interpreter	programming by path
compiler	looping structure	proper program
computer program	machine language	pseudocode
debug	macro instruction	selection structure
desk checking	mnemonic	sequence structure
documentation	module	source program
DOUNTIL loop	natural language	structured program
DOWHILE loop	object program	syntax
dump	problem-oriented language	top-down programming
error listing		

REVIEW QUESTIONS

1. What are the four phases of the programming process?
2. What traits do most good programmers have in common?
3. Describe the IF ... THEN ... ELSE ... mechanism.
4. Explain the difference between the DOWHILE and the DOUNTIL mechanisms.
5. Differentiate between a compiler and an interpreter.
6. How are procedure- and problem-oriented languages different?
7. What results when a source program is subjected to a compiler?
8. In what language are most business programs coded?
9. What language is most often available on microcomputers?
10. What new language is becoming very popular for writing microcomputer applications?
11. Name a problem-oriented language.

THOUGHT QUESTIONS

1. Describe the elements of good documentation. If you have access to documentation for a commercial program, critique it and make recommendations for its improvement.
2. Discuss the merits and demerits of using flowcharts and of using pseudocode.
3. What criteria should one use in selecting a language in which to write a program?

Point *Counterpoint*

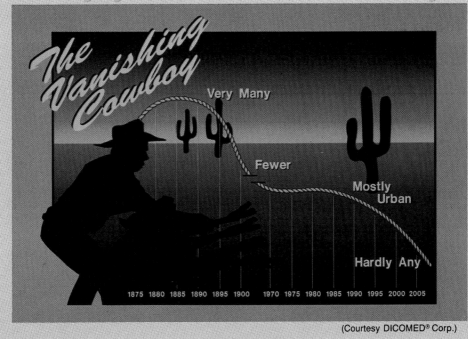

(Courtesy DICOMED® Corp.)

Chapter One traced the evolution of computers through four generations and anticipated that the fifth generation, characterized by artificially intelligent machines, would become operational realities by the 1990s. So, too, could the evolution of programming languages be described. The first generation offered only machine language. All programmers had to use the only language that the computer understood. The second generation made use of a primitive translator, the assembler, which was a program that converted the assembly language source program into machine language. Assembly language closely resembles machine language and each computer has its unique assembler. Third generation languages, the first of which were FORTRAN and COBOL, became known as "high-level" languages because they were further removed from machine language and were more or less independent of the computer on which they were to run.

The term *fourth generation languages* refers to those that accept human language as we speak or write it. They are, therefore, known as *natural* languages. Natural language is not yet widely used. Like the fifth generation of computers, we see it on the horizon, but it will be a while before it arrives. Most computer programming today is done using second and third generation languages. Indeed, the popular conception of computers leads people to believe that in order to use them, they must learn a programming language—a third generation language, that is, such as BASIC or Pascal.

The fact is, most computer users today do not write programs, nor do they need to. One writer asserts, with great exaggeration, that "Programmers are a dying breed...Future sales growth for mainframes and minis is projected to be bleak. But micro sales are brisk. And micros need no programming."[2]

Of course microcomputers *do* need programming. If we don't program them ourselves, we use someone else's programs. Those who write them sometimes do very well. Consider these programmers: Bill Gates founded Microsoft Corporation and was worth more than $100 million before he turned thirty. Mitch Kapor, psychiatric counselor-turned-programmer, founded Lotus Development Corporation to market his program *1-2-3*, the most popular spreadsheet of all time. Seymour Rubinstein wrote *WordStar,* the world's most used word processing program. Teenager Will Harvey wrote the *Music Construction Set,* a very successful program which allows the user to compose music with a microcomputer. Before he turned 20, Eric Hammond completed a program called *One-On-One,* a basketball simulation which grossed a million dollars in its first year on the market.

But you should not take up programming to get wealthy. Chris Crawford, manager of games research for Atari Corporate Research advises:

> Don't write a program to get rich on royalties; the Horatio Alger days of luck and pluck in software are over now. There's plenty of competition, and the only way to get rich is through hard work, talent, and experience, all in large measures.

Crawford comments generally about programming:

> I am not a programmer. Although I do write programs professionally and have written a number of successful programs, I do not consider myself a "real" programmer...What's more, I have never taken a single programming course.

> Contrary to the mystique that some programmers cultivate, programming is not some black magic accessible only to wizards or high priests — anyone can do it.

There are good reasons to learn programming, says Crawford: for the sheer joy of it, to learn logical thinking, to improve thinking skills, and to develop precise communication skills.[3] Probably because of the widespread use of microcomputers, many people are taking up programming who otherwise would not have.

> Once programming was deemed a relentless, exacting chore performed by people who were often considered socially inept, who could only communicate in BASIC, COBOL or assembly languages instead of plain English.

> Now that's all changed. Professionals from all walks of life, ranging from doctors and lawyers to businessmen and teachers, are boasting about their newly developed programming prowess as if they had just mastered the skill of hang gliding or water skiing.

> In fact, programming may well be the most intriguing intellectual sport since chess.[5]

Controlling a computer using a second or third generation language certainly requires intellectual skills. The logic of the program must be defined very carefully. The syntax of any second or third gener-

ation computer language is most unforgiving. A great deal of thought is required. Professional programmers understandably take great pride in their skills in such matters.

But if fourth generation, or natural, languages let us control computers using "plain" English, of what use are professional programmers? International Business Machines estimates that one out of every 30 employees in the United States is a programmer and that by 1990, the number will grow to one out of every 10. These are programmers skilled in the syntactical and logical requirements of second and third generation languages. Consultant James Martin, an industry watcher for more than 20 years disagrees. In an interview with the editors of *Business Computer Systems,* he made this comment:

> We're managing a *revolution,* not an evolution. Changes will occur very rapidly. Among other things, the languages for making computers do your bidding will change dramatically in the next few years...Don't you think it seems unlikely that there will ever be one professional programmer for every 10 workers? Application development without programmers is the most important revolution since the transistor was invented.[6]

Application development without programmers means that all of us will be able to control computers without the need to learn the intricacies of second or third generation computer languages. Instead, we will use natural languages.

> The natural languages translate human instructions — bad grammar and all — into code the computer understands. If it is not sure what the user has in mind, it politely asks for further explanation.

> Natural languages are aimed at managers and executives tired of obtaining their information secondhand from the data processing department.[7]

Obtaining information typically means retrieving information from a data bank. Says Steven Schwartz, Vice President of Software at Cognitive Systems Corporation,

> A lot of (non-computing) executives have shelves full of DP reports...When they want information that the reports don't cover, they have to ask data processing to generate another application for them. They get an answer in three weeks, and maybe it's the wrong answer.[8]

Using a natural programming language, managers and executives can order their own reports.

What happens is this. The language, a translator program that converts human-like instructions into machine language, uses a dictionary and a set of grammar rules to interpret such statements as "Give me all the salespeople who exceeded their quotas by 20 percent."

That's no easy trick.

To begin with, no program can encompass all possible queries users can think up, multiplied by the number of conceivable combinations of vocabulary and syntax with which they can express such queries... While a human being would understand the phrase "A hot cup of coffee" it is the coffee, not the cup, that is hot, a computer would assume that the cup was hot...The same phrase can mean entirely different things. Supposedly, for example, there are 17 possible interpretations of the phrase: "Mary had a little lamb." [9]

Despite these difficulties, a number of software firms are now marketing natural language programs. Intelligent Business Systems (IBS), for example, produces Easytalk, which runs on a Digital Equipment VAX 11/730. It acts as a user interface for an accounting system designed by Amcor Computer Corporation. Boasts an IBS executive, "Instead of spending many thousands a year for information support people, our users pay a one-time fee of $70,000 that lets everyone in the company use the system."[10]

That's a pretty hefty price tag, but it's also a pretty hefty program for a pretty hefty computer system. Microrim, producers of the R:base series of database manager programs for microcomputers, introduced Clout in 1984 as an English-like user interface to R:base. Clout lets users define "rich guys" as "employees making more than $40,000 per year" and "turkeys" as "companies that took a loss last year." In 1985, Microrim introduced Clout 2, which provides the same sort of user interface with such microcomputer programs as 1-2-3, dBASE-II, VisiCalc, PFS:File, and Multiplan.

Natural language development is an offshoot of research in artificial intelligence. The most effective programs require large computer systems with large amounts of on-line storage for dictionaries and grammar rules. As Microrim and a few other firms have demonstrated, however, limited versions of natural language processors can work quite well with microcomputers. Because natural language accepts wide variation in syntax and lets the user define his or her own phrases, dependence on professional programmers and their mastery of second and third generation languages is reduced.

QUESTIONS

1. Suppose that by 1990, most data inquiry and routine processing applications could be designed by end users. What roles would programmers and systems analysts then play in the organization?
2. What reasons can you give to expect other individual programmers like Will Harvey and Eric Hammond to produce best-selling programs? What personal qualities does that kind of success require?
3. If you were president of a firm with sales of $2 million to $4 million annually, would it be better to hire a programmer and an assistant or to purchase a natural language processor for data inquiry purposes? Why?
4. Human languages change over time. New generations coin new words and phrases. How will this affect natural language programming?

C H A P T E R   10

Data Base Management Systems

(Courtesy Wang Laboratories)

**PURPOSE AND DEFINITION OF
   DATA BASE MANAGEMENT
   SYSTEMS**

DATABASE STRUCTURES

**DATABASE MANAGEMENT
   SYSTEM PROGRAMS**

**USING A DATA BASE MANAGEMENT
   SYSTEM**

In Chapter Seven, we saw that the operating system component of the complete computer system is responsible for memory management, job control, input/output management, and file management. The chief responsibility of the operating system as a file manager is to keep track of the physical location of data and to make them available to the user either directly or through an application program. Access to data directly through the operating system is difficult at best. The user must remember the manner in which the data files are organized and the specific operating system commands needed to access information in them. What's worse, most operating systems (UNIX is an exception) make little provision for organizing data in a manner that would be comprehensible to users. Report formatting is left to application programs.

Individual users and many application programs frequently require the same data to perform different functions. The price of an item may be used to calculate accounts receivable by one program, sales commissions by another, and a sales analysis report by a third. If each of these programs uses a separate file for each item of merchandise, there's every chance that the price amounts will be different in each file. Furthermore, even though careful and elaborate mechanisms assure that the same data element in every file is consistently updated, there remains the problem of *redundancy*. The same element appearing in a number of files requires more file space than necessary.

PURPOSE AND DEFINITION OF DATA BASE MANAGEMENT SYSTEMS

Until the mid-1960s, this was the situation in most computer installations: the operating system kept track of the physical locations and addresses of the data files and each application program drew data from separate files that were unique to that application. This has been called the applications approach to data management because each application essentially had its *own set* of data files.

The data base management approach, which was developed in response to these inherent problems, integrates data in the computer system so that all applications and users have access to the same, and thus consistent, data. Using this approach, the price in the earlier example would appear just *once* in the computer's system of files.

At its simplest, a *data base* is nothing more than a collection of files. We know, from Chapter Two, that a file is a collection of records; a record is a collection of fields or data elements; and a field is a collection of characters. Data may be stored in and retrieved from a data base using the operating system alone or using the application programs. A *data base management system* is a program designed to store and retrieve data as effectively as possible.

File Organization and Access

In Chapter Six, we observed that certain secondary storage devices dictate the manner in which data files can be processed. Magnetic tape can only be processed sequentially. Magnetic disk, because it allows direct access to data, can be used in either sequential or direct access processing applications.

Note that there is a difference between the manner in which data are stored and the way in which they are processed. Data stored in non-sequential formats may be processed sequentially or not, depending on the needs of the application.

TABLE 10-1 *SPECIALTY PRODUCTS CORPORATION DATA FILES*

Product Master File

No.	Description	Cost	Price	On Hand	Vendor	Salesperson
P1	Gadget	125	215	20	GGU	S2
P2	Fortecye	138	230	18	PFF	S1
P3	Widget	160	210	35	WMI	S5
P4	Midget Widget	185	240	28	MMWMM	S4
P5	Gismo	86	125	62	GGU	S3

Salesperson Master File

No.	Name	Product	Price	Unit Sales	Total Sales	Rate	Commission
S1	C. Bow	P2	230	4	920	.15	138.00
S2	M. West	P1	215	5	1075	.12	129.00
S3	W. Fields	P5	125	5	625	.20	125.00
S4	B. Keaton	P4	240	6	1440	.10	144.00
S5	L. Costello	P3	210	5	1050	.10	105.00

Customer Master File

No.	Name	P1	Price	P2	Price	P3	Price	P4	Price	P5	Price	Total
C1	S. Greenstreet	3	215							2	125	925
C2	P. Lorre	2	215	3	230			6	240			2560
C3	H. Bogart			1	230							230
C4	L. Bacall					4	210			3	125	1215

Sales Transaction File

Customer	Product	Quantity	Price	Salesperson
C3	P1	2	230	S1
C1	P3	3	210	S5

Sequential Processing

Sequential processing involves processing records of a file in order. If the file is stored on a sequential device, such as magnetic tape, then *every* record must be processed in the order in which it is stored on the medium. Let's look at a simple example which illustrates the consequences of sequential processing using sequential storage.

Table 10-1 shows four sequential files used by Specialty Products Corporation (SPC). Three are master files: Product, Salesperson, and Customer. The fourth, Sales, is a transaction file. SPC uses data from the transaction file to update the three master files. The organization of the product and salesperson files is fairly straightforward. SPC employs five salespeople each of whom specializes in selling one of its products. Thus, W. Fields sells only gismos; L. Costello sells only widgets. Each salesperson record contains a commission field. The amount in this field is calculated by multiplying the number of products sold by the selling price and then multiplying that amount by the commission rate. When a product is sold, the amount of that product on hand, which is in the Product file, is updated.

Each customer record contains a field showing the number of each product purchased and a subordinate field showing the price of that product. Total sales to that customer are calculated by multiplying the number of each product purchased by the price of the product and adding the results. For exam-

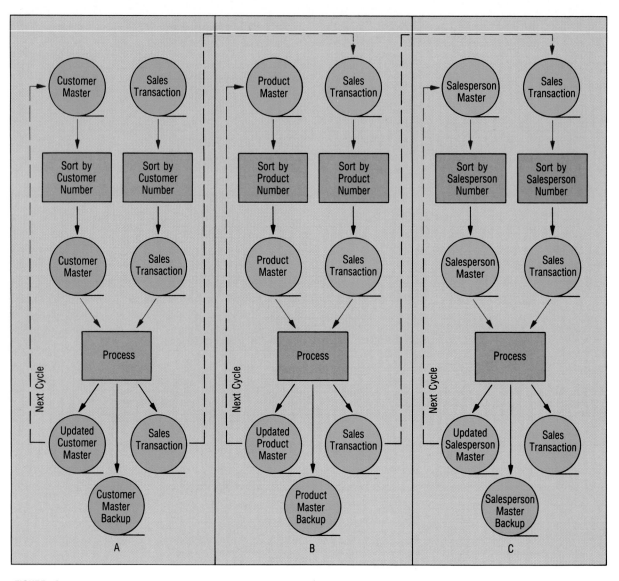

FIGURE 10-1
Sequential processing

ple, P. Lorre has purchased two units of Pl (gadgets), three units of P2 (fortecyes), and six midget widgets. Total sales to him for the period amount to $2,560.

The sales transaction file shows the customer, the quantity of each product purchased, its price, and the salesperson who made the transaction.

Each of the files is stored on magnetic tape, a sequential medium that requires sequential processing. Figure 10-1 shows the steps that must be undertaken to update all the files.

In part A of figure 10-1, the transaction file and the customer master file are sorted by customer number. The customer number functions as the *record key*, the means of identifying each customer. In sequential processing, all files must be arranged in the same order according to the appropriate record key. After they have been sorted, the records in the customer master file are processed. If the transactions file contains a transaction for the customer, the record is updated and written to the updated customer master file. If the transactions file has no transactions for the customer, the record is written without change to the updated customer master file. When the original customer master file has been completely processed in this fashion, it becomes the *backup* customer master file. The *updated* customer master file, which shows the results of the transactions, becomes the customer master input file for the next processing cycle.

Three tape drives are required for this updating operation: one for each of the two input files (after sorting) and one for the updated customer master file. Magnetic tape may be used for input or output, but it is infeasible to use it for both at once.

Parts B and C of figure 10-1 show a similar process for updating SPC's other two master files. In each case, both the master file and the transactions file must be sorted on the appropriate record key for the operation: product number for updating the product master file and salesperson number for updating the salesperson master file.

Indexed-Sequential Processing

Sequential processing, in general, is pretty clumsy. The introduction of direct access storage devices (DASDs) opened up other more flexible methods of processing. These devices make it possible to retrieve and store data records *directly*, without having to process the entire file. Of course, sequential processing is possible with DASDs, but it's not required.

Data access on direct access storage devices involves the use of an address which indicates exactly where the desired data are stored. For disk storage, this is known as the *disk address*.

Imagine that SPC's three master files are stored on disk, and that each file is arranged sequentially by customer number, product number, and salesperson number, respectively. To update a record in one of these files, the disk address of the record must be determined. In indexed-sequential processing, also known as the *Indexed-Sequential Access Method (ISAM)*, the disk must also include at least one index which shows the disk addresses of records in each file that is stored on the disk, much in the same way that the index to this book shows the page locations of various terms. Figure 10-2 shows what happens.

The first transaction requires updating of S. Greenstreet's customer record. He is customer number C3. The customer index file is consulted for the disk address (ADDR) of that customer's record. The record is retrieved for processing, updated, and then *rewritten back to the same disk location*. During the same pass through the sales transaction file, the other three master files are updated in the same manner.

Observe here that all three files can be stored on the same disk drive, making it possible to update all of them at once with each transaction. This avoids the three-pass-with-intervening-sorts situation in figure 10-1. In each case, the updated record is written back to its original location, destroying the status of the record prior to the transaction—there is no backup. If backup versions of the master files are required, and they always are, then they must be produced before the transactions are processed.

Using DASDs, files need not be kept in sequential order by record key. Individual records are retrieved and stored directly by disk address as determined by consulting an index. Application programs need not be concerned

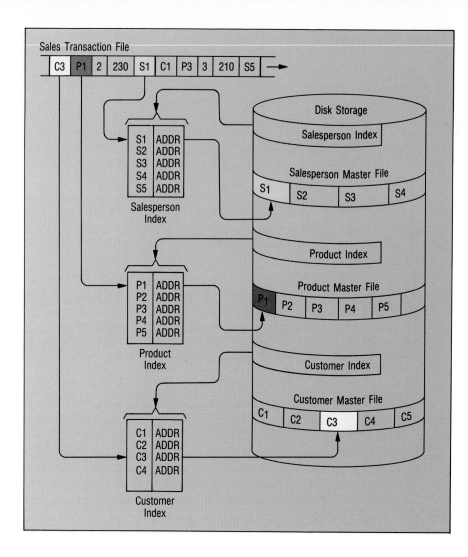

FIGURE 10-2
Indexed-sequential processing

with the arrangement of data on the disk at all. In fact, it is unnecessary for data to be arranged into files because any record can be stored anywhere on the disk so long as the address of that record is available in an index. Ordinarily, however, the term *indexed-sequential access method* or *ISAM*, refers to data storage techniques in which files are stored as contiguous series of records in order by record key.

Direct Access Processing

Using an index, a record's disk address is determined by comparing the record key of the desired record with each entry in the index. Sometimes two or more indexes are required to locate the address of a desired record. In another way of determining the address of a record, the record key itself becomes the basis for calculating the address.

If we were to devise an arithmetic routine or procedure—called an *algorithm*—to convert a product number (record key) into a disk address, then locating that record on the disk would not require an index. Access to it would be *direct*, meaning that it could be retrieved from and stored to the secondary medium without reference to any other record. Essentially, that's how direct access processing operates. Given a record key, a routine to translate the key into a valid disk address is executed and the record is retrieved or stored accordingly. *Direct access* is sometimes called *random access*, the word *random* arising from the notion that any record can be retrieved with as much ease as any other, without regard to sequence.

In figure 10-3, for example, a record from the transactions file requires the retrieval of a master file record identified, as always, by a record key. The record key is processed by a randomizer which converts it into a disk address. The data from that address are then brought into primary storage for processing, after which the updated record is rewritten to the same address.

The routine that converts the record key into an address is usually called a *hashing*, or *randomizing*, routine in recognition that, within specified limits, the record can be stored at random anywhere on the disk. For example, suppose that all customer numbers were four digits long. One procedure divides the record key by a prime number and takes the remainder as the track on which the record is located. For example, customer number 2969 divided by 17, a prime number because it can be divided without remainder only by itself and one, yields a track address of 11.

Randomizing algorithms are not easy to contrive. Sooner or later, the same scheme will use two different record keys to produce the same disk address. In the above example, customer numbers 2986 and 2952 will also yield track 11. Sooner or later the track will fill up. For this reason, when an address is determined, the record at that address must be examined to ascertain that it is, in fact, the one desired. If it is not, the record will contain a field that will point to another address where the desired record may be found. The use of *address pointers* in this fashion links various records together. Beyond being useful in coping with redundant disk addresses, the use of pointers to link records together will be seen shortly as an important ingredient in modern data base management systems.

FIGURE 10-3
Direct access processing

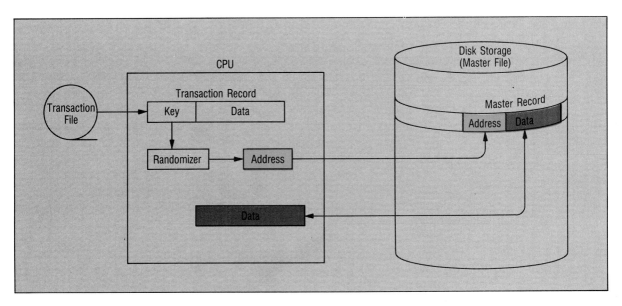

Virtual-Storage Access Method

From 1973 through 1975, work continued toward improving the effectiveness of these three primary file processing techniques. The use of absolute disk addresses in indexed-sequential and direct access processing usually meant that data base management programs and, often, the application programs too, were dependent on the hardware used to store the data.

During this period, much work, done chiefly by IBM, was devoted to preparing specialized programs that helped users organize and maintain their data files. These came to be called *data sets*. Loosely conceived, a data set consisted of a list of all of the data elements used in the computer installation, with little reference to file organization. The notion of the data set reflected the growing attitude that the concept of the file as a contiguous series of records was outgrowing its usefulness. These programs and modified versions of sequential, indexed-sequential, and direct access processing techniques were brought together into one package called the *Virtual-Storage Access Method*, or *VSAM*.

VSAM's chief contribution to the three basic file processing techniques was the use of *relative data addresses*. This meant that instead of determining and using actual or absolute hardware addresses, the location of each data element was determined relative to a fixed point within the disk system's addressing scheme. This released data base management programs from their dependence on storage hardware because only the base referent address needed to be used. All other addresses were determined as plus or minus so many sectors from the base.

Data Base versus Database

Data base is a general term that refers to any collection of data available to the computer system from secondary storage devices. Typically, one thinks of a data base in terms of files, not necessarily because the data are stored as files of contiguous records, but rather because the concept of the file as a group of related records is useful in organizing data processing tasks.

The term *database*, on the other hand, refers to data storage and retrieval techniques that do not organize data into files and records. Rather, they store and retrieve individual data elements (equivalent to fields) in the manner best suited to the needs of the user. The distinction between data base and database is by no means clear, for no matter how the data base management system works, users find it convenient to think of data as organized into files.

Database systems do not maintain specialized files for individual applications. The emphasis is on collecting and organizing data so that they best serve the application programs and the needs of individual users. A *database*, then, is an organized, integrated collection of data made available to all applications and users with little or no duplication or redundancy.

Table 10-2 shows the modifications possible to SPC's data files using the database approach to file processing. The redundancy has been eliminated. Each data element appears only once in the collection of data. In this scheme of things, the data in the sales transaction file can be used to update all of the other files in the system. Selling product P1 to customer C3, for example, provides links to the appropriate product master record and the customer master record. The product master record links to salesperson S2, the only salesperson who sells that product. It also provides the price information necessary to update both the customer master record and the salesperson master record.

TABLE 10-2 *SPECIALTY PRODUCTS CORPORATION DATABASE FILES*

Product Master File

No.	Description	Cost	Price	On Hand	Vendor	Salesperson
P1	Gadget	125	215	20	GGU	S2
P2	Fortecye	138	230	18	PFF	S1
P3	Widget	160	210	35	WMI	S5
P4	Midget Widget	185	240	28	MMWMM	S4
P5	Gismo	86	125	62	GGU	S3

Salesperson Master File

No.	Name	Unit Sales	Total Sales	Rate	Commission
S1	C. Bow	4	920	.15	138.00
S2	M. West	5	1075	.12	129.00
S3	W. Fields	5	625	.20	125.00
S4	B. Keaton	6	1440	.10	144.00
S5	L. Costello	5	1050	.10	105.00

Customer Master File

No.	Name	P1	P2	P3	P4	P5	Total
C1	S. Greenstreet	3				2	925
C2	P. Lorre	2	3		6		2560
C3	H. Bogart		1				230
C4	L. Bacall			4		3	1215

Sales Transaction File

Customer	Product	Quantity
C3	P1	2
C1	P3	3

DATABASE STRUCTURES

Modern database management systems offer a number of different processing structures, depending on the flexibility and complexity of the system. Note that these are processing structures, not storage techniques. How the data may be dispersed about the storage medium and how the database program locates them are of no concern. Nevertheless, the processing structures are reminiscent of the file organization and processing techniques discussed earlier.

File Management Systems

A sales manager may wish to maintain a file of prospective clients. Such a file might show the name and address of each prospect, the last time he or she was contacted, the field salesperson responsible for cultivating the prospect, and other such information. There is little need to relate any of the data in this file to other data, at least until a prospect becomes a client, so the data may well be viewed as a single file containing records all of the same format. This structure is called a *file management system* (FMS) or a *flat file*.

A *flat file* is an ordered collection of records, exactly like a sequential file. Flat files may be linked to others using a field or fields in each record that

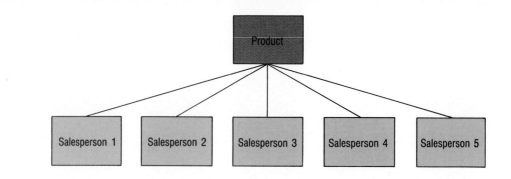

FIGURE 10-4
Hierarchical system

points to related records in other files. Indexes can be used to link files, or files can be connected as in figure 10-2.

File management systems (FMSs) are most widely used in microcomputer systems, although larger computer systems employ them also. For simple record-keeping tasks and elementary retrieval of data, they are inexpensive and effective. One such program, PFS:File, is used for business, professional, and personal needs. As is usual with microcomputer FMSs, there is no facility for linking one file to another.

Hierarchical and Networked Systems

A *hierarchical* system breaks records into logically related segments, or fields, which are connected to other segments by pointers in a tree-like arrangement. Suppose another sales organization, like SPC but much larger, has five salespeople specializing in just one of several products. In figure 10-4, the product record is said to be the *parent* for each of the salespeople records inasmuch as each salesperson sells only that product. The salesperson record is known

FIGURE 10-5
Networked system

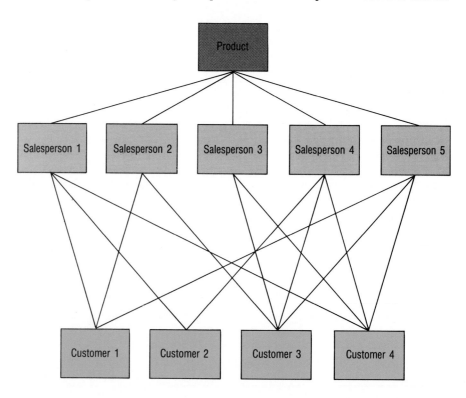

as a *child*. Access to information about salespeople in this arrangement can be had only through the product records. In this sense, the salesperson master file has disappeared.

A hierarchical system has only one parent for each child. *Networked* systems are almost identical to hierarchical ones, the chief difference being that in networks, any child may have more than one parent. As soon as we add customer records to the system, as in figure 10-5, we change the hierarchical arrangement into a networked system.

Notice that in figure 10-5 each of the customer records may have each of the salespeople as parents because any salesperson can work with any customer.

One should note here one of the differences between traditional data base systems and the database systems illustrated by figures 10-4 and 10-5. In database systems, data elements relate to each other in the same way that they relate to each other in the normal operation of the business. Information about a customer is related to the products the customer bought and the salespeople from whom he or she bought them. Similarly, because each salesperson specializes in the sale of one product, information about that person is directly related to that product.

Relational Systems

A relational database system escapes entirely from the concept of the data file, although most users of relational database management systems continue to think of data as being organized into files. It's easier that way. Turn back to table 10-2, and you'll see why. If SPC's data were organized as a relational database system, each of the three master files would be treated as a table, not as a file of records. For those accustomed to working with the terms *file*, *record*, and *field*, those words work quite well in describing the nature of the tables. Each row in the product master table, for example, can be considered a record, although in relational data base terminology, a row is known as a *tuple*.

Each column of the Product Master table can be considered a field, or data element. In relational database lexicon, the appropriate term for a column in a table is *attribute*. Finally, the total relationship among all the attributes and tuples is called a *relation*. Thus the term *table* is also inappropriate. Instead, we refer to data about products as the *product relation*.

Relational database systems do not process relations as series of records. Instead, they search out the attributes in each tuple throughout the system of relations to produce the information desired. For example, if SPC wished to know which salesperson had sold the greatest number of products to a single customer (table 10-2), it would set up a *query procedure* which would cause the system to perform these operations:

1. Scan the customer relation to determine the tuple with the highest number of sales in one product attribute. The result: attribute P4 in tuple C2.
2. Scan the product relation to determine the salesperson responsible for tuple P4. The result: attribute S4.
3. Scan the salesperson relation to determine the name attribute for tuple S4. The result: B. Keaton.

Notice how the attribute resulting from one scan, or search, becomes the tuple for the next search, which produces yet another attribute, which becomes the tuple for the following search, and so on. The relations are not treated as files from which records must be read, but rather as tables of relationships, hence the name *relational* database management system.

DATABASE MANAGEMENT SYSTEM PROGRAMS

A database management system program, known as a *DBMS*, consists of a set of instructions that causes the computer to perform the required functions. As we've seen, a DBMS offers four different processing structures: FMS, or file management systems; networked systems; hierarchical systems; and relational systems.

With mainframe DBMSs, a file management system almost always includes the ability to link one file to another through the use of a pointer, a data element in a record that provides the address of a record in another file.

Microcomputer users differentiate file management systems (FMSs) from "true" DBMSs by pointing out that FMSs for microcomputers can process but one file at a time. A DBMS, on the other hand, can process multiple files either through hierarchical and networking techniques or as a relational system.

When a DBMS supports other application programs written in such languages as COBOL, RPG, or PL/1, the languages are known as *host* languages. Ordinarily, the use of a DBMS to support other application programs and languages is limited to mainframe and minicomputer environments. Microcomputer users typically use a DBMS for independent data storage and retrieval purposes.

Paths and Schemas

DBMSs offer a number of independent functions that we will investigate shortly. In performing its functions, the DBMS essentially follows paths among the data that are stored on the secondary storage medium.

A *logical path* conceptually defines the routes to be followed in retrieving and storing data. The logical path is what the user has in mind: How many houses are listed for sale in Houston within the price range of $150,000 to $185,000? The *physical path* defines the hardware routes the system must follow through the various storage devices to answer the question. The logical path expresses in human terms the relationships among the data items to be retrieved. The physical path specifies the addresses and hardware devices on which they will be found.

The DBMS converts the logical path into the physical path. The description of the logical paths, the files, the relations, the links, and so on, is known as the *schema* of the data base and is usually broken down into *subschemas*. Individual users have access to specific subschemas of the database, and they may be restricted from access to other subschemas. Thus, from the user's viewpoint, the database contains only data to be processed by the user's applications. This serves the user well, because he or she need not be concerned with the entire spectrum of data in the database. It also acts as a security measure, preventing unauthorized access to sensitive data.

DBMSs use instruction sets to establish logical and physical paths. Logical paths, or logical data descriptions, are written in *Data Definition Language* (DDL); physical paths, or physical descriptions, are written in *Device Media Control Language* (DMCL). The data interrogation, or *query*, language, often called *System Query Language (SQL)*, is used to retrieve subsets of the data held in the data bank. The *Data Manipulation Language (DML)* provides a way of setting up standard processing routines, or *command files*, which automatically perform repetitive tasks.

As a program, a DBMS may be hard or easy to use depending on the type of database being maintained. Simple filing systems for microcomputers are relatively easy to use, but they provide little flexibility. Relational database programs, at the other shad of the spectrum, offer much flexibility but are difficult to use and to program.

DBMSs are very general programs and, consequently, can be used for many applications in place of several specialized programs. Several software publishers produce supportive languages which make DBMSs easier to use for these purposes. For dBASE-II and dBASE-III, the most popular relational database programs for microcomputers, such products as dBASE Window, dProgrammer, and Autocode offer *front-end programs* which help set up applications. They are called front-end because they are programs that are used to control other programs, that is, they stand in front of the main program.

Autocode and dBASE Window, for example, are known as *program generators* in that they prepare *command files*, which are sequences of instructions to the DBMS that set up specific applications such as customer billing and inventory control. Experienced users and database administrators often develop command files without the use of program generators. Their use, however, makes the job easier.

Microrim's Clout for RBASE-4000 and Ashton-Tate's Friday! for dBASE-II make those difficult programs easier to use by offering menus and other user friendly characteristics. They also limit the user's ability to take full advantage of the DBMS's power. It is a truism in computer work that the more powerful the system, the more difficult it is to use. Those users requiring the full power of computer systems must be prepared to spend time and effort in mastering the skills demanded by the application.

Salespeople can take their computers to their clients.
(Courtesy Hewlett-Packard, Inc.)

Functions of Data Base Management Systems

There are five primary functions of any data management program: creating files or relations, modifying them, adding data to them, deleting data from them, and selecting data according to some specified characteristics. The best way to appreciate how these functions work is to review a specific application.

The Richard Shaw Motorcar Rentals company maintains a small fleet of unique automobiles which are rented for fairly extended periods of time by customers who appreciate and need the type of transportation the autos provide. Table 10-3 shows a list of the autos in Rick's enterprise.

TABLE 10-3 *RICHARD SHAW MOTORCAR RENTALS AUTOMOBILE INVENTORY*

Lic. #	Make	Miles	Location	Fee	Customer
RSR001	Mercedes	4825	Los Angeles	250	J. Valentine
RSR002	Rolls	13497	Los Angeles	300	
RSR003	Rolls	2621	San Diego	350	J. Dillinger
RSR004	Bugatti	26825	Chino	475	W. Bonney
RSR005	Mercedes	8562	San Francisco	250	J. James
RSR006	Ferrari	3820	San Diego	200	A. Capone

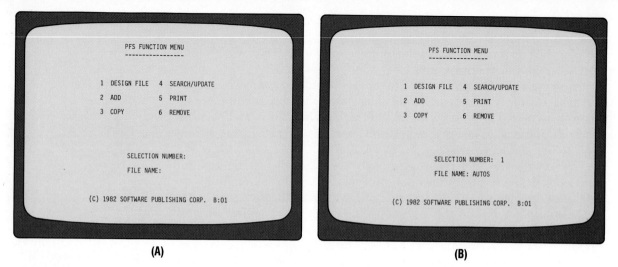

(A)   (B)

FIGURE 10-6
PFS:File startup menu

Rick uses PFS:File, a menu-driven file management system for microcomputer systems. When this program is started up, it offers the menu appearing in figure 10-6A.

Creating a File

Rick begins by selecting the Design File option and entering the filename he has chosen—AUTOS—figure 10-6B. PFS:File next presents him with another menu asking if he wants to create a file or change a file design. He picks the Create File option and is presented with a blank screen, which is similar to a clean chalkboard. Using the cursor control keys, Rick types in the name of each field that will appear in every record of the file, figure 10-7. Each field name is followed by a colon (:). He adds a general field, COMMENTS, which he will use to hold miscellaneous information about each auto and its present customer. When he's finished, PFS:File returns him to the main function menu, figure 10-6A.

Adding to a File

Now, Rick is ready to add data. Creating a file is one thing, adding data to it is another. After he picks the Add option from the function menu (figure 10-8A), PFS:File presents him with the next blank record, which it calls a *form*.

FIGURE 10-7
PFS:File file creation

(A)   (B)

Inasmuch as he has not yet entered data, the next blank form is form 1. Much as one might fill out index cards, Rick enters data into blank forms one at a time until all six autos in his fleet are represented by records in this file. The final record, form 6, containing the information about the Ferrari, appears in figure 10-8B.

FIGURE 10-8
Adding records to a file

Modifying a File

If Rick wanted to modify the *design* of his file, he would choose the Design File option from the PFS:File functions menu and then the Change Design option from the submenu that follows. For most DBMSs, changing the design or the structure of a file is a matter of setting up a new file with the fields required and then copying data from fields in the old file to those in the new. When this is finished, the old file can be discarded, presuming that the new one contains all of the needed data. This is the way that PFS:File works. Rick could set up a new file design with the same fields and, one would suppose, others besides. The program would then copy data from the old file into the new.

Although changing the design of a file is useful for creating additional applications for the file, it is usually time-consuming. It is much better to plan ahead and design the file initially for all probable uses, thus saving the time needed for file redesign.

Deleting Data

To delete a record using PFS:File or other database systems, Rick must identify the record he wishes to discard from the file. He selects the Remove option from the function menu, figure 10-6A. PFS:File then presents him with a screen showing the file design, figure 10-9, which he will use to identify the record to be removed from the file. If he wished, for example, to remove the record for the auto with license plate number RSR003, he would enter those characters in the LIC. # field. That record, or form, would then be deleted from the file.

Selecting Data

Suppose that Rick is interested in reviewing the records for all of the autos in his fleet that are in the city of Los Angeles. He picks option 4 on the functions menu, figure 10-6A, and he is presented with a blank retrieval form as

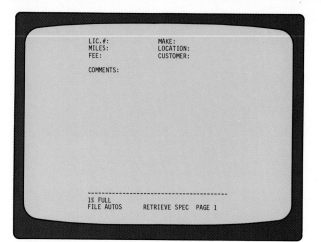

FIGURE 10-9
Retrieval specification screen

in figure 10-9. He enters Los Angeles in the location field and PFS:File displays, one at a time, the records for the two autos in that city, figure 10-10.

Selecting data for display or for some other operation is a matter of providing the DBMS with the selection criteria: the required content of one or more of the fields, or data elements. If Rick wants to review all of the autos with mileage greater than 20,000, he enters

>20000

in the MILES field in the retrieval specification screen (figure 10-9). If he were interested in just those Rolls that were in San Diego, he would specify Rolls in the MAKE field and San Diego in the LOCATION field.

In this way, DBMSs provide a number of logical alternatives in selecting data, which allow the user to specify all records within a range of values, all records *not* included in a range, all customers with the first initial J, and so forth.

The ability to select data based upon certain criteria leads to such functions as sorting records, merging selected files, removing groups of data from a data base, and creating new, specialized data bases. Even simple file management systems such as PFS:File offer great power and flexibility to the user

FIGURE 10-10
Selecting records

```
LIC.#: RSR002     MAKE: ROLLS
MILES: 13497      LOCATION: LOS ANGELES
FEE: 300          CUSTOMER:

COMMENTS: SERVICED AT 13495 MILES




------------------------------------
1% FULL
FILE AUTOS      FORM 2      PAGE 1
```

(A)

```
LIC.#: RSR001     MAKE: MERCEDES
MILES: 4825       LOCATION: LOS ANGELES
FEE: 250          CUSTOMER: J. VALENTINE

COMMENTS: CUSTOMER RECEIVED SEVERAL
DOUBLE-PARKING TICKETS IN FRONT OF BANKS



------------------------------------
1% FULL
FILE AUTOS      FORM 1      PAGE 1
```

(B)

because of operations involving data selection. In DBMSs that are inherently more powerful, such as relational systems, the selection function makes the programs enormously flexible.

Other Characteristics

Besides the major functional areas, computer installations, whether large or small, may require other features. Of these, *data security* surely ranks as most important. Even the casual database user who keeps nothing more critical than favorite recipes on a home computer wants to be sure that the data will not be inadvertently destroyed. DBMSs that offer ease of data backup, then, are highly valued.

Data security, however, involves more than protection from loss. It also involves protection from unauthorized access. Since the late 1970s, national attention has focused on the difficulty data base administrators have had in protecting sensitive information from invaders ranging from the idly curious to the intently criminal. The use of *passwords*, secret identifying codes that authorize access to a database, has been only partially successful. Indeed, it would seem that the only certain way of preventing unauthorized access to a database is to remove it physically from the computer system—but then, what good is it?

Many computer installations require that a database serve multiple users. Multi-user database systems add problems that single-user systems don't have. How shall the system handle situations in which more than one user wishes to work with the same data at the same time? Different levels of management require different access to sensitive data. How shall the system establish and enforce levels of authority with respect to retrieving data and updating data?

Managing the Database Manager

In large computer installations, data base management operations are usually supervised by an individual known as a *data base administrator*, not to be confused with the database manager which is a computer program. The administrator is responsible for establishing and maintaining the database and the data element dictionary (see Chapter Four) which users consult when retrieving or storing data.

In today's corporate world, thanks to the increasing recognition now given to the value of information, access to information carries the same status as does possessing the key to the executive washroom. For this reason, managers often want access to data for which they have no operational need. Balancing operational need with status motivation is no easy task. In working with this situation, the database administrator faces a tough job, one that involves not only the technical details of software and hardware, but the political considerations of the organization as well. It requires tact, diplomacy, and authority.

USING A DATA BASE MANAGEMENT SYSTEM

Stewart Potts, Inc., a firm specializing in the production of restaurant equipment, has just hired you to set up a database containing information about the firm's eighteen salespeople. The firm operates in four geographical areas in the United States and the salespeople are each assigned to one area. To start with, Stew wants a report showing the year-to-date (YTD) sales and the annual salary of each salesperson.

Creating the Database

You begin by studying the data that Stew currently has available for the salesforce. You determine that, for each salesperson, six attributes should be established in the database:

- Last Name   10 characters, alphabetic
- First Name   10 characters, alphabetic
- ID Number   5 characters, numeric
- Territory   10 characters, alphabetic
- Annual Salary   9 characters, numeric
- YTD Sales   10 characters, numeric

You have decided to use dBASE-II, a relational database program designed for microcomputers but modeled after mainframe database systems. The dBASE-II program is command-driven, as opposed to being menu-driven, which means that controlling it requires using commands rather than selecting from a list of alternatives, as in PFS:File.

When dBASE-II begins, it presents its prompt, a period (.). This is known among dBASE-II users as the *dot prompt*. The command to create a new database is

```
create
```

which you enter to the right of the dot prompt figure 10-11A. dBASE-II responds by asking for the filename of your database. You enter

```
slsmstr
```

as the filename for this database, standing for Sales Master. Note that dBASE-II accepts either upper or lower case letters for commands and filenames. This is true of most such programs. Data that require both upper and lower case letters are recorded as entered.

Next, dBASE-II asks for the structure of the database, by which it means the various fields, their type, and their length. It displays 001 as the first field (figure 10-11A) and waits for you to enter the specifications for that field. You enter

```
last,c,10
```

indicating that this field has the name of LAST, it is a character (alphabetic) field, and it will have no more than ten characters in it. After you press the Enter key, dBASE-II displays 002 and waits for the specifications for the next field.

You continue until all six attributes are specified. Notice field number 005. This is a numeric field (*n*), which has nine characters and two places to the right of the decimal point. When you are finished specifying the six fields of the database, you press Enter in response to the dBASE-II prompt for field 007. This indicates that you have finished designing the database. The pro-

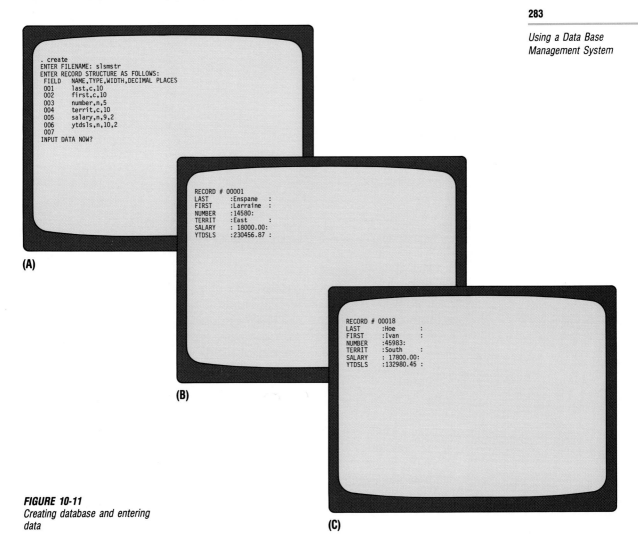

```
. create
ENTER FILENAME: slsmstr
ENTER RECORD STRUCTURE AS FOLLOWS:
 FIELD    NAME,TYPE,WIDTH,DECIMAL PLACES
 001      last,c,10
 002      first,c,10
 003      number,n,5
 004      territ,c,10
 005      salary,n,9,2
 006      ytdsls,n,10,2
 007
INPUT DATA NOW?
```

(A)

```
RECORD # 00001
LAST      :Enspane   :
FIRST     :Larraine  :
NUMBER    :14580:
TERRIT    :East      :
SALARY    : 18000.00:
YTDSLS    :230456.87 :
```

(B)

```
RECORD # 00018
LAST      :Hoe       :
FIRST     :Ivan      :
NUMBER    :45983:
TERRIT    :South     :
SALARY    : 17800.00:
YTDSLS    :132980.45 :
```

(C)

FIGURE 10-11
*Creating database and entering
data*

gram then asks if you would like to enter data at this time (bottom of figure
10-11A). You respond with *y* for *yes,* and dBASE-II clears the screen and
presents a format for record 00001.

Adding Data

Each field name in the record is shown on the CRT. Colons (:) bracket the
amount of space available for data entry. You enter the data for each field
in every record for each of the eighteen salespeople. Figure 10-11B shows the
entries for record 00001, Larraine Enspane; figure 10-11C shows the entries
for record 00018, Ivan Hoe.

After finishing the data entry for the last salesperson record, you press
the Enter key in response to the prompt for data for record 00019. This tells
dBASE-II that you have concluded entering data into the database. dBASE-II
responds by displaying the dot prompt which indicates that it is awaiting further instructions. Wishing to check your work, you enter the command

```
display all
```

and dBASE-II displays all of the records, or tuples, in the database, figure 10-12.

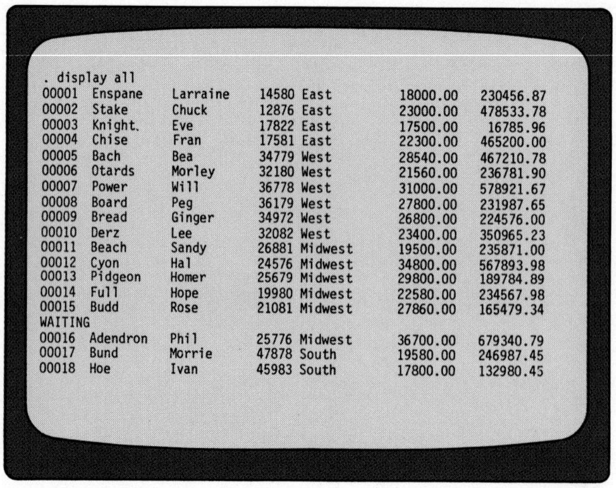

```
. display all
00001 Enspane   Larraine  14580 East      18000.00  230456.87
00002 Stake      Chuck     12876 East      23000.00  478533.78
00003 Knight.     Eve       17822 East      17500.00   16785.96
00004 Chise      Fran      17581 East      22300.00  465200.00
00005 Bach        Bea       34779 West      28540.00  467210.78
00006 Otards     Morley    32180 West      21560.00  236781.90
00007 Power      Will      36778 West      31000.00  578921.67
00008 Board       Peg       36179 West      27800.00  231987.65
00009 Bread       Ginger    34972 West      26800.00  224576.00
00010 Derz        Lee       32082 West      23400.00  350965.23
00011 Beach       Sandy     26881 Midwest   19500.00  235871.00
00012 Cyon        Hal       24576 Midwest   34800.00  567893.98
00013 Pidgeon    Homer     25679 Midwest   29800.00  189784.89
00014 Full        Hope      19980 Midwest   22580.00  234567.98
00015 Budd        Rose      21081 Midwest   27860.00  165479.34
WAITING
00016 Adendron   Phil      25776 Midwest   36700.00  679340.79
00017 Bund        Morrie    47878 South     19580.00  246987.45
00018 Hoe         Ivan      45983 South     17800.00  132980.45
```

FIGURE 10-12
Salesperson database

dBASE-II displays fifteen lines at a time on the screen and waits for the user to finish viewing them before continuing. That's why figure 10-12 shows the word *WAITING* after the record for Rose Budd. Displaying all of the data in this manner gives the user a chance to use dBASE-II's editing facilities to correct any errors. For the sake of brevity, we'll not consider these facilities here. Let's say that you entered all of the data perfectly and are now ready to design your first report.

Before launching into report preparation, we should emphasize that the design of the database is best accomplished with the various required output reports in mind. Report design and database design, in this sense, go hand in hand. Despite the ideal view that one should know all of the desired reports before beginning database design, eventually the database will be called upon to produce a report that was not anticipated. It is the beauty of modern database management systems that they can so easily facilitate the production of new reports.

Designing a Report

Like other DBMSs, dBASE-II includes procedures for designing report formats and for storing them on disk. Thereafter, they can be used any time with any file, or relation, that fits the specifications of the report. The dBASE-II command to create or produce a report is

```
report
```

which you enter to the right of the dot prompt, figure 10-13.

In response, dBASE-II asks for the filename of the report. If the filename entered is a report format already on disk, dBASE-II produces that report with data from the currently active database, SLSMSTR in this case. If no report format by that filename is stored on the disk, dBASE-II initiates a dialog asking you for format specifications for the new report. First, dBASE-II asks for options for page margins, lines per page, and page width as in figure 10-13. You accept the defaults for these values, which assume regular 8 1/2 by 11 inch paper, by pressing the Enter key. Next, dBASE-II asks if you wish a page heading. You respond with *y* and the program asks for the data to be shown in the heading. You enter *SALESFORCE REPORT*. Finally, dBASE-II asks if the report should be double-spaced and if totals are to be calculated. You

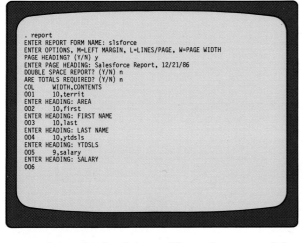

FIGURE 10-13
Report specifications

```
. report
ENTER REPORT FORM NAME: slsforce
ENTER OPTIONS, M=LEFT MARGIN, L=LINES/PAGE, W=PAGE WIDTH
PAGE HEADING? (Y/N) y
ENTER PAGE HEADING: Salesforce Report, 12/21/86
DOUBLE SPACE REPORT? (Y/N) n
ARE TOTALS REQUIRED? (Y/N) n
COL     WIDTH,CONTENTS
001     10,territ
ENTER HEADING: AREA
002     10,first
ENTER HEADING: FIRST NAME
003     10,last
ENTER HEADING: LAST NAME
004     10,ytdsls
ENTER HEADING: YTDSLS
005     9,salary
ENTER HEADING: SALARY
006
```

respond *n* to both of those. That takes care of the overall characteristics of the printed report.

Now dBASE-II is ready for you to specify the columns of data to be shown in the report. It prompts you by displaying

    COL   WIDTH,CONTENTS
    001

which asks for the width of column one (001) and the field name containing the data to appear in that column. You respond with

    10,territ

to the right of 001, figure 10-13. The program then asks for a column heading and you supply AREA. Notice that the column heading need not be the same as the name of the field containing the data to be shown in the column.

You proceed in this fashion for each of the five columns that will appear on the printed report. Figure 10-13 shows all of the entries needed to set up the report. In response to the prompt 006, asking for specifications for the sixth column, you press the Enter key and dBASE-II prints the report on the screen. After verifying that it is correct, you enter the commands

    set print on
    report

to which the program responds by asking for the filename of the report. You enter

    slsforce

and the report is printed on paper as shown in figure 10-14.

Modifying a Database

Potts now has a few modifications he wants you to make to the SLSMSTR database and a new report to prepare. He has acquired total control of Winner Industries, Ltd., a Canadian restaurant equipment manufacturer. Stew has absorbed Winner into the Potts organization and wants you to add its sales force to the SLSMSTR database.

```
PAGE NO. 00001

           Salesforce Report, 12/21/86


AREA           FIRST NAME     LAST NAME     YTDSLS       SALARY

East           Larraine       Enspane       230456.87    18000.00
East           Chuck          Stake         478533.78    23000.00
East           Eve            Knight         16785.96    17500.00
East           Fran           Chise         465200.00    22300.00
West           Bea            Bach          467210.78    28540.00
West           Morley         Otards        236781.90    21560.00
West           Will           Power         578921.67    31000.00
West           Peg            Board         231987.65    27800.00
West           Ginger         Bread         224576.00    26800.00
West           Lee            Derz          350965.23    23400.00
Midwest        Sandy          Beach         235871.00    19500.00
Midwest        Hal            Cyon          567893.98    34800.00
Midwest        Homer          Pidgeon       189784.89    29800.00
Midwest        Hope           Full          234567.98    22580.00
Midwest        Rose           Budd          165479.34    27860.00
Midwest        Phil           Adendron      679340.79    36700.00
South          Morrie         Bund          246987.45    19850.00
South          Ivan           Hoe           132980.45    17800.00
```

FIGURE 10-14
Salesforce report

Winner has five salespeople and Stew has provided you with information about their annual salaries and YTD sales so far. To add these records, or tuples, to the database, you use the following dBASE-II commands:

```
use slsmstr
append
```

The first of these tells dBASE-II that you wish to use the database with the filename SLSMSTR. The program *opens* that database so that it is currently active. The second command tells dBASE-II that you wish to add tuples to the active database. dBASE-II responds by displaying the data entry screen (figure 10-11B) and waiting for you to enter data for the nineteenth record, the next available empty one in the database. You enter the data for each of the five Canadian salespeople just as you did when you set up the database with Pott's original eighteen salespeople. Then you use the commands

```
set print on
report slsforce
```

to instruct dBASE-II to print the SALESFORCE REPORT, which appears in figure 10-15. The five added salespeople appear at the bottom of the report.

Stew believes that he can improve morale by giving salespeople a commission on all sales, retroactive for the current year. He also would like a means of evaluating the salespeople by comparing their annual sales with the total amount paid to each of them. To do this, you must add two fields to the database. COMM, the amount of commission, is calculated as one tenth of one percent of each salesperson's YTD sales. The comparison between total compensation (salary plus commission) and YTD sales is made by calculating total compensation as a percentage of YTD sales. This figure is put in a field named PRCNT for each salesperson.

This means that you must modify the structure of the database so that it includes the fields COMM and PRCNT. This is a little tricky, because when you modify a database structure in dBASE-II and other DBMSs, you routinely destroy all of the data in the database. To get around this, you enter the following commands:

```
use slsmstr
copy structure to temp
use temp
modify structure
```

The first opens the database SLSMSTR. The second copies the structure of SLSMSTR to a nonexistent, temporary database which has no data and which you decide to call TEMP. The third makes TEMP the active database and the last tells dBASE-II that you wish to modify the structure of the active database which is, of course, TEMP.

After receiving the last command, dBASE-II warns that all data in the database TEMP will be erased, figure 10-16A. Inasmuch as you know that TEMP has no data, this is O.K., so you enter *y*. dBASE-II then presents you with a listing of the attributes in TEMP, and you add the new attributes as Fields 07 and 08, figure 10-16B.

FIGURE 10-15
Salesforce report with added records

```
PAGE NO. 00001

            Salesforce Report, 12/21/86


AREA          FIRST NAME     LAST NAME      YTDSLS        SALARY

East          Larraine       Enspane        230456.87     18000.00
East          Chuck          Stake          478533.78     23000.00
East          Eve            Knight          16785.96     17500.00
East          Fran           Chise          465200.00     22300.00
West          Bea            Bach           467210.78     28540.00
West          Morley         Otards         236781.90     21560.00
West          Will           Power          578921.67     31000.00
West          Peg            Board          231987.65     27800.00
West          Ginger         Bread          224576.00     26800.00
West          Lee            Derz           350965.23     23400.00
Midwest       Sandy          Beach          235871.00     19500.00
Midwest       Hal            Cyon           567893.98     34800.00
Midwest       Homer          Pidgeon        189784.89     29800.00
Midwest       Hope           Full           234567.98     22580.00
Midwest       Rose           Budd           165479.34     27860.00
Midwest       Phil           Adendron       679340.79     36700.00
South         Morrie         Bund           246987.45     19850.00
South         Ivan           Hoe            132980.45     17800.00
Canada        Norm           Ahl            495837.46     31478.00
Canada        Roz            Inn            536879.92     29378.00
Canada        Judy           Shial          378462.21     17850.00
Canada        Rhett          Tyred          112629.47     42500.00
Canada        Juan           Ton            489521.48     21850.00
```

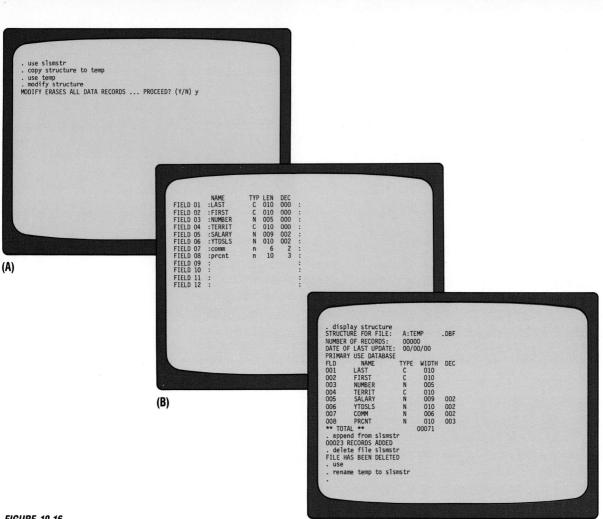

```
. use slsmstr
. copy structure to temp
. use temp
. modify structure
MODIFY ERASES ALL DATA RECORDS ... PROCEED? (Y/N) y
```

(A)

```
              NAME       TYP LEN  DEC
FIELD 01  :LAST       C   010  000  :
FIELD 02  :FIRST      C   010  000  :
FIELD 03  :NUMBER     N   005  000  :
FIELD 04  :TERRIT     C   010  000  :
FIELD 05  :SALARY     N   009  002  :
FIELD 06  :YTDSLS     N   010  002  :
FIELD 07  :comm       n     6    2  :
FIELD 08  :prcnt      n    10    3  :
FIELD 09  :
FIELD 10  :
FIELD 11  :                         :
FIELD 12  :                         :
```

(B)

```
. display structure
STRUCTURE FOR FILE:    A:TEMP      .DBF
NUMBER OF RECORDS:     00000
DATE OF LAST UPDATE:   00/00/00
PRIMARY USE DATABASE
FLD      NAME        TYPE  WIDTH  DEC
001     LAST         C     010
002     FIRST        C     010
003     NUMBER       N     005
004     TERRIT       C     010
005     SALARY       N     009    002
006     YTDSLS       N     010    002
007     COMM         N     006    002
008     PRCNT        N     010    003
** TOTAL **                00071
. append from slsmstr
00023 RECORDS ADDED
. delete file slsmstr
FILE HAS BEEN DELETED
. use
. rename temp to slsmstr
.
```

(C)

FIGURE 10-16
Modifying a database structure

At this point, TEMP has the structure you want, but no data. Figure 10-16C shows the steps for completing the database structure modifications. Transferring data from SLSMSTR to TEMP is not difficult. To be sure that the structure of TEMP is correct, you enter

> `display structure`

to see a listing of the characteristics of TEMP. Noting that it is correct, you enter

> `append from slsmstr`

and all of the data from SLSMSTR, twenty-three records worth, are added to TEMP.

Now that TEMP has all of the data and the desired structure, SLSMSTR is no longer needed so you remove SLSMSTR from the disk with the command

> `delete file slsmstr`

Then, these two commands rename TEMP as SLSMSTR:

> `use`
> `rename temp to slsmstr`

Without a filename, the first command, USE, closes all open databases. It is necessary because dBASE-II will not rename an active database. The second command does the renaming. After these commands have been executed, you have a database with the filename SLSMSTR which has the new structure and contains the data for the twenty-three salespeople.

We should observe at this point that it takes longer to read about these operations than it does to perform them. dBASE-II has something of a reputation for being difficult to use. We hope you see from this illustration that, at least for the type of work required for Potts, dBASE-II is straightforward. Of course, more complicated operations would require more complicated command sequences.

A Sorted Report with Group Totals

Up to this point, your report has been a simple listing of salespeople in the file. To be more useful, it should be categorized and summarized by geographic area so as to better meet management's needs. As it turns out, Potts wants a summary report that shows each of the five sales areas listed alphabetically with a subtotal, called a group total, for each and a grand total for the entire business.

You begin by displaying the structure of SLSMSTR (figure 10-17A) to help you remember the field names assigned to each attribute. Then you enter the command

        sort on territ to areasrt

which instructs dBASE-II to sort the active file, SLSMSTR, according to the data in the field TERRIT and put the sorted data in a new file called AREASRT. When this is finished, the disk will have *two* databases: SLSMSTR, which will be in order by the sequence with which the records were entered and AREASRT, which will be in order alphabetically by the names of the five sales areas that appear in the field TERRIT. Then the command

        use areasrt

which can be seen at the bottom of figure 10-17A makes AREASRT the active database, and you're ready to design the new report.

FIGURE 10-17
Sorting and report specifications

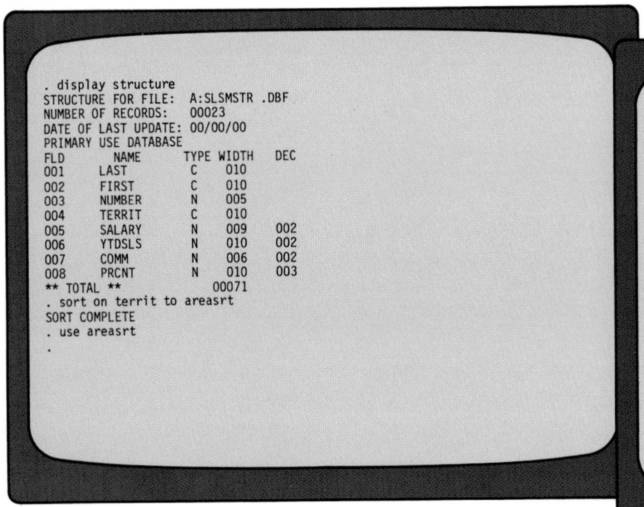

(B)

(A)

```
. display structure
STRUCTURE FOR FILE: A:SLSMSTR .DBF
NUMBER OF RECORDS:   00023
DATE OF LAST UPDATE: 00/00/00
PRIMARY USE DATABASE
FLD     NAME     TYPE WIDTH   DEC
001   LAST        C    010
002   FIRST       C    010
003   NUMBER      N    005
004   TERRIT      C    010
005   SALARY      N    009     002
006   YTDSLS      N    010     002
007   COMM        N    006     002
008   PRCNT       N    010     003
** TOTAL **            00071
. sort on territ to areasrt
SORT COMPLETE
. use areasrt
.
```

```
. report
ENTER REPORT FORM NAME: arearpt
ENTER OPTIONS, M=LEFT MARGIN, L=LINES/PAGE, W=PAGE WIDTH
PAGE HEADING? (Y/N) y
ENTER PAGE HEADING: STEWART POTTS AREA SALES SUMMARY 12/21/86
DOUBLE SPACE REPORT? (Y/N) n
ARE TOTALS REQUIRED? (Y/N) y
SUBTOTALS IN REPORT? (Y/N) y
ENTER SUBTOTALS FIELD: territ
SUMMARY REPORT ONLY? (Y/N) n
EJECT PAGE AFTER SUBTOTALS? (Y/N) n
ENTER SUBTOTAL HEADING: AREA TOTAL
COL     WIDTH,CONTENTS
001      10,last
ENTER HEADING: LAST NAME
002      10,first
ENTER HEADING: FIRST NAME
003       9,salary
ENTER HEADING: SALARY
ARE TOTALS REQUIRED? (Y/N) n
004      10,ytdsls
ENTER HEADING: YTD SALES
ARE TOTALS REQUIRED? (Y/N) y
005
```

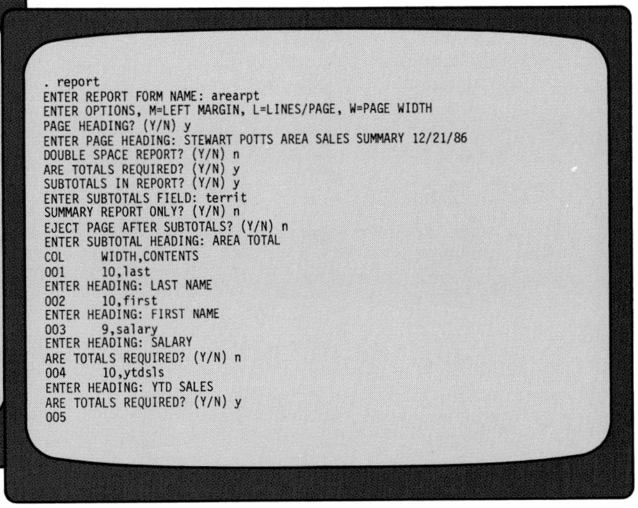

```
PAGE NO. 00001


STEWART POTTS AREA SALES SUMMARY 12/21/86


LAST NAME FIRST NAME  SALARY    YTD SALES

* AREA TOTAL Canada
Ahl         Norm      31478.00   495837.46
Inn         Roz       29378.00   536879.92
Shial       Judy      17850.00   378462.21
Tyred       Rhett     42500.00   112629.47
Ton         Juan      21850.00   489521.48
** SUBTOTAL **
                                2013330.54


* AREA TOTAL East
Enspane     Larraine  18000.00   230456.87
Stake       Chuck     23000.00   478533.78
Knight      Eve       17500.00    16785.96
Chise       Fran      22300.00   465200.00
** SUBTOTAL **
                                1190976.61


* AREA TOTAL Midwest
Beach       Sandy     19500.00   235871.00
Cyon        Hal       34800.00   567893.98
Pidgeon     Homer     29800.00   189784.89
Full        Hope      22580.00   234567.98
Budd        Rose      27860.00   165479.34
Adendron    Phil      36700.00   679340.79
** SUBTOTAL **
                                2072937.98


* AREA TOTAL South
Bund        Morrie    19850.00   246987.45
Hoe         Ivan      17800.00   132980.45
** SUBTOTAL **
                                 379967.90


* AREA TOTAL West
Bach        Bea       28540.00   467210.78
Otards      Morley    21560.00   236781.90
Power       Will      31000.00   578921.67
Board       Peg       27800.00   231987.65
Bread       Ginger    26800.00   224576.00
Derz        Lee       23400.00   350965.23
** SUBTOTAL **
                                2090443.23

** TOTAL **
                                7747656.26
```

FIGURE 10-18
Area sales report

Using the same procedures as before, you prepare the report specifications as shown in figure 10-17B. Because this report requires totals and subtotals, you respond *y* to those two dBASE-II prompts, lines 7 and 8 in the figure. The subtotal field, which is also known as the *control field*, is TERRIT. This means that as the data are printed on the report for each salesperson as *detail lines* (see Chapter Two), the content of the field TERRIT is examined to see if there has been a change. As soon as the area name changes, dBASE-II calculates and prints the total sales for the preceding area. Figure 10-18 shows the report produced by these specifications.

Calculating Field Contents

Now you're ready for Stew's last report, a listing of all salespeople in order by the percentage that their total compensation represents of their total YTD sales. Stew wants the list in descending order, with those with the highest percentage at the top. You remember him mumbling something about a hit list.

You begin by calculating the two fields you added earlier. Calculations in dBASE-II are simple. The fields COMM and PRCNT are now blank for each salesperson. The two commands that replace the blank contents with the results of the desired calculations follow:

```
replace all comm with (.001 * ytdsls)
replace all prcnt with ((salary + comm)/ytdsls * 100)
```

You enter these after displaying the structure of AREASRT, figure 10-19A. The first command multiplies, for all salespeople, the contents of YTDSLS by one tenth of one percent and puts the results in COMM. The second adds the contents of SALARY and COMM, divides that total by YTDSLS, and multiplies the result by 100 to convert it into a percentage. The parentheses add clarity and control the order of execution.

In two more quick steps, you'll be finished. First, you sort AREASRT by the contents of PRCNT in descending order. Sorting always prepares a new database to contain the results of the sort operation, so the command to do this is

```
sort on prcnt to evalsrt descending
```

where the filename EVALSRT stands for Evaluation Sort. In the final step, you design a report format that will use the database EVALSRT to prepare the desired report, figure 10-19B. The resulting report appears in figure 10-20.

From the evaluation report, Potts can see a listing in order by compensa-

FIGURE 10-19
Calculations and final report specifications

```
. display structure
STRUCTURE FOR FILE:  A:AREASRT .DBF
NUMBER OF RECORDS:   00023
DATE OF LAST UPDATE: 00/00/00
PRIMARY USE DATABASE
FLD       NAME      TYPE WIDTH   DEC
001      LAST        C    010
002      FIRST       C    010
003      NUMBER      N    005
004      TERRIT      C    010
005      SALARY      N    009    002
006      YTDSLS      N    010    002
007      COMM        N    006    002
008      PRCNT       N    010    003
** TOTAL **              00071
. replace all comm with (.001 * ytdsls)
00023 REPLACEMENT(S)
. replace all prcnt with ((salary + comm)/ytdsls * 100)
00023 REPLACEMENT(S)
.
```

(A)

```
. use evalsrt
. report
ENTER REPORT FORM NAME: slseval
ENTER OPTIONS, M=LEFT MARGIN, L=LINES/PAGE, W=PAGE WIDTH
PAGE HEADING? (Y/N) y
ENTER PAGE HEADING: SALESPERSON EVALUATION 12/23/86
DOUBLE SPACE REPORT? (Y/N) n
ARE TOTALS REQUIRED? (Y/N) n
COL      WIDTH,CONTENTS
001       10,last
ENTER HEADING: LAST NAME
002       6,number
ENTER HEADING: NUMBER
003       10,ytdsls
ENTER HEADING: YTD SALES
004       9,salary
ENTER HEADING: SALARY
005       6,comm
ENTER HEADING: COMMISSION
006       10,prcnt
ENTER HEADING: PERCENT
007
```

(B)

```
PAGE NO. 00001


         SALESPERSON EVALUATION 12/23/86

  LAST NAME    NUMBER   YTD SALES    SALARY     COMMIS    PERCENT
                                                 SION

  Knight       17822     16785.96   17500.00     16.78    104.353
  Tyred        56102    112629.47   42500.00    112.62     37.834
  Budd         21081    165479.34   27860.00    165.47     16.935
  Pidgeon      25679    189784.89   29800.00    189.78     15.801
  Hoe          45983    132980.45   17800.00    132.98     13.485
  Board        36179    231987.65   27800.00    231.98     12.083
  Bread        34972    224576.00   26800.00    224.57     12.033
  Full         19980    234567.98   22580.00    234.56      9.726
  Otards       32180    236781.90   21560.00    236.78      9.205
  Beach        26881    235871.00   19500.00    235.87      8.367
  Bund         47878    246987.45   19580.00    246.98      8.027
  Enspane      14580    230456.87   18000.00    230.45      7.910
  Derz         32082    350965.23   23400.00    350.96      6.767
  Ahl          51781    495837.46   31478.00    495.83      6.448
  Cyon         24576    567893.98   34800.00    567.89      6.227
  Bach         34779    467210.78   28540.00    467.21      6.208
  Inn          58715    536879.92   29378.00    536.87      5.571
  Adendron     25776    679340.79   36700.00    679.34      5.502
  Power        36778    578921.67   31000.00    578.92      5.454
  Stake        12876    478533.78   23000.00    478.53      4.906
  Chise        17581    465200.00   22300.00    465.20      4.893
  Shial        51265    378462.21   17850.00    378.46      4.816
  Ton          54601    489521.48   21850.00    489.52      4.563
```

FIGURE 10-20
Salesperson evaluation report

tion as a percentage of sales for each of the salespeople. Eve Knight, who was paid more than the amount of her total sales, would seem due for some attention. It is just this ability of data processing systems to organize data into meaningful reports that gives them their value to management.

SUMMARY

A *data base management system* is a program that maintains data on secondary storage devices and makes them available to application programs and to users. To a large extent today, as in the past, data are stored as *sequential, indexed-sequential* or *direct* files on secondary storage media. How the data are *processed*, however, is quite distinct from the manner in which they are *stored*. For the sake of ease of use, processing techniques often employ these same names: *sequential processing, indexed-sequential processing, direct access processing,* and *virtual-storage access method*, VSAM, which uses relative storage addresses.

The distinction between the terms *data base* and *database* is not always a clear one. Usually, the former is the more general of the two, referring to any collection of data, however organized and processed. The latter, however, refers to data storage and processing techniques in which no effort is made to store data as files of contiguous records. A database system concentrates on optimizing the processing of data, reducing data redundancy, and maintaining the data in a manner consistent with the way in which the organization works.

Database systems operate within four basic processing structures, depending upon the complexity of the database management system program, the DBMS. *File management systems (FMSs)* treat data as if they were processed as *sequential*, or *flat*, files. FMSs in large computer systems usually employ *pointers* to *link* separate files together. Microcomputer FMSs rarely have this linking ability, making only one file available to the user at one time. *Hierarchical* systems connect data elements in an arrangement in which access to records, *children*, is achieved by linking them to controlling records, or *parents*. *Networked* systems operate in the same fashion as hierarchical systems except that any child may have more than one parent. *Relational* database systems organize data according to tables, called *relations*. The rows of a relation are known as *tuples*; the columns as *attributes*. Processing data in a relational system links attributes and tuples in patterns to retrieve and store data as required by the application.

In performing its functions, the DBMS follows paths through the complex of stored data. Paths that describe physical routes to desired data are known as *physical paths*. The *logical path* describes the relationships among the data elements from the user's point of view. The DBMS program converts logical paths into the physical paths required by the operating system for data access. All of the paths and relationships are called the *schema* of the DBMS, which may be divided into *subschemas* for the purpose of making only the appropriate portions of the total database available to certain users.

DBMS programs perform five basic functions: *creating* databases, *modifying* them, *deleting data* from them, *adding data*, and *selecting data* according to specified criteria. In addition to these functions, DBMSs are often required to provide *data security*, especially in DBMS systems that serve multiple users.

Every day more small businesses are using computers on a regular basis. (Courtesy AT&T Information Systems)

KEY TERMS

algorithm	file management	program generator
attribute	system	query language
command file	flat file	query procedure
control field	front end program	record key
data base	hierarchical file	relation
data base	system	relational data base
administrator	host language	schema
data base management	indexed-sequential	sequential file
system (DBMS)	access method	sequential
data security	indexed-sequential file	processing
data set	master file	transaction file
direct access file	networked file system	tuple
disk address	password	virtual-storage access
		method

REVIEW QUESTIONS

1. What characterizes the "applications approach" to data management?
2. What is the data base management approach to data management?
3. Name three types of files.
4. What is the purpose of an address pointer?
5. Identify two types of redundancy.
6. What is the principal advantage of the virtual-storage access method?
7. Name four types of data base systems.

8. Explain a relational data base in terms of a table.
9. Differentiate between the two types of reports available on most database management systems.
10. What is the difference between the logical and physical data paths?

THOUGHT QUESTIONS

1. Discuss the importance of using passwords (and other security) in a large multi-user database management system.
2. Describe the importance of the philosophical change from the applications approach to the data base management approach of data management.
3. Describe how subschemas can be used to limit access to portions of a data base. Consider both reading data and modifying data in your answer.

(Courtesy CompuServe Inc., Columbus, Ohio/Photographer Michele Tcherevkoff, New York, New York)

The Computer as Liberator

Jim Stevens works at home as a computer programmer. He connects his IBM PC with a distant mainframe computer to enter his code. He is blind.[1] Henry Kiser, editor and columnist with the Chicago *Sun Times* conducts interviews using his computer and a modem. He is deaf.[2] Bill Battle has launched his own computer programming business which he operates at home. He is almost completely paralyzed from the neck down.[3] Deteriorating sight made reading impossible for writer Shell Talmy. He uses a speech synthesizer for preparing scripts and novels. It reads his writing back to him verbally. "I don't have to rely on people to read or write for me," he reports. "Writing can be a lonely job. My speech synthesizer makes me feel like somebody is talking to me."[4]

Dick Gage, blind since birth, is a staff member at IBM's Scientific Center at Cambridge. He works to develop computer input/output devices for the disabled. Judging from the results of his efforts, few if any handicaps can prevent a person from using a computer. About someone who couldn't see, hear, or speak, he says:

> The man had electrodes attached to his leg. When I typed messages on the keyboard, they were transformed into Morse code that vibrated on his leg. He typed his reply in Morse code on the keyboard.[5]

A number of equipment manufacturers have developed devices that enable the disabled to use computers. Koala Technologies has a digitizing pad, the KoalaPad, which can transform roughly drawn letters and symbols into recognizable characters. At Johns Hopkins Hospital, a boy with severe cerebral palsy learned to use one in just one day with a stylus strapped to his head. Techmar's Speech Master Board allows those with speech impediments to type messages on their computer keyboards. The computer does the talking. The firm's Voice Recognition Board can understand 100 spoken words that represent computer commands. Prentke Romich produces the Express III communications palette which can serve as a stand-alone computer or can be attached to other computer devices. The user can control it with sticks, light wands, sound, or body movement. The device includes a speech synthesizer which verbally verifies the entered information. A Stanford University engineering professor perfected the Opticon after his daughter lost her sight. It reads ordinary printed material and translates it into vibrating images that users feel with a finger. The Opticon helped his daughter earn a Ph.D. from Stanford and is today used by more than 9,000 people throughout the world.[6]

Employment opportunities for the disabled using such devices are growing rapidly, partly because of altruistic motives on the part of employers and, more importantly, because handicapped individuals make competent, reliable workers. In Stamford, Connecticut, thirty top U.S. corporations are giving money and consultation to Biped Corporation, a school for the disabled. The companies include American Can, Xerox, Reader's Digest, Texaco, and Union Carbide. Biped's graduates find jobs in a number of different businesses.[7]

In Palo Alto, California, Sensory Aids Foundation, a nonprofit training organization for the disabled, has placed more that 500 of its graduates. Says Susan Phillips, Director of the Foundation:

Technology is opening up a new world for disabled workers, who at long last can be genuinely competitive with the non-handicapped working population.

I believe that more employers would be willing to hire disadvantaged persons if they only realized the sophisticated aids that are now on the market.[8]

Gerald Schwartz quit his job as an aerospace engineer to devote full-time effort toward developing voice-recognition techniques and teaching the disabled how to use them.

I'm trying to make the handicapped no different from anybody else. So what if you don't play baseball? You can be the hottest computer programmer at 18.[9]

Occupations for the disabled need not be limited to computer programming and other related fields, as we've seen. A career carpenter who developed multiple sclerosis at age 57 uses a computer system to prepare materials requirements for construction projects as a consultant. Maria French, a victim of cerebral palsy who cannot use her fingers, teaches high school English and writes by striking keys with a pencil. She hopes some day to install a voice-activated system, even though it would cost nearly $10,000. "For me to use a regular computer is practically impossible, and yet I have the intellect and know-how to put it to good use."[10]

QUESTIONS

1. Does your school have special programs for disabled students? What are they? Are computers used in them? If so how?
2. Not only can computers offer employment opportunities, but they can also be used to restore lost functions. Discuss some possibilities for using computers to replace physiological functions.

Data Communication

(Courtesy Adage, Inc.)

Jennifer Lombardi, a sixth grader at Palisades Park's Lindbergh School in New Jersey says, "It's better than going to a book because it's easier to type into a keyboard than to flip through pages." "It" is the *Academic American Encyclopedia* made available to students by computer and telephone from Dow Jones News/Retrieval Service. Jennifer is one of many students who do their school work using telecommunications.[1]

Stephen Tillson is manager of clinical studies at the Medical Diagnostics Division of Syntex Corporation in Silicon Valley, California. Much of his work is done on an IBM PC XT microcomputer, but sometimes he needs more computing power than the XT can provide. He solved this problem by connecting it to a mainframe computer using telephone lines. His solution saved Syntex several thousand dollars over the alternative, running a cable from his office to a mainframe computer several buildings away.[2]

Photographers, too, often need specialized communications services. While they're off on a shooting assignment, perhaps in deepest Africa, a client may wish to contact them. Magazines such as *National Geographic,* for example, need to maintain contact with their staff while they are in the field. Photographers Len Kaltman and Patricia Woodson solved the problem by developing Photonet, a computerized *information utility* for the profession. Photonet links photographers with clients, camera repair services, and research professionals, providing a full range of services.[3]

Electronic mail links the President of the U.S. to Cabinet members and to staffs of key agencies. Secretary of Agriculture John R. Block carries a microcomputer when he travels. As he puts it, "Having...a portable computer terminal while we travel is more than a convenience—it has quickly become a necessity."[4]

The common factor in all of these stories is *data communication*. Data communication marries the technologies of computers and communications to provide information processing services throughout the office or around the world. *Data communication,* often called *telecommunication,* means transmitting data and information electronically from one point to another using the telephone, radio and microwave transmission devices, laser beams, optical cables, and direct wiring. This chapter looks at ways of connecting computers, things we can do when they are connected, and a few of the hundreds of telecommunicating services available to computer users. Finally, we will examine one computerized data base and information retrieval system in some detail. First, let's define data communications.

DATA COMMUNICATION

A data communication system consists of five parts. First, there is the *information source.* This is usually a database of some kind although it may be a person in the case of electronic mail or similar services. Second, there is a *transmitter.* This is a device (or group of devices) that sends information from one location to another.

Third, the *channel* is the logical connection between sender and receiver. The channel may use telephone wires, satellites, microwave towers, or other devices. The channel is not necessarily a physical device; it is the path over which data and information travel. A channel may employ several different communications devices and may change these from time to time. The user need not be concerned about this.

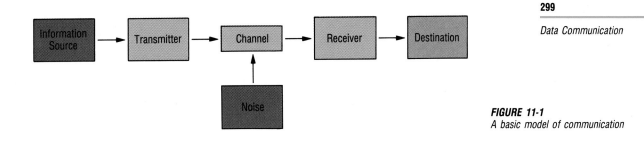

FIGURE 11-1
A basic model of communication

At times there may be *noise* along the path. Noise is an electronic signal that does not belong. Usually, noise is caused by some kind of electrical or electronic interference. Its effect is to change or obscure data. Although methods have been developed to detect and minimize noise, it remains a potential problem in electronic communication.

The fourth and fifth parts of the communication system are the *receiver* and the *destination*. For most computer applications, these are similar to the transmitter and the source. They may be another computer or terminal, a printer, or a person. Figure 11-1 shows a schematic diagram of a typical communication system.

The Nation's Data Communication System

The primary data communication system in most modern nations is the public telephone network which is government owned in almost all countries except the United States. In this country, telephone systems are owned by private, licensed monopolies. The best known of these is American Telephone and Telegraph, also known as AT&T, the Bell System, or Ma Bell.

For much of this century, Bell had total control of the phone network, including the devices that were connected to it. During this period, Bell was prohibited from entering the computer industry. The effect of these regulations was to impede progress in the development of computer communications, the marriage of two technologies.

In 1968, the Bell monopoly started to crack. The Federal Communication Commission (FCC) ruled in the Carterfone decision that Bell must allow non-Bell equipment access to the telephone system. This opened the door to a variety of ancillary telephone equipment such as automatic dialers, answering machines, and modems, the devices needed to connect computers via telephone.

About a decade after the Carterfone decision, the U.S. Department of Justice ruled that AT&T was to be broken into smaller organizations because of its monopolistic practices. The breakup was completed in 1984 with major effects on telephone service in the nation. Perhaps more importantly, AT&T was permitted to enter the lucrative computer market. They quickly developed a series of computers ranging in size and power from microcomputer to mainframe. The principal claim to fame for the new line of computers was their communication capabilities. In fact, Bell had developed the UNIX operating system (see Chapter Seven) with communication in mind. Late in 1984, IBM entered the data communications field with the purchase of Rolm, Inc., a nationwide telecommunications firm. The competition between these two giants, IBM and AT&T, illustrates the growing importance of telecommunications in today's world.

Common Carriers

Organizations like AT&T and Rolm are called *common carriers*. These are firms that have been authorized by the FCC or state public utility commissions to provide communication service to the public. There are several thousand common carriers and most, like AT&T, are investor owned and privately operated. Three important common carriers are Western Union, General Telephone and Electronics (GTE), and the Communications Satellite Corporation (COMSAT).

Specialized Common Carriers

In 1971 and 1972, the FCC made rulings that facilitated the development of a wide variety of new communications services offered by common carriers using land lines and satellite links. This broke the monopoly held by COMSAT since 1962.

These new common carriers are called *specialized common carriers*. These firms offer voice and data communications, often at less cost than that charged by AT&T. Prominent among them are MCI Telecommunications (MCI Mail) and Southern Pacific Communications (Sprint). In fact, many areas of the country allow telephone users to specify which carrier they use when dialing a long distance call.

Value-added Networks

Value-added networks, or VANs, such as GTE's Telenet, Tymshare's Tymnet, United Telecommunications' Uninet, and Lockheed's Dialnet use common carrier lines to provide additional services such as access to data banks and electronic mail. Because these networks provide additional service through the telephone, they are called value-added networks. These networks use special data handling techniques to provide low-error rate and fast response-time access to subscribers at low cost.

VANs provide economical service because they can make the most effective use of their equipment. For example, suppose that five companies want data communications service between their offices in Philadelphia and Los Angeles. Each would communicate about one hour each business day. The

FIGURE 11-2
Value-added network

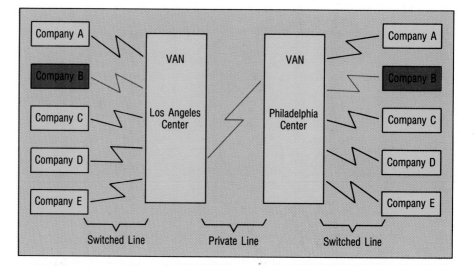

FIGURE 11-3
Point-to-point local area network

cost for this service through normal means would be prohibitive. Mann's VAN Company offers an alternative. Mann will provide a leased telephone line to be shared by the five companies. A leased line is economical if it is used more than three hours per day. The five companies will use the line for a total of about five hours daily and share in the cost savings of the leased line. Mann makes a profit and still has the capacity to add more firms to the network. Figure 11-2 shows this arrangement.

MAKING THE CONNECTION—A BRIEF REVIEW OF THE HARDWARE

Because computers are not standardized—they have different operating systems, hardware, and software—a variety of techniques is used to connect them. They can be connected with a wire cable, or *hard-wired* together. They can also be connected as needed by using ordinary telephone equipment. Hard-wiring permits fast data transmission but reduced flexibility. It might take several weeks to install new cable when a terminal is moved, for instance. Telephone hook-ups, on the other hand, provide flexibility because telephone lines are almost everywhere and can be quickly installed. Telephone line transmission is slower than hard-wire connections, but their advantages often outweigh this disadvantage.

Direct Connection

Computers that are permanently connected by a wire cable are said to be hard-wired together. Typically, devices are close together when they are hard-wired. A set of devices that is hard-wired and located within a small distance of each other (about one square mile) is called a *local area network,* or *LAN.* LANs can be assembled into a number of different configurations. Figure 11-3 shows a point-to-point arrangement and figure 11-4 shows a LAN with a *gateway computer* which provides all of the computers in the network access to computers outside the LAN.

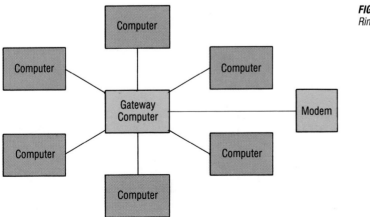

FIGURE 11-4
Ring network with gateway

FIGURE 11-5
Digital signal

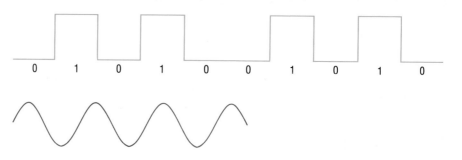

FIGURE 11-6
Analog signal

When computers are linked, rules or standards must be established so that all of the machines send compatible messages. These rules are called *protocols.* They specify, for example, the number of bits used to represent each character (seven or eight), the parity (odd or even), and so forth. A common protocol for LANs is *Ethernet,* a system developed by Xerox to be linked to as many as 1024 computers on a wire less than 8,000 feet long.

Computers that are connected directly send information as binary *digital* signals as shown in figure 11-5. In this circumstance, all of the devices in the communications link are digital. When computers are connected indirectly, using telephone lines, this is not the case.

Indirect Connection

With the proper equipment, computers can also be connected by telephone or by radio. Telephone links may be made by land line, microwave, or satellite. Data are sent by telephone in *analog* form, however, meaning that signals vary continuously instead of being just zeros and ones. Figure 11-6 shows an analog signal.

Modems

Because computers represent data in digital form and the telephone system transmits data using continuous, or analog, wave forms, their combination must include equipment that converts signals from one to the other. The unit that does this is called a *modem,* short for modulator-demodulator. *Modulation* converts digital signals into analog wave patterns. *Demodulation* reverses the process. Figure 11-7 shows what happens. Each computer is connected to the telephone network via a modem. Developments in telephone systems may soon eliminate the need for modems by combining analog and digital signals on the same line.

Computers work with several bits of data at a time (8, 16, 32, 48, or more bits) but modems send signals one bit at a time. Signals to and from the processor are transmitted in *parallel.* Think of them as the start of a 100 meter dash. All runners are next to each other and running in parallel. Signals to

FIGURE 11-7
Modulating a digital signal

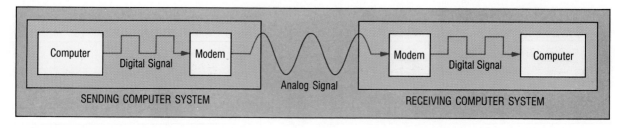

Computer — Digital Signal → Modem — Analog Signal — → Modem — Digital Signal → Computer

SENDING COMPUTER SYSTEM   RECEIVING COMPUTER SYSTEM

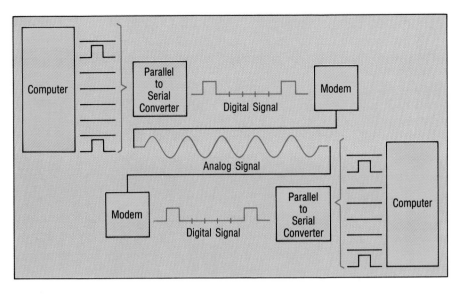

FIGURE 11-8
*Connecting two computers by
telephone*

and from the modem, on the other hand, are transmitted *serially*, that is, one bit follows another like cars on an assembly line. Thus, the processor and modem must be connected through parallel-to-serial circuitry. This is built in to some computers and must be added to others. The most commonly used standard serial protocol is called *RS-232*. Figure 11-8 shows the entire connection between two computers.

There are two types of modems: *acoustic* and *direct-connect*. Early modems required that a telephone handset be placed in a cradle with the computer signal being sent between the phone and the modem acoustically. In other words, the modem converted, or modulated, the computer's digital signals into sound signals, or pitches. This provided fairly slow data transmission with fairly high error rates. More recent equipment permits modems to be connected directly to the telephone system, somewhat like telephone answering machines. In fact, no telephone receiver is necessary when using such equipment. Direct connection allows higher transmission rates with better accuracy than does acoustic coupling.

*Acoustic couplers are modems
that connect computers to the
telephone system through a
telephone handset.* (Courtesy
Anderson-Jacobson Inc.)

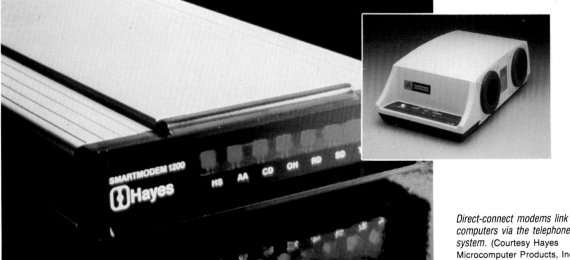

*Direct-connect modems link
computers via the telephone
system.* (Courtesy Hayes
Microcomputer Products, Inc.)

Transmission Characteristics

Acoustic and direct-connect modems can be used in the same communications link. Regardless of the type used, however, the two modems must have certain characteristics in common.

Baud Rate. Speed of transmission is measured in *baud*, which is equivalent to bits per second. Common baud rates are 110 (about 10 characters per second) which is used in teletypes; 300 (27 cps) and 1200 (110 cps) which are used by many information retrieval services such as The Source and Dow Jones News/Retrieval; 9600 (870 cps) and 19200 (1750 cps) which are used for high-volume, computer-to-computer communications that do not require human intervention.

There are three *transmission grades*, or *bandwidths*, which are also measured in baud. These are *narrow band* (45–90 bits per second), which is equivalent to the telegraph; *voice grade* (300–9600), like the telephone; and *broad band* (up to 120,000) which includes microwave and laser transmission as well as coaxial cable (cable on which several signals can be sent simultaneously).

Synchronization. Computers at each end of a data transmission must work together so that data that are sent can be properly interpreted. For instance, both computers must know when a message begins. Otherwise, the receiving computer may start interpreting data at a different bit than the sending processor. For example, the computer sends the message, "...send money immediately..." The bit pattern for this message begins

. . . 01110011 01100101 01101110 . . .
      s   e   n

If the receiving processor is not "in sync" with the sender, it might receive the same bit pattern but separate the bits into characters differently:

. . . 0 11100110 11001010 1101101 . . .

This bit pattern reads "...fj..." which is obviously garbled. This problem is solved by establishing a synchronization protocol that each computer must use.

We can coordinate the transmitting and receiving computers by establishing an *asynchronous transmission protocol* between them. In asynchronous transmission, the time interval between each transmission is not fixed. Instead, each set of bits is transmitted with a specific character preceding and following it. Thus, the receiving computer "knows" how to receive the message. Figure 11-9A shows this.

FIGURE 11-9
(A) Asynchronous transmission
(B) Synchronous transmission

```
S               S   S               S   S               S
T               T   T               T   T               T
A  01000001     O   A  01000010     O   A  01000011     O
R               P   R               P   R               P
T                   T                   T
```

(A)

01000001 01000010 01000011

(B)

*Monitors located away from their
computer provide an example of
simplex communications.*
(Courtesy New York Stock
Exchange)

The other technique employs a *synchronous transmission protocol*. Synchronous transmissions send data at a fixed rate. For that reason, they are sometimes called *locked transmissions*. No start or stop codes need be sent. A sample synchronous transmission is illustrated in figure 11-9B.

Synchronous transmission does not require start and stop characters; therefore, synchronous transmission is faster than asynchronous. It is also more expensive, however. Low-speed modems tend to support asynchronous transmission while high-speed ones often support synchronous transmission.

Direction of Transmission

When computers communicate with each other, they must use consistent speeds and synchronization methods. In addition, they must adhere to one of three transmission modes: simplex, half-duplex, or full-duplex.

Simplex is a rarely used mode of communication in which signals are sent in only one direction. Simplex transmission might be used in a computerized scoreboard at the local stadium.

Half-duplex transmission is also one-way, but the direction is changeable. Thus, a terminal can send a message to the host computer which then acknowledges receipt with a return transmission. After the acknowledgement, the terminal can send more data. Half-duplex transmission allows two-way communication but only in one direction at a time.

Full-duplex involves simultaneous two-way communication. This is a fast type of transmission which typically is used in computer-to-computer communication. A subscriber to a bibliographic service like NewsNet uses his or her computer to communicate with the NewsNet host computer in full-duplex mode.

All three types of transmission appear in figure 11-10.

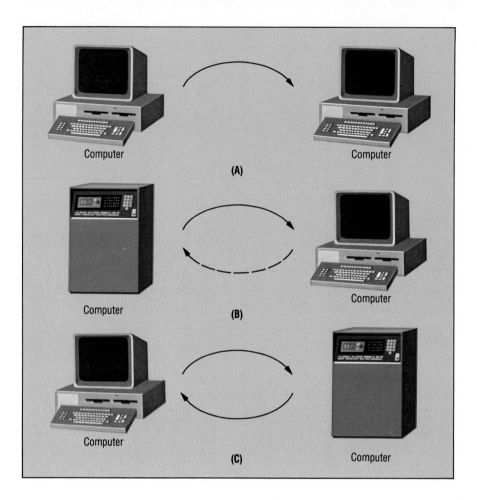

The Telephone Connection

There are several good reasons for using the telephone system to conduct computer communication. (1) Virtually any two points in the businessworld are already connected by telephone lines. (2) It is inexpensive to use—development costs have been shared by everyone already. (3) Although it is relatively slow (voice grade), it is fast enough for many applications.

When a message enters the telephone system, there are four paths it might travel to reach its destination: coaxial cable, microwave transmission, satellite transmission, and fiber optics cable.

Coaxial Cable

Underground and overhead copper wire carries much of the messages in the nation's telephone system. This *coaxial cable*, or *co-ax*, can carry hundreds of messages simultaneously by *multiplexing* the signals.

Multiplexing was invented in 1874 by Jean Emile Baudot to increase the message capacity of telegraph lines. In essence, multiplexing combines traffic from several low-speed data sources on one high-speed line. The signals are combined by a *multiplexor* at the source and are split back apart by a *demultiplexor* at the destination. These devices may or may not be combined with modems. Figure 11-11 shows a situation where several users are multiplexed together in communication with a host computer.

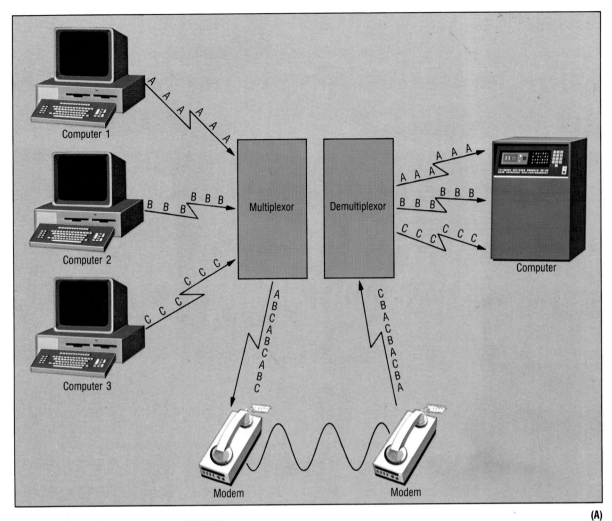

(A)

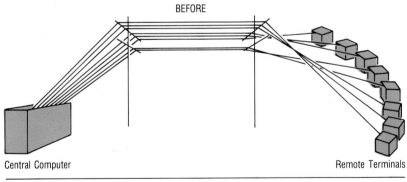

BEFORE

Central Computer

Remote Terminals

AFTER

Central Computer

Multiplexor

Multiplexor

Remote Terminals

(B)

FIGURE 11-11
(A) Multiplexed communication
(B) Typical multiplexor application

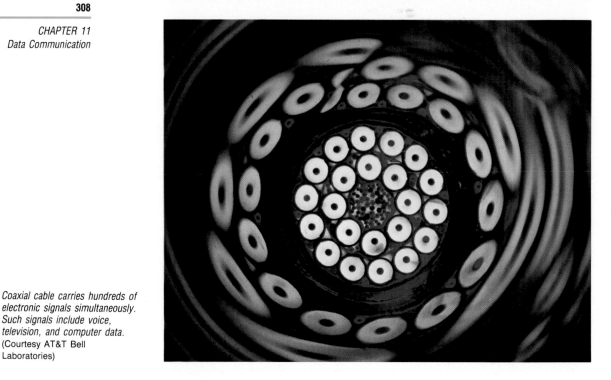

Coaxial cable carries hundreds of electronic signals simultaneously. Such signals include voice, television, and computer data. (Courtesy AT&T Bell Laboratories)

Microwave Transmission

Telephone messages can also be sent by high-frequency or microwave radio signals. Signals are sent by wire to a *microwave repeater* which amplifies the signal and sends it to another repeater and so on until the signal is returned to a wire or cable close to its destination. Due to the nature of microwaves, repeaters must be on a line of sight with each other and are typically about 30 miles apart. Figure 11-12 shows a microwave network.

FIGURE 11-12
Microwave network

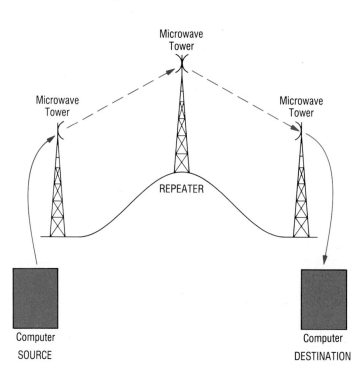

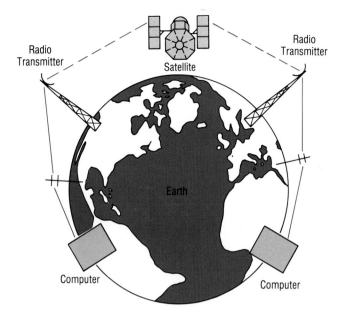

FIGURE 11-13
Satellite link

Satellite Transmission

Communications satellites currently circle the globe in *geosynchronous orbits* about 22,300 miles above the earth's surface. A geosynchronous orbit keeps the satellite over the same point on the surface of the earth at all times. This allows earthbound microwave antennas to aim at the satellite without continual adjustment (see figure 11-13).

Because of the distance to the satellite, signals take nearly one-half a second to transmit. This is too long for some real-time data communications applications, such as process control, but is satisfactory for most operations that transmit data to provide information.

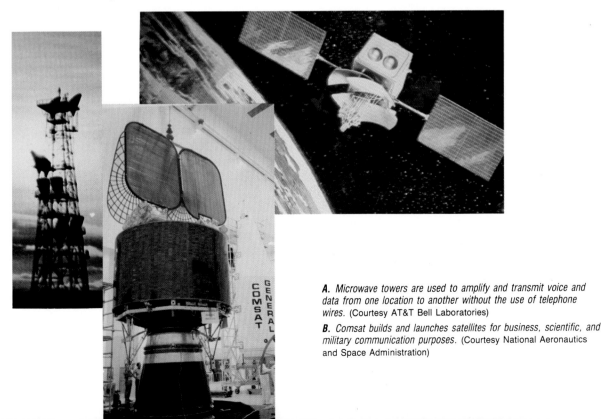

A. Microwave towers are used to amplify and transmit voice and data from one location to another without the use of telephone wires. (Courtesy AT&T Bell Laboratories)

B. Comsat builds and launches satellites for business, scientific, and military communication purposes. (Courtesy National Aeronautics and Space Administration)

Optical fibers transmit data by laser-generated light. Such systems are replacing the copper wire of the telephone network.(Courtesy AT&T Bell Laboratories)

Fiber Optics

With the cost of copper cable increasing dramatically, telephone systems now employ laser transmission using very fine optical glass cable for voice and data transmission. Since glass is easily and inexpensively made, cabling costs have been substantially reduced. In addition, optical fiber has the potential of carrying one billion bits of data per second. That's roughly equivalent to 6 million double-spaced typewritten pages every minute.

Much new telephone cabling is done with fiber optics. In fact, Los Angeles now has a major fiber optics installation, thanks to the tremendous need for information transmission — voice, television, and data — around the world for the 1984 Olympics.

Switched versus Private Lines

The telephones we use every day are connected to *switched lines.* These are normal telephone lines that are activated when someone dials a number. They are billed at a monthly service rate plus time and distance charges. Firms that do more than about three hours of teleprocessing per day should consider *private,* or *leased, lines* as an alternative. These are available on a full-time basis for a fixed rental rate. Private lines allow faster data transmission rates which allow better use of the computing facility. The savings are generally worthwhile and privacy is easier to maintain, although access to computerized services is somewhat limited. What's more, there are no busy signals on a private line. Computers on leased lines can also have a *gateway computer* to help maintain security from access by interlopers. A gateway computer allows a network access to external information sources.

OTHER HARDWARE, BRIEFLY MENTIONED

A *front-end processor* is a minicomputer that is connected to a mainframe or host computer to handle the details of connecting the host to other devices. This processor creates the link between terminals and their host by *handshaking,* a process whereby the computer acknowledges receipt of information and indicates its readiness to accept more. The front-end processor also establishes priorities for various system users, checks input, and disconnects a line when it is no longer needed. These minicomputers also deal with computer security, allowing access only to people with the proper user numbers and passwords. Front-end processors may also be called *terminal controllers*. Figure 11-14 shows a computer system with terminal controllers.

A *concentrator* accepts signals from a slow device and holds them until enough have been sent to keep the CPU busy. Essentially, a concentrator is a buffer. Concentrators also do some error checking, data compression, and other front-end processor tasks. Concentrators are frequently found in airline reservation systems in large cities. Figure 11-15 shows a concentrator and a concentrator/multiplexor.

FIGURE 11-14
*Terminal controllers connect
terminals to central processors*

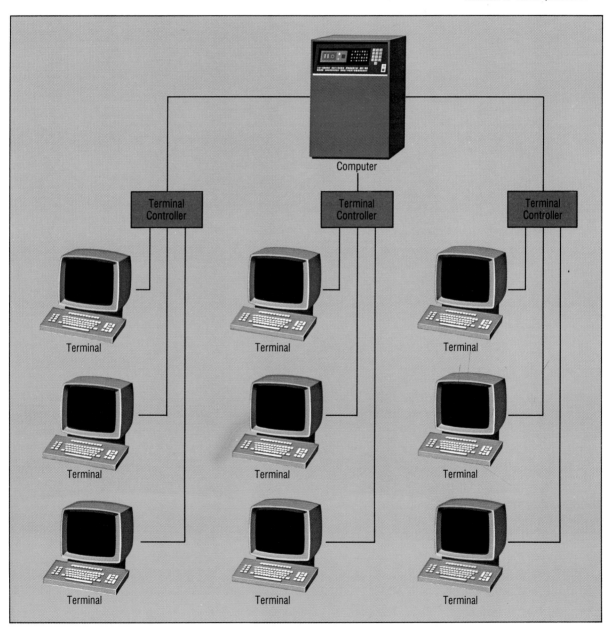

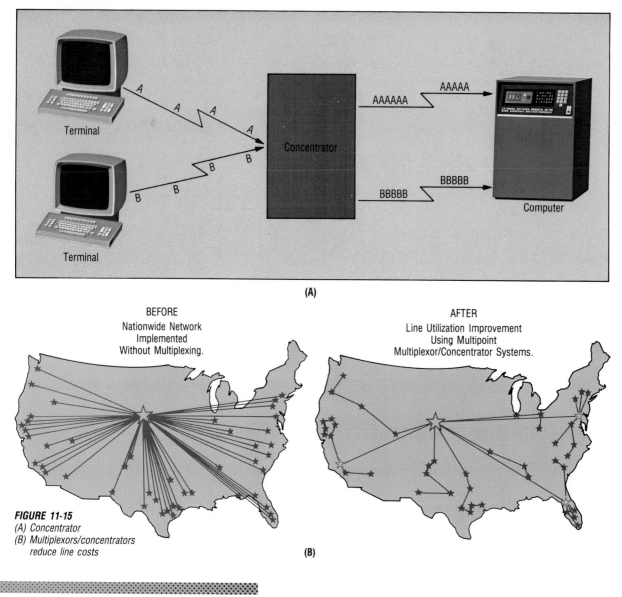

(A)

BEFORE
Nationwide Network
Implemented
Without Multiplexing.

AFTER
Line Utilization Improvement
Using Multipoint
Multiplexor/Concentrator Systems.

FIGURE 11-15
(A) Concentrator
(B) Multiplexors/concentrators
reduce line costs

(B)

NETWORKS

The ability of several computers to communicate with each other depends largely on the operating system which coordinates the transfer and storage of data, as we observed in Chapter Seven. Networks typically, but not always, involve on-line storage of great quantities of data, as was illustrated in figure

Hundreds of airlines reservationists work at their terminals in a worldwide system that is linked by leased telephone lines and switched lines.
(Courtesy American Airlines)

7-7. One computer, known as the *host* or *slave*, serves as a controller, providing access to mass storage and powerful processing resources to each of the other computers in the system. The controller is called a *file server* when it does no more than coordinate the delivery of data to the other computers. Figure 11-16 shows four typical configurations of networks: (A) point-to-point; (B) multi-drop line; (C) star; and (D) ring.

FIGURE 11-16
Networking

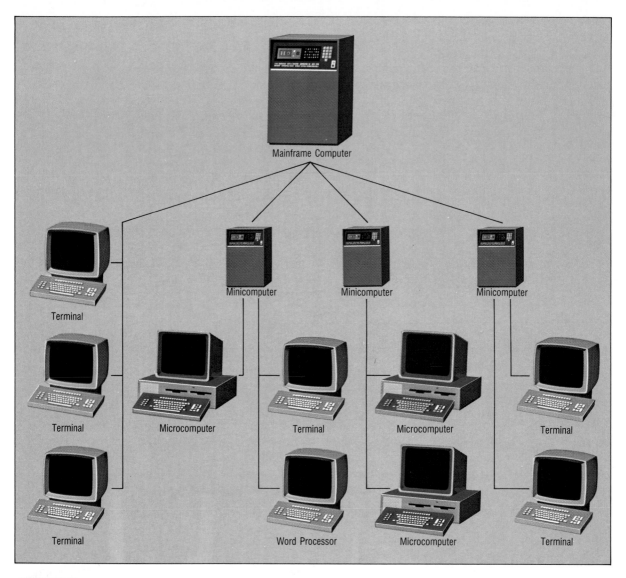

FIGURE 11-17
Hierarchical network

Point-to-point networks connect two or more devices with a single line. When only two CPUs or one CPU and one terminal are on the line, high-speed, high-volume communications can take place. Hospital bedside monitoring systems use this approach. When there are more than two devices, the line is called a *multi-drop line*. A multi-drop line set-up might be used in a sales office where several terminals are connected to a host computer at the corporate office.

The *star* configuration shows each computer in the network linked to a host which controls several peripheral devices such as high-speed printers and secondary storage devices. The *ring* arrangement connects several computers, but without a host or slave. Rings may or may not involve the sharing of common peripheral devices. If they do, as is illustrated in figure 11-16D, access to the peripherals is usually controlled by a small computer, which is associated with a central secondary storage unit.

Hierarchical networks look like the roots of a tree. There are several computing levels. *Distributed processing* is done using a hierarchical network. In distributed processing, we have access to the network via a terminal or a computer (typically a micro). That device is connected to a larger computer which may itself be connected to a still larger one. We do our computing on our "local" machine unless it is too limited. When necessary, the network provides access to the next level or the one above that. Figure 11-17 shows a hierarchical system.

Distributed processing also provides for sharing data among the computers in the network. The host computer may have a tremendous database. We can download some of these data from the host to our computer work station, as needed. *Downloading* means bringing data into a computer from another computer. Similarly, if the network protocols permit it, we can *upload* data; that is, we can send data from our computer to another.

In reality, few networks conform to the star, ring, point-to-point, or hierarchical forms exactly as illustrated here. Most networks are hybrids of these forms. Figure 11-18, for instance, shows the computer network of a manufacturing firm with its factory, main sales office, and corporate offices in Chicago and its sales offices on the East Coast and the West Coast.

One of the nation's largest banks, San Francisco-headquartered Bank of America, uses an elaborate distributed data processing system. Its network includes major operations centers in San Francisco and Los Angeles that are

FIGURE 11-18
Hybrid network

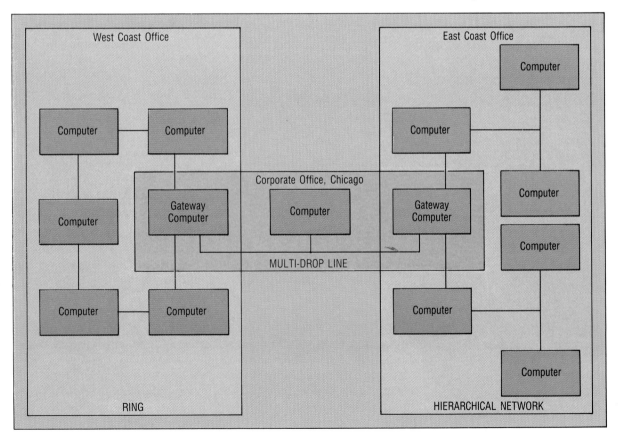

connected by leased and other lines to each branch office and automatic teller terminal. The system connects many computers with hundreds of phone lines. Terminals are assigned different priorities according to their functions. Thus, some terminals have instantaneous access to one of the main computers while other stations have lower priority.

DATA COMMUNICATION SERVICES

Government and private organizations offer an enormous breadth of services that cover all aspects of communications. Services that are currently available include electronic and voice mail, bibliographic information retrieval, teleconferencing, home banking, and electronic fund transfer to name a few. In the following pages, we will review these categories of service and look at some of the principal providers.

Electronic Mail

Electronic mail transmits and stores messages electronically. Electronic mail can be done on a local area network, over private lines, or over a value-added network. In the latter case, a third party, the VAN, becomes involved in the communication by storing messages and forwarding them to their destinations. Such a service is called a *store and forward* system, and it often involves the use of telephone equipment. To differentiate electronic mail from telephone conversation, the former is limited to messages sent digitally. After transmission, digital messages are stored in an *electronic mailbox* on the receiving computer until the recipient is ready to read them. Electronic messages can be read on a CRT, or they can be printed as hard copy.

The main advantage of electronic mail is speed. For instance, an insurance broker wrote a request for a policy and sent it to the home office. He had left out some important information, so the policy could not be issued. The home office tried to reach him by phone, but it took three days of "telephone tag" before they made contact. Meanwhile, the client went without insurance. Electronic mail would have solved the problem by allowing the revised policy language to be transmitted to and from the home office in a few hours or less.

Electronic mail also solves time difference problems. The Los Angeles office of a company can reach the New York office only between 9 a.m. and 2 p.m. Los Angeles time. The New York office can only reach Los Angeles from Noon until 5 p.m. New York time. With electronic mail, the L.A. office can send a written message at 4 p.m. It will be read at 9 the next morning in New York and a written response can be sent before the West Coast office opens for business. In situations in which action cannot be taken without written authorization, electronic mail does much to cut through red tape.

Electronic mail is not a new idea. It originated a century and a half ago when Samuel Morse invented the telegraph. Since then, electronic mail has expanded by using telephones via satellite, optical fiber, microwave, and coaxial cable and by using local area networks. In fact, we can expect the number of private electronic mail systems to increase as more and more local area networks are installed.

Computerized electronic mail was not developed until the 1960s, at which time it became available to users of large mainframe computers. In 1978, there were fewer than one-quarter million electronic mail terminals in the United States. The advent of the microcomputer and ready access to computing power broke the electronic mail market wide open. Studies show that over a million electronic mail terminals are in use today.[5]

Traditional Services

Traditional electronic mail services, which have been with us pretty much since the development of the telephone system, include telegrams, mailgrams, and telex/TWX. *Mailgrams* are telegrams that are sent to a recipient's local post office and then delivered by letter carrier. Mailgrams provide next-day delivery service at a reasonable cost. Telex/TWX uses the telephone system to transmit digital data which are typed out at the destination by a teletype machine.

Modern Services

Thanks to the computer's ability to produce digital information at enormous speed, other data communications techniques have been added to the traditional services mentioned. Examples of such services include E-Com, MCI Mail, and Western Union's Easylink.

E-Com is a pseudo-electronic mail system, which was developed by the U.S. Postal Service to facilitate mass mailing. Messages are transmitted to special post offices that print and mail the letters with guaranteed two-day delivery. A firm can arrange to send messages directly to the post office or can contract with a computer service bureau to do so.

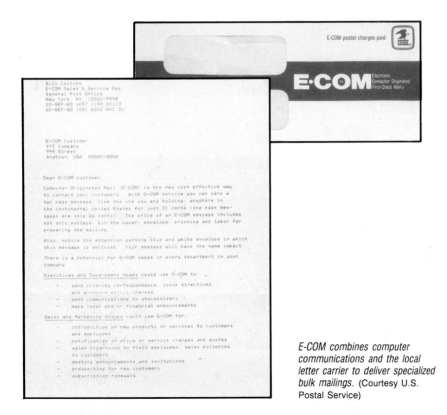

E-COM combines computer communications and the local letter carrier to deliver specialized bulk mailings. (Courtesy U.S. Postal Service)

Messages, which can be up to two pages long, can be sent in three categories: (1) *Single address messages* which have unique text going to each addressee; (2) *Common text messages* which have the same text going to several addressees; (3) *Text insert messages* which are sent to several addressees and which are essentially the same, except that unique information can be inserted into each message.

The Post Office claims that E-Com is a fast, economical, attention-getting alternative to standard, first-class mail. E-Com, however, has never made a profit, which suggests that business executives are not sold on its advantages.

Unlike E-Com, *MCI Mail* is a true electronic mail service. Customers can send mail to each other's electronic mailbox where it is held until the recipient disposes of it. No paper is involved, unless the recipient produces a hard copy of the electronic version. In addition, MCI will send letters to people who are not customers. Here's how it works. A client sends a letter to MCI electronically. MCI transmits it to a location near the destination, where it is printed and mailed to the addressee. Letters sent by MCI Mail may be printed on personal or company letterhead with the sender's signature. They arrive in bright orange envelopes which attract attention.

MCI provides four classes of service: (1) instant letters which are sent to electronic mailboxes; (2) MCI letters which are delivered by the post office; (3) overnight letters which are hand-delivered by noon of the following business day; and (4) four-hour letters which are hand-delivered within four hours in major cities. In addition, MCI Mail provides access to the Dow Jones News/Retrieval service which we describe later.

The following brief on-line session, between Gertrude Stein and MCI Mail, shows how electronic mail works. Gertrude wishes to determine if there are any messages awaiting her in her electronic mailbox. After making telephone connection, the CRT shows

```
Port: 27
Please enter your user name:
```

Gertrude can ignore the port. This tells how she is connected to the system and is useful if she has difficulty and must phone MCI Mail's Customer Serv-

FIGURE 11-19
Starting a session on MCI Mail

```
Port: 27

Please enter your user name: GSTEIN
Password: ????????          (Note: nothing displays
                            as you type here)
Welcome to MCI Mail!

    Your INBOX has 4 messages (1 PRIORITY, 1 RECEIPT)

You may enter:
SCAN        for a summary of your mail
READ        to READ Messages one by one
PRINT       to display messages nonstop
CREATE      to write an MCI letter
HELP        for assistance
EXIT        to leave MCI Mail

Your command:
```

FIGURE 11-21 Reading a letter

```
Your command: SCAN

You may enter:

INBOX          to SCAN your unread messages
OUTBOX         to SCAN messages you sent
DESK           to SCAN messages read before
DRAFT          to SCAN your DRAFT message
ALL            to SCAN ALL your messages
HELP           for assistance

Your command: INBOX
     4 messages in INBOX
No.    Posted          From              Subject          Size
1      JAN 27 15:23    R van Rijn        Portrait         244
                                         **PRIORITY
2      JAN 27 08:15    Al Steiglitz      Family Pictures  253
                                         **RECEIPT
3      JAN 27 10:29    S Roebuck         Paint            166
4      JAN 28 09:30    S. Postlethwaite  The Garden Club  2133
```

```
Your command: READ
Please enter scan numbers: 1
Date:     Mon January 27, 1986 3:23 pm EST          **PRIORITY
From:     Rem van Rijn/MCI ID: 244-9981
TO:       Gertrude Stein/MCI ID: 555-3449
Subject: Portrait
I am thrilled at the opportunity to paint your portrait. Per our discussion,
I recommend the rose-colored gown. I will plan to begin next Monday at
11:00 in the morning. Unless I hear otherwise, I will meet you in the
garden.
Regards, R
```

FIGURE 11-20 Scanning the mail

ice Department for assistance. First, she types her user name. Then the CRT requests a *password*. She must keep the password secret, so no one else can use her account. In fact, when Gert types it, the password doesn't even appear on the screen. Once she has entered the password, the screen appears as in figure 11-19.

This display tells her that there is one urgent (priority) letter, one that requires acknowledgement of receipt, and two others. Gertrude decides to find out what is in the mailbox. She types

        SCAN

and the results are shown in figure 11-20. Then she reads the priority letter (see figure 11-21). Having read van Rijn's letter, she decides to write him a letter using the CREATE command. She will send a copy to Arthur Teacher, president of the local art institute. This transaction is shown in figure 11-22. MCI Mail permits users to send the same letter to several people by just includ-

FIGURE 11-22
Sending a letter

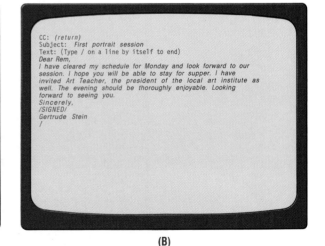

```
Your command: CREATE
TO:       RVANRIJN
There is more than one:
0  NOT IN THIS LIST
1       110-2322  Ralph van Rijn Livingstone, Inc. Westport, CN
2       244-9981  Rem van Rijn New Amsterdam, NY
Please enter the number: 2
TO: (return)
CC:       Arthur Teacher
          (Arthur Teacher not found; please enter address:)
          44433 Masters Circle
          New York, NY 10022
```

(A)

```
CC: (return)
Subject: First portrait session
Text: (Type / on a line by itself to end)
Dear Rem,
I have cleared my schedule for Monday and look forward to our
session. I hope you will be able to stay for supper. I have
invited Art Teacher, the president of the local art institute as
well. The evening should be thoroughly enjoyable. Looking
forward to seeing you.
Sincerely,
/SIGNED/
Gertrude Stein
/
```

(B)

ing their names after TO:. Each person receives a letter with only his or her name on it. Gertrude can also send any number of copies in the same way. At the bottom of the letter, she types

/SIGNED/

which signals MCI Mail to print a laser copy of her signature on the letter. Figure 11-23 shows the letter as it was delivered.

In many ways, Western Union's Easylink is like MCI Mail, except that it also includes two-way communication and direct communication between computers. Easylink is a worldwide system that gives its users two-way access to 1.5 million Telex machines in 154 countries of the world. As of 1985, there were over 100,000 users of the system.

By linking with the U.S. Post Office, Easylink is able to offer electronic access to mailgram, E-Com, telegram, and cablegram services. We can use Easylink, like MCI Mail, from any place where there is a computer: the office, home, or a hotel room, for instance. The Western Union service provides automatic electronic delivery of mail to a computer up to three times per day and will forward messages to other electronic mailboxes.

Easylink and other electronic mail services can be used in many ways. A factory manager, for example, can send quarterly reports to the corporate office. Salespeople can communicate with prospects, correspond with the sales

FIGURE 11-23
The printed copy

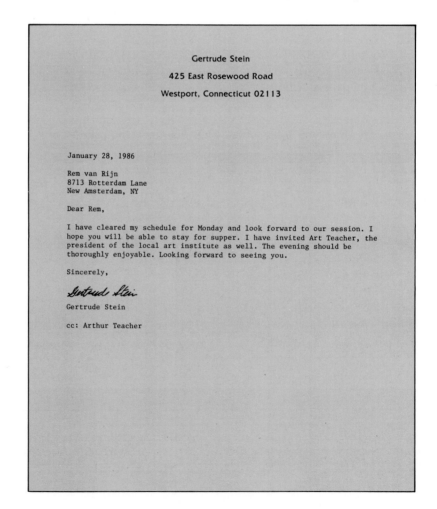

Gertrude Stein

425 East Rosewood Road

Westport, Connecticut 02113

January 28, 1986

Rem van Rijn
8713 Rotterdam Lane
New Amsterdam, NY

Dear Rem,

I have cleared my schedule for Monday and look forward to our session. I hope you will be able to stay for supper. I have invited Art Teacher, the president of the local art institute as well. The evening should be thoroughly enjoyable. Looking forward to seeing you.

Sincerely,

Gertrude Stein

Gertrude Stein

cc: Arthur Teacher

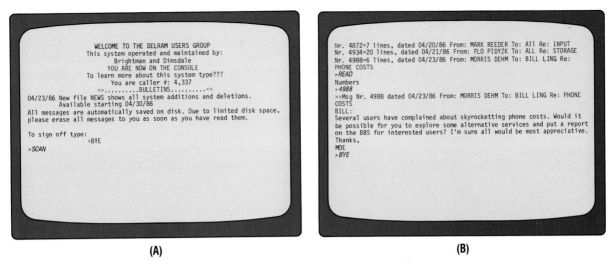

WELCOME TO THE DELRAM USERS GROUP
This system operated and maintained by:
Brightman and Dimsdale
YOU ARE NOW ON THE CONSOLE
To learn more about this system type???
You are caller #: 4,337
>>.........BULLETINS.........<<
04/23/86 New file NEWS shows all system additions and deletions.
Available starting 04/30/86
All messages are automatically saved on disk. Due to limited disk space,
please erase all messages to you as soon as you have read them.

To sign off type:
>BYE
>SCAN

Nr. 4872=7 lines, dated 04/20/86 From: MARK REEDER To: All Re: INPUT
Nr. 4934=20 lines, dated 04/21/86 From: FLO PIDYZK To: ALL Re: STORAGE
Nr. 4988=6 lines, dated 04/23/86 From: MORRIS DEHM To: BILL LING Re:
PHONE COSTS
>READ
Numbers
>4988
>>Msg Nr. 4988 dated 04/23/86 From: MORRIS DEHM To: BILL LING Re: PHONE
COSTS
BILL:
Several users have complained about skyrocketting phone costs. Would it
be possible for you to explore some alternative services and put a report
on the BBS for interested users? I'm sure all would be most appreciative.
Thanks,
MOE
>BYE

(A)	(B)

FIGURE 11-24
Using a bulletin board

manager, and process orders. All of this can be done from a hotel room, after sales calls have been made for the day. Travel agents can confirm reservations with hotels and airlines. A small business can send mailings to specialized lists of prospective customers. Writers can send articles to their editors and receive proof copy to be checked.

Virtually every profession can make use of an electronic mail service. In fact, several electronic mail systems specialize in serving specific industries. Photonet, which was described earlier, is one example. Another is REINET, a service developed by the National Association of Realtors and used by over 700 real estate offices throughout the country.

Bulletin Board Services

We introduced bulletin board services (BBSs) in Chapter Eight as a source of application software. A BBS can be considered a specialized electronic mail service. Bulletin boards are generally free services, which are offered by private individuals or computer equipment vendors.

The first BBS was developed in 1978 in Chicago to allow local computer users to communicate easily.[6] Today, most bulletin boards are aimed at a specific clientele such as Apple users, Pascal programmers, or WordStar users. BBSs typically provide a low-security electronic mail service. Many messages are provided for all users, others for specific ones, but there is no way to keep someone from reading another's mail.

Figure 11-24 shows a typical session on a computerized bulletin board service. Material in italics is our response. The rest was sent by the BBS system.

Voice Mail

Voice mail is a system in which a caller leaves a message for someone who is unable to come to the telephone. The message, which is sent in analog form, is converted to digital data and stored in the computer memory. This system has gained favor with those who feel the spoken word to be more effective for certain kinds of messages.

Other Techniques

In addition to voice mail, there are two other communications techniques that involve computer voice communications. The first is *speech synthesis* in which the computer generates human-like speech. This is used by many telephone companies for their information services. For example, we call 411 and an operator asks for our request. He or she types it into a computer terminal and the processor takes over, freeing the operator for the next call. The processor finds the required telephone number and instructs the speech synthesizer to "speak the number" to us. Many other applications of speech synthesis can be made as well, such as authorizing credit card purchases. In this case, a cashier sends credit card data by electronic mail and receives the response by voice. The entire transaction requires only a push-button phone at the point of sale.

Two-way voice mail requires computers that can recognize spoken words, a process called *speech recognition.* This is extremely difficult to do technically for several reasons. First, it requires tremendous amounts of memory. Second, although there are recognizable commonalities in the speech of all people, every human voice is different, and the computer must react accordingly. Third, virtually every language is ambiguous. The computer must decide which of several possible meanings the speaker intended. To date, speech recognition is available on a limited basis only.

Both speech synthesis and speech recognition represent exciting areas for future development.

Bibliographic Services

Bibliographic services, also known as *information utilities,* are libraries on disk. Unlike the public library, which may be located some distance away and open only a certain number of hours per week, bibliographic services are available virtually around the clock from any place where there is a computer with a modem. Through bibliographic services, hundreds of clients can use the same material at the same time; a big difference from the public library where materials are checked out, and thus rendered unusable to others.

This has obvious advantages, but reading a book or journal article on a CRT is hardly the most comfortable way. Instead, most clients use these services to find materials then have the services mail copies of the needed articles. Alternatively, users may have articles printed on their printers while they are on-line with the service. Users must balance speed of availability versus cost when deciding which alternative to take.

There are many information utilities that provide a broad range of services beyond bibliographic research. Many include electronic mail. Others offer electronic versions of current newspapers from around the world. Most information utilities make many different resources available to their clients.

Clients wishing to research a particular topic construct a *search strategy* which selects *key words* to be found in the text of various articles that are stored on the database. The client then uses the service to search through a specific database for articles that match all of the conditions described in the strategy. As is often the case, a client will need to examine several databases.

The following paragraphs describe a few of the major bibliographic services currently available. We will close this chapter with a discussion of search strategies and a research session conducted using The Source, one of the largest information utilities.

BRS and BRS/After Dark

BRS is an information utility maintaining about 70 databases in six categories: science and medicine; business and financial; reference; education; social sciences and humanities; and energy and environment. The service is aimed primarily at large users such as public libraries, universities, businesses, and professional offices. It is available 22 hours per day, seven days per week (the other two hours are used for maintenance and for adding information to the system). BRS/After Dark offers about half of the databases at a much lower cost but it is only available during "non-prime hours," from 6 p.m., users time, to 4 a.m., Eastern Standard Time.

Since BRS/After Dark was designed for the consumer instead of the information professional, it is easier to use than BRS. Because of this, it is more limited. For example, clients cannot order documents to be printed and mailed. They must get all their information on-line. BRS/After Dark, however, provides some services not available on BRS. These include an electronic mail program and a shop-at-home service.

Dialog

With over 200 databases, Dialog is one of the oldest and largest information utilities. Clients sign on to Dialog by direct connection or value-added networks such as Tymnet, Telenet, or Uninet. Dialog includes databases in the following categories:

- Business, industry, corporate
- Chemistry
- Medicine, biosciences
- Law, government, intellectual property
- Science, technology
- Energy, environment, agriculture
- Education, reference
- Humanities, social science
- People

It also provides non-bibliographic data from such sources as the *Electronic Yellow Pages* and files from the U.S. Bureau of Labor Statistics. Like BRS, Dialog is designed for large users and is available about 120 hours per week.

Dow Jones News/Retrieval

For over a century, Dow Jones (DJ) has been a principal purveyor of information to the business world through the *Wall Street Journal, Barron's,* and the *Dow Jones News Service,* or "ticker." Recently, DJ expanded into a business-oriented computerized information utility providing electronic access to current and historical business news, stock quotations, corporate data, and

The Dow Jones News/Retrieval Service provides financial news as well as individual stock quotations. (Courtesy Dow Jones & Company, Inc.)

even general news, weather, sports, and movie reviews. DJ also offers a computerized shopping service.

The Dow Jones information service is available 22 hours per day. While it is essentially a business-oriented system, Dow Jones News/Retrieval is becoming a more general information utility. It is the first utility with an electronic encyclopedia. It offers United Press International (UPI) news services and access to MCI Mail. In the early 1980s, DJ made a concerted effort to attract microcomputer users, making agreements with Apple, Tandy, and other producers. One of the first programs available for the IBM PC was software for the Dow Jones service.

NewsNet

NewsNet is a unique bibliographic service that provides over 200 newsletters in electronic form. The newsletters, which are also available by mail, can be read sooner when delivered via NewsNet. Furthermore, the NewsNet service includes automatic searching which puts all articles about any topic

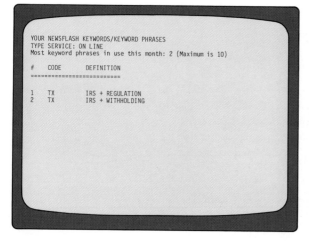

FIGURE 11-25
NewsFlash keywords

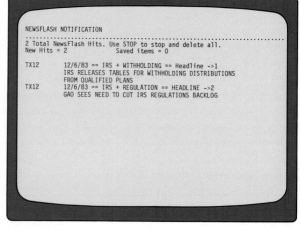

FIGURE 11-26
List of NewsFlash "hits"

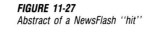

FIGURE 11-27
Abstract of a NewsFlash ''hit''

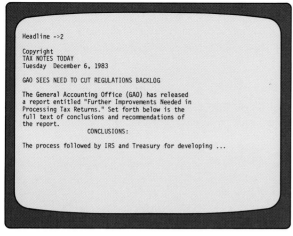

```
Headline ->2

Copyright
TAX NOTES TODAY
Tuesday  December 6, 1983

GAO SEES NEED TO CUT REGULATIONS BACKLOG

The General Accounting Office (GAO) has released
a report entitled "Further Improvements Needed in
Processing Tax Returns." Set forth below is the
full text of conclusions and recommendations of
the report.
                  CONCLUSIONS:

The process followed by IRS and Treasury for developing ...
```

the user specifies in an electronic mailbox. This is a tremendous time-saver for the busy executive. The utility does this on a daily basis. This service, called NewsFlash, is essentially an electronic clipping service which is unique to the industry. The user can run the same search hourly for even quicker updates.

Figures 11-25 through 11-27 show one such daily search. On the first screen (figure 11-25), we see a report of the topics we wish to find. The next screen (figure 11-26) shows the results of the latest search. The last screen (figure 11-27) shows an abstract of one of the "hits." We can see the entire article if we wish or have the item printed for further work.

Using the same search strategy, we can request NewsNet to find all stories about our choice of topics, either from the entire database or between any two dates. The results of this search are available to us virtually instantaneously.

The Source

The Source is one of the largest information utilities. It is a general interest service used by tens of thousands of subscribers who have access to over 800 databases. It is probably the most popular information utility among personal computer users.

THE SOURCE MAIN MENU

1. NEWS AND REFERENCE RESOURCES
2. BUSINESS/FINANCIAL REPORTS
3. CATALOGUE SHOPPING
4. HOME AND LEISURE
5. EDUCATION AND CAREER
6. MAIL AND COMMUNICATIONS
7. CREATING AND COMPUTING

ENTER ITEM NUMBER OR HELP

The Source can be used with a series of menus or by typing in commands to take users directly to the services they wish. New users often prefer to use the main menu, which provides easy and quick guidance to the many services of The Source.(Courtesy The Source)

The Source provides a full range of services that include shopping services, games, on-line conferencing (more about this later), bibliographic services, news, and computer programming. The services are grouped into six categories:

- Business and financial
- Communications
- Consumer services
- Games
- News and sports
- Travel services

Teleconferencing

When a group of people wishes to meet without all coming to the same location, they can do so by *teleconferencing*. The group may be as small as two or as large as several hundred. Typically, a teleconference involves from five to forty people. There may be several small clusters of people, say a group in Los Angeles, another in Chicago, and a third in New York; each cluster meeting at a convenient site. On the other hand, every conferee might be alone at home.

Teleconferencing is done electronically, by voice over radio or telephone conference call, by one-way or two-way television, or by computer. We will limit our discussion to computerized teleconferencing, also known as *computerized conferencing*, or *CC*.

CC started in 1975 with the development by Murray Turoff of the *Electronic Information Exchange System (EIES)*. A forerunner of this system was used during Richard Nixon's presidency to administer a wage and price freeze declared to control inflation. Teleconferencing is now readily available to information consumers via information utilities such as The Source.

CC is somewhat like a sophisticated electronic bulletin board in that participants send messages to a central file for other participants to read. While a BBS is accessible to anyone with a computer, a modem, and the appropriate software, a CC has three levels of control. A conference can be open to everyone (a public conference), it can be open only to a group of people given a specific password (a closed conference), or it can be limited, so that anyone can read the proceedings, but only participants can add comments to the messages (read-only conference).

Some teleconferencing systems allow participants to vote on issues, to prepare reports to send to other participants (a word processor is built in), to see who is currently participating in a conference, and to send one participant a message unseen by other participants.

Some teleconferences continue for years. Participants often develop a tremendous camaraderie even though they never see or hear one another. That's both good and bad. Ongoing CCs allow people to keep up to date whereas face-to-face conferences generally provide information that is six months to one year old. People cannot form judgements based on a participant's appearance. On the other hand, such face-to-face communication techniques as body language and voice inflection cannot come into play.

Teleconferencing is relatively inexpensive. There are no travel costs and time away from the office for conference attendance is kept to a minimum. On the other hand, many executives find that an occasional trip refreshes them and yields important contacts.

Teleconferencing has both detractors and advocates. Although ARCO has employed teleconferencing for many years, its executives often report that it does not always work out so well. On the other hand, one enthusiast explains that

> ...most important of all, (teleconferencing) makes you a part of a thriving electronic community—filled with ideas and personalities—that is probably unlike anything you have ever experienced before. For many people, computerized conferencing is one of the best reasons for buying a personal computer in the first place.[7]

Electronic Banking and Electronic Fund Transfer

One of the newest services offered by many banks, *electronic banking*, involves banking with either your own computer or with an automatic teller terminal.

Because they are generally located in the bank itself, automatic tellers may not appear to involve communications. In fact, they are usually connected to bank computers by private lines. Typical of automatic teller systems is Bank of America's Versateller. This system permits customers to withdraw up to $200 from checking or savings accounts by entering appropriate passwords. The Versateller also permits automatic deposits, payments to loan and credit card accounts, transfer of funds between accounts, and it provides information about account balances. Automatic teller machines work to the advantage of banks and their customers. Banks save money because there is less clerical work when the customer makes his or her own computer entries, and customers like the availability of banking services around the clock.

Banking by computer, often called *home banking*, lets customers complete

Automatic teller machines are generally linked to computers at a central location rather than to computers at branch offices. (Courtesy Bank of America NT & SA)

Home banking systems allow users to pay bills and maintain control over their accounts without leaving the house. (Courtesy Bank of America NT & SA)

most banking transactions without going to the bank. Customers can check their account balances and review checks that have cleared. They can find out interest rates on certificates of deposit. They can transfer funds among various accounts at the same bank, for instance, from a savings account to a checking account.

Customers can also order bills to be paid automatically on a certain day. The customer can establish a standing order to pay a particular company's bill on the same day each month. The bill can be paid in part or in full. He or she can command the bank computer to pay Master Card $25 on July 23 and American Express $113 on July 30.

Because home banking is a relatively new service, we can expect a number of additional services to be added as more banks embrace the idea. Some of the services we expect to see are checkbook balancing and home budgeting programs; computerized purchase of savings certificates, travelers checks, and securities; credit card monitoring; and on-line loan application.

Most transactions today do not involve the exchange of currency. Payment is made through the credit or checking systems. These systems keep track of monetary balances as records of numbers. From this standpoint, money today amounts mostly to data that can be translated electronically. This is the essence of *electronic fund transfer,* or *EFT.* Here's how it works.

The Chicago Manufacturing Company orders $1 million worth of parts from the Phoenix Fortecye Factory. Phoenix will discount the price five percent if payment is made immediately, in advance. To take the $50,000 discount, the Chicago firm contacts its bank which transfers the money electronically via the Federal Reserve Bank's computerized network centered in Culpeper, Virginia. The funds are deposited in the Fortecye Factory's bank account in a matter of minutes.

Banks throughout the country are trying to persuade their customers to embrace EFT for two reasons. First, it saves substantially on clerical costs since it reduces paperwork. Second, the bank has more access to funds because float is eliminated. The term *float* refers to the value of uncleared financial transactions outstanding at any time. By decreasing float one day for every transaction in the U.S., banks and other businesses would have $66 billion per year in additional funds for short term investments. This would generate several billion dollars in additional interest income each year.[8] There is little wonder that financial institutions are promoting EFT.

Each bibliographic service organizes its search patterns a little differently. Perhaps one uses the word "and," while another uses " + " to mean the same thing. Regardless of the specific commands, all search techniques are based on Boolean algebra, a method of combining sets that was developed by George Boole in the mid-19th century. To see how it works, let's start by considering a database as a *set* of related documents. We can define a *subset* as all documents that have some common characteristic, for instance, all documents about the Internal Revenue Service.

We begin our search by defining all terms that are important to our research. These terms are called *descriptors*. Each of them identifies one subset. Usually, the search program will report the number of documents in a subset, as follows:

```
1. INTERNAL REVENUE SERVICE
      2173 DOCUMENTS
2. TAX
      1004 DOCUMENTS
3. TAXATION
      693 DOCUMENTS
```

There is probably a lot of overlap in the articles we have found. This situation is shown in figure 11-28.

We can combine these subsets by using the first Boolean operator, OR:

```
4. 1 OR 2 OR 3
      2741 DOCUMENTS
```

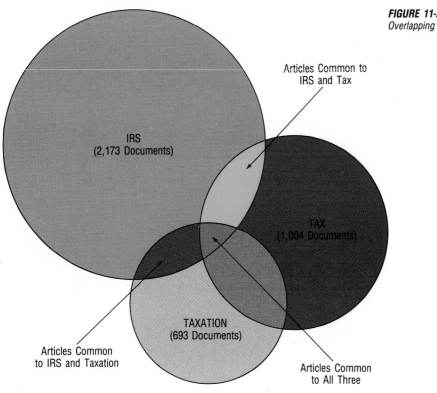

FIGURE 11-28
Overlapping subsets of a database

Articles Common to
IRS and Tax

IRS
(2,173 Documents)

TAX
(1,004 Documents)

TAXATION
(693 Documents)

Articles Common
to IRS and Taxation

Articles Common
to All Three

IRS or
TAX or
TAXATION
(2,741 Documents)

FIGURE 11-29
Combining subsets with "OR"

The new subset, number 4, includes all articles containing at least one of the three descriptors. Inasmuch as several of the documents include two or three of the descriptors, the number of documents in the combined subset will be less than the sum of the numbers of the first three subsets; that is, no article is counted more than once. This is shown in figure 11-29.

Since 2741 is a lot of documents to review, we probably should narrow our field. Perhaps we are interested in investment credits. Let's define a new subset.

> **5. INVESTMENT CREDIT**
> **689 DOCUMENTS**

Because investment credit might deal with taxation or with taking out a loan, we must link taxation with this subset. The Boolean operator *AND* will do this for us.

> **6. 4 AND 5**
> **399 DOCUMENTS**

Figure 11-30 shows that AND means "both." Documents in subset 6 include both the term *investment credit* and one of the taxation descriptors.

There are still too many documents to review. We need to narrow the field further. Not being interested in articles about real estate, let's eliminate the documents that deal with that subject.

> **7. 6 AND NOT REAL ESTATE**
> **103 DOCUMENTS**

NOT is the third Boolean operator. It takes all documents that do not include the phrase "real estate." Subset 7 includes taxation articles about the investment credit for everything except real estate.

Some searching services have additional operators that are not Boolean but function in the same fashion. In particular, these are used to limit the publication dates of articles selected. Perhaps we are only interested in articles about investment credit published during Jimmy Carter's presidency. We might request:

```
8.  7 BETWEEN JAN 20 1977 AND JAN 19 1981
    43 DOCUMENTS
```

or we might just want the most current information, having completed the same search a week ago:

```
9.  7 LAST 5
    5 DOCUMENTS
```

This will provide the five most recent documents in subset 7.

When we have finally narrowed our search sufficiently, we must determine what information we have found. Most data bases provide three options.

```
10.   TITLE 9
```

will provide a list of titles of subset 9.

```
11.  ABSTRACT 9
```

will provide the abstracts and bibliographic data about the five documents in subset 9.

```
12.  DOCUMENT 9
```

will provide a copy of each article in subset 9.

Because information utilities charge by the minute or the amount of information we use, it is important to plan carefully before going on line. It is also a good idea to look at titles before requesting abstracts and to look at abstracts before requesting full texts of articles. It is also important to know all of the

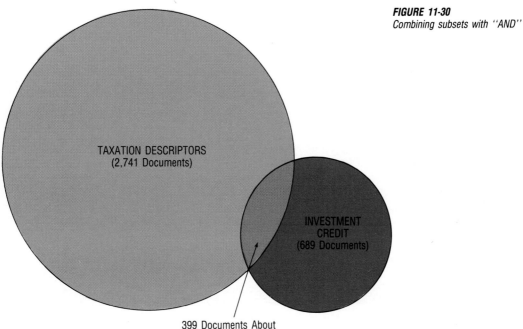

FIGURE 11-30
Combining subsets with "AND"

TAXATION DESCRIPTORS
(2,741 Documents)

INVESTMENT
CREDIT
(689 Documents)

399 Documents About
Both Taxation and Investment Credit

synonyms of a word before beginning to search. For instance, we might find information about cancer by using "cancer," "carcinogen," "oncology," or several other terms.

Information utilities can provide an incredible wealth of information but only if we are organized when we use them and only if we design our searches so they are neither too broad nor too focused.

USING DATA COMMUNICATION TO GATHER INFORMATION

Raymond Gunn is a regional sales manager for the Space Age Injection Molding Company, a firm that produces plastic products for home workshops. In the normal course of each working day, Ray allows an hour to work with The Source. Normally, he checks his electronic mailbox, sends letters to his sales force and other regional managers, and reads the business news.

Signing on to The Source

Ray signs on to The Source by booting ASCII Express "The Professional" on his Apple II. ASCII Express is a communications application program. Then he directs the program to dial The Source using the Uninet VAN the phone number of which is 555-3309.

Figure 11-31 shows the sign-on procedure which is a three-step process. After dialing and connecting, he types

RETURN.RETURN

This doesn't show on the screen, but it signals the VAN that he wants to make contact. After its response, he types

S14

which tells the VAN to connect him to The Source. Again he receives a response. Then he enters his identification number and password:

ID MKT058 BDJMRW

and receives a welcome message.

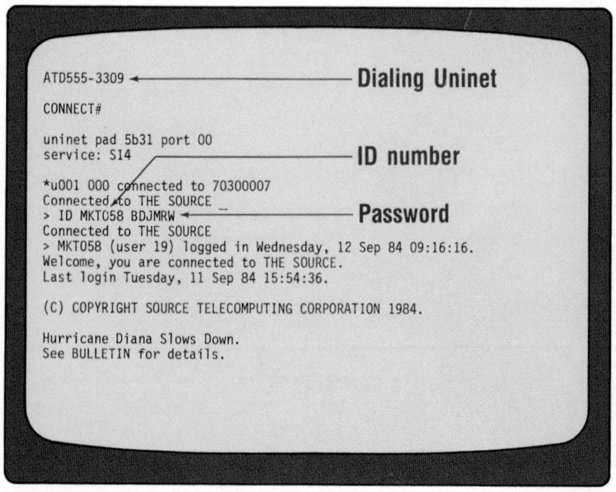

FIGURE 11-31
Sign-on procedure for The Source

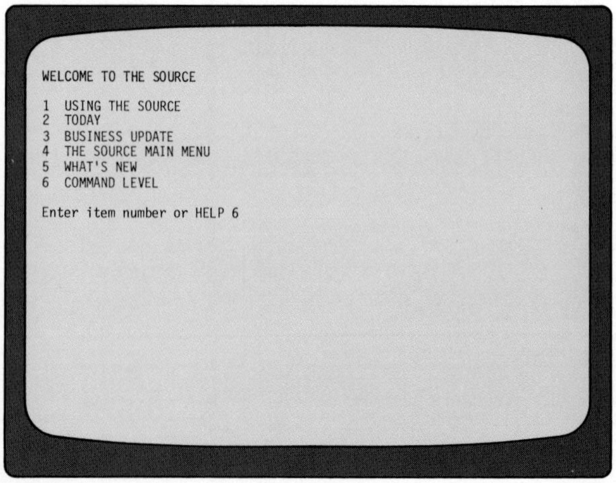

FIGURE 11-32
The Source entry menu

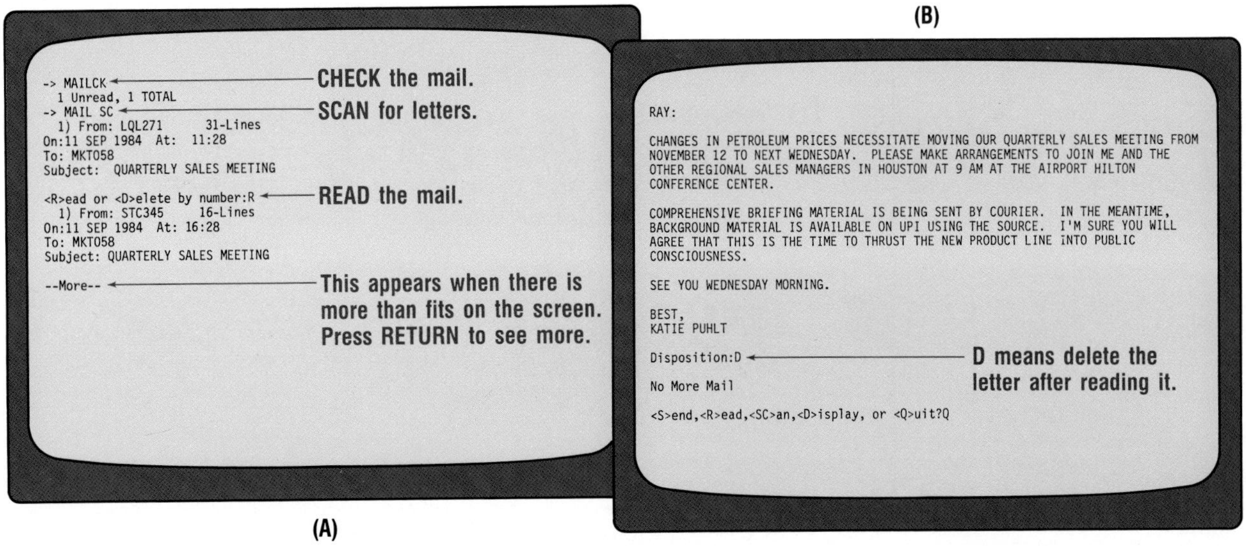

(B)

```
-> MAILCK ←─────────────────        CHECK the mail.
   1 Unread, 1 TOTAL
-> MAIL SC ←────────────────        SCAN for letters.
   1) From: LQL271      31-Lines
On:11 SEP 1984  At:  11:28
To: MKTO58
Subject:  QUARTERLY SALES MEETING

<R>ead or <D>elete by number:R ←    READ the mail.
   1) From: STC345      16-Lines
On:11 SEP 1984  At: 16:28
To: MKTO58
Subject: QUARTERLY SALES MEETING

--More-- ←──────────────────        This appears when there is
                                    more than fits on the screen.
                                    Press RETURN to see more.
```

```
RAY:

CHANGES IN PETROLEUM PRICES NECESSITATE MOVING OUR QUARTERLY SALES MEETING FROM
NOVEMBER 12 TO NEXT WEDNESDAY.  PLEASE MAKE ARRANGEMENTS TO JOIN ME AND THE
OTHER REGIONAL SALES MANAGERS IN HOUSTON AT 9 AM AT THE AIRPORT HILTON
CONFERENCE CENTER.

COMPREHENSIVE BRIEFING MATERIAL IS BEING SENT BY COURIER.  IN THE MEANTIME,
BACKGROUND MATERIAL IS AVAILABLE ON UPI USING THE SOURCE.  I'M SURE YOU WILL
AGREE THAT THIS IS THE TIME TO THRUST THE NEW PRODUCT LINE INTO PUBLIC
CONSCIOUSNESS.

SEE YOU WEDNESDAY MORNING.

BEST,
KATIE PUHLT

Disposition:D ←──────────           D means delete the
                                    letter after reading it.
No More Mail

<S>end,<R>ead,<SC>an,<D>isplay, or <Q>uit?Q
```

(A)

FIGURE 11-33
Receiving electronic mail

Ray is next presented with The Source main menu. Six choices are presented. Ray selects COMMAND LEVEL by entering 6 (see figure 11-32) which gives him access to all of The Source's services.

Reading the Mail

As is his daily habit, Ray Gunn starts the session by checking the mail. He enters

MAILCK

when he sees the system prompt, −>. He is told that there is one letter that he has not yet read. Although The Source will allow him to store his mail, it charges for the service, so he makes printed copies of the letters he wants to keep.

Ray decides to scan his mail. He enters

MAIL SC

at the next prompt. He is told there is a letter from account LQL271. He recognizes that number as belonging to Kathryn Puhlt, the national sales manager. He reads the letter, then deletes it, figure 11-33. Ms. Puhlt has asked Ray Gunn to come to Houston.

Selecting a Flight to Houston

Now Gunn must make arrangements to fly to Houston. He starts by checking on flight information. The Source includes information about scheduled domestic and international air travel. When prompted, Ray enters

AIRSCHED-D

Ray makes a note of the flights, figure 11-34, checks on return flights, and continues about his business. He will call his travel agent later to make the reservation. Next Ray must decide on lodgings. He'd like to find a top quality hotel near the airport.

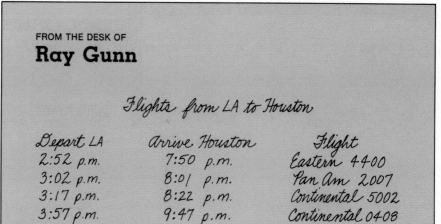

FROM THE DESK OF
Ray Gunn

Flights from LA to Houston

Depart LA	Arrive Houston	Flight
2:52 p.m.	7:50 p.m.	Eastern 4400
3:02 p.m.	8:01 p.m.	Pan Am 2007
3:17 p.m.	8:22 p.m.	Continental 5002
3:57 p.m.	9:47 p.m.	Continental 0408

FIGURE 11-34
Selecting a flight

Finding Lodging for the Trip

After entering

    QUIT

to get out of the flight schedule service, he enters

    USROOM

to check on accommodations through the Mobil Travel Guide. He is asked for the city and enters

    HOUSTON,TX

to which the Source responds with 57 entries. Ray enters

    F AIRPORT

to find listings that include the word *airport*. There are 25 of them. Since he stays in only the best places, he next enters

    F *

and The Source displays

    13 accommodation(s) with "AIRPORT", "*"**

which tells him that there are 13 hotels near the airport with ratings of three stars or better. Since Ray is a nonsmoker, he decides to find a hotel with rooms for nonsmokers. He enters

    F SMOK

and is informed that there is one accommodation rated with at least three stars, located near the airport that has rooms for nonsmokers. All of these transactions are shown in figure 11-35.

Ray wants to find out more about this ideal room so he enters

    P ALL

requesting The Source to print all the entries (only one) that meet the three criteria. The result is shown in figure 11-36. Ray notes the hotel and quits this service.

```
-> USROOM

Welcome to the Mobil Travel Guide, your window into fine lodging.

Enter "help" for further instructions.

City,State (for example, CHICAGO,IL):HOUSTON,TX

  57 accommodation(s) found in Houston, TX.   57 total.
City,State or <cr> to search:

  57 accommodation(s).
```

(A)

```
Select <S>can, <F>ind, <B>ackup, <P>rint,
<R>estart or <H>elp for more instructions:F AIRPORT
Searching...

  25 accommodation(s) with "AIRPORT".

Select <S>can, <F>ind, <B>ackup, <P>rint,
<R>estart or <H>elp for more instructions:  25 accommodation(s) with "AIRPORT".

Select <S>can, <F>ind, <B>ackup, <P>rint,
<R>estart or <H>elp for more instructions:F ***
Searching...

  13 accommodation(s) with "AIRPORT", "***".

Select <S>can, <F>ind, <B>ackup, <P>rint,
<R>estart or <H>elp for more instructions:F SMOK
Searching...

  1 accommodation(s) with "AIRPORT", "***", "SMOK".
```

FIGURE 11-35
Finding a room to meet Ray's needs

Reading the News

Having found all he needs about getting to Houston and staying there, Gunn is ready to check the news for background information. He signs on to UPI Datanews by entering

UPI

Ray notices the message

Type HELP or QUIT at any time.

He knows that he can get help with this service or any other whenever he needs it. He also knows that he can stop using a service very easily.

He is asked for the scope of news—national, regional, or state. He responds with

N

for national news. Then he is given the choice of general, business, sports, or miscellaneous news. He chooses business news by entering

B

FIGURE 11-36
A hotel listing

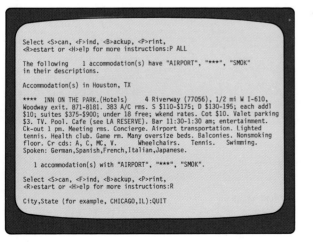

```
Select <S>can, <F>ind, <B>ackup, <P>rint,
<R>estart or <H>elp for more instructions:P ALL

The following    1 accommodation(s) have "AIRPORT", "***", "SMOK"
in their descriptions.

Accommodation(s) in Houston, TX

**** INN ON THE PARK.(Hotels)     4 Riverway (77056), 1/2 mi W I-610,
Woodway exit. 871-8181. 383 A/C rms. S $110-$175; D $130-195; each addl
$10; suites $375-$900; under 18 free; wkend rates. Cot $10. Valet parking
$3. TV. Pool. Cafe (see LA RESERVE). Bar 11:30-1:30 am; entertainment.
Ck-out 1 pm. Meeting rms. Concierge. Airport transportation. Lighted
tennis. Health club. Game rm. Many oversize beds. Balconies. Nonsmoking
floor. Cr cds: A, C, MC, V.      Wheelchairs.   Tennis.   Swimming.
Spoken: German,Spanish,French,Italian,Japanese.

  1 accommodation(s) with "AIRPORT", "***", "SMOK".

Select <S>can, <F>ind, <B>ackup, <P>rint,
<R>estart or <H>elp for more instructions:R

City,State (for example, CHICAGO,IL):QUIT
```

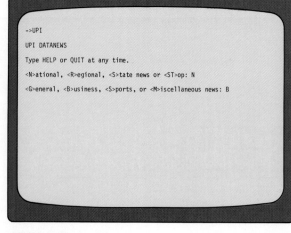

FIGURE 11-37
Beginning a news search

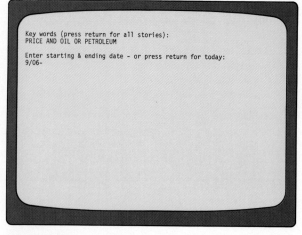

FIGURE 11-38
Specifying search characteristics

These responses put Ray into a database of news stories about business at the national level. They include the day's news as well as stories from the previous six days. These transactions are shown in figure 11-37.

There are hundreds of stories entered under national business each week. Like so many Source subscribers, Ray doesn't have time to read them all. So UPI Datanews provides limited Boolean searching capabilities. Users can search for articles containing up to three key words. Any words may be used and they may be connected by the conjunctions AND and/or OR (see figure 11-38). Ray wants stories about prices of oil products, so he enters

PRICE AND OIL OR PETROLEUM

when The Source prompts him with

Key Words (press return for all stories):

The Source also gives Gunn the option of selecting dates on which stories were entered. He can pick a first date and get all of the stories since then, a range of dates or any single date within the seven-day limitation of the service.

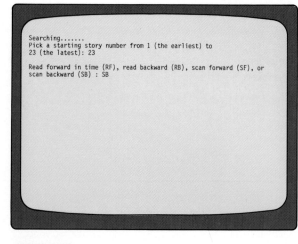

FIGURE 11-39
Viewing what's been found

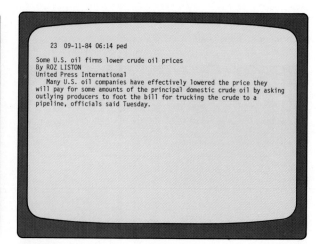

FIGURE 11-40
The most recent article

Ray decides to review all of the week's stories even though he's read many of them before. To the prompt

> Enter starting & ending date - or press return for today:

he responds

> 09/06-

The program begins the search.

Twenty-three "hits" have been made. The Source lets Ray select a starting point within that list (it is in order of date and time of story). Then he can read forward or backward in time from that point or scan in either direction. If he chooses to read, The Source will present Ray with the entire text of each article selected. If he decides to scan, Ray is shown headlines and first sentences. In figure 11-39, Ray decides to start with the latest article and scan backwards.

The first article he scans is dated September 6 (see figure 11-40). It discusses the price of crude oil. He makes note of that. He will want to read the entire article later. Other articles like number five (shown in figure 11-41) don't appear relevant. Even so, Gunn knows that the words *price* and either *oil* or *petroleum* appear somewhere in the article.

After he has scanned all 23 articles, Ray is presented the menu in figure 11-42. If he hadn't remembered what the letters stood for, he could have entered

> HELP

Instead, he enters

> G 23

This means he wants to read story 23. The Source presents the article in its entirety. Figure 11-43 shows the first few lines of the article.

When Gunn is finished with UPI Datanews, he types

> QUIT

and he is again able to select any Source service he needs.

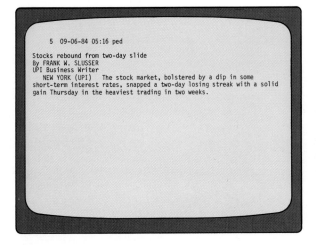

```
    5  09-06-84 05:16 ped

Stocks rebound from two-day slide
By FRANK W. SLUSSER
UPI Business Writer
    NEW YORK (UPI)   The stock market, bolstered by a dip in some
short-term interest rates, snapped a two-day losing streak with a solid
gain Thursday in the heaviest trading in two weeks.
```

FIGURE 11-41
Some articles don't seem to fit

```
    1  09-06-84 12:06 ped

    CHICAGO (UPI)   Grain and soybean futures were mixed to mostly
lower at midmorning Thursday on the Chicago Board of Trade.

We are on story 1.
Type R, S, N, B, or G and a Story Number: G 23
```

FIGURE 11-42
The last article, continuing the search

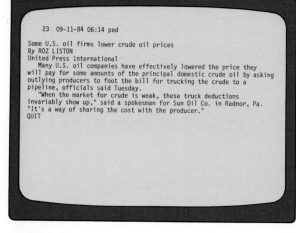

FIGURE 11-43
Articles are available in their entirety

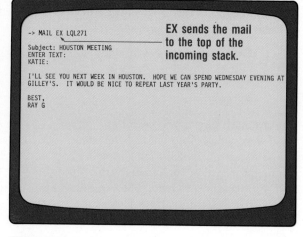

FIGURE 11-44
Sending electronic mail

Mailing a Letter

Having finished all he needs to do on The Source, Ray decides to send Katie Puhlt a letter so she knows he has received her communication. He enters

```
MAIL EX LQL271
```

The computer responds

```
Subject:
```

He types

```
HOUSTON MEETING
```

and is given the opportunity to type his letter. The entire letter is shown in figure 11-44. The letter as Katie received it is shown in figure 11-45.

FIGURE 11-45
Receiving express mail

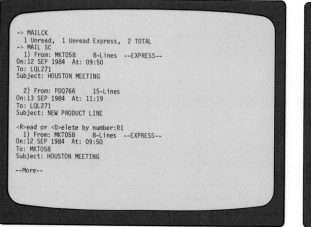

(A)

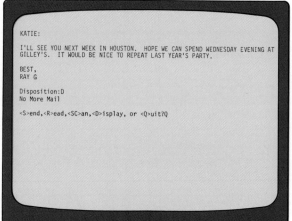

(B)

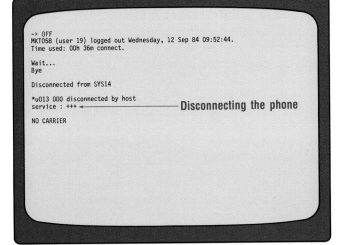

```
-> OFF
MKT058 (user 19) logged out Wednesday, 12 Sep 84 09:52:44.
Time used: 00h 36m connect.

Wait...
Bye

Disconnected from SYS14

*u013 000 disconnected by host
service : +++ ◄─────────────── Disconnecting the phone

NO CARRIER
```

FIGURE 11-46
Signing off

Signing Off The Source

At this point, Ray has finished and signs off from The Source. The sign-off procedure, shown in figure 11-46, indicates that Gunn spent 36 minutes to accomplish all that we've seen. Ray believes, as do his colleagues, that using The Source saves many hours of work and provides information that is otherwise very hard to acquire. He's so sold on The Source that he carries a lap computer when he travels so that he can use the electronic mail and have up-to-the-minute news.

SUMMARY

Communications is one of the fastest growing aspects of the information age. Computers are connected directly by *hard-wire* or *indirectly* through the telephone system. Computers that are connected by hard-wire and are close together form a *local area network*, or *LAN*, and use standard transmission *protocols* such as Ethernet. Computers that are connected by telephone may use *land lines*, *microwave*, or *satellite* links. Connections may be made by *private*, or *leased*, *lines* but more often they are made through *value-added networks* (*VANs*) such as Tymnet, Telenet, Dialnet, or Uninet.

Computers are connected to the telephone system by *modems* which turn *digital* information into the *analog* signals required for voice communication. Before entering the modem, data that move in *parallel* inside the computer are converted to *serial* signals and are outputted through an RS-232 peripheral device. In order to increase the amount of information transmitted, signals are often *multiplexed*, or *concentrated*. In order to increase computing power, special minicomputers called *front-end processors* collect and feed communicated data to mainframe computers.

Computers are used to provide numerous communication services. Among them are *electronic mail*, the sending of text and graphic data by computer; *voice mail*, the storage of voice messages in digital form; *bibliographic searching*, the gathering of information from an electronic library; and *home banking* and *electronic fund transfer* (*EFT*), the movement of money by electronic means.

We can expect great growth in the applications of computer communications, not only in the areas outlined in this chapter but in many other aspects of society, such as public safety, industrial control, and entertainment. Communications will become more important as the three foci of technological development, inflation, and the energy crisis expand.

KEY TERMS

baud rate	front-end processor	multiplex
common carrier	full duplex	protocol
data communication	gateway computer	speech recognition
demodulate	geosynchronous orbit	speech synthesis
demultiplex	half duplex	store and forward
distributed processing	hard-wired	switched line
download	hierarchical network	telecommunications
electronic fund	information utility	teleconference
transfer (EFT)	leased line	terminal controller
electronic mail	local area network (LAN)	upload
fiber optics transmission	modem	value-added network
file server	modulate	voice mail

REVIEW QUESTIONS

1. What part does the telephone play in the communication model shown in figure 11-1?
2. How is a VAN different from a common carrier?
3. Computer signals are digital, while telephone signals are _____. The _____ is the equipment used to make the signals compatible.
4. Is it better to use hard-wire or telephone connections when maximum transmission rates are important?
5. Computers move data internally in parallel, but data is moved in _____ between computers.
6. Sending several messages on one telephone line is the job of the _____.
7. Private, or leased, lines are not economical unless they are used at least _____ hours per day.
8. LANs can be constructed as rings, _____, _____, and _____.
9. What is the primary advantage of electronic mail?
10. What is the major difference between bulletin boards and teleconferences?
11. _____, _____, and _____ are the Boolean operators we use to develop search strategies.
12. _____ is an information utility that provides stock quotations.
13. _____ is an information utility that provides automatic daily searches.
14. _____ is the largest and most popular information utility among personal computer users.
15. Name one advantage for the bank and one for the customer of home banking.

THOUGHT QUESTIONS

1. Discuss the implications for data communication of government regulation of AT&T.
2. Explain the advantages and disadvantages of electronic mail.
3. Develop a search strategy for research about data communication hardware.

(Courtesy Hewlett-Packard Inc.)

Return of the Cottage Industries?

By 1990, it is predicted that nearly 40 percent of the American work force will be in the information industry and that one out of every five of those will be working at home.[9] Technically speaking, that makes a lot of sense. It's a whole lot easier to transport information from the workplace to the worker's home than it is to carry the worker from home to the workplace.

Countless millions of hours are wasted every working day as employees commute from home to workplace. If the average worker spends 30 minutes getting properly dressed, traveling to work, finding a parking place, entering the building, greeting coworkers, and preparing for the day's labors, then more than 10 percent of the worker's effort for the day is spent in commuting activity.* For the suburbanite manager or office worker, the amount of time spent on the road often exceeds two hours per day.

Telecommuting, the process of transporting information to the worker rather than vice-versa, requires that the worker have, at home, a computer or terminal and communications equipment to download information from the employer's data banks and upload the fruits of the employee's labors back to the office. Because telecommuting converts nonproductive commuting time to productive working time, it promises enormous benefits to both employer and employee.

By January of 1984, some 200 U.S. organizations had been experimenting with telecommuting. Blue Cross and Blue Shield of South Carolina found home-based clerical employees to be 50 percent more productive than office workers. Control Data's alternative work site program yielded productivity gains of 35 percent. Telecommuting also helps employers tap new sources of workers. Joseph Wynn,

*That's eight hours of work plus one hour of travel, round trip, for a total of nine. Of the nine, the one spent for travel counts for 11.1 percent.

a paraplegic who cannot travel to work, earns $1,100 per month as a word processing operator for American Express in New York City, a considerable difference from his $312 monthly Social Security check—not to mention the psychic benefit of being productively employed.[10]

California set aside $1.7 million for an experimental program to have 200 state employees work at home during 1985. In California's private sector, some 25,000 workers were already telecommuting by the start of that year. By 1990, estimates the University of Southern California's Center of Futures Research, nearly 10 million people will be working at home.[11] Other estimates reach as high as 18 million.

The self-employed, too, are quick to point out the advantages of working at home using computing and communications equipment. Dick and Jill Miller, founders of Miller Micro Services in Natick, Massachusetts, report that "We want to be available during extended hours to our customers. Also, most creative work is not done eight to five, but around the clock." Since establishing their business, the Millers have added twelve employees, all of whom telecommute.[12] Author Steven Roberts, who bicycles about the U.S. writing articles for USA Today on a battery-operated portable computer reports that "Some people don't work well in an office— they feel chained to their desks...Now it's clear that with all of these new technologies that provide portable computing horsepower, data communication can be used to run a business on the road."[13]

Some have likened the electronic office at home to cottage industries that arose during the early part of the industrial revolution. In those days, employers provided workers with sewing machines or other tools and paid them on a piece-rate basis, which led to accusations of exploitation and worker abuse. So too, does telecommuting draw its detractors. Labor leaders have expressed a strong distaste for the idea: "Put out of your mind the idea that the sewing machine is somehow different from a computer terminal," cautioned Donald Elisburg, Assistant Labor Secretary during the Carter Administration. In October of 1983, the AFL-CIO passed a resolution that called for a ban on computer home work, except for the disabled.[14]

Telecommuting can also be criticized on less ideological bases. Managers express discomfort with the idea of supervising workers who are not physically on the job. Employees working at home often report a sense of isolation, losing touch with office politics, and fear of being overlooked for promotions. Says Phillip Becker, an independent computer designer, "There just aren't that many jobs where you can work in total isolation...(Telecommuting)... doesn't move socially-interactive information such as body language or trust, based on a face-to-face conversation.[15]

QUESTIONS

1. Telecommuting clearly seems to require unique characteristics of both employer and employee. What are they?
2. What do you think will be the social and environmental consequences of having from 10 million to 20 million workers telecommuting by the year 1990?
3. Would you prefer working at home or at a place of business? Why?

C H A P T E R   12

Word Processing

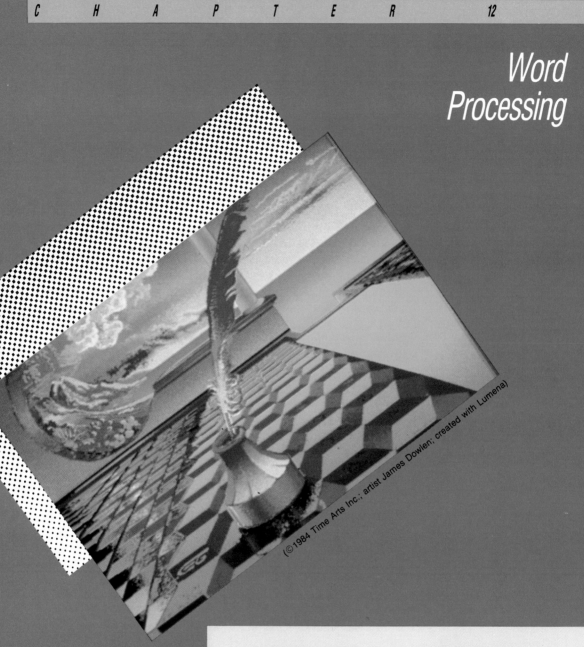

(©1984 Time Arts Inc.; artist James Dowlen; created with Lumena)

The Fredson and Fredericks Fine Furniture Factory has decided at the last minute to bid on furnishing a new government building in Fremont, Florida. It is a big job: bigger, in fact, than any Fredson has undertaken in the past. Managing partner Fanny Fredson received the bid specifications a week ago, almost two months after the government released them. There is little time left before the bid must be submitted. In preparation for a series of meetings with management, Fanny needs to send a package of written materials to each member of the management team. The package will include a letter to each of the twelve managers explaining the responsibilities of each and the details of the project.

Fanny's secretary, Frank Fowler, looks at the letter and other materials and says, "Each package, including the letter, will take about an hour to type. With everything else I have to do," he concludes a bit petulantly, "I can get these in the mail in about three days."

He types the same letter twelve times, varying only the name of the manager to whom it is addressed. Much of the other material is also repetitive, but the letter has enough unique information to prevent copying it with an office copier. Boredom sets in and errors increase. By the time the participating managers receive their packages, a full week has expired. The delay makes preparing a successful bid virtually impossible. When Fanny told Frank to call the managers and cancel the meetings, he had the distinct impression that she blamed him for the delay.

Of course, it was not Frank's fault. He could have produced the twelve letters in two hours or less if he used word processing equipment, merging information that changed from letter to letter with fixed information about the schedule. This chapter describes how this process works and how modern word processing techniques increase office and writing productivity to the extent that many professional secretaries and writers now assert that their work would be impossible without it.

WORD PROCESSING TODAY

Nobody who writes expects to produce perfect material on the first try. Nobody, that is, who expects the work to be read. Writing, whether it is technical exposition, business communication, news reporting, or creative writing, is ten percent expressing ideas and ninety percent editing to make them readable and understandable. The key to good writing, the kind people will read, is editing. Editing is known as *text manipulation*. For this reason, we define *word processing* as the manipulation, by machine, of characters, words, sentences, paragraphs, and documents to serve communication purposes.

Word processing is certainly the most commonly used application for microcomputers today (see figure 12-1). More word processing application programs are sold each year than any other type of computer software. Larger computer systems such as minicomputers and mainframes also use word processing programs. In addition to computer programs executed on general-purpose computers, a number of so-called dedicated word processing machines are used for the same purpose. A *dedicated* word processor is a computer that is devoted exclusively to word processing functions.

Newspapers and publishing firms have embraced word processing as a

more effective way to get their work done. In publishing newspapers in the not-too-distant past, for example, articles written by reporters were typeset by a Linotype machine, a device that drew on a reservoir of molten metal to cast the story into lines of type. After the reporter typed the article, the operator rekeyed it on the typesetting machine. Following the work of that operator, several other manufacturing steps were required to prepare the curved printing plate used by the presses. This technique, called the *hot-type* method, was cumbersome and labor intensive.

Today, reporters and editors work on a computer, that is, a word processor, which stores the article electronically as a string of characters. To produce a column of type, the computer draws each character with an electron beam or by photographic means, forming the completed newspaper column. The columns thus produced are pasted up, with photographs and other art, into a page that is photographed to produce the printing plate. For this reason, the method is called photocomposition.

Using the hot-type method, a good Linotype operator could set about sixty words a minute. Today, photocomposition gushes out some 7,600 words per minute and the final results need only be photographed to produce the printing plate. If you've ever wondered how a news story that broke at 10:00 p.m. could appear in the newspaper that was delivered at your door at 5:00 a.m. the next morning, give the credit to modern word processing.

THE GROWTH OF WORD PROCESSING

Setting aside the slate and stylus, the papyrus and quill pen (after all, our definition of word processing specified the use of machines), we mark the beginning of word processing with Johann Gutenberg who started the art of typesetting in 1437 when he invented the moveable-type printing press and produced the Mazarin Bible. His process involved taking blocks representing each letter and locking them into a frame. Pages were printed by inking the blocks and placing paper against the frame.

The invention of the typewriter, which was patented by Henry Mill in 1714, stands as the next most important development of word processing. The

FIGURE 12-3
IBM Model C electric typewriter
(Courtesy International Business
Machines Corp.)

THE FIRST COMMERCIAL TYPEWRITER
MODEL 1 REMINGTON, SHOP NO. 1.

65

FIGURE 12-2
Early typewriter (Courtesy Culver
Pictures, Inc.)

typewriter (see figure 12-2) was (and still is) an inexpensive device that increased the amount of writing that could be recorded on paper in a given amount of time while at the same time improving its appearance.

Since then, typewriters have seen many changes. Of special importance was the addition of electrical components. These improved the appearance of the typed page because all of the keys struck it with consistent force, not depending on evenness of the typist's stroke. Also, electric typewriters could be used without having to lift one's hand from the keyboard to return the carriage, thus increasing speed and reducing the chance of returning one's hands to the wrong keys.

Electric typewriters (see figure 12-3) were developed during World War II in response to the need to improve clerical speed during that period's burgeoning economic growth. The need for increased speed, not to mention more reliable and easily maintained machines, led eventually to the Selectric typewriter, which was developed by IBM in the early 1960s (see figure 12-4). It replaced the moving carriage with a moving type element. Not only does the Selectric increase typing speed, but, because it has fewer moving parts, it requires less maintenance than its electric counterpart with moveable carriage and individual type hammers. In the early 1970s, the daisy-wheel element (see figure 12-5) was installed in typewriters, increasing their speed and reliability even further.

In the midst of these mechanical developments, automated typing made its entry into the field. In 1968, IBM coined the term *word processing* to refer to methods of typing in which the typing machine could retype documents from data stored on magnetic storage devices. This led to the name *automated typing*.

IBM's Magnetic Tape Selectric Typewriter, also known as the MT/ST, was the first automatic typewriter, figure 12-6. As the user typed using the MT/ST, the device recorded the text on magnetic tape and printed it on paper at the same time. Each tape could store many documents, making it possible to retrieve any of them for typing again later and for repetitive typing of the same document. The MT/ST, then, was the first device to enable semi-automatic production of personalized form letters. The user typed individual names and addresses; the machine did the rest.

In 1969, IBM introduced the MC/ST, or Magnetic Card Selectric Typewriter. This unit differs from the MT/ST in that it stores data on magnetic cards rather than on magnetic tape. Because each card stores about a page of text, the cards are easier to use than tape when locating a particular

FIGURE 12-4
The Selectric typewriter with interchangeable type elements
(Courtesy International Business Machines Corp.)

FIGURE 12-5
Daisy wheel typewriter element
(Courtesy Diablo Supplies)

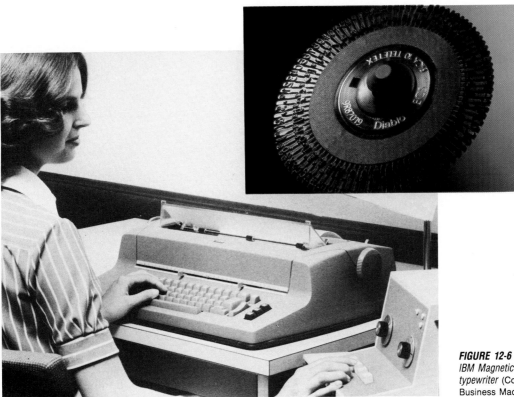

FIGURE 12-6
IBM Magnetic Tape/Selectric typewriter (Courtesy International Business Machines Corp.)

document for retyping. In 1974, IBM improved the MC/ST with the development of the Mag Card II, the first word processor to use internal storage along with external storage on tape or card.

All of these devices, granted their improvements over ordinary typewriters, suffered from the same fault: they were based on the Selectric, a mechanical device that prevented really fast typists from reaching their full potential.

Introduction of CRT-based word processing equipment (see figure 12-7) released operators from the constraints of mechanical printing devices altogether. These machines accept high-speed typing almost without limit, especially if they are equipped with *type-ahead buffers*, memory devices that temporarily store entered text while the computer performs such functions as screen formatting, line counting, and other chores. The user forges ahead at top speed with no notice of computer response except for an occasional brief delay in the characters appearing on the screen.

The ability to retrieve data electronically is provided by magnetic disk storage devices. A single disk can store up to several thousand pages of text, depending upon the page formats and the type of disk employed. This makes great volumes of text available to word processing systems. *Paragraph assembly*, or *boilerplating*, the process of preparing a new document by arranging paragraphs from others, becomes an easy task. Gone, now, are the paste pot and scissors, those familiar tools of writers and secretaries. Paragraph assembly is still known, however, as cut and paste. Menus for many word processing programs show a paste-pot icon as the indicator for this function, even though the work is done electronically.

Time-honored word processing techniques stay with us, even as our ability to write effectively and quickly improves, thanks to computers. We still carve words into stone for grave markers and other monuments. We still use the fountain pen, a more convenient version of the quill pen. Many creative writers prefer doing their work in longhand, arguing that most of their effort goes on in the head and heart anyway, and speed is not important.

Despite automated methods of producing hundreds and thousands of "personalized form letters," there is not yet any written communication more personal than a hand-written note. With the introduction of the humble typewriter many prophesied the collapse of personal communication, but this has not happened nor do we expect it to.

WORKING WITH A WORD PROCESSOR

By this time, you've probably developed something of an image of what working with a word processor is like. You sit before a standard typewriter keyboard that has a few additional keys used for swapping paragraphs, deleting text, inserting text in the middle of what you've already done, and so forth. Entering text is just like typing it except that your work appears on a CRT display rather than on a sheet of paper.

Furthermore, you need not worry about pressing the carriage return at the end of each line because the computer does that for you, formatting each line on the screen as you go. The carriage return is used primarily to start new paragraphs. As you work, the cursor moves along with your typing showing you where the next character entered will appear.

All those who type, even the least facile, detect most errors as soon as they make them. Backspacing and typing over automatically removes the error. Spotting a mistake in text several lines above, you move the cursor to the offending word or letter and make the correction. Then you return the cursor to where you were before and continue. In fact, many find their typing speed increases because they no longer fear making mistakes.

Believing that the sentence or paragraph you just typed would be better if it were inserted five paragraphs earlier in the text, you press a few keys and it is moved. Other adjustments to the text go as easily if not more so. Words are replaced with better ones, phrases deleted, spelling corrected, all simply by moving the cursor to the appropriate location and entering the changes.

Proofreading your work, which is always necessary, is done at the screen, making the corrections as you go. Inserting and deleting words, sentences, and paragraphs causes the system to reformat the entire document automatically so that margins, paragraphs breaks, new pages, and the like are of no concern. Many find that final proofing is best done from hard copy. Those who use word processors confess that they often spot errors on paper that they miss on the screen. These corrections are made on the screen, as before, prior to the final printing.

To print, you press a few more keys, specifying page length, margins, type size, and font (many word processors offer a variety of fonts, including Old English, cursive, and more esoteric options) and let the printer do its work while you continue to use the computer for other purposes.

Naturally, you save the document on disk, both as a way of filing it and in case you should need to print it again or use parts of it in other work you are doing.

That's essentially it. Producing many copies of a form letter, which requires retrieving addresses from an address file, also on your disk, is only a little more complex. You concentrate on what the letter should say and how to say it and let the machine do the drudgery of grinding the copies out.

Productivity

Word processors make text preparation quick and easy. They facilitate editing, correcting, revising, and making other changes without retyping. They encourage creativity to flow naturally, without worry of the appearance of the final printed document. The machines, that is, the computers, take care of that. They provide final output without erasures, crossouts, whiteouts, or typographical errors and can repeat this performance as many times as is necessary to prepare originally typed copies of the same document.

Word processors are found in many settings. The business executive without a secretary finds word processing an important tool for carrying on correspondence. It is invaluable for the office that produces a great deal of repetitive typing: contracts containing identical clauses, form letters, legal briefs, and so on. Professional writers often find their word processor to be their best friend. It was fine for Hemingway to write stories with pencil and paper in a Paris cafe. The modern writer uses modern tools which increase the speed with which ideas can be written down and the ease with which writing can be revised.

Word processors offer the writer the same advantages in manipulating words that a computer offers the accountant or the statistician in manipulating numbers. For those who already have a computer, word processing programs add substantial productivity to one's personal and working life at very little cost. The secretary, working in an office equipped with a computer that usually does accounting or analytical chores, can take great advantage of its word processing ability for producing personalized form letters, printing mailing labels, and preparing lengthy documents.

The office that has too much typing work for one secretary, but not enough for two, will often find that a modest investment in word processing equipment will make it possible for the lone secretary to do all the work with ease. Moreover, if the word processing is performed by a general-purpose computer, it can be used for other tasks when not required for secretarial work.

Word processors, however, aren't a perfect solution in every situation. If a secretary is very fast and accurate and types nothing but short notes and letters, a word processor probably won't increase productivity. If an office staff types little but fills out many forms, a word processor might, in fact, make that work go more slowly than when done by hand.

The remarkable productivity of word processing results from its automating many of the everyday typing functions and from the fact that it is easy to use. "...if you already know how to type, a few extra keystrokes is all you need to start entering text on a CRT screen...add a few more keystrokes...(and you) can print out the document."[1] Of all the computer software available today, surely it can be said of word processing that it was designed with the nontechnical user in mind.

Organizing for Word Processing

Organizations implement word processing systems in two ways: centralized and, as you might expect, decentralized. In the *centralized* arrangement, one location handles all word processing. The work is routed to the word processing department from wherever in the organization it originates. This works well in situations in which many people use the same data base to produce high volumes of written documents. Expensive equipment such as high-speed printers can be used with great effectiveness. Word processing operators can go about their jobs with few interruptions (answering telephones, intercepting visitors, and so forth) and work does not pile up because of the absence of one worker. What one does, all can do. Because centralized word processing operations are typically found in large organizations, operators see a more clearly defined path of career advancement with a concomitant positive effect on employee morale.

The *decentralized* arrangement has word processing units scattered throughout the organization as needed by individual work centers and offices. *Turnaround time,* that is, the time it takes to complete a job once given to the word processing operator, is usually faster because the operator works directly with the person requiring the work, thus easing personal communications and providing the ability to handle unique requirements for the job. Moreover, most people prefer to work in small groups in which they enjoy personal recognition and involvement with their work. The typing or secretarial "pool" has never been a favorite place for people to work.

There are hybrid organizational patterns that combine the best features of the centralized and decentralized situations. However organized, electronic word processing has revolutionized the office environment.

We should add that the distinction between a secretary and a word processing operator is rapidly disappearing. Increasingly, skill in using an electronic word processor is required by employers seeking secretaries. Most secretarial training institutions, including secondary schools and colleges, now require their students to take courses in word processing. Word processing is no longer a wave on the horizon. It is an operating feature of the modern office.

TYPES OF WORD PROCESSORS

Word processing equipment comes in four varieties: electronic typewriters, dedicated word processors, microcomputers, and mainframes or minicomputers.

Electronic Typewriters

At first glance, electronic typewriters look very much like electric ones (see figure 12-8). Closer inspection, however, reveals important differences, including a number of special keys, called *function keys,* and, on some models,

FIGURE 12-8
Electronic typewriter (Courtesy Brother International Corp.)

FIGURE 12-9
Dedicated word processor
(Courtesy Wang Laboratories,
Inc.)

a video display unit that shows a small portion of the text before it is typed on paper.

Electronic typewriters are great for typing one-of-a-kind documents that will not undergo massive editing and rewriting. They are not very good for composition that invariably requires much editing and revision. Some electronic typewriters may be upgraded to full-scale word processors with relative ease and modest expense, thus offering a fairly painless avenue for moving toward full-function word processing capability.

Dedicated Word Processors

A dedicated word processor, as we mentioned earlier, is a special-purpose computer that serves but one function: word processing. To be sure, some models also offer limited general-purpose computing ability, but as a rule they do not. As compared with word processing application programs run on general-purpose computers, these devices reduce the number of keystrokes required to prepare a document and minimize the degree of technical knowledge required by the secretary. They are particularly useful in small offices with one secretary or in offices where secretaries work quite independently of each other (see figure 12-9).

Microcomputers

The microcomputer (see figure 12-10) can be a word processor one minute, a data processor the next, and a tool for education and training at other times. For that reason, it is an economical device in situations in which neither a word processor nor a data processor is needed full time. This flexibility costs keystrokes. Word processing functions that require one keystroke on a dedicated machine may require two or three on a microcomputer. Most micro-

FIGURE 12-10
*Portable computer used as a
word processor* (Courtesy Texas
Instruments, Inc.)

computers today employ function keys that can be set up to work much in
the same manner as those on dedicated word processors. We suspect that in
a very few years, the use of dedicated word processors in the modern office
will yield almost entirely to general-purpose computers.

Mainframes and Minicomputers

Mainframes and minicomputers are faster than their smaller microcomputer
counterparts. More often than not, they are used for multi-user situations,
that is, situations where one large or medium central processor is used by
several people at terminals. When it is used for word processing, a minicomputer may do nothing but provide word processing capability to a number
of secretaries and others through its network of terminals.

Mainframe computers are large enough and fast enough to provide a
number of processing services to many users at once through multi-user networks (see figure 12-11). These services can, of course, include word processing. Both mainframes and minicomputers can accommodate much more data

FIGURE 12-11
Large word processing system
(Courtesy Texas Instruments,
Inc.)

than a microcomputer, but they often do this by employing data files that are shared by all users. Having confidential information accessible to the entire staff can lead to security concerns.

Mainframe computers, when employed for word processing functions, suffer from two disadvantages. First, word processing is not an efficient use of the mainframe's computing power. The speed at which data can be entered, edited, and manipulated depends entirely on the speed of the operator using the system, that is, the computer must wait for fingers to do their work before it can do its own. Mainframes are better employed in systems in which virtually all data input is automated, coming from disk or tape or over high-speed communications facilities. Mini and microcomputers are better suited to word processing from an economic point of view because the cost per unit of word processing output is much lower with smaller computers.

Second, mainframe word processing programs, reflecting their complex text editing forbears, are less easy to use than those available with minicomputers, microcomputers, and dedicated word processors. Even though they are proficient in word processing as an office skill, most secretaries prefer not to get involved with the technical details required when working with a multiuser mainframe system. The individually controlled work station remains the most popular in the modern office.

FUNCTIONS OF WORD PROCESSING SYSTEMS

There are no software packages that offer more different functions to the user than word processing programs. This is probably because writing, editing, preparing mailings, and boilerplating involve so many different operations: moving paragraphs, deleting words and sentences, correcting spelling and punctuation, and manipulating files of text, to name a few. The following paragraphs describe the essential functions of any word processing system.

Cursor Control

In word processing systems, the cursor is analogous to the point of a pen or pencil. It indicates where text will appear next when it is entered from the keyboard. It is used to identify text to be deleted, moved elsewhere in the document, or copied to multiple locations.

Modern word processing systems employ *full-screen* editing techniques, which means that editing is accomplished by moving the cursor anywhere on the screen to perform the needed functions. This is faster than *line editing* which requires that the user identify each line to be edited, one at a time.

In order for full-screen editing to be most effective, the user must be able to move the cursor about the screen easily. Cursor movement is accomplished with the use of cursor control keys, a mouse, or touch screens (see figure 12-12).

Deletion

Every word processor should allow for deleting material. This works in a number of ways. Some systems use dedicated keys for deleting characters, words, sentences or lines, paragraphs or blocks of text, and pages. The operator places the cursor anywhere in the text to be deleted and presses the appropriate keys. Other systems require that the total block of text: a word, paragraph,

FIGURE 12-12
*Special keys on a word
processing keyboard* (Courtesy
Wang Laboratories, Inc.)

or whatever, be identified by highlighting it or by bracketing it with unique characters. After identification, the delete keys perform the function. Many word processors save deleted material temporarily in a small memory buffer so that inadvertent deletions can be restored or so that deleted material can be moved to another location in the document.

Insertion

Like deletion, insertion is an essential feature of all modern word processing systems. *Insertion* means adding characters in the midst of existing text. There are several ways to do this. The operator may press an insert key or some combination of keys (e.g., CONTROL-I) that causes any subsequent keystrokes to be automatically inserted at the cursor until the insert key is depressed again. Some word processors insert characters and push the following text down the screen as the new text is entered. Others clear the screen below the cursor and restore that text after the insertion is completed.

Still other word processors automatically insert any text that is entered. The operator positions the cursor and begins typing. The characters push existing text at that location to the right, making room for the new material. This is known as *automatic insertion*.

Word processing systems almost always offer the option of automatic insertion or automatic type-over. *Automatic type-over* means that, when the cursor has been positioned, any new text will replace existing text at that location, in essence, typing over it.

Type-ahead Buffer

A word processor should permit the operator to type as quickly as possible. The machine should not impede the person. Some word processors, particularly older microcomputer versions, do not permit this. They allow typing only as fast as the CRT display can be updated with the new characters. Newer word processors have type-ahead buffers which allow top-speed data entry. The machine catches up when it can without losing characters.

Word Wrap

Every good word processor program employs *word wrap*, a method of forming lines on the screen and the final printed page automatically without breaking words in two. The program does this by wrapping whole words that extend beyond the margin onto the following line of text. Only paragraph endings must be denoted with the carriage return. This not only eliminates many keystrokes, but it relieves the operator from making line ending decisions or even paying attention to line length.

Page Formatting

Word processors use a set format to print each page. Information in this format includes the length of each line, the number of lines per page, the size of margins, spacing (single or double), pitch (number of typed characters per inch), paragraph indentation, and page numbering data. Typically, these specifications can be changed on a *format page* which defines the appearance of the printed document.

Page formatting amounts to specifying where words, sentences, and paragraphs will appear on the final page. The operator can change the page format specifications by using control codes, called *embedded commands*, in the text. Embedded commands make it possible for one document to have several different formats. With some word processing programs, the codes appear in the text as displayed on the screen. In others, they don't. The text is formatted on the screen as it will be printed on paper.

Normally, text in a document is *left-justified* meaning that each line starts even with the left margin and the right-hand ends of lines are jagged. Word processors can also right justify or fully justify text. *Right-justification* means aligning the right-hand edges and leaving the left jagged. *Full justification* means aligning both ends of each line. The first lines of paragraphs are often indented, meaning that they start a short distance to the right of all the other lines. Outdenting means starting the first paragraph line to the left of all of the other lines.

Centered text, such as might appear as section headings, is placed there automatically by the program after the operator identifies the text to be centered with the appropriate embedded commands.

Character Formatting

Word processing programs make it possible to vary the characteristics of the type font used when printing the document. Often, one document will require several different fonts, including boldface, italics, and underlined characters. As with controlling page formats, the operator identifies the characters or words to be printed using a particular font and enters control characters specifying which is to be used.

With respect to both page and character formatting, the best word processing systems display on the screen exactly what will be printed. Italic words appear just that way on the screen. So do centered text, outdented paragraphs, and all the rest. Such word processing programs do not display the control codes for formatting, although they are, in fact, part of the string of characters making up the document.

As a rule, microcomputer display screens and other computer video display terminals cannot show a complete page, 8 1/2 by 11 inches. To do so would make the characters on the screen too small to view comfortably. Instead, the word processing program indicates where pages break by showing a dotted line or some symbol in the margin.

Word processors allow great flexibility in designing output. (Courtesy Apple Computer, Inc.)

Search, Search and Replace

The search function seeks a group of specified characters anywhere in a document. Typically, it finds the required text string nearest to the cursor when the function is invoked. A *global* search inspects all occurrences of the text string, and if every occurrence of a phrase should be changed to another phrase, *global search and replace* performs the function. For example, it may be necessary to change the characters *Mrs.* and *Miss* to *Ms.* every time they appear in an old file of customer names and addresses. Using the global search and replace function is much easier than changing each one individually.

These features are very nice. They allow quick updating of information in a document, and they facilitate the correction of a word that has been consistently misspelled throughout a document.

Text Rearrangement and Boilerplating

Text rearrangement is an essential of word processing systems. One of the most important aspects of word processing is the ability to say, I don't like that paragraph there, it belongs over here. Word processing systems accomplish this task by identifying the text to be moved, placing it in a move buffer, placing the cursor where the text belongs, and emptying the move buffer.

Boilerplating is a related facility. Using it, paragraphs are stored on disk as parts of other documents or, perhaps, as a special file of pre-written paragraphs. The operator copies those paragraphs as needed for a document from the disk, makes any needed formatting adjustments, and prints the new document. Boilerplating is very valuable for organizations that produce a great number of more or less standard documents such as contracts, bid specifications, and promotional mailings.

PRINTING A DOCUMENT

There is little point in doing word processing work if the results cannot be printed. After all, the printed word, as opposed to the word displayed on a CRT, is the object of all this effort.

Printers

Printers used with word processing systems have many capabilities; the various types available were discussed in Chapter Six. As a rule, dot-matrix printers are best for fast printing of draft copy, and letter-quality printers are best for correspondence. As printers continue to improve, however, some dot-matrix printers produce fast copy of near letter-quality appearance.

Recent advances in word processing software and printers have introduced easily used multiple fonts. Figure 12-13, for example, illustrates some of the striking fonts available with the Macintosh computer using the Apple Imagewriter printer.

Many printers offer *proportional spacing.* In proportional spacing, different letters use different amounts of space. For instance, the *i* takes about one-fourth the space of the *w.* In a given space, you can print more information proportionally than you can using nonproportional type. Another feature of

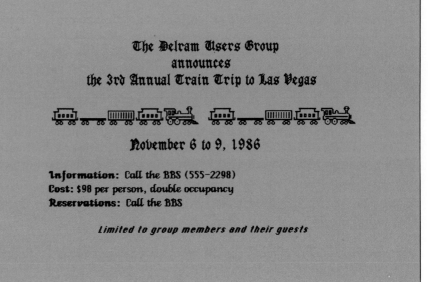

The Belram Users Group
announces
the 3rd Annual Train Trip to Las Vegas

November 6 to 9, 1986

Information: Call the BBS (555-2298)
Cost: $98 per person, double occupancy
Reservations: Call the BBS

Limited to group members and their guests

FIGURE 12-13
Fonts from Macintosh with
Imagewriter printer

proportional spacing is its ability to fully justify text attractively, without wide spaces between words on the line. The word spaces (space between words) can be different lengths to accommodate this requirement. Not all printers can provide proportional spacing and not all word processing programs can accommodate this feature. When it is available, proportional spacing gives the appearance of professional printing.

Print Buffering

A word processor or computer whose memory is divided into two distinct parts is said to have a foreground and a background (see Chapter Seven). If a word processor has both, it can do two things at once, or at least appear to. For instance, it can print one document, while the operator edits another. The editing takes place in the foreground of memory, while the printing takes place in the background which is also called the buffer (see Chapter Six). This feature increases productivity greatly.

Paper Feed

Some printers accept single sheets of paper. Others take continuous form paper. Many accept both. Cut-sheet feeders can be added to many printers, enabling the user to put a stack of single sheets of paper in the printer and have them fed as needed. Similarly, envelope feeders are available.

Printer Queuing

Some word processing systems allow several typing stations to use the same printer since it is used only part of the time. These systems contain queuing procedures which keep track of which document to print next according to a first-come, first-served basis or according to priority status. Simpler systems connect one printer to several word processing stations. The printer can be switched from one station to another, thus reducing the investment in printers while making one available to each of the stations.

So far, we've seen that word processing systems accomplish many of the more tedious chores, such as typing final copy, that writers must do. Since the late 1970s, a number of other programs have been prepared to add to the basic text editing and document producing functions of word processors. These programs fall into three categories: spelling checkers, grammar programs, and thesaurus programs.

Spelling Checkers

Everyone makes spelling mistakes. When using a keyboard, as compared to writing in longhand, spelling errors generally increase because of the opportunity to strike the wrong key. Proofreading for spelling errors is dull work at best—exactly the kind of detailed, repetitive work we would hope that a computer could do for us. It can.

Generally, spelling-checker programs are not included as parts of word processing programs. They are executed after the text is prepared by the word processor. Typical spelling programs for microcomputers work with several different word processing systems.

Spelling programs read word processing files and compare each word to a dictionary. If a word is not found in the dictionary, it is brought to the attention of the operator. Some programs just flag unrecognized words, others give suggested correct spellings. Some spellers make the corrections, others just point out the errors.

The best spelling checkers have a fairly large dictionary—80,000 words or more. The smallest have dictionaries of about 20,000 words. Good spelling checkers allow the addition of words to the dictionary, or perhaps to a supplemental dictionary, so that work that is laced with many technical terms and names not ordinarily found in standard dictionaries can be checked too.

Even the best spelling checkers cannot detect every mistake. Entering *in* instead of *it*, for example, will not signal an error to the checking program. The program cannot determine whether a sentence makes sense, only if a word is not in its dictionary. A sentence such as "Their are many weighs too right write" will escape attention. A correct sentence such as "Twas brillig and the slithy toves did gyre and gimble in the wabe" (from *Through the Looking Glass*), however, would produce many errors because many of its words are not in the dictionary.

Grammar Programs

An organization's image depends on how well its staff communicates, both orally and in writing. To insure use of correct grammar, several application programs that check for consistency of subject and verb number, verb tenses, punctuation, and other matters have been written.

No machine can detect all grammar and punctuation flaws. Too often, for example, punctuation is a matter of context. For example, both "When do we throw Mother?" and "When do we throw, Mother?" are grammatically correct. Most likely we mean the latter. What can grammar-checking programs do, then? They can identify and mark potential problems and let the operator decide what adjustments, if any, are necessary.

Style Programs

No computer will turn you into an Emily Dickinson, but style programs can help improve your writing. Style programs check for sexist gaffes ("Everyone protects his home and family."), and review text for excessive use of the passive voice, that is, too frequent use of the verb *to be*; awkward phrases, cliches ("The state-of-the-art in computer science..."), distracting, if not offensive and inaccurate expressions, and run-on sentences such as this one which you have just read.

Thesaurus Programs

The word *thesaurus* meant treasury or storehouse in the Latin and Greek from which it originated. A thesaurus is a reference book of synonyms and antonyms. Synonyms are words that have the same meaning. Antonyms are words that have the opposite meanings. We often find that the same word appears over and over in a document. We can enrich the style of our writing, and as a consequence, its interest level, by using a variety of words.

Here is how a computerized thesaurus works. After writing a word you don't like, place the cursor on it and strike a few specified keys to put the thesaurus program in control. First, the screen is split. The top shows the portion of the text containing the word; the bottom the thesaurus. The bottom of the screen lists all possible synonyms. You may choose the one you wish and automatically replace your word with it, or you may request that each choice be shown in the context of the sentence before you decide.

THE ECONOMICS OF WORD PROCESSING

Will word processing systems reduce the cost of correspondence and the preparation of written material? The answer depends upon the volume of material produced, the complexity of the text, the repetitiveness, the amount of revision, and the requirements for such ancillary functions as form letter mailings and telecommunications. To a great extent, costs depend on the system used. A dedicated word processor must be used for word processing almost all of the time to be cost effective, while a microcomputer can be used for other data processing tasks some of the time.

Many firms install word processing systems only to be disappointed because they either drastically underestimated the cost of getting started or held unreasonably high expectations of what could be done with word processing. As with the installation of any information system, word processing systems require careful analysis before their acquisition.

DEDICATED WORD PROCESSORS VERSUS MICROCOMPUTERS

Leaving mainframe word processing systems aside as generally uneconomical for most organizations, this chapter has presented material that compares differences between dedicated word processing systems and those implemented by general-purpose computers, especially microcomputers. This section makes the comparison more explicit.

Advantages of Dedicated Systems

Dedicated word processing systems require fewer keystrokes for most word processing functions, thus increasing typing productivity. Many systems can be linked together so that several input stations can serve one printer. Many systems can be directly connected with typesetting equipment and other sophisticated output devices. Dedicated systems normally come as a package with all equipment, service, and operator training available from one source.

Advantages of Microcomputer Systems

For the most part, microcomputer systems cost about half as much as dedicated systems, and more software, such as grammar and spelling checkers, is available. In return, many functions may require more keystrokes, although this does not seem to be a serious disadvantage. Most microcomputer word processing programs are simple enough so that extensive training is unnecessary. In addition, microcomputers readily communicate with distant computers. They are amenable to integrated software, permitting documents with graphics and tables to be easily produced. Finally, microcomputers can be used for other computational activities when they are not needed for word processing.

SPECIALIZED INPUT AND OUTPUT FOR WORD PROCESSING SYSTEMS

Earlier in this chapter, we suggested that input to a word processing program involves the use of a typewriter keyboard and output consists of printed pages. This is not always true. Because automated word processing systems are computer-based, there is no reason why they cannot take advantage of all electronic means of communication, and of course they do.

In addition to the standard forms of input and output used with a word processing system, there are three specialized formats. These are *optical character recognition* (OCR), *computer output microfilm* (COM), and *typesetting*.

Optical Character Recognition

OCR devices "read" typed material and convert it into code that the computer can understand. When an OCR reader is connected to a word processor or a microcomputer, every typewriter in the office can become an input device for the system. When executives write a report, their secretaries can type at top speed and send draft copy to the word processing center. This frees up word processing equipment and allows the traditional executive-secretary relationship to continue.

Computer Output Microfilm (COM)

One of the major problems facing business today is the explosion of paper. We use too much of it. We have to mail it, store it, and retrieve a copy of it at the most inconvenient times. The space requirements for file cabinets alone is astounding. One solution is to miniaturize output by recording it on microfilm.

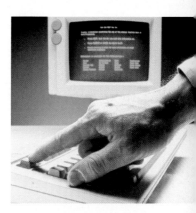

Special keys allow word processing operators to control the computer with a single keystroke. (Courtesy Wang Laboratories, Inc.)

Millions of microfilm records can be stored in a very small space and the computer can be used to retrieve any image, as long as it was properly indexed when it was stored. Images are stored on rolls of film or on cards called *microfiche*. As many as 700 pages can be stored on a 4 by 6 inch piece of film.

Typically, COM is too expensive for the small business. This will remain the case for the foreseeable future. COM equipment directly converts computer signals into film images by laser photography. COM devices such as Kodak's Komstar Microimage Processors require large mainframe computers for input.

In a large business, COM might be used to maintain backup records of invoices or copies of purchase orders. COM might even be used instead of carbon copies of letters sent to clients. In fact, any computer or word processing output can be printed on microfilm. The drawbacks to microfilm or fiche are their cost and the need for special equipment to read the images.

Typesetting

Most professional printing is typeset. It looks better and is easier to read than typewritten material. Typically, text to be typeset is entered on a keyboard much like the word processor's. The typesetting machine is really a special-purpose computer that behaves like a sophisticated word processor.

Because of the similarities between typesetters and word processors, they can be linked together through software. Thus, a typist can key a document, revise it, make sure it is perfect, and then have it typeset. Figure 12-14 shows a paragraph with typesetting commands embedded (printed in color here) and the result when the paragraph has been typeset.

FIGURE 12-14
Paragraph with typesetting codes and then printed

$FTB1$SZ10$PL012$LL2800$FS018There is no question that computerized accounting systems are a boon to business. Because of the cyclical nature of accounting procedures, they fit most amenably with the cyclical aspects of using computers to perform routine tasks. Creative Media Development, a producer of safety programs in Portland, uses a Texas Instruments Professional computer for its general ledger system. The firm has twenty employees and sales of about $1,000,000 annually. Says Philip Parshley of their accounting system:$SZ09$PL011$ILO018

Preparing financial reports used to take a few days. About a year ago we bought a Timberline General Ledger. Now she (the operator) plugs in the numbers, hits a key and they're done in a few hours.$SSQ

ICFS018$SZ10$PL012We hope that through the course of this chapter, you've come to understand that using an accounting system requires a bit more than plugging in the numbers and hitting a key. As with all computer applications, one must understand the work to be done before one can use a computer to do it.$RN

$FT4$SZ16$PL032SUMMARY

$SZ10$PL012$FT1An accounting system $FT2records, stores, classifies, summarizes,$FT1 and $FT1interprets$FT2 business transactions. Virtually everyone associated with business management must have at least a rudimentary knowledge of accounting. The accounting profession is among the oldest and, over the centuries, has established $FT2generally accepted accounting principles$FT1 which govern the manner in which all accounting systems, whether manual or automated, operate.

There is no question that computerized accounting systems are a boon to business. Because of the cyclical nature of accounting procedures, they fit most amenably with the cyclical aspects of using computers to perform routine tasks. Creative Media Development, a producer of safety programs in Portland, uses a Texas Instruments Professional computer for its general ledger system. The firm has twenty employees and sales of about $1,000,000 annually. Says Philip Parshley of their accounting system:

Preparing financial reports used to take a few days. About a year ago we bought a Timberline General Ledger. Now she (the operator) plugs in the numbers, hits a key and they're done in a few hours.[2]

We hope that through the course of this chapter, you've come to understand that using an accounting system requires a bit more than plugging in the numbers and hitting a key. As with all computer applications, one must understand the work to be done before one can use a computer to do it.

SUMMARY

An accounting system *records, stores, classifies, summarizes,* and *interprets* business transactions. Virtually everyone associated with business management must have at least a rudimentary knowledge of accounting. The accounting profession is among the oldest and, over the centuries, has established *generally accepted accounting principles* which govern the manner in which all accounting systems, whether manual or automated, operate.

Normally, it makes sense to use typesetting only for documents that will be produced in large quantities. Typeset pages not only look better than typed ones, but they are more economical when many copies are being printed. Each page of typeset material requires about 1 1/2 to 2 1/2 typed pages, thus a 100-page, typed manuscript would require between 40 and 67 typeset pages. Businesses usually typeset their sales brochures, instruction manuals, annual reports, and prospectuses.

USING WORD PROCESSING IN THE BUSINESS WORLD

Most organizations benefit from using word processing systems. The following brief descriptions show how various types of businesses make use of this important communications resource.

Lawyers

Lawyers use word processing systems for two primary purposes. First, they produce many contracts which must be typed error-free and which have many common paragraphs. Lawyers make great use of the boilerplate, or paragraph assembly, feature of a word processor by developing a library of paragraphs. They then merge variable data like names, dates, and amounts with the stock paragraphs to produce finished documents.

Second, they write briefs which are submitted to the court. These are highly technical documents that must meet strict court requirements. They are frequently rewritten on short notice. Often, a brief has been typed and, at the last minute before submission, a law clerk has discovered a new, important citation. Without the word processor, this could not be included in the brief. With it, perhaps, the case will be won.

The use of word processors in legal offices has improved the quality of clerical work. At the same time, it has increased productivity to the point that secretarial overtime, once a commonplace feature of working in a legal office, is almost a thing of the past.

Newspapers

Newspapers are the prime example of a multi-function, multi-user word processing system, as we saw earlier in this chapter. First, a reporter writes an article on the word processing system. The article is then stored in the central data file. An editor "calls up" the story. It is polished and readied for print. Finally, the computer is directed to typeset the article automatically. By using the computer this way, a story that would have been typed three times (reporter's original, edited version, typeset version) is only typed once.

Writers and Researchers

Standard operating procedure for writers, researchers, and students is to take notes about a topic, organize them, write an outline, and use this material to produce an essay, a book, a technical manual, or another product. This process cries out for a computer with word processing capabilities.

Here is how the system works. First, researchers gather their material from a library or other source. They take notes from the material and may develop an outline with an idea processor (see Chapter Sixteen) or a word processor. When the outline is completed, they use the word processor to compose their text. After rewriting and editing, the material is sent to the publisher, as often as not in the form of text recorded on magnetic disk. The publisher works with the text until finished copy is ready. Finally, much like the newspaper operation, the disk is sent to the typesetter for final copy.

Mail-order Companies

Mail-order houses promote sales by sending catalogs to potential buyers. Using a word processor, the seller can send personalized letters and specialized catalogs to specially targeted customers. Targetting of this kind goes well beyond the mail-order seller. Political candidates use the same techniques. They buy mailing lists from sympathetic causes and send targeted letters seeking funds and other support.

Other Businesses

Virtually every business is overwhelmed by paperwork. Much of the work is repetitive, either because of continual revision or because the same document is sent to many people. For example, slow-paying customers, as identified by the accounts receivable system (see Chapter Thirteen), can be sent personal letters (or so they appear) that ask for payment. A document that appears to be individually typed and includes personal references to names and dates of transactions is much more likely to produce payment from the delinquent account than the usual, mass-produced dunning notice.

Because word processing systems accomplish repetitive, not to mention boring, tasks with great facility, we expect that virtually every office and every business will be making extensive use of word processing systems in the next few years.

By the 1990s typewriters may well be a thing of the past, having been replaced by word processors. Granted its vested interest, Apple Computer has already banned all typewriters from its offices. In the immediate future, most colleges will require students to have access to a computer with word processing capability.

Where in the past, paper and pencil were common household and business artifacts, there seems every likelihood that word processing systems will be as pervasive within the next few years. After all, if a fairly complete word processing system can be easily carried about in a briefcase, why not?

USING A WORD PROCESSOR

Peter Odegard, impressario of the Irvine Symphony, maintains a file of donors to the Symphony using Applewriter IIe, a word processing program for his Apple IIe computer. Among other features, Applewriter includes a word processing language called WPL, which can prepare programs that perform a number of different functions.

One of Peter's WPL programs prepares personalized form letters to each of the donors on his list. He is about to prepare a letter to send to each donor announcing the annual benefit concert for the Symphony. The benefit is an important event that is used to raise the lion's share of the funds for the Symphony's annual budget.

FIGURE 12-15
Applewriter IIe screen

```
>   Z Mem:46043 Len: 802 Pos: 345 Tab:    0 File: benefit, d1

September 15, 1986

(Address)

Dear (Name),

The Irvine Symphony is about to start its 1986 season, and I wanted to contact
you about an exciting musical event coming up soon.  We have arranged for
Buddy Rich to come and play Vivaldi's Concerto for Drums, Orchestra and Boy's
Choir on October 31 for our annual benefit concert.

This will be the world premiere performance of the Concerto, (Name).  One of my
musicology students discovered it in the basement of a monastery near Milan
just last summer.  I know that you won't want to miss this important
performance.

To receive your tickets, just fill out the enclosed form and return it with
your check using the postage-paid envelope.  Many thanks, we'll see you on the
thirty-first!

Sincerely,
```

Peter begins by booting Applewriter and entering his letter. He proceeds in much the same fashion as if he were typing the letter on a typewriter except that his work appears on the monitor screen rather than on paper. Using cursor movement keys and the delete key, he corrects errors and organizes the letter into its final form, figure 12-15.

In figure 12-15, Peter has entered

(Address)

in the location in which the address of each donor is to appear in the letter and

(Name)

where the first name of each donor is to be printed. The WPL program will take the information for these parts of the letter from the file of donors on the disk. Notice that the donor's name appears twice. Using this program, officially known as a *mail merge* program because it merges information from an address file and a document, Peter can make each letter appear as if it were personally prepared for each donor. In fact, all of the letters will be produced at once under control of the program.

Peter's donor file appears in figure 12-16. Each entry begins with the number of the file entry in brackets. The program uses these identifiers to pick each name and address in order.

FIGURE 12-16
Donor file

```
<   Z Mem:46514 Len: 331 Pos:  96 Tab:    6 File: DONORS
<1>Sarah Vaughn
Suite 16
231 Campus Drive
Irvine, CA 92714
<2>Anita O'Day
1660 Krupa Ave.
Uptown, CA 92723
<3>King Pleasure
511 Moody Lane
Balboa Peninsula, CA 92628
<4>June Christy
1702 Alamo Crossing
Santa Ana, CA 92701
<5>Mel Torme
17 Velvet Fog Way
Tustin, CA 92680
<6>Billy Eckstine
567 Everything Ave.
Laguna Beach, CA 92776
```

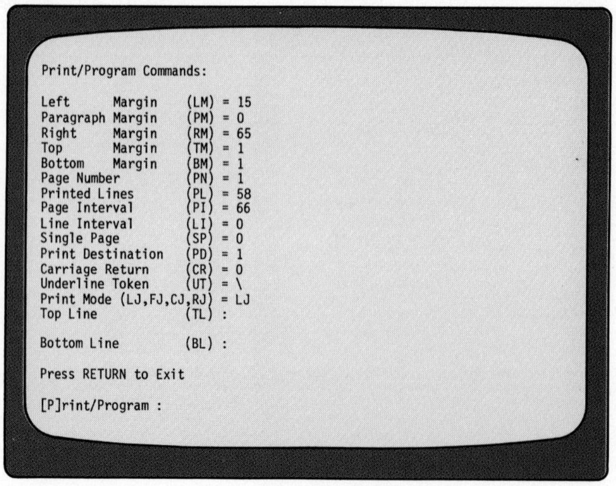

Having checked the list of donors, updated it, and added additional entries, also using Applewriter IIe, Peter is now ready to run off his letters. He loads his letter into memory by entering Control-L and the filename for the letter, benefit. Then, he reviews the printing options available by entering

FIGURE 12-18
Draft of form letter

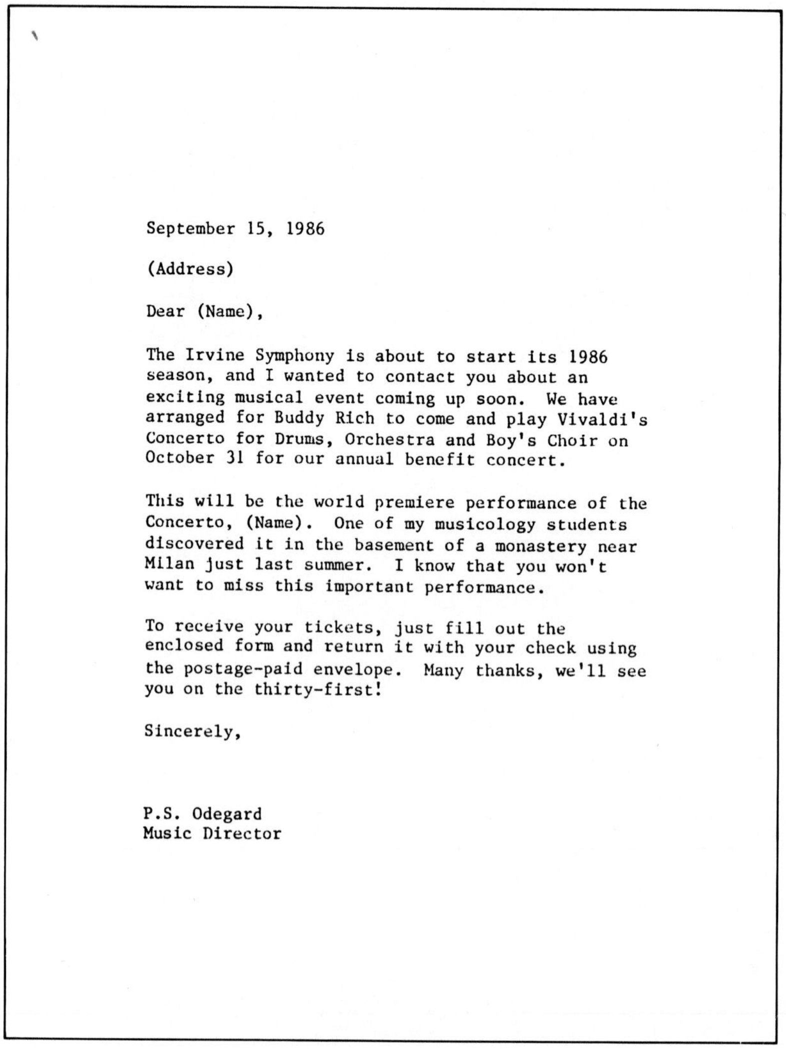

5082 Cinnamon, Irvine, California 92715 • Telephone 714/555-4237

September 15, 1986

Sarah Vaughn
Suite 16
231 Campus Drive
Irvine, CA 92714

Dear Sarah,

The Irvine Symphony is about to start its 1986 season, and I wanted to contact you about an exciting musical event coming up soon. We have arranged for Buddy Rich to come and play Vivaldi's Concerto for Drums, Orchestra and Boy's Choir on October 31 for our annual benefit concert.

This will be the world premiere performance of the Concerto, Sarah. One of my musicology students discovered it in the basement of a monastery near Milan just last summer. I know that you won't want to miss this important performance.

To receive your tickets, just fill out the enclosed form and return it with your check using the postage-paid envelope. Many thanks, we'll see you on the thirty-first!

Sincerely,

P.S. Odegard
Music Director

FIGURE 12-19
Finished letter

Control-P. In response, Applewriter displays the various printing options, figure 12-17. While reviewing these, Peter sets the left margin to 15 characters from the left edge of the page, and the right margin 65 characters from the left edge. The remaining settings he leaves as established by the program. These determine the length of the page, the spacing of lines, and other matters. When he is ready, he prints a draft copy of the letter for a last check of its appearance. The result appears in figure 12-18.

The entries (Address) and (Name), he knows, will be replaced by the addresses and first names of each donor as provided by the file. Now he's ready to set the computer system to preparing all of the letters. He enters Control-P and the command

```
do donor letter
```

where *donor letter* is the name of the program that merges the information from the donor file with the letter currently in memory. This causes the program to automatically execute and prepare one letter for each donor on the file.

When the letters are finished, Peter uses the same process to prepare address labels, one for each entry in the donor file. These are affixed to envelopes, and the letters are then stuffed and delivered to the Post Office. Figure 12-19 shows one of the finished letters.

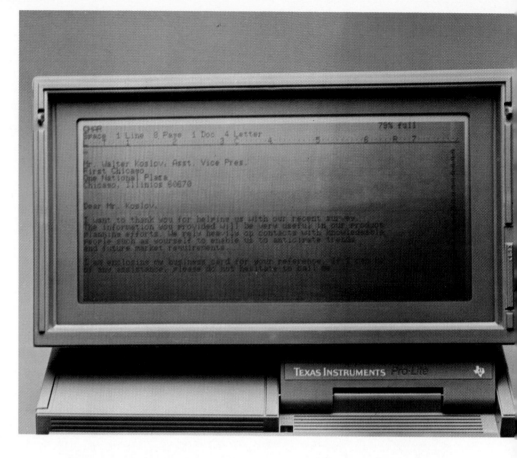

Microcomputers are used for word processing more frequently than are minis or mainframes. (Courtesy Texas Instruments, Inc.)

SUMMARY

Word processing, the manipulation by machine of alphabetic and numeric characters, words, sentences, and documents to serve communication purposes, is the most widely used application for computers today. Beginning with the invention of the Gutenberg press in 1437, word processing has evolved into its modern form which has two basic types of systems: *dedicated word processors* and word processing application programs for *general-purpose computers.*

A dedicated word processor is a computer that has no other application than word processing. Dedicated word processing systems have an advantage in reducing the number of keystrokes required of the operator because of their use of special function keys. Word processing programs prepared for use with general-purpose computers have an advantage in that the computer may be used for other data processing tasks when it is not required for word processing. Modern word processing programs for microcomputers, in addition, offer virtually all the features heretofore found only on dedicated machines.

General-purpose computers used for word processing purposes are usually either minicomputers or microcomputers inasmuch as it is economically unfeasible to use mainframe computers for word processing functions. Minicomputer word processing applications generally are *multi-user systems* in which several operators work at terminals sharing a central processing unit with a common data bank. Microcomputer word processing programs are typically used exclusively by one operator although microcomputer word processing networks are growing in popularity.

Word processing system functions found to be essential by virtually all users include the following:

1. Ease of cursor movement using *cursor control keys*, a *touch screen*, or a *mouse*.
2. Ability to *delete* characters, words, sentences, and paragraphs with one or two keystrokes.
3. Ability to *insert* characters, words, sentences, and paragraphs with one or two keystrokes.
4. A *type-ahead buffer* so that operator speed need not be limited to the computer's ability to keep up with fast typists.
5. *Word wrapping* to eliminate the need for the operator to press the carriage return at the end of each line.
6. *Embedded commands* to allow the operator to specify printing formats and changes in printing formats within the document itself.
7. Automatic *indenting* or *outdenting* of paragraphs as specified by the operator.
8. *Search* and *search and replace* functions to permit the operator to scan the document automatically for a specified group of characters (searching) for investigation. If it is known that all occurrences of the character group are to be replaced by another, automatic search and replace is used.
9. *Text rearrangement* to make it possible to move paragraphs, sentences, blocks of text from one point in the text to another. A closely related function, *boilerplating*, takes stored material and uses it to construct new documents.

So that documents can be printed while the operator is using the word processing system for continued editing or text entry, printing can be controlled by *background memory* while the *foreground memory* is used by the operator. Some systems employ *stand-alone buffers* for this purpose.

Printers use various paper feeding mechanisms including single sheet, continuous form, and automatic cut sheet or envelope feeders, depending upon the need of the applications.

Word processing systems are often enhanced with special programs that expand their power. These include *spelling; grammar, punctuation,* and *style checkers;* and *thesaurus* programs.

To be of the most economical benefit to the organization, word processing systems must be evaluated in terms of

1. staffing and personal considerations;
2. relative costs and benefits of dedicated versus general-purpose computer systems;
3. costs of hardware and software;
4. costs of staff training and implementation.

Even though the keyboard and the printer remain the primary input and output devices for word processing systems, other data handling techniques are gaining popularity. These include *optical character recognition (OCR), computer output microfilm (COM),* and *typesetting* directly from word processing system text files.

automatic insertion
automatic typeover
boilerplate
character formatting
computer output microfilm
  (COM)
cursor
embedded command
full-screen editing

global search and replace
insertion
line editing
optical character recognition
  (OCR)
page formatting
paragraph assembly
printer queuing
search and replace

text manipulation
touch screen
turn-around time
type-ahead buffer
typesetting
word processing
word wrap

1. What is the primary advantage of word processing?
2. When is a word processor not a productivity builder?
3. Identify two organizational structures used to provide word processing in a business.
4. What is the difference between a stand-alone word processor and a microcomputer with word processing software?
5. Cite a typical example of the use of paragraph assembly (boilerplate).
6. Name three supplementary programs that make word processing more productive.
7. How do spelling checkers build productivity?
8. How should you test a word processing system before buying it?
9. What technique is used to minimize nonelectronic storage techniques in a word processing environment?
10. List two storage media other than disk.
11. List at least five essential features and five nice features of a word processing program.
12. What equipment can be used to turn all office typewriters into computer input devices?

1. Compare and contrast the strengths and weaknesses of floppy diskette versus hard disk storage in a word processing system.
2. Rank your answers to review question 11 from the most important to the least important feature. Justify your answer.
3. Discuss the issues to be considered when deciding to buy word processing equipment for a business.

Point *Counterpoint*

Will Word Processing Take the "Creative" Out of Creative Writing?

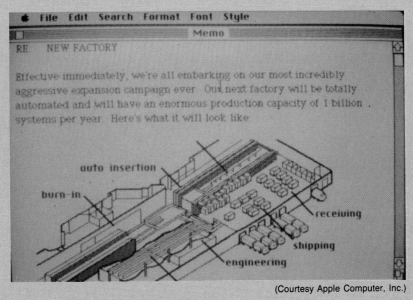

(Courtesy Apple Computer, Inc.)

The purist would observe that humans have been processing words ever since they began talking. Spoken words have several crucial failings. First, they require the addressee to be present and listening. Of what use is an inspirational speech to an empty auditorium? Second, unless they are outstandingly skilled, speakers use wrong words, incorrect inflection, and misleading body language and facial expression; they leave important information out and generally wish they had said it differently after it is too late. Third, as soon as they are uttered, spoken words are gone, remaining only in the imperfect memories of those who heard them.

Abraham Lincoln's address at Gettysburg was heard by few, but has been read by millions and memorized by thousands. That's because Honest Abe wrote his speech before delivering it. Writing, the act of committing words to paper, makes them permanent. Lincoln's words at Gettysburg, thanks to their context and his writing skill, are more than permanent. They are immortal, having been given life by generations who respond to their inspirational message.

Until recently, learning writing skills was pretty laborious. Children first learned to form characters with pencil or pen on paper. The expression of ideas

and thoughts had to await long months of penmanship practice. Later, when writing stories and papers, students would settle for poor work because rewriting by hand took so much time.

> Teachers of writing have said that children learn best when they copy work over and correct their mistakes at the same time. Many children do this to please a parent or teacher but will avoid the drudgery, left to themselves.[2]

Electronic word processing removes the drudgery of writing and rewriting. *Rewriting* means editing, the process of correcting errors and improving the manner in which the ideas are expressed.

> All "creative" writing is really editing, whether it is done before the words leave the brain or is carried out on paper or screen...
>
> There is no question that children who are given the opportunity to write with a computer, simple word processing software, and a little instruction tend to write more easily and eagerly than most other children do.[3]

Adults respond to electronic word processing with as much enthusiasm as children. Computer literature is replete with testimony from professional writers who claim that their work would be next to impossible without their electronic partner.

Electronic editing, however, is not without undesirable byproducts. Syndicated columnist Jack Smith observes that

> When a writer composes on a computer, his mistakes are instantly erased, without a trace, by his corrections, and there is no tortured original manuscript to betray the anguished trial and error behind the finished work.
>
> Writing on a computer screen is like writing in water. The literary manuscript will become a historical curiosity, like the quill pen.[4]

Smith quotes a professor who wrote a column for the *Monterey Peninsula Herald*:

> One wonders what will become of the craft of literary historians...To the writer whose study is the works of other writers, there are few thrills comparable to holding an original manuscript by a fine novelist or poet in his hands, the very words and paper that the great man himself sweated over.
>
> Something magic is involved in the craft of writing and to see the rough draft of a story or poem is to reexperience the creative process. The literary historian revels in detailing the words stricken out in favor of those that finally see print; the telltale blobs of ink and spots of blood, sweat and tears on paper.[5]

Visiting Los Angeles' Huntington Library, Smith examined the original manuscript of Robert Louis Stevenson's *Kidnapped*.

> And then he begins that famous story; words I hadn't read since I was 12:
>
> *I will begin the story of my adventures with a certain morning*...But he had crossed out *a certain* and made it *April*.
>
> Then he crossed out *April* and restored *a certain*. Then he had gone on to write *in the month of May in the year 1749*. But he had crossed out *May* and made it *June* and crossed out *1749* and made it *1751*. He scribbled on. *When I arose for the last time from my old bed*...But then he crossed that out and wrote *When I took the key for the last time out of the door of my father's house*...And so it went, page after page...
>
> From now on, a writer's agony will remain his secret. Nothing will remain for the archives but a letter-perfect printout and a floppy disk, from which, alas, no future historian will ever discover that his hero had feet of clay.[6]

So, electronic word processing will likely make it impossible to study the labors of creative writing.

Some think, in addition, that it may replace creativity itself, for all of word processors' prowess at making editing easier.

> In an environment in which rewriting and editing are so facilitated by technology, the mark of an individual writer may well be diluted. Original creative efforts may largely be abandoned in favor of a new literature of compilation and collage.[7]

Compilation and collage means taking material already written and reorganizing it. A paragraph from this, three more from that, a few sentences from something else, and a new work is complete.

But is it a new work, or is it just rehashing someone else's creativity? With enormous data bases easily available to anyone with the machinery that gives access to them, students, authors, and anyone else can pick and choose from a huge warehouse of written material.

> Public data bases are becoming centers for group novels and reports written by hundreds of people. Vast electronic libraries are opening up the world's literary treasures for extraction and editing by remote word processors.[8]

Think of the times that you, as a student, have had to write a book report. Have you discovered that there are volumes full of book reviews in the reference section of the library? Isn't it easier to write a book report after reading someone else's review? Maybe you've been tempted to use a few sentences of the reviewer's as your own. Wouldn't it be even easier if you could capture several reviews on a microcomputer and pick and choose paragraphs and sentences from them to compose your own report? You wouldn't even have to type it. The computer would do that. In fact, you wouldn't even have to read the book.

QUESTIONS

1. Write a short paragraph explaining why it's better to write originally than to copy and reassemble somebody else's work.
2. It's virtually impossible for a teacher to read and remember all reviews of every book students might read. If you were a teacher, what would you do to discourage plagiarism in preparing book reports?
3. What role do tape recorders play in recording the spoken word? Do we need printed transcriptions of tape recorded speeches? Why or why not?

C H A P T E R 13

Accounting Systems

(©1984 Time Arts Inc./Artist: James Dowlen/Created with Lumena)

A VERY OLD PROFESSION
ACCOUNTING PROCEDURES
THE GENERAL LEDGER
SUBSIDIARY SYSTEMS
USING AN ACCOUNTING SYSTEM

When I use a word, it means just what I choose it to mean—neither more nor less.—Humpty Dumpty[1]

Accounting is the language of business. We speak of assets, inventory, costs, expenses, liabilities, capital, and profits, to mention a few. While the layperson may use these terms casually, accountants use them very precisely. We'll turn to the precise meaning of accounting terms as we go along in this chapter. Meanwhile, Humpty Dumpty's admonition about the meaning of words will remind us to interpret them as accountants define them.

Accounting, however, is much more than attaching specialized words to routine ideas. *Accounting* is the process of recording, storing, classifying, summarizing, and interpreting business transactions. This definition should remind you of data processing which was defined earlier in this book. Because of the similarity in their nature, few business activities lend themselves as well to automated data processing as does accounting.

Accounting applications were among the first commercial uses of digital computers. In fact, it was their importance to accounting operations that caused data processing departments in organizations to be initially responsible to accounting and financial vice presidents. Although data processing departments, now called information systems departments, are concerned with more than just accounting, accounting remains an enormously important function that computers perform very well. More organizations use accounting programs than any other single type of program. In 1984, for example, small business purchases of software packages showed word processors to be the most often bought, accounting packages the next most often.

It's not a question of whether or not to use an accounting system. We have no choice. Records must be kept if for no reason other than that without them, we are likely to forget vital information or to violate the law. Reports must be prepared and information delivered to individuals and agencies outside the business. For this reason, virtually everyone associated with the management of business must have at least a rudimentary knowledge of the language of business: accounting. This includes managers as well as their clerical and support staff. It goes without saying that those who use computers in business must know about accounting processes in order to maximize computer effectiveness.

A VERY OLD PROFESSION

There's a good chance that the activity of writing itself got its start from the need to record business transactions. Record-keeping was practiced ages before the development of written history. Babylonian records dating back to 4500 B.C. show that scribes recorded sales contracts on clay tablets. In those days, of course, few people knew how to do this. Literacy was limited to a very few. The scribe, then, was the world's first accountant and the world's first data processor, too.

Clay tablets eventually yielded to papyrus, material made by glueing thin sheets of bark together. Scribes wrote using a calamus, a pen made from a reed or a feather quill. Interestingly enough, use of papyrus or parchment as the primary data recording medium continued until the fifteenth century. Long after that, the United States Constitution and the Declaration of Independence were written with quill pens on parchment.

Bookkeeping systems were first developed in ancient Babylon which also set up the world's first monetary system. Later, the Greeks developed inventory control systems and ledgers or day books in which all of the day's transactions were recorded. As we shall see, the idea of the ledger remains with us today as the heart of accounting systems.

In the tenth century, William the Conqueror gathered the largest accumulation of accounting data for the time. It recorded information about all of England's taxable property in a volume called the Domesday Book. The notions of "debit" and "credit," so familiar to those initiated into accounting processes and terminology, were contributed by the Italians in the fourteenth century.

Automated accounting first made use of pegboard systems with which a clerk would write down information. Thanks to a set of carbon paper interleaves, the entries appeared on a number of different documents. Many medical and dental offices still use such systems today.

The first automated accounting systems were developed during the 1950s by IBM, Remington Rand, and Royale-McBee. These used punched cards to record and store data in machine-readable form. Elaborate electrical and mechanical devices were incorporated in machines, called EAM equipment, that processed decks of punched cards. The initials stood for Electric Accounting Machines and in later years for Electronic Accounting Machines, although the degree of electronic sophistication used by them was not very high by today's standards.

A. Accounting machines were precursors of modern computers. (Courtesy International Business Machines Corp.)

B. The IBM 088 is used to sort data cards according to data keypunched into them. (Courtesy International Business Machines Corp.)

C. Special equipment was designed in the 1950s to manipulate data cards which, at that time, were the principal input medium for computers. (Courtesy International Business Machines Corp.)

A.

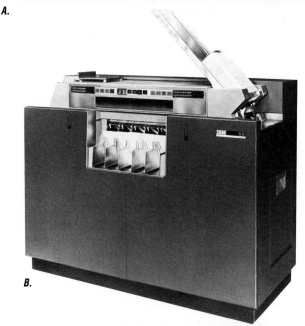

B.

C.

The first computerized accounting systems operated on mainframe computers. Those were the only computers around. Most mainframe installations today operate accounting systems. For large organizations that have much accounting data to process, the mainframe computer is the only feasible alternative.

Smaller organizations took advantage of the introduction of minicomputers in the 1970s to implement computerized accounting systems. Since the early 1980s, comprehensive accounting systems have been available for microcomputers as well. Microcomputer accounting systems offer virtually all of the features of those that operate on larger computers. Because of the inherent limitations of speed and volume of data storage, however, microcomputer accounting systems cannot handle the volume of work required by large organizations.

As things stand right now, no business, large or small, need operate its accounting system using manual methods. Indeed, considering the advantages that computerized accounting systems offer over manual methods, no business would want to.

ACCOUNTING PROCEDURES

In the United States, accounting programs must follow procedures and practices adopted by the Financial Accounting Standards Board (FASB) which establishes "generally accepted accounting principles." These principles assure that accounting information reported by one organization is consistent in form and terminology with that reported by all others and that the procedures that derive the information are similarly consistent.

For this reason, accounting programs must closely follow the procedures that have been used in manual systems for several centuries. Unlike other application software which can use whatever methods seem best to accomplish the task, accounting programs all follow the same pattern and produce the same results as governed by generally accepted accounting practices.

Given that generally accepted practices are followed, accountants are more concerned with using information than with the manner in which it is processed. Their work concentrates on that aspect of our definition of accounting that involves interpreting information and using it to further the interests of the enterprise.

Accounting software, on the other hand, concentrates on processing the data and producing information useful to those who will interpret it. It is helpful, then, to recognize that accounting programs are, in reality, bookkeeping programs. As bookkeeping programs, they maintain the data, leaving interpretation to management. Also, as bookkeeping programs, they produce reports and documents that otherwise would be nearly impossible to prepare.

Words, Words, Words

All accounting data for an organization are maintained in accounts. An *account* is a file containing financial data about something the organization owns, an amount it owes, the owner or owners of the organization, the revenues earned during a period of operation, or the costs and expenses incurred in earning those revenues. A file, as we know, consists of a number of records. In accounting systems, each record in an account file is called an *entry*. Now here come some more of those terms alluded to at the outset of this chapter.

Financial data are measured in monetary amounts. Accounting is concerned only with information that can be measured in terms of money. To be sure, accounting systems keep track of the names and addresses of customers, employees, vendors, and other assorted information, but the gist of the whole system is keeping track of financial information.

Things owned by the organization are called *assets*. Typical assets include land, buildings, cash, office supplies, and merchandise inventory. When money is owed to the organization in the form of accounts receivable, notes receivable, mortgages and bonds held, these, too, are assets.

Amounts of money the organization owes to others are known as *liabilities*. Liabilities include accounts payable, notes payable, mortgages, and bonds payable, and such other liabilities as taxes payable and salaries payable.

The degree to which the owner or owners of the organization have a financial interest in it goes by a number of names: *capital, proprietorship, equity,* and *owner's equity* being among the most popular.

Revenues, or *sales,* refers to money or promises to pay (accounts receivable) that the firm receives in exchange for providing goods and services to its customers.

The term *expense* refers only to those expenditures related to the conduct of the organization's normal operations. Expense must be distinguished from *cost* which refers to the amount paid for materials and merchandise acquired for resale to the firm's customers. Monthly rent is an expense. The purchase of electrical parts as components of products to be sold to customers is a cost.

Profit is calculated as the difference between revenues and the sum of costs and expenses for a specified time period. The profit formula looks like this

$$\text{PROFIT} = \text{REVENUES} - (\text{COST} + \text{EXPENSE})$$

or

$$\text{PROFIT} = \text{REVENUES} - \text{COST} - \text{EXPENSE}$$

You've probably run across these terms before. They are reviewed here to emphasize their precise definitions. Accountants don't use them casually and neither will the discussions that follow.

A System of Accounts

Chapter Three described an *accounting system* as a collection of subsystems under the control of a general ledger system (figure 3-10). These subsystems, called *subsidiary systems*, include accounts receivable, accounts payable, payroll, sales and invoicing, inventory control, and financial reporting. There may, of course, be other subsystems that meet specific needs of an organization, such as cost accounting and asset management, but the ones in figure 3-10 cover most accounting needs of all organizations.

The *general ledger*, or *G/L*, is the heart of any accounting system, regardless of what other subsystems are included. In fact, the general ledger system, by itself, is a complete accounting system. The subsidiary systems usually operate only in conjunction with the general ledger.

The Accounting Equation

The general ledger maintains a separate file for each of the assets, liabilities, capital, revenue, and expense accounts that the system maintains. These files, called *accounts*, are organized according to the *accounting equation*, which is

FIGURE 13-1
The accounting equation

FINANCIAL CONDITION   OPERATING RESULTS

Assets = Liabilities + Capital + Revenues − Expenses

an expression of the overall status and operational performance of the organization. The equation is very simple and is the fundamental basis of double-entry accounting, the standard procedure for all accounting systems. Figure 13-1 shows the equation.

As with all equations, the equal sign is the pivotal point. The total amount on the left must equal the total amount on the right. When this situation prevails, the accounting system is said to be *in balance*. In fact, by definition, accounting systems must *always* be in balance. If they are not, something is in error and must be corrected.

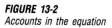

THE GENERAL LEDGER

The Chart of Accounts

An accounting system is a keeper of data and a producer of reports. Data are kept by the system in a number of accounts. An account shows all of the activity and the current status of individual Asset, Liability, Capital, Revenue, and Expense items in the accounting equation. Although accounting programs don't use paper to store data, it may help to visualize each account as a list or file of transactions maintained on a separate piece of paper. Manual account-

FIGURE 13-2
Accounts in the equation

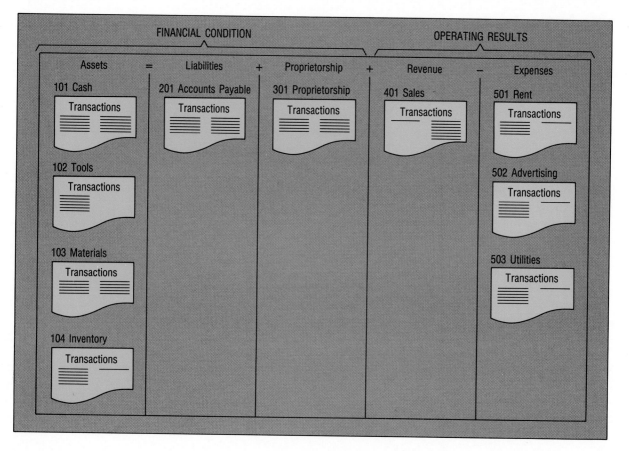

ing systems would call these *ledger cards.* The collection of all ledger cards, or accounts, is called the *general ledger,* not to be confused with the *general ledger system* which includes not only all of the accounts but also the system under which the accounts are kept up to date.

Each account in the system is assigned a number in a *chart of accounts* which is a listing by number of all the accounts in the system. The number identifies the type of each account in terms of the categories in the accounting equation: 100 for Assets, 200 for Liabilities, and so on. Figure 13-2 shows accounts in the accounting equation for a small business named Giapetto's Wooden Toys. Figure 13-3 shows Giapetto's chart of accounts.

Transactions

A *transaction* is an economic event that affects two or more accounts in the general ledger. Note the *two or more.* Every transaction is expressed in monetary terms and affects at least two accounts. This means that *every transaction consists of two or more entries.* That's what double-entry bookkeeping is all about. Furthermore, the entries have to balance, that is, their net effect on the accounting equation must leave it in balance.

Examination of figure 13-2 shows that each account is a file of entries, or records. Recording transactions to accounts is called *posting* to the account and adds records to at least two files in the system. Data entry techniques for accounting programs take advantage of all of the data entry devices available to computer systems as shown in figure 13-4.

Microcomputer systems usually employ keyboard input with prompting

Giapetto's Wooden Toys
Chart of Accounts
May 1, 1986

Account Number	Account Title	Type
101	Cash	Asset
102	Tools	Asset
103	Materials	Asset
104	Inventory	Asset
201	Accounts Payable	Liability
301	Giapetto, Proprie-torship	Capital
401	Sales	Revenue
501	Rent Expense	Expense
502	Advertising Expense	Expense
503	Utility Expense	Expense

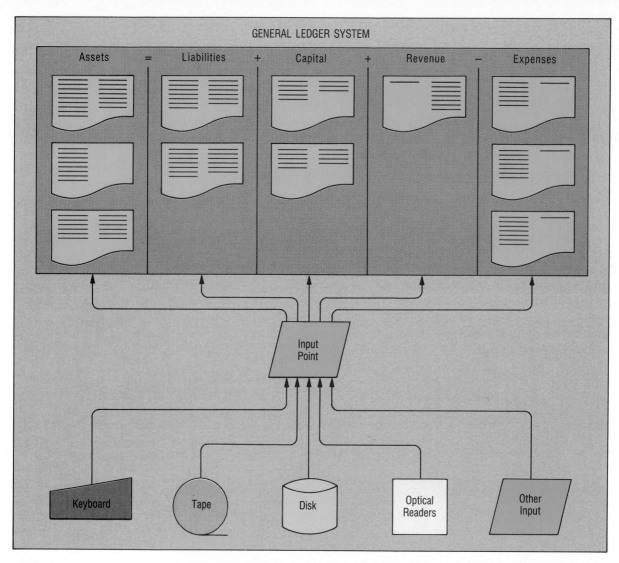

FIGURE 13-4
General ledger input

from screen menus. We will look at a typical system later on. Minicomputers and mainframes, because they process greater amounts of data, use faster input techniques including optical readers and off-line preparation of data which are then entered into the accounting program from magnetic tape or disk.

General Ledger Reports

Accounting systems prepare reports that adhere to fairly standardized formats. Each of the various subsystems, or subsidiary systems, produces its own family of reports which we will review later. The general ledger system also produces very standardized reports. In fact, these reports represent the fundamental output of all accounting systems. Whatever else an accounting program may do, it must produce these two documents: the balance sheet and the income statement.

The Balance Sheet
The balance sheet lists the balances in all of the accounts that reflect the financial condition of the enterprise and appear on the left of the accounting

equation in figure 13-1. Balance sheets are sometimes called *statements of financial condition,* reflecting this relationship. Figure 13-5 shows a balance sheet for Giapetto's Wooden Toys.

Every balance sheet lists the asset, liability, and capital accounts in separate sections and draws totals of each of these three categories as shown. The total of the assets must equal the sum of the total liabilities and capital according to the accounting equation. This is why this document is called a balance sheet.

The Income Statement

The income statement, like the balance sheet, lists account balances, those balances on the right in figure 13-1, that is, those that indicate operating results. Because the operational accounts contain data that describe what has happened over a period of time, making sales and incurring expenses, the income statement is an historical document and is dated accordingly.

Income statements are often called *Profit and Loss,* or *P&L statements,* because they summarize the profit-making activities. Figure 13-6 shows Giapetto's income statement for May.

Income statements present information in three major sections. The first, *revenues* (sales, in this case), lists all of the sources of operating revenues for the organization. The second section, *cost of revenues,* shows the costs of the goods sold. The difference between revenues (sales) and cost of goods sold is called *gross profit.* The final section lists the operating expenses incurred during the period in which the revenues were earned. The expenses are totaled

FIGURE 13-5
Balance sheet

```
            GIAPETTO'S WOODEN TOYS
                 BALANCE SHEET
                  MAY 1, 1986


              Assets

        Cash                      $ 5,000

        Tools                      12,000

        Materials                   2,500

        Inventory                   1,000

              Total Assets        $20,500


              Liabilities

        Accounts Payable          $ 2,500


              Capital

        Giapetto, Proprietorship  $18,000


              Total Liabilities
                 and Capital      $20,500
```

```
                         GIAPETTO'S WOODEN TOYS
                            INCOME STATEMENT
                      For the Month Ending May 30, 1986

          Sales                                    $ 825
          Cost of Goods Sold                         400

          Gross Profit                             $ 425

          Operating Expenses
              Rent Expense           $ 300
              Utility Expense           40
                    Total Expenses                   340

          Net Profit                               $  85
```

FIGURE 13-6
Giapetto's income statement
for May

and subtracted from gross profit to yield *net profit*. This is what is meant by
"the bottom line."

The balance sheet and the income statement, then, are the fundamental
financial documents of any general ledger system. The balance sheet is like
a snapshot. It expresses the financial status of the firm at an instant of time.
The income statement is a history. Two balance sheets and the income state-

FIGURE 13-7
Comparative income statement

```
                                  Gateway  Industries
                               COMPARATIVE INCOME STATEMENT
 As of : 10/28/81                  for All Departments                           Page No        1

                                            October                    Year to Date
 Account    Account Description   Current    Prior Yr.     %   Current    Prior Yr.       %

 Income :
    4000    Merchandise Sales     382545.97  310300.90  123.30  382545.97   310800.90   123.10
    4001    Repair Service         61750.00   57855.70  106.70   61750.00    57855.70   106.70

            Total Income          444295.97  368156.60  120.70  444295.97   368656.60   120.50

 Adjustments :
    4100    Discounts Given          -48.13     -25.16  191.30     -48.13      -25.16   191.30

            Total Adjustments        -48.13     -25.16  191.30     -48.13      -25.16   191.30

            Net Income            444247.84  368131.44  120.70  444247.84   368631.44   120.50

 Cost of Goods Sold :
    5000    Cost of Goods          71445.84   60898.51  117.30   71445.84    60898.51   117.30
    5001    Cost of Goods - Service 231234.90 199857.89 115.70  231234.90   199857.89   115.70

            Total Cost of Goods Sold 302680.74 260756.40 116.10 302680.74   260756.40   116.10

            Gross Profit          141567.10  107375.04  131.80  141567.10   107875.04   131.20

 Expenses :
    1300    Inventory Adjustments  17884.36   14755.00  121.20   17884.36    14755.00   121.20
    7100    Freight Expense         1845.00    1350.00  136.70    1845.00     1350.00   136.70
    7300    Office Supplies          427.00     399.50  106.90     427.00      399.50   106.90
    7350    Service Supplies         500.00     435.98  114.70     500.00      435.98   114.70
    7500    Postage Expense          153.00      89.90  170.20     153.00       89.90   170.20
    7510    Telephone Expense        250.00     201.90  123.80     250.00      201.90   123.80

            Total Expenses         21059.36   17232.28  122.20   21059.36    17232.28   122.20

            Operating Profit      120507.74   90142.76  133.70  120507.74    90642.76   132.90

 Other Income and Expenses :
    9000    Misc. Income           13772.18   10065.95  136.80   13772.18    10065.95   136.80

            Total Other Income and Expen 13772.18 10065.95 136.80 13772.18  10065.95   136.80

            Profit Before Tax     134279.92  100208.71  134.00  134279.92   100708.71   133.30
```

```
                          Gateway Industries
                      COMPARATIVE BALANCE SHEET
  As of : 10/28/81          for October                    Page No    1
  ====================================================================
                                    Current       Prior      % Chg
  Assets :
      Current Assets :
          Cash in Bank            18631.27      11256.54      65.5
          Petty Cash              -100.00          0.00       0.0
          Inventory              38884.90      23896.71      62.7
          Accounts Receivable - Trade  462260.93   407409.60   13.5
                                 -----------   -----------   ======

        * Total Current Assets   519677.10     442562.85      17.4
                                 -----------   ===========   ======
          TOTAL ASSETS           519677.10     442562.85      17.4
                                 ===========   ===========   ======
  Liabilities :
    . Current Liabilities :
          Accounts Payable - Trade    357169.27   301595.50   18.4
          Accounts Payable - Sls. Tax   3227.91     2550.90   26.5
                                 -----------   ===========   ======

        * Total Current Liabilities  360397.18   304146.40    18.5
                                 -----------   ===========   ======
          TOTAL LIABILITIES      360397.18     304146.40      18.5
  Capital :
      Owner Equity               25000.00      19800.00      26.3
                                 -----------   ===========   ======
      Earnings                   134279.92     118616.45      13.2
                                 -----------   ===========   ======

        * Total Capital          159279.92     138416.45      15.1
                                 -----------   -----------   ------
          TOTAL LIABILITIES & CAPITAL  519677.10   442562.85   17.4
                                 ===========   ===========   ======

  ====================================================================
```

FIGURE 13-8
Balance sheet

ment for the intervening period give a very good idea about a company's financial health and operations.

The statements for Giapetto's Wooden Toys are simplified. Figures 13-7 and 13-8 show more typical examples of income statements produced by an accounting system program.

Other Reports

General ledger systems produce a number of reports other than income statements and balance sheets. Figure 13-9 shows a chart of accounts report, similar to figure 13-3.

All of the transactions for an accounting period are entered electronically, using one or more of the input devices shown in figure 13-4. These transactions are stored on the secondary storage medium, usually disk, and are used by the accounting program to update the accounts. It will always be necessary to have a means of reviewing all of the transactions for a period. This is done by producing a *journal listing*. A journal listing will show all of the period's transactions, sorted by date, account number, or any of several criteria. The name *journal*, incidentally, comes from manual accounting systems in which all transactions were entered in a book, called the journal, and then

```
                    Account Listing                        Page 1
                   Gateway Industries
                     as of 10/28/81

  Account            Account Description              Account Type
  -------            -------------------              ------------
     1000    Cash in Bank                       Current Assets
     1001    Petty Cash                         Current Assets
     1100    Inventory                          Current Assets
     1200    Inventory Receipts                 Current Liabilities
     1300    Inventory Adjustments              Expenses
     2000    Accounts Receivable - Trade        Current Assets
     2010    Accounts Rec. - Deposits           Current Liabilities
     2100    Accounts Payable - Trade           Current Liabilities
     3000    Accounts Payable - Trade           Current Liabilities
     3100    Accounts Payable - Sls. Tax        Current Liabilities
     3900    Note Payable - B of A              Long Term Liabilities
     4000    Merchandise Sales                  Sales
     4001    Repair Service                     Sales
     4002    Maintenance Contracts              Sales
     4100    Discounts Given                    Sales Adjustments
     5000    Cost of Goods                      Cost of Goods Sold
     5001    Cost of Goods - Service            Cost of Goods Sold
     6000    Owner Equity                       Capital
     7000    Payroll Expense                    Expenses
     7100    Freight Expense                    Expenses
     7101    FUTA                               Current Liabilities
     7102    Tax Expense                        Expenses
```

FIGURE 13-9
Chart of accounts

posted by hand to each of the accounts affected. Figure 13-10 shows a sample detailed journal listing for the firm appearing in figures 13-7 through 13-9.

General ledger systems produce a great variety of reports, but we will not examine more than these few samples. Individual reports may be prepared for each account in the system, showing the entries during a period that affected each and the account balances. These are usually called *ledger account reports*. Some general ledger systems produce *budget reports* which compare costs and expenses with budgeted or planned costs and expenses. Other accounting programs include separate budgeting modules for this purpose. As shown in figure 3-10, some accounting programs include a separate module that does nothing but prepare financial statements of the type we have reviewed here.

Report Output

Because accounting reports are typically distributed on hard copy, all accounting programs must produce printed output. During the course of an accounting period, transactions are entered into the system. The current status of accounts, intermediate financial statements, and other reports can also be viewed on terminal screens, thus avoiding the necessity of printing a report everytime someone requires information. This is an important advantage that computerized accounting systems have over their manual forebears. Using manual systems, managers had to wait for the close of an accounting period to review operational statistics. Now, that information is available immediately and is as current as the data last entered into the system.

```
                                      Gateway Industries
As of : 10/28/81                     DETAIL JOURNAL LISTING                          Page No    1

Ref. No.  Transaction Description    Account  Account Description   Dept   Date        Debits         Credits  Type
--------  -----------------------    -------  -------------------   ----   --------     -------        -------  ----
   1  BALANCE FORWARD                1000  Cash in Bank             NA    10/27/81    25000.00                    1
                                     6000  Owner Equity             NA    10/27/81                   25000.00    1
                                                            TOTAL FOR REF. #       1  25000.00       25000.00 <--- **

   2  BEGINNING BALANCE              1000  Cash in Bank             NA    10/27/81      100.00                    1
                                     1001  Petty Cash               NA    10/27/81                     100.00    1
                                                            TOTAL FOR REF. #       2    100.00         100.00 <--- **

   3  PHONE BILL                     1000  Cash in Bank             NA    10/27/81                     250.00    1
                                     1000  Cash in Bank             NA    10/27/81                     427.00    1
                                     7300  Office Supplies          10    10/27/81      177.00                    1
                                     7300  Office Supplies          20    10/27/81      250.00                    1
                                     7510  Telephone Expense        10    10/27/81      250.00                    1
                                                            TOTAL FOR REF. #       3    677.00         677.00 <--- **

AP EOM  E.O.M.  Accts Pay Entries    1000  Cash in Bank             NA    10/27/81                    5540.73    6
                                     1000  Cash in Bank             NA    10/27/81                     251.00    6
                                     1100  Inventory                NA    10/27/81    14950.00                    6
                                     1100  Inventory                NA    10/27/81   194500.00                    6
                                     3000  Accounts Payable - Trade NA    10/27/81                   10454.27    6
                                     3000  Accounts Payable - Trade NA    10/27/81                  196715.00    6
                                     3100  Accounts Payable - Sls. Tax NA 10/27/81      160.00                    6
```

```
                                      Gateway Industries
As of : 10/28/81                     DETAIL JOURNAL LISTING                          Page No    2

Ref. No.  Transaction Description    Account  Account Description   Dept   Date        Debits         Credits  Type
--------  -----------------------    -------  -------------------   ----   --------     -------        -------  ----
                                     4000  Merchandise Sales        NA    10/28/81                  300000.00    4
                                     4001  Repair Service           10    10/28/81                   61750.00    4
                                     4100  Discounts Given          .NA   10/28/81       45.00                    4
                                     5000  Cost of Goods            NA    10/28/81    70454.47                    4
                                     5001  Cost of Goods - Service  10    10/28/81   231234.90                    4
                                     7100  Freight Expense          NA    10/28/81                     100.00    4
                                     7100  Freight Expense          NA    10/28/81                     500.00    4
                                     9000  Misc. Income             NA    10/28/81                     285.00    4
                                     9000  Misc. Income             NA    10/28/81                     345.00    4
                                                     TOTAL FOR REF. # AR EOM  764989.80  764989.80 <--- **

INV EOM  E.O.M. Inventory Transaction 1100  Inventory              NA    10/27/81                      56.03    2
                                     1100  Inventory                NA    10/27/81                     151.23    2
                                     1100  Inventory                NA    10/27/81                   17677.10    2
                                     1300  Inventory Adjustments    NA    10/27/81       56.03                    2
                                     1300  Inventory Adjustments    NA    10/27/81     1510.06                    2
                                     1300  Inventory Adjustments    NA    10/27/81                    1510.06    2
                                     1300  Inventory Adjustments    NA    10/27/81      151.23                    2
                                     1300  Inventory Adjustments    NA    10/27/81    17677.10                    2
                                                     TOTAL FOR REF. # INV EOM  19394.42   19394.42 <--- **
```

FIGURE 13-10
Journal listing

SUBSIDIARY SYSTEMS

The general ledger program is the basic controlling unit of an accounting system. Although it can be used by very small companies as a complete accounting system, the G/L is too limited to be used that way for firms of even modest size. Such general ledger accounts as accounts receivable, accounts payable, and inventory do not provide all of the information required. The accounts payable general ledger account needs to be supplemented with information about each vendor to whom the firm owes money. Similarly, the accounts receivable general ledger account must be backed up with information about each of the customers who owe money to the firm.

Figure 13-11, which shows how this works, is directly related to figure 13-4. All of the subsidiary systems—accounts receivable, accounts payable, sales and invoicing, inventory control, payroll, and other systems.

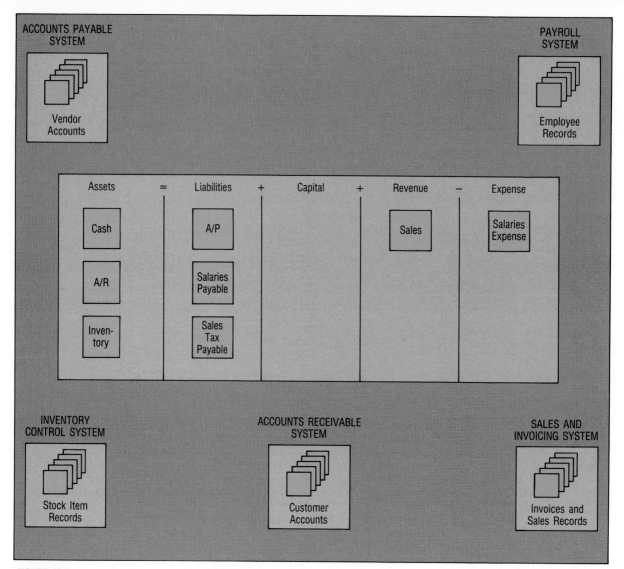

FIGURE 13-11
Subsidiary systems

First, they serve as input channels to the general ledger system and update the general ledger accounts. As sales are made, for example, the sales and invoicing subsidiary system records the sale amounts in the appropriate revenue accounts and updates the individual customer accounts in the accounts receivable subsidiary ledger for sales on account and the cash account for cash sales. It also updates inventory files to reflect both the quantity and cost of the inventory reduction. The accounts receivable and inventory control subsidiary systems, in turn, update the general ledger control accounts, accounts receivable and inventory.

Second, the subsidiary systems produce documents and reports directly related to the subsidiary ledgers. The accounts receivable system, for example, prepares customer statements and analyses of customer payment patterns. The payroll system produces payroll checks, various payroll tax reports, and reports summarizing payroll activity.

We turn now to a very brief review of each of these subsidiary systems.

Accounts Receivable

As we have just seen, the accounts receivable (A/R) system keeps individual customer accounts up to date. It is likely that lack of control over accounts receivable has led to the failure of more small businesses than any other single financial cause. Any business with more than a couple dozen customer accounts finds that keeping information about customer purchases and payments is very time consuming. Therefore, it is often not done very well with the consequence that money owed to the organization is not received promptly and is sometimes not received at all. Accounts receivable control, then, is a primary function of the accounts receivable subsidiary system.

Most businesses send *statements* to their account customers once each month. Statements summarize the period's transactions, indicate the total amount owed as of the date of the statement, and usually show how long the money has been due. Figure 13-12 illustrates a typical example.

Figure 13-13 shows an *aged invoice report*, also called an *aged accounts receivable report*. Probably no other A/R report is as important to the firm as one that indicates the amount of money due from each customer and the amount of time that it has been outstanding. This information is vital for initiating collection procedures for delinquent accounts and for making credit decisions regarding individual customers. Typically, aged accounts receivable reports break down the outstanding amounts by those that have been due 30 days or fewer, between 30 and 60 days, between 60 and 90 days, and more than 90 days.

These are by no means the only reports that accounts receivable systems prepare. They also produce reports showing customer activity, listings of cus-

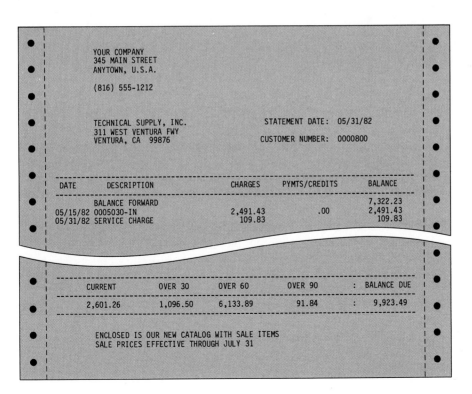

FIGURE 13-12
Customer statement

```
05/31/82                        YOUR COMPANY                    PAGE:   1
                            A/R AGED INVOICE REPORT
                                ALL INVOICES

   ---------INVOICE-----------
   DATE    NUMBER   DATE PAID    CURRENT      OVER 30      OVER 60      OVER 90


IRVINE INDUSTRIAL SUPPLY
01/31/82 0000102-IN 05/20/82       .00
02/28/82 0000301-IN 05/20/82       .00
02/28/82 0000315-IN 05/20/82       .00
02/28/82 0000425-IN 05/20/82       .00
02/28/82 0000510-IN 05/20/82       .00
02/28/82 0000531-IN 05/20/82       .00
02/28/82 0000605-IN 05/20/82                                           1,109.48
02/28/82 0000706-IN                                                    1,201.28
03/31/82 0001101-IN                                       1,166.00
04/01/82 0005000-IN                                       2,862.79
04/15/82 0005007-IN                           1,087.82
04/15/82 0005014-DM                             106.47
05/15/82 0005023-IN             373.65
                             ----------   ----------   ----------   ----------
0000100    TOTAL:   7,907.49    373.65     1,194.29     4,028.79     2,310.76

ABC DISTRIBUTION COMPANY
01/31/82 0000104-IN 05/20/82       .00
03/31/82 0001102-IN                                       1.066.46
                             ----------   ----------   ----------   ----------
0000200    TOTAL:   1,066.46       .00          .00     1,066.46          .00
CHICAGO PET SUPPLY
01/31/82 0000103-IN                                                   10,499.30
03/31/82 0001103-IN                                       3,313.40
04/01/82 0005001-IN                                       1,902.75
05/15/82 0005025-IN           3,539.00
                             ----------   ----------   ----------   ----------
0000300    TOTAL:  19,254.45  3,539.00         .00      5,216.15    10,499.30
ALLEN'S BAR AND GRILL       BF
0000400    TOTAL:   3,036.75     71.30      911.31       1,057.14       997.00
MORGAN INVESTMENTS          BF
0000500    TOTAL:  11,338.91    754.00         .00       1,594.88     8,990.03
REIDY AND COMPANY
01/31/82 0000100-IN 05/20/82                                           2,293.38
03/31/82 0001106-IN                                         272.27
04/01/82 0005003-IN                                         260.99
04/15/82 0005010-CM 05/15/82       .00
04/15/82 0005021-IN                             744.12
05/15/82 0005028-IN             927.08
                             ----------   ----------   ----------   ----------
0000600    TOTAL    4,497.84    927.08       744.12        533.26     2,293.38
```

FIGURE 13-13
Aged invoice report

tomers by salespeople, and detailed reviews of all sales on account. These examples should give you an idea of the usefulness of accounts receivable reports and the difficulty of trying to produce them using manual procedures.

Accounts Payable

Accounts payable (A/P) subsidiary systems perform three important tasks: they keep track of the amounts due to each vendor; they produce checks; and they provide forecasts of cash balances needed to make the payments.

The amounts due each vendor enter the A/P system when goods and services ordered are delivered and the vendor's invoice is approved for payment. Chapter Five discusses this process in some detail.

Paying the bills on time is of great importance, primarily because timely payment is required in order to take advantage of cash discounts offered by the vendors. Indeed, many retail organizations find that their total profits are equal to the amount of cash discounts taken.

Projecting cash needs is an important consideration in paying bills promptly. The firm does not keep great sums of money in a checking account in the bank; it prefers to invest in interest-bearing deposits. Because it can identify invoices to be paid in the future, the A/P system can project the amount of cash needed to do so. This makes for more effective funds management.

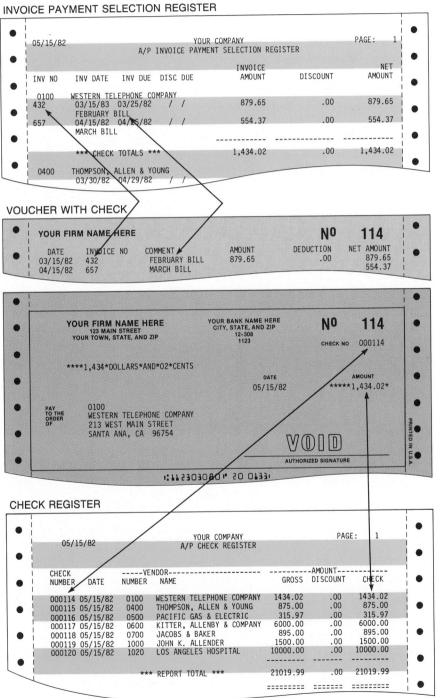

INVOICE PAYMENT SELECTION REGISTER

VOUCHER WITH CHECK

CHECK REGISTER

FIGURE 13-14
Invoice selection, voucher, and check register

Figure 13-14 shows four documents prepared by an accounts payable subsidiary system. Invoices are selected for payment according to the date they must be paid in order to qualify for the cash discount. This information is used to prepare a voucher authorizing payment. The system produces the check and the check register which lists all of the checks prepared.

Payroll

Producing the payroll is certainly one of the most critical accounting tasks that a firm must undertake. The deadlines are relentless. Payroll checks must be delivered to employees every week or two. Reports of tax withholding must be submitted to taxing agencies with frequencies ranging from every few days to every quarter, and summary reports must be submitted each year to the government and to the employees. Accuracy is essential. There are few errors as embarassing or more insistent on immediate correction as miscalculating an employee's pay.

In the United States, every organization with one or more employees is required to deduct federal income tax withholding and Social Security taxes from employees' pay and to submit these amounts periodically to the Internal Revenue Service. In addition, the employer is levied payroll taxes over and above the amounts deducted from the employees' pay for state and federal unemployment programs. Two thirds of the states also require state income tax withholding. Besides tax deductions, voluntary employee deductions for

FIGURE 13-15
Employee master listing

```
                                             GATEWAY INDUSTRIES
 As of: 10/ 8/82                           EMPLOYEE MASTER LISTING                                    PAGE:  1

  Employee ID : KEEPER  Empl. Status : ACTIVE       Taxation State     : CA
 ----------------------------------------------------------------------------   ---------------------------- QTD --------- YTD -----
 Empl. Name        : JAMES KEEPER                   No. Fed Exempt     :          1   Gross Pay          :   2425.80     7277.40
 Empl. Address 1 : 8274 JOHNSON AVE                 State Reg Exempt   :          1   Fed With. Tax      :    274.17      822.51
       Address 2 :                                  State Extra Exempt:           0   FICA Tax Withheld :    162.53      487.59
       Cty & St. : SAN JOSE, CA                     State Exempt Amt   :       0.00   State With. Tax    :     36.92      110.76
       Zip Code  : 95462                            St. Filing Status :      Single   State Disability   :     16.98       50.94
 Soc. Sec. No.     : 457-45-7900                                                      Local With. Tax    :      0.00        0.00
 Pay Rate          :       4.5600                                                     FICA Taxable Pay   :   2425.80     7277.40
 Department No.    :     20
 Empl. Pay Code    : (2)  Weekly Payroll --> Salaried, Exempt
 Marital Status    : Single
 FWT Exempt        : No
 FICA Exempt       : No
 Employee sex      : Male
 Empl Eth. Origin: Caucasian
 ----------------------------------------------------------------------------
 SL/Pay Period     :     0.8                        Accrued S/L        :    6.4
 Vac/Pay Period    :     1.5                        Accrued Vacation   :    9.4
 ----------------------------------------------------------------------------
 Date of Hire      : 11/25/81
 Last Review Date:  2/25/82
 Next Review Date:  3/25/83
 Rate Change Date:  2/25/82


  Employee ID : WAXTON  Empl. Status : ACTIVE       Taxation State     : CA
 ----------------------------------------------------------------------------   ---------------------------- QTD --------- YTD -----
 Empl. Name        : GEORGE WAXTON                  No. Fed Exempt     :          5   Gross Pay          :   6654.70    19964.10
 Empl. Address 1 : 3421 S. CHERRY LN                State Reg Exempt   :          2   Fed With. Tax      :    842.92     2528.76
       Address 2 :                                  State Extra Exempt:           3   FICA Tax Withheld :    445.86     1337.59
       Cty & St. : SANTA CLARA, CA                  State Exempt Amt   :       0.00   State With. Tax    :    121.42      364.26
       Zip Code  : 95654                            St. Filing Status : Mar-Joint    State Disability   :     46.58      139.74
 Soc. Sec. No.     : 857-70-9856                                                      Local With. Tax    :      0.00        0.00
 Pay Rate          :      10.6645                                                     FICA Taxable Pay   :   6654.70    19964.10
 Department No.    :     10
 Empl. Pay Code    : (2)  Weekly Payroll --> Salaried, Exempt
 Marital Status    : Married
 FWT Exempt        : No
 FICA Exempt       : No
 Employee sex      : Male
 Empl Eth. Origin: Caucasian
 ----------------------------------------------------------------------------
 SL/Pay Period     :     0.8                        Accrued S/L        :   15.0
 Vac/Pay Period    :     1.5                        Accrued Vacation   :   65.5
 ----------------------------------------------------------------------------
 Date of Hire      :  1/15/80
 Last Review Date:  4/15/82
 Next Review Date:  4/15/83
 Rate Change Date:  4/15/82
```

```
GATEWAY INDUSTRIES                        PAYROLL REGISTER SUMMARY                    As of: 10/ 8/82              PAGE   1

                            GROSS    REGULAR  OVERTIME  SICK LV  VACATION  HOLIDAY  ADDL PAY/     NET
    EMPL-ID EMPLOYEE NAME     PAY    PAY/HRS   PAY/HRS  PAY/HRS  PAY/HRS   PAY/HRS  TOTAL DED     PAY      ERROR MESSAGE
    -------  -------------  -------  -------  --------  -------  --------  -------  ---------   -------   -------------
    AKINS    JOHN AKINS      221.92   209.42                                          12.50     155.10
                                       40.0                                           66.82

    GREEN    MICHAEL GREEN   195.84   195.84                                                    139.49
                                       40.0                                           56.35

    KEEPER   JAMES KEEPER    182.40   145.92                     36.48                          131.05
                                       32.0                       8.0                 51.35

    MORTON   JAMES MORTON    418.24   418.24                                                    300.93
                                       40.0                                          117.31

    SMITH    STEVEN SMITH    253.00   253.00                                                    188.07
                                       40.0                                           64.93

    STEVE    NANCY STEVENSON 354.96   354.96                                                    211.12
                                       40.0                                          143.84

                            ========= ========= ========= ========= ========= ========= ========= =========
    ****  REPORT TOTALS **** 1626.36  1577.38    0.00      0.00     36.48     0.00     12.50    1125.76
                                       232.0      0.0       0.0       8.0      0.0     500.60
```

FIGURE 13-16
Payroll register

retirement and insurance plans, savings, union dues, payments to banks and credit unions must be taken and accounted for.

Without a payroll program, all this work must be done by hand. It's no wonder that computerized payroll systems are popular.

Payroll systems perform a number of tasks. They maintain information about each employee, including personal information as well as payroll histories. They produce payroll checks and payroll check registers. They account for all of the voluntary and involuntary withholdings from employees' pay and produce reports to be submitted to the government agencies that require them.

Figure 13-15 shows a listing of employees from a payroll employee master file. Personal data are maintained on the file, as is information about earned and used vacation, pay rates, evaluation reviews, gross pay earned for the quarter and the year, and taxes withheld.

In figure 13-16, the payroll register lists the payments and deductions for each employee for the current period.

These sample payroll reports do not include all of the reports that payroll systems produce. They do suggest, however, the complexity and laboriousness of payroll accounting if undertaken manually.

Sales and Invoicing

Sales and invoicing systems provide data for the accounts receivable and inventory control systems. They also maintain the general ledger revenue accounts and prepare invoices, shipping orders, and a wide variety of sales analysis reports.

Figure 13-17 illustrates an invoice prepared by a sales and invoicing system. It shows the customer's name and delivery instructions, the customer's purchase order number, the date, the shipping instructions, the discount terms, the merchandise ordered and the quantities, the unit price of each item purchased, and the extended amounts with totals and other information printed toward the bottom of the invoice form.

In figure 13-18, the system has prepared a detailed summary of sales over a period of time. The summary is organized by sales order number. The same information can be used to produce reports organized by customer, by merchandise item, by the salespeople who made the sales, or by groups of merchandise. This information is most useful in analyzing the activity of customers, analyzing products, and evaluating salespeople.

```
Gateway Industries - DEMO                              INVOICE NO.   1022
Bicycle Products Division
1278 Golden Gate Dr.                                   CUSTOMER NO.   IBS
San Francisco, CA  95123


   BILL TO:                                 SHIP TO:
      Inter. Bicycle Sales                     Inter. Bicycle Sales
      1238 Federal Bldg.                       1238 Federal Bldg.
      Avenue of the Americas                   Avenue of the Americas
      New York, NY                             New York, NY
                   11507                                    11507
```

DATE	SHIP VIA		F.O.B.	TERMS	
2/ 4/81			Origin	5.0% 10/Net 30 Days	

PURCHASE ORDER NUMBER		ORDER DATE	SALES PERSON		OUR ORDER NUMBER
1234		2/ 4/81	John		1011

QUANTITY			ITEM NUMBER	DESCRIPTION	UNIT PRICE	EXTENDED PRICE
ORDERED	SHIPPED	B.O.				
25	20	5	1001	26 in. BICYCLE	150.00	3000.00
10	8	2	1000	20 in. Bicycle	100.00	800.00
				Shipment Sub-Total		3800.00
				Discount Allowed		-380.00
				Freight Charges		96.00
				Invoice Total		3516.00

FIGURE 13-17
Sales invoice

```
                                     Gateway Industries                                               Page    1
As of :  3/29/81                SALES ORDER DETAIL BY SALES ORDER NUMBER
  SO                                                                     Unit                 Order  Open
Number Customer      Customer Name       Part Number    Part Description Price   Due Date      Qty    Qty  Ext Price

  1000 IBS           Inter. Bicycle Sales  1002 24 in. BICYCLE           120.00  5/ 9/80       50      0      0.00
                                           1002 24 in. BICYCLE           120.00  5/ 7/80       50     40   4800.00
                                           1002 24 in. BICYCLE           120.00  5/ 7/80       75     55   6600.00
                                           1001 26 in. BICYCLE           150.00  5/ 9/80       27     -4      0.00
                                           ***** SALES ORDER TOTAL *****                            11400.00

  1002 STANS         Stan's Cyclery      3965-1050 SPOKE REFLECTOR         3.00  4/28/80        2      1      3.00
                                         7600-50 CHAIN                     4.00  5/ 9/80        7      2      8.00
                                         1001 26 in. BICYCLE             150.00  5/ 6/80        2      0      0.00
                                         ***** SALES ORDER TOTAL *****                                 11.00

  1004 WHEEL         Wheelaway Cycle Center  1003 20 in. BICYCLE         100.00  5/ 6/80       20     20   2000.00
                                         ***** SALES ORDER TOTAL *****                               2000.00

  1005 IBS           Inter. Bicycle Sales  NON-STOCK  CHROME WHEEL NUTS    1.25  5/ 6/80      100      0      0.00
                                         4200-0020 STANDARD SEAT           8.00  5/ 7/80       20      0      0.00
                                         3974-1005 SPOKE                   2.50  5/ 9/80      300      0      0.00
                                         3970-1011 WHEEL - 26 in.         45.00  5/ 9/80       25      0      0.00
                                         3965-1050 SPOKE REFLECTOR         3.00  5/ 9/80       50      0      0.00
                                         ***** SALES ORDER TOTAL *****                                  0.00

  1006 RODEBYKE      Rodebyke Bic. & Mopeds  7600-50 CHAIN                 4.00  5/ 9/80       20      9     36.00
                                         1003 20 in. BICYCLE             100.00  5/ 7/80       20     10   1000.00
                                         ***** SALES ORDER TOTAL *****                               1036.00
```

```
                                     Gateway Industries                                               Page    2
As of :  3/29/81                SALES ORDER DETAIL BY SALES ORDER NUMBER
  SO                                                                     Unit                 Order  Open
Number Customer      Customer Name       Part Number    Part Description Price   Due Date      Qty    Qty  Ext Price

  1016 IBS           Inter. Bicycle Sales  1000 20 in. BICYCLE            80.00  3/ 4/81      100    100   8000.00
                                         ***** SALES ORDER TOTAL *****                               8000.00

  1017 RODEBYKE      Rodebyke Bic. & Mopeds  NON-STOCK  GREASE             1.00  3/10/81        1      1      1.00
                                         1001 26 in. BICYCLE             150.00  3/10/81      100    100  15000.00
                                         1000 20 in. BICYCLE              80.00  3/10/81       10     10    800.00
                                         ***** SALES ORDER TOTAL *****                              15801.00
```

FIGURE 13-18
Sales order report

Inventory Control

Taking inventory means counting the physical amount of goods and materials on hand. Such a count is called a *physical inventory*. Physical inventories must be taken from time to time by all businesses. Businesses also maintain *book inventories,* which are running counts of the quantities of merchandise on hand. A book inventory can be calculated at any time by adding the beginning inventory and quantities purchased and deducting quantities withdrawn for each merchandise item. Note that these calculations do not use monetary values, rather they employ physical counts of inventory items. Once the physical count of an item is determined, one need only multiply that by the cost of the item to determine the value of the inventory.

That's easy enough if the business has but a few items of inventory. An organization that has hundreds or thousands of inventory items could not do it without an inventory control program. Knowing the quantities of inventory on hand is vital to the successful operation of the firm. For most businesses, being out of stock guarantees that a sale will be lost. Running counts of inventory quantities provide essential information needed to purchase or manufacture replacements so that sales orders can be filled promptly.

Inventory control systems deduct sales quantities from the quantities on hand and use the resulting information to update the general ledger inventory accounts, prepare inventory status reports, and signal when additional stocks of inventory should be ordered. They also help to identify slow-moving inventory, thus suggesting special promotional efforts and product line changes or discontinuance. Figure 13-19, for example, calculates the cost value of each item of inventory.

We close this discussion of the general ledger and subsidiary accounting systems by repeating our observation that the information provided by these systems is both vital for the success of the organization and very difficult to produce using manual methods. Accounting system functions are operational

FIGURE 13-19
Inventory evaluation report

```
05/29/82              STATE OF THE ART OFFICE SUPPLY              PAGE:    1
* MEANS DISCONTINUED    I/C INVENTORY VALUATION REPORT
                         ALL ITEMS AT UNIT COST

-------ITEM----------              ON-HAND      UNIT       INVENTORY
  NUMBER    DESCRIPTION        UM  QUANTITY     COST        VALUE

010 DESK ACCESSORIES

   100      ASH TRAY - BLACK 8"   EA    31      11.00         341.00
   200      BOOK STYLE CALENDAR   EA    76      16.50       1,254.00
   300      DOUBLE LETTER TRAY    EA    19      44.50         845.50
   400      DOUBLE PEN SET        EA    11      26.00         286.00
                                                           -----------
                       PRODUCT LINE TOTAL                   2,726.50


020 RING BINDERS

   750      1" 3 RING FLEXIBLE COVER  EA  34    1.01          34.34
   850      1" 3 RING STIFF COVER     EA  80    2.50         200.00
                                                           -----------
                       PRODUCT LINE TOTAL                    234.34


030 SHIPPING ROOM SUPPLIES

 W3-1000A   KRAFT PAPER 18" WIDE   EA    45
 W3-2000A   KRAFT PAPER 24" WIDE   EA    94
 W3-3000A   KRAFT PAPER 36" WIDE   EA
 W3-4000A   JUTE TWINE - 2 PLY     EA
      A     JUTE TWINE - 4 PLY
```

necessities, and they produce documents that are required by law. No other application programs provide as much direct help in operating a business organization as do accounting systems.

USING AN ACCOUNTING SYSTEM

Robert Cratchit operates an accounting service bureau for small businesses. His clientele consists of business owners who have no experience or training in accounting, yet need to maintain a set of books for tax purposes and for general review of their business operations. His customers deliver accounting

FIGURE 13-20
Mighty Midget Widget Works
Chart of Accounts

```
                    MIGHTY MIDGET WIDGET WORKS
                 Chart of Accounts and Account Balances
                            July 1, 1986

        Current Assets
            001010      Cash                          $9,221.80
            001020      Petty Cash Fund                   50.00
            001040      Accounts Receivable              392.25
            001060      Inventory                      3,197.85
            001080      Supplies                         291.12
            001100      Prepaid Insurance                800.00

        Fixed Assets
            001230      Tools and Equipment           12,857.50
            001240      Accumulated Depreciation,
                          Tools and Equipment          2,571.50
            001270      Furniture and Fixtures         6,212.98
            001280      Accumulated Depreciation,
                          Furniture and Fixtures         887.50

        Liabilities
            002010      Accounts Payable                 472.85
            002020      Sales Taxes Payable               36.00
            002040      Notes Payable                  8,057.62

        Capital
            003010      J. Watt, Proprietorship       20,817.96
            003020      J. Watt, Drawing
            003030      Net Income/Loss

        Revenues
            004010      Widget Sales
            004030      Service Revenue

        Expenses
            005030      Utilities Expense
            005050      Telephone Expense
            005070      Rent Expense
            005090      Supplies Expense
            005100      Insurance Expense
            005130      Depreciation Expense,
                          Tools and Equipment
            005150      Depreciation Expense,
                          Furniture and Fixtures
            005170      Miscellaneous Expense
            005200      Insurance Expense
            006100      Purchases
            006200      Purchase Discounts
            007010      Cost of Sales
```

```
                    Mighty Midget Widget Works
Date: 070186              Ledger Chart of Accounts              Page  1

         Account Number         Type    Dept        Title

              001010              A        1         Cash
              001020              A        1         Petty Cash Fund
              001040              A        1         Accounts Receivable
              001060              I        1         Inventory
              001080              A        1         Supplies
              001100              A        1         Prepaid Insurance
              001230              A        1         Tools and Equipment
              001240              A        1         Acc. Dep. Tools & Equip.
              001270              A        1         Furniture and Fixtures
              001280              A        1         Acc. Dep. Furn. & Fix.
              002010              L        1         Accounts Payable
              002020              L        1         Sales Taxes Payable
              002040              L        1         Notes Payable
              003010              C        1         J. Watt, Proprietorship
              003020              C        1         J. Watt, Drawing
              003030              C        1         Net Income/Loss
              004010              S        1         Widget Sales
              004030              S        1         Service Revenue
              005030              E        1         Utilities Expense
              005050              E        1         Telephone Expense
              005070              E        1         Rent Expense
              005090              E        1         Supplies Expense
              005100              E        1         Insurance Expense
              005130              E        1         Dep. Exp. Tools & Equip.
              005150              E        1         Dep. Exp. Furn. & Fix.
              005170              E        1         Miscellaneous Expense
              005200              E        1         Interest Expense
              006100              M        1         Purchases
              006200              M        1         Purchase Discounts
              007010              M        1         Cost of Sales


          There are 30 ledger account entries on file.
```

FIGURE 13-21
Mighty Midget Widget Works Chart of Accounts

information to him, which he uses to prepare income statements, balance sheets, and a few other accounting documents. With few exceptions, all of his clients' needs are satisfied with the reports produced by a general ledger system that Bob uses with his microcomputer. This system, called the Multiple Journal Accounting Software System (MJA), supports multiple clients and is therefore ideal for Bob's operation, although it can be used as well by individual businesses.

During the month of June, Bob was contacted by James Watt, an inventor from Glasgow who perfected the midget widget, a miniaturized version of the well-known but clumsy widget.* Having sold the manufacturing rights to midget widgets, Watt now sells and maintains widgets in the greater Spokane metropolitan area.

* Invention of the widget is attributed to Elmer Fagan, for forty years Professor of Economics at Stanford University. On his retirement in 1961, his students presented him with the world's first operational widget. He was also awarded the coveted Dinklespiel Award for Excellence in Teaching.

Bob agreed to maintain Watt's books. Watt provided Bob with a chart of accounts and their balances as of the first of July, figure 13-20. At the end of each month, Watt will deliver a list of transactions for the month. Bob will prepare monthly income statements and balance sheets and a few other documents routinely prepared by the general ledger system.

Setting Up the Books

Bob's first task is to set up the books for Watt's company which is called the Mighty Midget Widget Works (MMWW). It takes less than two hours to do this using MJA's procedures. This short period resulted from the limited number of MMWW accounts and the fact that Watt had been careful in preparing the account balance figures shown in figure 13-20. Ordinarily, firms converting from manual to computerized systems find that the conversion takes a great deal of time, usually because the books are in poor shape. That's why they decided to use computers. Fortunately for Bob, that was not the case with MMWW.

For the last step in setting up the books, Bob uses the computer system to list the chart of accounts (figure 13-21) and a trial balance (figure 13-22). The *trial balance* shows all of the accounts used in MMWW's books and their current balances. The totals at the bottom of the first two amount columns show that the accounts, as set up, are in balance. The report also provides room to make notation of various entries that will be required when closing the books at the end of an accounting period.

Entering the Transactions

FIGURE 13-22
Mighty Midget Widget Works
Trial Balance, July 1

On the last day of July, Watt delivers the month's transactions for Mighty Midget Widget Works, figure 13-23. Bob enters these in preparation for producing the various general ledger reports Watt wants.

```
                              Mighty Midget Widget Works

As of: 07/01/86            T R I A L   B A L A N C E   W O R K S H E E T        Page 1     Rundate: 07/01/86

Account     Account Title         Trial Balance            Adjustments      Profit / Loss      Balance Sheet

001010 Cash                 *     9,221.80 :       *           :       *        :       *         :       *
001020 Petty Cash Fund      *        50.00 :       *           :       *        :       *         :       *
001040 Accounts Receivable  *       392.25 :       *           :       *        :       *         :       *
001060 Inventory            *     3,197.85 :       *           :       *        :       *         :       *
001080 Supplies             *       291.12 :       *           :       *        :       *         :       *
001100 Prepaid Insurance    *       800.00 :       *           :       *        :       *         :       *
001230 Tools and Equipment  *    12,857.50 :       *           :       *        :       *         :       *
001240 Acc. Dep. Tools & Equip. *          :    2,751.50       *        :       *         :       *         *
001270 Furniture and Fixtures *   6,212.98 :       *           :       *        :       *         :       *
001280 Acc. Dep. Furn. & Fix. *          :      887.57 *       :       *        :       *         :       *
002010 Accounts Payable     *            :      472.85 *       :       *        :       *         :       *
002020 Sales Taxes Payable  *            :       36.00 *       :       *        :       *         :       *
002040 Notes Payable        *            :    8,057.62 *       :       *        :       *         :       *
003010 J. Watt, Proprietorship *        :   20,817.96 *       :       *        :       *         :       *
003020 J. Watt, Drawing     *       0.00 :       *           :       *        :       *         :       *
003030 Net Income/Loss      *       0.00 :       *           :       *        :       *         :       *
004010 Widget Sales         *       0.00 :       *           :       *        :       *         :       *
004030 Service Revenue      *       0.00 :       *           :       *        :       *         :       *
005030 Utilities Expense    *       0.00 :       *           :       *        :       *         :       *
005050 Telephone Expense    *       0.00 :       *           :       *        :       *         :       *
005070 Rent Expense         *       0.00 :       *           :       *        :       *         :       *
005090 Supplies Expense     *       0.00 :       *           :       *        :       *         :       *
005100 Insurance Expense    *       0.00 :       *           :       *        :       *         :       *
005130 Dep. Exp. Tools & Equip. *   0.00 :       *           :       *        :       *         :       *
005150 Dep. Exp. Furn. & Fix. *     0.00 :       *           :       *        :       *         :       *
005170 Miscellaneous Expense *      0.00 :       *           :       *        :       *         :       *
005200 Interest Expense     *       0.00 :       *           :       *        :       *         :       *
006100 Purchases            *       0.00 :       *           :       *        :       *         :       *
006200 Purchase Discounts   *       0.00 :       *           :       *        :       *         :       *
007010 Cost of Sales        *       0.00 :       *           :       *        :       *         :       *

       Totals              *    33,023.50 :   33,023.50 *
```

```
            MIGHTY MIDGET WIDGET WORKS
            Transactions for July, 1986

  1.  Paid rent for July, $650.00

  1.  Received $22.85 from Barnaby Jones, payment on account

  6.  Deposited cash receipts for July 1 through 6
          Services $887.50
          Merchandise sales, 4 widgets @ $495.00, $1,980.00
          Sales tax collected $118.80

  8.  Paid utility bill for June, $63.14, check #1088

  9.  Paid Mammoth Midget Widget Manufacturing Multinational
      $472.85 on account, invoice #86-1020, less 2% discount,
      check #1089

  9.  Received 6 widgets from Mammoth Midget Widget Manu-
      facturing Multinational, invoice #86-1025, $1,620.00 on
      account

 10.  Paid telephone bill for June, $24.85, check #1090

 12.  Billed Downtown Diversions, Inc. $350.00 for monthly
      maintenance service (July) plus $83.12 for replacement
      parts and $4.99 sales tax, invoice #5702
```

```
 31.  Watt withdrew $900 for personal use, check #1094

 31.  Paid Richard Uncle Finance Company $77.20 interest on
      note payable, check #1095

 31.  Replenished cash fund for miscellaneous expenses paid,
      $32.15
```

FIGURE 13-23
Mighty Midget Widget Works Transactions for July, 1986

MJA is a menu-driven system, as are most accounting programs. From the Start Menu in figure 13-24, Bob selects the general ledger option. From the general ledger Main Menu, figure 13-25, he picks the second option which lets him enter transactions using an input screen as shown in figure 13-26. For each transaction he enters a reference, the date of the transaction, the

```
    Multi Journal Accounting System - Start Menu



        1)  General Ledger Accounting System

        2)  Payroll and Personnel System

        3)  Accounts Receivable System

        4)  Accounts Payable Software System

        5)  Sales Order Entry / Inventory

        6)  MJA System Managers Programs

        7)  Set / Reset Client Code:

        Select Number or (RETURN to exit):  1
```

```
    General Ledger Accounting System - Main Menu
                Mighty Midget Widget Works

        1)  Chart of Accounts (Add / Edit / List)

        2)  General Journal Transactions (Add & Edit)

        3)  General Journal Transaction Reports

        4)  General Ledger Reports

        5)  Company Financial Statements and Reports

        6)  Automatic Period Holdover

        7)  General Ledger System Utilities

        8)  System Managers Inquiry and Update
            Select Number or (RETURN to exit):  1
```

FIGURE 13-24
Start menu

FIGURE 13-25
General ledger menu

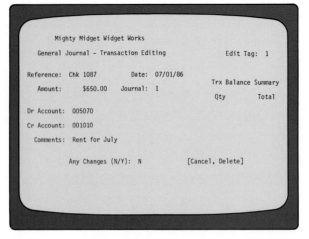

FIGURE 13-26
Transaction input screen

amount of the transaction, the journal number (1 for General Journal), the accounts to be debited and credited, and a descriptive comment. When he completes each input screen, the program asks for verification before processing the data.

Accounting transactions always have at least two entries. Each transaction must have at least one debit and one credit entry and the sum of the debit entries must equal the sum of the credit entries. That's how the system keeps the books in balance. The transaction shown in figure 13-26 is the first one for the month—payment of $650.00 rent—a debit to Rent Expense (Account 005070) and a credit to Cash (Account 001010).

The month's transactions provided by Watt included some end-of-the-month adjustments which Bob enters as transactions. These include entries to expense accounts for supplies used, depreciation accumulated, and insurance expired during the month, figure 13-27. These figures also include the value of inventory at the end of the month, which the accounting system needs to calculate cost of goods sold.

Producing the Reports

Having entered all of the transactions, Bob now uses the General Ledger Transaction Reports menu (figure 13-28), to prepare the reports Watt requires.

FIGURE 13-27
Mighty Midget Widget Works
adjusting entry data

```
              MIGHTY MIDGET WIDGET WORKS
              End-of-Month Adjusting Data
                     July, 1986


    1.  Value of inventory, $1602.02

    2.  Value of supplies used in July, $88.92

    3.  Depreciation of tools and equipment for July, $179.97

    4.  Depreciation of Furniture and Fixtures for July, $73.86

    5.  Insurance expense for July, $33.33
```

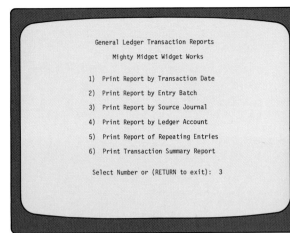

FIGURE 13-28
General ledger transaction reports menu

Figure 13-29 shows the transactions in the order in which they were entered. In addition to the transaction listings, Watt requires a report showing the activity of each account in the general ledger for the period. Using menu selection techniques, Bob produces this report as shown in figure 13-30.

The account activity report lists each entry and the account into which it was entered by the system. It also shows the beginning and ending balances of the accounts, the comments entered with the transactions, and, for each entry, the offsetting debit or credit account. It provides a thorough *audit trail* of each transaction, the means by which the recorded data for business activities can be verified for accuracy.

Finally, Bob produces the income statement and balance sheet for Mighty Midget Widget Works. These appear in figures 13-31 and 13-32.

FIGURE 13-29
Transaction register

```
                      Mighty Midget Widget Works

  As of: 07/31/86          G/L Transaction Register      Page 1          07/31/86

                                 -- Account --      Transaction Amounts
                                 Debit  Credit         Debit      Credit
   Tag Reference     Date    Src Debit  Credit         Debit      Credit      Comments

     1  Chk 1087   07/01/86   1  005070 001010        650.00      650.00    Rent for July
     2  Inv 5701   07/01/86   1  001010 001040         22.85       22.85    Barnaby Jones
     3  Cash       07/06/86   1  001010              2,986.30               Receipts, 7/1 - 7/6
     4  Cash       07/06/86   1         004030                    887.50    Receipts, 7/1 - 7/6
     5  Cash       07/06/86   1         004010                  1,980.00    Receipts, 7/1 - 7/6
     6  Cash       07/06/86   1         002020                    188.80    Receipts, 7/1 - 7/6
     7  Cash       07/06/86   1  002020                 70.00               Receipts, 7/1 - 7/6
     8  Chk 1088   07/08/86   1  005030 001010         63.14       63.14    Utilities for June
     9  Chk 1089   07/09/86   1  002010               469.39               MMWMM Inv. 86-10210
    10  Chk 1089   07/09/86   1         002010                    469.39    MMWMM Inv. 86-10210
    11  Chk 1089   07/09/86   1  002010               472.85               MMWMM Inv. 86-10210
    12  Chk 1089   07/09/86   1         001010                    463.39    MMWMM Inv. 86-10210
    13  Chk 1089   07/09/86   1  006200                 9.46                MMWMM Inv. 86-10210
    14  Chk 1089   07/09/86   1         006200                     18.92    MMWMM Inv. 86-10210
    15  86-1025    07/09/86   1  006100 002010       1,620.00    1,620.00   6 Widgets Received, MMWMM
    16  Chk 1090   07/10/86   1  005050 001010         24.85       24.85    Telephone for June
    17  Inv 5702   07/12/86   1  001040               438.11               Downtown Diversions Inc.
    18  Inv 5702   07/12/86   1         004030                    350.00    Downtown Diversions Inc.
    19  Inv 5702   07/12/86   1         004010                     83.12    Downtown Diversions Inc.
    20  Inv 5702   07/12/86   1         002020                      4.99    Downtown Diversions Inc.

    53  Chk 1095   07/31/86   1  005100 001010         77.22       77.22    July interest on note
    54  Chk 1096   07/31/86   1  005170 001010         32.15       32.15    To petty cash fund
    63  Chk 1095   07/31/86   1  005200 001010         77.22       77.22    Interest on M/R July

                                    Totals         16,846.31   16,846.31
  Cash Totals: Debit    82560.00    Credit         114110.00
```

Acct #	Description	Tag	Date	Jrnl#	Debit	Credit	Reference	Offset	Comments
									Mighty Midget Widget Works
									General Ledger Accounts Reports
As Of: 07/31/86								Page 1	Rundate: 07/31/86
001010	Cash				9,221.80				Beginning Balance
		1	07/01/86	GJ		650.00	Chk 1087	005070	Rent for July
		2	07/01/86	GJ	22.85		Inv 5701	001040	Barnaby Jones
		3	07/06/86	GJ	2,986.30		Cash		Receipts, 7/1 - 7/6
		8	07/08/86	GJ		63.14	Chk 1088	005030	Utilities for June
		12	07/09/86	GJ		463.39	Chk 1089		MMWM Inv. 86-10210
		16	07/10/86	GJ		24.85	Chk 1090	005050	Telephone for June
		21	07/13/86	GJ	947.56		Cash		Receipts, 7/7 - 7/13
		26	07/16/86	GJ	438.11		Inv 5702	001040	Downtown Diversions Inc.
		27	07/16/86	GJ		900.00	Chk 1091	003020	Watt Salary
		29	07/19/86	GJ	533.22		Cash		Receipts, 7/7 - 7/19
		34	07/19/86	GJ		1,587.60	Chk 1092		Inv. 86-1025
		37	07/14/86	GJ	47.85		Inv. 5703	001040	Cash McCall
		39	07/27/86	GJ	2,392.10		Cash		Receipts 7/20 - 7/27
		46	07/30/86	GJ	188.99		Chk 1093		Inv 86-11007 MMWM
		48	07/31/86	GJ	301.38		Cash		Receipts, 7/26 - 7/31
		52	07/31/86	GJ		900.00	Chk 1094	003020	Watt Salary
		53	07/31/86	GJ		77.22	Chk 1095	005100	July interest on note
		54	07/31/86	GJ		32.15	Chk 1096	005170	To petty cash fund
		63	07/31/86	GJ		77.22	Chk 1095	005200	Interest on N/R July
	Net Change:	3,082.79							
	Ending Balance:	12,304.59			7,858.36	4,775.57			
001020	Petty Cash Fund				50.00				Beginning Balance
	Net Change:	0.00							
	Ending Balance:	50.00			0.00	0.00			
001040	Accounts Receivable				392.25				Beginning Balance
		2	07/01/86	GJ		22.85	Inv 5701	001010	Barnaby Jones
		17	07/12/86	GJ	438.11		Inv 5702		Downtown Diversions Inc.
		26	07/16/86	GJ		438.11	Inv 5702	001010	Downtown Diversions Inc.
		28	07/18/86	GJ	47.85		Inv 5703	004030	Cash McCall
		37	07/14/86	GJ		47.85	Inv 5703	001010	Cash McCall
		38	07/25/86	GJ	329.00		Inv 5704	004030	Emily's Emporium
		44	07/28/86	GJ	990.00		Inv 5705	004010	Emily's Emporium
	Net Change:	1,296.15							
	Ending Balance:	1,688.40			1,804.96	508.81			
001060	Inventory				3,197.85				Beginning Balance
		59	07/31/86	ADJ		3,197.85	Adjust	007010	Beginning Inventory
		60	07/31/86	ADJ	1,602.02		Adjust	007010	Ending Inventory

FIGURE 13-30
Account activity report

FIGURE 13-31
Mighty Midget Widget Works
Income Statement

The income statement and balance sheet make use of the Multiple Journal Accounting system standard formats. Had Watt desired, Bob could have prepared a set of specifications to prepare these documents in a number of different formats.

Mighty Midget Widget Works
INCOME STATEMENT
for the Month ended 07/31/86

Revenue	Month to Date		Quarter to Date		Year to Date		:	Adjustments
Widget Sales	5,257.16	60.36 %	5,257.16	60.36 %	5,257.16	60.36 %	:	
Service Revenue	3,452.32	39.64 %	3,452.32	39.64 %	3,452.32	39.64 %	:	
Total Revenue	8,709.48	100.00 %	8,709.48	100.00 %	8,709.48	100.00 %	:	
Cost of Sales	Month to Date		Quarter to Date		Year to Date		:	Adjustments
Purchases	1,812.85	20.81 %	1,812.85	20.81 %	1,812.85	20.81 %	:	-1812.85
Purchase Discounts	-38.00	-0.44 %	-38.00	-0.44 %	-38.00	-0.44 %	:	38.00
Cost of Sales	1,595.83	18.32 %	1,595.83	18.32 %	1,595.83	18.32 %	:	11349.83
Total Cost of Sales	3,370.68	38.70 %	3,370.68	38.70 %	3,370.68	38.70 %	:	11349.83
Gross Profit on Sales	5,338.80	61.30 %	5,338.80	61.30 %	5,338.80	61.30 %	:	11349.83
Expenses	Month to Date		Quarter to Date		Year to Date		:	Adjustments
Utilities Expense	63.14	0.72 %	63.14	0.72 %	63.14	0.72 %	:	
Telephone Expense	24.85	0.29 %	24.85	0.29 %	24.85	0.29 %	:	
Rent Expense	650.00	7.46 %	650.00	7.46 %	650.00	7.46 %	:	
Supplies Expense	88.92	1.02 %	88.92	1.02 %	88.92	1.02 %	:	622.44
Insurance Expense	110.55	1.27 %	110.55	1.27 %	110.55	1.27 %	:	233.31
Dep. Exp. Tools & Equip.	179.97	2.07 %	179.97	2.07 %	179.97	2.07 %	:	1259.79
Dep. Exp. Furn. & Fix.	73.96	0.85 %	73.96	0.85 %	73.96	0.85 %	:	517.72
Miscellaneous Expense	32.15	0.37 %	32.15	0.37 %	32.15	0.37 %	:	
Interest Expense	77.22	0.89 %	77.22	0.89 %	77.22	0.89 %	:	
Total Expenses	1,300.76	14.93 %	1,300.76	14.93 %	1,300.76	14.93 %	:	
Net Profit and/or Loss	4,038.04	46.36 %	4,038.04	46.36 %	4,038.04	46.36 %	:	

```
                    Mighty Midget Widget Works

                    B A L A N C E    S H E E T

                          07/31/86


    Assets
      Misc Assets
        Cash                            12,304.59
        Petty Cash Fund                     50.00
        Accounts Receivable              1,688.40
        Supplies                           202.20
        Prepaid Insurance                  766.67
        Tools and Equipment             12,857.50
        Acc. Dep. Tools & Equip.                       2,931.47
        Furniture and Fixtures           6,212.98
        Acc. Dep. Furn. & Fix.                           961.53
      Total Misc Assets                                            30,189.34

      Inventory Assets
        Total Inventory                                             1,602.02

    Total Assets                                                   31,791.36

    Liabilities
      Misc Liabilities
        Accounts Payable                                 385.70
        Sales Taxes Payable                              292.04
        Notes Payable                                  8,057.62

      Total Misc Liabilities                                        8,735.36

      Owners Equity
        J. Watt, Proprietorship                       20,817.96
        J. Watt, Drawing                 1,800.00
        Net Income/Loss                                4,038.04

      Total Owners Equity                                          23,056.00

    Total Liabilities and Owners Equity                            31,791.36
```

FIGURE 13-32
Mighty Midget Widget Works
Balance Sheet

There is no question that computerized accounting systems are a boon to business. Because of the cyclical nature of accounting procedures, they fit most amenably with the cyclical aspects of using computers to perform routine tasks. Creative Media Development, a producer of safety programs in Portland, uses a Texas Instruments Professional computer for its general ledger system. The firm has twenty employees and sales of about $1,000,000 annually. Says Philip Parshley of their accounting system:

> Preparing financial reports used to take a few days. About a year ago we bought a Timberline General Ledger. Now she (the operator) plugs in the numbers, hits a key and they're done in a few hours.[2]

We hope that through the course of this chapter, you've come to understand that using an accounting system requires a bit more than plugging in the numbers and hitting a key. As with all computer applications, one must understand the work to be done before one can use a computer to do it.

An accounting system *records, stores, classifies, summarizes,* and *interprets* business transactions. Virtually everyone associated with business management must have at least a rudimentary knowledge of accounting. The accounting profession is among the oldest and, over the centuries, it has established *generally accepted accounting principles* which govern the manner in which all accounting systems, whether manual or automated, operate.

Accountants use words in a very precise sense. Accounting and financial data are always measured in *monetary* terms. *Assets* are the things the company owns; *liabilities* are the amounts the company owes to creditors. *Capital* means the financial interest the owners have in the business. *Revenues* is a term used to identify funds received in the form of cash or obligations to pay in return for goods and services provided by the business. *Expenses* represent the operating expenditures made in running the concern as opposed to *costs* which means the cost of goods sold. *Profits* are calculated as the difference in any one accounting period between revenues and the sum of costs and expenses. An *accounting period* is a month, quarter, or year over which operational profits are calculated.

An *accounting system* is a collection of subsystems under the control of the general ledger system. Accounting systems often employ *subsidiary systems* such as accounts receivable, accounts payable, payroll, invoicing, and inventory control. Each of these subsidiary systems performs specialized functions within the context of the general ledger. They serve as input to the general ledger and produce documents related to subsidiary ledgers.

Accounting system procedures conform to the requirements of the *accounting equation,* a simple formula that expresses the balance of accounts in the system. Maintenance of the balance of accounts is assured through the employment of *double-entry* transactions and the use of the notions of *debit* and *credit* which identify the effect of each entry on the account to which it is *posted.* A *transaction* is an economic event that affects two or more accounts in the system. Each transaction consists of two or more *entries.* The sum of the debit entries must equal the sum of the credit entries for any one transaction. An *account* is a file of entries maintained for each asset, liability, capital, revenue, and expense item in the accounting equation. The accounts used in an accounting system for a particular organization are specified in the *chart of accounts.*

The basic general ledger documents are the *balance sheet,* which expresses the financial condition of the firm at a particular moment in time and the *income statement* which summarizes operating transactions during an accounting period. The general ledger system also produces a number of working documents, including the *trial balance,* which verifies the balance of the account balances in the system, and reports of *journal transactions,* which provide *audit trails* by which transactions and entries can be traced through the system.

Subsidiary systems, all of which are related to the general ledger system, produce specialized reports and documents and maintain balances in the general ledger accounts. Subsidiary systems provide information on customers, vendors, payroll, inventory stocks, and other matters that the general ledger accounts cannot maintain easily.

Because of its cyclical nature, the accounting system lends itself very well to computerization. There is little reason for any business, unless it is very small indeed, to use manual accounting systems in preference to automated methods.

KEY TERMS

accounting
accounting equation
accounts
accounts payable
accounts receivable
asset
balance
balance sheet
capital
chart of accounts

cost
credit
debit
entry
equity
expense
financial condition
general ledger
income statement

inventory
journal listing
liability
payroll
profit
profit and loss statement
revenue
subsidiary system
transaction

REVIEW
QUESTIONS

1. In what ways are the definitions of accounting and data processing the same?
2. What is the heart of a modern accounting system?
3. How are financial data measured?
4. Differentiate between assets and liabilities.
5. What is the owner's financial interest in an organization called?
6. What is the difference between an expense and a cost?
7. Because we use double-entry accounting, every transaction affects at least _____ accounts.
8. A _____ entry always balances a credit entry.
9. What does a balance sheet show?
10. Income statements summarize _____.
11. Identify at least three subsidiary accounting systems.

THOUGHT
QUESTIONS

1. Describe an accounting system in terms of files, records, and transactions.
2. Why is it important for all businesses to have an accounting system?
3. Why do you think that so many small businesses purchase accounting software packages?

Corporate Piracy

(Courtesy Auto-Trol Technology Corp.)

Illegal copying of computer software costs the software industry staggering sums of money.

According to Chris Christiansen, a senior analyst at Boston's Yankee Group, the software industry lost $1.8 billion to pirates in 1983, an amount greater than the 1983 sales of such companies as Wang, MCI, Walt Disney and Federal Express. For every dollar's worth of legal software sold, he says, there is a dollar's worth of illegal copies made. And that is just the average. "For some of the more popular packages, like Lotus 1-2-3 or WordStar," says Christiansen, "I would estimate that there are anywhere from two to 10 stolen copies for every legitimate copy in use."[3]

During the winter of 1983–84, Lotus Development Corporation filed suit against Rixon Corporation in Maryland, alleging that it had made unauthorized copies of 1-2-3. The case was settled out of court with Rixon paying an undisclosed amount of money and agreeing to a permanent injunction

against unauthorized copying. In the summer of 1984, Lotus again sued, this time against Health Group, Incorporated (HGI), a southeastern operator of hospitals and nursing homes. Like Rixon, HGI settled out of court by paying Lotus a sum of money and agreeing to an injunction against further unauthorized copying.

Other software firms soon followed Lotus' lead. In January of 1985, MicroPro International sued Wilson Jones Company Office Products, a subsidiary of American Brands, Incorporated, a Fortune 100 company, for alleged copyright violations in making unauthorized copies of WordStar. Joining MicroPro in the suit was the Association of Data Processing Service Organizations (ADAPSO), which apparently intended to make an example of Wilson Jones Company and thus discourage corporate software piracy.

The stakes are high; the issues complex. Had

Lotus won all points of its suit against Rixon, for example, Rixon would have been out some $2 million. Here's a brief summary of the issues:[4]

1. *Copyright Violation* Making unauthorized copies of software violates copyright laws. In Lotus' interpretation, courts can award statutory damages of $50,000 for each infringement. This means $50,000 for *each* copy. Because software documentation is copyrighted separately, if a copy is made of the user's manual for the program, one for each disk, that's another $50,000 each.

   Some disagree with Lotus' position, believing the copyrights to have been violated only once. The courts did not have to decide.

2. *Trademark Infringement* Copying a program or its documentation violates the producer's trademark rights, whether the copy is sold or given away—it's only a matter of price. When a firm like Lotus spends millions of dollars each year advertising its products, its interest in the trademark is great and the courts can award damages accordingly for its unauthorized use. Lotus asserted that it was entitled to no less than $1 million in its claim against Rixon.

   In making copies for internal use, not resale, argue corporate users, no trademark infringement takes place. No use is made of the software vendor's trademark, only the product itself.

3. *License Agreement Violation* Software producers allege that purchasers buy the right to use the product, they do not own it. In their view, when purchasers open a software package by breaking its seal or shrinkwrap packaging, they agree to the terms of a license agreement. The agreement, included as part of the manual, forbids copying the programs or limits the number of copies that users can make.

   Detractors from this position claim that users purchase the product outright. Opening a package cannot constitute a contractual agreement. The copy they purchase becomes their property to use, give away, or sell as they wish. Furthermore, the 1980 Software Amendments to the 1976 Copyright Act specify that users may make backup copies or other copies and adaptations of the program necessary for its effective use.

4. *Unjustified Enrichment* By saving the cost of purchasing additional copies of a program, copiers enrich themselves at the cost of the software producer.

   Users have argued that in purchasing the program for use in their business, they should be able to use it with any and all computers owned by the firm without having to purchase separate copies of the same program for each work station.

The pressures on middle managers and operative personnel to use multiple copies of software can be great. The software budget is limited and perhaps exhausted. The work is piling up. Computer stations cannot contribute to getting the work out because the only copy of the appropriate software package is used all the time. Managers are rewarded for getting the job done, not for finding excuses for why it's unfinished. Who's going to know, in fact, who's going to care if an extra copy is made? The work gets out, the budget remains intact and everybody is happy.

Corporate executives care, but sometimes claim no control over how software is being used or misused among their many computer work stations even if their companies have policies forbidding unauthorized duplication.

> Two Chicago-area executives said no formal policy exists at their firms. One said he was not aware of any copying, "but then if somebody did, he wouldn't tell me." The other said, "We have no idea what they are doing with (software)," but added that his department controls acquisition of packages.[5]

Most, if not all corporations would prefer to avoid the publicity associated with being singled out for a lawsuit over unauthorized software copying. As one manager for a Chicago food products company said about preventing piracy in his organization and the fear of resultant litigation, "We never compromise anything that would bring our company to the forefront of negative publicity."[6]

Catching corporate pirates isn't easy. As often as not, software producers find out about corporate piracy from disgruntled employees or ex-employees. Informing on an employer who fired you would seem to be a fairly effective way to wreak revenge. Other employees suffer pangs of conscience when supervisors ask them to make unauthorized copies and contact the software vendor. Another occasion arises when a user of a program calls the vendor on the vendor's user-support hotline. While helping the user, the vendor representative discerns that he or she has a bootlegged copy. That's how Lotus detected the unauthorized disks in the Rixon situation. Lotus alleged that Rixon made 13 unauthorized copies.

Why so much fuss over 13 copies? It's a matter of principle, says Lotus president Mitchell D. Kapor. He says that the company's hard line is necessary to protect the very integrity of its products and—not incidentally—the economic strength of the company. By cracking down on Rixon, he says, Lotus is letting other pirates know that it does not take the matter lightly. "We got what we wanted out of it. In doing so, we have sent a message to a lot of other people and corporations."[7]

In June of 1985, Wilson Jones Company settled with Lotus and ADAPSO. As with Lotus' suit against Rixon and Health, details were not made public.

1. By 1985, the four software copying issues raised earlier in this Point/Counterpoint selection had not been tested in court. In fact, some believe that Lotus and other software producers would just as soon not see court precedents set until the industry, together with users, arrives at fair copy-protection procedures that meet the needs of both groups. If you were a judge, how would you rule on the issues?

2. If you were an executive in a large organization, what would you do to discourage software piracy?

C H A P T E R 14

(Courtesy Sperry Corp.)

NECESSITY IS THE MOTHER...
SING SOMETHING SIMPLE
SPREADSHEET CONTROL
SPREADSHEETS AT WORK
USING A SPREADSHEET PROGRAM

I had assumed that most of my applications were too involved to do with VisiCalc, but I've since discovered there's virtually nothing I can think of that I can't do with a spreadsheet...—John Klingel, magazine circulation consultant.[1]

NECESSITY IS THE MOTHER...

The story has become folklore among computer cognoscenti. As a student at Harvard's Business School, Dan Bricklin would spend hours each night analyzing case studies for his classes. Using a columnar tablet, a hand calculator, and a pencil, Bricklin would construct profit projections, cash flow analyses, and other financial models. A mistake meant recalculating all the figures that were based upon the erroneous value. Changing the analysis to accommodate possible events, such as increases in prices or reductions in interest rates, meant reconstructing the whole table, called a *spreadsheet* or *worksheet*, from scratch. In short, more time was spent in doing and redoing arithmetic than in analyzing and interpreting the results.

In 1978, that's what financial managers did. The tools of the trade included just those used by Bricklin: the pad, the calculator, several pencils, and, of course, a good eraser. Bricklin is said to have mumbled "there has to be a better way," just as Charles Babbage had 176 years earlier. Babbage's frustration led, ultimately, to the electronic computer; Bricklin's to the electronic spreadsheet.

Joining forces with friend Robert Frankston, a computer programmer, Bricklin set about preparing a computer program that would alleviate the tedium of spreadsheet analysis. After all, they must have reasoned, doing repetitive calculations is what computers do best. Their work resulted in a program they called VisiCalc, short for Visible Calculator. It was visible because the results of the computer's calculations appeared on a computer's video display screen as a sheet of columnar paper. In 1979, Dan Fylstra, who had acquired the rights to market VisiCalc, began his sales campaign.

> About the same time, Steven Jobs and Stephen Wozniak, operating out of a garage in Cupertino, California, introduced the Apple II computer, an improved version of the Apple I. Whereas the Apple I appealed primarily to computer hobbyists, the Apple II with disk drives and an operating system of considerable power was a fully-functioning computing tool. Bricklin and Frankston modified VisiCalc to run on the new desktop computer. The marriage was a perfect match. For the first time, there was a legitimate business and professional application for desktop computers. VisiCalc met a clear need in the business world for a personal analysis tool. The Apple II was an attractive, reliable, readily available vehicle for the program.[2]

The union of VisiCalc and the Apple II, you see, presented the world with a *complete computer system* which fit nicely on top of one's desk. Hundreds of thousands of the VisiCalc-Apple II systems were sold. Indeed, some industry observers credit this combination as the primary moving force behind the microcomputer revolution.

Today, there are dozens of spreadsheet programs available, not only for microcomputers but for minis and mainframes, too. Recognizing managers' needs to use electronic spreadsheets to analyze data available only from the data banks maintained by larger computers, software producers have been quick to prepare spreadsheet programs for them. Oxford Software Corporation's Maxicalc, for example, runs on the IBM 4341 mainframe under the DOS/VS operating system. Because of spreadsheet programs' popularity, virtually all general-purpose computers manufactured today will operate at least one.

To be sure, most spreadsheet programs are designed for microcomputers because microcomputer users represent the biggest market for them. Many observers of the microcomputer industry suggest that two applications packages are essential for any microcomputer user. One of these is a word processing program, the other is a spreadsheet program.

Earlier, we referred to the Big Six applications programs, each of which meets a distinct productivity need. If we were to identify the Big Two, they would surely be word processors and spreadsheets. As a general category, more word processing programs are used today than any other single application. As a specific software product, more copies of VisiCalc had been sold through 1983 than any other single program. By the end of 1984, 1-2-3, a spreadsheet program for IBM's PC, captured the title of the world's most popular program for microcomputers.

Since the Apple-VisiCalc alliance, many other software producers have introduced spreadsheet programs, each trying to outdo the others in power and flexibility. As a result, business managers and more casual users of computers have a wide spectrum of enormously powerful tools that can be used for a great number of different purposes.

Almost everybody in modern society is a financial manager. The sole proprietor is a financial manager and every other kind of manager, too. So is the homeowner. So, too, are the apartment dweller, the college student, and the military professional. One does not have to be a financial manager to make good use of a spreadsheet program, but a financial manager today would be lost without one.

SING SOMETHING SIMPLE[3]

Just A Piece of Paper

The spreadsheet program's greatest virtue is its simplicity. Think of it as a sheet of paper. It'll be easier to use if it's ruled into columns and rows. *Rows* march down the paper vertically; *columns* across it horizontally. It is just the kind of paper we can buy in pads from a stationery store. We'll call the intersection of a row and a column a *cell*. There's nothing much to using the sheet. One writes numbers in various cells, trying to organize them so that the sheet will be easy to interpret when finished.

The Electronic Worksheet

One uses an electronic worksheet, or spreadsheet, just like its paper counterpart. Values are entered into cells and calculations are performed. The results of the calculations also appear in cells. It's comforting to know that if you understand how to do this kind of work on paper, it's easy to learn how to do it on a computer.

The differences between paper worksheets and electronic ones are many. These differences make the electronic variety much easier to use. They also make spreadsheet analysis much more powerful than when done on paper.

Size

Columnar tablets have as many as 50 rows and a dozen or so columns. There's no reason why one can't paste many of these together to make a worksheet as large as needed. It might be easier to buy a roll of butcher paper.

If one ruled it off into 64 columns and 256 rows, it would be about the size of the smallest electronic worksheet, the original VisiCalc. Many electronic spreadsheets today are limited to that size and, indeed, having 16,384 cells, seem large enough to handle many applications.

Some others are much larger, challenging even the most dedicated user of butcher paper. Target Financial Modeling, for example, offers 50,000 rows and 10,000 columns, although the program will not support more than 50,000 cells at one time. SuperCalc3 sets up a worksheet with 9,999 rows and 127 columns. Lotus Development Corporation's 1-2-3, so named because, according to Lotus, it is as easy to use as "1-2-3," offers 250 rows and 2,000 columns, but of course, these limits are reduced by the size of the computer's RAM. Still other spreadsheets, such as BitsCalc, employ virtual memory techniques (see Chapter Seven) to establish worksheets that are limited in size only by the capacity of the computer system's on-line disk storage.

It's easy to see that electronic spreadsheets offer more working space than even the largest sheet of paper can reasonably accommodate. Still, it helps to think about an electronic spreadsheet as a program that converts the computer system's memory into a giant sheet of paper that is organized into columns and rows.

Viewing the Worksheet

You may remember seeing a hand-held magnifying glass attached to a flashlight that is used to read books typeset in very fine print. The book is open, the entire page is available, but the reader looks only at the portion under the glass. The glass is moved to view new sections of text.

That's just the way spreadsheet programs use the display screen. The user can *scroll* the screen right, left, up, and down to view any part of the worksheet. Figure 14-1 illustrates the idea.

On initial startup of a spreadsheet program, the screen is positioned in the upper left-hand corner of the sheet. Figure 14-2 shows screens from four spreadsheet programs: 1-2-3, VisiCalc, SuperCalc, and Multiplan for the Macintosh.

The similarity among these screens should come as no surprise. All spreadsheets operate in essentially the same fashion and all can be visualized as a rectangular sheet of paper divided into columns and rows. In the cases of 1-2-3, VisiCalc, and SuperCalc, the columns are identified by letters of the alphabet; the rows by numbers. For these, the *cell identifier,* or the *cell address,* of any cell consists of a letter (or letters) and a number. The cell in the upper left-hand corner of each of these three spreadsheets carries the identifier A1.

FIGURE 14-1
Scrolling around a worksheet

Area Viewed on the CRT   **Full Worksheet**

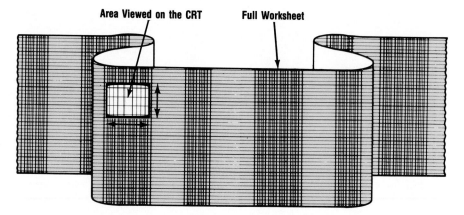

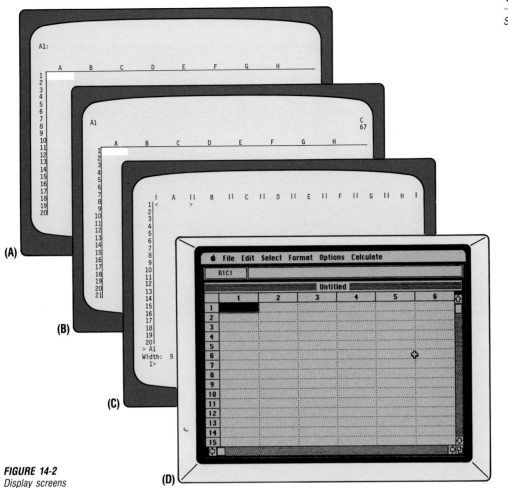

FIGURE 14-2
Display screens

Multiplan identifies cells a little differently, but the idea is the same. Both the columns and rows in that program are identified by numbers. Therefore, the upper left-hand corner cell address is R1C1 which stands for "Row 1, Column 1." The cell in the 27th column and the 15th row is identified in each of the first three spreadsheets by AA15 because after exhausting the 26 letters of the alphabet, the program adds a second letter and continues. Multiplan identifies that cell as R15C27.

Ordinarily, the *cursor* on an empty spreadsheet appears in the upper left-most cell when the program first starts. The cell on which the cursor is resting is known as the *active* or *selected* cell. For VisiCalc and 1-2-3, the cursor appears as a highlighted rectangle. SuperCalc uses the symbols < > to identify the active cell. In the Macintosh Multiplan, the active cell is filled with black. The cursor, or *pointer*, is the cross you see in figure 14-4D. We select a cell in this program by using a mouse to position the pointer on the desired cell and clicking the mouse button. This is called "clicking the cell."

Scrolling is accomplished by moving the cursor, or pointer, toward the desired cell. When the cursor reaches the edge of the screen, the spreadsheet begins to move, bringing other rows or columns into view. In effect, the user slides the window across or down the spreadsheet to see other parts of it.

With most spreadsheet programs, the user can also scroll a page or a screenful at a time in any direction. All spreadsheets can split the screen into

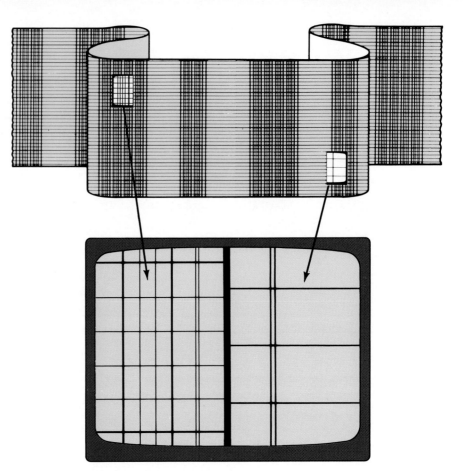

FIGURE 14-3
Screen split into windows

horizontal or vertical windows. Using windows, one can put an area of the spreadsheet into one window, another area in the other and scroll the windows independently so that widely separated areas can be compared easily. Figure 14-3 illustrates the use of windows.

Entering Data

Recording data in an electronic spreadsheet is much easier than writing them using paper and pencil. We need only select the desired cell and type the data. There are three kinds of data that can be recorded in a cell: character data, numeric data, and formulas.

Character Data

Character data consist of groups of letters, numerals, and special symbols, as you'll recall from Chapter Two. Because words are most usually employed in spreadsheets to identify the contents of rows and columns, a cell containing them is said to hold a *label* or *title*.

Numeric Data

Numeric data consist of combinations of the numerals zero through nine and may include a decimal point. A minus sign is used to identify negative numbers. When a cell contains a number, it is said to hold a *value*. Most cells in spreadsheets hold values that are entered directly by the user or are the result of some calculation.

Formulas

The ability to enter formulas into cells gives electronic spreadsheets their great power and usefulness. Suppose we want to add 137 to a value in cell C25. We decide that the best place for the result of this calculation would be cell C28. All we need do is select C28 and enter into it the formula

$$137 + C25$$

Immediately following this entry the result is displayed in the selected cell, C28. If C25 contained the value 28, we would see 165. Figure 14-4A shows how this looks on a VisiCalc screen. At the very top of the screen, the address of the active cell, C28, is shown. Then, in parentheses, the letter V indicates that the content of that cell is a value. The value is calculated by the formula shown to the right of the V. We see in the body of the sheet itself the content of cell C25 and the result of the calculation in cell C28.

If later we change or the program changes the content of C25 to some other value, say, 49.21, the value in C28 is immediately recalculated so it now contains 186.21 as shown in figure 14-4B.

The spreadsheet program does not record the results of the calculation in memory, it *stores the formula* that produces the results. That way, any time the content of one of the cells used in the formula is changed, the program can recalculate new results.

Our formula made use of a constant, 137, and a cell address, C25. Typically, formulas in spreadsheets consist primarily, if not exclusively, of cell addresses. Any constant numbers to be used in calculations are stored in their own cells so the user can change them easily. If we were to follow this practice and store our constant 137 in cell A19, we would change our formula to

$$+ A19 + C25$$

as shown in figure 14-5.

Look at the top line again. The plus sign in front of the cell address A19

FIGURE 14-4
Formulas and calculations

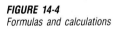

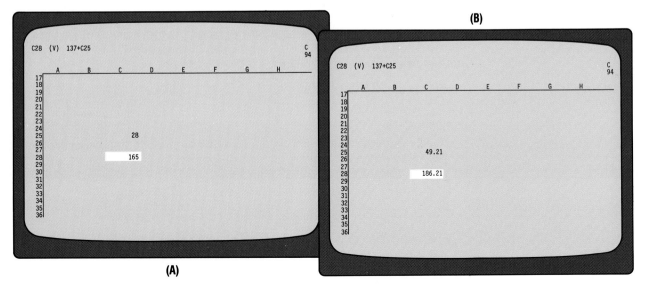

(A)

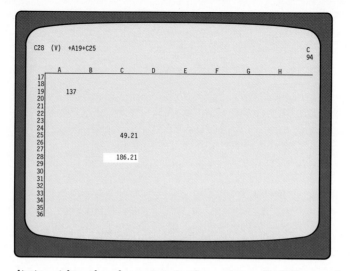

C28 (V)   +A19+C25

C
94

FIGURE 14-5
Using a constant in a cell

distinguishes the characters in the active cell, C28, as a formula as opposed to a label, or a title. Usually, spreadsheet programs assume that any entry that begins with a letter of the alphabet is a label, or a title, and any entry that begins with a number, a plus sign ($+$), a minus sign ($-$), or a parenthesis is a value or a formula.

Formulas in spreadsheets use the following symbols to specify arithmetic operations:

^ Exponentiation (raising to a power)

* Multiplication

/ Division

$+$ Addition

$-$ Subtraction

Spreadsheet programs perform exponentiation first, then multiplication and division, then addition and subtraction. Parentheses may be used to control the sequence of calculations. If, for instance, we want to multiply the content of cell Q67 by the sum of the contents of cells R56, R57, and R58, the formula

$$+Q67*R56 + R57 + R58$$

would be *incorrect* because the program will multiply the contents of Q67 and R56 first and then add to that product the contents of cells R57 and R58. The correct formula uses parentheses, just as in algebra:

$$+Q67*(R56 + R57 + R58)$$

Functions

You can imagine occasions when it's necessary to add the contents of a considerable number of cells to produce a total for an entire column or row of figures. If the first cell were E6 and the last P6, the formula to enter in cell Q6, where the total should appear, would look like this:

$$+E6 + F6 + G6 + H6 + I6 + J6 + K6 + L6 + M6 + N6 + O6 + P6$$

Entering this string of characters without error is no easy trick. If we wished to add the contents of several hundred cells, entering the formula would be next to impossible. For this reason, spreadsheet programs include a *function*, called the SUM function, which makes this much easier. Using it, we enter this formula into Q6:

@SUM(E6...P6)

That's all there is to it. The at sign (@) tells the program that what follows, SUM, is the name of a function, not a label. Inside the parentheses, the *range* of cells, E6...P6, specifies the cells containing the data to be added. The three dots are called an ellipsis.

Spreadsheet programs include a number of different functions besides SUM. As examples, an average function will calculate the average of the values in a number of cells; a sort function will sort a spreadsheet based upon the contents of a row or column.

SPREADSHEET CONTROL

Entering data and formulas into a worksheet is easy. Simply select the cell in which the data are to be recorded and type. Pressing the Enter key or selecting another cell causes the entry to be recorded in the cell that was active when the typing took place. When formulas are entered into a cell, the cell displays the results of the calculation.

There are many more things that we may need to do with a worksheet. These include copying the contents of a group of cells from one location to another or inserting empty rows or columns in order to modify the worksheet. Frequently, too, we need to duplicate formulas from one portion of a worksheet to another. There also must be a way to save worksheets to disk and retrieve them later.

Command Sequences

These activities are performed by entering commands. In spreadsheet programs, *command* or *command sequence* is a sequence of characters that initiates operations such as those mentioned in the preceding paragraph.

When we first boot up a spreadsheet program, the screen appears as in the examples shown in figure 14-2. Any characters typed at this point will be interpreted by the program as data to be entered into the active cell. To tell the program that what's being entered is a command rather than data, we use a special character to begin the command sequence. For many programs, such as VisiCalc, SuperCalc, and 1-2-3, this initial character is the slash (/).

Suppose we have a spreadsheet called Interest Table stored on our disk and we want to load it into memory. The command sequence would look something like this:

```
/SLInterest Table
```

The slash identifies the characters to follow as a command sequence. The S means Storage, the *L* means Load, and Interest Table is the filename of our spreadsheet. Now, you might be asking yourself at this point how we remember what the letters mean. For most spreadsheet programs all we have to remember is the slash. The program will prompt us through a series of brief menus to determine which characters should be entered next.

Let's see how it works. In figure 14-2B we saw the start-up screen for

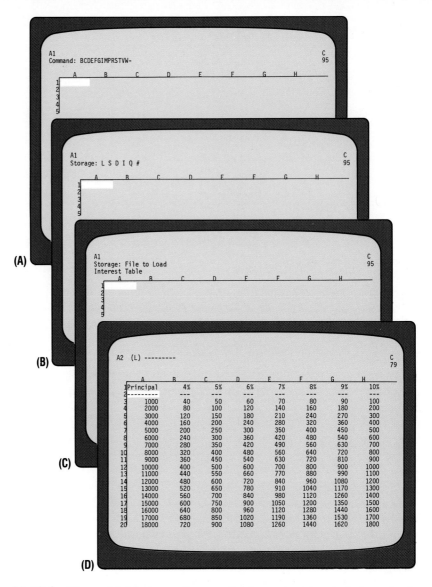

FIGURE 14-6
Executing a command sequence

VisiCalc. Figure 14-6A shows the result of pressing the slash key. At the top of the screen appears a menu: a sequence of characters each of which stands for a command. The S, which is fifth from the right, stands for Storage.

Pressing the S key yields yet another menu as shown in figure 14-6B. In this menu, the L stands for Load. On pressing L, the screen appears as in figure 14-6C, asking for the filename of the worksheet we wish to load into memory. Typing it in and pressing the Enter key causes the program to retrieve that file from disk and load it into memory, figure 14-6D. As a rule, the command character is the first character in the word that describes the operation: Storage and Load, in this example.

Help Screens

As software producers improved spreadsheet programs, they added "Help" screens for those who do not use the programs frequently enough to keep the command characters memorized. Pressing the slash key in SuperCalc, for example, produces the command menu at the bottom of the screen, figure 14-7. Entering the question mark (?), which is one of the choices in the menu,

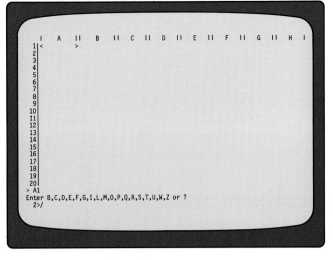

FIGURE 14-7
SuperCalc command menu

causes the program to display the help screen shown in figure 14-8.

Command characters used by one spreadsheet program are very similar to those used by all the others. One need only remember the character that initiates command execution (the slash, for example) to produce screen menus that help in entering the remaining characters of the command sequence. Most worksheet programs today include extensive help facilities, which reduce, if not eliminate, the need to search through the program's operating manual to figure out how to do something.

Command Power

Commands can affect the selected cell, several cells, called a *range* of cells, or the entire worksheet, in which case they are called global commands. Figure 14-6D, for example, shows an interest table displaying amounts of interest at various interest rates as applied to different amounts of principal. The numbers are shown in general format, which the program uses given no instructions to the contrary. In general format, whole numbers are shown without a decimal point and decimal fractions are shown with one. In this case, the general format is called the *default* condition, that is, the one most people would normally use. We use commands to change the default conditions to those we prefer.

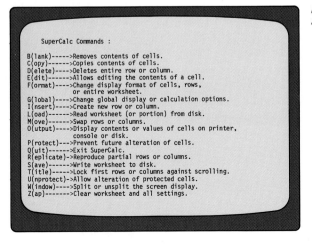

FIGURE 14-8
SuperCalc help screen

Suppose we wish to show a decimal point and two places to its right (including zeros) with every value. This is known as dollars and cents format. One way to do this is to select a cell, say B3, and change its format. Pressing slash gives us the same menu as that shown in figure 14-6A. The letter *F* stands for format. Pressing it gives the format menu in figure 14-9A.

The dollar sign ($) in the format menu stands for Dollars and Cents. Pressing it changes the format of the selected cell so that it displays 40.00, as you can see in figure 14-9B. Now it happens that this spreadsheet is 12 columns wide and 50 rows deep. If we were to use this technique, we would enter the command sequence

/ F $

FIGURE 14-9

Formatting with a global command

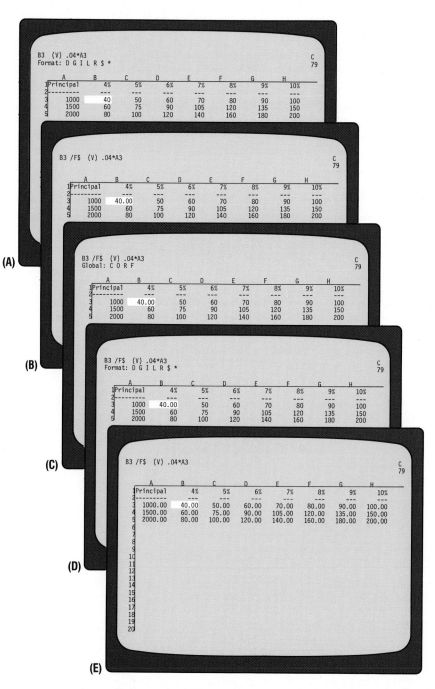

K33 (V) +J33+(.01*A33)   C
                                                                79

	A	B	C	D		J	K	L	M
1	Principal	4%	5%	6%	33	1920.00	2080.00	2240.00	2400.00
2	--------	---	---	---	34	1980.00	2145.00	2310.00	2475.00
3	1000.00	40.00	50.00	60.00	35	2040.00	2210.00	2380.00	2550.00
4	1500.00	60.00	75.00	90.00	36	2100.00	2275.00	2450.00	2625.00
5	2000.00	80.00	100.00	120.00	37	2160.00	2340.00	2520.00	2700.00
6	2500.00	100.00	125.00	150.00	38	2220.00	2405.00	2590.00	2775.00
7	3000.00	120.00	150.00	180.00	39	2280.00	2470.00	2660.00	2850.00
8	3500.00	140.00	175.00	210.00	40	2340.00	2535.00	2730.00	2925.00
9	4000.00	160.00	200.00	240.00	41	2400.00	2600.00	2800.00	3000.00
10	4500.00	180.00	225.00	270.00	42	2460.00	2665.00	2870.00	3075.00
11	5000.00	200.00	250.00	300.00	43	2520.00	2730.00	2940.00	3150.00
12	5500.00	220.00	275.00	330.00	44	2580.00	2795.00	3010.00	3225.00
13	6000.00	240.00	300.00	360.00	45	2640.00	2860.00	3080.00	3300.00
14	6500.00	260.00	325.00	390.00	46	2700.00	2925.00	3150.00	3375.00
15	7000.00	280.00	350.00	420.00	47	2760.00	2990.00	3220.00	3450.00
16	7500.00	300.00	375.00	450.00	48	2820.00	3055.00	3290.00	3525.00
17	8000.00	320.00	400.00	480.00	49	2880.00	3120.00	3360.00	3600.00
18	8500.00	340.00	425.00	510.00	50	2940.00	3185.00	3430.00	3675.00
19	9000.00	360.00	450.00	540.00	51	3000.00	3250.00	3500.00	3750.00
20	9500.00	380.00	475.00	570.00	52	3120.00	3380.00	3640.00	3900.00

FIGURE 14-10
Formatted worksheet with windows

600 times to modify the format of every cell. Obviously, it would be easier to change the format of every cell in the spreadsheet with *one* command sequence.

Commands that do this are called *global* commands. Once again, we enter a slash and see the menu at the top of figure 14-6A. The letter G stands for Global. Pressing it yields the menu in figure 14-9C. In this menu, the letter F means Format. Pressing F yields the same format menu as before, figure 14-9D. Selecting the dollar sign again, changes every value in the worksheet to the format we want, figure 14-9E. Figure 14-10 shows the formatted worksheet with vertical windows displaying the upper-left and lower-right corners.

SPREADSHEETS AT WORK

A Very General Program

Unlike other applications programs, spreadsheets do not focus on just one kind of processing task. Word processors, for example, do only word processing tasks. Data base managers concentrate on processing collections of data and information. Accounting systems do accounting, and so on. Spreadsheet programs, one way or another, can be used for all of these applications. The list of business applications for which spreadsheet programs are used is lengthy. Here is a sampling:

- Taxes
- Sales Management
- Accounting
- Manufacturing
- Production Scheduling
- Record Keeping
- Personnel
- Inventory Management
- Financial Analysis
- Sales Invoicing
- Payroll
- Statistical Analysis
- Budgeting
- Sales Analysis

These are just business applications. Besides them, spreadsheets are used for scientific and engineering purposes and a wide variety of personal and miscellaneous tasks. Little League batting averages are kept, checkbooks and household budgets maintained, and contributions received by charitable institutions analyzed, to name a few.

Templates

As a general application program, spreadsheets are similar to general programming languages in that they can be applied to many different tasks. Those who use spreadsheets for accounting, statistical analysis, budgeting and other applications find that in setting up their spreadsheet, they follow the same pattern as everybody else who uses the program for the same purpose. As a result, a subindustry has grown in which those who have developed a spreadsheet for a particular purpose market it to those who would use it for the same purpose. Such a spreadsheet is known as a template.

A *spreadsheet template* is a spreadsheet with no data. Many users develop their own templates so that a particular spreadsheet format can be used again and again, resulting in a series of identical spreadsheets each of which has different data.

Figure 14-11, for example, shows a simple check register template. To use it, we load it from disk, enter the beginning checkbook balance, and enter some checks. The program keeps a running balance of the amount in the checking account and has columns for the usual information kept in a check register. We enter the date and name and address at the top. Then the spreadsheet is saved to the disk as, say, AUG86.

At this point, there are *two* worksheets on disk, the empty template and the worksheet for August. At the beginning of September, the empty template is used to set up the check register for that month and is saved accordingly. At the end of the year, we have a separate check register for each month.

Purchasing a template relieves users of having to set up the worksheet and, therefore, is a great time-saver. Dozens of books that show spreadsheet templates for particular applications are available. Usually, the purchaser can also buy a disk containing the templates ready to load into memory.

What If...?

Spreadsheet programs are famous for their ability to answer "What if...?" types of questions. Once a spreadsheet is set up, we need only enter new data and

FIGURE 14-11
Check register template

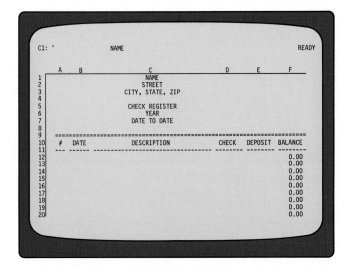

recalculate the spreadsheet to see the results of using different figures. If we were interested in an interest table based upon principals ranging upward from $10,000 rather than the $1,000 figure used in figure 14-10, changing the number in cell A3 and pressing return would produce the new table.

This is strong medicine. It means that spreadsheets showing financial relationships can be used to estimate the effects on a business enterprise of decreases in interest rates, increases in labor or material costs, changes in import or export tariffs, and the like.

Models

Financial analysts and business managers are understandably concerned with the future. That's why they prepare projected income statements, budgets, cash flow analyses, and the like. In the not-too-distant past, projections like these made on paper stayed as initially prepared. Modifying them to take into account new information was too time consuming.

Electronic worksheets have changed all that. Because spreadsheet programs perform mathematical operations so handily and because models are so often based on mathematical relationships, many users refer to their spreadsheets as "models."

A *model*, like a model airplane, simulates the real world. As models, spreadsheets are used in many different ways: to simulate job-shop production scheduling, to prepare cost estimates of construction projects, and to assess the effects of changing interest rates on investment portfolios, to mention a few.

Relationships with Other Programs

As general programs, electronic spreadsheets can use data from a number of different sources and produce data that other programs can put to good use for their specialized purposes.

At the insistence of managers armed with desktop computers running spreadsheet programs, data processing departments have made arrangements to download data maintained by mainframe computers to user's micros. In some instances, the arrangements include the ability to upload data from micros into the mainframe data bank as well. Retrieving data from mainframe data banks precludes the necessity to rekey data into the spreadsheet. Downloading techniques also increase the assurance that the data being analyzed by the spreadsheet user are up-to-date and accurate.

Linking micro-based spreadsheet programs with other micro-based applications programs has developed at a faster pace. Most spreadsheet programs include the ability to transfer data produced by the spreadsheet to data files with formats compatible with other applications programs. VisiCalc, for example, prepares data files following the Data Interchange Format (DIF) so that they may be processed by data base management, graphing, and statistical analysis programs. 1-2-3 uses the same technique. Multiplan prepares files under the SYLK (for SYmbolic LinK) format that can be processed by a number of different application packages. Similarly, many programs, particularly data base management applications, can prepare files in the DIF and SYLK formats, thus making the data readily available to spreadsheets that can use those formats.

Many spreadsheet programs have been developed as parts of integrated systems, meaning that in addition to spreadsheet operations, they offer graphics, word processing, data base management, and other functions. See Chapter Sixteen for a more detailed discussion of integrated systems.

Spreadsheet Limitations

For all their flexibility and general usefulness, spreadsheet programs are hardly the ultimate answer to every data processing need. Although some users employ them for such tasks as payroll, sales invoicing, and accounting, their usefulness in these high-volume applications is limited primarily to small firms.

Spreadsheet programs are bound by the limitations of the memory and disk storage of the hardware system on which they operate. The most powerful of the spreadsheet programs, particularly those that are integrated with other applications such as 1-2-3, MBA, and Framework, require 512K of memory to reach their potential. Symphony, for example, requires 320K of primary storage just for the program itself.

As the basis of integrated systems, spreadsheets are typically the most powerful of the programs in the package. Spreadsheet users who need full-featured word processors find the limitations of word processors in spreadsheet-based integrated packages too constraining. Those who need powerful graphics or data base management capabilities are better off using programs that specialize in graphics and data base management. These users employ file transfer techniques that produce files in DIF and SYLK formats to pass data back and forth among the spreadsheet and other applications.

Despite acclaims like the opening quotation of this chapter, spreadsheet programs cannot always do everything as well as everything must be done. Within their limitations, however, they are very productive tools.

There's not much question that spreadsheet programs, because of their general applicability and their ease of use, have had a profound impact on the manner in which computers are used in business today. Bringing a complete computer system into the office and home in the form of a microcomputer and a spreadsheet program has changed the professional and personal lives of millions of people.

USING A SPREADSHEET PROGRAM

Jill Tedd has decided to open a shop specializing in gifts, supplies, and rental equipment for weddings. Having had experience in the field, she knows that her average *gross margin* on retail sales will be 32%, that is, the difference between what she purchases goods for and what she sells them for will be 32% of sales. This means, of course, that her *cost of goods sold* will be 68% of sales.

A Purchases Budget

As a result of cash discounts her vendors offer, she knows that she will have to pay for each month's purchases of goods by the tenth of the month following the purchases. Furthermore, her vendors' delivery schedules dictate that she must have sufficient merchandise inventory on hand at the beginning of each month to provide for the next two months' sales.

Jill has already worked up her best estimate of monthly sales for the next six months and has ordered $6,800 of goods, enough to cover her first two months' expected sales: $4,000 for July and $6,000 for August. Therefore, she will have to pay her vendors $6,800 by the tenth of July, her first month in business.

Her husband, Mel, a CPA, advises her to prepare a monthly budget of cash outlays for purchases of goods so that she can plan her cash flow.

The Worksheet

Jill uses Macintosh Multiplan. When starting the program, it displays the empty worksheet shown in figure 14-2D.

Jill begins by setting up an *assumption table* in the upper left-hand corner, figure 14-12. An assumption table, in spreadsheet lexicon, is an area that holds values used throughout the sheet. Using the mouse, she selects cell R1C1 for the title Assumptions, and enters Gross Margin and its related value, .32, in their cells.

In figure 14-13, she enters Cost of Goods into the assumption table and the formula to calculate it in the adjacent cell. She could simply have entered .68, but one of the rules of thumb of spreadsheet use says that one always prefers formulas over constants.

Notice the formula in the second line of the display screen:

```
=1-R[-1]C
```

After selecting the cell, Jill indicates that it will contain a formula by first entering an equal sign (=).

Multiplan uses *relative* cell addresses. The selected, or target, cell in this case is R3C2. The cell containing the constant required for the formula is R2C2. Therefore, the cell address of the constant is

```
R[3-1]C2,
```

that is, one up from R3 in the same column. Multiplan refers to the selected or current row as *R* and the current column as *C*. For this reason, if the desired cell is in the same row, she need only enter *R*. If it's in the same column, she enters only *C*. The cell address

```
R[-1]C
```

means the same row but up one cell and in the same column as the selected cell. The completed formula

```
=1-R[-1]C
```

says subtract the contents of R2C2 from 1 and put the result in the selected cell.

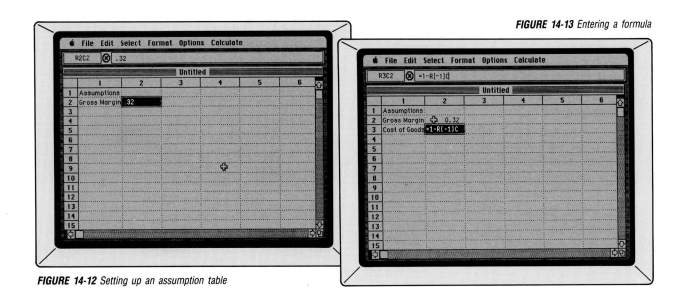

FIGURE 14-12 *Setting up an assumption table*

FIGURE 14-13 *Entering a formula*

The formula looks tough to type, and so it would be if Jill had to type it, but she doesn't. Instead, after entering

$$=1-$$

she simply selects the cell containing the constant, R2C2, by placing the pointer on it (notice the cross in figure 14-13) and clicking it in. Multiplan enters that cell address as a relative address in the formula being constructed at the top of the worksheet.

The second line down from the top of the Multiplan worksheet is called the *active formula bar*. To the left it shows the address of the current cell. To the right it shows the content of the current cell. The vertical line immediately to the right of the formula in the active formula bar is the *character insertion point*. That's where the next character entered into the current cell will appear. Editing of cell contents can be done easily by moving the character insertion point with the mouse to the characters to be changed and deleting and retyping just those characters as necessary. The circled X in the active formula bar is called the cancel icon. Clicking the cancel icon will delete the last entry from the current cell.

Having set up her formula in the active formula bar, Jill now presses the Enter key, and the results of the calculated formula appear in the current cell, figure 14-14.

Now Jill is ready to work up the body of her worksheet. She begins by clicking in cell R5C3 and, holding the mouse button down, drags the pointer downward to the bottom of the display to select a range of cells for data input, figure 14-15. When she releases the button, the top cell in the range is bordered in white, indicating that that cell is active and ready for input.

Now she enters each row title, leaving blanks between rows as she feels necessary to accommodate lines she will add later. After entering each title, she presses the Enter key, and Multiplan moves the cursor downward to the next cell in the selected range. The titles require more column width than is available, so she moves the pointer up to the line separating the column numbers in the fourth line from the top of the display, the *column head* line. Placing the pointer on the vertical line between columns, she holds the mouse

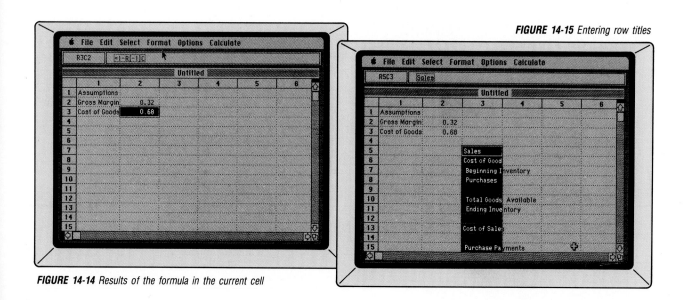

FIGURE 14-15 *Entering row titles*

FIGURE 14-14 *Results of the formula in the current cell*

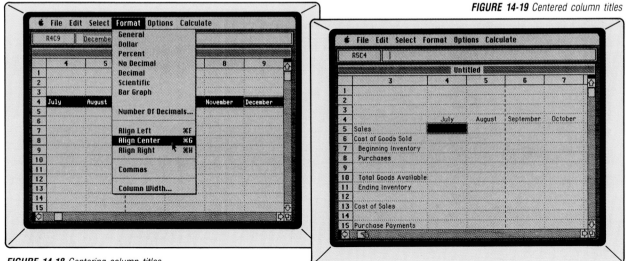

FIGURE 14-17 *Entering column titles*

FIGURE 14-16 *Adjusting column width*

button down and drags the line to the right until column three is wide enough to show the longest title, figure 14-16.

To enter column titles that will show the names of the months starting with July, she moves the pointer to R4C4 and drags it rightward, through column 10, holding the mouse button down. All of the cells in this range are now set up for data entry. Then she enters the names of the months, figure 14-17.

Wanting the column titles to be centered in each column, she makes use of the Format menu. This is one of six *pull-down menus* named in the very top line of the display in the *menu bar*. Moving the pointer to the word *Format* in the menu bar, she presses the mouse button and drags the pointer downward through the menu which appears until the Align Center selection is highlighted in black, figure 4-18. Notice, in that figure, that the cells containing the titles to be centered are still selected. Then she releases the button and Multiplan centers each title, figure 14-19.

FIGURE 14-19 *Centered column titles*

FIGURE 14-18 *Centering column titles*

FIGURE 14-21 Naming and saving a file

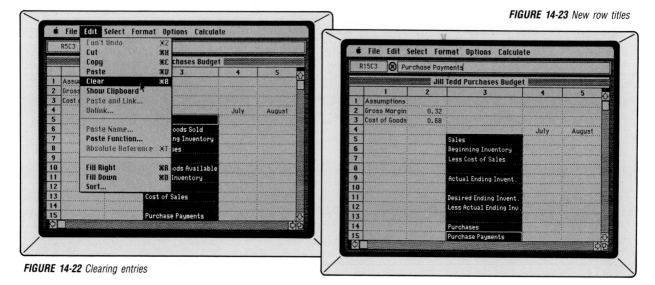

FIGURE 14-20 Selecting the Save As...function from the file menu

At this point, Jill is called away from her computer. An experienced user, she saves her work to disk every fifteen minutes so that if something goes wrong, such as a power failure, she will not lose more than a quarter hour's worth of effort. She also makes it a practice to save her work on each occasion when she must leave the computer unattended. Moving the pointer to the word *File* in the menu bar, she drags it down through the menu to the selection Save As... in figure 14-20. This option allows her to save a file that heretofore has never been saved and, consequently, has no filename. Notice the word *Untitled* in the line immediately above the column numbers.

Multiplan presents a *dialog menu,* figure 14-21. The character insertion point rests in the rectangle and she types in Jill Tedd Purchases Budget. This filename is longer than the rectangle can accommodate, so the last word is not shown, even though the full filename, as she typed it, will identify the file. After typing, she clicks the Save button in the dialog menu and the operating system saves the file on disk.

Returning the next day, Jill starts Multiplan and retrieves her file. Having decided to take a simpler approach, she selects the column of row titles she had previously entered, and using the Edit menu, clears them to blank (figure

FIGURE 14-23 New row titles

FIGURE 14-22 Clearing entries

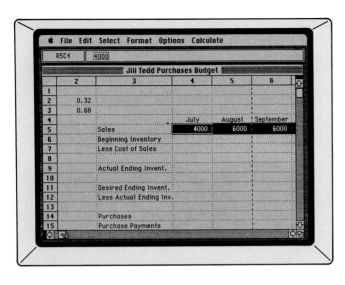

FIGURE 14-24
Entering projected sales

14-22) and enters the new row titles she will use (figure 14-23). Finally, she enters the expected sales for the first six months of operation, figure 14-24.

Now Jill is ready to set up the formulas to calculate her monthly payments for purchases. Her beginning inventory is 68% of the sum of the current and the following months' sales. In figure 14-25, she selects the target cell, R6C4, enters an equal sign, then clicks in R3C2, the cell containing her cost of goods percentage. Then she types the multiplication symbol (*) and a parenthesis and clicks in the cells containing the sales projections for July and August. This inserts those relative cell addresses into her formula. She concludes the formula with a closing parenthesis, as shown in the active formula bar.

She continues entering formulas by clicking in the cells and adding the arithmetic functions needed to perform her calculations through row 14 of the worksheet. Then she adds a couple of dotted lines to improve clarity, figure 14-26.

Multiplan sets up all formulas with relative cell address references. Because a couple of her formulas use the cost of sales ratio at R3C2, Jill needs to identify that cell address as *absolute*, that is, unchanged in a series of appearances. She selects each cell containing that address and moves the character insertion

FIGURE 14-26 *Completing the formulas*

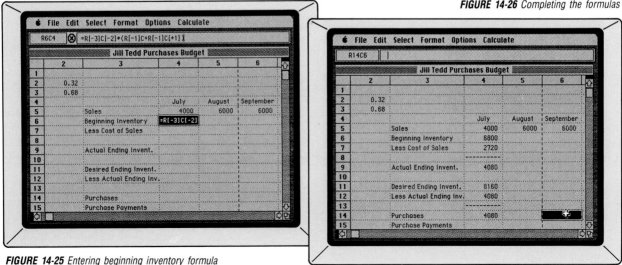

FIGURE 14-25 *Entering beginning inventory formula*

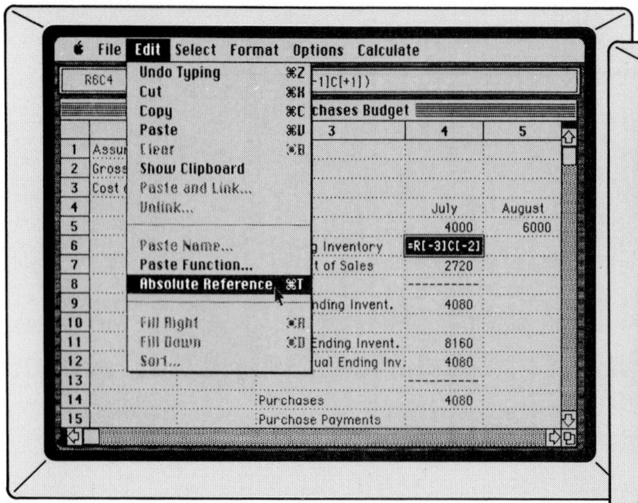

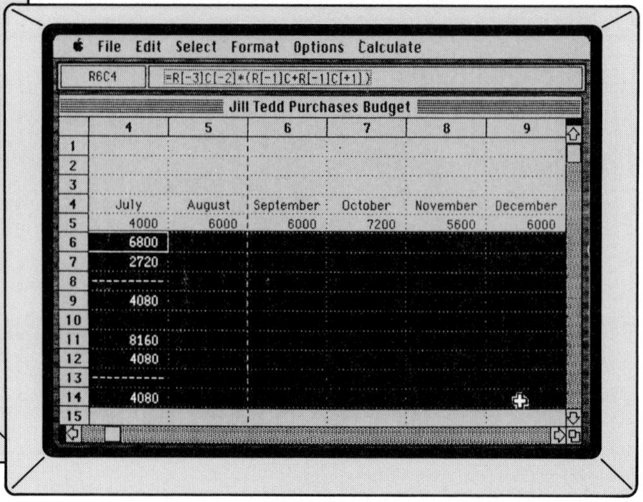

FIGURE 14-28 Selecting area into which formulas will be filled

FIGURE 14-27 Establishing an absolute cell reference

point in the active formula bar so that it rests on the cell reference to be made absolute. The she uses the Edit pull-down menu, figure 14-27, to set that cell reference as an absolute one. She does this for every formula that uses an absolute address.

At this point, Jill is ready to copy her formulas across to every month on her worksheet. She selects all the rows and columns that include Beginning Inventory and Purchases from July through December by placing the pointer on July's Beginning Inventory and dragging across and down to Purchases for December, figure 14-28. Then, using the Edit menu, she selects the Fill Right option to copy the formulas from column 4 to all the columns through December, figure 14-29. Multiplan fills in the formulas and calculates the results in something less than a second, figure 14-30.

This last operation represents one of the most powerful features of spreadsheet programs: the ability to *copy* or *replicate* formulas from a cell or range of cells to other cells. Multiplan uses the word *fill* to mean the same thing.

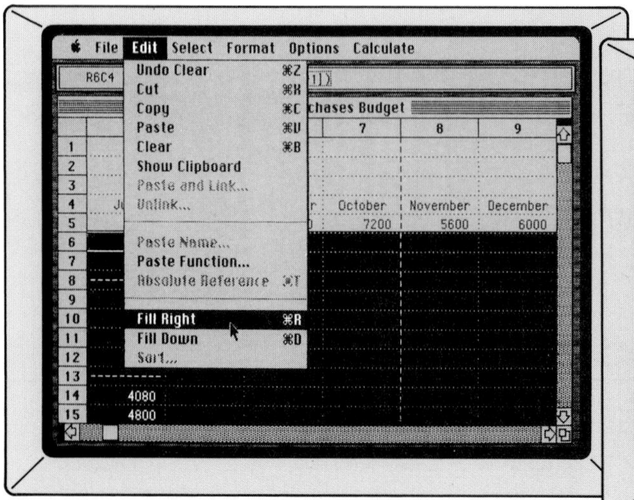

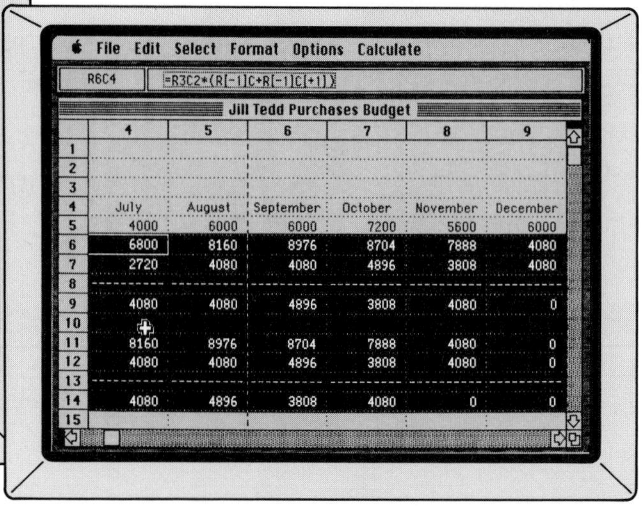

FIGURE 14-30 Calculation results

FIGURE 14-29 Filling formulas

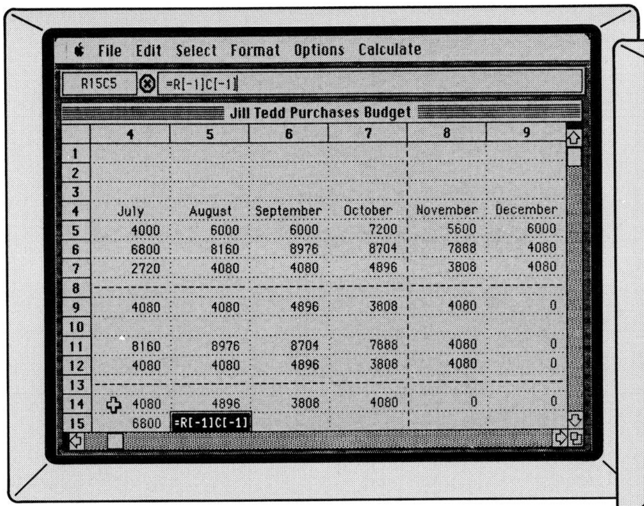

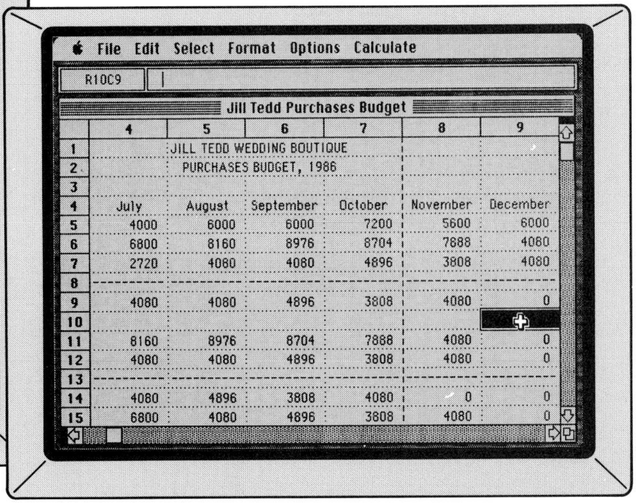

FIGURE 14-32 Results of filling purchase payments formula

FIGURE 14-31 Entering purchase payments

As the formulas are copied, the *relative* cell addresses in each are adjusted so that the results of the computations will be correct. For example, in Jill's spreadsheet, the desired beginning inventory (Row 6) is always calculated on the basis of sales for the following two months, that is, the value of R6C4 is based on the values in R5C5 and R5C6. The value for R6C5, on the other hand, must be calculated on the basis of the sales amounts shown in cells R5C6 and R5C7. The program adjusts cell addresses automatically when formulas are copied so that relative cell addresses as well as absolute ones will be correct.

In the last step in her calculations, Jill determines cash expenditures for purchases for each month. Jill knows that she must pay in July for the purchases she has already made, so she enters that amount, $6,800 in R15C5. During August and ensuing months she must pay for purchases in the month following them, so she enters the formula to indicate the amount to be paid in August is equal to the purchases made in July, figure 14-31. Following this, she fills the formula for purchase payments from August through December using the same techniques as described earlier. The results appear in figure 14-32.

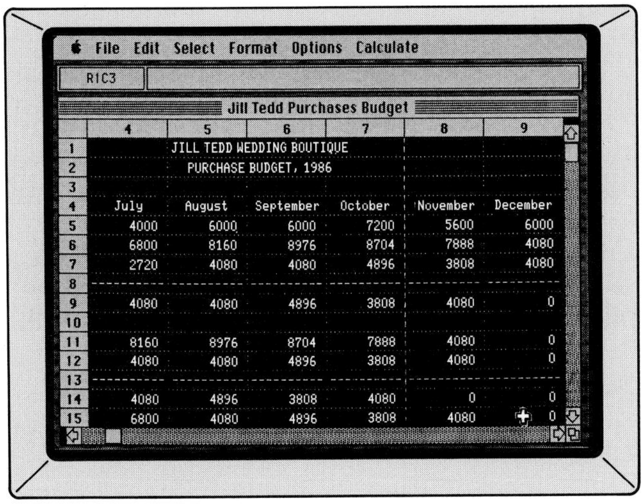

FIGURE 14-33
Selecting area to be printed

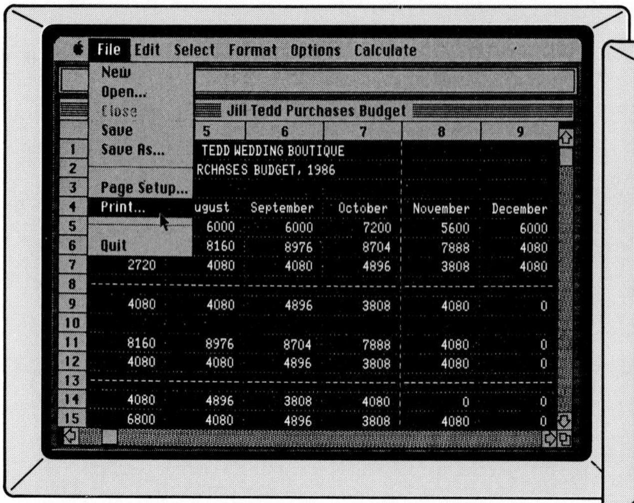

FIGURE 14-34 Selecting print option

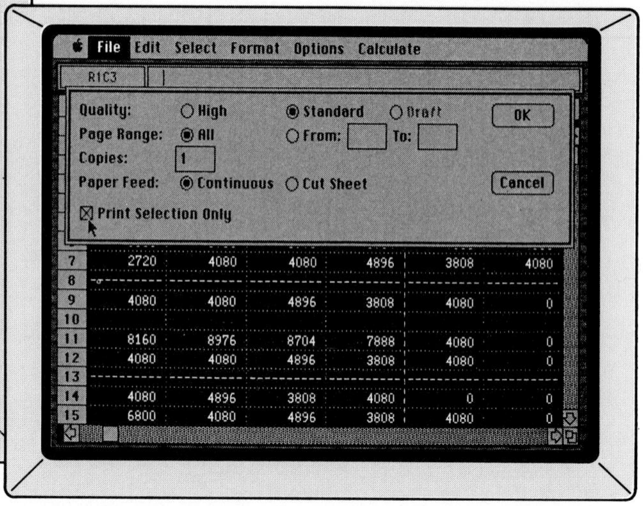

FIGURE 14-35 Print dialog menu

JILL TEDD WEDDING BOUTIQUE
PURCHASES BUDGET, 1986

	July	August	September	October	November	December
Sales	4000	6000	6000	7200	5600	6000
Beginning Inventory	6800	8160	8976	8704	7888	4080
Less Cost of Sales	2720	4080	4080	4896	3808	4080
Actual Ending Invent.	4080	4080	4896	3808	4080	0
Desired Ending Invent.	8160	8976	8704	7888	4080	0
Less Actual Ending Inv.	4080	4080	4896	3808	4080	0
Purchases	4080	4896	3808	4080	0	0
Purchase Payments	6800	4080	4896	3808	4080	0

FIGURE 14-36 Completed purchases budget

Printing the Report

Jill is ready to print her report. She begins by selecting the area she wishes to print, figure 14-33, leaving out the assumption table. Then she uses the File menu to select the Print option, figure 14-34. That option presents her with a dialog menu asking for specifics about the print operation, figure 14-35.

She clicks the Print Selection Only choice because she has selected the area in her worksheet she wants to appear on paper. Then she clicks the OK choice to initiate printing. The result appears in figure 14-36.

The purchases figures for November and December have not been calculated because projected sales figures are not available in the worksheet. As Jill operates her business, she can continue horizontally by adding sales projections to determine her cash outlays for purchases over time, thus calculating purchases figures for November and succeeding months.

SUMMARY

Spreadsheet programs are general programs as opposed to those that focus on specific applications. Because of their generality, they are applicable to many different types of processing tasks. Early in the 1980's, spreadsheets operating on microcomputers offered a complete computer system that would fit on a desk top. The system was easy to use and relatively inexpensive. As a result, spreadsheet programs are credited with being the single most powerful impetus behind the microcomputer revolution.

A *spreadsheet program* sets up the computer system's memory as if it were a huge sheet of paper divided into *rows* and *columns*. The intersection of a row and a column defines a *cell,* a location in memory into which data may be entered. Cells are identified by the *cell address* which locates the cell by the coordinates of the row and column in which it falls. Viewing the cells in a worksheet involves the use of *scrolling* techniques by which the user moves the cursor or pointer toward the cell to be examined.

To enter data into a cell, the user *selects* the cell by moving a *cursor,* or *pointer,* to it. This cell is known as the *selected, target,* or *current* cell. Three kinds of data may be entered into a cell: *character data,* called labels or titles, *values,* and *formulas.*

The most powerful aspect of spreadsheet programs relates to the use of formulas. A formula consists of arithmetic operators, functions, cell addresses, and, sometimes, constants. *Arithmetic operators* include addition, subtraction, multiplication, division, and exponentiation. *Functions* perform various tasks, including adding the contents of a *range* of cells, sorting, and executing mathematical operations. *Constants* are values that will not change. *Cell addresses* in a formula identify the locations of values to be included in the formula. When used in a formula, cell addresses may be *relative* to the line or column, changing as the target cell changes or *absolute,* always referring to the same cell.

Immediately upon entering a formula in a cell, the results are calculated. Thereafter, whenever one of the elements of the formula is changed, the program recalculates the results so that the cell showing the results is always up to date.

Spreadsheet operations are controlled by *command sequences* and *menus.* The commands are used for such operations as formatting the worksheet, dividing it into windows, saving and retrieving worksheets to and from disk, and other operations.

The most powerful command in spreadsheet programs *copies* or *replicates* data, including formulas, from one or more cells into one or more others. With this ability, users can set up very large worksheets with just a few formulas. Relative cell addresses in formulas that are copied are determined automatically by the program.

To aid the user, most spreadsheet programs display abbreviated *menus* listing the commands that are available. Many programs also offer extensive *help screens.*

Setting up a spreadsheet for a particular application often involves using *templates,* spreadsheets consisting only of formulas and titles. Using templates eliminates the need to set up formats repetitively for multiple versions of the same worksheet. Templates for many applications can be purchased.

Spreadsheet programs are best known for their ability to answer "*What if...*" types of questions and for keeping *projections* up to date as new data become available. Used in this manner, the spreadsheet becomes a *model* of the operation being studied.

Because of spreadsheet programs' ability to analyze data easily, users find that access to data from other applications in the organization's computer system is desirable. As a result, much work has been devoted to making data and file formats compatible among various application programs. Many spreadsheet programs produce and retrieve files in standard formats. Some spreadsheet programs are part of integrated systems that link spreadsheet, graphics, word processing, data base management, and other applications together.

Spreadsheet programs, although generally applicable to many processing tasks, are limited by the hardware constraints imposed by the computers on which they operate and by their ability to retrieve data from other applications. In addition, they are unsuited for high-volume operations done best by specialized programs operating on large computers. When used in a microcomputer environment, which is most common, specialized application programs for graphics, word processing, data base management, and other tasks are preferred by those who require full-powered programs for those purposes.

Nevertheless, spreadsheet programs offer tremendous power and flexibility within the constraints of their limitations. In the opinions of many, no desktop computer system is complete without one.

KEY TERMS

active cell	*character insertion point*	*selected cell*
active formula bar	*command sequence*	*source range*
assumption table	*default*	*spreadsheet*
cell	*model*	*target range*
cell address	*replicate*	*template*

REVIEW QUESTIONS

1. To what complete computer system can we attribute the microcomputer revolution?
2. What are the two essential business applications of microcomputers?
3. Describe scrolling.
4. What is the advantage of using windows with a spreadsheet?
5. What three types of items can we put into a spreadsheet cell?
6. How does a number entered as numeric data differ from one calculated as the result of a formula?
7. What is stored in memory when a formula is entered into a cell?
8. Describe the sum function in a spreadsheet.
9. What is the advantage of having global commands?
10. Cell B6 of a spreadsheet contains the number 34, A6 contains 2, and AD15 contains 20. What will be the result of the calculation +B6+A6*AD15?
11. What kind of question does a spreadsheet answer best?
12. How are spreadsheets that are not part of integrated systems linked to other types of programs?

THOUGHT QUESTIONS

1. Explain the differences between electronic and paper spreadsheets. Why is one more powerful than the other?
2. If you were designing a spreadsheet, what functions would you include? Why?
3. Discuss the value of spreadsheet templates.

Point Counterpoint

Who's the Pirate?

(Courtesy Apple Computer, Inc.)

The Point/Counterpoint selection for Chapter Thirteen outlined four issues concerning piracy of software. Consider the following situations in terms of those issues. Although the names are fictitious, the situations are real and fairly commonplace.

Stanley Straight

Small business owner Stanley Straight decided to purchase a computer system for accounting purposes and for word processing, especially for preparing personalized mailings to his growing list of customers. After shopping around carefully, Stan purchased a complete system from Quick Byte, a local computer store. The system included hard disk secondary storage and Quick Byte agreed to include with the package an accounting system with general ledger and accounts receivable and a word processing program that had a mail merge feature. The mail merge could use data from the accounts receivable files to prepare mailings.

Quick Byte installed the programs on Stan's hard disk and also provided tutorials on floppy disks to train Stan's office helper in using the programs.

After a few weeks spent in learning the new system and converting the manual accounting system to the new one, everything seemed to be going very well. Stan was delighted.

Not long after, however, Stan's office helper encountered minor difficulties in using the general ledger program and called the software producer for advice. During the ensuing conversation, the producer learned that Stan had not registered the software by returning the warrantee card. Subsequent inquiry revealed that Quick Byte had sold both the word processing and accounting programs with several computer systems but had only purchased one copy itself.

A few weeks later, both Stan and Quick Byte were served with notice of suit for copyright infringement and license agreement violations.

Prudence Fairweather, CPA

Certified public accountant Prudence Fairweather operated an income tax service. For her purposes, she purchased a $500 tax accounting program to prepare returns for her customers. The software came

433

with one program disk and a notice in the user's manual that a backup copy could be purchased from the software producer for an additional $50. The manual also detailed a license agreement that forbade users from copying the program disk. Being something of a computer hobbyist, she quickly defeated the disk's copy-protection scheme and made her own backup copy which she used for all of her work. She kept the original program disk in her bank's safe deposit vault.

One dark and stormy night, lightning struck the power lines serving her place of business while she was preparing a customer's return. The surge of current through the computer system destroyed the program disk. The next day she retrieved the original program disk from the bank, copied it again, stored the original back in the vault, and continued operations.

As her business grew, Prudence found it necessary to hire an assistant and, eventually, to purchase a second computer system. Making yet another copy of the tax program disk, she set her assistant to using it with the new computer.

R. Whimsy Bullroar

Author R. Whimsy Bullroar contracted with Expert Publishers, Incorporated, to write a college text. The agreement required Whimsy to deliver the completed manuscript in typewritten form and on floppy disk, as well. For that purpose, Whimsy purchased a copy of WordSmith, a word processing program produced by MarvelSoft Corporation.

After receiving the typewritten manuscript and the disks, Expert contacted Whimsy asking for a copy of MarvelSoft WordSmith. "We need the program to enter typesetting codes," explained an editor. "After all, you can't expect us to buy every word processing program our authors use, can you?"

Della Gate

Della Gate is a traveling sales executive with a large corporation. When she is in the office, she uses a microcomputer to keep track of her many contacts in the field. Because her office staff maintains her data files by updating customer accounts, she finds it necessary to purchase a portable computer and a communications software package so that she can retrieve information from the home office account files while traveling.

It quickly becomes apparent that in order for communications to work at all, both her portable computer and the computer in the office must be equipped with communications programs. Furthermore, the programs must be compatible. The simplest solution, Della reasons, is to make a copy of the communications program so that one operates the computer at the office while the other runs her portable. Accordingly, she instructs her assistant, Alfred Ways, to make a copy of the program disk. Al objects, asserting that copying the program disk would violate the licensure agreement.

QUESTIONS

1. Who is guilty of the charges: Stanley Straight or Quick Byte? Why?
2. Was Prudence Fairweather guilty of pirating by making her own backup disk? Why or why not?
3. Was Prudence guilty of pirating when using a backup disk with the second computer? Why or why not?
4. If you were MarvelSoft Corporation, how would you respond to Expert's arguments?
5. Should R. Whimsy Bullroar give Expert Publishers a copy of MarvelSoft WordSmith?
6. How should Della Gate respond to Alfred Ways?

C H A P T E R 15

Computer Graphics

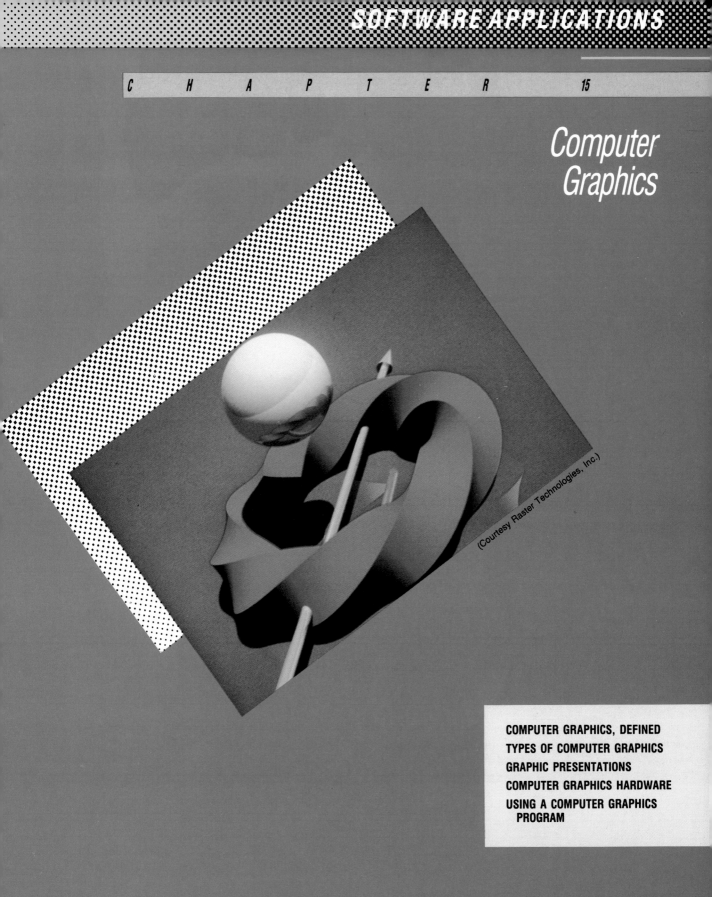

(Courtesy Raster Technologies, Inc.)

COMPUTER GRAPHICS, DEFINED

TYPES OF COMPUTER GRAPHICS

GRAPHIC PRESENTATIONS

COMPUTER GRAPHICS HARDWARE

USING A COMPUTER GRAPHICS PROGRAM

Computer art that uses ray tracing to study reflections and color. ("Colorplay" by Patricia Search, Rensselaer Polytechnic Institute. Copyright 1984 by Patricia Search. All rights reserved.)

"I don't see it that way," says one manager when listening to an explanation from another. "Try to get the big picture," says a third. "If Sam doesn't understand these labor cost figures, draw him a picture," vents an exasperated accountant. "Why don't you sketch out your ideas during lunch?" suggests the account executive.

The plant manager, proposing the purchase of new equipment, prepares cost and production comparisons carefully and approaches the company president with a folder full of facts and figures neatly typed in orderly rows and columns. One look and the president knows that it will take more time to review the material than she can spend now. "Ahh...How about getting together next week. It'll take some time for me to study these reports. As soon as I get the complete picture, I'll give you a call."

So much for the new equipment. Chances are that if the manager had prepared the complete picture for the president, things would have gone much better. Preparing the complete picture is the crucial step in business communication. The data processing work was done well, the facts supported the manager's proposal for additional investment, all that remained was to get the idea across to the person who makes the decisions. Communication failed.

Summarizing, often overlooked by those like our plant manager who work with a lot of detail all the time, is an essential element in the process of communicating. There is nothing that summarizes as well as a picture. If this sounds like another way of expressing the platitude about a thousand words, you're right. After all, if the final and crucial step of information and data processing is that of communication, we would be ill-advised to slight the power of visual presentation.

Although the written word is often the only effective way to relate complex information, reading or listening to words is a slow process. The average person can speak only 110 to 120 words per minute, yet the mind is capable of understanding many times that number.

What's more, the mind retains a visual representation of data with greater accuracy and for a longer period of time than it does a written equivalent.

With reams of computer printouts full of data to present, today's business professional is crippled without the use of conceptual shortcuts.[1]

Lucky for us, the very same computers that produce our tables of figures and our pages of text can also produce pictures, graphs, and other illustrations. Ideally, the computer uses the very data that appear in our financial analysis reports to produce the visual versions. Thus, a table of numbers that measures the cost per unit difference between the current production equipment and the proposed new machine can be summarized in a graph by the same computer that initially processed the data. Computer software systems that link graphics programs with other data processing programs represent an important aspect of integrated software. The linkage provides easy-to-use techniques for communicating the results of the analysis most effectively, through pictures.

COMPUTER GRAPHICS, DEFINED

The term *computer graphics* embraces all techniques of using computers to prepare visual presentations. The results of these efforts take the form of graphs and drawings printed on paper, displayed on video display units, or presented before an audience as slides and transparencies. These may make use of color and sound and motion as well. The motion is *animated* and is produced by the computer itself.

In computer graphics, the computer, under the control of various programs, produces the images directly. As you might expect, the programs that do this work are quite elaborate. Using the programs is generally easy. Commercially-available software readily converts data into a variety of graphic forms. Some software products permit the sketching of shapes and designs, which the computer then puts into finished form. The sketching can be done using

CAD programs allow wire-frame models to be rotated in three dimensions. (Courtesy Enertronics Research, Inc.)

The object is the finite element mesh for the crankshaft of a single cylinder engine. (Courtesy Mark A. Yerry, Rensselaer Polytechnic Institute's Center for Interactive Computer Graphics)

Designers create parts using sophisticated computer-aided design programs on computer systems. (Courtesy McDonnell Douglas Automation Co.)

a light pen to trace the design on a computer display monitor or using a graphics tablet, so called because one uses it just in the same way that one uses a tablet of drawing paper. Still other programs use mathematical techniques to fit lines and curves to data.

Some of the more tangibly productive and technologically exciting computer graphics software enables the user to design mechanical parts, such as the transmission housing for an automobile. Once designed, the computer system can, at the will of the designer, rotate the part's image on the screen, thus providing views from any perspective. It can also produce three-view mechanical drawings of the art and construct perspective renderings as well.

As if that were not enough, the designer can retrieve the specifications for the transmission itself and cause that assembly to be illustrated on the same screen that shows the transmission housing. Then he or she can "assemble" the parts on the screen to be sure that, indeed, the transmission fits properly into its housing. If it doesn't, either part can be adjusted as necessary.

Moreover, the same computer system can also produce the specifications and control tapes needed to govern the operation of the machining equipment that will produce the actual parts. These two aspects of computer graph-

Computers are used to create three-dimensional architechtural images. (Courtesy Computervision Corp.)

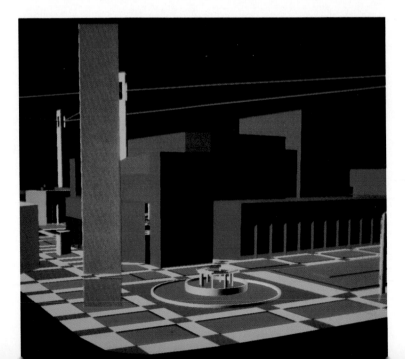

ics—*computer-aided design* and *computer-aided manufacturing*—are known as CAD/CAM. They are now revolutionizing such areas as product design, processing, manufacturing, electronics, and architecture, to name a few.

Perhaps the most dramatic use of computer graphics is in the preparation of visual presentations. Such presentations can be for informative purposes, as with a report of operations to the corporate Board of Trustees; for inspirational purposes, such as a pep talk to the company's marketing force; or for entertainment, as in the 1983 movie *Tron* which was produced in its entirety using computer graphics techniques.

TYPES OF COMPUTER GRAPHICS

With that brief survey of the roles of computer graphics in business today, we turn now to the varieties of graphic illustrations and products currently available to computer users. As a rule, microcomputers provide all of these capabilities. Larger computers won't do more, but, as we shall see in a later section of this chapter, they can produce higher quality imagery.

Business Graphics

To depict business information, we use a handful of tried and true images. The most popular of these include line plots, bar charts, and pie charts, all of which are subsumed under the general rubric of *histograms*.

Line Plots

We construct a line plot by graphing points on a two-axis grid and then connecting the points together with a line. Consider, for example, a marketing budget for a medium-sized corporation. It consists of three categories: promotion, travel, and advertising. The company is interested in comparing

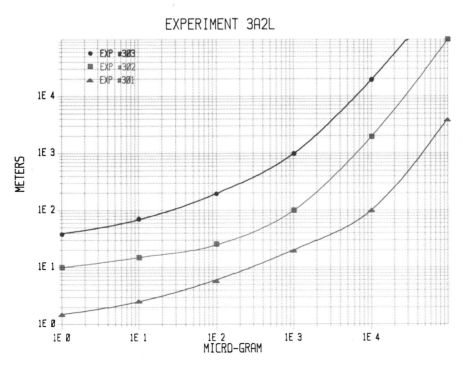

FIGURE 15-1
Line plot (Courtesy Enertronics
Research, Inc.)

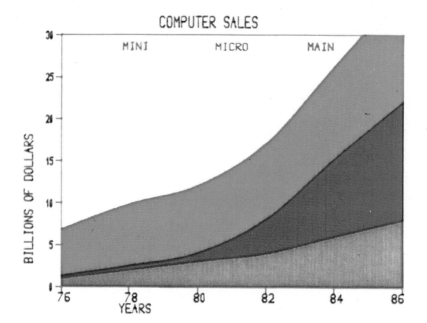

FIGURE 15-2
Area plot (Courtesy Enertronics
Research, Inc.)

changes in these budget categories over time. Time is the uncontrollable element and is known as the *independent variable*. In general, uncontrollable variables or input values are known as independent variables. They are plotted along the horizontal axis. Budget expenditures for each of the three categories are plotted by dollar amount along the vertical axis. These are known as the *dependent variables* because their values depend on the values of the independent variable, which is time in this case.

Figure 15-1 shows a graph. The points, each technically called a *vertex* are connected by lines. To aid understanding, the lines are often differentiated by drawing them as dashes (----), dots (....), or asterisks (****). As shown in figure 15-1, using color differentiates lines even better.

Area Plots

In an important variation of the line plot known as an area plot, we shade the area under each line. This suggests that all of the values under the line should be considered in the analysis. Figure 15-2 shows such a picture.

Bar Charts

Line plots and area plots illustrate changes over time quite well and facilitate comparisons among dependent variables. Bar charts are somewhat more emphatic in appearance. They represent the values of the dependent variables as two-dimensional rectangles. Figure 15-3, for example, compares productivity increases among twelve industrial nations over a ten-year period of time. Bar charts in which the bars are vertical rather than horizontal are sometimes called *column charts*, although they, too, are really bar charts, figure 15-4.

Pie Charts

Pie charts depict the relative proportion that each part contributes to the whole as shown in figure 15-5. In this example, the graph is called an *exploded* pie chart because a portion of it is singled out for special attention.

International Market Segment
(in Thousands)

FIGURE 15-3
*Bar chart comparing
manufacturing productivity.
Created on the DICOMED
IMAGINATOR Design Console and
imaged on the D148SR Image
Recorder.* (Courtesy DICOMED
Corp.)

FIGURE 15-4
*Column chart created on the
DICOMED IMAGINATOR Design
Console and imaged on the
D148SR Image Recorder.*
(Courtesy DICOMED Corp.)

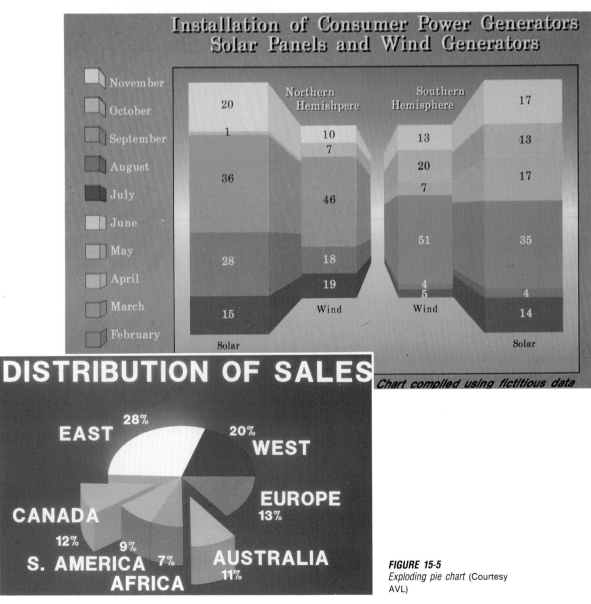

FIGURE 15-5
Exploding pie chart (Courtesy
AVL)

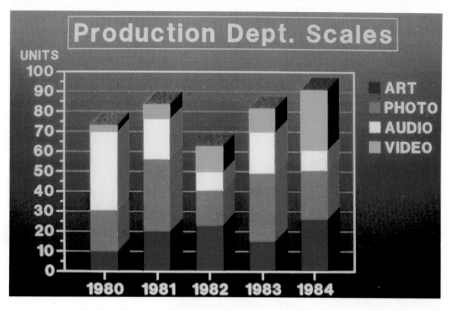

FIGURE 15-6
Three-dimensional bar graph
(Courtesy AVL)

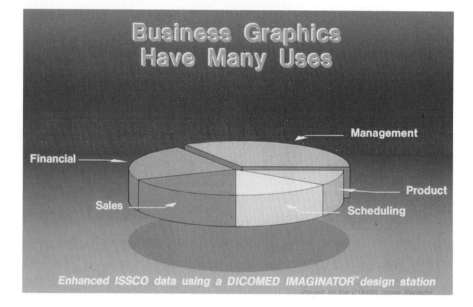

FIGURE 15-7
Three-dimensional pie chart
created on the DICOMED
IMAGINATOR Design Console and
imaged on the D148SR Image
Recorder. (Courtesy DICOMED
Corp.)

Variations and Combinations

Essentially, line plots, bar graphs, and pie charts make up the total of business graphics techniques. Several combinations and variations of these histograms add measurably to their effectiveness. Consider, for example, the bar graph in figure 15-6. It adds a third dimension to each bar, and to the picture generally, thus making the presentation more dramatic.

Figure 15-7 shows a three-dimensional pie chart. In this example, management is singled out by exploding the pie.

The different combinations and variations on the three basic types of business graphs offer many ways to communicate the results of data and information processing. Figure 15-8, for example, shows an operator preparing a three-dimensional graph.

Graphics for Analysis and Planning

Business graphics, as discussed above, aids analysis and display of past activities. Much use can be made of computer graphics tools for the purpose of planning for the future, as well.

Statistical Analysis

Much of statistical analysis involves predicting the future: How long will production tools last before wearing out? What will monthly sales be for the next four months? Answering these questions requires one to analyze past data carefully and then to project what the data will be in the future. One "fits" a curve to the past data and then projects that curve into the time to come.

Fitting a curve to data amounts to plotting the data on a two-axis grid. The horizontal axis represents variation in the independent variable such as time, number of parts produced, or distance travelled. The vertical axis represents variation in the dependent variable being studied: sales growth, machine wear, or fuel consumption. Figure 15-9 shows two varieties of data analysis of this type. Data points are plotted on the grid. A line is then drawn in an effort to summarize the direction of the changes in the data points over time.

Flowcharting

Planning how things work is greatly aided by pictorial representations. That's why programmers and systems analysts use them. These pictures, called flowcharts, can be produced by computer graphics systems. Figure 15-10, for example, illustrates a program flowchart.

To be sure, programmers prepare program flowcharts before doing the program coding. By the time the program is finished, debugged, and tested, however, it is likely that the flowchart will have changed. Modifying the initial

FIGURE 15-8
Three-dimensional graph
(Courtesy Sperry Corp.)

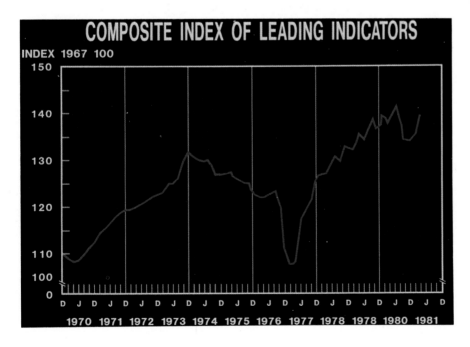

FIGURE 15-9
Statistical analysis created on the DICOMED D38E Design Station and imaged on the D148SR Image Recorder. (Courtesy DICOMED Corp.)

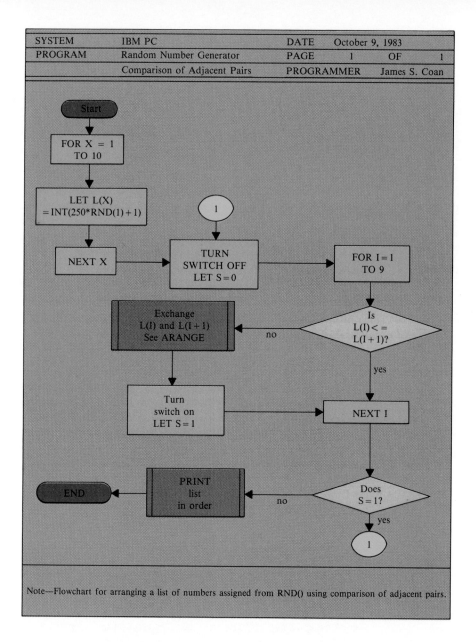

SYSTEM	IBM PC	DATE	October 9, 1983	
PROGRAM	Random Number Generator	PAGE	1	OF	1
	Comparison of Adjacent Pairs	PROGRAMMER	James S. Coan	

Note—Flowchart for arranging a list of numbers assigned from RND() using comparison of adjacent pairs.

FIGURE 15-10
Program flowchart (Courtesy
Enertronics Research, Inc.)

flowchart may require redoing it completely—not something that programmers like to do. Computers can be used to produce initial flowcharts and to modify them easily during program testing and debugging. Graphics systems that analyze a program and produce its logical flowchart prepare accurate documentation in a very timely manner. Similarly, systems flowcharting is greatly aided by graphics programs that specialize in producing systems flowcharts. Figure 15-11 shows a data flow diagram produced by such a program.

Scheduling

The computer has done much to replace the magnetic scheduling board on the production manager's office wall. Planning techniques such as Program Evaluation and Review Technique (PERT), production scheduling, and Gantt

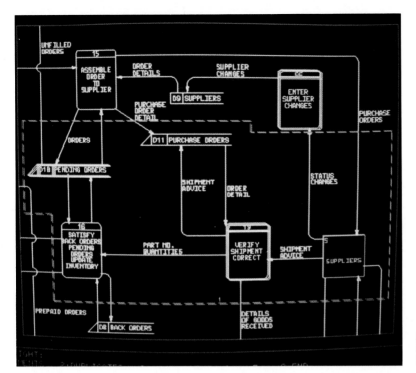

FIGURE 15-11
Data flow diagram (Courtesy
McDonnell Douglas Corp.)

charts are all available as computer programs, most of which include graphics output. Chapter Sixteen reviews a typical project planning application program. Project planning and control, production scheduling, and equipment and facilities utilization analysis are all made considerably easier with software developed for those purposes.

Facilities Planning

It used to be that planning an office or a manufacturing plant was a matter of pushing paper cutouts of furniture and equipment around on a scale drawing of the floor plan. For elaborate facilities, three-dimensional models were made, and still are, to make sure that all of the equipment fit properly. Because many new office buildings are being constructed with movable walls, the job of the office planner becomes more difficult. Now, not only can furniture be rearranged, but so can walls. Programs aiding in these planning processes make good use of the computer's ability to prepare scale drawings. Figure 15-12, for example, shows floor plans produced by such programs.

Some facilities planning programs convert overhead floor plan views into side views and perspective renderings to better aid in visualizing the completed facility. Still more elaborate facilities planning programs use animated techniques to take the planners on a "walk" through the facility by depicting three-dimensional views of its interior. What if we were to move that couch over there, relocate the file cabinets along that wall, then shift this desk back three feet? This is the sort of query that gives the custodial crew backaches if the furniture actually has to be moved. Moreover, the crew suspects, there is a good chance that yet more furniture shifting will be done before the matter is settled. Using computer graphics facilities planning tools is clearly a more effective way of doing this work.

FIGURE 15-12
Floor plan and interior design
(Courtesy Auto-Trol Technology
Corp.)

Computer graphics provides tools for preparing visual presentations. So far in this chapter, we have considered the computer as a device that draws images using data that it processes. The computer today is also considered by many as an art medium itself: the means by which visual presentations are prepared by an artist as if using oil on canvass. Using the computer as an art medium is a fairly new development, primarily because computer output devices have been, up until the last few years, character-producing rather than image-producing.

The Computer as an Art Medium

With the advent of computer systems that can produce pictorial images, the use of computers as an art medium has attracted much attention. Indeed, computers have been hailed by the *Los Angeles Times* as "The most significant technological advance in the visual arts since the invention of film."[2] In the first of a four-part series on computer graphics published by the *Times*, Harry Marx, operator of a computer animation studio is quoted as follows:

> We're rapidly approaching the point where computer-generated imagery will be indistinguishable from reality...Except a computer has virtually no visual limitations, so we can take you where it's physically impossible to go. If you want to see what it would look like to sail the Queen Mary through the eye of a needle, we can show you—in perfect detail.[3]

The *Times* series concludes with some comments from Ed Emshwiller, Dean of the School of Film and Video at California Institute of the Arts in Valencia, California:

> More recently, I've been working with computer graphics systems at the New York Institute of Technology and CalArts. I still use the painterly skills I developed, but I'm using new tools to make the images...While I prefer the image film produces, I like the immediacy and plasticity of video. It's like painting to me—I can see what I've done immediately and can make changes with great flexibility using the devices of keying and matting. I feel you work within the limits of any system, whether it's a piece of charcoal, an oil brush, a $50 computer or a million-dollar computer: Each of them has its own characteristics and capabilities and you use those to the hilt.[4]

The modern computer, then, cannot only prepare visual manifestations of the data it processes, but can also produce effective illustrations and art work. Many of the illustrations in this chapter are of the art variety.

Presentations to Groups

Presentations at the annual stockholders' meeting, before a management group, or at a professional conference are greatly enhanced by visual representations of the information being delivered. Of course, any of the graphics output illustrated in this chapter can be so presented. By *presentation graphics* we mean preparing informational graphic images for presentation to a group of people.

> Let us in no way minimize the opportunity, or the danger, involved. The 30 minutes an executive spends on his feet formally presenting his latest project to corporate superiors are simply and absolutely the most important 30 minutes of that or any other managerial season.[5]

With that comment in mind, let us review some of the computer graphics techniques available to be used for group presentations.

Video Display Terminals

One way to show graphics images to an audience is to gather the people around a computer video display terminal and run the programs that produce the images. If the group is moderately large, video projection units employing screens of forty inches or larger, or several terminals, will be needed to afford everyone a satisfactory view. This is awkward. Setting up computers and video terminals is time consuming. It takes even more time during the presentation for the computer to produce the images, and image production requires considerable computer time. Furthermore, one would often prefer to have the images printed on paper for distribution to the audience.

Photography

A fairly straightforward way of using the computer to prepare visual images for large audiences is to display the image on the video terminal and photograph it using a 35 millimeter camera with color slide film. The slide can then be projected on a large screen before the audience with far greater effectiveness and ease than one could expect from the video terminal itself. The slide can also be reproduced as hard copy for handing out to the audience, if necessary. Figure 15-13 shows some color slides made from computer images.

Printers and Plotters

Another way of producing projection images is to use a color printer or plotter that will write on transparent acetate, as illustrated in figure 15-14. This

FIGURE 15-14
Color printer producing overhead projector transparency (Courtesy Hewlett-Packard Co.)

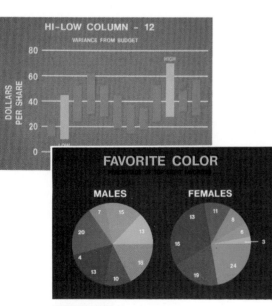

FIGURE 15-13
Computer-generated color slides created with DICOMED's Presenter PC Software and imaged on the D148SR Image Recorder. (Courtesy DICOMED Corp.)

FIGURE 15-15
Animated flight training (Courtesy Microsoft Corp.)

produces a much larger original image that can be projected using an overhead projector. Overhead projectors work well in an undarkened room, which makes it easier for the audience to take notes and the speaker to face the audience. Finally, the speaker can write or draw on the transparency during the presentation. This, of course, would be impossible when using slides.

Animation

Certainly one of the most dramatic uses of computer graphics is animation. Animated graphics programs used in flight training, for example, produce realistic, if not hair-raising, simulation of reality, figure 15-15.

Such programs for entertainment purposes are readily available. Video game arcades often have one or more racing simulators that give surprising realism, even to "feeling" the centrifugal force when roaring around a bend in the road.

Scenes from a computer-generated animation depicting the deployment of a space antenna. (Courtesy Alan Barr, Beth Conk, Bruce Edwards, and Jeff Goldsmith, Rensselaer Polytechnic Institute's Center for Interactive Computer Graphics)

Animation is very effective in business and professional graphics presentations. The exploding pie chart not only shows a piece outstanding from the rest, but makes it move away, as well. Showing sales growth as a series of larger bars on a bar graph is O.K., but having an area representing sales actually increase in size on the screen gets much more attention. Some business graphics programs also include animated cartoon characters that will point to aspects of the presentation to be emphasized.

Presentation graphics, especially the use of animation, will doubtless enjoy increased use in the immediate future. Audiences get a sense of immediacy and realism when viewing information presented graphically on a video terminal and invariably are pleased and excited about the experience.

COMPUTER GRAPHICS HARDWARE

Computer-generated images can be produced on many different types of peripheral devices. These include video display units, printers and plotters. As we observed earlier in this chapter, computer-generated images can also control machine tools as output devices, thus converting the image into the actual product being designed. This section reviews some technical aspects of hardware devices used in computer graphics work.

Video Display Units

Almost all computers today employ video display units for graphics output. Although they look like home television sets, these terminals are quite different. Their difference lies in the number of phosphorescent dots that can be illuminated on the screen.

Look closely at a video screen and you will see that the image is made up of thousands of little dots. Officially, they are known as *pixels*, which is shorthand for "picture elements." The greater the number of pixels, the higher the *resolution* of the image appearing on the screen. In effect, the pictures appear more in focus. Resolution is measured by the number of pixels used to make up the longest line that can be drawn on the screen. Typically, a computer CRT or monitor has much greater resolution than a home television screen, thus accounting for why those who work even moderate amounts of time at a video terminal prefer monitors over television sets.

Virtually every computer today can be equipped with the internal hardware and operating system features required for graphics output. Moreover, almost all computers also offer the ability to produce graphics images in color and can use their color capabilities to produce graphic images on a monochrome screen if a color screen is unavailable. Differences in color on monochrome screens can sometimes be discerned as variations in the textures of the colored areas.

Two kinds of color CRTs are used with computers today. The usual variety, and the less expensive, operates much like a home television set. Color is represented by illuminating one or more of three closely spaced pixels. Each pixel, when illuminated by an electron gun shows its particular color: red, green, or blue. The computer sends a composite color signal through one set of wires; the electron gun aims the electron stream or streams toward those pixels to be lit up. Because of their close proximity on the screen, the eye combines the individual pixel colors into the single color to be represented: green and red make yellow, for example; red and blue make magenta. This is called a *composite color CRT.*

Using three pixels to display a dot of color, of course, does much to reduce the resolution of the image, resulting in a fuzzy picture that is O.K. for many graphics images, but quite unacceptable for presentations that require displaying both images and text. A better, albeit more expensive, alternative is the second type of CRT, the *RGB* (for red, green, blue) *monitor.* This device receives separate color signals for each of the three colors from separate sets of wires, recording the desired color by illuminating just one pixel. Naturally, the resolution is much higher. Using an RGB monitor, very carefully controlled colors can be represented using the highest resolution possible with the computer system. The resulting high quality is expensive, but many believe the price to be worthwhile.

Given a computer with color graphics capabilities, the number of colors available depends on its storage capacity and the desired image resolution. The larger the number of colors available, the greater the storage needed. Similarly, the higher the resolution, the greater the storage requirement. Obviously, one can trade off these variables and their associated costs to arrive at the best compromise concerning color availability and resolution. One company, PC Plus of Frederick, Maryland, for example, produces a color adapter card for the IBM PC that offers two alternatives: sixteen colors at medium resolution (320 × 200 pixels); or four colors at high resolution (640 × 200 pixels).

Probably the artistically ideal CRT graphics system would use a full-color matrix of 2000 by 2000 pixels on a 9-inch screen: 4,000,000 picture elements. Resolution this high is equivalent to the grain of photographic film. At today's prices, such systems would be very expensive and would require mainframe computers. As prices of storage and software decrease, however, the industry is moving toward producing very high resolution even with microcomputers. The Apple Macintosh computer uses a 512 × 342 pixel matrix that produces black and white images of near-publication quality (publication quality with a laser printer). The IBM PC, which offers only four colors, can be modified into a full-color system by using a hardware and software kit that provides the

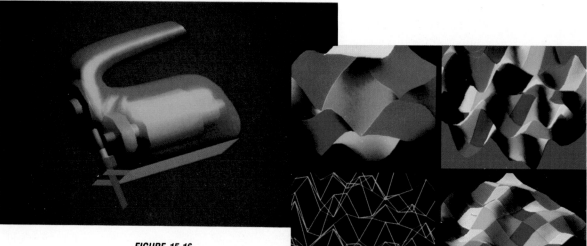

FIGURE 15-16
Full-color moderate resolution graphics (Courtesy Adage, Inc.)

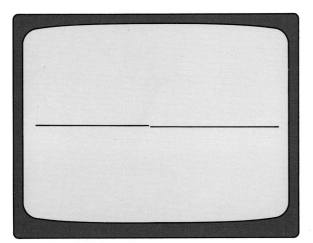

FIGURE 15-17
*Angled line approximated by a
raster-scan display*

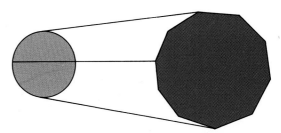

FIGURE 15-18
*Straight line approximation of a
curve*

artistic capability of systems costing over eight times as much, according to its manufacturer. Figure 15-16 shows a few examples of the work that this system can do. Rated as a moderate resolution system, the fuzziness introduced by the individual pixels is still evident.

At the high end of the cost spectrum for color graphics computer systems, one finds matrices of 600 × 500 pixels and more than 256 colors. WICAT, a Utah-based company, markets a multi-user graphics system for educators that includes animation capabilities. Interleaf, in Massachusetts, sells a computer system that produces publications and reports, incorporating business graphics. It has a very high resolution: 900 × 1152 pixels.

Sacrificing aesthetic appearance for the sake of reducing cost probably does little to damage the communicative effectiveness of moderately priced microcomputer graphics systems.

When CRTs display pictures using pixels, the picture takes the form of many dots. Look at figure 15-17, for example. It shows what happens when such a screen tries to represent a line at a very slight angle to the horizontal, specifically, a line that goes from the left-most dot on one line to the right-most dot of the line immediately beneath. The line is broken. This happens as the computer tries to fit the line to the available dots on the two rows used. Such a system is called a *raster-scan* system. The electron gun which records the pixels on the screen scans one row of pixels at a time horizontally.

Images in raster-scan systems are composed of a series of horizontal lines. Another type of graphics output, known as the *vector-stroke* system, uses a series of straight lines connecting any pairs of points in the graphics field, the area in which the image is to be constructed. Because of this, the lines can be drawn in virtually any direction, so long as they terminate at defined points. Thus, the fundamental picture element in vector stroke systems is the line. All is not perfect, however, as curves must still be approximated by short straight line segments, resulting in jagged edges of curved figures in the image, particularly when the curved figures are small or are enlarged, in which case they appear as polygons. Figure 15-18 illustrates this problem.

One attempt to cope with the problem involves using mathematical formulas derived from the cone. Using these formulas, curves can be derived to produce almost any shape that is required. Because the geometric figure of the cone is used, this technique has been named *conography* by its developer. Figure 15-19 shows how various curves, including the circle, the ellipse, and

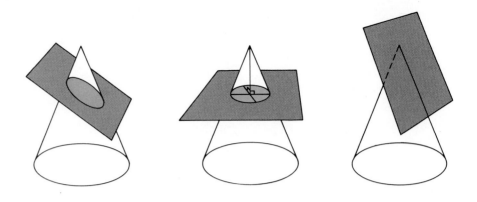

FIGURE 15-19
Calculating curves as the
intersection of a cone and a
plane

the straight line can be calculated as the intersection of a plane and a cone.

Using conography requires fewer program steps than would approximating the same curves with straight line segments. Figure 15-20 shows a drawing of an automobile using the conography technique. The specifications for this drawing are eighty percent fewer in number than they would be using straight-line approximations for the curves.

Printers

Taking a photograph of a computer monitor is one way of getting hard copy of the output being displayed. Photographs are expensive to duplicate in quantity and the time and trouble required to produce just one photograph discourages most people from using this technique. Using a printer to draw the image on paper is much more feasible.

Dot-Matrix Printers

Generally, dot-matrix printers are used to produce graphic images. Dot-matrix printers, both impact and ink-jet, print across the page in lines, just as the electron gun in the monitor scans the screen as it registers the images. The resulting picture consists of several hundred horizontal lines across the page. As often as not, graphics images are produced on paper by first constructing or displaying the image on a monitor. Then, with the press of a key or two, the image, which is contained in an image buffer in the computer's memory, is also displayed on the printer, that is, it is printed.

FIGURE 15-20
Using conography, this car image was created with less than 10% of the calculations required with conventional techniques.
(Courtesy Conographic Corp.)

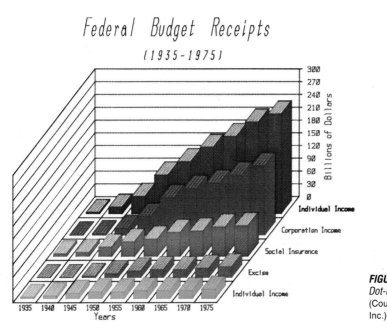

Dot-Matrix, Impact Printers. Dot-matrix printers can do a commendable job of reproducing the CRT's image on paper. Figure 15-21 shows such output. This printer's advantage over a letter quality printer for graphics lies in the way in which it prints: as a column of dots. The picture is formed as a number of horizontal broken lines across the page. The shortest line is one dot, the longest is governed by the resolution of the system and the width of the page. Dot-matrix printers, then, print images made up of pixels; they simulate the raster-scan system.

So far, so good. Introducing color is a matter of equipping the printer with a multicolored ribbon, the necessary mechanics to move it, and the appropriate circuitry to control it all. Color printers come with ribbons of anywhere from three to seven colors. The color for a particular dot is established by raising the ribbon so that the required color band on the ribbon is between the print head and the paper at the time of printing. Figure 15-22 shows a sample output

FIGURE 15-22
*Sample output of dot-matrix color
printer* (Courtesy International
Business Machines Corp.)

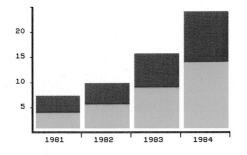

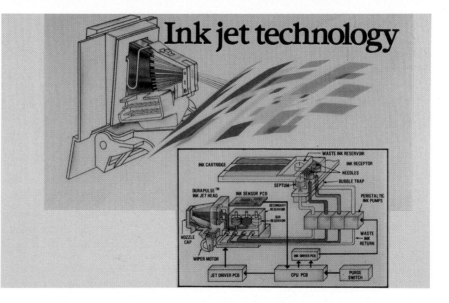

FIGURE 15-23
Color ink-jet printer mechanism
(Courtesy Advanced Color
Technologies)

from a color dot-matrix printer. Both text and graphics are printed in various colors as controlled by the software employed. Software that can print graphics on the same page on which text is printed is available from a number of software producers.

Dot-Matrix, Non-Impact Printers. For the purpose of producing graphics hard copy, ink-jet printers offer the advantage of being able to change the color of the ink cartridges easily, thus having more practical control over the colors being printed.

Figure 15-23 shows a schematic of a color ink-jet printer. This printer makes use of three primary colors—red, blue, and yellow—to produce a wide variety of colors and shades, as can be seen from figure 15-24.

Laser printers also produce graphic images, although not in color.

FIGURE 15-24
Tapestry design produced by ink-jet printer (Courtesy Advanced Color Technologies)

Plotters

Plotters, not limited by the pixel or raster scans, are able to draw any line or approximate any curve that the computer can specify. Computer techniques to generate various shapes are available right now.

There are two types of plotters. On one, paper is fixed and an arm holding a moving pen slides back and forth describing the image, see figure 15-25. In this fashion, the turret holding the pens moves in both dimensions.

The second type of plotter moves the paper in one dimension while the turret moves in the other. One of these is illustrated in figure 15-26.

The fixed-paper plotter has the advantage in that its turret can hold many pens, thus allowing for pictures with several colors or line widths. It can accommodate paper of limited size, however. The movable-paper plotter, on the other hand, will accept paper of any length, but generally such plotters use only one pen at a time. Figure 15-27 shows the pen turret of the Apple Computer's color plotter. Four pens of different colors or widths are available at one time on this movable-paper plotter, making it a very versatile output device.

FIGURE 15-25
Fixed paper plotter (Courtesy Radio Shack, a division of Tandy Corp.)

FIGURE 15-27
Apple plotter showing pen turret (Courtesy Apple Computer, Inc.)

FIGURE 15-26
Movable paper plotter (Courtesy Hewlett-Packard Co.)

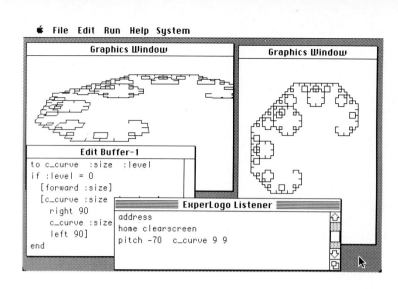

Input Devices

Generally, graphics images displayed by computers either on a monitor or as hard copy are generated by the computer itself, under program control. Using the computer as an art medium, in which the image is drawn by the artist, as opposed to being calculated by the computer, requires input techniques to record the desired image in the input buffer of the computer's main memory. From there it can be stored on disk or tape and reproduced on the screen or printed as hard copy when needed.

Keyboards and Mice

One input technique involves using a cursor to describe the outlines of the image and to specify the colors to fill the various areas. Spinnaker Software of Cambridge, Massachusetts, for example, markets its Delta Drawing program for microcomputers at a modest cost. Using a triangular-shaped cursor, hence the product's name Delta, one defines lines and areas by moving about the screen using keys on the keyboard: *D* for draw, *L* to turn left, and so forth. Other cursor-using graphics systems such as Apple's MacPaint program employ a mouse to control the cursor's movement on the screen.

A number of graphics drawing programs offer a simple programming language that moves the cursor under program control. This facilitates preparing geometric and trigonometric designs. The Logo language is one such program.

Light Pens

In another input technique, we use a light pen to draw the image on the screen itself, as if using a pencil. We can also use the pen to point to various areas to be colored, and we can specify the colors by entering codes on the keyboard. Figure 15-28 shows a light pen being used.

Graphics Tablets

Finally, entering graphics data into the computer can be accomplished by using any one of a variety of graphics tablets, so called because we use

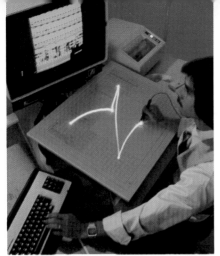

FIGURE 15-28
Light pen graphics input
(Courtesy Paradyne Corp.)

them much in the same manner as we use a tablet of drawing paper. These devices use a pressure-sensitive surface on which we draw the figure. Alternatively, the surface can be electrically charged so that moving an object such as one's finger about on it will create the image. Still others use arms resembling a drafting table parallel arm that measure movement of the stylus in two or sometimes three dimensions. The measurements are sent to the computer's memory and displayed on the monitor as the image. Such a system works well for tracing figures and patterns. Figure 15-29 illustrates a graphics tablet device.

USING A COMPUTER GRAPHICS PROGRAM

Let's look at the use of a business graphics program: VisiPlot, a menu-driven, commercial software package for microcomputers. Bill Ding, the operator of a construction firm specializing in aluminum siding and solar water heating

FIGURE 15-29
Graphics tablet device (Courtesy
McDonnell Douglas Information
Systems)

systems for homes, has used VisiCalc to analyze the effects on his operation of introducing insulation installation. The analysis used sales projections Bill had made. The data indicated that, because it could be installed indoors, home insulation would be a good complement to his other two lines of home improvement activity. A year later he prepared an income statement using actual sales and compared the actual results of the year's operation with his projections.

Now, Bill wants to prepare some graphs to share with potential investors in his firm. He wants to show them how well the introduction of insulation to his line helped to smooth out his monthly profits. Thanks to inclement winter weather, Bill's profits in December, January, February, and March traditionally went into the red every year—so much so that he feared losing his business. He thinks that the 1985–86 year foretells a bright future and is seeking expansion into yet other home improvement lines, but he needs additional capital.

Bill decides to prepare three graphic presentations. First, a line graph will show sales for all three of his products, thus illustrating how the new product, insulation, has an annual sales cycle that complements the other two. Second, a pie chart will show the degree to which insulation accounted for total sales volume. Third, a comparative bar graph will show projected and actual profits for the year.

Data Entry

In doing his earlier analysis, Bill had used VisiCalc to project profits for 1985–86 as well as to prepare his actual income statement for the same period. The actual income statement appears in figure 15-30. On the monitor screen, not all of it is visible, of course, and he has to scroll about to see all of the data.

The VisiPlot program offers the ability to enter data directly into the system. Thus, Bill can type in the sales and profit figures for each month, as well as the year's total profit figures on the far right of the spreadsheet. This will require some time. Worse, it is easy to make mistakes doing this kind of work. Fortunately, VisiPlot will accept data from files that adhere to the Data Interchange Format (DIF) and VisiCalc will prepare DIF files (see Chapter Fourteen). It's not really the same as having an integrated software package including both spreadsheet analysis and graphics, but it's what Bill has and it will work just fine.

FIGURE 15-30
Bill Ding spreadsheet

```
VARIABLE EXPENSES
  LABOR       0.35
  MATERIAL    0.20                                    BILL DING CONSTRUCTION COMPANY
  COMMISS.    0.08                                         INCOME STATEMENT
  OTHER       .035                                         FOR PERIOD ENDING
FIXED EXPENSES                                               JUNE 30, 1986
  SALARIES 1800.00
  RENT      850.00
  OTHER     800.00


                 JULY     AUGUST     SEPT.      OCT.      NOV.      DEC.       JAN.      FEB.     MARCH     APRIL      MAY      JUNE    TOTAL

        SALES
     ALUMINUM  5176.89   5534.43   7132.69   4572.87   2978.12   1967.56    956.34    427.59    934.67   2536.98   5278.46   6539.31  44035.91
     SOLAR     2645.70   1867.50   2147.00   3100.50   3245.57   3187.68    746.48    380.00    679.16   1745.27   2465.88   4973.44  27184.18
     INSULATE  4328.67   4997.12   6089.14   6578.00   7025.50   7457.98   7649.00   8145.67   7439.00   6349.65   4762.90   3872.15  74694.78
                -------   -------   -------   -------   -------   -------   -------   -------   -------   -------   -------   -------  --------
     TOTAL SLS 12151.26  12399.05  15368.83  14251.37  13249.19  12613.22   9351.82   8953.26   9052.83  10631.90  12507.24  15384.90 145914.87

        EXPENSES
     VARIABLE  8080.59   8245.37  10220.27   9477.16   8010.71   8387.79   6218.96   5953.92   6020.13   7070.21   8317.31  10230.96  97033.39
     FIXED     3450.00   3450.00   3450.00   3450.00   3450.00   3450.00   3450.00   3450.00   3450.00   3450.00   3450.00   3450.00  41400.00
                -------   -------   -------   -------   -------   -------   -------   -------   -------   -------   -------   -------  --------
     TOTAL EXP 11530.59  11695.37  13670.27  12927.16  12260.71  11837.79   9668.96   9403.92   9470.13  10520.21  11767.31  13680.96 141883.39

     PROFIT     620.67    703.68   1698.56   1324.21    988.48    775.43   -317.14   -450.66   -417.30    111.69    739.93   1703.94   4031.48
               ========= ========= ========= ========= ========= ========= ========= ========= ========= ========= ========= =================
```

DING SALES.DIF

BILL DING CONSTRUCTION COMPANY
INCOME STATEMENT
FOR PERIOD ENDING
JUNE 30, 1986

DING TOTALS.DIF

	JULY	AUGUST	SEPT.	OCT.	NOV.	DEC.	JAN.	FEB.	MARCH	APRIL	MAY	JUNE	TOTAL
SALES													
ALUMINUM	5176.89	5534.43	7132.69	4572.87	2978.12	1967.56	956.34	427.59	934.67	2936.28	5278.46	6539.31	44035.91
SOLAR	2645.70	1867.50	2147.00	3100.50	3245.57	3187.68	746.48	380.00	679.16	1745.27	2465.88	4973.44	27184.18
INSULATE	4328.67	4997.12	6089.14	6578.00	7025.50	7457.98	7649.00	8145.67	7439.00	6349.65	4762.90	3872.15	74694.78
TOTAL SLS	12151.26	12399.05	15368.83	14251.37	13249.19	12613.22	9351.82	8953.26	9052.83	10631.90	12507.24	15384.90	145914.87
EXPENSES													
VARIABLE	8080.59	8245.37	10220.27	9477.16	8810.71	8387.79	6218.96	5953.92	6020.13	7070.21	8317.31	10230.96	97033.39
FIXED	3450.00	3450.00	3450.00	3450.00	3450.00	3450.00	3450.00	3450.00	3450.00	3450.00	3450.00	3450.00	41400.00
TOTAL EXP	11530.59	11695.37	13670.27	12927.16	12260.71	11837.79	9668.96	9403.92	9470.13	10520.21	11767.31	13680.96	141883.39
PROFIT	620.67	703.68	1698.56	1324.21	988.48	775.43	-317.14	-450.66	-417.30	111.69	739.93	1703.94	4031.48

DING ACT PROF.DIF

FIGURE 15-31
Cursor placement for building DIF files

Preparing a DIF file from a VisiCalc spreadsheet is easy. Bill loads his actual income statement into his VisiCalc program, uses the commands to initiate the storage routines, indicates that he wishes to build a DIF file and follows the VisiCalc prompts. He places the cursor on the upper left-most cell of the spreadsheet to be copied into a DIF file, presses the RETURN key, and names the file DING SALES.DIF which will remind him of both the data content (sales) and the fact that it is a DIF file. In response to additional VisiCalc prompts, he places the cursor in the lower right-hand corner of the area to be copied and presses RETURN again. The file is built.

See figure 15-31. It shows the cursor placement for building the three DIF files to be taken from the spreadsheet of actual sales for 1985–86.

To build the DING SALES.DIF files, Bill defines the upper left-hand corner of the spreadsheet as the word *ALUMINUM*. Each row of numbers is known as a *series* and is distinguished from the rest of the series in the file by the name in that row. He defines the lower right-hand corner of the spreadsheet area to be included in the DING SALES.DIF file by placing the cursor over the value 3872.15. He then presses RETURN and follows the VisiCalc prompts to store that file with its three separate series of numbers on his diskette. All this takes about two minutes.

Similarly, Bill identifies the bottom line of the spreadsheet as a file by first placing the cursor on the word *PROFIT*, defining the upper left-hand corner, then on the June Sales value, 1703.94, to define the lower right-hand corner. To be sure, these numbers are on the same line, but that's the way the system works. By pressing RETURN and following the screen prompts, Bill builds that file, consisting of the one series labeled PROFIT, which he names DING ACT PROF.DIF. Then he uses the same techniques to build a file he names DING TOTALS.DIF which consists of the sales figures for each of his lines for the year.

Bill then proceeds to load the projected income statement into the VisiCalc program and to define the PROJ.PROF row on that spreadsheet as a DIF file named DING PROJ PROF.DIF containing the single series named PROJ PROF. Building these various DIF files takes about five minutes.

Thus armed with DIF files on a diskette that the VisiPlot program can use, he exits VisiCalc and boots up VisiPlot.

FIGURE 15-33 Directory listing

```
LOAD SERIES
LOAD    ->PLOT  LOOKUP  CLEAR   <MORE>
EDIT    ->TREND SAVE    QUIT    DRIVE
SLOT: 6 DRIVE: 2

        VISITREND/VISIPLOT 1.00
        C 1981 MICRO FINANCE SYSTEMS

* USE ARROW KEYS, SPACE TO MOVE CURSOR

* PRESS RETURN TO SELECT A MENU ITEM
```

```
LOAD SERIES
<-, ->, SPACE BAR, OR RETURN

SLOT: 6  DRIVE: 2

DING PROJ
DING SALES DIF
DIN PAY
DING ACT
DING TOTALS DIF
MIGHTY MIDGET WIDGET W
DING ACT PROF DIF
DING PROJ PROF DIF
HEADING TEMPLATE
EXPENSE REGISTER TEMPL
CHECK REGISTER TEMPLAT
JAN CHECK REGISTER
[NONE]
```

FIGURE 15-32 VisiPlot main menu

Preparing the Line Plots

It takes a while for VisiPlot to boot up, perhaps ninety seconds or so. Once all of the initialization activities are completed, the system presents Bill with the main menu, figure 15-32.

Using the menu options is a matter of using the arrow keys and the space bar to place the cursor, the highlighted rectangle, over the appropriate choice. In order to use the VisiPlot program, data must first be loaded from the files on the diskette into the computer's main memory or RAM. Using the arrow keys, Bill positions the cursor over LOAD and presses RETURN. The program responds by providing a list of the files available, figure 15-33.

Because Bill wants to plot data from the file named DING SALES.DIF, he uses the arrow keys to position the cursor on top of the name of that file and presses RETURN. The data from that DIF file are then read from the diskette into memory. During the process, the system asks him for specifics about the series in the file. He responds by entering 1985 as the beginning year; 12 as the number of periods per year; and 7, indicating that the first period is July. After data loading is completed, he is returned to the main menu, figure 15-32.

Now he's ready to plot the three series of data in the DING SALES.DIF file: ALUMINUM, SOLAR, and INSULATE. He uses the arrow keys to position the cursor over the word *PLOT* in the main menu and presses the RETURN key. The computer responds with the message "ONE MOMENT PLEASE" while it loads the plotting program into memory. When the program is ready, it presents Bill with the select menu, figure 15-34.

The select menu offers several graphing options. The one Bill wants is LINE, so he positions the cursor over that word and presses RETURN. After Bill does this, the select menu disappears and a listing of the various data point series in the BILL DING.DIF file is displayed, figure 15-35.

Wanting to plot lines for aluminum siding, solar installations, and insulation, Bill places an asterisk by each of these series names, just as he did when selecting a file to be loaded into RAM. Then he presses RETURN again and the main plot menu appears on the screen, figure 15-36.

FIGURE 15-35 Series listing from BILL DING.DIF

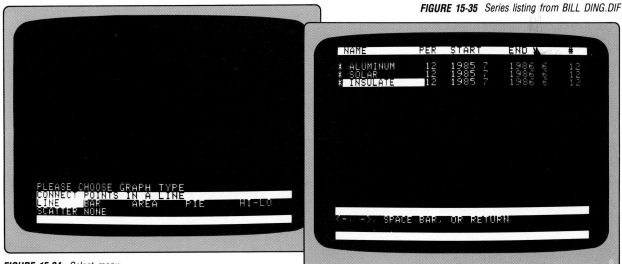

FIGURE 15-34 Select menu

Making sure the cursor is over the word PLOT, Bill presses RETURN. The computer flashes a message about scaling on the screen and eventually the graph showing the three data series appears, figure 15-37.

The graph appears with no menu and shows a legend at the bottom which identifies each of the three lines. If Bill wanted this just for his own perusal, it would probably be sufficient. Inasmuch as he wants to show it to prospective investors, he will take advantage of the several cosmetic options available. Pressing any key on the keyboard restores the main plot menu at the bottom of the screen, obscuring the legend. Using the main plot menu, Bill positions the cursor over OPTIONS and presses RETURN. In response, the program offers the OPTIONS menu at the bottom of the screen, figure 15-38.

Bill wants to add titles to the graph, so he selects the TITLE option, resulting in that menu appearing at the bottom of the screen, figure 15-39. Following VisiPlot's menu prompts, he adds titles to the graph. The final result appears in figure 15-40.

FIGURE 15-37 Initial plot of sales for three series

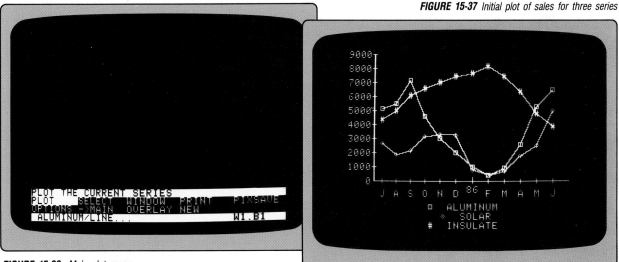

FIGURE 15-36 Main plot menu

FIGURE 15-39 Graph with titles menu

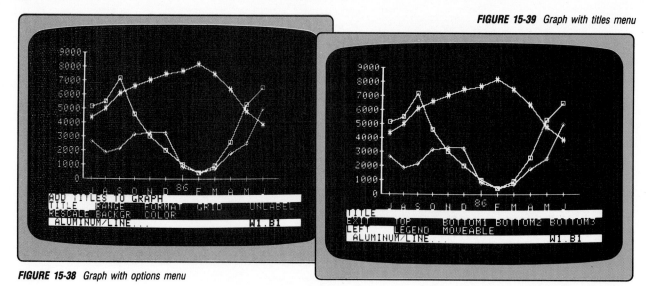

FIGURE 15-38 Graph with options menu

Bill concludes the preparation of the line plot of sales of each of the three products by printing the graph. This is done by selecting the PRINT option from the main plot menu. The final graph is prepared by his printer.

Preparing the Pie Chart

Bill's pie chart should show the relationship of sales of each of his lines to total sales for the year. Constructing it follows the same pattern as that used in preparing the line chart. Exiting from the titles menu, he selects the MAIN option from the main plot menu. He's asked to confirm this, because all of the work that he's done so far will be destroyed. He accedes by pressing Y and the system shows him the main menu again, as in figure 15-32.

He uses the LOAD option and loads the file DING TOTALS.DIF from the displayed list of available files. This file shows data as of June 30, 1986. Bill responds with a 0 to all the prompts concerning year, periodicity, and starting period.

Now that the data file DING TOTALS.DIF is stored in RAM, Bill chooses the PLOT option from the main menu. Eventually the main plot menu appears. Bill moves the cursor over SELECT, presses RETURN, and sees the

FIGURE 15-40
Final line plot

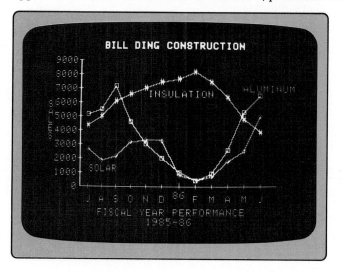

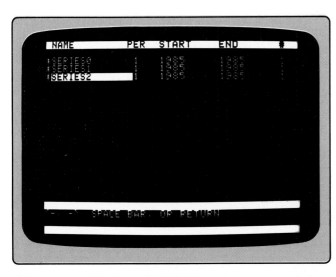
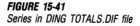

FIGURE 15-41
Series in DING TOTALS.DIF file

select menu. He chooses PIE. The system responds by providing a list of the three series included in the DING TOTALS.DIF file, figure 15-41.

In this case, the series are named SERIES0, SERIES1, and SERIES2. This results from the manner in which Bill placed the cursors on the spreadsheet when building the DIF file, figure 15-31. Because the cursor placement did not include titles for the three numbers, VisiPlot provided its own. The three titles refer to the sales values for each of the product lines, so Bill uses the space bar and the arrow keys to register an asterisk to the left of each one. When he is finished, he presses RETURN and the system presents him with the main plot menu as it did in figure 15-36. This time, he has already selected a PIE chart. With the cursor over the PLOT option, he presses RETURN and the basic graph appears on the screen, figure 15-42.

The pie chart appears with a legend to its right showing the percentage of sales for which each product accounted. A menu does not appear at the bottom of the screen, but, as with the line chart, it can be restored by pressing any key. Bill does this and the title menu appears. Wishing to shade the areas in the pie with color before adding titles, Bill exits the title menu and the shading menu replaces it, figure 15-43.

FIGURE 15-43 *Pie chart with shading menu*

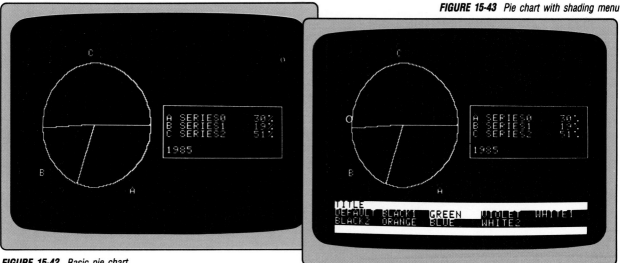

FIGURE 15-42 *Basic pie chart*

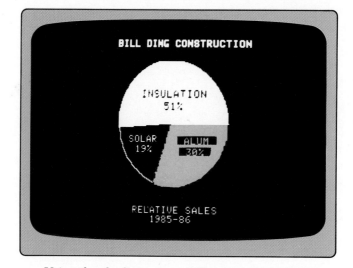

FIGURE 15-44
Final pie chart

Using the shading menu, Bill enters the letter A, indicating which of the segments he wishes to color. Then he specifies the color he wants by locating the cursor over the various colors available and presses RETURN. He repeats this procedure for each of the three segments of the pie. When he exits the shading menu, VisiPlot asks him to confirm that he has completed the shading because after exiting from the shading menu there is no return. He confirms by entering Y and is returned to the title menu. Now, using the same techniques he employed when preparing the line chart, Bill adds titles. He finishes by locating the cursor over the word LEGEND in the title menu and pressing RETURN. This removes the legend from the picture. Since Bill added his own titles, the legend is no longer needed. Figure 15-44 shows the final version of the pie chart. Bill prints it using the PRINT option from the main plot menu, as before.

Preparing the Bar Graph

The final step in Bill's project is to prepare a bar graph that will compare actual profits for the year with projected profits. With a couple of exceptions, he uses the very same techniques and menus as with the other graphs. First, he returns to the main menu and clears all of the existing series from RAM. Then he loads two files, DING ACT PROF.DIF and DING PROJ PROF.DIF. Each of these files has one series; therefore, memory now contains two series, one entitled PROJ PROFIT, the other PROFIT. Now he selects the PLOT option from the main menu in preparation for plotting the data.

Actually, Bill will plot two graphs, one for projected profits, the other for actual profits. VisiPlot allows him to overlay one graph on top of another and that is what Bill will do. From the main plot menu, Bill selects BAR and is presented with some choices, figure 15-45.

Does he want NORMAL, LEFT, or RIGHT bars? A NORMAL bar occupies the full width available for each time period, in this case a month. Because he will plot two bars for each month (actual and projected sales) he picks LEFT, knowing that later he will use RIGHT when plotting the second graph on top of the first. Having done that, the system presents him, as usual, with the list of series available, PROFIT and PROJ PROFIT. He selects PROFIT and is returned to the main plot program. He then selects PLOT, and the system prepares the bar graph shown in figure 15-46.

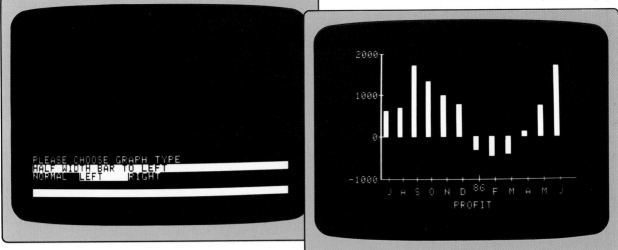

FIGURE 15-45 Bar graph options

FIGURE 15-46 Half of comparative bar graph

Notice, in figure 15-46 that profits drop below zero. This presents Bill with a minor problem, because he knows that his projected profits never dropped that low and, in fact, were substantially higher than actual profits in every month. This means that if he were to try to plot projected profits on the same graph as actual profits, he couldn't do it because the graph in figure 15-46 doesn't extend as high as projected profits.

To remedy the problem, Bill rescales the graph he now has. He selects the OPTIONS choice from the main plot menu and the RESCALE choice from the OPTIONS menu, figure 15-47.

The system asks him for the minimum value for the Y-axis, that is, the vertical one. He enters −1000. It then asks him for the maximum value. Because projected profits per month occasionally exceed $3,000, he enters 4000. Finally, the system asks for the number of divisions to be shown on the vertical axis. Bill enters 4 and is returned to the main plot menu. Executing the PLOT option redraws the graph with the new scaling factors, figure 15-48.

Now Bill is ready to add the second bar graph. He selects BAR from the main plot menu and RIGHT from the bar graph menu. Once again, the sys-

FIGURE 15-48 Rescaled bar graph

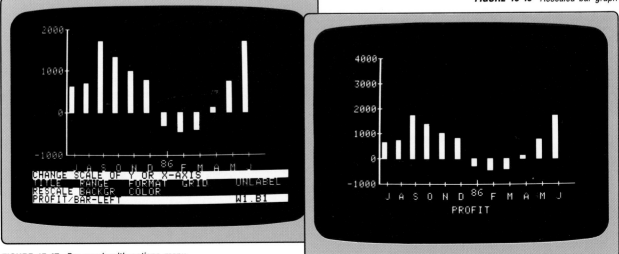

FIGURE 15-47 Bar graph with options menu

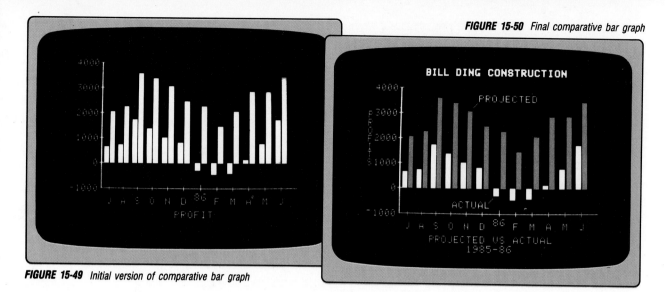

FIGURE 15-50 Final comparative bar graph

FIGURE 15-49 Initial version of comparative bar graph

tem presents him with the list of available series. He selects PROJ PROFIT and is returned to the main plot menu.

Now, he selects OVERLAY because he wants to plot right on top of the existing bar graph. Inasmuch as the existing one was plotted using the left half of the bar space for each month and the new one uses the right half, they will appear adjacent to each other. The result is shown in figure 15-49.

All that remains to be done is the same cosmetic treatment that Bill applied to the other graphs. He colors the PROJ PROFIT bars so as to make them more easily distinguishable from the PROFIT bars and puts titles in place. The final result, which Bill prints, appears in figure 15-50.

The Project Completed

It took Bill about an hour to complete all of the graphs he needed. In order to do the work quickly, Bill had to be familiar with his tools: VisiCalc and Visi-Plot. He spent about two days learning to use these two programs, an investment of time that he feels is well worth the effort.

VisiPlot is an excellent example of a complicated program made easy by menus. Menus, however, suffer the disadvantage of limiting the flexibility of the system. Other graphics programs, more difficult to use and to learn, offer many more capabilities, too.

SUMMARY

The picture is an excellent device for communicating. Because they can use the data resulting from processing operations, computer graphics programs are marvelous tools for preparing pictorial versions of the results.

The term *computer graphics* embraces all techniques of using computers to prepare visual presentations. The uses include *business graphics, presentation graphics,* and *computer-aided design and manufacturing, (CAD/CAM).*

Business graphics include several basic varieties: *line plots, area plots, bar charts,* and *pie charts.* Variations and combinations of these techniques provide many alternatives for preparing visual representation of information.

In addition to preparing informational pictures, computer graphics techniques are widely used for purposes of analysis and planning, including statistical analysis, flowcharting, scheduling, and facilities planning.

Presentation graphics is one of the more exciting developments in the computer graphics field, one that recognizes the computer as an art medium. Effective use of presentation graphics requires close attention to how the visual presentations are delivered to the audience. The alternatives include the use of video display terminals (VDTs), photographs of monitor screens, and hard copy as produced by graphics printers and plotters. *Animation* adds drama and excitement to presentation graphics.

Using computers to prepare graphic presentations requires certain hardware features. These include reasonably high *resolution* of images on screens and on paper. Computer images are usually made up of *pixels*, or picture elements. The greater the number of pixels a device can display, the higher the resolution, the higher the cost, and the greater the required memory and processing capacity of the computer.

Color is essential today for effective graphics presentation. The greater the range of colors available, the lower the resolution. This is a result of the storage requirements for color representation. Most graphic systems reach a satisfactory compromise between color flexibility and resolution within the constraints of cost.

Output devices currently used in computer graphics production include monitors or video display terminals, dot-matrix printers, ink-jet printers, and plotters. Each has its characteristic advantages and disadvantages.

Input devices include, in addition to the computer itself as it processes data, keyboards, mice, light pens, and graphics tablets. These devices make drawing images for processing by computer graphics systems as easy as using any other art medium, maybe even easier for some purposes.

KEY TERMS

composite color CRT
computer-aided design
computer-aided manufacture
computer graphics
conography
graphics tablet

hard copy
histogram
impact printer
light pen
pixel
plotter

presentation graphics
raster-scan system
resolution
RGB monitor
vector-stroke system
video display terminal

REVIEW QUESTIONS

1. What is computer graphics?
2. What are the differences between CAD and CAM?
3. How are CAD and CAM related?
4. What is the difference between images produced on microcomputers and those produced on larger machines?
5. Most business graphics involve _____, _____, and _____, which are subsumed under the rubric of histograms.
6. What is the relationship between spreadsheets and computer graphs?
7. Describe two inputting techniques for computer graphics.
8. What are the advantages of using a computer to create a flowchart?
9. In addition to flowcharting and graphing, major uses of computer graphics include _____ and _____.
10. How do presentation graphics differ from art graphics?
11. Why is it likely that animation will be used increasingly in future business graphics presentations?
12. How is resolution related to image quality?
13. Differentiate between composite and RGB color CRTs.
14. Describe two kinds of plotters.

1. Describe how you might use computer graphics to prepare a presentation for an annual stockholders' meeting.
2. Compare raster-scan graphics to vector-stroke graphics. Include a discussion of relevant hardware and image quality.
3. More and more, businesses are including graphics in their correspondence. What implications does this have for the purchasing agent buying equipment and for the hardware designer?

Point *Counterpoint*

(Courtesy Gerard Crum, New York Institute of Technology)

If this chapter has a Big Message, it's this: Graphic illustration does wonders for communication. Mark Skiba, Director of Software Engineering for the American Programmers Guild sums it up this way:

> We are bombarded daily by magazines, memos, and reports, and at least part of the blame for this phenomenon can be traced to personal computers. Word processing, spreadsheet, and data base programs have made the task of generating information dramatically less time consuming. Yet our capacity to absorb this knowledge has not increased. We find ourselves drowning in a sea of information while asking the question, "Haven't you read my memo?"[6]

Graphics offer an obvious aid to this dilemma. Graphics presentations were used before computers came along. In fact, some companies have continued producing graphs by hand long after computer graphics became available. Turning to computers to prepare graphs has yielded some remarkable successes. At General Motor's Chevrolet Division, for example, experimental autos are tested every Tuesday. Thousands of items of data are collected. It takes a full week for corporate artists to present this information graphically, in its most useful form. After installing a computer graphics system, the graphs are ready for review the day after the tests were run, saving a week's work for every test.[7]

At Dow Chemical, the decision to buy petroleum is made jointly by three executives. One is in Houston, another in New Orleans, and the third in Midland, Michigan. Tens of millions of dollars depend on their good judgement. Using computers, Dow sends information to the decision-makers graphically. Each decision must be made within 60 minutes—impossible if numbers had to be analyzed.[8]

Until 1984, business computer graphics programs took data from spreadsheets, data bases, and other sources and were used primarily as informative tools. Now they are used as on-the-spot analytical tools, too. Michael Mizen analyzes markets for medical products with a Chicago consulting firm.

> When you can get a graph with just two keystrokes, graphics become a decision tool you can change as fast as you can think of ways to analyze the data...

469

One problem you have with entering the numbers into a spreadsheet is that you're concentrating on the numbers themselves, not on what they mean.

Two keystrokes produce a graph from his numbers.

Once I see the graph, it's immediately obvious that all the market growth is taking place in the Class 5 products, and then I can go back to the actual numbers and have a look at what's going on.[9]

With the introduction of the Apple Macintosh in 1984, new kinds of graphics programs became available. These allow the user to paint pictures on the screen. The pictures can then be printed on paper. The Macintosh uses a program called Mac-Paint which comes with the machine. Soon after MacPaint's introduction, other painting programs were marketed for other computers, and for the Mac, too. Although the Mac had black and white output in 1984, other computers could take advantage of color screens, color printers, and color plotters.

Computer graphics programs that are used for artistic expression are not uncommon, as many illustrations in this chapter attest. The Macintosh-MacPaint combination brought exciting computer graphics techniques into the home and business. No longer are these tools available only to professionals. The Mac made good its promise to be "The computer for the rest of us."

Painting programs turned out to be enormous fun from the very beginning. Crowds still surround Macintosh demonstrations in computer stores and would-be customers stand in line to experiment with MacPaint. There's no question that more than a few purchased Macs just for that program alone.

Now painting programs have found their way into corporate offices. Jeffrey Erlich, Manager of Applied Technology for General Electric asks why:

I really can't see even the remotest use for any of these programs…I've seen people making cute little signs for birth announcements or sign-ups for softball games, but really, you can't call that a business use, now can you? The painting programs have curiosity value, but that's about it.

You know, if one of the people working for me were to come to a presentation with a whole bunch of beautifully illustrated drawings, my first reaction would be "I'm paying you to be a chemist or engineer or whatever, not an artist. What kind of judgement about the way you spend your time does this indicate?"[10]

But within six months of the introduction of everyman's painting programs, business people had already found uses for them. Apple grower John Biele uses MacPaint to help control irrigation of his orchards in Oroville, Washington. MSS, Inc., an engineering tool design firm in Lafayette, Louisiana, found that the Mac with MacPaint reduced its work force by two draftspeople. Jeri Laizure, a partner with the advertising firm of Laizure/Woodward & Wise in Charlotte, North Carolina tells this story:

The other day I was in Atlanta for a client meeting on an animated commercial. I had all our visual notes for the storyboard on MacPaint files. Then, after the meeting, I went back to my hotel room, changed things around the way we had all discussed, and the next morning took it back to them and had it approved. There's no way that we could have done it that quickly before—it's the way we've speeded the whole process that has made the difference in our profits.[11]

QUESTION

1. Suppose that you were an engineer and had used a painting program to prepare initial sketches of a new light fixture. How would you answer Jeffrey Erlich's question about how you manage your time?

C H A P T E R 16

More Productivity: Specialized Tools

(Courtesy Lotus Development Corporation)

PROJECT MANAGEMENT

TIME MANAGEMENT

STATISTICAL ANALYSIS

MODELING

EXPERT SYSTEMS

INVESTMENT PORTFOLIO
  MANAGEMENT

IDEA PROCESSORS

PROGRAM GENERATORS

INTEGRATED SYSTEMS

In the past few chapters, we've examined the big six business programs: accounting, communications, database managers, graphics, spreadsheets, and word processing. In addition to these, there are at least eight other important types of general-purpose programs business people use. We could well call them the Little Eight.

The little eight can be broken into three main categories. First, *management tools* help managers and other individuals control their work. In this chapter, we examine project management and time management as examples of management programs. Second, *analysis tools* perform comparisons and answer "What if...?" types of questions. The third, fourth, and fifth examples in this chapter include statistical analysis, modeling, and expert systems. The sixth example, investment portfolio management, has both management and analysis aspects. The third category, *creativity tools*, facilitates the development of thoughts and logic patterns. In this chapter, we discuss two such tools: idea processors and program generators.

In addition to the little eight, some programs combine application packages into *integrated systems*. An integrated system joins many of the big six, the little eight, and other programs into one unified package. Each part of an integrated system has access to the same data so that documents can be produced with text, graphics, and spreadsheets. These documents can then be transmitted by electronic mail to anyone with appropriate hardware.

With this background, let's look at nine examples of these programs—the little eight and integrated systems.

PROJECT MANAGEMENT

Virtually every business is involved in project management whether the project is remodeling a store, planning a new product line, or printing a sales catalog. Complex projects involve many people using different resources in numerous activities, some of which are dependent on other project activities. For example, consider a remodeling job. The painter cannot paint until the carpenter has built the partitions. The carpenter cannot finish his job until the building inspector has approved the electrical wiring, and so forth.

It is the manager's responsibility to insure that a project moves swiftly to completion. This means that he or she must know how long each phase will take and what resources are needed as well as the resource costs and the relationship between various aspects of the project. This can be a tremendous job as evidenced by the several million dollars spent by the Los Angeles Airport Department just to manage the 1981–84 renovation project for Los Angeles International Airport.

Most project management software performs *critical path analysis*, a procedure for analyzing projects in terms of the amount of time required for the completion of each of the projects' individual parts. Programs such as Microsoft Project, Harvard Project Manager, and Micro Planner help managers organize projects, control time and resources, assess progress and simulate project activities.

Let's start with a few definitions. A *project* is a group of related activities with a specific start and end. The activities are directed at a specified goal that must be reached within a specific time period. Thus, running an assembly line does not qualify as a project because it is an ongoing operation. Directing a political campaign, on the other hand, is a project since it has specific beginning and ending dates.

A *critical path* is the set of project activities that determine the minimum amount of time the total project will take. If one activity in the critical path set takes longer than expected, the project will also take longer than planned. *Slack* is the amount of extra time available to complete an activity. For instance, if an activity requires three days to complete and five days are available, the slack is two days. Activities *on the critical path* have zero slack. The real benefit of critical path analysis is that it shows where to spend time and money managing a project, keeping critical path activities on schedule.

Project management software has long been available on mainframe computers but it is so unwieldy that its use has been restricted to very large projects. Project managers agree that microcomputer-based programs are more accessible, easier to use, and more functional. They provide immediate answers whereas mainframe programs often do not. They allow the user to maintain control of the system rather than vesting control in the computer. They are also cost effective. Francis Webster of Western Carolina University points out that it costs as much annually to run a critical path program on a mainframe as it costs to buy the software and a microcomputer.[1] The savings on a three- or five-year project can amount to thousands of dollars.

Using Project Management Software

Samantha Browne, a graduate in computer science, has been recently hired by Lars Senny Enterprises as a junior systems analyst. For her first assignment, Sam has been asked to prepare an operating schedule for a project to design a new cash receipts accounting system. The project has been quite extensive, not to mention expensive. Senny Enterprises provides special asset protection services to entertainment establishments in Atlantic City, Las Vegas, Reno, Lake Tahoe, and Biloxi, Mississippi. The services are paid for in cash which is delivered to Senny's Chicago headquarters daily by special air couriers. The cash accounting system requires elaborate controls and procedures.

AT&T's UNIX PC was released in the Spring of 1985. (Courtesy AT&T)

The systems development project has been under way for some time. The preliminary investigation and analysis stages have been completed and Sam reviews the situation by studying the feasibility report. Armed with that preparation and with information from interviewing various people in the organization and observing the current cash receipts system in operation, Sam concludes that the system design phase of the project, which prepares the final specifications for the new system, will consist of seven activities. These, and the anticipated times for their completion are as follows:

1. Design the forms and reports: 30 days
2. Design the files and databases: 15 days
3. Prepare the personnel procedures and training programs: 10 days
4. Design the computer programs: 45 days
5. Conduct a final analysis of alternative systems to meet Senny's cash control needs: 5 days
6. Work up a final cost-benefit analysis: 5 days
7. Document the new system: 45 days

Each of these activities will use certain resources over the time required for their completion. Designing the forms and reports, for example, will require two full-time forms designers, a full-time systems engineer, and a full-time systems analyst for the thirty days required for that activity. Sam is reassured by Lars himself, who seems to have considerable personal interest in the project, that all the resources needed will be provided. The payroll

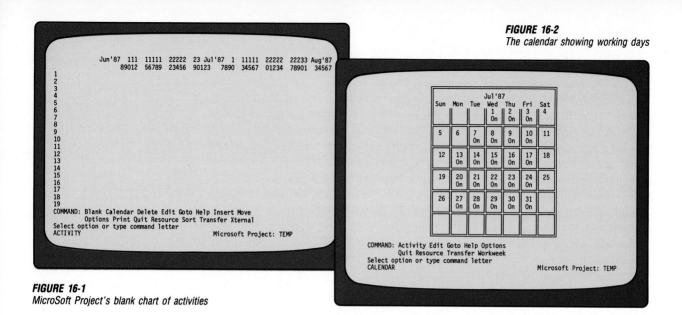

FIGURE 16-2
The calendar showing working days

FIGURE 16-1
MicroSoft Project's blank chart of activities

department gives her the current daily pay rates of the various personnel needed for each of the seven activities.

Working up an operating schedule and preparing cost estimates promises to be a formidable task if undertaken by hand. Sam decides to use Microsoft Project, a microcomputer-based scheduling and cost-estimating program. This program will produce cost estimates of each activity, will summarize the costs of each type of resource needed by the project, will prepare a Gantt chart for it, and can be used to monitor progress while the system design work is being done. A Gantt chart, named after Henry L. Gantt, a turn-of-the-century industrialist and management consultant, provides a graphical representation of the times and sequences of activities in a project. Gantt charts have long been a standard tool of project control and analysis.

Setting up the project, now that the resource requirements and costs for each of the activities have been gathered, goes very quickly. There are four basic steps: set up the calendar; describe the seven activities and the relationships among them; enter the resources needed for each activity and their costs; and produce some summary reports.

Calendar

On starting up, Project presents Sam with a blank schedule or chart of activities, figure 16-1. Down the left margin are spaces for the names of various activities each of which is numbered. Across the top, the chart is broken into days each of which is identified by month and date. The dates are numbered vertically to conserve space.

Sam selects Calendar from the menu at the bottom of the chart and is shown the calendar for June, 1987, the current month. Inasmuch as the project will get under way on June 8 and will continue for several weeks, Sam will identify the holidays that are not working days: July 6 (Independence Day) and September 7 (Labor Day). She pages to the month of July, figure 16-2, and removes the word ON from the sixth of that month to indicate that it is not a working day. She does the same thing for September 7.

Activities

Next, Sam returns to the activities chart and uses the Edit option from the menu at the bottom of the chart to describe each of the seven activities. Figure 16-3 shows the entries for the seventh activity, Documentation. At the left-hand margin, each of the previously entered activities is listed. At the bottom, the information for Documentation shows that it will require 45 days and that activities 1, 2, and 3 must be completed before it can start, that is, those activities are *predecessors* of the Documentation activity. Any changes in the predecessors will cause Project to adjust the documentation activity.

Because the project will take several weeks, the entire Gantt chart, which appears in the upper portion of the display screen, will not show on one screen and Sam must scroll back and forth to see it all. To condense the chart so that it fits on one screen, she modifies the time frame option so that the schedule is broken down into months rather than days, figure 16-4.

Resources

Each activity requires certain resources, typically personnel in this type of project though supplies and equipment can be included. Figure 16-4 shows the use of the Edit option with the activity screen to enter the resources for Activity 7: Documentation. This activity requires two full-time programmers, two full-time programmer/analysts, one full-time systems analyst, one full-time word processing operator, and one half-time word processing operator, each with word processing equipment. Sam enters these data in the spaces provided at the bottom of the activity screen.

After Sam has entered all of the resources for each activity of the project, the program will summarize all of the various resources needed by all of the activities, figure 16-5A. Then, using an edit option for the resource screen, she enters the daily cost for each resource, e.g., $190.00 per day for programmers, $600.00 per day for the Vice President of Finance, and so on. The program calculates the total cost of each resource and the sum of these costs as the total cost of the system design project, figure 16-5B.

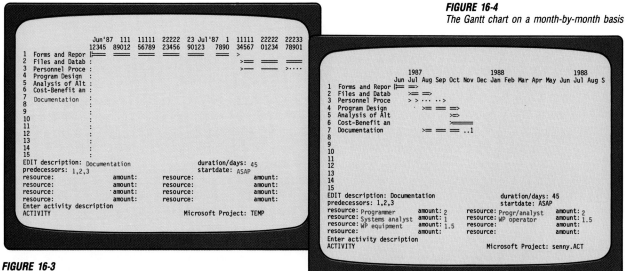

FIGURE 16-4
The Gantt chart on a month-by-month basis

FIGURE 16-3
Describing activity 7: Documentation

FIGURE 16-5
List of resources for the project
(A) Before adding cost data
(B) After adding cost data

FIGURE 16-6
Detailed report for the Personnel
Procedures activity

At this point, we should observe that the lion's share of Sam's efforts so far has been devoted to gathering the data about resources, costs, and activities. Entering the data into the computer takes less than an hour. Furthermore, as the project progresses, modifications to the data are easy to make and are instantly reflected in the Gantt chart and the project cost figures.

```
                      LARS SENNY ENTERPRISES
                       Cash Receipts System
                         Design Project


Activity: #3    Personnel Procedures                    Date: 06/01/1987

Early Start: 07/14/1987                     Early Finish: 07/27/1987
Late Start : 08/04/1987                     Late Finish : 08/17/1987

Resources Allocated:

Name            Duration   Amount      Cost        Cost      Cost to
                (Days)     used                    Basis     Complete

Training spcl.     10       1.0      $175.00       Day       $1750.00
Office super.      10       1.0      $100.00       Day       $1000.00
Acct. clerk        10       1.0       $75.00       Day        $750.00
Forms designer     10       1.0      $150.00       Day       $1500.00
                                                            -----------
Total                                                        $5000.00

Predecessors:

   # Activity:                       EARLY         LATE        SLACK
                                     FINISH        FINISH      AVAIL
   1   Forms and Reports           07/13/1987    07/13/1987      0

Successors:

   # Activity:                       EARLY         LATE        SLACK
                                     START         START       AVAIL
   6   Cost-Benefit analysis       10/14/1987    10/14/1987      0
   7   Documentation               08/04/1987    08/18/1987     10
```

```
                        LARS SENNY ENTERPRISES
                         Cash Receipts System
                           Design Project

  Project: senny.ACT                                    Date: 06/01/1987
  ----------------------------------------------------------------------
  #   Activity              Duration   Early      Early     Slack  Critical
                            (Days)     Late       Late      Avail
                                       Start      Finish
  ----------------------------------------------------------------------
  1 Forms and Reports          30   06/01/1987  07/13/1987    0      *
                                     06/01/1987  07/13/1987

  2 Files and Databases        15   07/14/1987  08/03/1987    0      *
                                     07/14/1987  08/03/1987

  3 Personnel Procedures       10   07/14/1987  07/27/1987   15
                                     08/04/1987  08/17/1987

  4 Program Design             45   08/04/1987  10/06/1987    0      *
                                     08/04/1987  10/06/1987

  5 Analysis of Alternatives    5   10/07/1987  10/13/1987    0      *
                                     10/07/1987  10/13/1987

  6 Cost-Benefit analysis       5   10/14/1987  10/20/1987    0      *
                                     10/14/1987  10/20/1987

  7 Documentation              45   08/04/1987  10/06/1987   10
                                     08/18/1987  10/20/1987
```

FIGURE 16-7
Summary of all activities

Reports

Now that Sam has entered the data, Project will prepare a number of different reports. Figure 16-6 shows a detailed report for Activity 3, Personnel Procedures. It shows the various resources allocated to the activity, their costs, and the total activity cost, $5,000. The report also shows information about the activity's predecessors and successors, that is, those other activities that must be completed before this one can start and those that cannot start until this one is finished. A report like this prepared for each of the seven activities.

Figure 16-7 shows a summary of all activities which indicates the starting and ending dates of each, their durations, and whether or not the activity is critical. A *critical* activity is one for which a delay means the whole project will be delayed. Activity 3, Personnel Procedures, for example, is not critical. It can be delayed as much as 15 days (the slack time) without affecting the completion date of the entire project. Program design, on the other hand, is critical. One day's delay in that activity will mean one day's delay in completing the systems design effort.

Figure 16-8 shows a Gantt chart prepared by the program. Using a dot-

FIGURE 16-8
The Gantt chart showing the
critical path

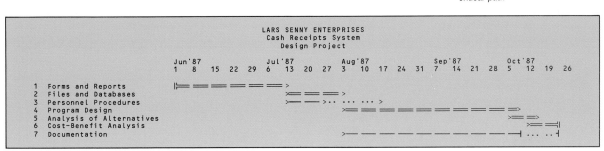

matrix printer with graphics capability, the program will print the chart sideways, along the length of continuous paper so that lengthy charts need not be pasted together. Critical activities are identified with bold double lines, noncritical ones with single lines. Dots indicate slack time.

Conclusion

In the past, project control and monitoring was done manually. Gantt charts took the form of magnetic boards hung on managers' walls. Activities were adjusted by shifting magnets around; costs were recalculated using manual methods. With programs such as Project, changes in project data such as an increase in programmers' pay, can be entered once into the computer and all calculations using those data are modified immediately. If it requires an extra week to complete an activity, one entry causes all the costs to be recalculated and the time schedule for the entire project to be modified accordingly.

Many managerial jobs require the careful monitoring of projects: building houses, ships, roads and bridges; remodeling offices and factories; designing automobiles and aircraft; and producing an employees' handbook are but a few examples. Project management programs, then, are good examples of how modern computer systems provide the tools needed for better management.

TIME MANAGEMENT

One of the most important things an executive can do is manage his or her time effectively. Computers can help to accomplish this task. There are numerous calendar programs available that keep track of appointments, meetings, and things to do. An effective program should do more, however. Good time management programs, can in fact, create more time for important executive functions.

Programs like Habadex and Sidekick do this by providing automatic telephone dialers, notepads, desk calculators, and small data bases. For users with hard disks, Habadex automatically loads up to two dozen programs quickly and easily. This is very important for the user who is involved with several applications of a microcomputer, say, a word processor, a spelling checker, and a data base. Some programs such as these even provide mini report generators and automatic telephone cost data for billing clients.

Time management programs typically warn the user when it's time to go to the next meeting. The programs do this by ringing a bell built into the computer. This means that the programs must be running all the time. This can tie up the computer unless the program is designed to run simultaneously with other programs. Without this feature, a time management program is of little value. Fortunately, many time management programs offer this capability.

Controlling an Executive's Time

Cliff Dweller is the manager of a real estate firm in Yuma, Arizona. He spends a great deal of time on the phone, talking to other brokers. He also has weekly staff meetings and monthly meetings of the Real Estate Association which he serves as secretary. He still enjoys selling homes, so he spends a lot of time with clients. Like so many real estate offices, Cliff's has no clerical help—no

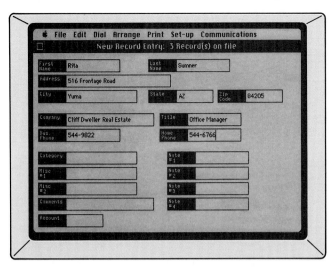

FIGURE 16-9
Habadex standard record format

one to maintain a calendar or make telephone connections. Cliff found himself spending too much time on time management housekeeping so he bought a copy of Habadex for his Macintosh.

Establishing a Data Base

When Cliff got the program, he entered the names of all of the members of the association into the data base. The Habadex data base allows twenty fields per record including standard address book items, notes, comments, and others. The standard record format is shown in figure 16-9. Cliff decided he wanted to add data beyond name, phone, address, and company. He also wanted the records in a different format. With figure 16-9 still displayed on the screen, Dweller used the mouse to point to a field he wanted to move. He clicked the mouse and dragged the field elsewhere on the screen, figure 16-10. He repeated this procedure for each field he wanted to move. The result is shown in figure 16-11. Cliff also wants to rename some of the fields. He

FIGURE 16-11
Revised record format

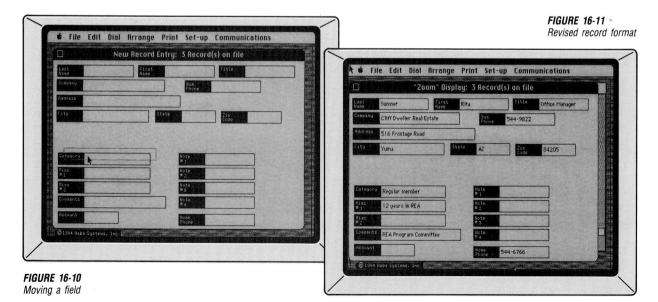

FIGURE 16-10
Moving a field

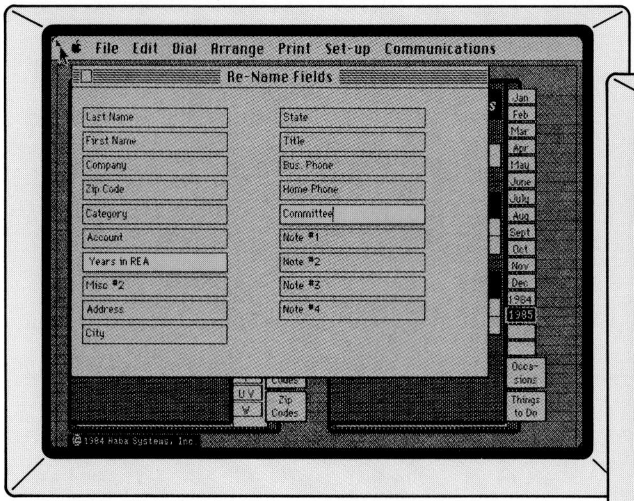

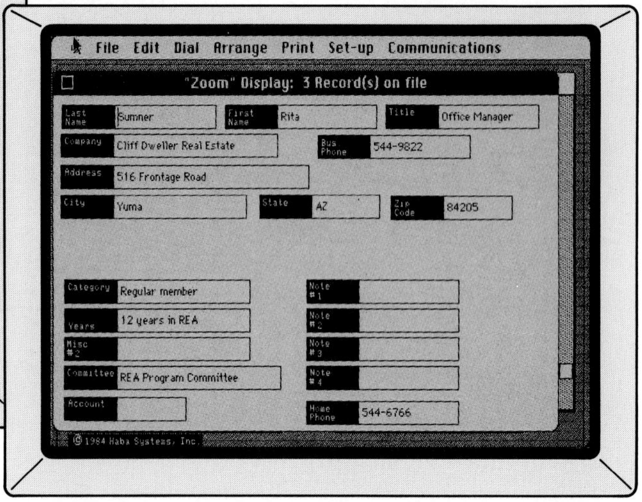

FIGURE 16-13
Sample record

FIGURE 16-12
Renaming fields

did this with the rename field command which produced figure 16-12. All records were then displayed as shown in figure 16-13.

Printing a Directory

Each year, Cliff produces a membership directory. Because it is so easy, this year the directory will include two listings, one by name alphabetically, the other by company (figures 16-14 and 16-15). He can create as many directories as he wants, changing the order in which information is printed as easily as he rearranged the record format.

Producing Form Letters

Once he had the directories printed, Cliff used the mailing label feature to design and prepare envelopes in ZIP Code order to minimize postage costs.

FIGURE 16-14
Directory: alphabetical listing

```
                    Last Name Listing
    Last Name/First Name    Company                    Bus. Phone    Home Phone
                            Address/City/State/Zip Code              Title

    Adams, Alex             City Real Estate Service   433-9888      433-1000
                            123 No. Main St. Yuma, AZ 84207          Agent
    Morless, Sarah          City Real Estate Service   433-9888      619-552-5612
                            123 No. Main St. Yuma, AZ 84207          Broker
    Smith, Jason            Cliff Dweller Real Estate  555-4031      667-9913
                            5223 Sixteenth Ave. Yuma, AZ 84200       Agent
    Sumner, Rita            Cliff Dweller Real Estate  544-9822      544-6766
                            516 Frontage Road Yuma, AZ 84205         Office Manager
    Winston, Evan           City Real Estate Service   433-9888      641-9822
                            123 No. Main St. Yuma, AZ 84207          Agent
    Worley, Richard         Cliff Dweller Real Estate  544-9822      566-9981
                            516 Frontage Road Yuma, AZ 84205         Agent
```

```
                            Company Listing
                            Last Name/First Name                 Title
         Company            Address/City/State/Zip Code
                            Bus. Phone/Home Phone


  City Real Estate Service  Adams, Alex                          Agent
                            123 No. Main St. Yuma, AZ 84207
                            433-9888 433-1000
  City Real Estate Service  Morless, Sarah                       Broker
                            123 No. Main St. Yuma, AZ 84207
                            433-9888 619-552-5612
  City Real Estate Service  Winston, Evan                        Agent
                            123 No. Main St. Yuma, AZ 84207
                            433-9888 641-9822
  Cliff Dweller Real Estate Smith, Jason                         Agent
                            5223 Sixteenth Ave Yuma, AZ 84200
                            555-4031 667-9913
  Cliff Dweller Real Estate Sumner, Rita                         Office Manager
                            516 Frontage Road Yuma, AZ 84205
                            544-9822 544-6766
  Cliff Dweller Real Estate Worley, Richard                      Agent
                            516 Frontage Road Yuma, AZ 84205
                            544-9822 566-9981
```

FIGURE 16-15
Directory by company

He can use a standard mailing label (figures 16-16 and 16-17) or design a special one. Habadex stores up to three label formats for future use.

He also used the mail merge feature to prepare individual form letters for each Association member using a word processing program. Dweller

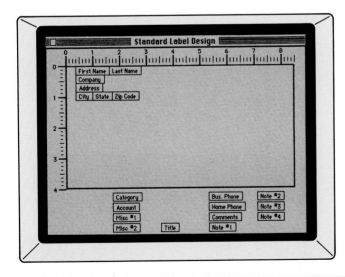

FIGURE 16-16
Standard mailing label

FIGURE 16-17
Printed labels

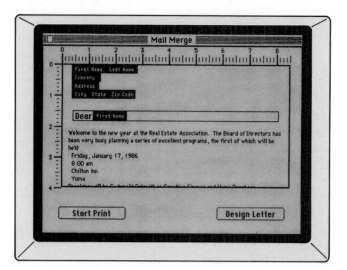

FIGURE 16-18
Designing a form letter

FIGURE 16-19
The form letter

designed the letter, figure 16-18, and the computer generated letters for all association members, figure 16-19.

Maintaining a Calendar

Cliff was then ready to use Habadex on a daily basis, starting with December, 1985. He entered all of the appointments he had scheduled. The monthly calendar shows the first two on each day, figure 16-20. It shows the next two for the current date. Then he "clicked" December 27th. That brought an appointment list onto the screen, figure 16-21. As he added new appointments, they were placed in the proper order, according to time. When he closed that page and returned to the main Habadex screen, it showed his next two appointments as well as a list of things to do, things he had entered earlier, figure 16-22. Habadex rings an alarm when an appointment time arrives, so Cliff enters his appointments with enough advance time to allow him to travel to his meetings and not be late.

FIGURE 16-21
Daily appointment log

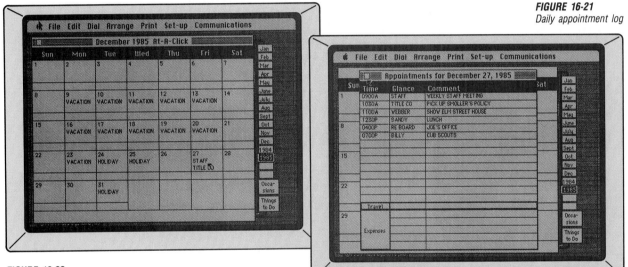

FIGURE 16-20
Monthly calendar

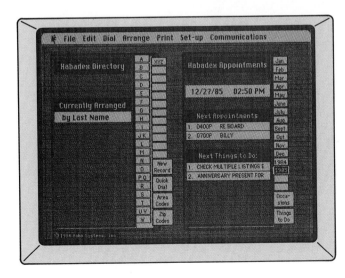

FIGURE 16-22
Habadex main screen

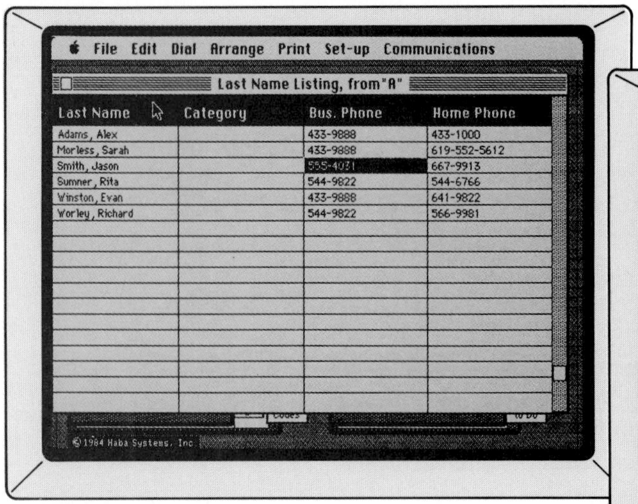

FIGURE 16-24
Automatic dialing

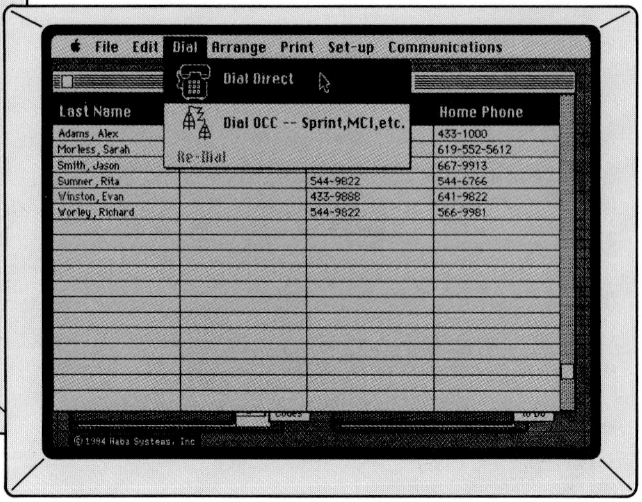

FIGURE 16-23
Telephone directory

Dialing the Telephone

Cliff had just over an hour until his meeting with the Real Estate Board so he decided to make some phone calls. He brought up the telephone directory, figure 16-23, and selected the number he wanted. Then he selected the Dial Direct option from the Dial menu, figure 16-24. Habadex dialed the number for him. Since the line was busy, Habadex set up the redial option, figure 16-25. That only required a click of the mouse to reach his number.

Cliff Dweller Real Estate is part of a nationwide syndicate of brokers. One of Cliff's many services is home finding for clients moving away from Yuma. This requires many long distance phone calls. To save money, Cliff has subscribed to Sprint, a secondary common carrier (see Chapter 10). This requires him to dial a local phone number, then a long access code, and finally the number he wishes to reach. All told he has to dial nearly 30 digits. Habadex does this automatically at the click of the mouse, figure 16-26.

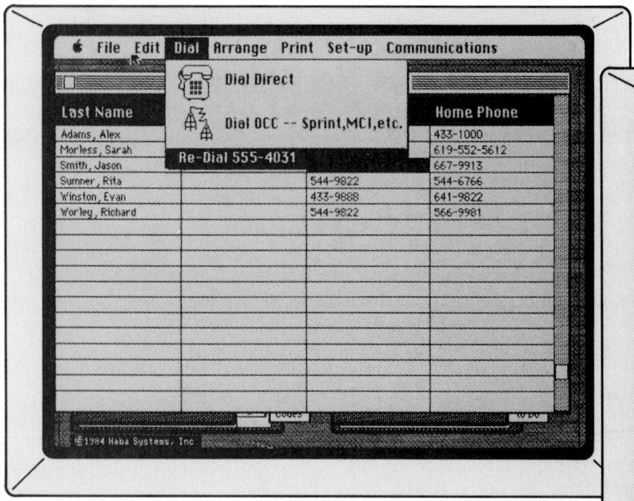

FIGURE 16-26
Dialing a VAN

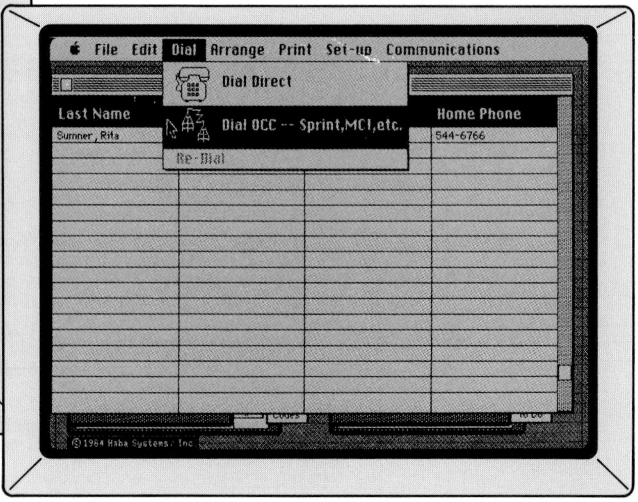

FIGURE 16-25
Automatic redial

Inasmuch as Cliff spends a lot of time on the phone, he finds the telephone aspects of Habadex are great time savers. He no longer has to remember numbers, he doesn't reach wrong numbers, and he doesn't spend wasted time trying to reach correspondents.

Conclusion

Time management programs may include the features of Habadex and other features as well. For example, attorneys need billing systems that record the time spent for each client and produce invoices. Whatever features a time management program has, it can lead to a major increase in executive productivity if it is used consistently and if it does not limit other uses of the computer. The wise business executive will consider time management programs early when developing a computerized office.

STATISTICAL ANALYSIS

Statistical analysis plays a big role in business planning. This is particularly true in quality control applications in which products are sampled to determine the percentage of faulty goods in an entire production run or in making comparisons between two products, several sales territories, a chain of markets, and so forth. This analysis is based on *sampling*—checking one of every ten products, selecting one phone number at random from each page of the telephone book, or performing similar procedures. Companies use samples to determine if their manufacturing, marketing, or other processes are working correctly. In fact, any process that requires sampling is a statistical procedure and is amenable to computerized analysis.

Many statistical analysis packages, such as the Statistical Package for the Social Sciences (SPSS), have long been available on mainframe computers. Recently, these packages have been reprogrammed for microcomputers. Newer packages combine statistical power with graphic output.

One of the first such programs designed for micros was VisiTrend/VisiPlot. As we saw in Chapter Fifteen, VisiPlot is a fairly standard graphics program. VisiTrend adds substantial statistical power to enable us to identify trends within the data we have.

Using Statistics for a Market Survey

Eta Bulls works for her father who owns a chain of grocery stores serving affluent urban areas just north of Los Angeles and near Phoenix and San Francisco. She is currently a regional manager. She feels that it is very important to provide enough checkers so customers don't wait in line too long. She decides to complete a statistical study to determine if her belief is correct.

To simplify matters, Eta selects two typical stores from her chain for an experiment. She will assign a certain number of checkers each day and ask customers to rate their satisfaction with the store. For customers making small purchases, there will be a quick-check line at each store. These customers will not be part of the survey. Eta will begin the experiment by looking at one time period, 5:00 p.m. to 7:00 p.m., the busiest time of the day.

FIGURE 16-28
Selecting VisiTrend

```
LOAD SERIES
CONTINUE PRINT

NAME        PER   START    END      #

CHKR        12    1   1    1   12   12
SAT1        12    1   1    1   12   12
SAT2        12    1   1    1   12   12

SERIES: 3/16   DATA POINTS: 36/645
```

```
GO TO VISITREND PROGRAM
LOAD     ->PLOT  LOOKUP  CLEAR   <MORE>
EDIT     ->TREND SAVE    QUIT    DRIVE
SLOT: 6  DRIVE: 2
```

FIGURE 16-27
VisiTrend data series

The Experiment

The experiment will last for 12 days. The number of checkers will vary from three to eight. Customers will rate their satisfaction from one (poor) to three (average) to five (excellent).

Entering the Data

After collecting the data, Eta boots VisiPlot/VisiTrend. She enters the data just as we did in Chapter Fourteen. Her three data series are CHKR, the number of checkers assigned to work; SAT1 and SAT2, customer satisfaction ratings at the two stores. See figure 16-27.

Then she selects − >TREND from the menu, figure 16-28. The computer takes a moment and presents another menu. Wanting to check her data, Eta selects ANALYZE and TABLE, then selects the three series. She is shown the data in figure 16-29. After verifying that all of the data were entered correctly, she continues.

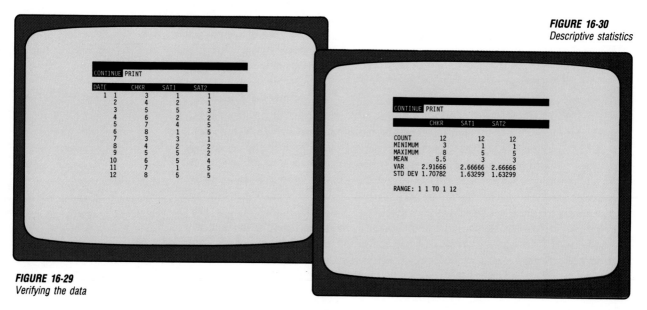

FIGURE 16-30
Descriptive statistics

```
CONTINUE PRINT

DATE      CHKR    SAT1    SAT2
  1  1     3       1       1
     2     4       2       1
     3     5       5       3
     4     6       2       2
     5     7       4       5
     6     8       1       5
     7     3       3       1
     8     4       2       2
     9     5       5       2
    10     6       5       4
    11     7       1       5
    12     8       5       5
```

```
CONTINUE PRINT

           CHKR      SAT1      SAT2

COUNT       12        12        12
MINIMUM      3         1         1
MAXIMUM      8         5         5
MEAN        5.5        3         3
VAR      2.91666   2.66666   2.66666
STD DEV  1.70782   1.63299   1.63299

RANGE: 1 1 TO 1 12
```

FIGURE 16-29
Verifying the data

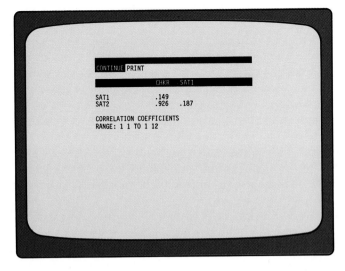

FIGURE 16-31
Inferential statistics

The Analysis

Now Eta is ready to analyze her data. She will use various statistics that fall into two categories: *descriptive statistics* which describe a set of data but do not lend themselves to drawing conclusions about the data and *inferential statistics* which enable Eta to make inferences.

Descriptive Statistics.   Returning to the VisiTrend Menu, she selects ANALYZE again, followed by STATS. Selecting all three series, she is presented with the screen shown in figure 16-30. The *means*, or averages, of SAT1 and SAT2 tell her that, taken as a whole, the customers' satisfaction levels are about the same. The *variance* (VAR) and *standard deviation* (STD DEV) tell Eta that many customers rate her service "excellent" while many others rate it "poor." Judging from these items, the customers do not agree on the quality of the service. In other words, there is a great deal of variance among individual customer responses and the mean response score.

Inferential Statistics.   The *correlation coefficients* tell the real story. Correlation coefficients tell us how nearly two lists of items are related. A perfect correlation coefficient is 1.0. If two lists have a correlation coefficient of 1.0, knowing an item on the first list tells us what item corresponds on the second list. CHKR and SAT2 have a coefficient near 1.0, see figure 16-31. This means that number of checkers and customer satisfaction scores are closely related. According to this, Eta's customers (in store two) will be happy if she keeps them in line the shortest possible time. So, if she knows how many checkers are on duty, Eta can tell how satisfied the customers will be.

Store one is different however. The correlation coefficient is near zero. A zero correlation coefficient means that there is no relationship between two lists. This means that the number of checkers is not very important in maintaining customer satisfaction. Even if Eta knows how many checkers are on duty, she can make no inference about customer satisfaction.

The third correlation coefficient relates the two satisfaction series. This measure shows that the groups of customers are quite different, which confirms Eta's suspicions. If shorter waiting periods make one group happy but have no affect on the other, the groups are dissimilar, at least so far as their satisfaction relates to waiting in line.

Conclusion

Eta Bulls completed her statistical analysis in minutes. Manual means would have increased the required time dramatically. The results of her work were very positive so she extended the survey to all the stores in her region. Within a few months, she had increased customer satisfaction in most of her stores from average to above average.

VisiTrend, like other statistical analysis programs, offers a range of sophisticated routines for calculating moving averages, linear regressions, and other important measures. Like correlation, they require considerable time to calculate manually. Statistical analysis programs allow the business person to concentrate on the statistics themselves instead of the process of calculating them.

This simple example of the use of a computer program to calculate statistical measures skirts many important requirements of statistical analysis. The point is that the calculations are performed by the computer system. The validity of the interpretation depends upon many factors that go beyond our purposes here.

MODELING

A model is a physical or hypothetical representation of some real-world phenomenon. A model airplane, for example, is a physical model of the real thing. Model airplanes, like all models, are useful in predicting the behavior of the real thing. That's why they are used.

Frequently, physical models are very useful in predicting real-world behavior. Other models used for predictive purposes are abstract and take the form of mathematical expressions of relationships.

Use of models, whether physical or abstract, offers a number of advantages. They are safer, less expensive, and easier to control than their real-world counterparts. Consider flight simulators used to train pilots. For many practical purposes practicing "flying" in a simulator is just as good as doing it in an actual aircraft.

Those who use computers are particularly interested in mathematical models because computers can use mathematical expressions to predict behavior.

Modeling, then, means making a mathematical description of a process. For example, we can model something as simple as interest earnings on a savings account or something as complex as the operation of an entire factory or landing astronauts on the moon. Developing mathematical models requires a great deal of skill and knowledge. Many books are available that provide ready-made models, often for use with spreadsheet and other programs.

Once models have been developed, it is not always easy to solve them. Programs now exist to assist in this effort. Examples include Encore and TK!Solver. Modeling programs use two methods for finding the solution of a system of equations that make up a model: direct solution and iterative solution.

Direct solution is used for problems the variables of which are defined in terms of other variables. For example, simple interest is calculated by the formula

$$\text{Interest income} = \text{Principal} \times \text{Rate of interest} \times \text{Time}$$

If we know any three of these four variables, we can solve directly for the fourth using standard algebraic methods. If principal is $5,000, rate of interest is .17 (17%), and interest income is $1,275, we can solve for time (the length of the investment) by "plugging in" the known values

$$1275 = 5000 \times .17 \times time$$

and manipulating the equation

$$time = 1275 / (5000 \times .17)$$

to yield 1.5 years.

Iterative solution is used if a variable is defined in terms of a variable the value of which we don't know. An example of such a circular definition involves calculating bonuses as a percentage of net profit. Here are the formulas:

Bonus = Net profit × Rate of bonus
Net profit = Gross profit − Bonus

In this problem, we don't know the bonus even though we must use it to define net profit. We can see the circular nature of the problem by combining the two equations:

Bonus = (Gross profit − Bonus) × Rate of bonus

For this example, let's assume that gross profit is $50,000 and the rate of bonus is 12 percent. The formula now looks like

Bonus = (5000 − Bonus) × .12

This problem can be solved by direct calculation, but let's examine an iterative technique. We begin the process by guessing a value for the bonus, say, $10,000. The program tests that value and finds that the bonus is too large so it picks a smaller value to test. It continues to test values until the computer comes up with an answer that is close enough (most iterative solutions are only approximate) at which time it presents the answer. In our case, the computer tells us the answer is $5,357. This repetitive process is called *iteration*. If the computer cannot come up with an answer within a specified number of iterations, we must provide a better first guess or redefine the model.

Programs such as TK!Solver answer "What if..." questions much like spreadsheets do. A problem that might take an hour with a hand calculator takes minutes with the computer. An analyst can examine many more cases with this tool. He or she will be able to find the "right" combination of factors to solve a problem. This is shown in the next example which demonstrates the usefulness of modeling programs.

The Cray II, one of the world's most powerful computers, increases productivity on a grand scale. (Courtesy Cray Research Inc.)

Using TK!Solver

One of Cliff Dweller's clients, William Pair, visits him one day to discuss the financial arrangements for a home that they found in the real estate section of the local newspaper. The home was listed for $185,000 and required a down payment of twenty percent with terms of 30 years at 13.8 percent.

"What would my monthly payments be on this deal?" asks Bill.

"Hang on for a couple of minutes while I set up a model for you," answers Cliff. He knows that his model will serve more than just Bill's immediate question. He begins by booting up TK!Solver, a program designed for various modeling and calculation applications.

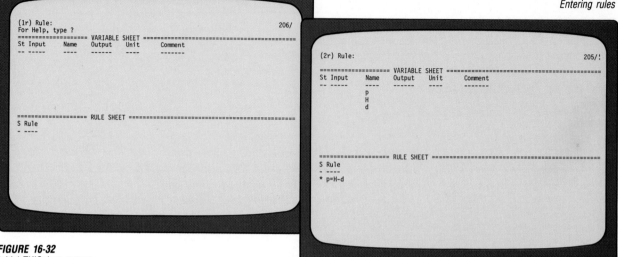

FIGURE 16-33
Entering rules

```
(1r) Rule:                                                206/
For Help, type ?
==================== VARIABLE SHEET ====================
St Input      Name     Output    Unit      Comment
-- -----      ----     ------    ----      -------




==================== RULE SHEET ====================
S Rule
- ----
```

FIGURE 16-32
Initial TK!Solver screen

```
(2r) Rule:                                                205/!

==================== VARIABLE SHEET ====================
St Input      Name     Output    Unit      Comment
-- -----      ----     ------    ----      -------
              p
              H
              d




==================== RULE SHEET ====================
S Rule
- ----
* p=H-d
```

Defining Rules and Variables

The initial TK!Solver screen, figure 16-32, displays the two fundamental sheets or definition forms used by the program. The lower sheet, called the rule sheet, is used to define arithmetic and mathematical relationships used by the model. The upper sheet, the variable sheet, will show the various variables used by the model and will be used for the input of values for the various variables.

Cliff begins by entering the first rule, an algebraic expression that describes one of the relationships in his model:

$$p = H - d$$

where p represents the principal of the loan, H the price of the home, and d the amount of the down payment. This rule says that the amount of the loan, the principal (p), is equal to the price of the home (H) less the down payment (d). When he presses the Enter key, each of the variables in this expression appears in the variable sheet, in the upper portion of the screen, figure 16-33.

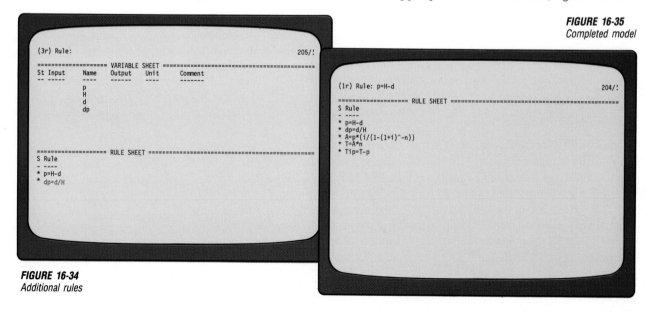

FIGURE 16-35
Completed model

```
(3r) Rule:                                                205/!

==================== VARIABLE SHEET ====================
St Input      Name     Output    Unit      Comment
-- -----      ----     ------    ----      -------
              p
              H
              d
              dp




==================== RULE SHEET ====================
S Rule
- ----
* p=H-d
* dp=d/H
```

FIGURE 16-34
Additional rules

```
(1r) Rule: p=H-d                                          204/!

==================== RULE SHEET ====================
S Rule
- ----
* p=H-d
* dp=d/H
* A=p*(i/(1-(1+i)^-n))
* T=A*n
* Tip=T-p
```

Cliff's next rule or expression describes the manner in which the down payment is calculated as a percent of the price of the home:

$$dp = d / H$$

where dp stands for the down payment as a percent, d the down payment as an amount of money, and H the price. After entering this expression, the new variable, dp, is added to the variable sheet, figure 16-34.

Cliff continues in this fashion defining the relationships in his model. Figure 16-35 shows all of the rules or expressions. The monthly payments, A, are determined by a formula which uses the amount of the principal, p, the interest rate, i, and the time period in months, n:

$$A = p * (i / (1 - (i + 1) \hat{} - n))$$

which Cliff found in one of his college financial management texts. Mathematical expressions in TK!Solver follow the usual computer conventions in which

^ means exponentiation (raising to a power)

* means multiplication

/ means division

+ means addition

− means subtraction or negative values

The total amount paid by Bill Pair over the term of the loan is established by the fourth equation

$$T = A * n$$

where T represents the total of all payments, A the amount of the monthly payment, and n the number of monthly payments.

The last equation,

$$Tip = T - p$$

defines the total amount of interest paid over the term of the loan (Tip) as the difference between the total payments (t) and the principal of the loan (p).

As Cliff enters each of these rules or expressions, the variables required for the calculations are entered automatically into the Variable Sheet. Figure 16-36 shows the Variable Sheet after entering each of the rules and after Cliff

```
(1i) Input:                                                    204/!

==================== VARIABLE SHEET ====================================
St Input      Name    Output    Unit      Comment
-- -----      ----    ------    ----      -------
              H                 dollars   House price
              d                 dollars   Down payment
              dp                percent   Down payment percentage
              p                 dollars   Mortgage
              n                 years     Term
              i                 percent   Interest rate
              A                 dollars   Monthly payment
              T                 dollars   Total of payments
              Tip               dollars   Total interest payments
```

FIGURE 16-36
Variable sheet

defined the units of measure (dollars, percent, and years) for each variable. On the right of figure 16-35, Cliff has entered comments associated with each variable that explain what the variables represent.

Answering "What if...?"

"How much will our monthly payments be if I buy this house?" asks Bill.

"Well, let's see," says Cliff. "We'll enter a value for the price of the house in the Variable Sheet, and do the same for the term of the loan, the interest rate, and the percent of the down payment." The entries appear in figure 16-37 under the column labeled Input.

Having entered the input values, Cliff now enters an exclamation point (!) to calculate the results. They appear in the output column of figure 16-37.

"My goodness," exclaims Bill, "I can't afford a monthly payment of $1,730 per month."

After considerable financial counseling, Cliff and Bill decide that Bill's financial situation warrants monthly payments of $950 for housing.

"What price house will that buy at today's interest rates?" asks Bill.

To answer, Cliff enters 950 as an input amount for monthly payment, 13.8 as the current rate of interest and 20000, the maximum that Bill can afford to invest as a down payment in a home, figure 16-38. Then he enters an exclamation point to calculate the new results.

"As you can see," says Cliff, "Your financial situation dictates that the maximum price you can pay for a home today is $101,261.89."

"But we really want that $185,000 home," says Bill. "What if I were to swing a deal through my father-in-law's bank to get a loan for 50 instead of 30 years?"

"Won't make much difference," responds Cliff. "You see, the key to home financing is how much you can afford to pay each month. Let's enter 50 as the number of years in our model and see what difference it makes." Cliff enters the new term of the loan, figure 16-39.

"Extending the period of the loan by 20 years increases the price of the home that you can afford only by roughly $1,000. It hardly seems worth it."

"I don't understand," says Bill. "Almost doubling the period of the loan doesn't seem to make much difference. How come?"

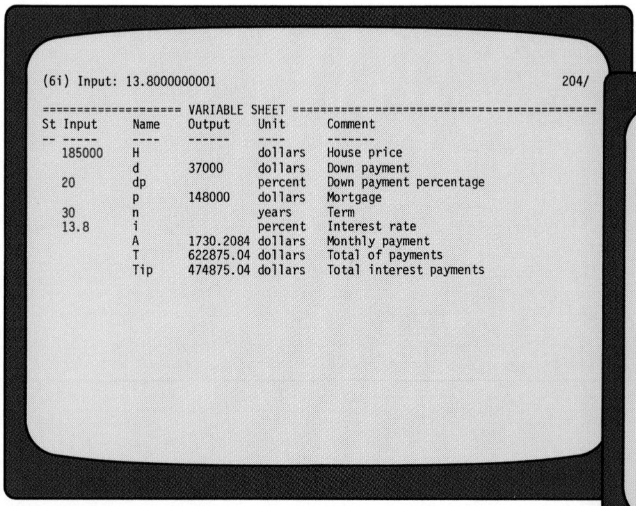

FIGURE 16-38
Results

```
(6i) Input: 13.8000000001                                    204/

=================== VARIABLE SHEET =========================================
St Input    Name    Output      Unit      Comment
-- -----    ----    ------      ----      -------
   185000   H                   dollars   House price
            d       37000       dollars   Down payment
   20       dp                  percent   Down payment percentage
            p       148000      dollars   Mortgage
   30       n                   years     Term
   13.8     i                   percent   Interest rate
            A       1730.2084   dollars   Monthly payment
            T       622875.04   dollars   Total of payments
            Tip     474875.04   dollars   Total interest payments
```

FIGURE 16-37
Entering values

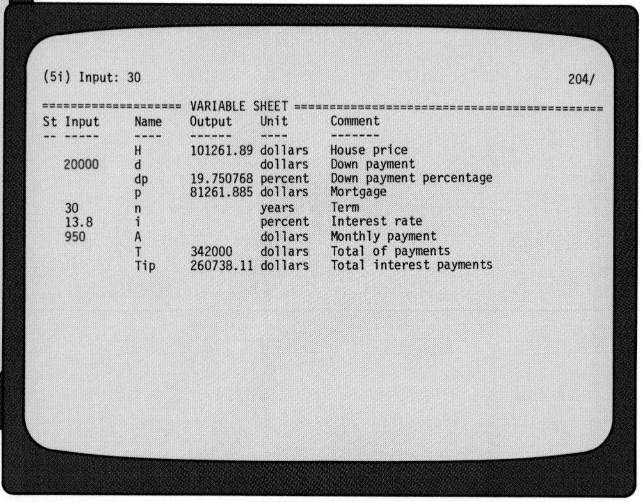

```
(5i) Input: 30                                               204/

=================== VARIABLE SHEET =========================================
St Input    Name    Output       Unit      Comment
-- -----    ----    ------       ----      -------
            H       101261.89    dollars   House price
   20000    d                    dollars   Down payment
            dp      19.750768    percent   Down payment percentage
            p       81261.885    dollars   Mortgage
   30       n                    years     Term
   13.8     i                    percent   Interest rate
   950      A                    dollars   Monthly payment
            T       342000       dollars   Total of payments
            Tip     260738.11    dollars   Total interest payments
```

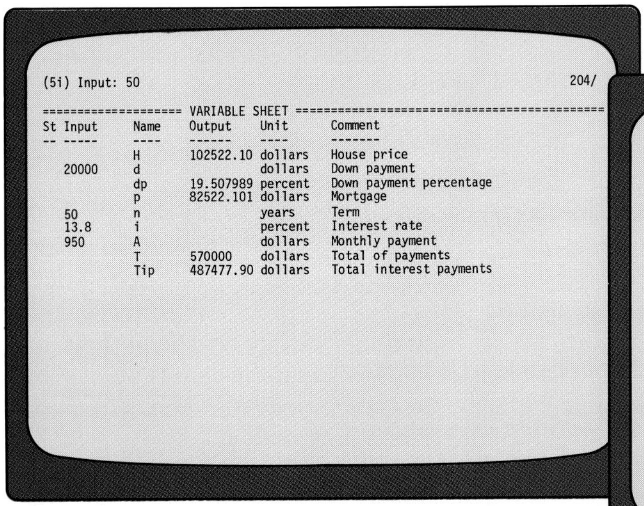

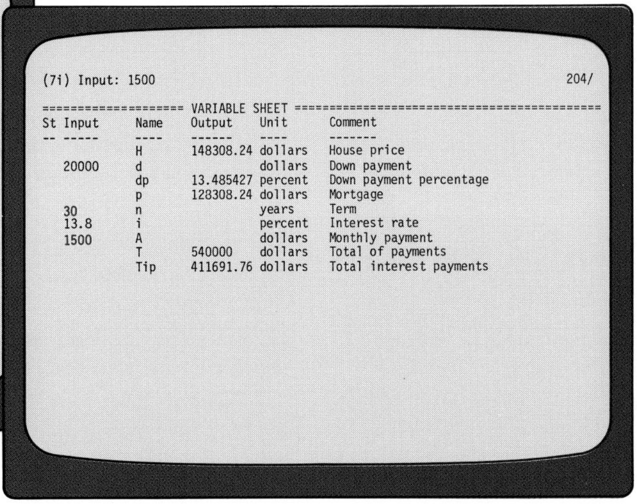

FIGURE 16-40
Changing values again

```
(5i) Input: 50                                                        204/

==================== VARIABLE SHEET ==========================================
St Input      Name   Output      Unit      Comment
-- -----      ----   ------      ----      -------
              H      102522.10   dollars   House price
   20000      d                  dollars   Down payment
              dp     19.507989   percent   Down payment percentage
              p      82522.101   dollars   Mortgage
   50         n                  years     Term
   13.8       i                  percent   Interest rate
   950        A                  dollars   Monthly payment
              T      570000      dollars   Total of payments
              Tip    487477.90   dollars   Total interest payments
```

```
(7i) Input: 1500                                                      204/

==================== VARIABLE SHEET ==========================================
St Input      Name   Output      Unit      Comment
-- -----      ----   ------      ----      -------
              H      148308.24   dollars   House price
   20000      d                  dollars   Down payment
              dp     13.485427   percent   Down payment percentage
              p      128308.24   dollars   Mortgage
   30         n                  years     Term
   13.8       i                  percent   Interest rate
   1500       A                  dollars   Monthly payment
              T      540000      dollars   Total of payments
              Tip    411691.76   dollars   Total interest payments
```

FIGURE 16-39
Changing values

"It's because your monthly payments are eaten up by interest on the loan," responds Cliff. "Look here. Let's say that you could afford monthly payments of $1,500 instead of $900."

Cliff enters this monthly payment and recalculates the model, figure 16-40.

"There, what did I tell you," announces Cliff. "If you could afford $1,500 monthly house payments, you could buy a house at a price of $148,000. That's not quite the same as the $185,000 home you had in mind, but it gives you an idea of your financial situation."

Conclusion

Like spreadsheets, modeling programs answer "What if...?" questions. These programs use techniques from the simplest arithmetic to extremely complex mathematical functions, functions that allow the modeling of complicated economic, financial, and other situations.

EXPERT SYSTEMS

Expert systems are computer programs designed to provide information normally available from highly skilled specialists. These systems typically do not replace expert humans. Instead, they provide information that is fairly mundane and routine from the expert's point of view, yet not obvious to the user. As such, they are available in many fields such as medicine and business. By the 1990s, expert systems will be available for home consumption and will provide information on how to plant a garden, how to build an energy efficient home, and how to set aside funds for the childrens' education, among other things.

By 2000, according to James Johnson, president of Human Edge Software Corporation and a leading authority in this field, "Expert systems and data bases will be the only reason to buy a computer."[2] For businesses, expert systems now provide advice on handling a range of personal relationships such as sales, negotiations, personnel management, and the like.

Expert systems have several distinct characteristics. They have access to a body of information in a given field and a method to select appropriate information for specific situations and circumstances. In those respects, they "think" like human experts do.

In reality, expert systems imitate human thought by comparing facts, looking for similar cases in their historical data bases, looking at the probable implications of various conclusions, then offering "expert" opinions. Current efforts at developing expert systems start from scratch for each program. Some expert systems vendors have developed expert system program generators. Using one, a company that markets expert systems programs each "expert" separately. A human expert, say in marketing, will input a large base of marketing information including many "what if" situations into the program generator. Then that program will generate a computerized expert system for use by those requiring marketing information and analysis.

Human Edge produces a series of expert systems. One of them is the Sales Edge. The Sales Edge compares many personality factors of each party (the seller and the prospective buyer) in a sales situation, factors in environmental considerations, then provides a strategy that will be beneficial to both the seller and the buyer.

Using the Sales Edge

Cliff Dweller has bought a copy of Sales Edge to help his sales force deal with their clients. Cliff first uses the program to analyze his interactions with Homer Beier who wants a palatial mansion in the ritzy part of town.

Self-Assessment

Cliff boots the program, figure 16-41, and begins to assess himself. The program asks him to agree or disagree with nearly 100 statements about himself, figure 16-42. Using the Macintosh, he merely points with the mouse and clicks. If he wants to change an answer, Cliff pages forward or back to the correct statement and clicks a different answer. When he has responded to all of the statements, the program continues.

FIGURE 16-41
Booting Sales Edge

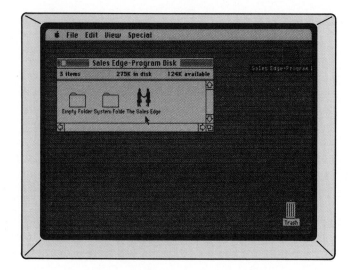

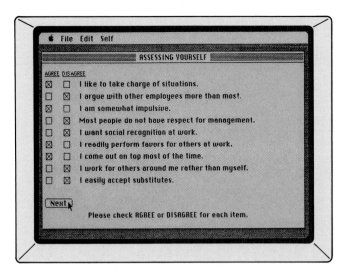

FIGURE 16-42
Assessing the seller

Assessing the Buyer

Next the program begins an assessment of the client. Cliff responds to 50 adjectives that might describe Homer. Figure 16-43 shows a sampling. Because changing answers is easy, he can experiment with different buyer characteristics—what if Mr. Beier were very reserved, what if he were outgoing, and so forth. This is important, because Cliff learns more about Homer during the course of negotiations, updating Homer's data file created by the Sales Edge program will provide Cliff with further information to help him close the sale.

Presenting a Strategy

Once the data have been entered, the program takes over. Cliff is asked to save to disk the data he has entered, figure 16-44. Then the program presents its sales strategy, a three- to ten-page report. Portions of the report are

FIGURE 16-44
Saving the data

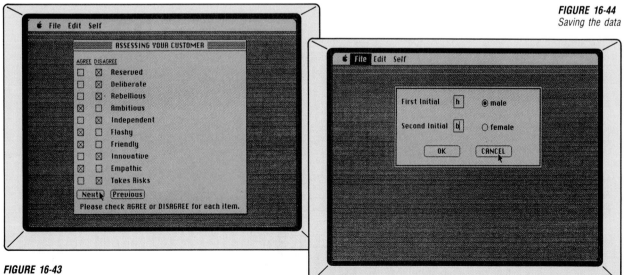

FIGURE 16-43
Assessing the customer

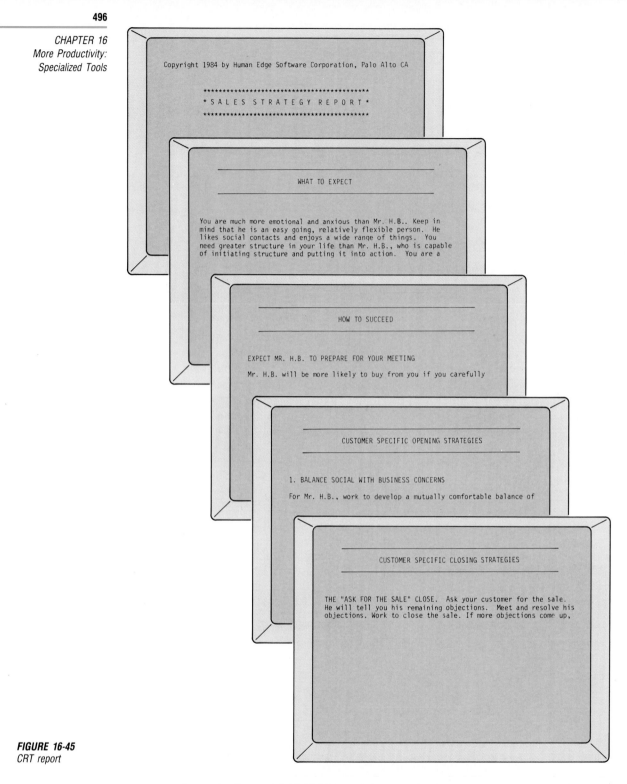

Copyright 1984 by Human Edge Software Corporation, Palo Alto CA

****
* S A L E S   S T R A T E G Y   R E P O R T *
****

WHAT TO EXPECT

You are much more emotional and anxious than Mr. H.B.. Keep in
mind that he is an easy going, relatively flexible person. He
likes social contacts and enjoys a wide range of things. You
need greater structure in your life than Mr. H.B., who is capable
of initiating structure and putting it into action. You are a

HOW TO SUCCEED

EXPECT MR. H.B. TO PREPARE FOR YOUR MEETING

Mr. H.B. will be more likely to buy from you if you carefully

CUSTOMER SPECIFIC OPENING STRATEGIES

1. BALANCE SOCIAL WITH BUSINESS CONCERNS

For Mr. H.B., work to develop a mutually comfortable balance of

CUSTOMER SPECIFIC CLOSING STRATEGIES

THE "ASK FOR THE SALE" CLOSE. Ask your customer for the sale.
He will tell you his remaining objections. Meet and resolve his
objections. Work to close the sale. If more objections come up,

FIGURE 16-45
CRT report

shown in figure 16-45 (CRT) and figure 16-46 (printed output). Armed with
this information, Cliff is better able to close a deal because he knows how
to meet Mr. Beier's needs and desires.

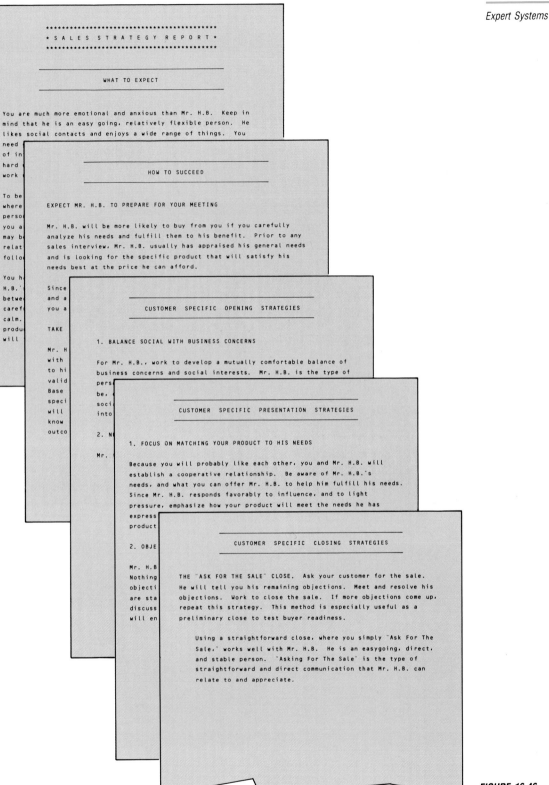

```
**********************************************
* S A L E S   S T R A T E G Y   R E P O R T *
**********************************************
```

WHAT TO EXPECT

You are much more emotional and anxious than Mr. H.B. Keep in
mind that he is an easy going, relatively flexible person. He
likes social contacts and enjoys a wide range of things. You
need
of in
hard
work

To be
where
perso
you a
may b
relat
follo

You h
H.B.'   Since
betwe   and a
caref   you a
calm.
produ   TAKE
will
                 Mr. H
                 with
                 to hi
                 valid
                 Base
                 speci   soci
                 will   into
                 know
                 outco   2. N

                          Mr.

HOW TO SUCCEED

EXPECT MR. H.B. TO PREPARE FOR YOUR MEETING

Mr. H.B. will be more likely to buy from you if you carefully
analyze his needs and fulfill them to his benefit. Prior to any
sales interview, Mr. H.B. usually has appraised his general needs
and is looking for the specific product that will satisfy his
needs best at the price he can afford.

CUSTOMER SPECIFIC OPENING STRATEGIES

1. BALANCE SOCIAL WITH BUSINESS CONCERNS

For Mr. H.B., work to develop a mutually comfortable balance of
business concerns and social interests. Mr. H.B. is the type of
pers
be,
soci
into

2. N

CUSTOMER SPECIFIC PRESENTATION STRATEGIES

1. FOCUS ON MATCHING YOUR PRODUCT TO HIS NEEDS

Because you will probably like each other, you and Mr. H.B. will
establish a cooperative relationship. Be aware of Mr. H.B.'s
needs, and what you can offer Mr. H.B. to help him fulfill his needs.
Since Mr. H.B. responds favorably to influence, and to light
pressure, emphasize how your product will meet the needs he has
express
product

2. OBJE

Mr. H.B
Nothing   CUSTOMER SPECIFIC CLOSING STRATEGIES
objecti
are sta
discuss
will en   THE "ASK FOR THE SALE" CLOSE. Ask your customer for the sale.
                   He will tell you his remaining objections. Meet and resolve his
                   objections. Work to close the sale. If more objections come up,
                   repeat this strategy. This method is especially useful as a
                   preliminary close to test buyer readiness.

                      Using a straightforward close, where you simply "Ask For The
                      Sale," works well with Mr. H.B. He is an easygoing, direct,
                      and stable person. "Asking For The Sale" is the type of
                      straightforward and direct communication that Mr. H.B. can
                      relate to and appreciate.
```

**FIGURE 16-46**
*Printed report*
```

Conclusion

The Sales Edge is an easy program to use, requiring virtually no knowledge of computers. In fact, the Macintosh version used the mouse for all input except the initials of the client. Entering Cliff's and Homer's profiles and printing the report took about 15 minutes.

According to a survey taken in July of 1984, more than half of all small businesses will be using microcomputers by 1987.[3] As they become more conversant with computers, managers of both small and large businesses will use many tools beyond the big six. Because small firms often are unable to afford high-priced consultants, it is reasonable to expect that expert systems will become more prevalent in the business world.

INVESTMENT PORTFOLIO MANAGEMENT

Portfolio managers, whether they are professionals handling dozens of clients, or amateurs handling only their own investments, have a common goal—to make money by identifying security market trends at the earliest possible time. This necessitates analyzing masses of investment data. For this reason, analysts have only dealt with a small number of issues until the advent of analysis software. Now an investment analyst can effectively deal with broader segments of the market.

There are many aspects to investment portfolio management. Programs may be used to track performance of stocks or bonds, possibly downloading information from the Dow Jones News/Retrieval Service (DJN/R) described in Chapter 10. They may be called upon to analyze performance. They may be used to maintain records of one or more investment portfolios, keeping track of stock and bond purchases and sales, profits, and losses. They can even produce tax forms at the end of the year.

Because there are so many aspects, investment software tends to be complex and varied. Before buying such software, the buyer must decide how big a system to use. Will there be more than one portfolio? How many issues will there be in each portfolio? How many transactions can we expect? Does the package handle the types of investments to be made—stocks, bonds, futures, and so forth? Will it handle margin and short positions? Can it retrieve data from the Dow Jones information utility?

Using an Investment Management Program

Tyrone Kuhn considered these questions and others before buying one program from a series of programs produced by Dow Jones (DJ).

Analysis

Market Analyzer provides access to DJN/R. It also keeps daily price histories of the stocks, bonds, mutual funds, and options in their portfolios. The program does complex mathematical computations so investors can use the extensive charting and graphing functions so important to market analysis. These investors are able to compare issues, study volume indicators, oscillator charts, and trend lines, and use other analytical tools.

Industry Group Numbers

```
Intl Controls (A).......INC      Mohawk Data (N).........MDS      Matrix Cp (A)...........MAX
Kamen Corp A (O)........KAMNA    Network Sys (O).........NSCO    Optical Coatg Lab (O)...OCLI
Lundy Elec (A)..........LDY      NBI Inc (N).............NBI      Perkin-Elmer (N)........PKN
Moog Inc (A)............MOGA     Onyx IMI Inc (O)........OINX    Sargent-Welch (N).......SWS
OEA Inc (A).............OEA      Prime Computer (N)......PRM
Raytheon Co (N).........RTN      Printronix (O)..........PTNX         181 Mechanical Devices
Rockcor Inc (O)........ROCK      Recog Equip (N).........REC
Rohr Industries (N).....RHR      Rolm Corp (N)...........RM       Badger Meter (A)........BMI
RSC Indus (A)...........RSC      Sci Systems (O).........SCIS    Gen Signal (N)..........GSX
Sargent Indus (A).......SGT      Seagate Tech (O)........SGAT    Millipore Corp (O)......MILI
Sierracin Corp (A)......SER      Sperry Corp (N).........SY      Moore Products (O)......MORP
Simmonds Prec (N).......SP       Storage Techni (N)......STK     Pall Corp (A)...........PLL
Sundstrand Cp (N).......SNS      Sykes Data (O)..........SYKE    Precian Castpart (O)....PCST
TransTechnol (A)........TTK      System Industries (O)...SYSM    Ranco Inc (N)...........RNI
TRE Corp (N)............TRE      Tab Products (A)........TBP     Varo Inc (N)............VRO
Watkins Jhnan (N).......WJ       Tandem Cpt (O)..........TNDM    Wstn Pac Ind (N)........WPI
                                 Tandon Cp (O)...........TCOR
                                 Telex Corp (N)..........TC        182 Electronic Cntrls, Instr.
    162 Aircraft Mfg.,Parts.Svc  Threshold Tech (O)......THRS
                                 Topaz Inc (A)...........TPZ     AccuRay Cp (O)..........ACRA
Advance Ross (O)........AROS     TEC Inc (A).............TCK     Ametek Inc (N)..........AME
Aero Systems (O)........AESM     TRW Inc (N).............TRW     Autom Switch (A)........ASV
Aeroflex Labs (A).......ARX      Ultimate Cp (A).........ULT     Bowmer Instr (A)........BOM
Aerosonic Corp (A)......ASON     Vector Graphic (O)......VCTR    Clarostat Mfg (A).......CLR
Breeze Corp (A).........BRZ      Vermont Reech (A).......VRE     CompuDyne (A)...........CDC
Butler Intl (N).........BTL      Vernitron Corp (A)......VRN     Conrac Corp (N).........CAX
Cdn Marconi (A).........CMW      Visual Tech (O).........VSAL    Daniel Inds (N).........DAN
Cessna Aircrft (N)......CEA      Wang Labs (A)...........WANB    Dranetz Engin (O).......DRAN
Gates Learjet (A).......GLJ      Wespercorp (A)..........WP      Dynascan CP (O).........DYNA
Hiller Aviation (A).....HIL      Zentec (O)..............ZENT    Electron Cp A (A).......ECA
IPM Technology (A)......IPM                                      Energy Conversion (O)...ENER
Macrodyne Ind (A).......MCT          171 Office Machines         EIP Microwave (O).......EIPM
Pioneer Sys (A)........PAE
```

FIGURE 16-47
Predefined industry groups

Market Microscope, like Analyzer, provides access to DJN/R. Once the investor has downloaded historical data about a portfolio and other issues being considered for purchase, he or she can complete in-depth analysis, selecting up to 20 technical indicators from a list of 68 provided by DJ. These indicators help make decisions about buying and selling. Microscope is organized to deal with predefined industry groups of stocks as shown in figure 16-47. Users can also define their own groups of stocks to analyze.

Management

Kuhn decides these programs are more advanced than he needs. He decides to start with a portfolio management program. Ty buys Market Manager. Not surprisingly, this DJ product also connects with DJN/R. This program maintains a transaction audit trail, produces tax records, evaluates portfolios, and generates a variety of reports about the holdings in a series of portfolios. Kuhn is not a very experienced investor. Most of his holdings are in mutual funds in which he invests the same amount each month. He decides to follow the same strategy with several individual issues he will buy.

Tyrone buys many stocks, so he establishes four separate portfolios, one each for industrial, transportation, utility, and computer companies. We will examine six months of his computer portfolio.

Starting Market Manager

Each time Ty completes a transaction, he updates his files. To do this, he boots the Market Manager diskette, enters the date (figure 16-48), selects "portfolio maintenance" from the main menu (figure 16-49) and the appropriate choice from the secondary menu (figure 16-50).

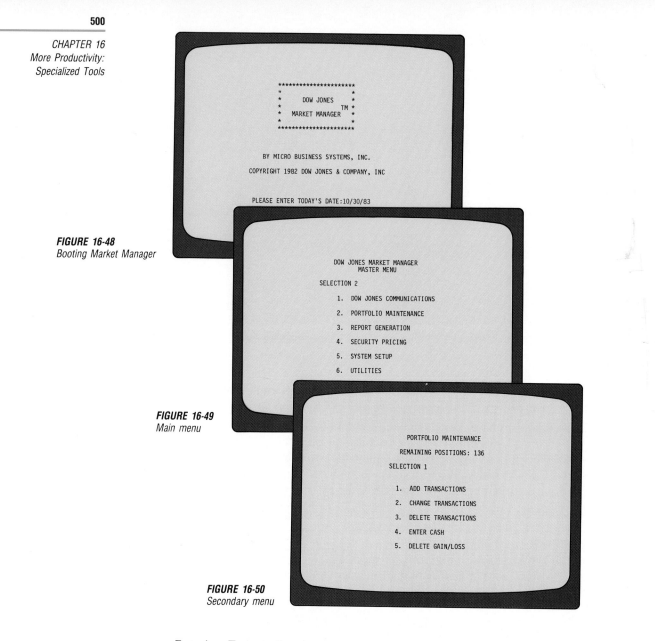

FIGURE 16-48
Booting Market Manager

FIGURE 16-49
Main menu

FIGURE 16-50
Secondary menu

Entering Transactions

When he selects "add transaction," he is presented with the screen in fig-ure 16-51. He enters the seven items of data required and the program calcu-lates the price per share. He is allowed to change any items. This is shown in figure 16-52 which tells us that on October 3, 1983, Ty bought 87 shares of Apple Computer, Inc. stock for $2012, a price of $23 1/8 per share.

Ty continues to enter his purchase transactions, one for IBM stock and one for Apple stock each month from October 1983 to March 1984. In April, he decides to sell all of his computer stock. He requests a printout of all the holdings in his computer portfolio, Portfolio D. This is shown in figure 16-53. According to this report, an immediate sale would mean a net profit of nearly $5000. Before the sale is consummated, this is called an *unrealized gain*.

Ty sells the stock in April. He enters the sale transaction just like the pur-

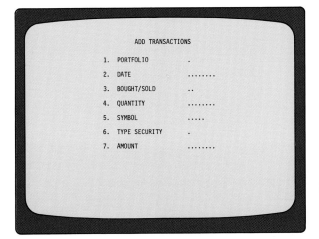

FIGURE 16-51
Transaction entry menu

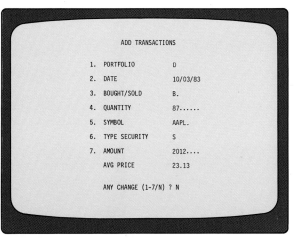

FIGURE 16-52
Transaction

FIGURE 16-53
Portfolio holdings

```
                          HOLDINGS BY PORTFOLIO

  TODAY'S DATE      3/30/84
  ================================================================================

  C         T
  O         Y
  D         P B                  =======TRANSACTION========   ====07/22/83=====  UNREALIZD   L
  E SYMBOL  E SS    DATE     QUANT    $COST     PRICE    $VALUE    PRICE    GAIN/LOSS   S
  - ------  - --  --------  -----   -------   -------   -------   ------   ---------   -

  D AAPL    S B    1/03/84    82     1,999     24.37     2,624      32          625    S
  D AAPL    S B   12/02/83    99     2,005     20.25     3,168      32        1,163    S
  D AAPL    S B   11/01/83    89     2,014     22.62     2,848      32          834    S
  D AAPL    S B   10/03/83    87     2,012     23.12     2,784      32          772    S
  D AAPL    S B    2/01/84    81     2,005     24.75     2,592      32          587    S
  D AAPL    S B    3/01/84    77     2,021     26.24     2,464      32          443    S


  *TOTAL AAPL          515    12,056              16,480                4,424

  D IBM     S B   12/02/83    17     2,021    118.88     2,108     124           87    S
  D IBM     S B   11/01/83    16     2,028    126.75     1,984     124          -44    S
  D IBM     S B    3/01/84    18     1,984    110.22     2,232     124          248    S
  D IBM     S B   10/03/83    16     2,030    126.87     1,984     124          -46    S
  D IBM     S B    1/03/84    16     1,952    122.00     1,984     124           32    S
  D IBM     S B    2/01/84    18     2,054    114.11     2,232     124          178    S


  *TOTAL IBM           101    12,069              12,524                  455


  VALUED SECURITIES LONG    616    24,125         29,004              4,879
  VALUED SECURITIES SHORT     0         0              0                  0
  CASH BALANCE = -24125
```

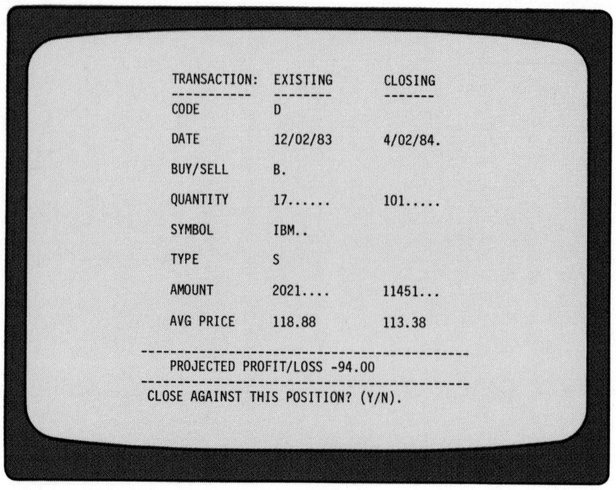

FIGURE 16-54
Unrealized profit/loss

```
TRANSACTION:   EXISTING        CLOSING
-----------    --------        -------
CODE           D

DATE           12/02/83        4/02/84.

BUY/SELL       B.

QUANTITY       17......        101.....

SYMBOL         IBM..

TYPE           S

AMOUNT         2021....        11451...

AVG PRICE      118.88          113.38

---------------------------------------------
 PROJECTED PROFIT/LOSS -94.00
---------------------------------------------
CLOSE AGAINST THIS POSITION? (Y/N).
```

chase except the B (Buy) in figure 16-52 is replaced by an S (Sell). Kuhn's first sale is for 101 shares of IBM stock, all he owns. The sale is compared against each purchase to show the impact on his assets. Figure 16-54 shows that Tyrone will lose $94 if he sells the 17 shares he bought in December, but he decides to sell anyway.

Generating Reports

After the sale is complete, Tyrone wants reports printed to help him prepare income tax forms. Figure 16-55 shows realized gains (actual profit or loss) instead of the unrealized (paper) gains shown in figure 16-53. Figure 16-56 shows all transactions he completed.

FIGURE 16-55
Realized profit/loss

REALIZED GAINS/LOSSES

C O D E	SYMBOL	QTY	PURCHASE DATE	PRICE	$COST	SALE DATE	PRICE	PROCEEDS	GAIN/LOSS	L / S
D	IBM	17	12/02/83	118.88	2021	4/02/84	113.35	1927	-94	S
D	IBM	18	3/01/84	110.22	1984	4/02/84	113.38	2041	57	S
D	IBM	18	2/01/84	114.11	2054	4/02/84	113.38	2041	-13	S
D	IBM	16	11/01/83	126.75	2028	4/02/84	113.37	1814	-214	S
D	IBM	16	10/03/83	126.87	2030	4/02/84	113.37	1814	-216	S
D	IBM	16	1/03/84	122.00	1952	4/02/84	113.37	1814	-138	S
D	AAPL	82	1/03/84	24.37	1999	4/02/84	24.74	2029	30	S
D	AAPL	99	12/02/83	20.25	2005	4/02/84	24.74	2450	445	S
D	AAPL	89	11/01/83	22.62	2014	4/02/84	24.75	2203	189	S
D	AAPL	87	10/03/83	23.12	2012	4/02/84	24.74	2153	141	S
D	AAPL	81	2/01/84	24.75	2005	4/02/84	24.75	2005	0	S
D	AAPL	77	3/01/84	26.24	2021	4/02/84	24.75	1906	-115	S
TOTALS		616			24125			24197	72	

```
                         YEAR-TO-DATE TRANSACTIONS

TODAYS DATE    4/30/84
======================================================================================

   DATE    CODE  TRANSACTION              DESCRIPTION                    AMOUNT
 ---------  ----  -----------  ------------------------------------    --------

 10/03/83    D   BUY          87 AAPL     @     23.13                      2012
 10/03/83    D   BUY          16 IBM      @    126.87                      2030
 11/01/83    D   BUY          16 IBM      @    126.75                      2028

 11/01/83    D   BUY          89 AAPL     @     22.63                      2014
 12/02/83    D   BUY          17 IBM      @    118.88                      2021
 12/02/83    D   BUY          99 AAPL     @     20.25                      2005
 1/03/84     D   BUY          82 AAPL     @     24.38                      1999
 1/03/84     D   BUY          16 IBM      @    122.00                      1952

 2/01/84     D   BUY          18 IBM      @    114.11                      2054
 2/01/84     D   BUY          81 AAPL     @     24.75                      2005
 3/01/84     D   BUY          18 IBM      @    110.22                      1984
 3/01/84     D   BUY          77 AAPL     @     26.25                      2021
 4/02/84     D   SELL         17 IBM      @    113.35                      1927

 4/02/84     D   SELL         18 IBM      @    113.39                      2041
 4/02/84     D   SELL         18 IBM      @    113.39                      2041
 4/02/84     D   SELL         16 IBM      @    113.37                      1814
 4/02/84     D   SELL         16 IBM      @    113.37                      1814
 4/02/84     D   SELL         16 IBM      @    113.37                      1814

 4/02/84     D   SELL         82 AAPL     @     24.74                      2029
 4/02/84     D   SELL         99 AAPL     @     24.75                      2450
 4/02/84     D   SELL         89 AAPL     @     24.75                      2203
 4/02/84     D   SELL         87 AAPL     @     24.75                      2153
 4/02/84     D   SELL         81 AAPL     @     24.75                      2005

 4/02/84     D   SELL         77 AAPL     @     24.75                      1906
```

FIGURE 16-56
Transaction summary

Ty reviews the reports he has printed to learn that waiting until April to sell the stock cost him about $4800. He should have taken his profits in March. A simple but important lesson can be learned from this. Use of a computer is no guarantee of winning. Human judgement and intuition still contribute heavily to human success stories.

Conclusion

As Ty Kuhn found out, market management programs help greatly with record keeping, but they do not help decide when to buy and sell. Tools for this purpose are the market analysis programs. These are very complex programs that require a great deal of skill to be used properly. They are powerful tools for the serious investor with the proper knowledge.

IDEA PROCESSORS

Idea processors help users organize their thoughts. They are useful for creating outlines of letters, reports, speeches, and other documents. Basically, idea processors are special-purpose word processors that automatically format infor-

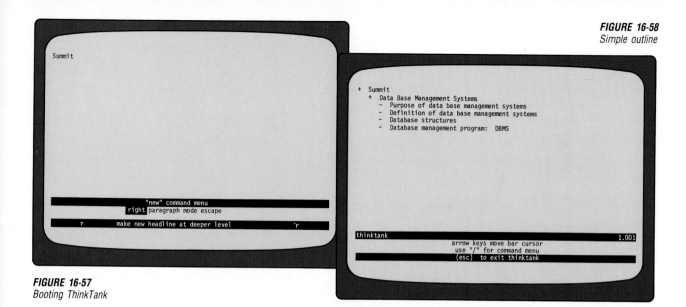

mation in outline form and provide limited capability to include paragraphs within the outline. They create text files that can then be used with many common word processors to expand an outline into a full blown article. The first idea processor, ThinkTank, was produced by Living Videotext. Fastware, Inc. also produces an idea processor called Thor.

ThinkTank, currently available for a range of machines including IBM PCs, Apple IIs and IIIs, and the Macintosh, not only produces an outline with up to 1000 levels of headings, it also can incorporate text under each heading. Thus, the program can be used for many short word processing tasks. Files created with ThinkTank can also be edited and expanded with many common word processors. With its search command and other powerful tools, ThinkTank can be used for many purposes. Among them are maintaining client records and preparing presentation outlines, memos, catalogs, resumes, and telephone directories.

Using ThinkTank

Morris Dehm is an expert in the use of databases in small business applications. A faculty member at the state university, he is in much demand as a speaker at Chambers of Commerce and other groups of business people. Most of his consulting contacts are made at these luncheons and breakfast meetings. Professor Dehm used ThinkTank to develop the presentation he makes. Here is the process he used.

Creating an Outline

After booting the ThinkTank diskette, Dehm sees the screen in figure 16-57. The summit is the top of the outline. The hyphen indicates that Mo hasn't entered any information yet. He selects "right" by typing R to enter the first headline of the outline. After a carriage return, he repeats the process for each succeeding headline. Figure 16-58 shows the outline after he has entered the major headline (Data Base Management Systems) and four subordinate ones. The plus sign preceding any headline indicates that it has subordinate headlines.

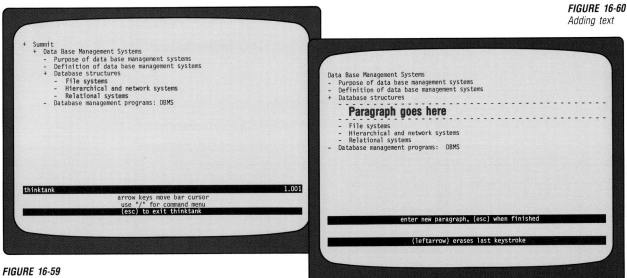

FIGURE 16-60
Adding text

FIGURE 16-59
Extending outline

Adding Text

Next, Morris must "fill out" the outline, providing more data for each of the topics listed. He extends the Database structures headline as he has done before, figure 16-59, deciding to add some text to the headline. The program presents the screen in figure 16-60. Mo types whatever he wishes and the revised outline appears in figure 16-61. Because the outline now has several levels of headlines, the screen shown has been scrolled to the right. Text data under any headline can be as long as two kilobytes (2048 characters).

Dehm continues this procedure with each headline, adding paragraphs and new headlines in a hierarchy as complex as he needs. One section of the outline, which requires four levels, is shown in figure 16-62.

Printing the Outline

Once Mo is satisfied with the outline, he can produce a printed copy. The program keeps him informed of progress with the display in figure 16-63. Sev-

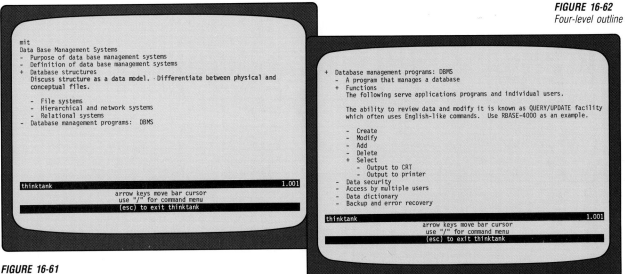

FIGURE 16-62
Four-level outline

FIGURE 16-61
Including a paragraph

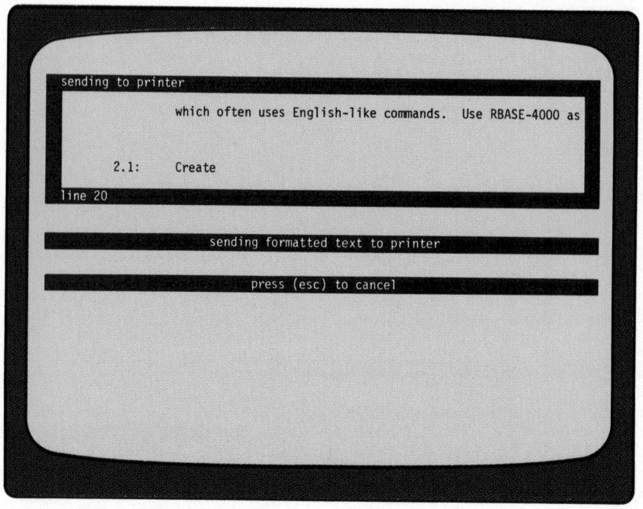

```
sending to printer

                which often uses English-like commands.  Use RBASE-4000 as

     2.1:     Create
line 20


          sending formatted text to printer

             press (esc) to cancel
```

FIGURE 16-63
Screen display of printing
operation

eral options are available to him. Figure 16-64 shows three of these printing options. The program also prints tables of contents as shown in figure 16-65. These may include only the major headlines or as many levels as Morris specifies.

Once he is satisfied with the outline, Dehm will save it to a diskette, where it will reside until he needs to revise it.

FIGURE 16-64
Three printing options
(A) Indented without line numbers
(B) Indented with line numbers
(C) Flush left with levels

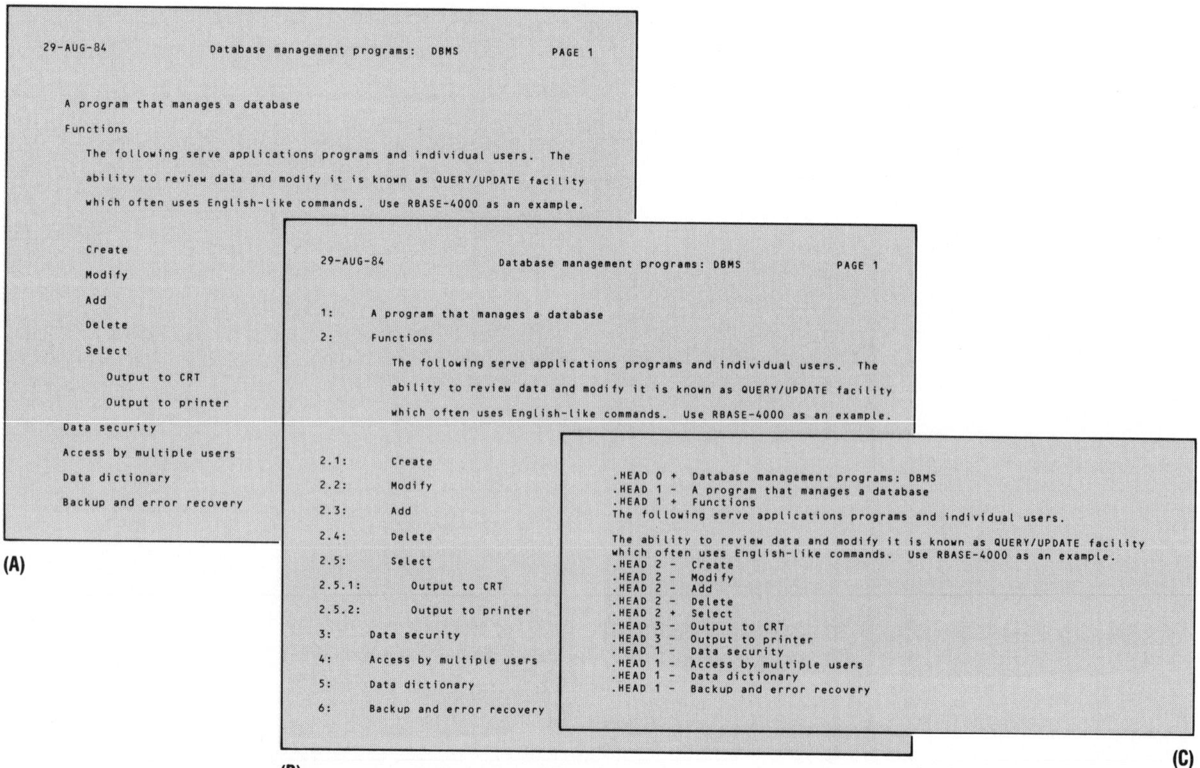

Conclusion

ThinkTank does much more than develop an outline with great ease. It allows one to look at only major headlines, thus placing the skeleton of an outline

```
29-AUG-84         Database management programs:  DBMS          PAGE 1


     A program that manages a database
     Functions
          The following serve applications programs and individual users.  The
          ability to review data and modify it is known as QUERY/UPDATE facility
          which often uses English-like commands.  Use RBASE-4000 as an example.


          Create
          Modify
          Add
          Delete
          Select
               Output to CRT
               Output to printer
     Data security
     Access by multiple users
     Data dictionary
     Backup and error recovery
```

(A)

```
29-AUG-84         Database management programs:  DBMS          PAGE 1


1:     A program that manages a database
2:     Functions
          The following serve applications programs and individual users.  The
          ability to review data and modify it is known as QUERY/UPDATE facility
          which often uses English-like commands.  Use RBASE-4000 as an example.

2.1:      Create
2.2:      Modify
2.3:      Add
2.4:      Delete
2.5:      Select
2.5.1:         Output to CRT
2.5.2:         Output to printer
3:     Data security
4:     Access by multiple users
5:     Data dictionary
6:     Backup and error recovery
```

(B)

```
.HEAD 0 +  Database management programs: DBMS
.HEAD 1 -  A program that manages a database
.HEAD 1 +  Functions
The following serve applications programs and individual users.

The ability to review data and modify it is known as QUERY/UPDATE facility
which often uses English-like commands.  Use RBASE-4000 as an example.
.HEAD 2 -  Create
.HEAD 2 -  Modify
.HEAD 2 -  Add
.HEAD 2 -  Delete
.HEAD 2 +  Select
.HEAD 3 -  Output to CRT
.HEAD 3 -  Output to printer
.HEAD 1 -  Data security
.HEAD 1 -  Access by multiple users
.HEAD 1 -  Data dictionary
.HEAD 1 -  Backup and error recovery
```

(C)

```
29-AUG-84              Database management programs: DBMS              PAGE i

                                                                         PAGE

A program that manages a database. . . . . . . . . . . . . . . . . . . .   1
Functions. . . . . . . . . . . . . . . . . . . . . . . . . . . . . . . .   1
   Create. . . . . . . . . . . . . . . . . . . . . . . . . . . . . . . .   1
   Modify. . . . . . . . . . . . . . . . . . . . . . . . . . . . . . . .   1
   Add . . . . . . . . . . . . . . . . . . . . . . . . . . . . . . . . .   1
   Delete. . . . . . . . . . . . . . . . . . . . . . . . . . . . . . . .   1
   Select. . . . . . . . . . . . . . . . . . . . . . . . . . . . . . . .   1
      Output to CRT. . . . . . . . . . . . . . . . . . . . . . . . . . .   1
      Output to printer. . . . . . . . . . . . . . . . . . . . . . . . .   1
Data security. . . . . . . . . . . . . . . . . . . . . . . . . . . . . .   1
Access by multiple users . . . . . . . . . . . . . . . . . . . . . . . .   1
Data dictionary. . . . . . . . . . . . . . . . . . . . . . . . . . . . .   1
Backup and error recovery. . . . . . . . . . . . . . . . . . . . . . . .   1
```

(A)

```
29-AUG-84              Database management programs: DBMS              PAGE i

                                                                         PAGE

A program that manages a database. . . . . . . . . . . . . . . . . . . .   1
Functions. . . . . . . . . . . . . . . . . . . . . . . . . . . . . . . .   1
Data security. . . . . . . . . . . . . . . . . . . . . . . . . . . . . .   1
Access by multiple users . . . . . . . . . . . . . . . . . . . . . . . .   1
Data dictionary. . . . . . . . . . . . . . . . . . . . . . . . . . . . .   1
Backup and error recovery. . . . . . . . . . . . . . . . . . . . . . . .   1
```

(B)

FIGURE 16-65
Printing the table of contents which can be shown to any depth (A) Four levels (B) One level

on the screen. Any of these categories can be expanded to show the entire hierarchy underneath it. This is done with one keystroke. The program automatically date-stamps each outline so we always know the most current version. The program can search for a phrase, either replacing it automatically or not as the user sees fit. Outlines can be reorganized with relative ease, moving items and changing their levels as necessary. The program also has a limited editing facility. Most important, particularly for a rapidly changing field, ThinkTank allows the user to update an outline easily.

Perhaps it seems that ThinkTank and other idea processors are just like word processors. In many respects they are. Their functions are all word processing ones but lack many of the standard operations available in all word processors. On the other hand, they do what typical word processors don't, they handle the outline form with ease.

PROGRAM GENERATORS

Despite the great number of software packages sold to businesses every day, there probably will always be a need for specialized programs. As we have seen in earlier chapters, the cost of developing such programs can be prohibitive. In the early 1980s, programs were developed to write other programs. In essence, these *program generators* take the requirements of a particular application and prepare a program to meet them. They still require users to define a problem thoroughly in terms of its solution, but they eliminate the time-consuming and error-prone task of coding.

Although program generators are advertised as programs anyone can use, this probably is not true. The fact is that no one can use a computer to solve a problem unless he or she can first solve it without one. For example, one cannot write a simple program to prepare a report from a data file without knowing how the file is organized.

On the other hand, program generators, as tools for people with programming knowledge, can be great productivity builders. In writing this book, we experimented with The Last One, an early microcomputer program generator that builds BASIC programs. We established a problem and defined the logic—steps that must be taken whether we use a generator or write the program from scratch. Then the experiment began. Coding and debugging the program by traditional means took about ten hours. The program generator took less than four.

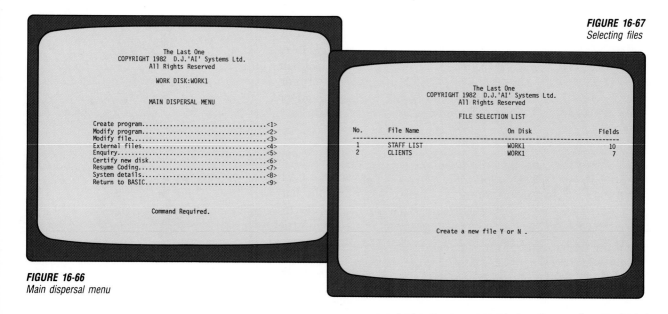

FIGURE 16-67
Selecting files

FIGURE 16-66
Main dispersal menu

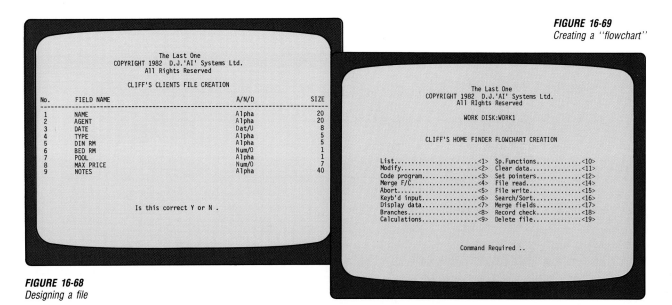

FIGURE 16-69
Creating a ''flowchart''

FIGURE 16-68
Designing a file

Using The Last One

Cliff Dweller uses The Last One (TLO) to write a computerized homefinder service. The program will list all clients and their desires—number of bedrooms, separate dining room, pool, house or condominium, and so forth. Then, when a home comes on the market, he will enter its description into the computer which lists all interested clients. He knows this could be done with a database program, but he wants something special for advertising purposes.

Defining Files

After designing the logic of the program, Cliff sits down at his computer and boots the TLO disk. He selects "Create program" from the first menu presented, figure 16-66, then tells the program that he will require files. He is presented with a list of existing files and given the option of using them or creating new ones, figure 16-67. He chooses CLIFF'S CLIENTS as a file name. The program then asks Cliff to define the fields in each record of CLIFF'S CLIENTS. There are nine. He gives each field a name and length and decides whether its contents will be alphabetic, numeric, or a date, figure 16-68. Dweller next specifies that this will be the only file used for this program.

Creating a ''Flowchart''

After he has defined all of the files, Cliff is presented with another menu, figure 16-69. This one is called the FLOWCHART CREATION MENU although it actually creates pseudocode instead of a flowchart.

Cliff wants to make his program easy to use, so he decides to make it menu driven. He selects a three-option menu (data entry, data retrieval, and end) then continues with 16 more pseudocode statements, figure 16-70.

In statement 2, Dweller will begin the data entry phase of the program. Wanting to add new records to the end of the file, he sets the file pointer there. Each time he uses the file, Cliff will have to set the pointer. Cliff con-

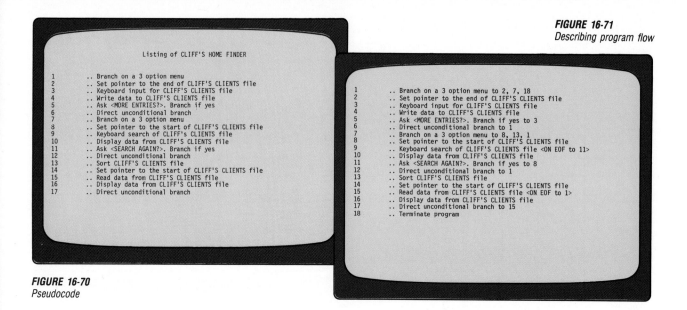

FIGURE 16-71
Describing program flow

FIGURE 16-70
Pseudocode

Listing of CLIFF'S HOME FINDER

```
1    .. Branch on a 3 option menu
2    .. Set pointer to the end of CLIFF'S CLIENTS file
3    .. Keyboard input for CLIFF'S CLIENTS file
4    .. Write data to CLIFF'S CLIENTS file
5    .. Ask <MORE ENTRIES?>. Branch if yes
6    .. Direct unconditional branch
7    .. Branch on a 3 option menu
8    .. Set pointer to the start of CLIFF'S CLIENTS file
9    .. Keyboard search of CLIFF'S CLIENTS file
10   .. Display data from CLIFF'S CLIENTS file
11   .. Ask <SEARCH AGAIN?>. Branch if yes
12   .. Direct unconditional branch
13   .. Sort CLIFF'S CLIENTS file
14   .. Set pointer to the start of CLIFF'S CLIENTS file
15   .. Read data from CLIFF'S CLIENTS file
16   .. Display data from CLIFF'S CLIENTS file
17   .. Direct unconditional branch
```

```
1    .. Branch on a 3 option menu to 2, 7, 18
2    .. Set pointer to the end of CLIFF'S CLIENTS file
3    .. Keyboard input for CLIFF'S CLIENTS file
4    .. Write data to CLIFF'S CLIENTS file
5    .. Ask <MORE ENTRIES?>. Branch if yes to 3
6    .. Direct unconditional branch to 1
7    .. Branch on a 3 option menu to 8, 13, 1
8    .. Set pointer to the start of CLIFF'S CLIENTS file
9    .. Keyboard search of CLIFF'S CLIENTS file <ON EOF to 11>
10   .. Display data from CLIFF'S CLIENTS file
11   .. Ask <SEARCH AGAIN?>. Branch if yes to 8
12   .. Direct unconditional branch to 1
13   .. Sort CLIFF'S CLIENTS file
14   .. Set pointer to the start of CLIFF'S CLIENTS file
15   .. Read data from CLIFF'S CLIENTS file <ON EOF to 1>
16   .. Display data from CLIFF'S CLIENTS file
17   .. Direct unconditional branch to 15
18   .. Terminate program
```

tinues to write. Statements 2 through 6 correspond to the first menu choice. Statements 7 through 17 correspond to the second (there is a three-option menu within this section as well). Inasmuch as the last option in statement 1 is to end, there are no statements for this option.

After completing the pseudocode, Cliff must describe the program flow. For instance, he tells the computer that the three options on the first menu branch to lines 2, 7, and 18 (the computer added a new line, "terminate program."). All of the branches are shown in figure 16-71. TLO even knows to ask what to do if it runs out of data when reading a file, called EOF or End-of-file (see line 9).

Designing CRT Displays

Next, TLO allows Cliff to design each screen display in this program. It takes about five minutes per display while standard programming can take

FIGURE 16-73
Resulting program: Screen 2

```
              CLIFF DWELLER'S HANDY HOME FINDER SERVICE
              ==========================================


         ENTER NEW CLIENT...........................<1>
         MATCH HOME TO CLIENT.......................<2>
         END PROCESSING.............................<3>




                    COMMAND REQUIRED 1
```

FIGURE 16-72
Resulting program: Screen 1

```
                      ENTER NEW CLIENT DATA
                      =====================

         NAME         JONES MARY
         AGENT        SMITH
         DATE         07.21.86
         TYPE         HOUSE
         DIN RM       SEP
         BED RM       3
         POOL         N
         MAX PRICE    100000
         NOTES



                      MORE ENTRIES? Y
```

an hour or more. Cliff's initial menu is shown in figure 16-72. His data entry screen and search screens are shown in figures 16-73 through 16-75.

Coding the Program

Finally, TLO is ready to create the BASIC program, figure 16-76. After a few moments, Cliff and his staff can use their new homefinder system.

All of the agents take turns entering their clients into the system and they are ready to go. When a new listing becomes available, Cliff enters it into the

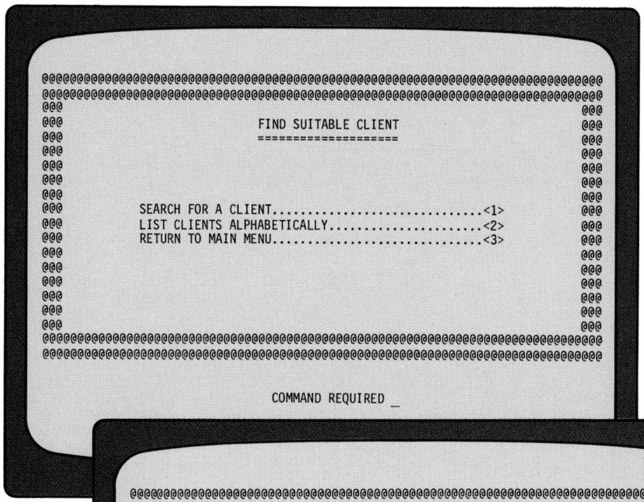

FIGURE 16-74
Resulting program: Screen 3

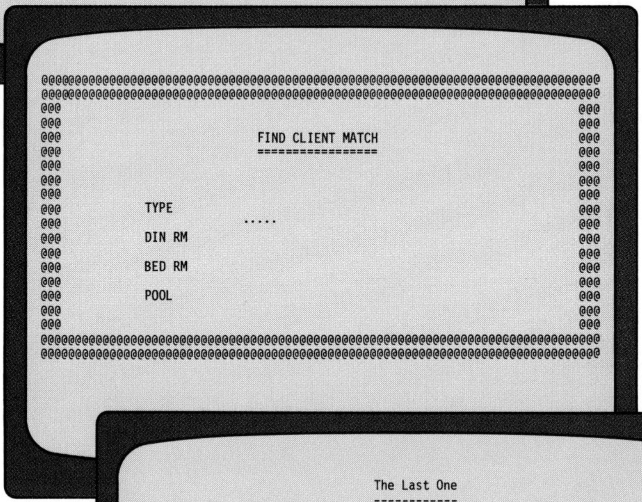

FIGURE 16-75
Resulting program: Screen 4

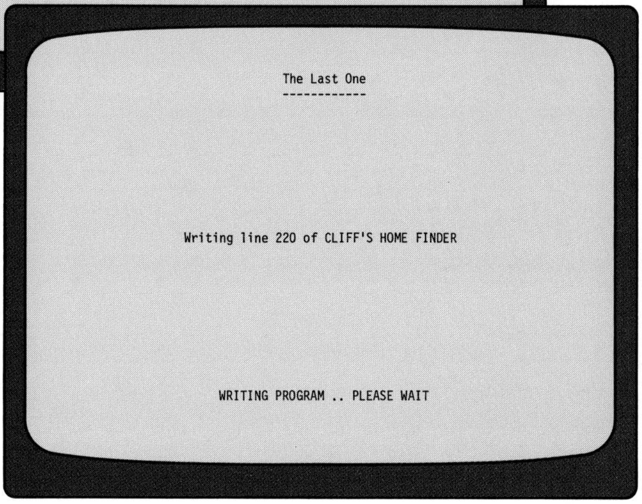

FIGURE 16-76
TLO created BASIC program

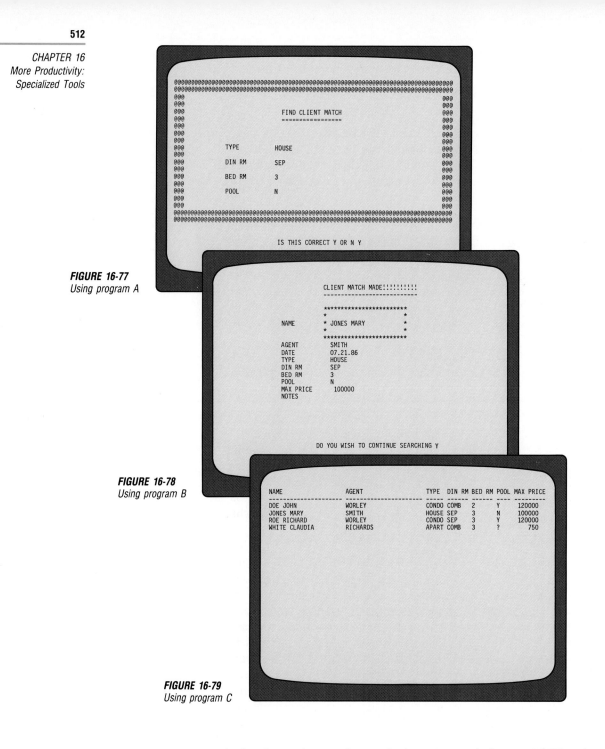

FIGURE 16-77
Using program A

FIGURE 16-78
Using program B

FIGURE 16-79
Using program C

computer which selects clients who might be interested, figures 16-77 and 16-78. Cliff also keeps a list of all clients, which the program prepares, figure 16-79.

Conclusion

Program generators will provide programs for less common or specialized business applications. They will become easier to use, approaching natural language input, as advances are made in artificial intelligence. For the foreseeable future, however, they will require some knowledge of programming concepts by people who create programs with them.

INTEGRATED SYSTEMS

In a late 1970s survey of managers who used microcomputers, Booz, Allen and Hamilton, a management consulting firm, concluded that above all, managers wanted a single program to perform more than one task.[4] Thus was born the world of integrated software with the development of MBA from Context Management Systems. Soon after, Lotus Development Corporation announced 1-2-3 which rapidly became the most popular business software package in the history of microcomputers. This program included database, graphics, and spreadsheet capabilities in one program.

Demand soon spread for word processing and communications. Lotus released a new program, Symphony, which included all five modules and the ability to add spelling checkers and additional software. On the same day, Ashton-Tate, producers of dBASE II and dBASE III, introduced Framework, another integrated package. This program included the features of Symphony but added an idea processor for outlines. It appears that future versions of integrated systems will include other business productivity products such as time and project managers.

Types of Integrated Systems

There are two ways to form an integrated system. We can build a series of independent programs that use a common data base or we can build a single program that performs many functions. The Visi series—VisiCalc, VisiPlot/Visi-Trend, and so forth—and the PFS series—PFS:File, PFS:Report, PFS:Write, etc.—are examples of multiple-program integrated systems, while 1-2-3, Symphony, and Framework are single-program systems.

In the first case, less RAM is required and modules can have great capabilities. In the latter case, large computers are necessary, typically with 256 kilobytes of RAM or more, and the segments of the program tend to be limited in their capabilities. For instance, we can do less with the graphics in 1-2-3 than with a stand-alone program. In the first case, each program tends to have its own command structure requiring the user to master several sets of instructions. In the second case, there is a common command structure, making it easier for the user to master. On the other hand, single program integrated systems tend to be very complex, so there is still a lot to learn.

Early attempts at integration produced only multiple-program systems. Because of size requirements, programs like 1-2-3 had to await the introduction of the 16-bit microprocessor. Thus, it was the entry of IBM into the microcomputer market with its 16-bit PC that started the development of these very popular programs.

The Structure of an Integrated System

Integrated systems usually base their operations on one of the modules. Consider two products that have received considerable publicity: Symphony and Framework. Lotus Development Corporation's Symphony is based on a spreadsheet and all other functions including word processing, graphics, communications, and data base management operate within the spreadsheet context.

Ashton-Tate's Framework organizes its functions around an idea processor.

Symphony uses one large spreadsheet for the entire document and cannot, therefore, permit the loading of separate spreadsheets into memory concurrently. Framework uses separate outlines in each frame; however, specific linkages must be defined to cause a change in one outline to be reflected in the others.

The systems differ in other ways as well. Symphony is a very powerful "number cruncher." Framework deals with text much better because of the close working relationship between word processors and idea processors. Its hierarchical form and the outlining module let the user shuffle individual sections of a document while viewing its entire structure. Framework is particularly useful for major reorganizations of large documents. So we can see that Symphony is probably better for analysts, while Framework is better for writers.

Symphony does not integrate printing of text and graphics though there is promise of add-on programs to accomplish this. Adding this capability, according to Lotus, would slow the program down too much. Framework does permit fully integrated printing.

Introduced in the Fall of 1984, the Software Group's Enable represents another approach to integrating several applications into one program. Instead of being a spreadsheet program that also does word processing, data base, and communication (Symphony) or an idea processor that also does the others (Framework), Enable uses five separate programs—word processing, telecommunications, spreadsheet, graphics, and data base management—under the control of a driver program called the Master Control Module (MCM). The MCM operates in such a manner that the user can view several applications at once through screen windows and transfer data from one to the other with great ease. The MCM also makes use of virtual memory techniques which reduce the total amount of memory required for the program. For this reason, Enable runs on a smaller machine than either Symphony or Framework.

It is clear from these paragraphs that substantial differences exist between the various programs currently available. It is likely that publishers of integrated systems will continue to add capabilities to their products. It is also clear that for many businesses, one integrated program may be a better solution to the firm's data processing needs than half a dozen or more separate programs that cannot share data.

Using an Integrated System

When her father Mandy died, Eta Bulls inherited the supermarket chain. Heeding her father's advice to emphasize advertising and promotion, Eta has recently hired a marketing expert, Chauncy Gardiner. Chauncy's first assignment is to evaluate the relative effectiveness of three advertising media in the Phoenix region: the local daily newspaper, a throw-away, once-a-week newspaper, and weekly direct-mail advertising.

Assessing the Media

For each of the three media, Chauncy places an advertisement offering a substantial discount for those who clip out a coupon and bring it to one of Eta Bull's stores. Each coupon is coded so that Chauncy can tell in which of the three media it appeared.

Because the throw-away is delivered every Thursday, Chauncy decides to place his ad in the daily newspaper on the same day and to deliver the direct-mail matter to the post office on Wednesday, so that every household will receive the three ads (one from each medium) on the same day.

As the returns come in, Chauncy records them, using a spreadsheet template he developed using Enable, an integrated data processing program, figure 16-80. Figure 16-80 shows part of the entries for the first week of Chauncy's two-week, experimental advertising campaign.

Using the Spreadsheet

The beauty of the Enable program, in Chauncy's opinion, is its ability to join various kinds of data processing functions. As he works up his presentation for Eta, he will take advantage of the program's ability to integrate spreadsheet, word processing, and graphics functions into one memorandum which he feels is bound to assure his rapid climb up the corporate ladder.

Once all of the returns are in from the promotional experiment, Chauncy completes his worksheet, figure 16-81. After reviewing it, he is most confident that the local newspaper promises the best way in which to spend Bull's advertising budget.

His next step is to compose a memorandum to Eta that will announce his convictions and, at the same time, illustrate why he has come to his conclusions.

Text and Graphics

When his spreadsheet is finished, he uses Enable to draft a memorandum to Eta, figure 16-82. At the appropriate point in his exposition, Chauncy calls up the spreadsheet and includes it in his memorandum, figure 16-83. Having done that, it is a simple matter to use the graphics functions of Enable to include a bar graph of the coupon return results as well.

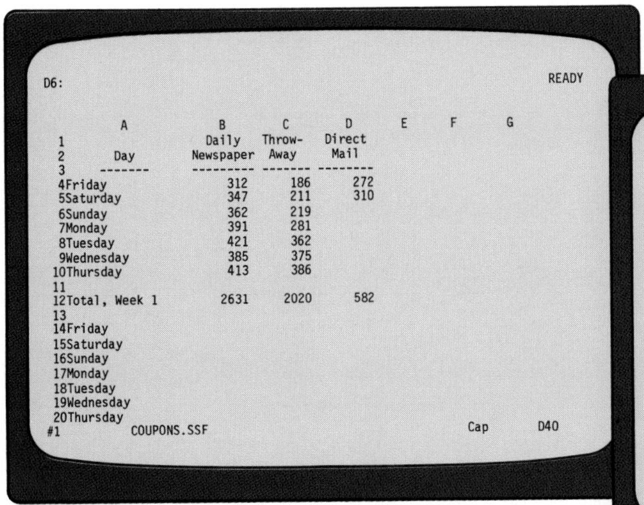

D6: READY

	A	B	C	D	E	F	G
1		Daily	Throw-	Direct			
2	Day	Newspaper	Away	Mail			
3	-------	---------	-------	--------			
4	Friday	312	186	272			
5	Saturday	347	211	310			
6	Sunday	362	219				
7	Monday	391	281				
8	Tuesday	421	362				
9	Wednesday	385	375				
10	Thursday	413	386				
11							
12	Total, Week 1	2631	2020	582			
13							
14	Friday						
15	Saturday						
16	Sunday						
17	Monday						
18	Tuesday						
19	Wednesday						
20	Thursday						

#1 COUPONS.SSF Cap D40

FIGURE 16-80
First week entries

FIGURE 16-81
Completed worksheet

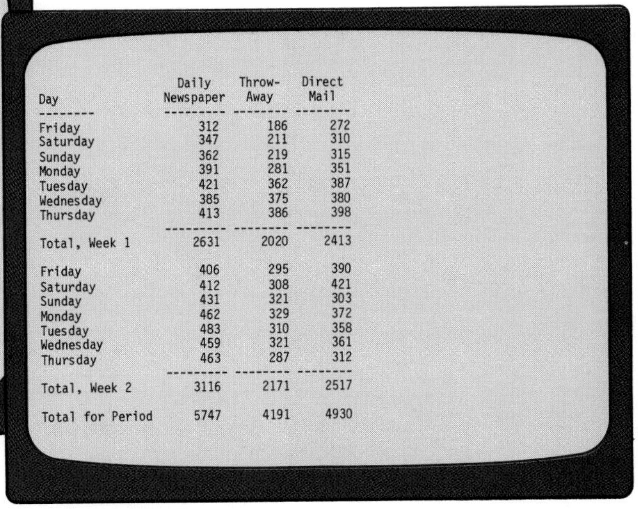

Day	Daily Newspaper	Throw-Away	Direct Mail
Friday	312	186	272
Saturday	347	211	310
Sunday	362	219	315
Monday	391	281	351
Tuesday	421	362	387
Wednesday	385	375	380
Thursday	413	386	398
Total, Week 1	2631	2020	2413
Friday	406	295	390
Saturday	412	308	421
Sunday	431	321	303
Monday	462	329	372
Tuesday	483	310	358
Wednesday	459	321	361
Thursday	463	287	312
Total, Week 2	3116	2171	2517
Total for Period	5747	4191	4930

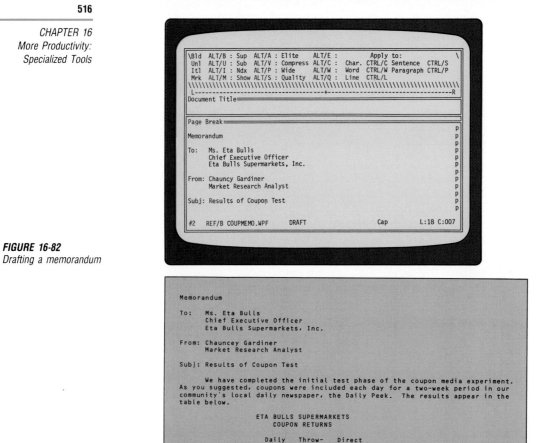

FIGURE 16-82
Drafting a memorandum

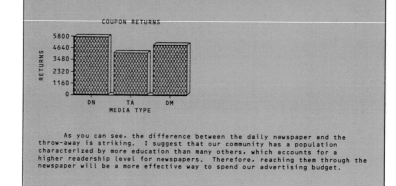

FIGURE 16-83
The finished memorandum

Admitting to himself that his memo to Eta may be something of an over-kill, Chauncy nevertheless prints it up and sends it off.

Chauncy's simple assignment illustrates the extraordinary flexibility that modern computer systems offer to those who must manipulate data in a manner that best serves those who must interpret them for decision-making purposes. He is able, thanks to his program, to express the results of his experiment in a number of different ways: in writing; as a table of figures; and as a graphical presentation which illustrates visually the relative effectiveness of the three advertising media options in question.

Conclusion

Using an integrated program such as Enable is not difficult, but it does require a few hours to learn. Once this initial investment in learning time has been made, the rewards in terms of increased personal productivity deliver a many-fold return.

SUMMARY

There you have it. The big six and eight other business productivity tools. The big six include *data base management, communications, word processing, accounting systems, spreadsheets,* and *graphics.* Each is described in its own chapter.

This chapter discussed the other business productivity tools. Eight of these tools fall roughly into three categories: management, analysis, and creativity.

There are two types of management programs. *Project management* programs schedule activities and keep track of resources when managing processes with clearcut beginnings and endings. *Time management* programs schedule time, keeping track of appointments and things to do. Time managers often include telephone modules to maintain phone records and provide automatic dialing service.

The chapter also investigated three analysis programs. *Statistical packages* help analyze data using standard statistical techniques. *Modeling* software solves systems of equations that describe business and other situations. *Expert systems* use preprogrammed information and their "experience" to analyze situations described by the user. Expert systems can help determine optimum strategies in sales, negotiating, and other situations.

One of the programs bridges management and analysis. *Investment portfolio* programs keep records of investments, receive current price quotations, and analyze markets to help investors make security purchase and sales decisions.

The final category, programs to aid productivity, includes two examples. *Idea processors* formulate and manipulate text information in outlines. *Program generators* create computer program code from a description of the problem and the desired results.

Various of the big six and the little eight can be combined to form *integrated systems,* the most popular software of the mid 1980s. Integrated systems perform many different functions on the same set of data. The results of one process are available to the other functions. As time goes on, we expect to see more and more integration with programs containing more segments, eventually leading to a complete computer system with hardware, operating system, and programs self-contained.

KEY TERMS

artificial intelligence
critical path analysis
descriptive statistics
expert system
heuristic

idea processor
inferential statistics
integrated system
investment portfolio
    management

model
program generator
project management
statistical analysis
time management

REVIEW QUESTIONS

1. The big six business programs include _____, _____, _____, _____, _____, and _____.
2. Identify two management tools among the little eight.
3. Identify three analysis tools among the little eight.
4. Identify two creativity tools among the little eight.
5. Into what categories might investment portfolio programs be placed?
6. Project management programs identify activities whose timely completion is essential to the success of a project. These activities fall on the _____.
7. What is the advantage of microcomputer project management software over its mainframe counterpart?
8. What functions should a time management program accomplish?
9. What is the basis for statistical analysis?
10. The two categories of statistics are _____ and _____.
11. What two methods are used for solving modeling problems? How are they different?
12. On what three facts are expert systems dealing with personality analysis based?
13. Name three functions of investment portfolio management programs.
14. The _____ is a special-purpose word processor.
15. Describe the output of an idea processor.
16. Under what circumstances should a program generator be used?
17. What is the advantage of using integrated software instead of separate programs for each data processing function?
18. What functions are included in the popular integrated systems?

THOUGHT QUESTIONS

1. Of the fifteen categories of programs discussed in this book, which is probably the greatest productivity builder? Why?
2. Select one program from each of the three categories in this chapter. Describe how it might be used in a business environment. Describe its effects on productivity.
3. Of the fifteen types of programs, which are of primary benefit to executives and which are of primary benefit to support personnel? Are any of equal benefit to both groups? Justify your answers.

Point Counterpoint

Graphics: The Way We Really Think?

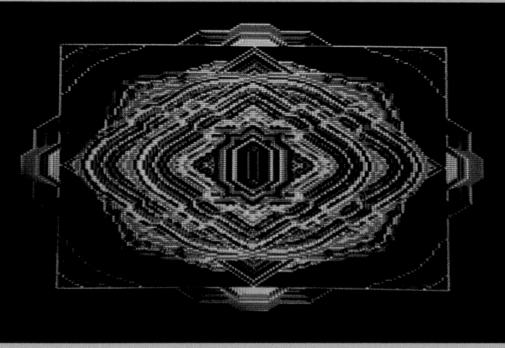

(Courtesy Synapse Software)

This chapter reviewed nine productivity tools in detail. One of those, ThinkTank, and other so-called idea processors have been hailed as the most significant software development since the spreadsheet. Indeed, as a representative of that genre, ThinkTank was named Software Product of the Year in *InfoWorld*'s 1985 annual award issue.[5]

It's no wonder. Idea processors help us organize thoughts. The ability to record ideas as they occur and to organize them easily for presentation to others increases personal productivity markedly. In describing the use of one such program, The Idea Processor, Paula Giese, President of a Minneapolis consulting firm specializing in information services for law firms, reports enthusiastically that

> Good lawyers can increase their leverage from the program by storing and referencing their past work and becoming adept in mustering everything relevant to the matter at hand. The text data management system employed in The Idea Processor can help you

improve the quality of your work, not just the speed.

> For knowledge workers, personal computers represent the opposite of office automation. They provide aids to working more intelligently rather than breaking tasks down into automated routines that can be done without thought.[6]

Most of us, as students, have prepared outlines for papers and reports. Our teachers give us course and lecture outlines. There's no question that the outline is indispensable for organizing thoughts.

But our teachers also draw on the chalkboard and use films, overhead transparencies, and physical models to illustrate ideas, and so do we. In 1953, James Watson and Francis Crick used a physical model to visualize the structure of the DNA molecule and revolutionized modern biology. It has been argued that human thought is more visual and relational than it is textual. That's why this book has so many figures. No less a luminary than Albert Einstein wrote that

The physical entities which seem to serve as elements in thought are certain signs and more or less clear images which can be "voluntarily" reproduced and combined...Conventional words or other signs have to be sought laboriously only in a secondary stage, when the mentioned associative play is sufficiently established and can be reproduced at will.[7]

In other words, ideas and concepts come first. Words to describe them and the organization of the words come, with great labor, afterward.

Can we use computers to develop ideas without the use of words, as Watson and Crick did using brass and wire? We must, argues Bill Benzon, Professor at Rensselaer Polytechnic Institute. He uses Apple's Macintosh and MacPic, a file of screen images, to express concepts and relationships, much as the classroom teacher does when using the chalkboard.

> Writing and drawing provide external support for thought...Learning the mechanics of writing—how to form the letters or use a keyboard—is relatively easy...However, images, whether two or three-dimensional, are different. Becoming proficient in the mere mechanics of freehand drawing...is difficult.

> By making it easy for us to create images and work with them, the Macintosh can help us to think...We have a large number of proverbs and countless stories, such as Aesop's fables, which we learn and use for thinking...Why not have a pool of images that we can use in the same way?

The main problem, Benzon continues, is that writing and drawing are two different skills. Yet we need both in order to conceive of ideas and express them to others. Computers with powerful graphics capability will, he asserts, "...lead to deeper thinking and more effective communication. It is easy—and it is fun."[8]

QUESTIONS

1. Make a short list of proverbs, catch phrases, and slogans we use frequently to express complex thoughts. "A picture is worth a thousand words" is an overworked example.
2. Write a description of how to steer an automobile without using the words "clockwise" and "counterclockwise." What communicative function do those words provide?
3. How many human emotions can you depict using a simple happy face sketch with eyebrows? Here are a couple of examples:

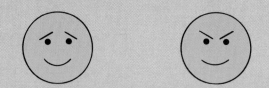

Chapter Five investigated the characteristics of that part of the complete computer system that does the actual data processing work: the central processing unit, or CPU. In operation, a computer system reads data from any of a number of input devices. These data are placed into the primary memory of the CPU. Also stored in memory is the program, a set of sequential instructions that control the computer's operation. The arithmetic/logic unit of the CPU performs the arithmetic and logical manipulations on the input data to prepare the output results. These results are then transferred to primary memory for eventual output.

All of the activity of the CPU and the input/output devices is controlled by the CPU's control unit. As figure 5-3 (Chapter Five) illustrates, the primary memory of the CPU is the heart of the hardware system. In it resides the program of instructions that controls the data processing application. Also in it are two buffers: one for input data; the other for output data.

This appendix traces the operations of preparing a computer program, loading it into primary memory, and executing it. The discussion uses a simulated computer, the DELRAM computer, which was designed specifically to illustrate how digital computers operate. Additional information, including programming exercises for the DELRAM computer can be found in the supplementary study materials for this text. The DELRAM computer is not hypothetical. It is operational and programs prepared for it may be executed on either IBM PC computers or Apple II computers.

THE DELRAM COMPUTER

Figure A-1 shows the DELRAM computer. The central processing unit has primary storage containing 64 separate memory locations. Each memory location can contain one unit of data: a value or a series of alphabetic or special characters. The values are decimal numbers. The alphabetic characters include all those from A to Z in our alphabet. The special characters include such things as asterisks (*), question marks (?), pound signs (#), and so on. In short, each memory location can contain either a number or a series of nonnumeric characters.

Each memory location is identified by a memory *address*, a number that uniquely identifies each location or cell from all the others. Memory addresses for the DELRAM computer range from 00 to 63. It's important to distinguish the numerical address of a memory location from the contents of that location. Thus, memory cell 46 may contain the value 72.76 or it may contain the characters HI THERE! There is no relationship between the address of a memory location and its contents. The address serves only to permit retrieving the contents of a memory cell for processing and storing the results of processing into a memory cell. Memory addresses provide a means of keeping track of things. They have no more relation to the contents of a memory cell than does the street number to the occupants of a house.

The DELRAM computer arithmetic/logic unit consists of an *accumulator*. The accumulator is a specialized unit of memory used to perform arithmetic and logical operations. Using the accumulator, the computer can perform the arithmetic operations of addition, subtraction, multiplication, and division. If the accumulator contains a value, for example, the computer multiplies the accumulator contents by the contents of some

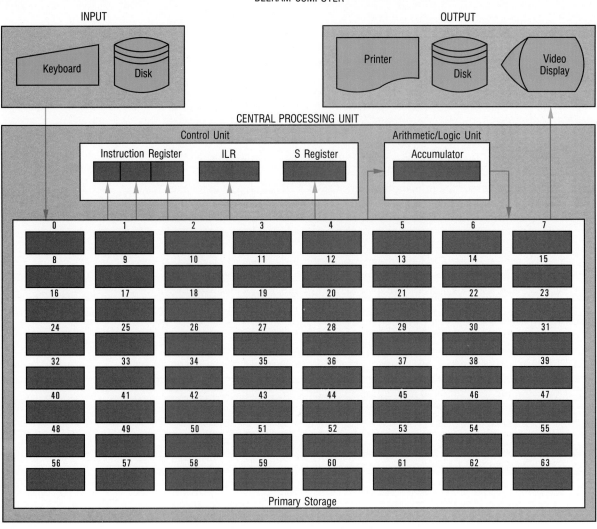

FIGURE A-1
DELRAM computer

memory cell. The product is contained in the accumulator. For logical operations, the computer can compare the contents of the accumulator with some specified value.

The accumulator, which is used for arithmetic and logical operations, is a type of *register*. In the CPU, a register is a specialized, small unit of memory with circuitry designed to perform certain operations such as adding and comparing. Registers are also used for the temporary storage of data being processed.

Programs enter memory from a disk storage unit or may be typed in directly from the keyboard. As is usual with computer operations, programs are prepared and tested before any attempt is made to execute them using actual data. Once the program has been thoroughly checked, it is stored, *saved* is the trade term, in secondary storage, almost always disk. DELRAM computer programs are stored on magnetic disk so that once a program is entered into the computer system, it can be loaded directly into memory from the disk mechanism without having to retype it.

Input data enter the DELRAM computer memory from the keyboard. Output is displayed on a video display terminal or is printed on paper.

The control unit coordinates all of the components of the computer system. For the DELRAM computer, the control unit has an *instruction location register (ILR)* which contains the memory address of the next instruction to be executed. Modern computers are *stored program* computers, meaning that the programs that control them are stored in primary memory. As with other computers, each cell in DELRAM's memory contains one instruction. Another part of the control unit, the *instruction register*, contains the instruction being executed at the time.

The process works like this. The control unit fetches an instruction from the address specified by the ILR and puts it into the instruction register. That instruction is analyzed and the required operations are carried out. Meanwhile, the value in the ILR is incremented by one so that the next sequential memory address shows in it. When execution of the current instruction is completed, the control unit consults the ILR for the address of the next instruction to be loaded into the instruction register. In this fashion, the computer fetches and executes instructions sequentially, exactly in the order in which they appear in memory by their cell addresses.

If this seems laborious to you, be comforted by the fact that computers are exceptionally stupid. They do one thing at a time, exactly as directed by the contents of their control unit registers. Computers do this tremendously quickly, which makes them look smart. A computer that can perform the process described above several million times per second will look much more clever than it really is.

A DELRAM MACHINE LANGUAGE PROGRAM

Because computers operate under the control of programs, we can best understand how they work by seeing how a computer executes a program. We'll use a program prepared by I. William Cell, top salesman for Pets and Unusual Pet Procurements, Inc. (PUPPI) as our example. Will wants a program for PUPPI's DELRAM computer that will calculate his sales commission earnings each week. He earns various commission rates on sales of different pets. His sales for the past week, which he'll use to test his program, are listed in figure A-2.

In planning his program, Will prepares the program flowchart shown in figure A-3. It uses the standard ANSI flowcharting symbols.

Because his program must refer to specific memory addresses, Will lays out the areas of memory that will contain the input and output data and his program. This takes the form of a chart, known as a memory map, which appears in figure A-4.

The memory map shows that Will picked memory positions 01 and 02 to contain the input data SALES AMOUNT and COMMISSION RATE. Position 04 will contain the sum of all of the commissions calculated as the sales transactions are processed.

The program itself, Will decides, will occupy memory starting in position 21. Because he has not yet written it, he is not sure how much memory it will require, but his experience tells him that there will be sufficient space.

FIGURE A-2
I.W. Cell sales figures

```
              PETS AND UNUSUAL PET PROCUREMENTS
                         Sales Report
                    For Week of July 1, 1986


       I. W. CELL


                                              COMMISSION
       _____PRODUCT_____  SALE_AMOUNT    _%____
       Slithy Toves                   1,800.00       15
       Momraths                       3,800.00       12
       Borogroves                     4,650.00       18
       Jabberwocks                    1,475.00       12
```

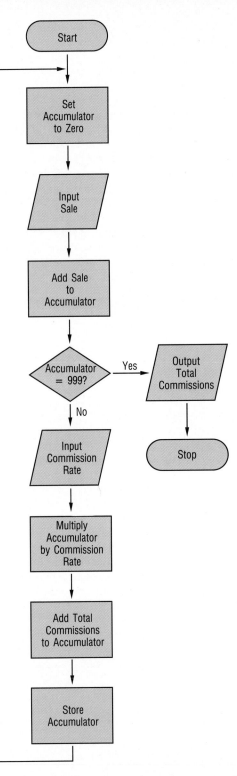

FIGURE A-3
I.W. Cell program flowchart

Note that the computer's memory stores three types of data: *input* (positions 01 and 02), *output* (position 04), and the *program* itself (position 21, etc.). Also note that all input data come directly into memory and must be moved to the accumulator for processing. All output data must be moved to the output device from memory. Thus,

```
                              DELRAM
                           MEMORY MAP

    Add          Contents              Add          Contents

    00                                 19
    01    Sale Amount: Input           20
    02    Commission Rate: Input       21    LDA:0
    03                                 22    STA:4
    04    Commission Amount: Output    23    RDN:1
    05                                 24    ADD:1
    06                                 25    BRN:32:999
    07                                 26    RDN:2
    08                                 27    MPY:2
    09                                 28    ADD:4
    10                                 29    STA:4
    11                                 30    LDA:0
    12                                 31    BRN:23:U
    13                                 32    PRN:4
    14                                 33    END
    15                                 34
    16                                 35
    17                                 36
    18                                 37
```

FIGURE A-4
DELRAM computer chart of memory use

output results, which are calculated in the accumulator, must be stored in memory before they can be sent to an output device.

Computer memory and other electronic and magnetic data storage media are *non-destructive-read* and *destructive-write* devices. This means that data may be read from a memory location and added to the accumulator, for example, and still remain recorded in the memory location from which they were read. It also means that inputting a second transaction, consisting of sales amount and commission rate into memory positions 01 and 02, will destroy the old values left over from the previous transaction.

Having planned the memory layout of the computer, Will next codes his program using a program coding sheet, figure A-5. He programs the computer using *machine language*, the only language that the computer understands.

Every computer responds to one and only one language, machine language. Every computer, furthermore, has its unique machine language. Machine language programs prepared for an IBM computer will not run on a VAX or an Apple or a Hewlett-Packard. Programs prepared in such languages as FORTRAN or BASIC must first be translated into the machine language of the computer that is to execute them. This process is discussed in Chapter Nine.

The DELRAM Machine Language Coding Sheet in figure A-5 provides space for Will to write each instruction and to identify the memory cell in which the instruction is to be stored in memory. It also has room to write comments about the program which will serve as memory aids when Will or anyone else wants to review them later.

In coding his machine language program, Will must adhere to the *syntax* requirements of the language, that is, the rules governing how instructions are to be written.

**DELRAM
MACHINE LANGUAGE CODING SHEET**

PROGRAM	PROGRAMMER	DATE
I.W. CELL COMMISSIONS	I.W. CELL	7-1-86

LOCATION	INSTRUCTION	COMMENT
21	LDA : Ø	Accumulator = Zero
22	STA : 4	Set commissions to Zero
23	RDN : 1	Sale amount to location 1
24	ADD : 1	Sale amount to accumulator
25	BRN : 32 : 999	EOJ Test
26	RDN : 2	Commission rate to location 2
27	MPY : 2	Multiply accumulator by commission rate
28	ADD : 4	Add total commissions to accumulator
29	STA : 4	Store new total commissions to location 4
30	LDA : Ø	Reset accumulator to Zero
31	BRN : 23 : U	Loop back for next sale
32	PRN : 4	Print total commissions
33	END	

FIGURE A-5
DELRAM computer coding sheet

DELRAM has nineteen machine language instructions. Each is specified in figure A-6. Each instruction consists of an operation code and zero, one, or two operands. The operation code tells the control unit what is to be done. The operands indicate what is to be used in doing it. The ADD instruction, for example, has the format

```
ADD:LL
```

where ADD indicates that the contents of a memory position are to be added to whatever is in the accumulator and LL is the address of the memory position to use. The BRN instruction has two operands. The functions of the operands are explained in figure A-6.

Having decided to allocate his program in memory locations starting with 21, Will proceeds to code his program using his program flowchart as a guide. The first instructions, in locations 21 and 22, set the accumulator and memory location 04 to zero. The instructions in locations 23 and 24 read a sales amount from the keyboard into memory and then add the contents of that memory cell (01) to the zero contained in the accumulator. The result is stored in the accumulator; memory cell 01 is unchanged.

The instruction in location 25 tests to see if the amount entered is 999. If not, processing continues with the instruction in cell 26 which reads the commission rate into memory cell 02.

The accumulator is then multiplied by the contents of cell 02. The total commissions calculated thus far, stored in cell 04, are added to the figure in the accumulator and the contents of the accumulator are then stored back into cell 04, thus replacing the amount in that cell with the new total commission. In location 30, the accumulator is reset to zero. Finally, in location 31, the program branches back to the instruction in cell 23 so that the next transaction can be processed.

The instruction in cell 25, BRN:32:999, is known as a *conditional branch*, as compared with the *unconditional branch* in cell 31. In both cases, the branch is accomplished by replacing the contents of the ILR with the address of the next instruction to be executed. In the case of the unconditional branch, BRN:23:U, the next instruction to be executed is located in memory position 23. That instruction will always be executed.

In the case of the conditional branch, BRN:32:999, the instruction at the address

FIGURE A-6
DELRAM computer instruction set

Operation	Code	X-operand	Y-operand	Description
Load accumulator	LDA	constant		Replaces contents of accumulator with X-operand
Store accumulator	STA	location		Stores contents of accumulator in location
Add	ADD	location		Adds contents of location to accumulator, stores result in accumulator
Subtract	SUB	location		Subtracts contents of location from accumulator, stores result in accumulator
Multiply	MPY	location		Multiplies accumulator by quantity in location, stores result in accumulator
Divide	DIV	location		Divides quantity in accumulator by quantity in location, stores result in accumulator
Branch	BRN	location	U, +, -, #	Branches to instruction indicated in X-operand, unconditionally if Y-operand equals U or on accumulator positive, negative, or any number according to Y-operand
Branch to subroutine	BRS	location	U, +, -, #	Branches as per BRN, stores location of instruction after branch in S-register
Return	RET			Branches to location stored in S-register
End program	END			Stops program execution
No operation	NOP			Place holder
Route output	RTO	P or C		Sends program output to printer or CRT, unless otherwise set, output goes to CRT
Read numeric	RDN	location		Reads number from Keyboard and stores it in location
Read alphabetic	RDA	location		Reads up to 16 characters from keyboard and stores them in location
Print numeric	PRN	location		Prints number stored in location on CRT or printer
Print alphabetic	PRA	location		Prints characters stored in location on CRT or printer
Print space	PRS	number		Prints number of spaces
Print carriage return	PRR	number		Prints number of carriage returns (equivalent to number-1 blank lines)
Store character	STC	location	characters	Stores up to 16 characters in location

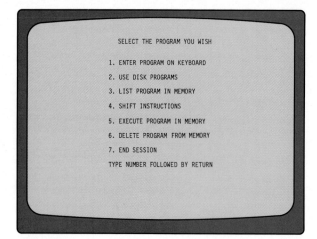

SELECT THE PROGRAM YOU WISH

1. ENTER PROGRAM ON KEYBOARD

2. USE DISK PROGRAMS

3. LIST PROGRAM IN MEMORY

4. SHIFT INSTRUCTIONS

5. EXECUTE PROGRAM IN MEMORY

6. DELETE PROGRAM FROM MEMORY

7. END SESSION

TYPE NUMBER FOLLOWED BY RETURN

FIGURE A-7
DELRAM computer menu

specified in the X-operand, 32, will be executed only on the condition that the accumulator contains 999. After executing a branch instruction, which replaces the address in the ILR, the ILR is incremented as usual each time an instruction is executed. After the branch is taken, processing continues sequentially by the addresses of the cells containing the instructions.

We're sure that this seems cumbersome to you, and so it is. It is, however, the way computers work. Fortunately, writing programs has been made considerably easier through the development of so-called high-level programming languages which relieve us of the need to understand in great detail how computers work internally. This is indeed fortunate because modern computers are considerably more complex than the DELRAM computer. They have more registers, larger instruction sets and are more flexible in their operation, all of which means writing programs in machine language for real-life computers is a whole lot more difficult than this simple example suggests. Nevertheless, we stress that the only language any computer understands is its unique machine language.

Loading Will's program into DELRAM's memory and executing it is fairly simple. He turns the computer on. The video display unit presents him with a menu of options as shown in figure A-7.

Selecting the Enter Program option, he keys in the instructions, just as they appear on the machine language coding sheet, except that he does not enter the comments. Having accomplished that, he returns to the menu of options (figure A-7) and selects Execute Program. As the program executes, he enters the sales and commission rate data. After the data for the last transaction have been entered, he enters 999 as if it were the sales amount for yet another transaction. Because that is the end-of-job (EOJ) signal, the program terminates after printing his total sales commissions for the week, 1740, on the screen.

Execution of the program by the computer is simple. When Will selected the Execute Program option from the menu, he also entered the address of the first instruction to be executed, which is 21. This value was placed in the ILR. The control unit consulted the ILR, fetched the instruction at the address shown in it, placed that instruction in the instruction register, executed it, and returned again to the ILR for the address of the next instruction. Because the ILR is incremented by one each time an instruction is executed, it then had 22, the address of the second instruction. Processing continued in this fashion until Will entered the EOJ code, which caused the instruction in location 25 to replace the contents of the ILR with 32, the instruction that caused the total commissions (in location 04) to be printed. After that instruction was executed, the ILR had the address of the END instruction. This was fetched by the control unit accordingly, placed in the instruction register and executed.

In executing a program, the computer's CPU, under the control of the *control unit*, fetches one program instruction at a time and places it in a register known as the *instruction register*. There the instruction is analyzed and its function carried out. Meanwhile, the *instruction location register (ILR)*, which contains the address of the next instruction to be executed is incremented by one. When instruction execution is complete, the control unit consults the ILR for the address of the next instruction. In this fashion, instructions are executed in sequence as they are stored in primary memory.

SUMMARY

The execution of a branch instruction changes the contents of the ILR so that it contains the address of the instruction, out of sequence, that should be executed next.

During program execution, primary memory contains three things: the *program*, areas for *input* of data, and areas for receiving the results of processing the data from the *arithmetic/logic unit* prior to their *output*.

For DELRAM, the arithmetic/logic unit consists of one accumulator. In full-scale computers, the arithmetic/logic unit consists of many accumulators, called *registers*.

Programming in machine language, the only language that a computer understands, requires that the programmer keep careful track of memory locations and their contents, including those memory locations occupied by individual program instructions. The development of higher-level programming languages makes computer programming a much easier task. Programming DELRAM in this fashion, however, illustrates the manner in which all digital computers work.

KEY TERMS

accumulator	instruction location register (ILR)	register
address	instruction register	syntax
conditional branch	machine language	unconditional branch

A computer program is a logical set of instructions that tells the computer what steps to take to solve a problem. There are many different ways to give these instructions to the computer. Each way uses a *programming language* as we saw in Chapter Nine. But *programming* is more than just using a particular language correctly. After we have identified a problem we will use the computer to solve, there are three steps involved in writing a correct program: designing the logic, coding, and debugging.

First, we design the *logic of the program*. This involves specifying every step the computer must take. We will use a device called a *flowchart* to describe the steps and the order in which they are to be taken. To see how specific we must be, consider an everyday experience we've all had thousands of times: getting ready for the day. Most people, when asked how they prepare for the day, say something like, "I get out of bed, get washed, dress, have breakfast while I'm reading the paper, and leave for work." We understand this description. A computer, on the other hand, would be totally lost.

Let's take one small block of this process and see what the computer would need to know.

> Each morning I check the closet and select a shirt to wear. I put my right arm through the right sleeve and my left arm through the left one. Then I pull the shirt on and button it. If I am going to wear a necktie, I select one from the closet. If it matches the shirt, I put it under the collar, button the top button of my shirt, and tie the tie (describing that process would take another paragraph). If it doesn't match the shirt, I select other ties until one matches. If it is a button-down and the collar buttons are not buttoned, I button them. I check the sleeves; if they are short, I can skip to the next phase of this project. If they are long, I button them or select cuff links and fasten them to the cuffs. Finally, I fill my shirt pocket with the items I will need today.

This type of detail must be repeated with every part of the morning routine.

Second, we *code* the program in a language the computer understands. As we saw in Chapter Nine, the computer can use many languages each of which has its own characteristics, strengths, and weaknesses. The language we will use here is *BASIC* (Beginners All-purpose Symbolic Instruction Code). BASIC was developed in the early 1960s by John Kemeny and Thomas Kurtz of Dartmouth College. It was designed as a teaching language but became one of the most popular general programming languages of all time. From a very limited language with few capabilities it has been extended until, today, it allows a wide range of programming from strictly mathematical applications to graphics to business applications and many other things. BASIC is the most common language available on microcomputers. It is available on virtually every computer produced.

There are many versions of BASIC. The standard is called ANSI (*American National Standards Institute*) BASIC. Because ANSI BASIC is somewhat limited, we will discuss two extended versions. *Applesoft* is BASIC for Apple II computers. *Microsoft BASIC* appears on IBM PCs and many other machines.

Third, once the program is designed and coded, we must make sure it works correctly. This process is called *debugging*. This name allegedly arose in the early days of computers when a programmer had difficulty with a program because a moth had flown into the machinery. The term is obviously much older because Thomas Edison used it in his correspondence describing errors in the operation of his inventions. There are three parts to the debugging process. First, we check the logic of our flowchart. Second, we make sure that our code is correct. This is called checking the syntax of

Thomas Kurtz and John Kemeny
developed BASIC around 1960.
They have just created a new
structured form call True BASIC.
(Courtesy Dartmouth College)

each BASIC statement. Usually, the computer will tell us if we have made a syntax error. Then we must check the logic of our code. This involves using test data to be sure the program behaves as it is supposed to. This process can be difficult and time consuming unless proper care is taken in the logic design phase.

In this appendix, we will concentrate on the first two aspects of programming although some discussion of debugging will occur as well. We will begin by defining the flowcharting process. After that, we will develop a series of programs of increasing complexity, all based on a cash register system. By the end of this appendix, you should have a fairly good understanding of the coding process and logic design for simple problems. You should be able to extend your knowledge by completing the programs at the end of the appendix and by reading a book that discusses BASIC for the particular machine you use.

This appendix is different from the chapters in the book. In the chapters, we asked you to learn a body of facts and to master a set of ideas. In this appendix, you will develop a skill in programming. For this reason, you must approach the material differently.

As you read the appendix, you will notice specific lines of computer code (instructions to the computer). You should determine what these lines cause the computer to do before continuing with the text. You will also find exercises within the text. Do them before continuing to read. You will find the answers to all of the exercises at the end of the appendix. If you have access to a computer, complete the exercises with paper and pencil before trying them on the computer.

There are numerous programs for you to write at the end of the appendix. These are keyed throughout the text. Try writing at least one program after you have completed each numbered example (except example 7) in the text. Be sure to spend enough time planning the program before you sit down at the computer.

We have placed each of the Sugarman's Candy Emporium examples (1 through 6) on a disk that accompanies this book. If you want to test the programs or see the effects of modifying them, they are called EX1, EX2, and so forth. Later in the appendix, we show you how to retrieve the programs from the disk and execute them or look at them.

Each time you try something new, you will want to clear the computer memory so the old coding will not affect the new. You can do this by typing NEW followed by a carriage return. When you do this, however, *everything you have not saved will be lost. Be sure to review the pointers on saving programs in box B-4.*

PROGRAM LOGIC AND FLOWCHARTING

The most important aspect of computer programming is designing proper logic at the beginning of a project. *Structured programming* is a logical style that was developed by Dutch computer engineer Edsger Dijkstra in the 1960s. A structured program is made up of a series of *proper segments*. A proper segment has only one input path and one output path. The true value of structured programming lies in the ease of logic checking and debugging and of changing a program to meet revised needs. One way to write structured programs is to use independent modules that can be controlled by a *driver* program. This is known as *modular programming*. The Sugarman's Candy Emporium example in this appendix illustrates the development of a modular program.

Computers really cannot do many things. They can do arithmetic, compare words and numbers, and move data. These three things can be shown clearly on a flowchart. Complex flowcharting systems use many symbols to represent the various parts of a computer and the actions that they take. Figure 4-4 shows these symbols. We will use a simplified system that requires only five of them. We will show these symbols as we build the logic for the following problem:

Many stores sell at a discount when customers buy in quantity. Our problem is to design a program that will calculate the unit selling price of an item. We will provide the computer with the list price and the quantity sold. The computer should give us the list price if fewer than 15 units are sold, 90 percent of list if 15 or more are sold.

Generally, procedures must have a beginning and an end. A process that never begins is not a process at all. A process that never ends but keeps repeating is called an *infinite loop*. Infinite loops, while seldom intended, often sneak into computer programs. We can tell an infinite loop exists because our program will keep repeating the same steps over and over. Sometimes procedures end before meeting their goals. These procedures are called *uncompleted paths*. Our program must have a beginning and an end. These are shown as ovals.

Because our flowchart will consist of a number of symbols of various shapes, we must have a way of showing the logical sequence in which they are connected. This sequence, called the *flow of the program*, is shown with arrows or *flow lines*. To make flowcharts more readable, flow lines are drawn top to bottom and left to right whenever possible.

Virtually every procedure requires input and produces output. As you have seen in an earlier chapter, input and output can take many forms. For the purposes of our system, all input will take place from the keyboard and all output will be to the screen or a printer. Input and output are represented as parallelograms in our flowcharts.

Decisions are indicated by diamonds. These are the only boxes from which more than one flow line exits. There are no boxes into which more than one flow line enters.

Arithmetic, storage, and all other computer operations are described in rectangles. You may put more than one operation in a box, but that means the operations must be executed in sequence.

Many flowcharts are so complex that it is inconvenient to draw all of the flow lines. They would make the chart too hard to read. To solve this problem and the problem of flowcharts spanning two or more pages, we use connectors. They take the form of circles and always come in pairs. One shows where the flow originates. The other shows its destination. Connectors are circles with letters or numbers inside. By matching the symbols, we can see the flow.

FUNDAMENTAL PRINCIPLES FOR WRITING BASIC STATEMENTS

We will discuss both Applesoft and Microsoft BASIC in this appendix. These versions are very similar, but there are minor differences between them that we will point out.

Modes

BASIC has two operational modes. In the *immediate execution mode*, the computer acts like a sophisticated desk calculator by performing instructions immediately as we enter them and press the RETURN or ENTER key (from now on, we'll refer to both as the RETURN key). The computer does not process what we type until the RETURN key is pressed. This means that we can type characters and correct them if necessary before we hit the RETURN. Alternatively, in this mode, we may direct the computer to execute a program of instructions entered earlier.

We write programs in *deferred execution mode*. These programs can be stored for later use and the statements that we write are not executed at the time they are written.

Most BASIC statements can be used in either immediate or deferred mode. In the forms of BASIC discussed here, deferred execution statements must begin with line numbers, while immediate execution statements never have line numbers.

Syntax

There is a specific *syntax* or set of grammatical rules that make BASIC statements intelligible to the computer. There are similar rules in English. Every sentence must obey certain rules to make sense. For example, "John runs red" makes no sense, while "John runs hard" is meaningful. BASIC statements are single directions from the programmer to the computer. One aspect of BASIC syntax is to separate each part of a statement with at least one blank space. Some versions require this, while others make it optional. For the sake of simplicity, we will always include these spaces. Another syntax rule stipulates that every BASIC statement must end with a carriage return. This tells the computer that we have completed the statement. Beyond these two rules, every BASIC statement has its own syntax.

Reserved Words

Reserved words have special meaning in BASIC. They can only be used in that context within a program. Every BASIC statement must have a reserved word in the proper place. Reserved words generally describe the operations they cause the computer to execute. For example, PRINT causes the computer to print something and INPUT causes the computer to request information from the keyboard. For every reserved word, we have to use a specific syntactic rule so that we will be understood by the computer. We will see many reserved words and learn how they operate in this appendix.

Line Numbers

Line numbers tell the computer the order in which to execute a series of statements. A line number can be any whole number as long as it is not negative and not too big. The largest allowable line number in Applesoft is 63999; in Microsoft, it is 65529. Line numbers are the first item on a statement line. It is good practice to number lines 100, 110, 120, and so forth. That way when we debug the program, there is room to insert statements, if necessary. We also leave room at the beginning of a program (lines 0 to 99) for documentation.

BOX B-2: EDITING ON THE IBM PC

In order to change a BASIC statement, we must display it on the screen. Then we must move the cursor to the location of the change. After we have made the change, we must press the ENTER key (↵).

We use the LIST command to display a line. Typing LIST followed by ENTER lists the entire program. Typing LIST followed by a line number and ENTER displays that one line:

```
LIST 450
```

To display a range of lines, we type LIST and the first and last line numbers separated by a dash. As always, we end with ENTER.

```
LIST 340 - 400
```

To change a line that has already been ENTERED, we display that line using LIST, use the cursor keys (see next paragraph) to move the cursor to the correction, make the correction, and press ENTER.

We move the cursor up, down, left, and right with the four arrow keys (8, 2, 4, and 6) on the numeric keypad at the far right side of the keyboard.

The INS (insert) key (0 on the numeric keypad) allows us to insert characters immediately before the cursor. Pressing the key once begins insert, pressing it again or pressing an arrow key ends insert. The DEL (delete) key (decimal point on the numeric keypad) deletes the character at the cursor location. In both cases, the screen is altered to show the changes we have made.

Using the arrow keys, DEL and INS requires that NUMLOCK (numeric lock) be off. The NUMLOCK key toggles the numeric keypad (where the arrow keys, DEL, and INS are located) on and off. If these keys don't work, try pressing NUMLOCK once.

To delete a line, we type its line number followed by a carriage return. To delete several lines, type DELETE XX–YY where XX is the line number of the first line to be deleted and YY is the line number of the last line to be deleted. After you press ENTER, the entire range of lines will be deleted.

BOX B-3: EDITING ON THE APPLE

It is easy to correct typing mistakes when you are programming on the Apple. There are essentially two ways to make corrections, depending on where you are in the coding process.

If you recognize a typing mistake while you are typing a line, before pressing the RETURN key, you can back up to the mistake by using the arrow key that points to the left. Then retype the corrected line from the error rightward. If you just want to change a few characters without adding any, back up to the changes, make them, then use the right arrow key to retype the characters that show on the screen. This procedure works because the Apple accepts as input everything you see on a line up to the cursor. By moving the cursor to the right, you are "showing" the computer the characters you have already typed.

Once you have pressed the RETURN, however, the process is a little more difficult. You can always retype the whole line. Just type a BASIC statement with the same line number as the one you want to replace. Typing a line number followed immediately by a carriage return will eliminate the line from your program completely.

If you want to change part of a line, start by listing the line:

```
LIST 30
```

Then press ESC (left side of the keyboard). The I, J, K, and M keys form the cursor control diamond. To move up, press the I. To move to the left, press the J. Use these keys to locate the cursor on the first character of the line. Then press ESC again. These steps are called the *escape sequence*. Now you are ready to edit the line. Use the arrow keys and the character keys to restructure the line as you want it. You can leave extra blanks if you wish, as long as they are not within quotation marks.

Adding extra characters is more difficult on the Apple. Use the arrow keys to bring the cursor to the place where you want to add characters. Press ESC. Move the cursor to an empty line on the CRT (use the I, J, K, L keys). Press ESC again. Then type the additional characters. When you are done, use the *escape sequence* to bring the cursor to the next position on the line being edited. Finish other editorial changes as described above.

Be careful when editing character strings: Don't inadvertently add blanks to character strings. When the Apple lists a statement that is too long to fit on one screen line, it lists the statement with indentations on the second and following lines. When you use the right arrow across these indentations, the computer sees blanks. If they are within quotation marks, your text gets changed. To avoid this problem, use the escape sequence to move the cursor over the indentations.

Listing an entire program is done by typing

```
LIST
```

while listing the range of lines is done by typing

```
LIST XX, YY
```

where XX is the first line number to be listed and YY is the last.

Deleting a line is done by typing its line number, followed by a RETURN. To delete a range of lines, type

```
DEL XX, YY
```

Let's look at some examples. In each case, we must press the carriage return to complete the statement. The PRINT statement will be discussed momentarily. For now, understand that it causes the results of the value or number to its right to be displayed on the screen. If we type

```
110 PRINT 3 + 4
```

(deferred mode because there is a line number) the computer will wait for its next instruction. If we type

```
PRINT 3 + 4
```

the computer will respond

```
7
```

because this is an immediate instruction (no line number).

Let's type another statement

```
120 PRINT 10 - 6
```

Since this statement is in the deferred execution mode thanks to the line number, the computer is waiting for further direction.

Listing a Program

To see a list of the statements in a program, type

```
LIST
```

The computer will respond

```
110 PRINT 3 + 4
120 PRINT 10 - 6
```

on the CRT. LIST is a command that displays the BASIC program in memory. We can list a single line by typing the line number after the word LIST:

```
LIST 510
```

or a range of lines by typing the first and last line numbers, separated by a dash in Microsoft or a comma in Applesoft:

```
LIST 200 - 250     or     LIST 200, 250
     (Microsoft)                (Applesoft)
```

Running a Program

To make the computer run the program, we use another immediate execution mode statement,

```
RUN
```

The computer will respond

```
7
4
```

and wait for instructions from the programmer. At this point, the program is still in memory because we haven't removed it or replaced it with another program. We can execute it again with the command RUN.

TABLE B-1 *VARIABLE NAMES*

Name	Legal?	Numeric or Character	If Illegal, Why?
AD	legal	numeric	
A.1	illegal		only numbers and letters allowed
X$			
1W			
PRICE			
DEPT$			
$NAME			
TYPE			

Variables

The BASIC interpreter (see Chapter Nine) identifies memory locations with names. The names are like labels on a post office mailbox. The name on a memory location does not tell us what is stored there. Variable names must start with a letter and can be followed with other letters or numbers. Some versions of BASIC limit the programmer to names with one or two characters, the first character being a letter and the second a number. Others allow longer names but only use the first two characters. In such a system, the variables AX1 and AX2 represent the same storage location. If we assign a value of 54 to AX1 and a value of 10 to AX2, the value of AX1 becomes 10 because BASIC always takes the last value entered. Applesoft BASIC behaves like this. Still other BASIC systems, such as Microsoft BASIC, allow long names, as many as 40 characters. In Microsoft BASIC, if we store 54 in AX1, then store 10 in AX2, the value represented by AX1 remains 54 while AX2 represents 10.

In addition to identifying storage locations, variable names are used to identify the type of data being stored. Although there are several types of data, we will only consider two. Variable names like the ones above represent whole numbers or decimals, either positive, negative, or zero. They are called *numeric variables*. Variable names can also be used to represent character data. Character data includes all of the things we can type on the keyboard. *Character variable names* are names just like numeric variable names except that they must have a dollar sign ($) at the end. For example, ALPHA$ is a legitimate character variable name, as are W$, A1$, and XA$. The variable names A$ and A do not represent the same storage location! Character variable names refer to memory locations containing *character strings*: collections of characters that are sometimes called *string variables*. The symbol $ stands for string. Not only does a $ appear at the end of the name of every character variable name, it also appears at the end of almost every reserved word that deals with strings.

When we select a name for a variable, two things should be considered. First, remember that we will need to type the name every time we want to use it, so we need to keep names as short as possible. Second, as a memory aid, it is a good idea to select a name with some meaning. For example, TTL might represent a total, TX might be the sales tax, and so forth. As we program, it is a good idea to keep a list of variables and what they represent. This can be done on a separate piece of paper or in the program itself (we'll see how later).

Exercise 1

We have listed a set of names in table B-1. Decide which ones are legal variable names. Explain why the illegal ones are unacceptable. Identify the numeric and character variables. Answers for this and other exercises appear at the end of the appendix.

BASIC PROGRAMMING STATEMENTS

With this background, let's look at four essential concepts: assignment of values to variables, arithmetic, inputting data via the keyboard, and printing output.

Assignment

The equal sign is used for assignment. In addition, many computers require or allow the reserved word LET. In the assignment statement, LET, if it is used, comes first (after the line number in deferred execution mode). The variable name to which a value is assigned comes next, followed by an equal sign. To the right of the equal sign is any expression that has a value. For example, the following are all valid assignment statements.

```
100 LET AS = 3 + 4
120 X4 = 5
130 PW = 9 - X4
```

The equal sign has a different meaning in BASIC than the one we're used to in math. Instead of "is the same as," it means "is replaced by." Thus, line 120 tells us that the contents of storage location X4 is replaced by the value 5. The operations in lines 110, 120, and 130 place a 7 in the location identified as AS, a 5 in X4, and a 4 in PW. Line 130 is of particular interest. Notice that there is a variable name, X4, to the right of the equal sign. Before PW is assigned a value, the computer replaces X4 with 5 then subtracts 5 from 9.

Variable names can be used anywhere in an assignment statement. This means that if we execute the same statement more than once in a program, we may get different results each time. If we use a variable name on the right side of an equal sign, we must be sure we have assigned a value to it earlier in the program. Otherwise, the computer will assign it a value or print an error message and stop executing. Normally, the value assigned is zero, but it is sometimes something else.

Arithmetic Operations

Arithmetic in BASIC works just like the arithmetic of algebra. There are five operations, table B-2. In addition to these operations, BASIC uses parentheses to determine which operation to do first.

This table shows a hierarchy of operations. It is important to know the hierarchy. Otherwise, you are likely to get incorrect results when you write a program. In BASIC

TABLE B-2 ARITHMETIC OPERATORS

Level	Operation	Symbol	Examples	
1	Raising to a power	^	3 ^ 2 is 9	2 ^ 3 is 8
2	Multiplication	*	4 * 3 is 12	2.5 * 4 is 10
	Division	/	12 / 6 is 2	24 / 16 is 1.5
3	Addition	+	5 + 4 is 9	2.4 + 4.3 is 6.7
	Subtraction	−	6 − 3 is 3	9.3 − 14.5 is −5.2

Complete all operations at level 1 before attempting any at level 2.
Complete all operations at level 2 before attempting any at level 3.

TABLE B-3 *ARITHMETIC EXPRESSIONS WITHOUT PARENTHESES*

In each example, the second line shows the order in which operations are completed.

	Expression	Value
1.	3 + 2 − 5 + 8 1 2 3	8
2.	2 * 6 / 4 * 5 1 2 3	15
3.	18 / 3 + 5 * 2 1 3 2	16
4.	4 + 3 ^ 2 * 5 − 40 / 10 − 20 4 1 2 5 3 6	25

as in arithmetic, operations are completed from left to right unless parentheses are involved.

Expressions without Parentheses

To evaluate an expression that has no parentheses, there are three steps. First, do all of the exponentiations in the order that they occur from left to right. Second, do all of the multiplications and divisions in the order that they occur from left to right. Finally, do all additions and subtractions in the order that they occur from left to right. Table B-3 shows several examples of BASIC expressions. Written below the expressions is the order in which the operations are completed.

Exercise 2

For each expression in table B-4, write the order in which the operations are to

TABLE B-4 *EVALUATING ARITHMETIC EXPRESSIONS*

	Expression	Value
1.	3 * Z1 + 4 __ __	_____
2.	A * Z1 + A ^ 2 __ __ __	_____
3.	F * A ^ 3 − 6000 __ __ __	_____
4.	Z1 / 2 + A + F * 10 __ __ __ __	_____
5.	A ^ 2 + A * Z1 − 200 __ __ __ __	_____

be completed. Then evaluate the expressions. In this table, assume that the following three statements have been executed.

```
10 Z1 = 14
20 A = 10
30 F = 6.287
```

Expressions with Parentheses

If there are parentheses in an expression, the rules are only slightly modified. Take what is inside the parentheses and evaluate it first, using the above rules. Then evaluate the entire expression. If there are more than one set of parentheses, evaluate from left to right and from inside to outside. Here are two examples using the variable names from exercise 2. The information in the boxes shows the order in which to do the steps.

```
A + 3 * (Z1 - 10)^2

   4    3    └─1─┘  2

10 + 3 * (14 - 10)^2
10 + 3 *      4^  2
10 + 3 *      16
10 +     48
58
```

and

```
3 + 4 * (2 + 5 * (1 + 2))

      5   4   └─3──2─      └─1─┘

3 + 4 * (2 + 5 *   3   )
3 + 4 * (2 +   15      )
3 + 4 *       17
3 +       68
71
```

Exercise 3

Write the order in which the operations in table B-5 will be completed and then evaluate the expressions using the rules of BASIC. Use A1, Z1, and F from exercise 2.

TABLE B-5 EVALUATING EXPRESSIONS WITH PARENTHESES

	Expression	Value
1.	(3 + 4) * (5 + 1)	
	— — —	___
2.	(A − 3) ^ 2	
	— —	___
3.	2 * (1 + Z1 * (2 + A))	
	— — — —	___

Exercise 4

What will be stored in AX3 when the following program has been executed? Answer for Applesoft BASIC and Microsoft BASIC.

```
100 AX3 = 4 + 3 * (15 - 2 * (2 + 5))
120 AX4 = 20 - 12 * 2 ^ 2 / 6
```

Remember, in BASIC, the equal sign means assignment or replacement. This allows BASIC statements that make no sense in algebra. For example, $X = X + 1$ is meaningless in algebra, but in BASIC, it means, "Replace the value in location X by one more than it now contains."

Exercise 5

What value is stored in COST and PRICE by each line of this BASIC program?

	COST	PRICE
10 COST = 100	_____	_____
20 PRICE = 1.5 * COST	_____	_____
30 COST = COST * 2	_____	_____
40 PRICE = PRICE * 2	_____	_____

The INPUT Statement

Most computer programs are designed to be run many times, each time working with different numbers. These numbers are the input data for the program. They can be input directly to the program during execution by using the keyboard. As we will see later, character data can be input in the same way. Information is taken in by the INPUT statement. The syntax of the input statement is

```
10 INPUT X
```

When this statement is executed by the computer, a prompt (usually a question mark) is displayed on the CRT telling the operator to provide data. The data provided is stored in the location called X. Some programs need more than one piece of data. There are two ways to solve this problem. First, we could use multiple INPUT statements:

```
10 INPUT X1
20 INPUT X2
30 INPUT A1
```

Second, we could use one INPUT statement with multiple variables:

```
10 INPUT X1, X2, A1
```

In this case, we separate the variables with commas (,). The commas are called *delimiters* and serve to separate parts of a BASIC statement. With multiple statements, each value input will be displayed on a separate line on the CRT. With one INPUT statement, all three values will be displayed on the same line. When we enter the data, we also separate the numbers by commas. In either case, the computer will insist that we provide the correct number of data items. If we provide too few, it will prompt for more. If we provide too many, it will ignore the extra.

Most people who write programs write them for other folks to use. Since the *end user* might not know what the programmer had in mind when a question mark prompts input, BASIC provides another type of prompt. This can include anything we can type except the quotation mark ("). We type the prompt in quotation marks:

```
10 INPUT "PRICE: "; P        or        10 INPUT "PRICE: ", P
```
    (Applesoft)   (Microsoft)

In this form of the INPUT statement, the prompt is separated from the variable name(s) by a semicolon (Applesoft), another form of delimiter, or a comma (Microsoft). When the statement is executed, the question mark prompt is replaced by

```
PRICE:
```

and a cursor. It is considered good programming practice to prompt all input requested by a program. We can also prompt input format:

```
20 INPUT "LAST NAME, FIRST NAME, RETURN "; N$
```
                    (Applesoft)   or
```
20 INPUT "LAST NAME, FIRST NAME, RETURN ", N$
```
                    (Microsoft)

From now on, we will only show the Microsoft version of the INPUT statement. We leave it to you to remember to change the comma to a semicolon for Applesoft.

The PRINT Statement

Central to the output phase of any BASIC program is the PRINT statement. This statement causes information to be sent to the CRT screen. In addition, some BASIC versions, like Applesoft use the PRINT statement in conjunction with other code to use a printer. Other versions, notably Microsoft, use LPRINT to print hard copy.

There's a great deal to learn about PRINT statements, so we will discuss them in several small sections. First, the fundamentals.

To PRINT the value of a variable named A, use the following statement:

```
10 PRINT A
```

This will place the value stored at A on the left hand margin of the CRT. Like the INPUT statement, PRINT can be used with more than one variable:

```
20 PRINT A, B
```

The comma is used to separate what is printed into *zones* which are like tabs on a typewriter. The number of zones varies from computer to computer. Most display 80 characters per line, divided into five zones. The Apple II+ has a 40-column screen with print zones starting in columns 1, 17, and 33. In Microsoft, the screen is 80 characters wide and print zones are 14 characters wide.

The output from the following program is shown in figure B-1.

```
10 A = 20
20 B = 30
30 C = 40.7
40 D = -23.1
50 PRINT A, B, 2 * A, 2 * B, 3 * A, 3 * B
60 PRINT C, D
```

20	30	40
60	60	90
40.7	-23.1	

(A)

20	30	40	60	60
90				
40.7	-23.1			

(B)

FIGURE B-1
(A) Output in Applesoft with a 40-column display (B) Output in Microsoft with an 80-column display

In line 50, the arithmetic is done before any printing. Because that line includes more elements than there are print zones, the computer wraps data around and takes two lines to print the information. Notice also that the columns do not line up as we might expect. There are several ways to control output in BASIC, but we will not worry about them at this time.

Sometimes we need to skip a zone when printing a line. Perhaps we want to print A in zone 2, B in zone 3, C in zone 1, and D in zone 3. We can add lines 70 and 80 to the preceding program as follows:

```
70 PRINT , A, B
80 PRINT C, , D
```

The results are shown in figure B-2.

Two more statements should be discussed before we write our first program. These are the END and the REM statements.

ENDing a Program

Every program has an end. In BASIC, this is signified by the END statement. The syntax is

```
100 END
```

Some forms of BASIC require the END statement to be the statement with the largest line number. In other BASICs, the END can be anywhere the program logically ends. Still others do not require an END statement at all. Both Applesoft and Microsoft BASIC allow END statements anywhere in the program.

The REM Statement

Programmers often need to make notes to themselves in a program. These notes may tell what a variable name represents, what a segment of code does, or any other pertinent information about the program. These notes are inserted in the program as remarks. Remarks are made in REM statements. Although a REM statement stays in the program until the programmer removes it, it is never executed. We can put any information we want into the REM:

```
10 REM THE FOLLOWING 20 LINES CALCULATE WITHHOLDING TAX
```

Microsoft BASIC offers an additional variety of the REM statement. Using Microsoft BASIC, we can enter remark statements preceded by an apostrophe ('). What's more important, this kind of remark statement may be appended to a BASIC line without affecting its execution. For example, the statements

FIGURE B-2
(A) Output in Applesoft
(B) Output in Microsoft

20	30	40		
60	60	90		
40.7	-23.1			
	20	30		
40.7		-23.1		

(A)

20	30	40	60	60
90				
40.7	-23.1			
	20	30		
40.7	-23.1			

(B)

```
500 REM DEDUCT WITHHOLDING FROM GROSS
510 NET = GROSS - WITHHOLDING
```

are equivalent to

```
500 NET = GROSS - WITHHOLDING 'DEDUCT WITHHOLDING FROM GROSS
```

The equivalent statement in Applesoft is

```
500 NET = GROSS - WITHHOLDING:  REM DEDUCT WITHHOLDING FROM GROSS
```

In the Sugarman's Candy Emporium examples that follow, we'll find the ability to add remark statements to program instructions very helpful in documenting the programs and in understanding them.

It is important to place plenty of remarks in all programs. You never know when you will have to return to a program to change it or when some other programmer will be asked to work on your code.

Clearing the CRT Screen

Before we run a program, we'll often want to start with a clear CRT screen. We can clear the screen by typing

```
        HOME        or        CLS
```
    (Applesoft)   (Microsoft)

These commands put the cursor in the upper left corner of the screen and leave the rest of the screen blank. It is always a good idea to clear the screen before running a program. We can do this by including CLS or HOME in the program listing. In our program that should be done before the first INPUT statement.

Let's now look at the first part of the development of a cash register program we'll prepare for Sugarman's Candy Emporium.

Example 1

Our first example is a system that processes single-item transactions. A purchase amount is entered at the keyboard and the computer calculates the tax (we'll assume a tax rate of six percent on all items), then prints the purchase amount, the tax, and the total. Figure B-3 shows the flowchart for this problem.

The Logic.   This program is about as simple as one can be. There is an input box, a process box, and an output box in a simple sequence. No decisions are needed. In fact, this program could be done more easily on a pocket calculator. All we have to do is decide what formulas to use to calculate the tax and the total cost.

The Coding.   The coding for the program is as simple as the flowchart. In fact, only eight of its fifteen lines do any work. The rest of the program consists of remarks identifying the program's main sections and explaining the function of each BASIC statement. Throughout the development of the Sugarman's example in this appendix, we'll divide the programs into modules identified by remark statements such as the one in line 2000:

```
2000 REM *** PROCESS ROUTINE ***
```

The modules will each fall into specific ranges of line numbers: 1000s for the IN-PUT ROUTINE, 2000s for the PROCESS ROUTINE, 3000s for the OUTPUT ROU-TINE, and 4000s for the end of the job. We'll use lines 100 through 999 for program identification, variable name identification, and initial program housekeeping chores. Line 800, for example, clears the screen.

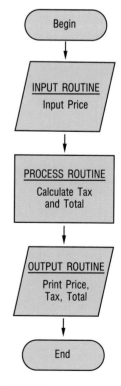

FIGURE B-3
*Flowchart for Sugarman's
examples 1 and 2*

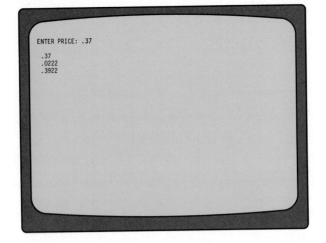

All of the programs in the Sugarman's example are written in Microsoft BASIC. With only three modifications, they will run with Applesoft BASIC, too. First, the CLS statement must be changed to HOME. Second, the apostrophe in remarks such as the one on line 2010,

```
2010 TX = .06 * PR      'CALCULATE TAX
```

must be changed to

```
2010 TX = .06 * PR:   REM CALCULATE TAX
```

Finally, the syntax of INPUT statements must be changed by replacing a comma with a semicolon, as explained earlier.

Now read the program carefully. Pay attention to the remark statements. Line 100 identifies the program. Lines 110–130 list the variable names and their functions. These initial lines form an important part of the program's documentation. The apostrophe remarks explain the purpose of each of the commands.

Ordinarily, we won't explain each command in a program, but we have in this first example. Part of the value of the Sugarman's examples is to help you learn to read a program. As we work through the examples, study each one carefully. We'll leave much of the program's explanation to the remark statements and the flowchart. Figure B-4 shows the program's output.

```
100 REM SUGARMAN'S CANDY EMPORIUM, EXAMPLE 1
110 REM PR = PRICE OF ITEM
120 REM TX = SALES TAX AT 6%
130 REM TL = TOTAL TRANSACTION INCLUDING TAX
800 CLS                              'CLEAR SCREEN
1000 REM *** INPUT ROUTINE ***
1010 INPUT "ENTER PRICE: ",PR         'RECEIVE PRICE FROM KEYBOARD
2000 REM *** PROCESS ROUTINE ***
2010 TX = .06 * PR                    'CALCULATE TAX
2020 TL = PR + TX                     'CALCULATE TOTAL
3000 REM *** OUTPUT ROUTINE ***
3010 PRINT PR                         'PRINT PRICE
3020 PRINT TX                         'PRINT TAX
3030 PRINT TL                         'PRINT TOTAL
4000 END                              'END PROGRAM
```

Programming problems 1–5 at the end of the appendix require the skills we have discussed up to this point.

Since most programs are written to be used over and over, we need a technique for storing them where they will be available when we need them but not be in the way when we don't. We solve the problem by storing our programs on disk.

In order to do this, we must assign a name to each program. These are called *filenames*. Like the names of variables within programs, filenames must start with a letter of the alphabet for Applesoft; any valid character except the period for Microsoft DOS (MS DOS). After the first character, they can be a combination of letters, numbers, and certain special characters except periods and blanks in Microsoft, commas in Apple DOS. A filename must be eight characters or fewer in Microsoft. It can be considerably longer in Applesoft.

Saving a Program to the Disk

Let's say we chose EXAMPLE as the filename of our program. To save it on the disk, we would enter one of the following lines. We would want to be sure not to use a filename we had already used for another program.

```
SAVE "EXAMPLE"          (MS DOS)
SAVE EXAMPLE            (Apple)
```

Retrieving a Program from the Disk

After we have stored a program on the disk, we will want to use it at a later time. In order to retrieve a program, either to execute it or to continue writing its code, we use the following lines, again concluded by a carriage return.

```
LOAD "EXAMPLE"          (MS DOS)
LOAD EXAMPLE            (Apple)
```

Using the Second Disk Drive

When you start a session, the active drive will be Drive 1 (Apple DOS) or Drive A: (Microsoft). Changing from one drive to another is accomplished by these commands:

```
SAVE "B:EXAMPLE"        (MS DOS)
LOAD "A:EXAMPLE"
SAVE EXAMPLE,D2         (Apple DOS)
LOAD EXAMPLE,D1
```

Executing the Program

Once it is loaded into the computer, we can execute the program by entering RUN.

PRINT, Revisited

As with the INPUT statement, we can include character data in a PRINT statement. The text we want to include is entered in quotation marks. This information can be placed in any zone.

For example,

```
10 TX = 1.59
20 PRINT "5% SALES TAX =", TX
```

will generate the line

```
5% SALES TAX =    1.59
```

The extra space to the right of the equal sign is caused by the comma delimiter. If we do not like the spacing in this line, we can ignore print zones by using semicolons instead of commas. Changing line 20 to

```
20 PRINT "5% SALES TAX ="; TX
```

changes our output to

```
5% SALES TAX =1.59           or        5% SALES TAX = 1.59
```
             (Applesoft)   (Microsoft)

While this is acceptable in Microsoft, it still isn't quite right in Applesoft. We need a blank space between TAX = and 1.59. It turns out that Microsoft always displays the sign of a number: blank for positive; minus sign for negative. Applesoft displays the sign only for negative values.

In a computer, a blank space is just like any other character. If we want space, we must put it into the statement using the space bar at the bottom of the keyboard. For the Apple, line 20 should look like this:

```
20 PRINT "5% SALES TAX = "; TX
```

The output will be just what we need:

```
5% SALES TAX = 1.59
```

We could even be fancy.

```
20 PRINT "5% SALES TAX = $"; TX
```

will provide the following output.

```
5% SALES TAX = $1.59         or        5% SALES TAX = $ 1.59
```
             (Applesoft)   (Microsoft)

We can include dollar signs in output but *never* in numeric input!

We can also include both semicolons and commas in the same PRINT statement. The semicolons will place things next to each other while the commas will skip to the next zone.

```
10 PR = 100
20 TX = 6
30 TL = 106
40 PRINT "PRICE: "; PR, "TAX: "; TX, "TOTAL: "; TL
```

produces this output in Microsoft BASIC:

```
PRICE:  100    TAX:  6       TOTAL:  106
```

In Applesoft with 40 columns, the output will be

```
PRICE: 100       TAX: 6           TOTAL: 1
06
```

because the zones are different and we run out of room on the 40-column screen. The computer automatically *wrapped around* and finished its work on the next line. We can avoid this problem by using separate PRINT statements and printing all output on the left margin of the CRT.

Exercise 6

Table B-6 shows various PRINT statements. Use the rows of boxes to write the expected output from each statement. Each box represents one character on the CRT. For the purpose of this exercise, we will use Microsoft print zones (positions 1, 15, 29).

Exercise 7

Table B-7 shows various printed lines on a CRT. Each box represents one character. Write a PRINT statement for each example, using print zones whenever possible. For the purpose of this exercise, we will use Applesoft 40-column print zones (positions 1, 17, 33).

Example 2

Let's now revise the program in example 1 to include labels in the output.

The Logic. There is no change in the logic between examples one and two.

TABLE B-6 *PRINT STATEMENTS*

```
1   PRINT 10, 20, 30
                        1 1 1 1 1 1 1 1 1 1 2 2 2 2 2 2 2 2 2 2 3 3 3 3 3 3 3 3 3 3 4
    1 2 3 4 5 6 7 8 9 0 1 2 3 4 5 6 7 8 9 0 1 2 3 4 5 6 7 8 9 0 1 2 3 4 5 6 7 8 9 0
```

```
2   PRINT "TAX "; 1.59, "TOTAL "; 27.09
                        1 1 1 1 1 1 1 1 1 1 2 2 2 2 2 2 2 2 2 2 3 3 3 3 3 3 3 3 3 3 4
    1 2 3 4 5 6 7 8 9 0 1 2 3 4 5 6 7 8 9 0 1 2 3 4 5 6 7 8 9 0 1 2 3 4 5 6 7 8 9 0
```

```
3   PRINT "COST:"; "TAX:"; "TOTAL:"
                        1 1 1 1 1 1 1 1 1 1 2 2 2 2 2 2 2 2 2 2 3 3 3 3 3 3 3 3 3 3 4
    1 2 3 4 5 6 7 8 9 0 1 2 3 4 5 6 7 8 9 0 1 2 3 4 5 6 7 8 9 0 1 2 3 4 5 6 7 8 9 0
```

```
4   PRINT "COST:"; 26.00; "TAX:"; 1.56; "TOTAL:"; 27.56
                        1 1 1 1 1 1 1 1 1 1 2 2 2 2 2 2 2 2 2 2 3 3 3 3 3 3 3 3 3 3 4
    1 2 3 4 5 6 7 8 9 0 1 2 3 4 5 6 7 8 9 0 1 2 3 4 5 6 7 8 9 0 1 2 3 4 5 6 7 8 9 0
```

```
5   PRINT "DATE:  JANUARY 12", 1986
                        1 1 1 1 1 1 1 1 1 1 2 2 2 2 2 2 2 2 2 2 3 3 3 3 3 3 3 3 3 3 4
    1 2 3 4 5 6 7 8 9 0 1 2 3 4 5 6 7 8 9 0 1 2 3 4 5 6 7 8 9 0 1 2 3 4 5 6 7 8 9 0
```

1

```
          1 1 1 1 1 1 1 1 1 1 2 2 2 2 2 2 2 2 2 2 3 3 3 3 3 3 3 3 3 3 4
1 2 3 4 5 6 7 8 9 0 1 2 3 4 5 6 7 8 9 0 1 2 3 4 5 6 7 8 9 0 1 2 3 4 5 6 7 8 9 0
C O S T   =     2 5 . 5 0           T A X   =     1 . 5 3
T O T A L   =     2 7 . 0 3
```

(USE TWO PRINT STATEMENTS)
10 PRINT _____
15 PRINT _____

2

```
          1 1 1 1 1 1 1 1 1 1 2 2 2 2 2 2 2 2 2 2 3 3 3 3 3 3 3 3 3 3 4
1 2 3 4 5 6 7 8 9 0 1 2 3 4 5 6 7 8 9 0 1 2 3 4 5 6 7 8 9 0 1 2 3 4 5 6 7 8 9 0
C O S T   =     3 4             T A X   =     2 . 0 4           T O T A L   =
3 6 . 0 4
```

(USE ONE PRINT STATEMENT)
20 PRINT _____

3

```
          1 1 1 1 1 1 1 1 1 1 2 2 2 2 2 2 2 2 2 2 3 3 3 3 3 3 3 3 3 3 4
1 2 3 4 5 6 7 8 9 0 1 2 3 4 5 6 7 8 9 0 1 2 3 4 5 6 7 8 9 0 1 2 3 4 5 6 7 8 9 0
A = 4 7 . 8 3                                                B = 3 1 6 . 2
```

30 PRINT _____

4

```
          1 1 1 1 1 1 1 1 1 1 2 2 2 2 2 2 2 2 2 2 3 3 3 3 3 3 3 3 3 3 4
1 2 3 4 5 6 7 8 9 0 1 2 3 4 5 6 7 8 9 0 1 2 3 4 5 6 7 8 9 0 1 2 3 4 5 6 7 8 9 0
P R I C E :     1 5 . 7 5       Q U A N T I T Y :     1 2       T O T A L :     1 8 9
```

40 PRINT _____

5

```
          1 1 1 1 1 1 1 1 1 1 2 2 2 2 2 2 2 2 2 2 3 3 3 3 3 3 3 3 3 3 4
1 2 3 4 5 6 7 8 9 0 1 2 3 4 5 6 7 8 9 0 1 2 3 4 5 6 7 8 9 0 1 2 3 4 5 6 7 8 9 0
P R I C E :                 T A X :
                                                        T O T A L :
```

(USE TWO PRINT STATEMENTS)
50 PRINT _____
55 PRINT _____

The Coding. Because only the output routine has been modified, let's just look at it.

```
100 REM SUGARMAN'S CANDY EMPORIUM, EXAMPLE 2
   .
   .
   .
3000 REM *** OUTPUT ROUTINE ***
3010 PRINT                          'PRINT BLANK LINE
3020 PRINT "SUGARMAN'S CANDY EMPORIUM"
3030 PRINT
3040 PRINT "PRICE: "  ,  PR
3050 PRINT "TAX:    "  ,  TX
3060 PRINT , "---------"            'PRINT UNDERSCORE
3070 PRINT "TOTAL: "  ,  TL
```

Note that the commas in the PRINT statements line up the output from PR, TX, TL, and the underscore line in the second print zone on the screen. Figure B-5 shows

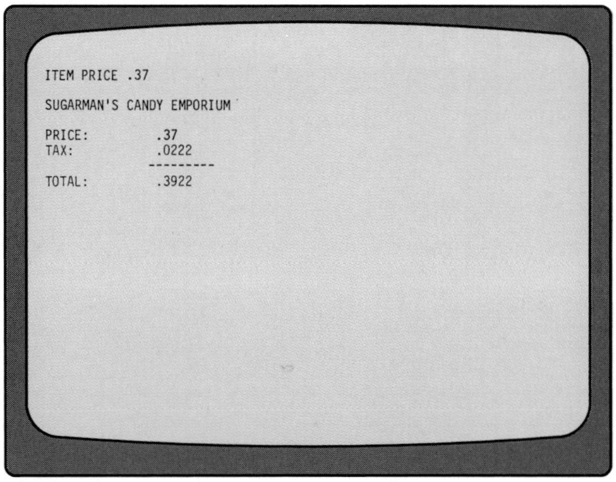

```
ITEM PRICE .37

SUGARMAN'S CANDY EMPORIUM

PRICE:        .37
TAX:          .0222
              ----------
TOTAL:        .3922
```

FIGURE B-5
Display from Sugarman's example 2

the resulting program output. Line 3020 produced the line identifying the store that appears just above the price, tax, and total listings. The blank lines in the output are produced by a PRINT statement that does not have any specified output, as in line 3030.

Programming problems 6–10 at the end of the appendix require the skills we have discussed up to this point.

There is much more to BASIC than just this. The rest of our examples will include arithmetic procedures and decision-making. Input and output will be nearly the same as what we already are using. Program flow, the order in which instructions are executed, is the next topic of discussion. There are several ways to modify program flow. In the first method, we use a BASIC command that compares values or character strings. Based on the results of the comparison, the command will direct the program flow to perform alternative tasks.

The IF ... THEN Statement

An IF ... THEN statement in BASIC instructs the computer to execute an instruction only if a certain condition is met. For example,

```
IF Y = 7 THEN PRINT X
```

prints the value of X only if Y = 7. In either case, the computer executes the next sequential instruction after completing the IF ... THEN statement. In most versions of BASIC, any instruction can follow THEN. For instance, we could code

```
10 INPUT X, Y
20 IF Y < 10 THEN X = X - Y
30 IF Y >= 10 THEN X = X + Y
40 PRINT X
50 END
```

In line 10, we enter two numbers into the computer. Line 20 tells the computer to replace the first number by the first minus the second only if the second number is less than ten. Line 30 tells the computer to replace the first number by the sum of the two numbers if Y is greater than ten or Y equals ten. Line 40 prints the result of this arithmetic.

Relations

Lines 20 and 30 show *relations*. These are two of the six relations available in BASIC. Relations are always surrounded by variable names, numbers, or expressions.

TABLE B-8 RELATIONS

Symbol	Meaning	Examples		
=	Is equal to*	A = 2 (true)	A = 4 (false)	A = B − 2 (true)
< > or > <	Is not equal to	A < > 2 (false)	A > < 4 (true)	A > < B − 2 (false)
<	Is less than	A < C (true)	A ^ 2 < B (false)	A < A (false)
>	Is more than	A > C (false)	A ^ 2 > B (false)	C > B (true)
< = or = <	Is less than OR is equal to	A ^ 2 < = B (true)	A < = B (true)	C < = B (false)
> = or = >	Is more than OR is equal to	A ^ 2 > = B (true)	A > = B (false)	C > = C (true)

*The symbol = has two meanings in BASIC. When used as part of a condition, it means "equals." When used in an assignment, it means "is replaced with."

A relation and its surrounding expressions (expressions can be single numbers, variable names, or combinations) make up a statement that is either true or false. When the IF part of an IF ... THEN statement is true, the THEN part is executed. When the IF part is false, the THEN part is ignored.

Table B-8 shows the six relations, their meanings, and examples of their use. For the purposes of this chart, assume that A = 2, B = 4, and C = 5.

Exercise 8

Write the output for each of the programs in table B-9.

IF ... THEN ... ELSE

Some versions of BASIC (including Microsoft BASIC but not Applesoft) have an IF ... THEN ... ELSE statement. This works just like an IF ... THEN except that the ELSE portion is executed if the THEN portion is not. In other words, when the condition following the IF is true, the THEN portion is executed. When the condition is false, the ELSE portion is executed. Consider this program

```
10 INPUT Y
20 IF Y <> 10 THEN PRINT Y ELSE PRINT "BINGO"
30 END
```

If we input 12, the program prints 12. If we input 10, the program prints BINGO.

The GOTO Statement

Often when we use an IF ... THEN statement, one condition causes the computer to execute the next line of code while another condition requires it to execute some code elsewhere in the program. In order to move to the code that doesn't follow the IF ... THEN, we need an *unconditional branch* statement. GOTO is such a statement. Every time the computer encounters a GOTO statement it branches to the indicated line regardless of any conditions in the program. The syntax is

```
10 GOTO 40
```

TABLE B-9 USING RELATIONS IN PROGRAMS

```
1.        10 X = 10
          20 Y = 20
          30 IF X = 10 THEN PRINT Y
          40 IF Y < = 10 THEN PRINT X
          50 END

2.        10 S = 5
          20 T = 9
          30 IF 2 * S < T THEN PRINT "HELLO"
          40 PRINT "GOODBYE"
          50 END

3.        10 D = 9
          20 W = 4
          30 Z = 8
          40 IF D <> 10 THEN PRINT "D NOT EQUAL 10"
          50 IF 2 * W < = Z THEN PRINT W, Z
          60 IF 2 * W < = D THEN PRINT W, D
          70 END
```

where the number following the GOTO is any line number. GOTO can be a statement by itself or part of an IF ... THEN statement. Structured programming uses GOTOs only for the structures described in Chapter Nine, DOWHILE, DOUNTIL, and IF ... THEN ... ELSE.

Consider this example program:

```
10 IF Y <> 10 THEN GOTO 40
20 PRINT "ELSE"
30 GOTO 50
40 PRINT "THEN"
50 END
```

Here, if the value stored in location Y is *not* ten the computer prints THEN at line 40. Statement 10 is a *conditional branch*. If the value is ten, the program "falls through" the IF ... THEN statement and prints ELSE at line 20. THEN is not printed because of the unconditional branch at line 30.

End-of-Job Indicators

One of the problems with Sugarman's cash register program so far is that the register operator must execute, or RUN, the program for each item purchased by a customer. Then the individual tax and total amounts must be added by hand to arrive at the total bill for the customer. Obviously, this will not do. We'll modify the program so that it operates a loop. Each time through the loop, it will receive the quantity and price of each item purchased by the customer as input. When all of the quantities and prices are entered, the program will print out the totals.

In order to prepare this program, we need a way to indicate that the last quantity and price have been entered so that the program will print out the totals. We'll do this with an *end-of-job indicator*, also called a trailer, flag, or sentinal record. Each time the computer executes the loop, it receives the data to be processed. If the input data indicate that there are no more items to process, the program will exit the loop.

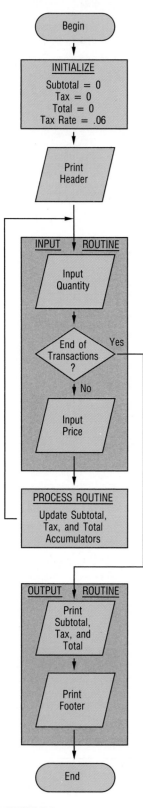

FIGURE B-6
Flowchart for Sugarman's
example 3

One way to make an end-of-job indicator is to input a value that cannot be mistaken for valid data. For instance, respond –4 to a request for age. Our cash register application does not ask for the customer's age, so we must come up with something else. How about entering a zero in response to a request for the quantity of an item purchased? When it executes an IF ... THEN statement, the program will determine if the quantity entered is zero; if it is zero, the computer will exit the input loop and print the totals.

Example 3

The third version of our program for Sugarman's will let the cash register operator enter any number of transactions. When the last transaction has been entered, the program will output the required totals.

The Logic. In order to do this, it must add or accumulate the totals each time it executes its loop. We will use three variables in the program to act as *accumulators*: ST, the subtotal of the values of each entry; TX, the total of the taxes calculated for each entry; and TL, the sum of the subtotal and the taxes.

Updating an accumulator makes use of the way the equal sign (=) works in a BASIC assignment statement. As we've noted, it does not mean equal, it means "is replaced by." To update the subtotal accumulator, ST, for example, we'll use the command

```
2020 ST = ST + AMT
```

where AMT is the variable name representing amount. Amount is calculated as the product of the quantity entered times the item's price. The command can be expressed as follows: replace ST with itself plus AMT. Therefore, if ST begins at zero, as it should for a customer, and the sale amount for the first item is $0.56, executing the command for the first time will change the value in ST from zero to .56. If the second sale amount for that customer is $1.44, executing the command again will change the value in ST from .56 to 2.00 (actually, just 2, since the computer does not store values in dollars and cents format). In this way, each time through the loop, ST will be updated by adding the amount of the last transaction to its previous value.

Figure B-6 depicts the logic of the modified program. Study it carefully so that you'll find the coding easier to understand.

The program begins by *initializing* the totals to zero. Although most versions of BASIC will automatically set the value of a numeric variable to zero when the program starts, it is preferred practice to include commands to do so. In later versions of this program, initializing the totals to zero will be required. The initialization process also sets the tax rate, TR, to six percent. Notice here that computers do not perform calculations with percentages. We are responsible for converting percentages to their decimal fraction equivalents or writing program instructions that will do that for us. In this example, TR is initialized to .06.

Following initialization, a header is printed: SUGARMAN'S CANDY EMPORIUM. Because it will be printed at the top of every customer's report, we'll consider its printing as part of the general housekeeping functions performed at the beginning of the program rather than as part of the output module.

Figure B-6 shows each of the three main modules in color, thus illustrating the modular nature of our program. The input and processing modules are executed as part of a loop until the input value for quantity of item purchased is zero. The diamond in the input routine represents an IF ... THEN statement that examines each quantity entered. As soon as the quantity entered is zero, control is passed to the output module and from there to the end of the job.

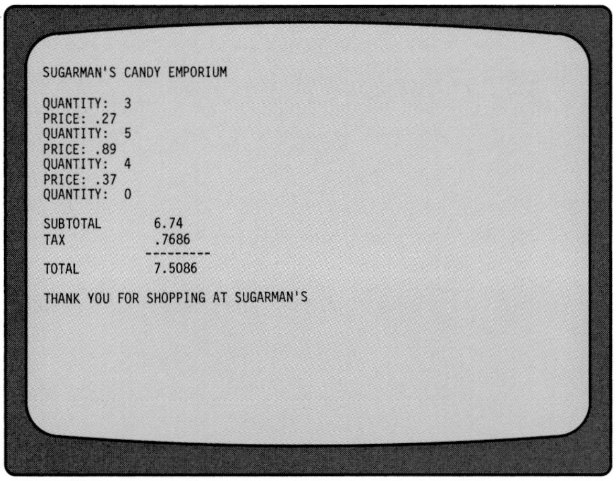

```
SUGARMAN'S CANDY EMPORIUM

QUANTITY:  3
PRICE: .27
QUANTITY:  5
PRICE: .89
QUANTITY:  4
PRICE: .37
QUANTITY:  0

SUBTOTAL      6.74
TAX           .7686
             ----------
TOTAL         7.5086

THANK YOU FOR SHOPPING AT SUGARMAN'S
```

FIGURE B-7
*Display from Sugarman's
example 3*

The Coding. Compare the coding of example 3 carefully with the flowchart in figure B-6. Be sure to acquaint yourself with the variable name definitions in lines 110–160. Notice in line 2040 that variable TL is not treated as an accumulator. Because ST and TX are both accumulators, we need only *replace* the contents of TL with the sum of ST and TX in order for TL to contain the correct figure.

Rather than repetitively updating the total variable, TL, it might make more sense to calculate the total in the output routine. This could be done by modifying line 3050 as follows:

```
3050 PRINT "TOTAL" , ST + TX
```

and deleting line 2040. The PRINT statement in line 3050 would print the sum of ST and TX, along with the word TOTAL. In modular programming, however, we keep all calculations in the process module to every extent possible. Similarly, all input takes place in the input module and all output in the output module. Exceptions can be made from time to time, as in printing the header in this program, but we'll avoid them if possible. As we'll see in example 6, this will make the final modification of our program very easy.

Figure B-7 shows the output from this program. The customer purchased three items in the quantities shown. Both the quantities and the prices were entered in response to INPUT statements. The final quantity entered, 0, ended the job.

```
100 REM SUGARMAN'S CANDY EMPORIUM EXAMPLE 3
110 REM PR = PRICE
120 REM QN = QUANTITY
130 REM AMT = SALE AMOUNT FOR EACH ITEM (= PR * QN)
140 REM ST = SUBTOTAL (= TOTAL SALES OF ALL ITEMS)
150 REM TR = TAX RATE
160 REM TX = AMOUNT OF TAX
170 REM TL = TOTAL SALE AMOUNT
800 REM *** INITIALIZE ACCUMULATORS AND TAX RATE ***
810 ST = 0
820 TX = 0
830 TL = 0
840 TR = .06
900 CLS
910 PRINT "SUGARMAN'S CANDY EMPORIUM"
920 PRINT
```

```
1000 REM *** INPUT ROUTINE ***
1010 INPUT "QUANTITY: ", QN      'RECEIVE QUANTITY FROM KEYBOARD
1020 REM END OF JOB CHECK
1030 IF QN = 0 THEN GOTO 3000 'IF QUANTITY = 0 THEN GOTO OUTPUT
1040 INPUT "PRICE: ", PR          'RECEIVE PRICE FROM KEYBOARD
2000 REM *** PROCESS ROUTINE ***
2010 AMT = PR * QN                'CALCULATE AMOUNT OF SALE
2020 ST = ST + AMT                'ADD SALE TO SUBTOTAL
2030 TX = TX + ST * TR            'CALCULATE TAX
2040 TL = ST + TX                 'UPDATE TOTAL
2050 GOTO 1000                    'RETURN FOR ANOTHER ITEM
3000 REM *** OUTPUT ROUTINE ***
3010 PRINT
3020 PRINT "SUBTOTAL" , ST
3030 PRINT "TAX" , TX
3040 PRINT , "---------"
3050 PRINT "TOTAL" , TL
3060 PRINT
3070 PRINT "THANK YOU FOR SHOPPING AT SUGARMAN'S"
4000 END
```

Programming problems 11–12 at the end of the appendix require the skills we have discussed up to this point.

FOR ... NEXT Loops

As we've seen from example 3, it is often necessary to execute the same instructions many times. A payroll program, for example, might input an employee's time card, calculate regular hours worked and overtime hours, calculate gross pay, calculate deductions, record this information for later use, and print a check. It would repeat these operations for every employee. The second way to modify program flow is the FOR ... NEXT loop which allows us to specify this easily. FOR and NEXT are reserved words that appear in separate statements and serve as the beginning and end of a loop of repeated instructions.

The FOR statement initiates the loop. Its syntax is

```
10 FOR I = 3 TO 11 STEP 2
```

I is called the *index variable*. It is given the value 3 for the first "trip" through the loop. Then it is *incremented* (increased) or *stepped* by 2 to the value 5 for the next trip. The index value is incremented by the *step value* for each loop until the index exceeds 11. In this case, the index variable assumes the values 3, 5, 7, 9, and 11. The index variable limits (3 and 11 in this example) and the step variable (2) can be any number or numeric variable. The step variable can even cause the index variable to *decrement* or decrease. This is done by using a negative step value.

```
20 FOR X = 3.2 TO 2.1 STEP -.4
```

Here the index variable will assume the values 3.2, 2.8, and 2.4 because the initial value of X, 3.2, is used. Then −.4 is added to it (result 2.8) and so forth. The next value would be 2.0, but this is outside the limits for the index variable so execution terminates.

In most loops, the step value is 1. To save time and space, BASIC allows us to eliminate the STEP if it is 1. It's as if we asked you to count from one to 100. We don't say "Count by ones." That's assumed. The following two lines of code have the same effect.

```
DR. VERA BORING
APPOINTMENT LOG
8
    ----------------------
9
    ----------------------
10
    ----------------------
11
    ----------------------
12
    ----------------------
```

FIGURE B-8
Output of appointment program

```
30 FOR W3 = 2 TO 8
30 FOR W3 = 2 TO 8 STEP 1
```

Following the FOR statement, write all of the code to be repeated. Then end the loop with the NEXT statement. The syntax is

```
50 NEXT W3
```

in which W3 is the index variable. The index variable can be any valid numeric variable name. The NEXT statement specifies where the end of the loop is and what the index variable is. This is quite important in a complex program with many loops. Some versions of BASIC, however, allow you to omit the index variable from the NEXT statement. This is a dangerous practice in programs that use many FOR ... NEXT loops. It is considered good programming practice to include the index variable reference with every NEXT statement.

The NEXT statement tells the computer something else as well. It says change the index value and test it against the variable limits. If the index value is between the limits or at the second limit, go back to the statement after the FOR. If the index value is outside the limits, execute the statement after the NEXT. This is called *falling through the loop.*

Here is a simple program to make one day's appointment book for a dentist who sees patients every hour throughout the morning. To help you see the structure of this and the following programs, we have indented statements within loops and other structures. Microsoft allows this, but Applesoft does not.

```
110 PRINT "DR. VERA BORING"
120 PRINT "APPOINTMENT LOG"
130 FOR I = 8 TO 12
140    PRINT I
150    PRINT " ----------------------"
160 NEXT I
170 END
```

The output of this program as run with Applesoft is shown in figure B-8.

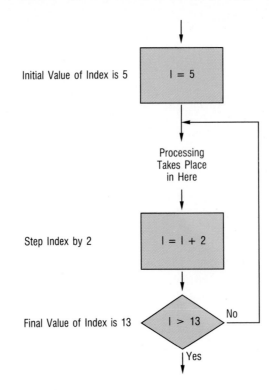

Initial Value of Index is 5 — I = 5

Processing Takes Place in Here

Step Index by 2 — I = I + 2

Final Value of Index is 13 — I > 13 — No

Yes

FIGURE B-9
FOR ... NEXT loop

The flowchart for a FOR ... NEXT loop is shown in figure B-9. The upper rectangle indentifies the index variable and assigns its first value. The diamond defines the second index variable limit. The lower rectangle sets the step value.

Exercise 9

Determine the number of times each loop in table B-10 will be executed and the final value of the index variable.

TABLE B-10 *FOR ... NEXT LOOPS*

1.
```
10 FOR I = 1 TO 10
20    PRINT I
30 NEXT I
40 END
```

2.
```
10 FOR Z = 10 TO 1 STEP -2
20    PRINT Z
30 NEXT Z
40 END
```

3.
```
10 FOR K = 3 TO 14 STEP -1
20    PRINT K
30 NEXT K
40 END
```

4.
```
10 FOR D = 1 TO 10
20    D = 20
30 NEXT D
40 END
```

```
DR. VERA BORING
APPOINTMENT LOG
8:00
        ----------------------
8:30
        ----------------------
9:00
        ----------------------
9:30
        ----------------------
10:00
        ----------------------
10:30
        ----------------------
11:00
        ----------------------
11:30
        ----------------------
12:00
        ----------------------
12:30
        ----------------------
```

FIGURE B-10
*Output of modified appointment
program*

Nested FOR ... NEXT Loops

Many programs require loops within loops. These are called *nested FOR ... NEXT loops*.
The inner loop must be completely contained in an outer loop. Each time the computer executes the outer loop, it executes the inner loop as well. It is important to
be sure that the NEXT statement for the inner loop occurs before the NEXT for the
outer loop. The next example improves Dr. Boring's appointment book to allow appointments every 30 minutes.

```
110 PRINT "DR. VERA BORING"
120 PRINT "APPOINTMENT LOG"
130 FOR I = 8 TO 12
135   FOR J = 0 TO 3 STEP 3
140       PRINT I;":";J;"0"
150       PRINT "  ----------------------"
155   NEXT J
160 NEXT I
170 END
```

The output of this program as run with Applesoft is shown in figure B-10.

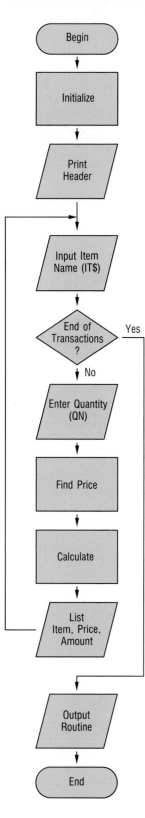

FIGURE B-11
Block diagram for Sugarman's example 4

Exercise 10

What are the first and last lines printed in this program:

```
10 FOR I = 0 TO 3
20    FOR K = 1 TO 9
30        PRINT I; K
40    NEXT K
50 NEXT I
60 END
```

Up to this point, all of the data our program has available have been entered from the keyboard in response to INPUT statements. FOR ... NEXT loops help us enter successive items of data as necessary. Frequently, we want to incorporate data that seldom change as an integral part of our program so that they can be used without requiring the user to enter them manually every time the program is run. This is accomplished through the use of DATA statements. In conjunction with DATA statements, the program will use READ statements to make the data available for processing.

The DATA Statement

The DATA statement allows us to store fixed character and numeric data in a BASIC program easily. A DATA statement can have one piece of data or several, and each is called a *data element*. Data elements are separated by commas in a DATA statement:

```
10 DATA 1, 2, 3, 4, 5
```

As in the PRINT and INPUT statements, the commas serve as delimiters separating individual data elements. If we have more data than can fit in one DATA statement, we can type several DATA statements. The computer treats

```
20 DATA 1, 2
30 DATA 3, 4, 5
```

just as it does line 10. DATA statements can intermix character and numeric data:

```
40 DATA JAN, 31, FEB, 28, MAR, 31, APR, 30, MAY, 31, JUN, 30
```

The DATA statement is the only place where character strings do not have to be surrounded by quotation marks. We may include quotation marks if we need to, for example, if the first character of a character string is to be a blank:

```
50 DATA " RED", BLUE
```

We also use quotation marks if we want to include a comma as part of a character string:

```
60 DATA 36 West St., "New Orleans, LA"
```

DATA statements are not executed, they just provide information to the program. For that reason, they can be placed anywhere in a program: at the beginning or end or with their corresponding READ statements. As a matter of style, we will place all DATA statements at the beginning.

The READ Statement

In order to make use of data elements in DATA statements, our program must use READ statements. The syntax of a READ is just like an unprompted INPUT:

```
100 READ M$, D
```

We can put one or more variables in a READ statement.

```
110 READ K, L$
```

READ and DATA statements always go hand-in-hand. If statements 100 and 110 are combined with

```
120 DATA SAM, 86.1, -8, 23SKIDOO
```

in a program and executed, M$ is assigned the character string SAM, D is assigned the value 86.1, K is assigned −8, and L$ is assigned 23SKIDOO.

The Data Pointer

BASIC maintains a *data pointer* that keeps track of the next data element to be read. DATA statement elements are always read in the order that they appear in the program. If we try to READ beyond the last data element, the computer will send an error message. Therefore, it is important to be sure not to run out of data when using READ statements.

The RESTORE Statement

When the computer tries to read beyond the available data, an error message is generated. While we don't want this to happen, we may want the program to read the same data more than once. Listing the data twice solves this problem, but not very well. What if the data are to be read many times? Then, we can reset the pointer.

The RESTORE statement resets the data pointer to the first element in the first DATA statement of our program. RESTORE can appear anywhere in the program. Its syntax is

```
120 RESTORE
```

Although RESTORE is valuable in various applications, it is particularly useful for tables. We'll modify the third example of our Sugarman's Candy Emporium program to use DATA statements to store the names and prices of each item the store sells. Then a READ statement will consult the DATA statements to find the price of each item sold.

Example 4

Many of Sugarman's customers complain that the cash register operator enters incorrect prices when calculating their bills. The operator complains, too, about having to remember the price of each item and also suggests that the output display show the name of the products purchased as well as the quantities, prices, and totals. We'll modify the program to take these new requirements into account.

The Logic. The modifications require only two adjustments to the overall program logic in example 3. In figure B-11, you'll see that the logic is very similar to that in figure B-6. The input routine in figure B-11 begins by inputting the name of the item sold, IT$. The program will use that name to find the item's price. Because the operator will input a name, a character string, rather than the quantity purchased, a number, the program's end-of-job test must use an IF ... THEN statement that will compare character strings. Let's use the character string DONE as the end-of-job signal. Our IF ... THEN command will appear as follows:

```
1010 IF IT$ = "DONE" THEN GOTO 3000
```

where IT$, as mentioned earlier, is the name of the item entered by the operator. Notice that the character string DONE is surrounded by quotation marks (") in the command.

As when using PRINT and INPUT statements, character strings require quotation marks in IF ... THEN statements, as they do for almost all BASIC commands. Line 3000, as usual, is the beginning of the output routine.

For the other modification, we'll add a routine that uses the name of the item just entered by the operator to find the item's price. The name of that routine or module is FIND PRICE. You'll find it just following the ENTER QUANTITY (QN) symbol in figure B-11.

Figure B-11 shows a general diagram of our program logic, but it does not show all of the details. Such diagrams are frequently called *block diagrams*. Figure B-12 presents

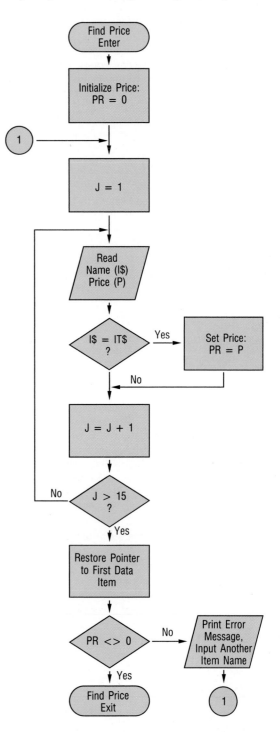

FIGURE B-12
Detail flowchart for FIND PRICE
routine of Sugarman's example 4

the details of the FIND PRICE module. Such a diagram is often called a *detailed flowchart* or *program flowchart*. Modular programming usually takes this form when flowcharts are employed. The general logic of the program appears in a block diagram. The details of each of the block diagram's modules appear in program flowcharts.

In figure B-12, the FIND PRICE module begins by initializing PR to zero. PR is the variable name for the price used to calculate the amount of each item transaction. Following that, a FOR ... NEXT loop reads each item name (I$) and price (P) from DATA statements. When I$ matches IT$, the item name entered by the operator in the input routine, PR is replaced by P, the price associated with I$ in the DATA statements. The FOR ... NEXT loop executes fifteen times, once for each of the fifteen items Sugarman's has for sale. After that, the data pointer is restored to the first data item in preparation for the next transaction.

If PR remains at zero after reading and comparing all fifteen I$s in the DATA statements with the IT$ entered by the operator, the operator entered an incorrect item name. In this case, an error message is printed and a new item name is requested. If PR is not equal to zero, the item name entered was found in the DATA statements (programmers call this a *hit*) and the FIND PRICE module exits to the calculate module (figure B-11) which calculates the sale amount for that item based upon the price that was found.

The calculate module is followed by one that lists the item name, the price, and the amount of the transaction. Then the main loop continues by returning to the input routine for another item.

There is, as the saying goes, more than one way to skin a cat. Our FIND PRICE module has the shortcoming that it must read all of the data in the DATA statements before processing can continue, even if a hit occurred with the first item name. Many programs will exit the FOR ... NEXT loop immediately upon finding a hit. This avoids unnecessary reading and comparing, but violates the principle of structured programming that stipulates that every loop or module must have but one entry and one exit. Exiting a FOR ... NEXT loop on a hit gives the loop two exits: one at the hit, the other at the NEXT statement.

Still other programs will force an exit from the loop on a hit by, in our example, setting the index variable, J, equal to sixteen, the value that causes the loop to conclude. This ignores the warning that we may use the index variable for any number of purposes, but we should not modify it as it controls the execution of the loop.

In any case, using DATA statements as look-up tables is not the best way of accomplishing our task. In example 5, we'll see a much more effective method.

The Coding. Our program uses lines 500–570 for DATA statements. The REM statements preceding the DATA statements add the new variable names we'll use in the program. The apostrophe remarks in the FIND PRICE and CALCULATIONS routines explain the function of each statement.

We've made additional modifications to the output routine. In it, the program will place all totals and underscores in the third print position on the screen so that they will line up vertically with the transaction listing produced by line 2170. This is accomplished by adding additional commas as shown. Line 3060 draws a double underscore (a series of equal signs) under the final total.

```
100 REM SUGARMAN'S CANDY EMPORIUM, EXAMPLE 4
110 REM P = PRICE READ FROM DATA STATEMENTS
120 REM PR = PRICE USED IN CALCULATIONS
130 REM QN = QUANTITY ENTERED FROM KEYBOARD
140 REM AMT = SALE AMOUNT FOR EACH ITEM (= PR * QN)
150 REM ST = SUBTOTAL (TOTAL SALES OF ALL ITEMS)
160 REM TR = TAX RATE
170 REM TX = TAX
180 REM TL = TOTAL (= ST + TX)
190 REM IT$ = ITEM NAME ENTERED FROM KEYBOARD
```

```
200 REM I$ = ITEM NAME READ FROM DATA STATEMENTS
210 REM J = INDEX VARIABLE FOR FOR...NEXT LOOPS
220 REM
500 DATA LOLLIPOPS, 0.20, CHOCOLATE BARS, 0.50
510 DATA CHOCOLATE DROPS, 1.50, TOFFEE, 0.95
520 DATA RED HOTS, 0.25, LICORICE, 0.37
530 DATA PEANUT BRITTLE, 1.42, TAFFY, 0.89
540 DATA KISSES, 1.25, NUT BARS, 0.74
550 DATA BON BONS, 2.95, HARD CENTERS, 1.98
560 DATA NUTTY FUDGE, 2.15, PLAIN FUDGE, 1.97
570 DATA WHITE CHOCOLATE, 1.75
580 REM
700 REM *** INITIALIZE ACCUMULATORS AND TAX RATE ***
710 ST = 0
720 TX = 0
730 TL = 0
740 TR = .06
750 CLS
800 PRINT "SUGARMAN'S CANDY EMPORIUM"
810 PRINT
1000 REM *** INPUT ROUTINE ***
1010 INPUT "ENTER ITEM NAME:  ", IT$
1020 IF IT$ = "DONE" THEN GOTO 3000      'IF NO MORE ITEMS, GOTO OUTPUT
1030 INPUT "ENTER QUANTITY:  ", QN
2000 REM *** PROCESS ROUTINE ***
2010 REM FIND PRICE
2020 PR = 0                              'SET PRICE TO ZERO
2030 FOR J = 1 TO 15                     'FIND PRICE FOR ITEM
2040    READ I$ , P                      'READ NAME AND PRICE
2050    IF I$ = IT$ THEN PR = P          'SET PR = PRICE
2060 NEXT J
2070 RESTORE                             'RESET POINTER
2080 IF PR <> 0 THEN GOTO 2120           'GOTO CALCULATIONS
2090 PRINT "ITEM NOT FOUND"              'ITEM NOT FOUND
2100 INPUT "ENTER ITEM NAME: " , IT$     'REQUEST CORRECT NAME
2110 GOTO 2030                           'RETURN TO PROCESS
2120 REM CALCULATIONS                    '  NEW ITEM NAME
2130 AMT = PR * QN                       'CALCULATE AMOUNT
2140 ST = ST + AMT                       'CALCULATE SUBTOTAL
2150 TX = TX + TR * AMT                  'CALCULATE TAX
2160 TL = ST + TX                        'CALCULATE TOTAL
2170 PRINT QN; IT$ ; "@" ; PR , AMT      'LIST ITEM SOLD
2180 GOTO 1000                           '   AND AMOUNT
3000 REM *** OUTPUT ROUTINE ***
3010 PRINT
3020 PRINT "SUBTOTAL" , , ST
3030 PRINT "TAX" , , TX
3040 PRINT , , "---------"
3050 PRINT "TOTAL" , , TL
3060 PRINT , , "========="
3070 PRINT
3080 PRINT "THANK YOU FOR SHOPPING AT SUGARMAN'S"
4000 END
```

```
SUGARMAN'S CANDY EMPORIUM

ENTER ITEM NAME: HARD CENTERS
ENTER QUANTITY:  4
 4 HARD CENTERS @ 1.98     7.92
ENTER ITEM NAME: TAFFEE
ENTER QUANTITY:  4
ITEM NOT FOUND
ENTER ITEM NAME: TAFFY
 4 TAFFY @ .89            3.56
ENTER ITEM NAME: BON BONS
ENTER QUANTITY:  6
 6 BON BONS @ 2.95        17.7
ENTER ITEM NAME: DONE

SUBTOTAL              29.18
TAX                    1.7508
                     ---------
TOTAL                30.9308
                     =========

THANK YOU FOR SHOPPING AT SUGARMAN'S
```

FIGURE B-13
*Display from Sugarman's
example 4*

Figure B-13 shows the output of our program. Note that each item transaction is listed. Also, when entering the second item purchased, the operator misspelled taffy, resulting in an error message. Compare the construction of line 2170 with the item transaction listings in figure B-13. Note how the semicolons and commas in the PRINT statement control the appearance of the output.

Our program will process negative input, too. Suppose a customer approaches the register with three nutty fudges and the operator inadvertently enters five. At the customer's indignant urgings, the operator corrects the error by entering another transaction for nutty fudge with a quantity of −2. The resulting output is shown in figure B-14.

Programming problems 13–23 at the end of the appendix require skills we have discussed up to this point.

Subscripted Variables

It is often valuable to be able to store many things under the same variable name. While these data are not stored in the same memory locations, they have a common identifier. Subscripted variables allow us to do this. Subscripted variables, either numeric or character, are identified by the parentheses immediately following their names. Inside the parentheses is a number that identifies which of the variables we wish to use. For example, ITEM$(1) may represent lollipops while ITEM$(2) represents chocolate bars. PRICE(0) may be 50 cents.

```
SUGARMAN'S CANDY EMPORIUM

ENTER ITEM NAME: NUTTY FUDGE
ENTER QUANTITY:  5
 5 NUTTY FUDGE @ 2.15    10.75
ENTER ITEM NAME: NUTTY FUDGE
ENTER QUANTITY:  -2
-2 NUTTY FUDGE @ 2.15    -4.3
ENTER ITEM NAME: DONE

SUBTOTAL              6.45
TAX                    .387
                     ---------
TOTAL                6.837
                     =========

THANK YOU FOR SHOPPING AT SUGARMAN'S
```

FIGURE B-14
*Display from Sugarman's
example 4, showing quantity
correction*

The number in the parentheses is called the *subscript*. It can be any number, zero or bigger. When fractions are used, they are rounded to the nearest whole number. The subscript can be a number, numeric variable, or an arithmetic expression. The following example shows all of these possibilities.

```
10 FOR G = 1 TO 5 STEP 2
20    Z(G) = G + 5
30    Z(G + 1) = G * 5
40 NEXT G
50 Z(7) = 19
60 END
```

Tracing through this program, we find that G is assigned the value 1 and G + 5 or 6 is stored in Z(1) with G * 5 stored in Z(2). Then G is stepped to 3. Eight (3 + 5) is stored in Z(3) while 15 (3 * 5) is stored in Z(4). Finally, G is stepped to 5 and the BASIC interpreter assigns 10 (5 + 5) and 25 (5 * 5) to Z(5) and Z(6), respectively.

A set of variables with the same name and different subscripts is called an *array*. To help you differentiate between variable names and array names, we will use parentheses with all array names. Think of an array as an apartment building with one family on each floor. The number in parentheses indicates what floor to visit to find a particular family (value). When we use arrays, we are limited to the 11 subscripts from zero to ten. If we want to use more, we must include a DIMENSION statement.

The DIMension Statement

We can reserve a specific number of storage locations in an array if we use the DIM statement. The statement

```
10 DIM ST(6)
```

reserves seven positions because the first position saved is ST(0). Then ST(1), ST(2), and so on up to ST(6) are reserved. If we want seven positions starting at position one, we enter

```
10 DIM ST(7)
```

even though this will reserve eight positions [we just won't use ST(0)]. We can put more than one variable in the same DIM statement if we separate them with commas.

```
10 DIM ST(12), PR(4), ITEM$(9)
```

Good programming practice requires us to place all dimension statements at the beginning of a program. We never put the same variable name in more than one dimension statement. BASIC will not accept that since it allocates space the first time a variable is dimensioned and cannot reallocate the space. If we dimension a variable twice, the computer responds with an error message:

```
?REDIM'D ARRAY         or      DUPLICATE DEFINITION
```
      (Applesoft)   (Microsoft)

Exercise 11

Write a program (eight statements plus REMs) to input 12 names into an array called NME$( ) then print the names in reverse order.

Exiting a FOR ... NEXT Loop Early

We often require a program to exit or to drop through a loop before completing all its cycles. Consider, for instance, the situation in which we don't know how much data to input into an array. We would use the following code to dimension the array sufficiently to take care of all realistic cases.

```
10 DIM N$(500)
20 J = 500
30 FOR I = 1 TO 500
40   INPUT N$(I)
50   IF N$(I) <> "DONE" THEN GOTO 80
60   J = I - 1
70   I = 500
80 NEXT I
```

In this code, we use I as the loop index and J to keep track of the number of entries to the array. Here's how it works. Line 20 sets J to its maximum value, 500, in case there is no end-of-job indicator. Line 60 sets J to the number of entries in N$( ), eliminating the last entry which is the indicator. These two statements, taken together, insure that J will be set correctly in every case. Finally, line 70 sets I to the ending value of the loop so control will pass out of the loop and into the next block of code.

From this point in the program, we use J as the ending value of the index when we use the array. I no longer stores data of any value to us, so we can use it for other purposes.

More on Variable Names

BASIC allows us to use the same characters for four different names: a numeric variable, a numeric array, a character variable, and a character array. Thus, A, A(3), A$, and A$(9) can all exist in the same program. Changing one of them has no effect on the others. Each of them represents a different memory location in the computer. It's not a good idea to use names like this though. That only leads to confusion.

Logical Operators

Because decisions are often made on the basis of several conditions, an important aspect of BASIC is the ability to combine relational conditions (X < 7, Y = 10, etc.) using *logical operators*. We will consider three logical operators: OR, AND, and NOT.

OR

When two conditions are connected by an OR, the resulting *compound condition* is true if either or both of the original conditions is true. In other words, the compound condition will only be false if both conditions are false. Table B-11 shows examples of OR.

TABLE B-11 THE LOGICAL OPERATOR OR

Expression	Calculation	Value
2 < 3 OR 3 < 6	TRUE OR TRUE	TRUE
2 < 3 OR 3 > 6	TRUE OR FALSE	TRUE
2 > 3 OR 3 <> 6	FALSE OR TRUE	TRUE
2 = 3 OR 6 <= 4	FALSE OR FALSE	FALSE

TABLE B-12 THE LOGICAL OPERATOR AND

Expression	Calculation	Value
2 < 3 AND 3 < 6	TRUE AND TRUE	TRUE
2 < 3 AND 3 > 6	TRUE AND FALSE	FALSE
2 > 3 AND 3 <> 6	FALSE AND TRUE	FALSE
2 = 3 AND 6 <= 4	FALSE AND FALSE	FALSE

TABLE B-13 THE LOGICAL OPERATOR NOT

Expression	Calculation	Value
NOT 3 < 5	NOT TRUE	FALSE
NOT 3 >< 5 – 2	NOT FALSE	TRUE

AND

When two conditions are connected by an AND, the resulting compound condition is true *only* if both original conditions are true. Table B-12 shows examples of AND.

NOT

NOT precedes a condition. If a condition is true, having NOT precede it makes the expression false. When NOT precedes a false condition, it makes that expression true. See table B-13 for examples of this logical operator.

Compound relational conditions linked by logical operators can be used wherever single conditions are allowed. For example, the following code transfers control to statement 100.

```
10 X = 5
20 Y = 8
30 Z = 3
40 IF X < Y AND Z <> Y/2 THEN GOTO 100
```

We are not limited to using two relational conditions. We can combine several, as long as there are appropriate logical operators between each. When we combine more than two conditions with different logical operators, it is important to use parentheses to tell the computer the order in which to do the operations indicated. In the following example, the computer evaluates the expressions in the parentheses first, then determines whether the entire expression is true or not.

```
10 X = 5
20 Y = 15
30 Z = 8
40 IF X < Z AND NOT (Z + 7 = Y OR 2 * Z > Y) THEN PRINT "TRUE"
50 PRINT "DONE"
```

In line 40, the program first evaluates (Z + 7 = Y OR 2 * Z > Y), which is true. The NOT changes this to false. Then X < Z is evaluated. It is true. The entire expression is

true AND false

which is false. The computer does not execute the THEN part of line 40. The program's output is

DONE

Exercise 12

Decide whether the THEN part of the IF ... THEN statements in table B-14 will be executed. Assume X = 1, Y = 8, and Z = 11.

After using our cash register program for a few days, the register operator has even more suggestions. First, the output display is cluttered with input dialog. In figure B-13, we can see that the input prompts and responses are interspersed with the transactions listing. It would be much nicer if the program listed the transactions separately, after the inputting operation concludes. Second, if a customer purchases three licorices, four white chocolates, and then two more licorices, and the operator enters the items in that order, the output listing shows three transactions. It would be better, the operator points out, if the listing showed two transactions: five licorices and four white chocolates. Third, the operator, not being a skilled typist, frequently misspells the item names. This causes delays at the register counter. Fourth, the program must be RUN separately for each customer. We should fix it so that after a customer has been billed, the operator can either process another customer or close the register for the day. Finally, after entering transactions for a customer, the operator occasionally misspells the end-of-job indicator. The only way to recover from this error is to process a dummy transaction with zero entered as the quantity and then try to enter DONE again at the next item name prompt. Study the FIND PRICE module in figure B-12 carefully, and you'll see why this happens.

As if that weren't enough, Sugarman's must now charge an additional tax. For years, the Concerned Citizens Committee for Restriction of Chocolate Consumption (CCCROCC) has lobbied Congress to levy an excise tax on chocolate, believing it to be addictive, just like alcohol and tobacco. This year, CCCROCC met with partial success. Congress has established a 12 percent excise tax on fudge, considered to be the most addictive chocolate product of all.

Example 5

Our cash register program must solve the five problems identified by the operator and calculate the total state sales tax of six percent on all items purchased and an additional 12 percent tax on fudge products, namely nutty fudge and plain fudge. The state tax and the federal excise tax must be listed separately.

The Logic. It sounds as if there are a lot of changes, but it's not really so bad. Our program will include four arrays: IT$( ), a table of item names; PR( ), a table of prices for each item; QN( ), a table of quantities of each item purchased; and AMT( ),

TABLE B-14 COMPOUND CONDITIONS

```
10 IF Y + 3 * X < Z OR X > 0 THEN PRINT "ROMEO"
20 IF Y < Z AND X > 4 THEN PRINT "JULIET"
30 IF (Y = X + 7) AND (X > Z OR Z <> 100) THEN PRINT "CAPULET"
40 IF Y < 10 AND (X > 0 OR NOT Z = 11) THEN PRINT "MONTAGUE"
```

TABLE B-15 TABLE FOR EXAMPLE 5

Position I	Item Name IT$(I)	Price PR(I)	Sales Quantity QN(I)	Sales Amount AMT(I)
1	lollipops	0.20	0	0
2	chocolate bars	0.50	0	0
3	chocolate drops	1.50	0	0
4	toffee	0.95	0	0
5	red hots	0.25	0	0
6	licorice	0.37	0	0
7	peanut brittle	1.42	0	0
8	taffy	0.89	0	0
9	kisses	1.25	0	0
10	nut bars	0.74	0	0
11	bon bons	2.95	0	0
12	hard centers	1.98	0	0
13	nutty fudge	2.15	0	0
14	plain fudge	1.97	0	0
15	white chocolate	1.75	0	0

a table containing accumulators for the sales amounts of each item the customer purchased. Table B-15 shows the relationships among these tables.

Instead of entering an item name for each transaction, the operator will enter an item number from 1 through 15. We'll use the variable name I to represent the entry. The quantity purchased is also entered and is represented by the variable name Q. Let's say a customer buys 3 red hots. The operator enters 5 for the item number, I, and 3 for the quantity purchased, Q. From table B-15, you can see that IT$(5) contains the item name, red hots, and that PR(5) contains its price, 0.25. Our processing routine will update the sales quantity accumulator for red hots, QN(5), by adding the sales quantity, Q, to it:

```
2010 QN(I) = QN(I) + Q
```

Note that I = 5 because that's the item number the operator entered. Similarly, we'll update the sales amount accumulator by adding the product of the quantity of the item purchased times the item's price to it:

```
2020 AMT(I) = AMT(I) + Q * PR(I)
```

Because, in this example, I equals 5, the quantity purchased, QN(5), and the amount of the item sale, AMT(5), are both updated with the appropriate values for the product red hots, IT$(5).

In figure B-15, the program begins by building the item name and price tables using READ ... DATA. Then it prints the header and initializes the total accumulators, including the tables QN( ) and AMT( ), to zero in preparation for a new customer.

Because the operator will now enter item numbers instead of names, our end-of-job code will be zero. If, in response to the INPUT prompt ENTER ITEM NUMBER, 0 FOR NO MORE ITEMS, the operator enters a non-zero number, the program will check it to assure that it is a valid item number. To be valid, the number must be from 1 through 15. If the operator enters 16, say, the program will show an error message and ask for another number. Our test for a valid item number uses, as you would expect, an IF...THEN statement:

```
1030 IF I >= 1 AND I <= 15 THEN GOTO 1060
```

Line 1060 continues the input routine for valid item numbers. The statement in line 1030 uses the logical operator AND. *Both* the I > = 1 and I < = 15 conditions must be true for processing to continue.

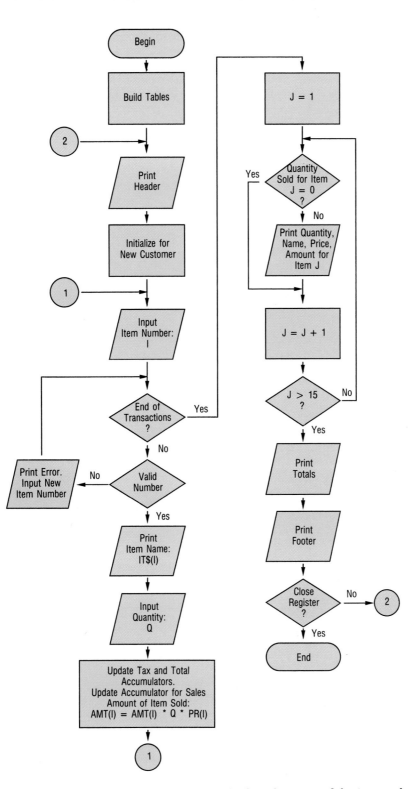

FIGURE B-15
Flowchart for Sugarman's
example 5

Given a valid item number, the program displays the name of the item and requests the quantity purchased. Then it updates the accumulators and returns for another item.

On receiving the end-of-job code, 0, the program transfers control to the output routine. The output routine uses a FOR ... NEXT loop to list the transaction for each item purchased. Within that loop, if the quantity purchased for an item is zero, the program skips it without printing. This way the transaction listing shows only those items purchased.

The output routine prints the totals, as usual, but now includes the excise tax, too. The end-of-job routine then asks if the register is to be closed with the INPUT prompt

```
CLOSE REGISTER? (Y/N):
```

If the response is N, for No, the program returns to the initialization routine and prepares for the next customer. If the response is Y, for Yes (or any other character besides N), the program ends.

The Coding. Leaving out the DATA statements, which are identical to those in the example 4 program, here is the program listing. Study it carefully and compare it with the flowchart in figure B-15.

```
100 REM SUGARMAN'S CANDY EMPORIUM, EXAMPLE 5
110 REM I = ITEM NUMBER ENTERED FROM KEYBOARD
120 REM PR(I) = PRICE READ FROM TABLE
130 REM IT$(I) ITEM NAME READ FROM TABLE
140 REM Q = QUANTITY ENTERED FROM KEYBOARD
150 REM QN(I) = QUANTITY SOLD ACCUMULATORS FOR ITEMS PURCHASED
160 REM AMT(I) = SALE AMOUNT ACCUMULATORS FOR ITEMS PURCHASED
170 REM ST = SUBTOTAL (TOTAL SALES OF ALL ITEMS)
180 REM T6 = TOTAL AMOUNT OF TAX AT 6%
190 REM T12 = TOTAL AMOUNT OF TAX AT 12%
200 REM TL = TOTAL (= ST + T6 + T12)
210 REM J = INDEX VARIABLE
         .    .    .
700 DIM PR(15), IT$(15), QN(15), AMT(15) 'SET UP ARRAYS
710 FOR J = 1 TO 15              'BUILD TABLES
720   READ IT$(J), PR(J)
730 NEXT J
800 REM *** START NEW CUSTOMER ***
810 CLS
820 PRINT "SUGARMAN'S CANDY EMPORIUM"
830 PRINT
840 ST = 0                      'SET TOTAL
850 TL = 0                      'ACCUMULATORS
860 T6 = 0                      'TO ZERO
870 T12 = 0
880 FOR J = 1 TO 15             'SET ITEM SALES
890   QN(J) = 0                 'ACCUMULATORS
900   AMT(J) = 0                'TO ZERO
910 NEXT J
1000 REM *** INPUT ROUTINE ***
1010 INPUT "ENTER ITEM NUMBER, 0 FOR NO MORE ITEMS: ", I
1020 IF I = 0 THEN GOTO 3000    'IF NO MORE ITEMS, GOTO OUTPUT
1030 IF I >= 1 AND I <= 15 THEN GOTO 1060  'VALID NUMBER CHECK
1040 INPUT " ITEM NUMBER FROM 1 THROUGH 15, PLEASE: ", I
1050 GOTO 1020                  'RETURN TO CHECK ITEM NUMBER
1060 PRINT IT$(I)
1070 INPUT "QUANTITY: " , Q
```

```
2000 REM *** PROCESS ROUTINE ***
2010 QN(I) = QN(I) + Q                'UPDATE SALES QUANTITY ACCUMULATOR
2020 AMT(I) = AMT(I) + Q * PR(I)      'UPDATE SALES AMOUNT ACCUMULATOR
2030 T6 = T6 + .06 * Q * PR(I)        'UPDATE TAX ACCUMULATORS
2040 IF I = 13 OR I = 14 THEN T12 = T12 + .12 * Q * PR(I)
2050 ST = ST + Q * PR(I)              'UPDATE TOTAL ACCUMULATORS
2060 TL = ST + T6 + T12
2070 GOTO 1000                        'RETURN FOR NEXT ITEM
3000 REM *** OUTPUT ROUTINE ***
3010 PRINT
3020 FOR J = 1 TO 15
3030  IF QN(J) = 0 THEN GOTO 3050     'SKIP ITEM IF NO SALES
3040  PRINT  QN(J) ; IT$(J) ; " @" ; PR(J) , AMT(J)
3050 NEXT J
3060 PRINT , , "---------"
3070 PRINT "SUBTOTAL" , , ST
3080 PRINT "6% TAX" , , T6
3090 PRINT "12% TAX" , , T12
3100 PRINT , , "---------"
3110 PRINT "TOTAL" , , TL
3120 PRINT , , "========="
3130 PRINT
3140 PRINT "THANK YOU FOR SHOPPING AT SUGARMAN'S"
4000 REM *** END OF JOB ROUTINE ***
4010 PRINT
4020 INPUT "CLOSE REGISTER? (Y/N): ", C$
4030 IF C$ = "N" THEN GOTO 800
4040 END
```

The loop in lines 710–730 builds the item name and price tables. Notice that we use the variable name J as the index variable. Our earlier programs used I as an index variable. Because this version uses I to represent the item number, we'll use J for the index variable. It's a good idea to list index variables in the documentary REM statements at the beginning of a program, as we've done in line 210.

The loop in lines 880–910 initializes the QN( ) and AMT( ) accumulators to zero.

Lines 2030 and 2040 update the tax accumulators. T6 is the variable name for the six percent tax accumulator; T12 for the 12 percent tax accumulator. Line 2040 determines if I = 13 or I = 14, the item numbers of the two products that are subject to the excise tax. If either condition is true, the T12 accumulator is updated by the amount of the tax.

Lines 3020–3050 select and list the transactions for those items that have been sold. Figures B-16 and B-17 show the output from this program.

Programming problems 24–33 at the end of the appendix require the skills we have discussed up to this point.

Subroutines

Often, it is useful to code BASIC in independent sections, and then connect the sections with a set of instructions or block of code called a *driver*. The sections of code are called *subroutines*. When we do this, we are using a form of structured program-

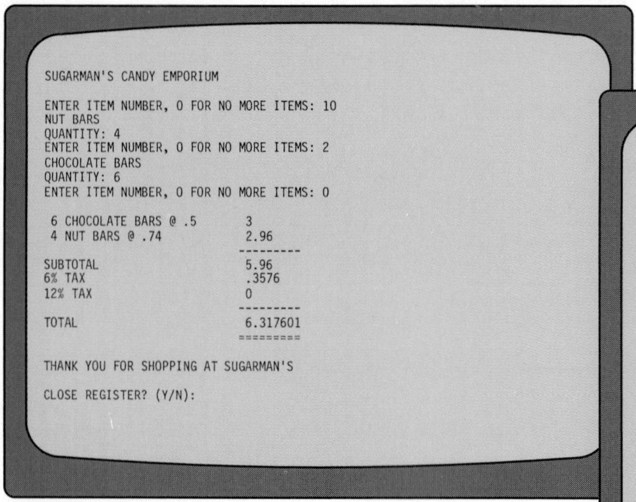

```
SUGARMAN'S CANDY EMPORIUM

ENTER ITEM NUMBER, 0 FOR NO MORE ITEMS: 10
NUT BARS
QUANTITY: 4
ENTER ITEM NUMBER, 0 FOR NO MORE ITEMS: 2
CHOCOLATE BARS
QUANTITY: 6
ENTER ITEM NUMBER, 0 FOR NO MORE ITEMS: 0

 6 CHOCOLATE BARS @ .5       3
 4 NUT BARS @ .74            2.96
                             ---------
SUBTOTAL                     5.96
6% TAX                       .3576
12% TAX                      0
                             ---------
TOTAL                        6.317601
                             =========

THANK YOU FOR SHOPPING AT SUGARMAN'S

CLOSE REGISTER? (Y/N):
```

FIGURE B-16
Display from Sugarman's example 5

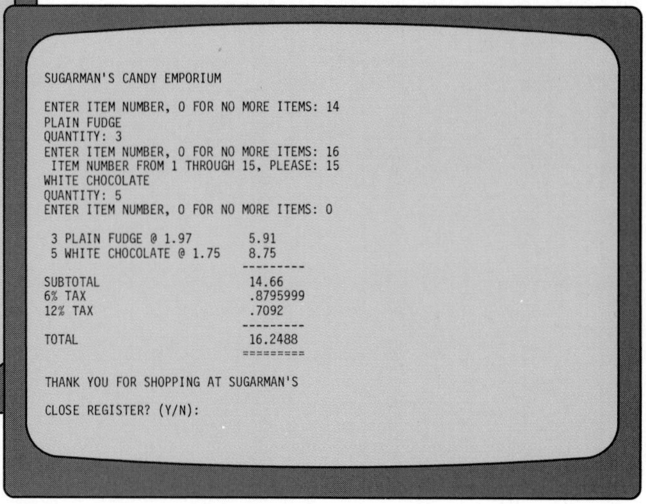

```
SUGARMAN'S CANDY EMPORIUM

ENTER ITEM NUMBER, 0 FOR NO MORE ITEMS: 14
PLAIN FUDGE
QUANTITY: 3
ENTER ITEM NUMBER, 0 FOR NO MORE ITEMS: 16
 ITEM NUMBER FROM 1 THROUGH 15, PLEASE: 15
WHITE CHOCOLATE
QUANTITY: 5
ENTER ITEM NUMBER, 0 FOR NO MORE ITEMS: 0

 3 PLAIN FUDGE @ 1.97        5.91
 5 WHITE CHOCOLATE @ 1.75    8.75
                             ---------
SUBTOTAL                     14.66
6% TAX                       .8795999
12% TAX                      .7092
                             ---------
TOTAL                        16.2488
                             =========

THANK YOU FOR SHOPPING AT SUGARMAN'S

CLOSE REGISTER? (Y/N):
```

FIGURE B-17
Display from Sugarman's example 5, showing incorrect item number correction and excise tax listing

ming called *modular programming.* The modules form a structure chart (see Chapter Nine). The driver is a controlling module in a structure chart.

A subroutine is a block of code that performs one task each time it is executed. A set of subroutines might be used when the computer must take one of several options, then return to a standard program flow. Figure B-18 illustrates the idea. We can also build a library of subroutines to use in many different programs, thus increasing programming efficiency. The subroutine is indistinguishable from the code around it except that there is a clear endpoint. It is a good idea to indicate the beginning of a subroutine with a REM statement. We end a subroutine with a RETURN statement:

```
130 RETURN
```

Transferring Control to a Subroutine

The GOSUB statement transfers control to a subroutine. The syntax is

```
100 GOSUB 500
```

When the computer encounters this statement, it immediately executes the statement with the line number following the word GOSUB. The computer continues execution from that statement until it encounters a RETURN. The next statement executed is the one immediately following the GOSUB statement. For example, output from

```
10 PRINT 10
20 GOSUB 100
30 PRINT 30
40 END
100 REM SUBROUTINE STARTS HERE
110 PRINT "SUBROUTINE"
120 RETURN
```

would be

```
10
SUBROUTINE
30
```

Exercise 13

Determine the output produced by the following program when the values entered as X are 5, 6, 7, and 99.

```
10  INPUT X
20  IF X = 99 THEN END
30  IF X < 6 THEN GOSUB 70
40  IF X > 6 THEN GOSUB 100
50  IF X = 6 THEN GOSUB 130
60  GOTO 10
70  REM SUBROUTINE FOR X SMALL
80    PRINT "SMALL"
90  RETURN
100 REM SUBROUTINE FOR X LARGE
110   PRINT "LARGE"
120 RETURN
130 REM SUBROUTINE FOR X = 6
140   PRINT "RIGHT IN THE MIDDLE"
150 RETURN
```

Our example 5 program prints to the nearest 1/100,000 of a penny. We need to develop some technique for rounding off the amount. To do this, we will use one of the many built-in functions provided by BASIC. This one is called the INTeger function.

The INTeger Function

The integer function returns the number if it is an integer; otherwise, it returns the next lower number. For example, INT(12.3) is 12, while INT(4) is 4, and INT(0) is 0. The number or expression in the parentheses of a function is called an *argument*. So far, so good. When we consider negative numbers, though, things get a little less clear. First, some examples: INT(-1) is -1; INT(-2.7) is -3; INT(-3.1) is -4. The answers don't seem right. But if we visualize all of the numbers on a line and pick a number on that line, the INT of that number is the selected number if it is whole or the next whole number to the left of the selected number. Thus, INT(12), INT(12.001), and

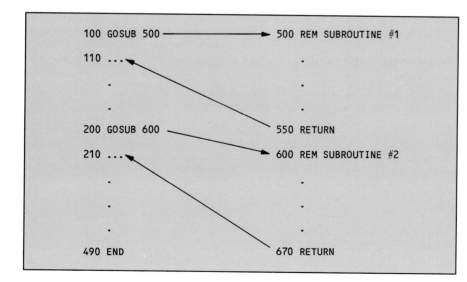

FIGURE B-18
Using subroutines to alter program flow

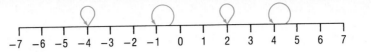

INT(12.999) all result in the value 12. Figure B-19 shows such a number line. On it we have selected several numbers. The arrows point to the corresponding INTs of the numbers.

Exercise 14

Determine the value stored in Z for each of these BASIC statements.

```
1 Z = INT(-2.774)
2 Z = INT(14.7)
3 Z = INT(0)
4 Z = INT(-5)
```

Rounding Off

The integer function is especially useful for rounding off numbers. Rounding is almost like throwing away unneeded digits. The INT function does this, but it throws away too many. We'd like to save two digits to the right of the decimal point. What we must do is move the decimal point two places, use INT to drop off places to the right of the decimal point and then move the decimal point back:

```
INT(TAX * 100) / 100
```

This is almost correct. Instead of always throwing away digits, or *truncating*, the program must sometimes round up and sometimes round down. If we add one half after multiplying by 100, we increase the integer portion of our number by one only for numbers that should be rounded up. Our round off expression looks like this:

```
INT(TAX * 100 + .5) / 100
```

Let's see how to evaluate this expression. Say we want to round 87.537 to the nearest hundredth. Then the BASIC statement is really

```
INT(87.537 * 100 + .5) / 100
```

Using BASIC's rules of arithmetic, we evaluate the expression in parentheses first:

```
INT(8754.2) / 100
```

Use the function next:

```
8754 / 100
```

Finally, we do the division:

```
87.54
```

Thus, the value is rounded to the nearest cent. Try exercise 15.

Exercise 15

Determine the printed output of the following program.

```
100 PRINT INT(21.234)
110 PRINT INT(21.234 * 100)
120 PRINT INT(21.234 * 100) / 100
130 PRINT INT(21.234 * 100 + .5) / 100
140 PRINT INT(21.546 * 100 + .5) / 100
150 END
```

TABLE B-16 BUILT-IN FUNCTIONS

Function	Reserved Word	Purpose	Availability*
Greatest integer	INT	Gives the closest whole number not greater than the argument.	A, M
Signum	SGN	Gives 1, 0, or −1 if the argument is positive, zero, or negative respectively.	A, M
Absolute value	ABS	Gives the value of the argument without regard to sign.	A, M
Square root	SQR	Gives the square root of a nonnegative number.	A, M
Random number	RND	Gives an unpredictable fractional number in the range 0–1.	A, M
Sine	SIN	These functions deal with cyclical processes like inflation and recession.	A, M
Cosine	COS		A, M
Tangent	TAN		A, M
Inverse tangent	ATN		A, M
Exponential	EXP	These functions deal with growth processes like mortgage interest.	A, M
Logarithm	LOG		A, M
Left segment	LEFT$	These functions deal with character strings.	A, M
Right segment	RIGHT$		A, M
Middle segment	MID$		A, M
ASCII value	ASC		A, M
Select character	CHR$		A, M
String length	LEN		A, M
Numeric value	VAL		A, M
Convert to string	STR$		A, M
Space	SPC	These functions control the location of the next character on the CRT.	A
	SPACE$		M
Tabulate	TAB		A, M
Horizontal tab	HTAB		A
Vertical tab	VTAB		A
Position cursor	LOCATE		M
Date	DATE$	Provides the current system date.	M
Time	TIME$	Provides the current system time.	M

*A = Applesoft, M = Microsoft

There are numerous other functions available in BASIC. Although we will not use them in this book, we will describe some of them briefly in table B-16.

Example 6

The new program works so well that Sugarman wants to show it to some of his friends. Because they are computer professionals and because Sugarman has heard from them about the virtues of modular and structured programming, he wants it modified so that a driver program controls the various modules as subroutines. He also wants the program modified so that it rounds the output amounts to the nearest penny rather than to the nearest 1/100,000 of a penny as it now does. Also, as it now stands, the program prints the header as part of the initialization activity. When a customer buys more than three items, it scrolls off of the top of the screen. Sugarman would like it to show at the top of the transaction listing rather than at the top of the input dialog.

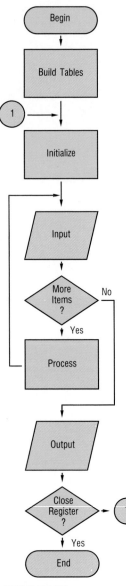

FIGURE B-20(A)
Block diagram for Sugarman's
example 6

The Logic.   The program logic of the modules in our program will change very little. Figure B-20(A) shows a block diagram for the driver program. It is very simple, as you can see. Each of the modules — BUILD TABLES, INITIALIZE, INPUT, PROCESS, and OUTPUT — operate as subroutines which are called as necessary by the driver program. Each module would ordinarily be described by its own program flowchart, but we will not show them here. The logic of the modules appears in the flowchart for example 5. Figure B-20(B) shows a structure chart for the program. Structure charts are often used to show the organization of modular programs. This one is very simple. The driver program, CASH REGISTER, controls all of the modules connected to it from below. Structure charts do not show logic, only controlling organization. The driver calls the submodules from left to right unless its logic dictates otherwise.

The Coding.   Having already prepared the program in modular fashion, there's not much to converting it. From the listing for the example 5 program, we can see that the BUILD TABLES module begins with line 700 and the new customer INITIALIZATION module begins with line 800. As we know, the INPUT, PROCESS, and OUTPUT modules start in lines 1000, 2000, and 3000, respectively. Armed with this information, we add the driver routine to the example 5 program starting in line 300:

```
300 REM *** DRIVER ***
310 GOSUB 700                         'BUILD TABLES ROUTINE
320 GOSUB 800                         'NEW CUSTOMER INITIALIZATION
330 INPUT "ENTER ITEM NUMBER,          0 FOR NO MORE ITEMS: " , I
340 IF I = 0 THEN GOTO 390            'TO OUTPUT
350 GOSUB 1000                        'INPUT ROUTINE
360 IF I = 0 THEN GOTO 390
370 GOSUB 2000                        'PROCESS ROUTINE
380 GOTO 330                          'RETURN FOR NEXT ITEM
390 GOSUB 3000                        'OUTPUT ROUTINE
400 REM *** END OF JOB ROUTINE ***
410 PRINT
420 INPUT "CLOSE REGISTER? (Y/N): ", C$
430 IF C$ = "N" THEN GOTO 320   'RETURN FOR NEXT CUSTOMER
440 END
```

Line 310 calls the BUILD TABLE module or routine. After BUILD TABLE finishes, it returns control to the next line of the driver, 320, which calls the INITIALIZE routine. When INITIALIZE is finished, it returns control to the driver at line 330. Because the driver must control the execution of the other modules, the item number input and end-of-job test will be part of the driver. Lines 330 and 340 take care of that operation. If the item number entered in response to the INPUT prompt is not zero, the driver calls the INPUT routine and the PROCESS routines in order.

Line 360 takes care of a special circumstance that may arise if the operator enters an invalid item number. The INPUT module will check it and ask for another. If a 0 is entered at this time, the INPUT module returns control to the driver at line 360 which transfers control to the OUTPUT module and then, eventually, to the END-OF-JOB routine.

Line 380 loops back for the next item number. An item number of zero will cause

FIGURE B-20(B)
Structure chart for Sugarman's
example 6

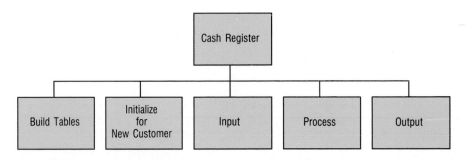

a branch to line 390 which calls the OUTPUT routine. When it finishes, it returns control to the driver in line 400, the END-OF-JOB module. We do not treat the END-OF-JOB module as a subroutine because the driver, not a subroutine, should control whether or not the program will end.

Modifying the modules in the body of the program is even easier. For the BUILD TABLE module, we simply add a RETURN command in line 740 of the exercise 5 program. Similarly, we add a RETURN command in line 920, the end of the INITIALIZE module. Continuing in this fashion, we add RETURN commands in lines 1080, 2070, and 3150 of the INPUT, PROCESSING, and OUTPUT modules. Notice, from the example 5 listing, that the RETURN command will replace the GOTO 1000 in line 2070. We delete the END-OF-JOB routine from lines 4000–4040 because the driver program has it starting at line 400.

That's just about all there is to it. The INPUT module in the exercise 4 program requires some minor adjustment. Here's the modified version:

```
1000 REM *** INPUT ROUTINE ***
1010 IF I >= 1 AND I <= 15 THEN GOTO 1060  'VALID NUMBER CHECK
1020 INPUT "ITEM NUMBER FROM 1 THROUGH 15, PLEASE: " , I
1030 IF I = 0 THEN GOTO 1080
1050 GOTO 1010
1060 PRINT IT$(I)
1070 INPUT "QUANTITY: " , Q
1080 RETURN
```

The commands to receive an item number and check for the end-of-job signal have been moved to the driver. If the item number entered there is not zero, the driver calls the INPUT routine, as we've seen. Line 1010 of the INPUT routine checks for a valid number. If the number is valid, control is transferred to line 1060 where processing continues. If the item number is invalid, line 1020 prints an error message and requests a new item number. If the new item number is not zero, line 1010 checks it for validity. If the item number is zero, this customer's transactions are completed and control returns to the driver through line 1080.

The PROCESS module remains unchanged except for replacing the GOTO 1000 instruction on line 2070 with RETURN.

The OUTPUT module is also unchanged, so far as its operation as a subroutine is concerned, but the output amounts have been rounded to the nearest penny using the INT function in lines 3040–3110. We've also deleted the header printing operation in line 820 of the example 5 program and added it with a CLS to the beginning of the OUTPUT routine in lines 3002 and 3004.

```
3000 REM *** OUTPUT ROUTINE ***
3002 CLS
3004 PRINT "SUGARMAN'S CANDY EMPORIUM"
3010 PRINT
3020 FOR J = 1 TO 15
3030  IF QN(J) = 0 THEN GOTO 3050   'SKIP ITEM IF NO SALES
3040 PRINT QN(J) ; IT$(J) ; " @" ; PR(J) , INT(AMT(J) * 100 + .5) / 100
3050 NEXT J
3060 PRINT , , "---------"
3070 PRINT "SUBTOTAL" , , INT(ST * 100 + .5) / 100
3080 PRINT "6% TAX" , , INT(T6 * 100 + .5) / 100
3090 PRINT "12% TAX" , , INT(T12 * 100 + .5) / 100
3100 PRINT , , "---------"
3110 PRINT "TOTAL" , , INT(TL * 100 + .5) /100
3120 PRINT , , "========="
3130 PRINT
3140 PRINT "THANK YOU FOR SHOPPING AT SUGARMAN'S"
3150 RETURN
```

FIGURE B-21(B)
Display from Sugarman's example 6 showing header,
transaction listing, and rounded output

```
TOFFEE
QUANTITY: 7
ENTER ITEM NUMBER, 0 FOR NO MORE ITEMS: 2
CHOCOLATE BARS
QUANTITY: 35
ENTER ITEM NUMBER, 0 FOR NO MORE ITEMS: 7
PEANUT BRITTLE
QUANTITY: 10
ENTER ITEM NUMBER, 0 FOR NO MORE ITEMS: 10
NUT BARS
QUANTITY: 20
ENTER ITEM NUMBER, 0 FOR NO MORE ITEMS: 14
PLAIN FUDGE
QUANTITY: 40
ENTER ITEM NUMBER, 0 FOR NO MORE ITEMS: 1
LOLLIPOPS
QUANTITY: 30
ENTER ITEM NUMBER, 0 FOR NO MORE ITEMS: 9
KISSES
QUANTITY: 100
ENTER ITEM NUMBER, 0 FOR NO MORE ITEMS: 5
RED HOTS
QUANTITY: 45
ENTER ITEM NUMBER, 0 FOR NO MORE ITEMS:
```

```
SUGARMAN'S CANDY EMPORIUM

30 LOLLIPOPS @ .2          6
35 CHOCOLATE BARS @ .5     17.5
50 CHOCOLATE DROPS @ 1.5   75
7 TOFFEE @ .95             6.65
45 RED HOTS @ .25          11.25
10 PEANUT BRITTLE @ 1.42   14.2
25 TAFFY @ .89             22.25
100 KISSES @ 1.25          125
20 NUT BARS @ .74          14.8
40 PLAIN FUDGE @ 1.97      78.8
                           ---------
SUBTOTAL                   371.45
6% TAX                     22.29
12% TAX                    9.46
                           ---------
TOTAL                      403.19
                           =========

THANK YOU FOR SHOPPING AT SUGARMAN'S

CLOSE REGISTER? (Y/N):
```

FIGURE B-21(A)
Display from Sugarman's example 6 after
entering ten transactions

Figure B-21(A) shows the screen after entering ten transactions for a customer who was stocking up on candy in anticipation of a sugar shortage. The first three transactions have scrolled off the top of the screen. Figure B-21(B) shows the screen as it appears after the operator entered the end-of-job code. The header and all transactions appear, and the output amounts are rounded to the nearest penny.

Programming problems 34–40 at the end of this appendix require the skills we have discussed up to this point.

There you have an introduction to BASIC, a powerful language for solving business problems. As you've seen with INT, a little creative thought enables you to accomplish tasks not originally planned for BASIC. There are many features we have not discussed. But we have presented enough to give you a good start. Work some of the problems at the end of this appendix. When you feel confident, get a book about BASIC and continue to learn. The best way to do this is by using a computer to write programs. Before we turn you out into the cold cruel world, though, let's talk about debugging.

DEBUGGING A BASIC PROGRAM

There are essentially two phases in the debugging process. First, we make sure that our logic is correct. Then we check the coding.

The Logic

The logic is readily checked if we have made a flowchart. Basically, we play computer, called *desk checking*. In desk checking, we trace program logic, keeping track of all variable assignments and arithmetic. Consider the problem of averaging three scores. A flowchart appears in figure B-22(A). The *trace* of the program is shown in figure B-22(B). As you can see, there is a flaw in our logic. We've added only two numbers together instead of three. We must correct the flowchart and repeat the desk check.

Exercise 16

Correct the flowchart in figure B-22(A) and desk check the logic.

We must make test cases to check every possible data path to make sure we get the correct answers, being particularly careful to try cases that test decision points. For instance, in a statement like

```
IF X <= 2 THEN PRINT "TEST CASE"
```

does the program behave correctly if X = 2? Later, when we are debugging the code, we can use the same test cases to check that.

Example 7

In California, food is not taxed, while other goods are. We are to write a cash register program to total a sale and charge the correct sales tax.

For the sake of this example, we will assume that item codes under 1000 are non-food items and codes 1000 and above are foodstuffs. Let's consider only that portion of the program that calculates the tax and total. We will assume that the item number and price are stored in IT(I) and PR(I) and the quantity purchased will always be one. The number of items purchased is stored in N.

We start by drawing the flowchart shown in figure B-23.

For completeness, make three test cases. Check an item that is taxable, an item that is nontaxable, and item number 1000 (is this one taxed or not?), the boundary case. The first two cases work just fine, but the boundary case is taxed even though it shouldn't be. Adjust the flowchart as shown in figure B-24 and retest all three cases.

The Coding.   Once the logic is correct, we can code the program. Using modular programming techniques, code a small section and debug it before starting the next portion of the code. By the time the coding process is complete, we will only have to debug the linkages.

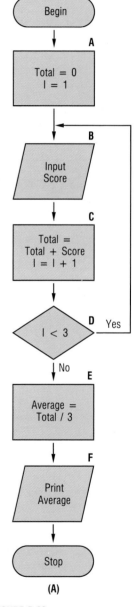

(A)

FIGURE B-22
*(A) Flowchart for exercise 15
(B) Desk checking the logic of a
program*

BOX	TOTAL	I	SCORE	AVERAGE	NOTES
A	0	1			
B			21		
C	21	2			
D					Loop back to B
B					
C	33	3			
D					Drop through to E
E				11	
F					Print 11

(B)

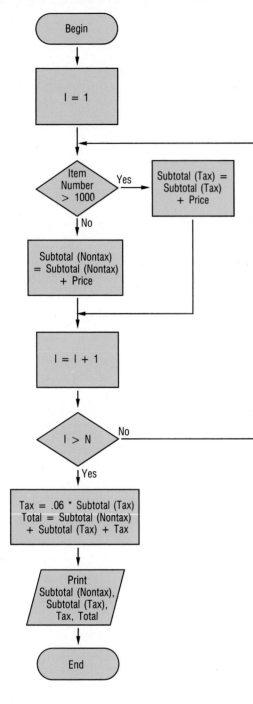

FIGURE B-23
Flowchart for example 7

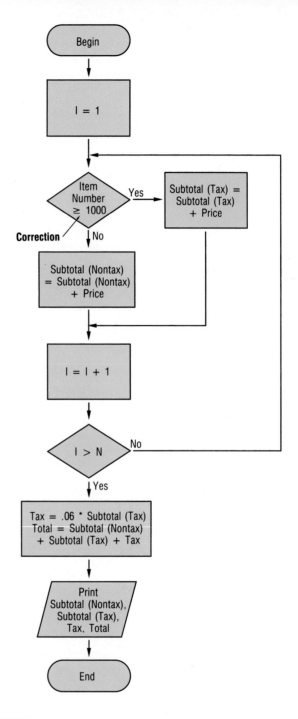

FIGURE B-24
Corrected flowchart for example 7

Using a Listing

Once the code is entered into the computer, we can start debugging by making a listing of the program. We look at every line to be sure it represents what was intended. We

TABLE B-17 *COMMON ERROR MESSAGES*

Message	Meaning	Availability*
Syntax Error	A statement does not follow the rules of BASIC. Examine the statement indicated for a syntactic error.	A, M
Division by Zero	You are not allowed to divide by zero. Check any variables used in a division to be sure they do not equal zero.	A, M
Duplicate Definition Redim'd Array	The same array name appears twice in DIM statements.	M A
Bad Subscript Subscript out of Range	You have used a subscript that is too large according to the DIM statement.	A M
Illegal Quantity	You have used an inappropriate number with a BASIC statement. The number may be too big, too small, or a fraction when only a whole number is allowed.	A
Extra ignored	You have provided too many items in response to an INPUT statement.	A
NEXT without FOR	You have either omitted a FOR statement or used a GOTO or GOSUB to skip a FOR statement.	A, M
FOR without NEXT	Your program encountered a NEXT statement without reference to a preceding FOR statement.	M
RETURN without GOSUB	You entered a subroutine without using a GOSUB statement.	A, M
Out of Data	You have used READ statements too many times for the number of data elements in the program.	A, M
Undef'd Statement Undefined Line Number	A GOTO or GOSUB statement points to a line number that does not exist in the program.	A M
Type Mismatch	You have assigned a character string to a numeric variable or a number to a string variable.	A, M

*A = Applesoft, M = Microsoft BASIC

often find two types of errors: typographical mistakes and inadvertent use of reserved words. For example, in using an Apple II, we might use

```
10 PRINT TOTAL
```

and the listing shows

```
10 PRINT TO TAL
```

We have forgotten that TO is a reserved word in Applesoft.

The First RUN

When a program is first run, it is likely that something will not work. We might get the error message

```
SYNTAX ERROR IN 10
```

This says to examine line 10 for an error. Occasionally, the line reference is wrong. When this happens, we must look for a "linked" statement. For instance, DATA and READ statements or FOR and NEXT statements are linked logically.

Some of the other common error messages are shown in table B-17.

After all of the syntax has been corrected, the program still may not run correctly. This is an indication that even though the logic is correct on the flowchart, we have translated it into BASIC incorrectly. The next step is to add some debugging statements that will monitor the flow of the program. Select critical places in the program and insert PRINT statements to show the value of certain variables. Be sure to print the line number on any such statement to show where the values came from. Statement 120 shows this approach:

```
120 PRINT "LINE 120 "; V1, V2, V3
```

If V1, V2, and V3 contain 12, 33, and 10 respectively, the CRT will show

```
LINE 120 12              33              10
```

Try putting extra GOTOs, GOSUBs, and STOPs into the program to control the flow. STOP statements work like END statements, but the computer prints their line numbers before stopping execution. Entering CONT resumes execution after a STOP has been encountered. By trying various combinations of these statements, we can isolate problems in coding and logic and correct the difficulties, then remove all the extra statements.

Be sure to retry all test cases after correcting any problems encountered. Correcting one problem can give rise to another.

SUMMARY

BASIC is a computer language used to write programs that solve problems we can describe in a step-by-step process. The language consists of a series of reserved words that tell the computer what to do. These reserved words, variables, constants, and special symbols make up the syntax of the language. Syntax is the specific form in which BASIC statements must be written for the computer to understand them.

The process of writing programs involves three intertwined steps. The first involves deciding how to attack the problem: determining what steps to use whether or not there is a computer available. It is important to thoroughly analyze the solution to the problem to be sure it describes the steps in complete detail. After establishing the logic of a solution, simulate the computer to debug the logic. The test cases used for this phase also can be used for further debugging in later stages of the development process.

Once convinced that the logic solves the problem at hand, we convert the flowchart into BASIC coding. Having completed this phase, we debug the program again. When we are sure that there are no typographical errors and that all of the syntax is correct, we can start checking to see that the program gives correct answers. We do this by using the test cases we established to check the logic. If there is a problem, we can insert temporary coding to help locate the difficulty. Later, we must be sure to remove the temporary coding.

Finally, when we believe that all errors have been eliminated, we must make a last test. We try all the test cases to be sure no new errors have been built into the coding as we solved another problem.

We have only considered the elementary aspects of BASIC in this appendix. With this background, you should be able to complete the programming exercises at the end of the chapter. If you want to extend your knowledge of BASIC, there are many excellent books to help you, including those that follow. Ask at the library, bookstore, or computer store for these books or others.

For Further Study

1. Coburn, Edward J. *Advanced BASIC: Structured Programming for Microcomputers.* Albany, N.Y.: Delmar Publishers Inc., 1986.

2. _____. *An Introduction to BASIC: Structured Programming for Microcomputers.* Albany, N.Y.: Delmar Publishers Inc., 1986.

3. _____. *Microcomputer BASIC: Structures, Concepts, and Techniques.* Albany, N.Y.: Delmar Publishers Inc., 1986.

4. Morrill, Harriet. *BASIC Programming for the IBM Personal Computer.* Boston: Little, Brown and Company, 1984.

5. Presley, Bruce. *Guide to Programming in Applesoft.* Lawrenceville, N.J.: Lawrenceville Press, 1984.

6. _____. *A Guide to Programming the IBM Personal Computers.* Lawrenceville, N.J.: Lawrenceville Press, 1985.

7. Quasney, James and John Maniotes. *BASIC Fundamentals and Style.* Boston: Boyd and Fraser, 1984.

KEY TERMS

argument
character string
conditional branch
debug
decrement
deferred execution mode
delimiter

driver
end-of-job indicator
immediate mode
increment
index variable
infinite loop
initialize

proper segment
relation
step value
string variable
subscript
uncompleted path
unconditional branch

PROGRAMMING EXERCISES

The following exercises are grouped by required skills. The groups correspond to the major examples in the appendix. After you have completed each example, try some of the corresponding problems before you continue with the appendix.

Problems 1–5 correspond to example 1

1. Print the following list with the first day of the season on one line, the date on the next. Print two blank lines between each entry.

First day of season	Date
vernal equinox	March 21
summer solstice	June 21
autumnal equinox	September 22
winter solstice	December 22

2. A newspaper advertised a computer for $1194 with a disk drive for $450 and a monitor for $250. Print the total cost of this computer system including 6.5% sales tax.

3. While at the computer store, you saw diskettes at several prices. Write a program to input unit price, quantity, and tax rate then print the cost of the diskettes. Use the following unit costs per box of ten diskettes: 22.95, 15.80, 41.75. Use these corresponding quantities: 30, 20, and 40. Use a tax rate of 6% for all transactions.

4. Calculate and print the cost to carpet a room. Input length and width of the room in feet and cost of carpet per square yard. Use the formula

   Total Price = Length × Width / 9 × Cost per Yard.

   Find the cost to carpet a 9 × 12 foot room with carpet costing $17.95 per square yard.

5. The United States Post Office limits packages it delivers to 108 inches in length plus girth (the distance around). Calculate and print the size of a package using the formula

   Size = Length + 2 × (Width + Height)

   The package is 12 × 30 × 20 inches.

Problems 6–10 correspond to example 2

In all further work, please include a PRINT statement to identify the problem and one for your name.

6. Revise programs 1–5 so all output is labeled.

7. Write a program to input your first name, last name, address, city, state, ZIP code, and telephone number. Print the information in the following format.

```
Print zone 1        Print zone 2
↓                   ↓

NAME:               JONES, MARY
ADDRESS:            123 W. BROADWAY BLVD.
                    WHITEHORSE, MT  83423
PHONE:              555-3998
```

8. Callendar's Date Growers wants to find out how much fruit the average tree yields. With hundreds of trees, the growers decided to sample three trees each week during harvest. Write a program to input the weight (in pounds) of fruit from each tree and print the three weights and the average. Label all output and include a header to identify the company and program used. The sampled trees yield 57, 32, and 61 pounds of fruit.

9. The city council has decreed that all houses on Sunset Lane shall have their addresses increased by 100. Write a program that inputs a street number on Sunset Lane and prints the revised address. Use a numeric variable for the number and a string variable for "SUNSET LANE." Sample input:

```
NUMBER:  51
```

Sample output:

```
151 SUNSET LANE
```

Current addresses on Sunset Lane are 33, 37, 44, and 48.

10. Business was bad for the bank so Mort Gauge decided to discount his loan fee. He wanted to cut the cost of getting a home loan by 20%. Write a program to input the normal loan processing fee and print it with the reduced fee. Be sure to label all output and include a header. Input $1968 as the normal loan fee.

Problems 11–12 correspond to example 3

11. Write a program that inputs a number between 1 and 100. If the number is less than 30, print SMALL and ask for another number. If the number is over 60, print LARGE and ask for another number. If the number is less than 1 or greater than 100, print ERROR and end the program. Test for 1, 10, 29, 30, 31, 59, 60, 61, 100, 105.

12. Input a denomination of U.S. coins (use P, N, D, Q, H, and S for penny, nickel, dime, quarter, half-dollar, and silver dollar) and a number of coins. Print the value of the coins. Request additional input until 0 is input as a number of coins. Test with 11 pennies, five nickels, seven dimes, three quarters, four half-dollars, and eight silver dollars.

Problems 13–23 correspond to example 4

13. You have been hired to complete a survey of grocery prices in several stores. Use nested FOR ... NEXT loops to create the following form which you need for data collection:

```
ITEM 11    ----------------------
ITEM 12    ----------------------
ITEM 13    ----------------------
STORE 1    ITEM 11 (          )
           ITEM 12 (          )
           ITEM 13 (          )
STORE 2    ITEM 11 (          )
           ITEM 12 (          )
           ITEM 13 (          )
STORE 3    ITEM 11 (          )
           ITEM 12 (          )
           ITEM 13 (          )
                  SURVEY DATE
                  ----------
```

14. Input a number, P. Print a two-column table. Column one contains 1.1, 1.2, 1.3, ..., 1.8. Column two contains P% of column one. (For example, if P = 120, then column 2 is 120% of column 1.) Use P = 130 for the test run.

15. A grower has 40 orange trees on a plot of land. Each tree yields 380 pieces of fruit per year. For each new tree the grower plants, the yield per tree will decrease by 8 oranges. Produce a table showing the total yield of the orange grove if the grower has 40 trees, 41 trees, ..., 55 trees.

16. Use nested FOR ... NEXT loops to print tax tables for 5%, 6%, 7%, and 8% tax rates. Column one should contain dollar amounts from $1 to $10. Column two should contain the appropriate tax. Label each column and include the tax rate in a header for each table.

17. Use two FOR ... NEXT loops to input five items of character data and print them in the order inputted and in reverse order.

18. Rewrite problem 8 using FOR ... NEXT loops.

19. Write a program to input 12 items and the total sales for each in each of two sales regions, West and East. Create a report showing these data and total sales of each product and each region:

PRODUCT	REGION 1	REGION 2	TOTAL
PAPER	500	412	912
PENS	...	...	...
TAPE	234	333	567
TOTAL	8734	9210	17944

Use the following data:

Item	Region 1	Region 2
Pens	870	210
Pencils	450	750
Erasers	320	100
Envelopes	810	460
Tape	510	500
Glue	400	470
Paper Clips	300	250
Brads	240	300
Rulers	600	175
Ink	290	455
Notebooks	635	700
Pads	500	300

20. Input total sales in millions (5 means 5 million) for 15 divisions of a company. Then print a bar chart to compare them:

```
DIVISION        SALES ($MILLIONS)
   1            ###
   2            ########
   3            #####

                .
                .
                .

   15           ##########
```

Select sales between $1 and $20 million for each division.

HINT 1: Ending a PRINT statement with a semicolon will cause the program to print on the same line with the next PRINT statement. For example,

```
10 PRINT "#";
20 PRINT "#"
```

will print

```
##
```

HINT 2: Use a variable index in a FOR ... NEXT loop.

21. Create a printed telephone directory of at least twelve people.

22. Write a program to READ four numbers and print their sum, product, and average. Use 3.5, 8.4, 1.1, and 6.2 for your data.

23. Write a program to READ a set of numbers of unknown length and calculate their average. A zero in the data list will indicate the end of data.

HINT: Do not include zero in your calculation.

Use the following two sets of data:

2.3, −1.1, 8.8, 4.5, 0
6.1, −3, −4, 7, 9, 10, −3.9, 2.4, 6.6, −4.7, 0

Problems 24–33 correspond to example 5

24. The Restinhaus Motel has 13 rooms. Write a program that the registration clerk will use to enter the name of each customer and the room assigned. Then print a report showing room number and customer name. Vacant rooms should be listed as VACANT. The following guests are staying at the motel:

Dan Sur, room 4
Sandy Beach, room 8
Hope Fuhl, room 10
Ben Twud, room 13

HINT: Start by using a FOR ... NEXT loop to store the guest's name or a blank entry for every room in the customer name array. If the name is blank, replace it with the word VACANT.

25. Create arrays for 500 names and numbers. Input the names and years of service of at least 8 employees of the BMOC Clothiers for Big and Tall Men. Use DONE as an end-of-data indicator. Then print a table like the following.

```
                         YEARS OF SERVICE
      NAME               0-4      5-8      9+
      ------------------------------------------
      FRED SMITH          3
      MARY JONES                    8
      BILL WILLIAMS                         15
      SALLY EVANS                   7
      ------------------------------------------
      TOTAL YEARS         3        15       15
      NUMBER OF
        EMPLOYEES         1         2        1
```

Use the preceding four names and at least four other employees of your choice.

26. I. Strane and Sons Book Publishers pay royalties at the following rates.

Total Sales	Royalty as a percentage of total sales
$15,000 or less	13%
$15,001 – $30,000	15%
$30,001 – $40,000	17%
$40,001 or more	18%

Write a program to input up to 100 author's names and their total sales. Print a report showing name, sales, and royalty. Be sure to use an end-of-data indicator. Use the following data:

Twain, 20500
Dickens, 31000
Shakespeare, 50000
Chaucer, 12050

27. Input employee records of these people:

Last Name	First Name	Sex	Years with Company
FORTH	SALLY	F	12
DEHR	WILLIAM	M	25
KAAT	ROBERT	M	4
DARMES	JONATHAN	M	20
BEACH	SANDRA	F	8
RELLA	CYNTHIA	F	27

Print the following lists:

Females
Males
Number of employees with more than 20 years of service

28. Use DATA and READ statements to build the following table.

Code	Service	Fee
32	REPLACE WASHER	23.00
41	CLEAR DRAIN	29.00
52	INSTALL DISPOSER	45.00
56	INSTALL DISHWASHER	90.00
67	INSPECT ALL PLUMBING	99.00

Input a client name and services rendered (by code). Print an invoice for the Walter Fawcett Plumbing Company. Use the following input:

Esther Williams, replace two washers, inspect all plumbing
Buster Crabbe, install dishwasher and disposer
Sammy Lee, one of each service

29. Five DATA statements include the names of five stocks, their current values, and the number of shares held. Print a table showing these data, the total value of each stock held, and the total value of the portfolio. Use the following DATA statements:

```
DATA GFR, 23.25, 200
DATA FRA, 12.50, 50
DATA PRC, 17.50, 100
DATA URS, 10.75, 300
DATA GBR, 21.25, 250
```

30. Print a table that shows the total additional annual cost of salary increases of 5, 10, and 15 percent raises. Use the following DATA statements in which the first value is the number of salaries and the following values are annual salaries.

```
DATA 12
DATA 15050, 22500, 16750, 28000, 42000, 36400
DATA 30750, 40950, 28900, 38790, 31000, 34560
```

31. Use DATA and READ statements to provide a list of scores between 1 and 100. Use an end-of-job indicator to end the READing. Print a report showing the number of scores between 1 and 25, 26 and 50, 51 and 75, 76 and 100. Use the following scores: 49, 50, 51, 27, 39, 58, 100, 75, 90.

32. Write a program to merge two lists of, at most, 100 numbers (ascending order) in DATA statements so the resulting list is also in ascending order. Zero is the end-of-data indicator. Both lists will be of the same length. Print the resulting list. Use the following data to run the program:

```
DATA 5, 7, 9, 11, 12, 15, 17, 0
DATA 3, 4, 6, 7, 14, 20, 30, 0
```

Rerun the program with the DATA statements interchanged.

33. Ten salaries are listed in the following DATA statements. Calculate and print the average salary and print each salary that is more than $800 above or below the average.

```
DATA 23400, 28000, 26000, 24000, 26100
DATA 26200, 25800, 26000, 25500, 35000
```

Problems 34–40 correspond to example 6

34. A data list contains pairs of scores (end-of-data indicator is 0, 0). Print a report in which the lines show the pairs of numbers and the algebraic and geometric averages.

The formulas for the algebraic and geometric averages are (X + Y)/2 and (X*Y) ^ .5. Assume a maximum of twelve pairs of numbers. Use subroutines to calculate each type of average. Use this DATA statement:

```
DATA 7, 11, 6, 8, 10, 90, 7, 0, 40, 50, 0, 0
```

35. Modify problem 34 to test X and Y to see if one is positive and one negative. If so, leave the geometric mean column blank. If both are positive or both negative, proceed with the calculation. Use this DATA statement:

```
DATA 7, 11, 6, 8, 10, 90, 5, -7, -8, -10, -4, -7, 40, 50, 0, 0
```

HINT: Test to see if X*Y < 0.

36. Input a selling price and the word SALE or REGULAR. For regular items, print the selling price. For sale items, use a subroutine to change the price to 75% of the selling price, then print the new price. Continue inputting until a selling price of zero is entered. Use the following input:

```
9.55, REGULAR, 8.84, SALE, 0.
```

37. Kerry's Kitchen, a local restaurant, surveyed 15 people about a new dish on the menu. The dish was rated +2, +1, 0, −1, or −2. Use the SGN(X) function to count the number of positive, negative, and neutral responses. SGN(X) generates a +1 if X is positive, a 0 if X is zero, and a −1 if X is negative. Use the following statement for the survey data:

```
DATA -2, 0, 2, 2, 2, 1, 0, 0, -1, -1, -2, 0, 2, 2, 1
```

38. The DELRAM Computer Users Group sponsored a raffle. Tickets numbered from 101 to 1000 were sold for $5 each. The grand prize was a new computer. Use the RND(X) function to select the winning number. RND(1) generates a random number between 0 and 0.999999999.

HINT 1: If you are using Microsoft BASIC, complete and debug the program, then add a statement at the beginning of the program to turn on the random number generator. This statement is

```
RANDOMIZE TIMER
```

No such statement is needed in Applesoft BASIC.

HINT 2: You will have to scale the number and "INT" it as we did in the round-off example.

39. Sales people at Sarah Dipity's boutique receive 4 7/8% commission on all sales with the monthly total rounded to the nearest dollar. Write a program to input total sales and print the commission. Continue to input data until a negative total sales is input. Use the following sales figures:

```
455, 387, 1023, -1
```

40. Produce a table showing a set of numbers from a DATA statement in one column and their deviations from an input number in a second column. Deviation from a number is calculated using the absolute value function, ABS (X − I) where X is the number in the DATA statement and I is the number input. Use the following DATA statement and run the program for I = 0, I = 2, and I = 5:

```
DATA -5, -4, -3, -2, -1, 0, 1, 2, 3, 4, 5
```

Sample output:

```
INPUT NUMBER IS 0
DATA            DEVIATION
----            ---------
-5              5
-4              4
.               .
.               .
.               .
0               0
.               .
.               .
5               5
```

ANSWERS TO THE EXERCISES

Exercise 1

X$, legal, character; 1W, illegal, first character must be alphabetic; PRICE, legal, numeric; DEPT$, legal, character; $NAME, illegal, first character must be alphabetic; TYPE, legal, numeric.

Exercise 2

Order	Value		
1. 1–2	46	4. 1–3–4–2	79.87
2. 2–3–1	240	5. 1–3–2–4	40
3. 2–1–3	287		

Exercise 3

Order	Value		
1. 1–3–2	42	3. 4–3–2–1	338
2. 1–2	49		

Exercise 4

Applesoft: 12 because AX3 and AX4 represent the same storage location.
Microsoft: 7 because AX3 and AX4 represent different locations.

Exercise 5

Line 10: COST = 100   Line 20: PRICE = 150
Line 30: COST = 200   Line 40: PRICE = 300

Exercise 6

Position:	1	15	29
1.	10	20	30
2.	TAX 1.59	TOTAL 27.09	
3.	COST:TAX:TOTAL		
4.	COST: 26.00 TAX: 1.56 TOTAL: 27.56		
5.	DATE: JANUARY 12		1986

Exercise 7

1.
```
10 PRINT "COST = 25.50", "TAX = 1.53"
15 PRINT "TOTAL = 27.03"
```
2.
```
20 PRINT "COST = 34", "TAX = 2.04", "TOTAL = 36.04"
```
3.
```
30 PRINT "A = 47.83" , , "B = 316.2"
```
4.
```
40 PRINT "PRICE: 15.75 QUANTITY: 12 TOTAL: 189"
```
5.
```
50 PRINT "PRICE:", "TAX:"
55 PRINT , , "TOTAL:"
```

Exercise 8

1. 20
2. GOODBYE
3. D NOT EQUAL 10

4	8
4	9

Exercise 9

	Number of times	Final value of index
1.	10	11
2.	5	0
3.	1	2
4.	1	21

Exercise 10

01
39

Exercise 11

```
10   REM PROGRAM TO INPUT NAMES THEN
20   REM LIST THEM IN REVERSE ORDER
100 DIM NME$(12)
110 FOR I = 1 TO 12
120    INPUT NME$(I)
130 NEXT I
140 FOR I = 12 TO 1 STEP -1
150    PRINT NME$(I)
160 NEXT I
170 END
```

Exercise 12

10 executed	20 not executed
30 executed	40 executed

Exercise 13

SMALL
RIGHT IN THE MIDDLE
LARGE

Exercise 14

1. -3 2. 14   3. 0   4. -5

Exercise 15

21   2123   21.23   21.23   21.55

Exercise 16

Change box D to I $\leq$ 3

Box	Total	I	Score	Average	Notes
A	0	1			
B			21		
C	21	2			
D					Loop back to B
B			12		
C	33	3			
D					Loop back to B
B			15		
C	48	4			
D					Drop through to E
E				16	
F					Print 16

This glossary contains over 700 terms. There are three types of listings. Many terms are defined as if they were in a dictionary. For many terms, you are referred elsewhere. If a term has no definition and you are referred to another term, that one is a synonym. If a term has a definition and you are asked to "see also," the reference is a related word that may or may not be a synonym. Some terms have two meanings. These terms will be followed by two numbered definitions. These numbers do not indicate the most frequently used definition.

Access arm Device to which disk read/write heads are attached.

Access arm movement delay Time required to position the read/write head over a specified disk cylinder or track.

Access width The amount of data that can be transferred along the bus in one cycle.

Accumulator A register that contains the result of arithmetic operations of the ALU.

Acoustic modem A modem that sends and receives signals from the handset of a telephone.

Active cell The cell of a spreadsheet that currently can be changed.

Active drive See Default drive.

Active formula bar See Formula bar.

Ada An extremely powerful high-level structured language designed by the United States Department of Defense to ensure transportability of programs. Ada has not yet become the major force that it promises to be. Ada was named after the first programmer, Augusta Ada Byron, Countess of Lovelace.

Address The identifier of the location at which particular data are stored.

Address pointer Data that link records in a file.

Address register A storage location in the CPU that stores the location of data being used.

Algorithm A mathematical procedure to solve a problem.

Alternate key A special-purpose key on the computer keyboard. Works like a control key. See also Control key.

ALU See Arithmetic/logical unit.

Analog computer A computer that uses continuous data. Analog computers measure things. See also digital computer.

AND The operator which has the value true if both statements it connects are true and the value false otherwise.

ANSI American National Standards Institute, the organization that publishes standards for various aspects of the computer industry.

APL A Programming Language, a computer language with extremely powerful mathematical capabilities. It is difficult to use because of its heavy reliance on abstract symbols.

Apple DOS An operating system for the Apple II series of computers.

Application program See Application software.

Application software Programs that control the work a user wants done. See also Program, System software.

Applications programmer A programmer who specializes in application software.

Argument The expression on which a BASIC function operates.

Arithmetic/logical unit The part of the CPU that does arithmetic and makes comparisons.

Artificial intelligence Computer processing that functions like the human mind in arriving at logical conclusions to problems that are posed to it.

ASCII American Standard Code for Information Interchange, a seven (binary) digit coding scheme for representing numbers, letters, and special characters in the computer. Most microcomputers use ASCII.

Assembly language A low-level computer language that replaces machine language instructions with mnemonics like ADD and that uses labels to identify memory addresses.

Asynchronous transmission Data transmission at a variable rate of speed in which special signals indicate the start and end of a transmission. See also Synchronous transmission.

Attribute A column in a relational database.

Autoboot See Autoload.

Autoload Automatic loading and execution of a program when a system is started.

Automated system Any system that requires a computer in order to function. See also Manual system.

Automatic insertion A method of text insertion in which text is added in the middle of existing text.

Automatic typeover A method of text insertion in which the existing text is replaced by the text being entered.

Background An area of memory where a program of secondary priority may be running. See also Foreground.

Backtracking See Programming by path.

Bandwidth The range of frequencies that can be transmitted over a communication channel. This affects the amount of data that can be sent each second.

Bar code An encoding scheme to enter data into a computer. Bar code is a series of parallel lines of differing widths separated by differing distances.

Base referent address The address against which everything is compared in a virtual system.

BASIC An early all-purpose language. BASIC (Beginners All-Purpose Symbolic Instruction Code) is the most popular language for personal computers.

Batch entry Loading a series of programs with their data into a computer, then executing them one at a time.

Batch file A file of system commands.

Batch processing Collecting transaction data for processing all at once as opposed to processing each transaction as it occurs. See also Real time processing.

Baud rate The rate at which data are transmitted. Typical baud rates for interactive transmissions are 300 and 1200. Computer-to-computer transmission is often at 19,200 and higher baud rates.

BBS See Bulletin board service.

BCD Binary coded decimal, a four- or six-bit data encoding scheme used in early computers. BCD has since been replaced by EBCDIC. See also EBCDIC.

Belt printer A line printer in which the characters to be printed lie on a revolving belt.

Binary digit Either of the numerals 0 or 1.

Binary system Numeration system based on two symbols, 0 and 1.

Bit A single binary digit.

Block A group of logical records that form a physical record.

Block diagram See Macroflowchart.

Blocking factor The number of logical records per physical record. See also Logical record, Physical record.

Boilerplate See Paragraph assembly.

Boot disk See System disk.

Bootleg software See Pirated software.

Boundary An area that separates two or more systems or subsystems.

Bubble A symbol for data processing used on a data flow diagram.

Bubble memory Volatile memory in which data are stored in magnetic bubbles. Bubble memory is sequential.

Buffer (1) An area in RAM from which data are written to secondary storage or to which records are written from secondary storage. (2) An area in RAM to which input is read or from which output is sent.

Buffer card A peripheral card for temporary storage of data to be printed, thus freeing primary storage for other uses. Buffer cards occupy expansion slots in microcomputers.

Bulletin board See Bulletin board service.

Bulletin board service (BBS) A service whereby people can communicate via computer and telephone, generally at no cost.

Bundled system A system in which hardware and software are sold as a package.

Bus The electronics that connect the parts of a computer. The internal bus connects the parts of the CPU. The external bus connects peripheral devices to the CPU.

Byte Eight binary data bits. A byte contains one character of data.

C A computer language designed by Bell Labs to serve as a transportable assembly language.

CAD/CAM Computer-aided design and computer-aided manufacture.

Calculating Performing mathematical operations on data.

Card punch operator A person who produces punched cards for computer data entry.

Case-control structure A mechanism on a flowchart that indicates several alternative logical paths a program can take at the same decision point.

Catalog See Directory.

Cathode ray tube (CRT) A television-like device for viewing computer output.

CC See Computerized conferencing.

Cell (1) The location of a piece of data within a spreadsheet. (2) The intersection of a row and a column in a spreadsheet.

Cell address The name that enables a user to select a cell of a spreadsheet.

Cell identifier See Cell address.

Central processing unit (CPU) The part of the computer where all activity takes place. The CPU is made up of primary storage, the arithmetic/logical unit, and the control unit. See also Primary storage, Arithmetic/logical unit, and Control unit.

Chain printer A printer with all printable characters on a print chain. Hammers strike the chain when one of its characters is in the proper print position.

Channel (1) The logical connection between the sender and the receiver of data. (2) A special processor (with a buffer) that connects an I/O device to a computer.

Character A single letter, numeral, or special symbol (/, ?, ., etc.).

Character formatting Specifying the type style, font, and size for characters printed in a document. Examples of specification include boldface, underlined, and italic.

Character insertion point The point on the CRT at which the next typed character will be displayed. A cursor normally denotes this point.

Character printer A device that prints characters one at a time.

Character set The symbols available in an encoding scheme.

Character string A group of characters.

Chief information officer The director of an information center and the manager of corporate data and information.

Child In a data base, a relation or record that is pointed to by another relation or record called the parent.

Classify Categorize by common characteristics.

Clock A device that coordinates data movement and operations in the CPU.

Clocked transmission See Synchronous transmission.

Closed architecture computer A computer into which additional peripheral boards cannot be placed. See also Open architecture computer.

COBOL The earliest business-oriented computer language. COBOL (COmmon Business-Oriented Language) is still the most widely used business computer language because of its transportability and focus on solving business-oriented problems.

Coding In programming, the process of converting logical statements into computer language instructions.

COM See Computer output microfilm.

Command disk See System disk.

Command-driven A program is command-driven if it operates under direction of typed commands or batch files. See also Menu-driven.

Command file A file of data manipulation language instructions for outputting a standard report.

Command sequence A set of instructions to an application program.

Common carrier A standard communications network such as the Bell System.

Communicating Transferring data from one computer to another.

Communication See Data communication.

Compiler A program that converts other programs into machine language before they are executed.

Composite color CRT A CRT that receives one signal and breaks it into its constituent colors. See also RGB monitor.

Computer-aided design (CAD) Using computers to develop specifications and draft plans for products to be manufactured.

Computer-aided manufacture (CAM) Using computers to control the machinery that manufactures a product.

Computer crime Illegal access to or use of data stored in computerized data bases.

Computer graphics The use of a computer to create a visual image.

Computer operator A person who runs the computer.

Computer output microfilm (COM) Microfilm images that are generated by computer.

Computer program See Program.

Computer system The combination of equipment and programs required to computerize a task.

Computer technician A person who repairs electronic equipment.

Computerized conferencing (CC) Teleconferencing by computer.

Concentrator A device that combines the signals of several slow devices to fully use the capacity of a high-speed device. A concentrator eliminates the time between transmissions of data.

Conditional branch A computer instruction that tells the computer to execute the next sequential instruction unless a specified condition is met. In that case, the computer is directed to execute some other instruction.

Conography The use of curves from a cone to develop graphic images.

Control field See Key field.

Control key A special key that functions like a shift key. Thus a computer may have upper case A, a lower case *a*, and a control-*a*.

Control unit The part of the CPU that manages data movement and processing.

Controller See Interface.

Conversion The changeover period when one system is phased out and another phased in.

Copy-protect Making a program difficult or impossible to duplicate so illegal copying (in violation of copyright) will not occur.

Core dump See Dump.

Core memory An early form of memory based on small iron "donuts."

Correspondence processing Creating individually addressed and typed form letters using electronic techniques.

CP/M An early microcomputer operating system.

CPU See Central processing unit.

Critical path The set of project activities that determines the minimum amount of time the total project will take.

CRT See Cathode ray tube.

Cursor An on-screen indicator of where the next character will be placed in a computer program or word processor.

Cursor-control keys Keys for moving the cursor on the CRT. Cursor-control keys are normally signified by arrows.

Cybernetics The theory of control and communication as it applies to animals, including humans, and machines.

Cyberphobia The fear of computers.

Cylinder The collection of tracks available with one positioning of the access mechanism in a multiple disk drive.

Daisy wheel The print element of certain letter-quality printers.

DASD See Direct-access storage device.

Data Raw facts.

Data analysis chart A listing of data elements and the files that use them.

Data base administrator A person responsible for maintenance and organization of all data in a firm's data base.

Data base management system A program designed to store and retrieve data and information as effectively as possible.

Data buffer See Buffer

Data cartridge High-volume magnetic tape data storage devices.

Data communication Transmission of data from one computer to another.

Data control supervisor A person responsible for distribution of computerized reports.

Data definition language (DDL) A language used to describe logical data paths in a database management system.

Data element See Field.

Data element dictionary A complete description of all data elements in a system.

Data entry clerk See Data entry operator.

Data entry operator A person who prepares data for input into a computer. See also Card-punch operator, Key-to-disk operator, Key-to-tape operator.

Data entry supervisor A person who supervises data personnel.

Data flow diagram (DFD) A pictorial representation of data flow through a system.

Data manipulation language (DML) A language for retrieval of standard data sets. Part of a data base management system.

Data media control language (DMCL) A language used to describe the physical data path in a database management system.

Data processing The process of converting raw data into information.

Data retrieval Locating and making data available for processing or reporting.

Data retrieval system A system that retrieves and manipulates data.

Data security Protection of data from loss, alteration, or unauthorized access.

Data set A data file.

Data storage Recording data so they are available for later use.

Database A collection of data that provides data access to all applications and users with minimal redundancy.

Datapath The set of directories and subdirectories used to locate data in a secondary storage medium.

DDL See Data definition language.

Debug Testing a program to ensure that its logic and coding are error-free.

Decision support system (DSS) A management information system that distributes control of data and information processing activities to the users.

Decoding Converting encoded data into their original form.

Decrement To decrease by a fixed amount.

Dedicated word processor A microcomputer the only purpose of which is word processing.

Default The choice from a series of options that is preselected by a program. The user can change this choice at will.

Default drive The disk drive that will be used next unless instructions to the contrary are given.

Deferred execution mode The mode in BASIC in which programs are written.

Delimiter A character that separates parts of a computer instruction or data.

Demand report A report generated only on request.

Demodulate Convert a signal from analog to digital. See also Modulate.

Demultiplex To restore a set of multiplexed signals to their original state as separate signals. See also Multiplex.

Density A measure of how compactly data are stored on tape or disk.

Descriptor An item, all mentions of which are sought in a computerized search of a data bank.

Design report (1) A set of operating procedures, including computer programs and hardware specifications needed to implement a new system. (2) The documentation of the system design phase.

Desk checking Manually testing a program before trying to execute it on a computer.

Destructive write Writing data into a storage location or register destroys data that were already stored there.

DFD See Data flow diagram.

Digit code The right-most nibble in the bit representation of a character.

Digital computer A computer that uses discrete data. Digital computers count things. Most business computers are digital. See also Analog computer.

Direct-access file A file in which any record can be read or written without regard to what has been written before it.

Direct-access storage device (DASD) A device from which any record can be read regardless of when it was written.

Direct connect modem A modem that is hard-wired into the telephone network.

Directory A list of files on a disk. The directory typically contains additional information such as address, size, and creation date of each file.

Disk access time The amount of time required to store or retrieve data on a disk.

Disk address The physical location on a disk where data are stored.

Disk drive A secondary storage device that stores data on flat magnetic surfaces. Disk drives are direct or random access devices.

Disk operating system (DOS) An operating system that is based on the use of disk drives.

Disk pack A set of disks mounted on a common hub and used in a drive with multiple read/write heads.

Diskette See Flexible disk.

Display memory That portion of RAM that controls the video display.

Distributed data processing See Distributed processing.

Distributed information system (DIS) A system with decentralized decision making and a centralized data bank.

Distributed processing A hierarchical system of computers that provides each user only as much computing power as is needed to complete whatever task is at hand. Typically, each department has access to a central database and is responsible for some of its own programming.

Distribution-oriented system A system that emphasizes distribution of information.

DMCL See Device media control language.

DML See Data manipulation language.

DOUNTIL loop A group of instructions that are to be repeated until a given condition is met.

DOWHILE loop A group of instructions that are to be repeated as long as a given condition is met.

Document retrieval system A system that retrieves forms and documents but not individual data.

Documentation (1) The description, specifications, and operating instructions of a system. (2) The written material that describes a program or system and how to use it.

DOS See Disk operating system.

DOS command A job control language instruction in a disk operating system.

Dot-matrix printer A character printer that creates symbols by printing selected points in a square array (matrix). Many dot-matrix printers can also be used to print graphic images.

Download To receive a file from another computer. See also Upload.

Drive A machine that stores data off-line.

Driver A program module that controls other modules.

Drum printer A printer in which a revolving drum moves letters into position to be struck and printed.

DSS See Decision support system.

Dump A listing of the contents of primary memory.

Dvorak keyboard A modern keyboard designed to increase input speed.

EBCDIC Extended Binary Coded Decimal Interchange Code, the standard (eight bit) code for medium and large scale computers.

EFT See Electronic fund transfer.

Electronic banking Transacting bank business (deposits, withdrawals, loan payments, etc.) by computer, either by telephone or at an automatic teller machine.

Electronic digital computer See Digital computer.

Electronic fund transfer (EFT) The transfer of funds by electronic means.

Electronic mail The transmission of text and graphic data by electronic means, the storage of such data in electronic media, and the retrieval of such data by electronic methods.

Electronic typewriter A typewriter with minimal storage, editing, and formatting capabilities.

Electrostatic printer A printer in which images are formed by fusing carbon to paper by heat.

Embedded command An instruction to a word processing program that is placed within the text.

Emulator A program that makes one computer behave as if it were another.

Encoding Converting data into another form without changing its meaning.

End-of-job indicator A signal to the computer that there are no more data to input.

EPROM Erasable Programmable ROM. A PROM that can be erased and reprogrammed under controlled conditions.

Error listing An error report generated by a language translator.

Escape key A special key on the computer keyboard. When depressed, it sends a special character to the memory. It is often used in application programs to initiate or terminate special commands.

Ethernet A common local area network protocol.

Even parity See Parity.

Exception report See Triggered report.

EXEC file See Batch file.

Expansion slot An electronic outlet in the computer through which I/O controlling peripheral electronic boards are connected.

Expert system A program designed to provide information normally available from skilled specialists.

External bus See Bus.

Feasibility study The result of the detailed analysis phase of the system analysis. Systems analysts make recommendations regarding changes to a system in feasibility studies.

Feedback A process to evaluate system output.

Fiber optics transmission Transmission of data along glass fiber by optical means.

Field A specific item of data within a record.

File (1) A collection of data. (2) A series of related records.

File chaining Linking several small files together to give the appearance of having one large file. See also Virtual memory.

File format The organizational characteristics of a file.

File maintenance The process of keeping data on a file up to date.

File management system A simple database management system commonly found on microcomputers. Generally limited to using one file at a time.

File manager A device (usually an operating system) for keeping track of the physical location of files and making them available to applications programs as needed.

File merge A technique in word processing in which data from two files are combined. This is particularly useful for creating personalized form letters.

File server A computer that coordinates data communication and controls mass storage in a network of computers.

File structure See File format.

Filename The name by which the computer identifies a file.

Filename extension A set of characters appended to the end of a filename. Generally used to categorize files.

Filter A program that affects data after input and before output.

Firmware Programs that have been built into ROMs, PROMs, or EPROMs.

Flag See End-of-job indicator.

Flat file See Sequential file.

Flexible disk Thin Mylar disks used mainly in micro- and minicomputers. Flexible disks (also known as floppies) are removable from the disk drive.

Floppy disk See Flexible disk.

Flowchart A graphic representation of an algorithm or a process.

Foreground An area of RAM where the primary program is run. When system resources are needed, foreground programs have priority over background programs. See also Background.

Formatting Organizing the form of I/O.

Forms flowchart A pictorial representation of the movement of forms and documents through a system.

Forms program A word processing feature that enables the user to complete forms easily.

Formula bar The area of a spreadsheet that shows the formula for the currently selected cell.

FORTH An intermediate level language that the programmer can extend by defining new functions. FORTH is especially good for industrial control processes.

FORTRAN An early high-level language especially suitable for scientific applications. FORTRAN (FORmula TRANslation) is still widely used.

Front end processor A minicomputer connected to a mainframe to control data receipt and transmission.

Front end program A program that helps in the use of another program.

Full duplex A communications protocol that permits simultaneous two-way transmission of data.

Full-screen editing A text editing technique in which the cursor can be moved anywhere on the display screen for editing purposes.

Function See Subroutine.

Function keys Special keys that are used by programs to cause complex events to happen. Function keys are normally labelled F1, F2, etc.

Gateway computer The computer within a network that permits the network to communicate with other computer systems.

Geosynchronous orbit A satellite orbit that ensures that the satellite will always be over the same point on the earth's surface.

Gigabyte (GB) One billion bytes.

Global command A spreadsheet command that affects the entire spreadsheet.

Global search and replace Finding every occurrence of a passage in text and replacing each with a new passage.

Glossary A feature of a word processor in which a brief string of characters can be entered for repetitive insertion within a document.

Graphic tablet A pressure sensitive device for inputting graphic images into a computer.

Graphics software A program that processes pictorial data.

Half duplex A communication protocol in which data can be transmitted in two directions but only one way at a time.

Handshaking A procedure for transferring data in which one device informs another when it is ready to receive data, then the second device transmits them.

Hard copy Nonelectronic output, either film or paper.

Hard disk A rigid disk that is installed in a drive semipermanently.

Hard disk drive Semipermanent secondary storage.

Hard wired Two devices that are physically connected by electric wires.

Hashing routine See Randomizing routine.

Head switching delay Time required to activate the read/write heads in a disk operation.

Help screen Information that is available on the CRT as a program is being used. This documentation is designed to assist the user.

Heuristic program A program that "learns" or improves its performance as it is used.

Hexadecimal system A numeration system based on 16 symbols: 0, 1, 2, 3, 4, 5, 6, 7, 8, 9, A, B, C, D, E, F. Most modern computers work easily with hexadecimal numbers because 16 is a power of two (binary).

Hierarchical file system A database management system in which all data are linked in a tree-like structure.

Hierarchical network A computer network in which all devices are connected, but there are no closed loops, i.e., there is only one path between any two devices.

Hierarchy chart A diagram that depicts the procedures of an operation in a hierarchical or tree-like fashion.

High-touch trend The desire for increases in interpersonal communication caused by heavy reliance on high technology.

High-level language A computer language that is closer to natural language than to machine language.

High-tech revolution (1) The introduction of electronic devices for processing and communication of information and data and control of mechanical and electronic devices. (2) The advent of sophisticated electronic equipment using integrated circuitry.

HIPO diagram Pictorial representation of the input, processing, and output functions of a module in a visual table of contents.

Home banking See Electronic banking.

Horizontal program A program that can be used by many industries. See also Vertical program.

Host computer See File server.

Host language A language such as COBOL in which programs are supported by a DBMS.

I/O Input and output.

I/O-bound A program is I/O-bound if the CPU waits idly while I/O is done. See also Process-bound.

Icon Pictorial representation of a computer command or file.

Idea processor A special-purpose word processing program for creating outlines.

IF...THEN...ELSE mechanism An element of a flowchart that shows alternative logical paths a computer program might take depending on a decision made by the computer.

ILR See Instruction location register.

Immediate mode The mode in BASIC during which execution of an instruction is done as soon as a carriage return is sent.

Impact printer A printer that creates an image by striking the paper.

Increment To increase by a fixed amount.

Indexed-sequential access method (ISAM) Storage and retrieval of records on a file in order by record key.

Indexed-sequential file A file the records of which are sequenced by an index.

Index variable The controlling variable in a BASIC FOR ... NEXT loop.

Industry-nonspecific See Horizontal program.

Industry-specific See Vertical program.

Infinite loop A set of computer instructions that repeat forever.

Information Data in a useful form.

Information center A corporate department that controls company data and information and provides training in the use of computers.

Information explosion The uncontrolled growth of information.

Information processing Applying data processing techniques to information.

Information revolution The combination of the exponential growth of information and the high-technology equipment to manage it.

Information system A system in which input is data or information and output is information.

Information utility A company that sells information.

Initialize To set a variable to a known beginning value.

Ink-jet printer A printer in which ink is blown onto paper. Ink-jet printers are very quiet and have few moving parts.

Input (1) The process of providing data to a computer or to a system. (2) The data that are provided to a computer.

Input/output analysis The analysis of data that move through a system.

Input/output control system (IOCS) The set of input/output programs in an operating system.

Insertion See Automatic insertion.

Instruction location register (ILR) A storage location that tells the CPU which instruction to execute next.

Instruction register The part of the control unit in which the machine language instruction currently controlling the computer is stored. See also Machine language.

Integrated software A computer program that combines two or more functions, such as word processing, spreadsheet, graphics, etc.

Integrated system See Integrated software.

Interactive language A computer language that permits the programmer to converse with the computer, entering instructions, testing them, changing them, etc. Many languages have both interactive and noninteractive versions.

Interblock gap The space between physical records on secondary storage.

Interface (1) The channel through which information passes between systems. (2) A device that enables two otherwise incompatible computers or components to be connected.

Internal bus See Bus.

Interpreter A language translator that converts higher-level language programs into machine language as the instructions are executed.

Interrecord gap See Interblock gap.

Interrupt Cessation of processing one program so another can be executed.

IOCS See Input/output control system.

IPO diagram A pictorial representation of input, processing, and output of a module of a system. See also HIPO diagram.

ISAM See Indexed-sequential access method.

JCL See Job control language.

JCL cards See Batch file.

JCL program See Batch file.

Job control language (JCL) A programming language for controlling the monitor or operating system.

Job sheet A description of jobs to be performed by a computer system over a period of time.

Kernel See Monitor.

Key field A field around which a file is structured.

Keypunch operator See Card punch operator.

Key-to-disk Direct entry of data to a disk from a keyboard.

Key-to-disk operator A person who types data directly to magnetic disks.

Key-to-tape Direct entry of data to a magnetic tape from a keyboard.

Key-to-tape operator A person who types data directly to magnetic tape.

Keyword A word or phrase that is used to identify records of interest in a computerized search.

Kilobyte (K or KB) Approximately 1000 bytes. Actually 1024 (2^{10}).

LAN See Local area network.

Lead programmer A senior programmer on a project to whom other programmers on the same project report.

Leased line A telephone line that is reserved for use by the lessee.

Left justify Placing characters in a field to the far left.

Letter-quality printer A printer the print of which appears to have been typed by a conventional electric typewriter. Typical letter-quality printers have daisy wheels or thimbles as print heads.

Librarian A person responsible for maintenance and organization of data stored off-line.

Light pen A device for drawing images using the CRT as the graphic field. Also used for menu selections.

Line code See Bar code.

Line editing A text editing technique in which the user must specify the line to be edited.

Line printer A device that prints an entire line at a time.

Link editor A program in the operating system that links application programs with necessary input/output programs.

LISP LISt Processor, a special-purpose language for writing artificially intelligent programs.

Local area network (LAN) A group of interconnected computers located within a limited geographic region.

Logged drive See Default drive.

Logical path The path for storage or retrieval as defined by the user who may not know the physical location of the data.

Logical record A data record on secondary storage as created by an application program. See also Physical record, Blocking factor.

Looping structure A mechanism on a flowchart that indicates that a block of code is to be repeated several times.

Machine language A computer language expressed in binary notation. All other languages must be converted to machine language before the computer will understand them. Each computer has its own unique machine language written in binary code. See also Binary system.

Machine-readable data Data in a form that allows a computer to store them in primary storage.

Macro See Macro instruction.

Macro instruction A high-level language statement such as INPUT that signals the link editor to call a series of IOCS programs. See also Subroutine.

Macroflowchart A flowchart showing the major tasks to be completed by a program.

Magnetic ink character reader A device for converting magnetic printing such as the numbers on a bank check into machine-readable form.

Magnetic ink character recognition (MICR) A means of entering data into a computer system using characters printed with magnetic ink.

Magnetic tape drive A drive that reads from and writes to magnetic tape.

Main memory See Primary storage.

Main storage See Primary storage.

Mainframe A large computer installation that typically handles the computing needs of several dozen to hundreds of users simultaneously.

Management information system (MIS) (1) A system that provides information for operational, tactical, and strategic decision making. (2) Electronic linkage between all subsystems of an organization, generally implemented on large mainframe computers.

Manual system Any system that does not involve a computer. See also Automated system.

Master file A file containing accumulated data gathered in all processing cycles.

Megabyte (MB) Approximately 1,000,000 bytes. Actually 1,048,576 bytes (2^{20}).

Memory See Primary storage, Secondary storage.

Memory dump See Dump.

Memory map A listing of the location in RAM or ROM of various programs.

Menu A computer display that provides the user with a series of options.

Menu-driven A program that is controlled by a user making choices from a menu. See also Command-driven.

MICR See Magnetic ink character recognition.

Microcomputer A small computer designed for a single user. Microcomputers typically fit on a desk top, or even in a briefcase. They can be linked to other computers. See also Minicomputer.

Microprocessor The processor in a microcomputer. See also Processor.

Microsecond One millionth of a second.

Microwave repeater A device that receives microwave transmissions, amplifies them, and rebroadcasts them.

Millisecond One thousandth of a second.

Minicomputer A small computer that can usually handle the computer needs of several people. The distinction between mini- and microcomputers is blurred. See also Microcomputer.

MIPS Millions of Instructions Per Second, a measure of CPU speed.

MIS See Management information system.

Mnemonic An abbreviation that represents a computer instruction, e.g., MPY for multiply. Literally a "memory aid."

Model A hypothetical representation of a real-world phenomenon.

Model base See Database.

Modem Modulator-demodulator. A device for connecting a computer to the telephone system. See also Modulate, Demodulate.

Modulate Converting a signal from digital to analog. See also Demodulate.

Module An element of a structure chart or an independent segment of a computer program or a system.

Monitor (1) A program that supervises the execution of other application programs. (2) A CRT display unit. See also Cathode ray tube.

Monitoring report A regularly scheduled report from a computer system.

Mother board The main circuit board of a computer.

Mouse A device rolled on a desk-top to control cursor movement and other computer functions.

MS-DOS See PC-DOS.

Multi-drop line A communication line to which several computers are connected.

Multi-part form Computer paper designed to print several copies of a document at the same time.

Multiplex Combining several signals into one to increase the rate of transmission. See also Demultiplex.

Multiprocessing See Multitasking, definition 2.

Multiprogramming Programming an operating system to run several programs simultaneously.

Multitasking (1) Having several programs resident in RAM simultaneously. (2) Simultaneous use of several processors in one computer system.

Nanosecond One billionth of a second.

Natural language Spoken or written language as used in normal communication.

Networked file system A database management system in which each data element may be directly linked to every other element.

Networking Connecting several computers together.

Nibble Four binary data bits or one-half byte. A nibble corresponds to one hexadecimal digit.

Node (1) Any computer in a network. (2) The intersection of two paths in a data structure.

Noise Electronic interference in a communication channel.

Non-destructive read Reading data from a storage location without changing the data.

Nonimpact printer A device that prints without physical contact with the paper. Ink-jet, laser, and thermal printers are examples.

Non-volatile memory Memory that is not dependent upon electric power to store data.

NOT An operator that changes the value of the expression that follows it from true to false or vice versa.

Numeric keypad A set of keys laid out like an adding machine keyboard. Many computers have numeric keyboards in addition to alphabetic ones.

Object program The machine language program that results from compiling a source program. See also Source program.

OCR See Optical character reader, Optical character recognition.

Odd parity See Parity.

Off-line See Secondary storage.

Office automation The integration of office functions through electronic processes.

OMR See Optical mark reader.

On-line A term used to signify that disks or tapes are ready for use by the CPU.

On-line operation Direct entry of input into a computer without intermediate steps.

On-line query system A system for immediate retrieval of information.

Open architecture computer A microcomputer designed so the user can add peripheral boards. See also Closed architecture computer.

Operating cycle (1) The time during which one operation is executed by the CPU. (2) The normal cycle of activity undertaken during the life of an organization.

Operating system (OS) A set of programs that standardize the way a computer's resources are made available to application programs.

Operational information system (OIS) A system that provides information for routine operations.

Operational manual Instructions in the use of a system.

Operations department The department responsible for the day-to-day functions of a data processing department.

Operations supervisor A person who supervises the day-to-day operation of a data processing center.

Optical character reader (OCR) A device that converts written information into machine-readable form.

Optical character recognition (OCR) The ability to convert typed documents to machine-readable form directly.

Optical disk A disk on which information is stored by laser. Optical disks can be used in video, audio, and computer applications.

Optical mark reader (OMR) A reader that senses the presence or absence of a mark made on paper with a pen or pencil.

OR An operator the value of which is true if at least one of the expressions it connects is true and the value of which is false if both expressions are false.

Origination Recording data for the first time.

OS See Operating system.

Output (1) The process of gathering data from a computer. (2) The data and information gathered from a computer.

Overlap Simultaneous input, output, and processing by an operating system.

Page A section of a program loaded into primary memory. Pages are used for programs that are too large to load all at once.

Page formatting Specifying the layout of text on a printed page.

Page printer A machine that prints an entire page at one time.

Pageframe See Page.

Paragraph assembly Creation of a document from a set of predefined paragraphs. Particularly useful in developing legal contracts.

Parallel Able to move several bits of data simultaneously. See also Serial.

Parent A piece of data or record in a data base that points to another piece of data or record called the child.

Parity The number of bits with the value one in a specific byte of data. Often, data are transmitted with an additional bit called the parity bit. This bit is set to one or zero to ensure either an even or odd number of ones in a set of data to make sure data are correctly transmitted.

Parity bit See Parity.

Partition That portion of RAM allocated by the operating system to a single user in a time-sharing environment.

Pascal A powerful, structured language designed for teaching but used for many microcomputer applications, named after the seventeenth century mathematician Blaise Pascal.

Password A security device used to prevent unauthorized access to a computer or to data stored in it.

Path See Data path.

PC-DOS The operating system for the IBM PC and compatibles.

Peripheral devices Input and output devices that are connected to a computer.

Peripheral storage See Secondary storage.

Personal computer See Microcomputer.

Physical path The actual electronic path used to store or retrieve data within computer hardware.

Physical record A record as stored on secondary storage

by the operating system. See also Logical record, Blocking factor.

Pipe A series of system commands in one instruction.

Pirated software Programs that have been illegally copied and distributed.

Pixel Picture element. The smallest element on a graphic display.

PL/1 Programming Language 1, an all-purpose extensive language developed in the 1960s.

Planning report A report used for planning.

Plotter A printing device that draws pictures as a series of lines. Most plotters can use pens of different width and/or color to create images on paper or acetate.

Point-of-sale terminal (POS) A remote data entry terminal for recording sales. Bar code readers are one type of point-of-sale terminal.

Point-to-point network Two or more computers connected along a multi-drop line.

Pointer A piece of data that links other data such as file records together.

Poll Querying each terminal in a time-sharing system to determine if there is any input.

Portable computer A computer small enough to be carried easily.

Power A measure of the size and speed of a computer.

Pre-defined process A program routine or module that is to be used by a program but has already been written.

Predictive report See Planning report.

Presentation graphics Informational graphic images produced by a computer.

Primary storage Memory that is used for current computational activity. Primary storage is part of the CPU. See also Secondary storage.

Printer queuing Scheduling a printer to accommodate several work stations.

Priority interrupt Cessation of program execution because a higher priority program requires the processor.

Private line See Leased line.

Problem-oriented language A language in which users specify what is to be accomplished.

Procedure The most basic element of a system.

Procedure-oriented language A language in which programmers specify how to solve a problem.

Process-bound A program is process-bound if I/O devices sit idly while the CPU is operating. See also I/O-bound.

Process box An element of a flowchart in which serial instructions are represented.

Processing Execution of a set of procedures to meet the objectives of a system.

Processing cycle A sequence of computer procedures used repetitively.

Processor The combination of the control unit and the arithmetic/logical unit. See also Central processing unit.

ProDOS An operating system for Apple II computers.

Program A set of instructions that controls a computer's actions.

Program generator A program that writes other programs from logic provided by the user.

Program library A set of programs available on a particular computer. A monitor determines which program to execute. See also Monitor.

Program stub Dummy code used to simulate a missing module.

Programmer/analyst A programmer who is also involved in design.

Programming by level One technique of developing a structured program. Also called top-down programming. See also Programming by path.

Programming by path Programming all elements of a program on the same branch before programming any elements on another branch. See also Programming by level.

Programming manager An individual responsible for all programming services in a data processing department.

Programming supervisor A person in charge of a group of programmers.

PROM Programmable read-only memory. Memory that becomes indestructible after it has been programmed.

Proper program A program with only one entry point and one exit point.

Proper segment A part of a computer program with only one entry point and one exit point.

Protocol The specifications that define the technical requirements to transmit data.

Pseudocode An informal code in natural language that shows program logic.

Public-domain program A computer program that has not been copyrighted and is available to anyone at no charge.

Publically supported software A program available to the public for a nominal charge.

Pull-down menu A menu that is made visible when it is selected by mouse, light pen, or function key. Pull-down menus behave like window shades. They remain out of sight until needed.

Query language (SQL) A user's language for retrieving data from a database management system.

Query procedure The process by which a computer finds specified information in a database.

QWERTY keyboard Standard typewriter or terminal keyboard.

RAM Random access memory. See also Primary storage.

Random access file See Direct access file.

Random access memory See Primary storage.

Randomizing routine An algorithm to convert a record key into a storage address on a direct-access storage device.

Range A group of cells in a spreadsheet.

Raster-scan system A system that creates an image with a series of parallel lines of pixels. See also Vector stroke system.

Read-only memory (ROM) Non-volatile memory that can be read but not written over or destroyed.

Read/write head That part of a disk or tape drive that transfers data between the disk or tape and primary memory.

Real-time processing Processing of transactions as they occur. See also Batch processing.

Record A unit of information about someone or something.

Record key Data that identify a record within a file.

Recording Expressing data so they are recognizable at a later time by a person or machine.

Redundancy (1) Storing the same data in two or more files. (2) Using the same storage location for two or more keys. (3) Storing several programs to accomplish the same task.

Register A special area of primary memory used by the CPU.

Relation (1) The relationship between tuples and attributes in a relational database. (2) A mathematical expression that compares two quantities.

Relational data base A database in which data are organized in related rows and columns.

Relative data address The location of a piece of data in a virtual system relative to a base referent address.

Replicate To generate a set of related formulas in a range of spreadsheet cells.

Reset key A button on the computer that restores the computer to the status it was in when it was first turned on. Usually does not affect current contents of primary storage.

Resident device See System resident device.

Resident system program A program that is always available to the user or to other programs.

Resolution The number of pixels on the longest line that can be placed on a CRT. The higher the resolution, the sharper the image.

Response time The amount of time until a computer responds to a request from a user.

RGB monitor A CRT that receives separate signals for each of the primary colors: red, green, and blue. RGB images are cleaner than composite ones. See also Composite color CRT.

Right justify Placing characters in a field to the far right.

Ring network A network in which each computer is connected directly to the computer on each side of it and all connections, taken together, form a closed loop.

ROM See Read-only memory.

Root directory The highest level directory in a hierarchical directory structure.

Rotational delay Time required for a specific disk sector to pass under the read/write head.

RPG Report Program Generator, a problem-oriented language for printing reports using existing data files.

RS-232 (1) A connector for wiring computers and equipment together for serial data transmission. (2) A common protocol for transmitting serial data.

Run book Documentation for mainframe operators that shows how to start, run, and terminate a program.

Run sheet See Job sheet.

Sandwich principle Separating any two sinks by bubbles and any two bubbles by sinks except at the beginning and end of a data flow diagram. See also Bubble, Sink.

Scheduled report See Monitoring report.

Schema The description of logical relationships between data in a database management system.

Screen See Cathode ray tube.

Scrolling Moving the cursor to see different data on the CRT.

Search and replace Finding a passage in text and automatically replacing it with another passage.

Secondary storage Non-volatile storage that is not part of the CPU.

Sector A portion of a track on a disk. The sector is used for blocking logical records into physical ones.

Sector address The location by sector and track of specific data on a disk.

Segment A self-contained part of a program that is loaded into a computer when the entire program is too large to be loaded at one time.

Segmentation and paging Combining segments and pages to use a program that is too large to load into a computer at one time.

Selected cell See Active cell.

Sequence structure See Process box.

Sequential file A file in which a record can be read or written only after all records written earlier have been read.

Sequential processing Processing records in order by record key.

Serial A transmission format in which data are sent bit-by-bit. See also Parallel.

Service bureau A company that sells computer services.

Set A group of related documents in a data bank.

Shell A multi-layered system of programs in which outer programs control inner ones.

Shell command A JCL instruction in the UNIX operating system.

Shell program See Batch file.

Simplex One-way data transmission.

Simulator See Emulator.

Sink A source of information in a data flow diagram.

Slave computer See File server.

Software Computer programs that accomplish specific applications. See also Program.

Sort Placing items in predetermined numerical or alphabetic order.

Sorting See Sort.

Source document The document that provides data to be entered into a computer.

Source program A program in a higher-level language that is compiled into an object program. See also Object program.

Source range The cell or range of cells in a spreadsheet that contains data or formulas to be copied to other cells. See also Target.

Speech recognition Computer control by spoken command.

Speech synthesis Production of speech-like sounds by computer-controlled electronic devices.

SPOOL Simultaneous Peripheral Operations On Line, a technique whereby the CPU is freed for computation while other devices control I/O.

Spreadsheet (1) A program that creates a table of data and allows any piece(s) of data to be defined mathematically in terms of any other data within the table. (2) A computerized columnar pad.

SQL See Query language.

Stacked-job processing See Batch processing.

Stand-alone buffer A printer buffer that is external to a microcomputer.

Star network A network configuration in which each node is directly connected to every other node.

Status line The part of a CRT display that provides information about the program currently running. Such information might include which of several modes is currently operative, available storage, etc.

Step value The amount by which a variable is incremented or decremented.

Storage See Primary storage.

Storage dump See Dump.

Storage-oriented system A system that emphasizes safekeeping of data and information.

Store and forward Electronic mail in which a value-added network stores messages and sends them to the recipient at a later time.

Stored program A program that is presented to the computer as data instead of being presented as switch settings. All modern programs are stored.

Strategic information center See Information center.

String variable A variable that is made up of character data.

Structure A term used to refer to one of three logic patterns used in preparing computer programs: sequence, looping, or selection.

Structure chart See Hierarchy chart.

Structured program A program in which each block of code conforms to one of three logical structure patterns: sequence, looping, or selection.

Subdirectory A directory that is part of a set of directories.

Subroutine A block of code that is designed to be used in several programs or several times in the same program.

Subscript An indicator that tells which of a series of variables is to be used.

Subset All documents of a set that have some common characteristic.

Subsystem A system that is an element of a larger system.

Summarizing Condensing data or information into a more concise form.

Supervisor A program that supervises and controls computer activities.

Switched line A normal telephone line that is activated when a telephone number is dialed.

Synchronous transmission Data transmission at a fixed rate. See also Asynchronous transmission.

Syntax The rules for writing a computer instruction. Syntax is different for every language.

Sys-res See System resident device.

System A set of procedures used to accomplish a unified set of tasks to achieve some objective.

System administrator See System manager.

System analysis The study of how systems should and do work.

System analyst A person who performs system analysis and development.

System command A JCL instruction. See also Job control language.

System design The determination of what a system will do and how; the compilation of all of the particulars of a new system.

System development The division of a data processing department that provides systems analysis and programming.

System development cycle An orderly procedure to evaluate systems and effect changes when necessary.

System device See System resident device.

System disk A disk containing the operating system for a microcomputer.

System environment The sum of all external forces affecting a system.

System evaluation Checking a system to see how well it meets its goals.

System flowchart A pictorial representation of the processes used in a system.

System implementation Bringing a new system into operation.

System program A computer program designed to control a computer. Operating systems are made up of system programs.

System query language (SQL) See Query language.

System resident device The peripheral device, usually a disk drive on which the operating system is stored.

System software Programs that make up the operating system. See also Application software.

Systems department The division of a data processing department that provides systems design, development, and maintenance.

Systems maintenance The division of a data processing department that maintains hardware and software for day-to-day operations.

Systems manager A person responsible for management of the systems division of a data processing department.

Systems programmer A programmer who specializes in system software.

Systems support The division that provides production services for the systems personnel of a data processing department.

Tape drive A machine that stores data on magnetic tape. Such devices are sequential.

Target The cell or range of cells in a spreadsheet that will receive data. See also Source range.

Telecommunications The combined fields of computers and communications. See also Data communications.

Teleconference A meeting in which participants are geographically separated but are linked by electronic means.

Template A spreadsheet format with all of the necessary formulas for a particular application. Users can add their own data to a template without having to design the spreadsheet.

Terminal The set of input/output devices at a computer work station.

Terminal controller A front end processor that links terminals to a mainframe computer.

Text Data made up of numbers, letters, and special characters.

Text manipulation Electronic alteration of text stored on computer media.

Text processing Electronically creating and correcting text without the use of paper.

Thermal printer A printer that prints by burning specially coated paper.

Thimble The printing element of certain letter-quality printers.

Thought processor See Idea processor.

Thrashing Excessive transfer of pages or segments between RAM and disk.

Throughput (1) The time it takes from submission of a computer job to return of the output. (2) The amount of production of a system in a given time period.

Time-sharing Concurrent independent use of a single computer system by several individuals.

Time slice The amount of time allocated to each time-sharing user as the computer cycles from user to user. Time slices may vary among users depending on their priority.

Top-down programming See Programming by level.

Touch screen A CRT bordered by photoelectric cells that sense the location of an object placed on the screen.

Track Parallel or concentric paths along which data bits are stored on tape or disk.

Trailer See End-of-job indicator.

Transaction file A file of updates to be added to the master file.

Transient See Transient system program.

Transient system program A system program that must be loaded from peripheral storage before it can be executed.

Transmission grade See Bandwidth.

Transportable computer An easily movable computer about the size of a small suitcase.

Tree See Hierarchical network, Hierarchical file system.

Triggered report A report triggered by an unusual occurrence in a system.

Tube See Cathode ray tube.

Tuple A row in a relational database.

Turn-around time The time required from submission of a job to return of results.

Type-ahead buffer An input buffer that allows data entry at a rate faster than the CRT can react.

Uncompleted path A set of computer instructions that do not complete the task they are to accomplish.

Unconditional branch An instruction that requires the computer to execute some instruction other than the next sequential one.

Universal product code (UPC) Bar code data placed on most items sold in the United States to identify the product and manufacturer.

UNIX An operating system developed by Bell Labs.

UPC See Universal product code.

Upload To send a file from one computer to another. See also Download.

User (1) One served by a computer system through the services of a data processing department. (2) One who uses a computer or computer terminal.

Users group A club of computer users with some common interest, generally the type of equipment used, the type of program used, or geographic location.

Utility A general-purpose program that can be used in conjunction with many application programs, e.g., file copying programs, sorting programs.

Value-added network (VAN) A common carrier that provides services in addition to communications lines.

VAN See Value-added network.

Variable-length record A record that has an undetermined number of characters.

VDT See Video display terminal.

Vector-stroke system A system that creates images as a series of lines connecting any two points within the image. See also Raster-scan system.

Verifying Checking that data have been entered into a system correctly.

Vertical program A program that was designed for one particular industry.

Video display terminal (VDT) An input/output terminal. The VDT consists of a CRT and a keyboard. "Smart VDTs" include microprocessors and limited primary storage.

Virtual machine A computer designed to use virtual memory techniques.

Virtual memory (VM) A system whereby limited memory appears to be infinite. This is accomplished by breaking programs into segments or pages and loading each as it is needed.

Virtual-storage access method (VSAM) Technique of assigning relative addresses to records in a file.

Visual table of contents (VTOC) Structure chart with identifying numbers assigned to each module.

VM See Virtual memory.

Voice actuation Control of the computer by spoken commands.

Voice input See Voice actuation.

Voice mail Computerized storage and retrieval of voice messages.

Voice output Computer output simulating human speech.

Volatile memory Memory that requires continuous electrical power to store data.

Volume directory See Volume label.

Volume label Identifying data on a disk or tape.

VSAM See Virtual-storage access method.

VTOC See Visual table of contents.

Walkthrough An exercise in which systems analysts and people who use a system simulate operation of a new system to see if there are any problems with it.

Winchester drive See Hard disk drive.

Window Segmentation of the display screen to show the results of two or more programs or several aspects of a software package.

Word processing Preparation of correspondence and documents by electronic means. See also Text processing and Correspondence processing.

Word processor (1) A program for manipulating text. (2) A special-purpose computer for word processing.

Word wrap Automatic movement of text to the next line so that words are not broken in the middle.

Worksheet See Spreadsheet.

Work space See Partition.

Write-it-once principle Principle that data should be entered into an information system only once.

Zone (1) The left-most nibble (half-nibble in 6-bit BCD) in bit representation of a character. (2) Tab regions in a BASIC PRINT statement.

Notes

Chapter 1. Computers and Society: The Information Revolution

1. *Los Angeles Times*, 4 January, 1983. 2. John Naisbitt, *Megatrends*, Warner Books, 1982. 3. *Time*, 30 January, 1984. 4. *Scientific American*, December 1982. 5. Naisbitt, *Megatrends*. 6. Aaron Goldberg, "Micros, Mainframes, and You, the User...," *InfoWorld*, 6:19. 7. *Business Week*, 25 April, 1983. 8. "Bridging the Gap," *InfoWorld*, 5:48. 9. Quoted in Charles Rubin, "Computing in High Places," *Personal Computing*, November 1983. 10. David B. Schock, "Detroit Does It Different," *Personal Computing*, October 1983. 11. "A New World Dawns," *Time*, 3 January, 1983. 12. Ibid. 13. *California Penal Code*, Section 502. 14. Gene McMahon, "Putting a Lid on Software Piracy," *Management Technology*, June 1984. 15. Quoted in Joseph L. Galloway, "Computers Record Your Every Move," *U.S. News and World Report*, 24 April, 1984. 16. Seymour Rubinstein, "Opinion," *Interface Age*, June 1983. Rubinstein is president of MicroPro International and developer of the popular software program WordStar. 17. *InfoWorld*, 19 December, 1982. 18. *ComputerWorld*, 7 May, 1984. 19. "Portables—1984 and Beyond," *Byte*, January 1984. 20. G. Williams and K. Sheldon, "The Data General/One," *Byte*, November 1984. 21. G. Hartman, "Molecular Computer," *Popular Computing*, March 1984. 22. A. Fluegelman, "In Quest of True BASIC," *PC World*, November 1984. 23. *Time*, 3 January, 1984. 24. Ken Greenberg, "Executives Rate Their PCs," *PC World*, September 1984.

Chapter 2. Data and Information Processing: The Essentials

1. These observations are reported in detail in several articles in *The Computer Teacher*, April 1984, an issue with the theme "Computer Equity." 2. Marlaine E. Lockheed and Steven B. Frakt, "Sex Equity: Increasing Girls' Use of Computers," *The Computer Teacher*, April 1984. 3. Jane G. Schuberr and Thomas W. Bakke, "Practical Solutions to Overcoming Equity in Computer Use," ibid. 4. Anthony J. Alvarado, "Computer Education for ALL Students," ibid. 5. Jo Shuchat Sanders, "The Computer: Male, Female or Androgynous?," ibid. 6. Sanders, ibid. 7. Frederick W. Miller, "Women and MIS," *Infosystems*, January 1984. 8. Ibid. 9. Russ Adams, "Women in Meeting the Challenges," *Interface Age*, December 1983. 10. Judith Larkin, "Women in Computer Services," *ComputerWorld*, 12 November, 1984. 11. Ibid. 12. Miller, "Women and MIS."

Chapter 3. Business Information Systems: The Essentials at Work

1. *Time*, April 1964. 2. *Management Technology*, November 1983. 3. *Modern Office Technology*, February 1984. 4. Edward L. Unterberg, quoted in Kalbacker, Warren, "Trying to Find Tomorrow's Information Executive Today," *Management Technology*, February 1984. 5. *ComputerWorld*, 30 July, 1984.

Chapter 4. System Development: Building Information Systems

1. Frank Greenwood, *Profitable Small Business Computing*.

Chapter 5. Computer Hardware: The CPU and Memory

1. Charles Babbage, *Passages*. 2. P. and E. Morrison, *Charles Babbage and His Calculating Engines*. 3. Christopher Evans, *The Micro Millenium*, 1979. 4. Richard O'Reilly, "Crichton Envisions New Art Form," *Los Angeles Times*, 23 December, 1984.

Chapter 6. Computer Hardware: Secondary Storage and Input/Output

1. Warren Kalbacker, "Trying to Find Tomorrow's Information Executive Today," *Management Technology*, February 1984. 2. Ibid.

Chapter 7. Operating Systems: Managing Computer Resources

1. Isaac Asimov, *I, Robot*, Gnome Press, 1950. 2. Dana Blankenhorn, "Personal Robots: The PC on Wheels," *PC World*, January 1985. 3. Edward Cornish, "You Could Be Replaced by a Smarter, Cheaper Robot," *Los Angeles Times*, 11 January, 1985. 4. Blankenhorn, "Personal Robots"

Chapter 8. Applications Programs

1. Thomas Carlyle, *Past and Present*, 1984. 2. E. Brown and J. Faulkner, "Computers Ride the Range," *PC World*, May 1984. 3. Greg Stone, "The Electronic Gumshoe," *Softtalk*, November 1983. 4. Michael Ferris, "What Really is the Fruit of the Loom," *Softtalk*, December 1983. 5. Paul Gillin, "Packaged Software, Micros, OA Spearheading DP Budget Rise," *ComputerWorld*, 1 October, 1984. 6. Eds., "Computer," *Time*, 16 April, 1984, 60. 7. Poole et al., Osborne/McGraw-Hill, 1981. 8. Elsevier/International Software Database, published biannually. 9. Galen Bruman, "Home Computer: A Waste of Money?," *Los Angeles Times*, 20 February, 1984. 10. Dan Gutman, "Praising Weirdware," *InfoWorld*, 26 November, 1984. 11. John Unger Zussman, "My Computer Isn't Dumb, It Just Acts That Way," *A+ Magazine*, November 1984.

Chapter 9. Programming and Programming Languages

1. C. Bohm and G. Jacopini, "Flow Diagrams, Turing Machines and Languages with Only Two Formation Rules," *Communication of the Association for Computing Machinery*, May 1966. 2. Doug Clapp, "Clapp-Trapp," *InfoWorld*, 6 February, 1984. 3. Chris Crawford, "Why You Should Learn to Program," *Popular Computing*, September 1984. 4. Ibid. 5. Kathy Chin, "Professionals Turn Programmers," *InfoWorld*, 6 February, 1984. 6. Eds., "We're Managing a Revolution," *Business Computer Systems*, January 1985. 7. Elisabeth Horwitt, "Natural Languages Improve the User-Computer Dialog," *Business Computer Systems*, November 1984. 8. Ibid. 9. Ibid. 10. Ibid.

Chapter 10. Data Base Management Systems

1. Jonathan Littman, "Open Doors," *PC World*, March 1984. 2. *InfoWorld*, 19 March, 1984. 3. Lynn Smith, "Science Opens New Vistas for Disabled," *Los Angeles Times*, 28 September, 1984. 4. Littman, "Open Doors." 5. Ibid. 6. Wendy Lea McKibbin, "High-Tech for the Handicapped," *Infosystems*, January 1984. 7. *ComputerWorld*, 17 December, 1984. 8. McKibbin, "High-Tech." 9. Smith, "Science Opens Vistas." 10. Ibid.

Chapter 11. Data Communication

1. *Time*, 13 June, 1983. 2. *Business Software*, July 1984. 3. *InfoWorld*, 30 April, 1984. 4. *Management Technology*, November 1983. 5. S. Connel and I. Galbraith, *Electronic Mail: A Revolution in Business Communication*, 1980. 6. A. Glossbrenner, *The Complete Handbook of Personal Computing*, 1983. 7. Ibid. 8. George Reynolds, *Introduction to Business Telecommunications*, 1984. 9. Marvin Cetron, author of *Jobs for the Future: 500 Jobs, Where They'll Be and How to Get Them*, quoted in *ComputerWorld*, 30 July, 1984. 10. *Business Week*, 23 January, 1984. 11. *InfoWorld*, 31 December, 1984. 12. *InfoWorld*, 23 April, 1984. 13. *Personal Computing*, December 1984. 14. *Time*, 30 January, 1984. 15. *Link-Up*, November 1983.

Chapter 12. Word Processing

1. H. Glatzer, *Introduction to Word Processing*, 1981. 2. Adeline Naiman, "In the Beginning is the Word," *Personal Computing*, February 1985. 3. Ibid. 4. *Los Angeles Times*, 18 July, 1982. 5. Ibid. 6. Janette Martin, "New Dimensions in Word Processing," *PC World*, January 1985. 7. Ibid.

Chapter 13. Accounting Systems

1. Lewis Carroll, *Through the Looking Glass.* 2. Dan Post, "General Ledger's Bottom Line," *Business Computer Systems*, July 1984. 3. Gene McMahon, "Putting a Lid on Software Piracy," *Management Technology*, June 1984. 4. S. Greene and P. Saidman, "Copying Mass-Marketed Software," *Byte*, February 1985. 5. P. Bartolik, M. McEnaney, and D. Raimondi, "Firms Take Different Routes to Curtail Software Piracy," *ComputerWorld*, 4 February, 1985. 6. Ibid. 7. McMahon, "Putting Lid on Piracy."

Chapter 14. Spreadsheet Programs

1. Charles Rubin, "Power Spreadsheeting," *Personal Computing*, July 1984. 2. Thomas B. Henderson et al., *Spreadsheet Software from VisiCalc to 1-2-3.* 3. Herman Hupfeld, *Sing Something Simple*, Warner Brothers Music/ASCAP.

Chapter 15. Computer Graphics

1. David L. Wilcox, "The Boom in Business Graphics," *PC World*, August 1984. 2. *Los Angeles Times*, 29 October, 1983. 3. *Los Angeles Times*, 31 October, 1983. 4. *Los Angeles Times*, 3 November, 1983. 5. Walter Kiechel, *Fortune*, quoted in Wilcox, "Business Graphics." 6. Mark Skiba, "Correspond in Color," *PC World*, November 1983. 7. Alan Paller, "The Executive Palette," *ComputerWorld*, 14 November, 1984. 8. Ibid. 9. Michael Mizen, quoted in Charles Rubin, "Visual Decision Support," *Personal Computing*, February 1985. 10. Jeffrey Ehrlich, quoted in Jeffrey Young, "Computer Graphics: Toys or Tools?," *Personal Computing*, February 1985. 11. Young, "Computer Graphics: Toys or Tools?"

Chapter 16. More Productivity: Specialized Tools

1. *Personal Computing*, December 1983. 2. Interview, 6 September, 1984. 3. *ComputerWorld*, 3 September, 1984. 4. *Business Computer Systems*, June 1984. 5. *InfoWorld*, January 1985. 6. Paula Giese, "Due Processing," *PC World*, January 1985. 7. Jacques Hadamard, *The Psychology of Invention in the Mathematical Field*, 1973. 8. Bill Benzon, "The Visual Mind and the Macintosh," *Byte*, January 1985.

Index

Access width, 130
Accounting and accounting systems, 374-406
  general ledger, 378-85
    reports, 380-84
  history of, 374-76
  operational information systems, 64-65
  procedures, 376-78
  programs for, 218-19
  subsidiary systems, 385-94
  using, 394-401
Ada, 254-56
Aiken, Howard, 5, 17, 119
Algorithm, defined, 231
American Standard Code for Information Interchange. *See* ASCII
Analytical Engine, 119, 120
Analytical Machine, 5
APL, 251-52
Application software, 200-24
  commercial, 213-21
  firmware, 205-6
  hardware constraints, 202-3
  operating system constraints, 204-5
  sources of, 206-12
Architecture, computer, open and closed, 167
Artificial intelligence, 18-19
ASCII, 137-38
Assembly language, 243-45

Babbage, Charles, 5, 118, 119
BASIC computer language, 247-48
BASIC, programming in, B-1-B-63
  arithmetic operations, B-9-B-12
  assignment, B-9
  built-in functions, B-47
  clearing the CRT screen, B-15
  data pointer, B-31
  debugging a program, B-50-B-54
  editing on the Apple, B-6
  editing on the IBM PC, B-5
  end-of-job indicators, B-23-B-24
  error messages, B-53
  exercises, B-55-B-62
    answers to, B-62-B-64
  INTeger function, B-45-B-46
  line numbers, B-5-B-7
  logical operators, B-37-B-39
    AND, B-38
    NOT, B-38-B-39
    OR, B-37-B-38
  modes, B-4
  program logic and flowcharting, B-3-B-4
  reserve words, B-5
  running a program, B-7
  statements
    DATA, B-30
    DIM, B-36
    END, B-14
    FOR . . . NEXT loops, B-26-B-29
    FOR . . . NEXT loops, early exit of, B-37

    FOR . . . NEXT nested loops, B-29-B-30
    fundamental principles of, B-4-B-9
    GOTO, B-22-B-23
    IF . . . THEN, B-21-B-22
    IF . . . THEN . . . ELSE, B-22
    INPUT, B-12-B-13
    PRINT, B-13-B-14, B-17-B-18
    READ, B-30-B-31
    REM, B-14-B-15, B-36
    RESTORE, B-31
  subroutines, B-43-B-45
  syntax, B-4-B-5
  variables, B-8-B-9
    names, B-9, B-37
    subscripted, B-35-B-36
Batch files, 193
Batch processing, 74
Baudot, Jean Emile, 306
Billing in business, 61
Binary Coded Decimal (BCD), 138
Binary coding, 130, 136
Binary numbering system, 132-34
Binary system, 119
Bits, 130
  defined, 140
Block
  on a disk, 151
  on magnetic tape, 149
Block diagrams, 94
  example of, 93-94
Blocking factor on magnetic tape, 149
Bottom-up approach to system design, 106-7
BRS, 323
Bubble memory, 132
Buffer card, 169
Buffering, 181-82
Buffers, 150
Bulletin boards, electronic, 211-12, 321
Bus, 130
  external, 130
  internal, 130
Business information systems, 50-84
  management information systems (MIS), 69-80
  types of, 51-69
Business operations, operational information systems, 60-64
Byron, Augusta Ada, 119, 120
Byte, defined, 130, 140

C programming language, 253-54
CAD/CAM, 67
Calculating, defined, 33
Cathode ray tubes (CRT), 155-57
Central processing unit (CPU), 127-32
Channel, 168
Character, defined, 42, 46
Character printers, 159, 161
Character set, 136
Classification, defined, 33
Classifying data, 30, 32-33
Closed architecture, 167

COBOL, 246-47
Code of Fair Information Practices, 13, 86
Coding in programming, 228
Coding schemes, 136-39
  ASCII, 137-38
  BCD, 138
  EBCDIC, 139
Collecting in business, 61-62
Communicating data, 35-36
Communications
  computer, 165
  intrafirm, 63
  networking, 185
  programs, 216-17
Computer-Aided Design (CAD), 67
Computer-Aided Manufacturing (CAM), 67
Computer architecture, 166-68
  open and closed, 167
Computer crime, 12-13
Computer graphics, 436-68
  defined, 437-39
  hardware, 449-57
  presentations using, 446-49
  programs, 217-18
  types of, 439-42
    analysis and planning, 443-45
    business, 439-42
  using programs for, 457-66
Computer hardware
  architecture, 166-68
  coordinating diverse speeds of, 168-69
  data representation and, 132-41
  history of, 118-22
  input/output devices, 155-65
  secondary storage, 146-55
  software constraints and, 202-3
  system components, 127-32
  types of, 122-27
Computer languages, 240-54
  Ada, 254-56
  APL, 251-52
  assembly, 243-45
  BASIC, 247-48
  C, 253-54
  Cobol, 246-47
  Forth, 252-53
  FORTRAN, 245-46
  LISP, 251
  machine, 243
  Pascal, 252
  PL/1, 249
  RPG, 249-51
  types of, 240-43
Computer memory, 130-32
  allocation, 186-87
  bubble, 132
  core, 131
  erasable programmable read-only (EPROM), 132
  management, 186-89
  programmable read-only (PROM), 132
  random access (RAM), 131
  read-only (ROM), 132
  virtual, 187-89
  volatility of, 131

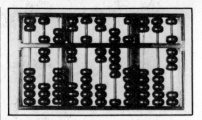

3000 B.C.
Abacus (p. 118)

1617
Napier's Bones (p. 118)

1944
Mark I computer (p. 17, p. 120)

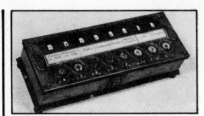

1642
Blaise Pascal's Arithmetique (p. 118)

1833
Charles Babbage's
Difference Engine
(p. 119)

Ada Augusta Byron
(Lady Lovelace)
develops the first
"program" (p. 254)

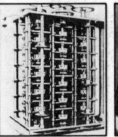

1951
UNIVAC installed at
US Bureau of Census
(p. 28, p. 176)

1948
Transistor invented
(p. 121)

1804
Punch-card operated
Jacquard Loom (p. 118)

1890
Herman Hollerith uses punched cards
and a tabulating machine to collate
the 1890 census (p. 50, p. 119)

1946
ENIAC computer (p. 16, p. 120)